Informed by Knowledge

Expertise: Research and Applications

Series Editors

Robert R. Hoffman, K. Anders Ericsson, Gary Klein, Michael McNeese, Eduardo Salas, Sabine Sonnentag, Frank Durso, Emilie Roth, Nancy J. Cooke, Dean K. Simonton

Informed by Knowledge

Expert Performance in Complex Situations

EDITED BY

Kathleen L. Mosier and Ute M. Fischer

Psychology Press
Taylor & Francis Group

New York   London

Psychology Press
Taylor & Francis Group
270 Madison Avenue
New York, NY 10016

Psychology Press
Taylor & Francis Group
27 Church Road
Hove, East Sussex BN3 2FA

© 2011 by Taylor and Francis Group, LLC
Psychology Press is an imprint of Taylor & Francis Group, an Informa business

Printed in the United States of America on acid-free paper
10 9 8 7 6 5 4 3 2 1

International Standard Book Number: 978-1-84872-911-7 (Hardback)

Library of Congress Cataloging-in-Publication Data

Informed by knowledge : expert performance in complex situations / editors, Kathleen L. Mosier, Ute M. Fischer.
       p. cm. -- (Expertise: research and applications)
    Based on presentations from the 8th International Conference on Naturalistic Decision Making.
    Includes bibliographical references and index.
    ISBN 978-1-84872-911-7 (hbk. : alk. paper)
    1. Decision making. 2. Expertise. I. Mosier, Kathleen L. II. Fischer, Ute M. III. International Conference on Naturalistic Decision Making (8th)

    BF448.I54 2011
    003'.56--dc22   2010027742

Visit the Taylor & Francis Web site at
http://www.taylorandfrancis.com

and the Psychology Press Web site at
http://www.psypress.com

Contents

Part IV: Outlook: New Methods and Approaches

Series Editor's Preface

The previous title in the Expertise Series was *Expertise Out of Context* (2007). It was formed around the proceedings of the 6th International Conference on Naturalistic Decision Making, which was held in 2003. The present volume has been formed around selected papers presented at the 8th International Conference on Naturalistic Decision Making (NDM8), which was held in June 2007. The presentations, posters, and demonstrations given at the meeting were unanimously regarded as being engaging as well as valuable. While the venue—the Asilomar Conference Center in Monterey, California—certainly contributed to the upbeat spirit of the meeting, its substance, and the many discussions and debates that were triggered, made NDM8 especially noteworthy and memorable. As in past NDM meetings, there were presentations on current work in the field of cognitive systems engineering, but there were also talks on topics drawn from outside the community of practice, and talks by invited speakers coming from other communities of practice. Everything converged, naturally, on phenomena of reasoning and knowledge as they occur in cognitive work, or complex sociotechnical systems.

Thematically, the sections of the present volume discuss the challenges to sensemaking that experts face (e.g., many sources of information, ambiguous and contradictory information, changing conditions), strategies they employ for discovering and integrating information, technical support and training for knowledge management, and new theoretical and methodological approaches and research paradigms for studying expert knowledge management in complex situations.

There was consensus that NDM8 was one of the most interesting conferences that attendees had been a part of, and that it did indeed showcase a great many high-quality presentations. This made the production of a book difficult, actually, in terms of the desire to emphasize breadth and diversity of coverage. The editors, Kathy Mosier and Ute Fischer, did a fine job of integrating the material and ensuring that each chapter was succinct as well as informative and valuable. Issues covered include coping with the challenges of team and organizational collaboration, coping with the complexity of cognitive work, coping with extreme environments, and coping with uncertainty in net-centric domains. Phenomena of macrocognition that are discussed include anticipatory thinking and sensemaking. Domains of study span a wide range, as one would expect and hope, including inventing, military command, healthcare, investment banking, and public safety.

This volume makes the Expertise Series coverage of cognitive engineering and decision making and naturalistic decision quite current. On behalf of all of the series editors, I thank the volume editors for their efforts, and the contributors for providing chapters on their most recent and intriguing research.

Robert R. Hoffman
Pensacola, FL
February 2009

Preface

The focus of this book is on how experts adapt to complexity. A primary tenet that emerged from presentations at the 8th International Conference on Naturalistic Decision Making, on which this volume is based, was the notion that a critical facet of expertise is the ability to synthesize and interpret information in context, transforming or "fusing" disparate items of information into coherent knowledge. This is true across experts (e.g., global leaders, individuals in extreme environments, managers, police officers, pilots, commanders, doctors), across contexts (e.g., corporate organizations, command and control, crisis management, air traffic control, the operating room), and for both individual and team performance. Successful information integration is a key factor in the success of diverse endeavors, including team attempts to climb Mt. Everest, product development, crowd control in the Middle East, and remote drilling operations.

Naturalistic decision making (NDM) has evolved considerably over the past 20 years, and several new themes appear across the chapters in this volume. *Uncertainty* figures prominently in several chapters, and issues regarding its management and representation are introduced. Questions are also posed: Is uncertainty good or bad—or is it a matter of how much uncertainty should be tolerated? How should uncertainty be displayed so that experts can make sense of the situation? Sensemaking, that is, generating knowledge through the interpretation and integration of information, is now recognized as an important component of expert performance in complex environments, and the chapters highlight the fact that technology today must support sensemaking if it is to effectively aid decision making. A third theme that emerges from the present chapters is the importance of teams. Researchers in the field of NDM are expanding their focus to include team issues such as collaboration and coordination when teams are *ad hoc*, multilayered, or distributed. Distributed teams require technological tools to support information sharing among team members, and several authors in this volume discuss design requirements as well as limitations in the use of team-ware. Boundary spanning, another recurrent theme in the volume's chapters, is both an individual- and a team-level phenomenon. At the individual level, it refers to the ability of experts to rise above intellectual molds or discipline- and culture-based explanations. At the team level, boundary spanning concerns the collaboration across professional and organizational groups and the delicate balance of multiple and at times conflicting goals. Lastly, it is clear that we are still learning about expert performance in complex situations, and new or overlooked issues are discussed in this book.

The volume is divided into four sections, each with its own specific focus on an area of expert performance. Chapters in Section I, "Managing Complexity: Discussions From Various Fields and Decision Contexts," cover a wide range of domains, many of which have not been addressed in previous publications on expertise, such as space and space analogs (Orasanu and Lieberman), global leadership (Osland), inventor cognition (Mieg), healthcare (Perry and Wears), the military (Hutchins and Kendall; Thunholm), product development (Badke-Schaub), and crowd management (Sieck, Smith, Grome, and Rababy). Chapter authors discuss the challenges their domain poses and the strategies experts use to manage knowledge, work within organizational and team structures, and adapt to complexity within them. While domains share characteristics typical of NDM task contexts—for instance, highly complex and ill-structured problems, time criticality, and high stakes—novel aspects were addressed. Orasanu and Lieberman discuss how environmental stressors such as danger, radiation, fatigue, sleep deprivation, and isolation may impact individual and team performance during space explorations. Sieck et al.'s chapter on U.S. and Lebanese personnel managing Middle Eastern crowds shows that successful intervention rests on an accurate understanding of the social factors and cultural models that shape crowd members' behavior. Chapters by Mieg, Badke-Schaub, and Perry and Wears point to an issue rarely considered in the expert decision-making literature: How do experts cope with nonroutine situations that do not fit learned responses, or, more generally, how do experts create novel solutions? Work by Osland and also Badke-Schaub demonstrates that in a team context, experts' domain knowledge and problem-solving and strategic thinking skills need to be complemented by interpersonal competence. The iterative nature of decision making in real-world contexts is highlighted in the chapters by Hutchins and Kendall, who examined distributed teams, and by Thunholm, who analyzed the planning process of military commanders.

In Section II, "Technological Support and Training for Knowledge Management," authors present technological and training approaches to facilitate knowledge management by individual experts and expert teams. Kirschenbaum addresses the issue of how to display uncertainty (i.e., probabilistic data) so that it can be interpreted and managed appropriately. Contemporary team configurations include hybrid teams, in which members interact both face-to-face and virtually in more than one location (Lauche and Bayerl); *ad hoc* teams formed to address specific issues or problems (Strater et al.); and teams in which members are distributed across organizations, time, and space, as in the National Airspace System (Smith, Spencer, and Billings). Chapters 9 to 12 describe procedures, displays, or technological support targeted toward facilitating team processes and cognition, including an awareness of the big picture; Chapter 13 describes a technological solution to pass essentials of planning, coordinating, allocating, and tasking joint air operations from senior to junior commanders (Zimmerman, Sestokas, and Burns)

New or neglected perspectives are presented in Section III, "Overlooked Issues in Expert Decision Making." Snowden introduces a narrative research tool to facilitate sensemaking and the discovery of "novel and beneficial" solutions. Klein, Snowden, and Chew discuss the need for anticipatory awareness and anticipatory thinking—that is, of preparing in time for problems and opportunities in order to have a resilient capacity to deal with surprising events. Fiore, Rosen, and Salas demonstrate the relevance of group communication theories to macrocognition in teams. The last two chapters in this section address pressures or blind spots that may produce ineffective expert decision processes, such as organizationally imposed accountability (Alison, Eyre, and Humann), and present a tool to diagnose shortcomings in expert mental models (DiBello, Missildine, and Lehmann).

The final section of this volume, Section IV, "Outlook: New Methods and Approaches," highlights the importance of modeling expert performance through techniques and frameworks such as cognitive task analysis (Militello et al.), computational architectures based on the notion of causal belief mapping, such as "convince me" (McAndrew and Gore), or the data/frame model of sensemaking (Stewart, Way, and Dominguez). Caldwell and Garrett introduce a framework of team-based event detection and task management to describe expert performance in time-critical team-based environments. Falzer discusses how NDM expertise can influence the practice of violence risk assessment by joining with structured professional judgment in developing, implementing and monitoring strategies to reduce violent behavior. Lastly, the volume returns to the theme of uncertainty, as Cohen presents a model for managing time and uncertainty in expert performance.

This book would not have been possible without the thoughtful comments and suggestions by all the individuals who helped us review the chapters. Our thanks go to Anne Adams, Cheryl Bolstad, Margaret Chrichton, Anna Cianciolo, Elliot Entin, Karen Feigh, Rhona Flin, Simon Henderson, Robert Hoffman, Raanan Lipshitz, Jean MacMillan, Jim McLennan, Susannah Paletz, Jan Maarten Schraagen, Daniel Serfaty, Jim Staszewski, Barbara Torell, Alex Wearing, and Yan Xiao.

Kathleen L. Mosier and Ute M. Fischer, Editors

Part I

Managing Complexity
Discussions from Various Fields and Decision Contexts

1

NDM Issues in Extreme Environments

Judith Orasanu
NASA Ames Research Center

Phil Lieberman
Brown University

Summing Mt. Everest. A three-year mission to Mars. Fighting the World Trade Center inferno. Coast Guard rescue at sea. Urban warfare. Overwintering in Antarctica. What do these activities have in common? They all are cases of human performance in extreme environments. Decision making in these environments is critical to both the survival of the participants and the completion of the mission.

Why should we care about these environments? We care because we know that stressors of many types associated with extreme environments can significantly influence cognitive processes in general and decision making in particular. While these environments may appear exotic, in fact they are ubiquitous in our modern society. People routinely choose to work or play in these environments for a variety of reasons. Humans push the frontiers in search of knowledge, personal achievement, and maintenance of peace and security. As noted by the Society for Human Performance in Extreme Environments (HPEE), "Endeavors under the earth and sea, at the Earth's poles, and in space have afforded numerous benefits to humankind and illustrate some of our greatest achievements" (HPEE, Web site).

Extreme environments are the next frontier of naturalistic decision making. These environments add new dimensions to expert decision making and performance in terms of physical and psychological stressors, interpersonal issues, and threats to cognitive functioning and general mental health. Understanding the impact of features of these environments on human functioning will also enhance our knowledge of naturalistic decision making.

In this chapter we define extreme environments (EEs) and discuss their effect on individual and team cognitive processes and decision making. We summarize the existing research on EEs, including studies from past space missions, simulations, and analog environments. Our focus then turns to the issues of what principles can be learned and generalized across different extreme environments, and what current knowledge and principles from NDM can inform future research in extreme environments. In addressing these issues, we will use human functioning during long-duration space missions as our primary focus.

Extreme Environments

Manzey and Lorenz (1998) define extreme environments as "settings that possess extraordinary physical, psychological, and interpersonal demands that require significant human adaptation for survival and performance." While many dimensions have been used to characterize various extreme environments (Sells, 1973), we find the following three to be most useful: the *ambient* environment, the *social* environment, and the *nature of the task*. Sauer, Wastell, and Hockey (1997) also include the technological environment. Several categories can be identified on the basis of these three factors, as shown in Figure 1.1.

Ambient Extremes

When we think of extreme environments, we typically imagine those that are inhospitable to life in the absence of life-sustaining technologies. These include outer space, underwater, deserts, polar regions, and high altitudes, as well as transient extreme environments, such as wildfires or urban fires and infectious disease areas (see Figure 1.1d). By requiring life-sustaining or protective habitats and equipment, these environments impose a number of constraints on human well-being and performance, and can be further subcategorized by several features that will be described in the next section. People sometimes place themselves in these extreme environments for reasons other than work, namely, for sport or the experience of being there, such as climbing Mt. Everest or scuba diving (Figure 1.1c).

Social Extremes

Other ambient environments are not inherently inhospitable to life, but the social environment is hazardous, such as working in a prison, hostage negotiations, human intelligence work, crisis management, mob control, peacekeeping operations, and all aspects of war (Figure 1.1b).

Task Extremes

The final category includes those in which the human activity itself is extreme, even though the ambient and social environments might not be inherently dangerous were

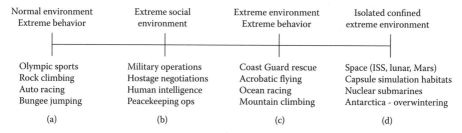

FIGURE 1.1   Categories of extreme environments from least (a) to most (d) extreme.

participants not engaged in the extreme activity. Examples include rock climbing, bungee jumping, auto racing, Olympic athletics, and other extreme sports (Figure 1.1a).

In this chapter we are most concerned with environments and activities in Figure 1.1c and d because of their relevance to space missions.

Space as an Extreme Environment

Space missions epitomize extreme work environments. Outer space is completely inhospitable to human life and requires a technologically sophisticated habitat and life support system. Kanas and Manzey (2003) note four primary classes of stressors in space—physical, habitability, psychological, and interpersonal.

Physical stressors are those associated with traveling in or being in the space environment: acceleration changes, microgravity, ionizing radiation, impacts from meteoroids or space debris, and the nature of light-dark cycles.

Habitability stressors arise from the space vehicle and habitat: constant noise generated by onboard equipment, vibration, temperature, lighting (typically low), and air quality.

Psychological stressors include isolation from family and friends, confinement in a limited space, ever-present dangers of working in a hostile environment and the potential for life-threatening system failures, restricted sensory cues, monotony of routine, crowding, and limited privacy and personal space.

Interpersonal stressors may be associated with enforced social contact with other crewmembers, gender or culture of crewmembers, personality conflicts, crew size and leadership.

Space-specific stressors are in addition to those transient stressors that may be found in many high-risk environments on earth: high workload, time pressure and imminent danger in the face of critical system failures, inadequate or ambiguous information, or novel events with uncertain outcomes. One of the most pervasive and significant physiological issues in space missions is sleep and circadian disruption: Sleep tends to be limited and of poor quality, in part due to the constant ambient noise and limited privacy in the habitat, but also due to "slam shifting," or shifting to the time schedule that matches earth time when a shuttle crew arrives at the station. Astronauts average about six hours of sleep per night, a level considered chronic deprivation for most people on earth and associated with decrements in cognitive performance (Mollicone, Van Dongen, Rogers, & Dinges, 2008).

During missions to the moon and ultimately to Mars, crews are likely to encounter problems that do not have scripted solutions. Problems may arise with the habitat, equipment, automated systems, science procedures, EVA gear, or health of the crew. Coping with unforeseen problems most likely will require team effort. Mission Control has significant resources to assist with problem resolution, but communication lags during Mars missions of up to 20 minutes (each way) or even total disruption mean that, on occasion, crews will need to function on their own. Another stressor unique to Mars missions is the fact that the crew will be the first space travelers who will not be able to see the earth or distinguish it from other dots of light in the vastness of space.

NASA's challenge is how to prepare crews for long-duration space missions, that is, how to select, compose, and train teams for effective performance, teamwork, and good psychosocial adjustment. In addition to premission preparation, technologies will be needed to monitor the crew's functional capability during missions and to provide countermeasures that support performance and well-being.

Findings that form the basis for expectations about how individuals and crews might perform in long-duration missions come from three primary sources—prior space missions, ground-based space simulations, and space analogs.

Prior Space Missions

The history of space missions to date indicates that crews may adapt quite well to these unusual circumstances (see Harrison, 2001; Suedfeld, 2005, for discussions of the salutogenic consequences of space travel). However, in some cases negative impacts have been found for cognitive, social, and emotional functioning.

Modern space missions can be separated into two major categories: (1) relatively brief shuttle missions that are about two weeks long and are used to transport replacement and visiting crewmembers to an orbiting vehicle, such as the Russian Mir or the International Space Station (ISS), and (2) long-duration missions. The longer-duration orbital missions typically last around six months, although actual durations have varied for both planned and unplanned reasons. Valeri Polyakov's 14-month stay aboard Mir, beginning in January 1994, still holds the record for the longest continuous spaceflight by a single person. The initial crew size while the ISS was being built was three; following September 11, 2001, it was reduced to two, but in 2006 it increased again to three. When shuttles arrive the crew can grow to 10 or 11. Since expansion of the ISS living quarters in 2009, the crew size has grown to its full complement of six. Mir and the ISS were designed as research laboratories for long-term studies, including long-term biomedical research on the human crew.

Cognitive Effects

Research on short (six-day) shuttle and Mir missions found no significant impairment of cognitive functioning associated with being in space (Kanas & Manzey, 2003). However, these initial studies only tested simple cognitive processes. This situation was remedied by including complex cognitive tasks drawn from the Standardized Tests for Research with Environmental Stressors (STRES) (AGARD, 1989). The single-subject study conducted during an eight-day Mir mission compared in-flight performance with pre- and post-mission measures. Again, no impairments of speed or accuracy of basic cognitive functions were found, but decrements emerged on a complex psychomotor task (unstable tracking) and in a dual task that made greater demands on attentional control (unstable tracking plus memory search) (Manzey & Lorenz, 1998).

The same instrument battery was used in a long-duration Mir mission (in fact, the 438-day record-setting one). Measures were taken 41 times and compared with baseline and post-mission performance. Initial decrements were observed during the first month on the tracking task and the dual task while the cosmonaut went through an adaptation period, but then returned to baseline levels. Performance on some measures actually improved over time. The performance decrements were closely coupled with perceptions of workload and subjective mood ratings (Manzey & Lorenz, 1998). Similarly, Nechaev (2001) reported that crew "errors" were likely to occur when there were disturbances in the usual work-rest schedule, high workload, or psychosomatic distress. These studies suggest that cognitive functioning of well-adjusted and highly trained space travelers might be expected to be robust despite the stressors of space, at least over the periods studied.

Behavioral Health Effects

Short-duration space missions do not induce significant behavioral/mental health issues. Given that these missions are only two weeks in duration, the general wisdom is that crewmembers can basically "tough it out" for that brief period and deal with any problems after returning to terra firma.

In contrast, anecdotal reports indicate that adjustment problems and somatoform disorders (i.e., psychosomatic reactions) occurred in long-duration Mir missions (Kanas & Manzey, 2003). For instance, Valentine Lebedev (1988) reported that his "nerves were always on the edge, I get jumpy at any minor irritation." After his experience on board the Russian orbiter Mir, U.S. astronaut John Blaha commented that he never anticipated the situation would be so stressful—or that it would interfere so much with his performance (Burrough, 1998).

The most systematic study on individual and crew functioning in space was conducted by Kanas and his colleagues (Kanas et al., 2001a). They collected weekly data from both U.S. and Russian crewmembers aboard the Mir and Mission Control personnel in both countries using several scales tapping individual mood and group climate. Compared to the normative sample, the space crews expressed less dysphoria and higher cohesion, leadership, and management control (Kanas et al., 2001b). When stress and mood disturbance were experienced, crewmembers tended to displace it to outside supervisors (Kanas et al., 2001c).

Interpersonal Issues and Crew Cohesion

Interpersonal tensions were rarely a problem on brief shuttle missions, but tended to emerge about six weeks into longer missions, after the crew had become adjusted to life in the space environment (Kanas & Manzey, 2003). Analysis of the critical incident logs in the shuttle/Mir study (Kanas et al., 2001a) revealed that U.S. crews reported more interpersonal problems than Russians (e.g., feeling unsupported by other crewmembers or conflicts with Mission Control personnel). The fact that the Americans were guests on Mir with two Russian cosmonauts and with Russian Mission Control being the lead control center may explain this finding. These relatively positive results led Kanas and Manzey to conclude that "negative interpersonal phenomena that occur during long-duration space missions are related more to psychosocial pressures from the stressful and confined conditions than to individual personality weaknesses" (Kanas & Manzey, 2003, p. 96).

Simulated Space Missions

Given the limited number of crewmembers from past space missions and the absence of systematic data from those crews, space agencies have turned to realistic simulations of space missions to study issues associated with crew functioning. These missions in hyperbaric chambers, which mimic the habitat and operations of the shuttle, Mir, or ISS, have run for durations from 4 days to 240 days.

One simulation of note that addressed crew decision making was a 60-day study run by the European Space Agency (ESA) in 1992, the Experimental Campaign for the European Manned Space Infrastructure (EXEMSI) (Hockey & Sauer, 1996). In addition to collecting biomedical and physiological data (as during a real space mission), the four crewmembers also performed a decision task every workday (40 trials each) using a simulated task that involved monitoring the cabin air quality to determine whether one of a set of possible contaminants exceeded safety criteria. This task required memory and strategic skills in order to maintain accuracy. The study found different strategies for adapting to the stress of continued isolation and confinement. Two of the four crewmembers were able to maintain low error rates throughout the two months of the study, but at a cost of increased cognitive effort and slowing of performance. The other two crewmembers' performance accuracy decreased over time, with little evidence of increased cognitive effort. While this was a realistic decision task, it was more structured than those typically used in NDM studies. However, an important contribution of this methodology is its finding that cognitive stress effects are not always evident in the product, but must be sought in indirect measures, such as response time, information search, or subjective ratings of effort or fatigue (Hockey & Sauer, 1996). The EXEMSI study also provided observations related to crew psychosocial adjustment. Despite composing the crew based on a theoretical framework for crew compatibility, two dominant crewmembers exhibited conflict over leadership. However, overall the crew adjusted well to the two-month isolation.

A longer isolation study conducted by the Russian Institute for Biomedical Problems (IBMP) in its ground simulator during 1999 resulted in much more interpersonal friction and behavioral health problems (Sandal, 2004). The Simulation of Flight of International Crew on Space Station (SFINCSS-99) included four Russian males who were onboard for 240 days; a second crew (one German and three Russian males) stayed in an adjoining chamber for 110 days, followed by a third multicultural gender-mixed crew for another 110 days. In addition, three shuttle crews visited for four or seven days. Several critical interpersonal incidents occurred during this mission, presumably resulting from lack of a common language as well as cultural differences concerning gender norms and conflict management strategies (Sandal, 2004).

Lessons learned from these and other simulation studies prepared IBMP and ESA to conduct the first Mars preparatory study, Mars-105 (ESA, 2009). A six-member male crew of four Russians, one French, and one German lived in the Russian simulator for 105 days, performing in scenarios as if they were actually traveling to Mars. Realistic crew tasks, including simulated emergencies and communication lags of up to 20 minutes, provided opportunities for researchers to observe how the crew performed under isolation and confinement for this duration. This is the first simulation study that included tasks to elicit naturalistic decision making. After analyzing data from this study (which was completed on July 14, 2009), a full Mars mission simulation will be conducted lasting 520 days, about half the duration of an actual round-trip to Mars.

To summarize, simulations of crews in the extreme environment of space have provided considerable information on interpersonal interactions, sources of tension, strategies for coping with isolation and confinement, and some evidence of effects on cognitive functioning. Simulations are valuable because of the control over scenarios, crew selection and composition, and living conditions they provide the researchers. Their biggest limitation is that it is impossible to generate the threats associated with real space missions. While it is easy to create isolation and confinement, it is not possible to introduce realistic threats associated with system failure or environmental hazards, for example, meteorites, radiation, or weightlessness. These studies also may suffer from the problem of small n, as they are expensive to conduct.

Space Analogs

One way to overcome many of the limitations of space simulations is to use analogs, which are other extreme environments that have elements in common with space missions, in which people with domain expertise and motivation engage in real work under various kinds of threats. Sells (1973) developed a taxonomy of environments and social contexts for comparing analogs with space environments, and concluded that submarines, exploration parties, naval ships, bomber crews, and remote duty stations were most similar to space systems. Similarly, Sauer et al. (1997) identified nuclear submarines as the best analog for space. Antarctica (over-wintering crews), underwater habitats (e.g., NASA's Extreme Environment Mission Operations [NEEMO] program), and mountaineering were judged to be good space analogs in terms of ambient and social environments. More recently, several other analogs have become available. The Mars Society has instituted the Mars Analog Research Station (MARS) project, to include four Mars base-like habitats located in deserts in the Canadian Arctic, the American southwest, the Australian outback, and Iceland.

Nuclear Submarines

Submarines exhibit many similarities to space vehicles and operations: Both operate unsupported in inherently hostile environments, where a small breach in the hull or in the seawater piping system can threaten the ship and its crew. Both must create and purify their own atmosphere, distill water, and maintain climate control. Their closed atmospheres create risks associated with fires and toxic fumes. Psychological stressors also are similar in many ways: Crewmembers work in the absence of day-night cues, and under conditions of disrupted sleep-wake cycles, sleep deprivation, varying noise levels, atmospheric composition and pressure constraints, and the lack of habitable space.

Sandal and her colleagues (Sandal, Endresen, Vaernes, & Ursin, 1999) identified several factors that contributed to crews' vulnerability or resilience in coping with the isolation and confinement typical of submarine missions. Crewmembers who employed problem-focused coping strategies, showed interpersonal sensitivity, and had strong achievement motivation were found to be more resilient and to experience less stress (as reflected in lower cortisol levels). Interpersonal sensitivity, moreover, was important for maintaining crew harmony and cohesion.

In contrast to the normal missions studied by Sandal and colleagues, other researchers have focused on reactions of crewmembers to life-threatening accidents at sea. These studies consistently showed that prior exposure to critical life events and a subjective experience of not coping with the immediate accident were sources of vulnerability. Resilience was predicted by a problem-oriented habitual coping style and by unit cohesion, in addition to emergency response training (Berg, Grieger, & Spira, 2005). These findings suggest that acute stress exposures have a cumulative effect on ability to cope with subsequent crisis events. They also demonstrate the power of training to reduce stress effects. How these factors may have influenced individual or crew decision making in coping with the threats was not studied.

Antarctica—Overwintering

Life on "The Ice" (Palinkas, 1990) is fraught with risks associated with the extreme environment, especially over the astral winter. "The Antarctic plateau is more similar in climate to Mars than to the rest of the earth. It is a frozen desert, much above 10,000 feet, where little in the way of natural life forms can exist" (Grant, 2009). Presently, 47 stations are operated by 20 nations. Station populations range from 14 to 1,100 in the summer and 10 to 250 over the winter (March to September) (Antarctica, Web site). Crewmembers typically stay for one year. The stations are physically isolated; during the winter months there is no possibility of quick rescue because flights cannot get in or out due to weather conditions. Communications with family and normal support networks are limited due to satellite coverage. Winters are dark all the time—hence artificial day-night cycles. The environment is physically stressful, with high altitude (the South Pole Station is at 2,835 meters or 9,300 feet), extreme light-dark cycles, low humidity, and extreme cold (some outdoors work must be done, even in winter). Life at the stations is confined: Personnel are in constant contact with other crewmembers, as in space and submarines; there is a lack of privacy, monotony, social conflicts, and gossip, with no escape.

These conditions are associated with a "winter-over syndrome" (Strange & Youngman, 1971) characterized by varying degrees of depression, irritability, hostility, insomnia, and cognitive impairment, specifically concentration and memory problems, absentmindedness, and mild hypnotic states known as long-eye or the Antarctic stare (Palinkas, Gunderson, Johnson, & Holland, 2000). This syndrome is similar to seasonal affective disorder. About 5% of wintering-over crewmembers exhibit psychiatric symptoms, which is about the same as in the general population.

Adjustment in part is related to the station's social structure, which has been found to vary across years. Significantly higher levels of anger-hostility, depression, and tension-anxiety were evident in crews characterized by a clique structure based on members' interests. The highest adjustment was observed in teams with a core-periphery structure; that is, most members identified with the team core, while others had close ties to the core but were somewhat more independent (Palinkas et al., 2000).

Leadership was a primary factor in maintaining team cohesion (Schmidt, Wood, & Lugg, 2004; Wood et al., 2005).

Empirical data on the cognitive effects of the astral winter are lacking, especially with respect to decision making. Only self-reports of cognitive impairment, specifically concentration and memory problems, absentmindedness, and mild hypnotic states are available, along with leader and peer ratings (Palinkas et al., 2000). Decision making data are needed because of the physiological responses that are common to Antarctic winters: complete absence of stage 4 sleep, reductions in stage 3 and REM sleep, and disruption of circadian rhythms. Decision making following sleep deprivation in normal environments is characterized by increased risk taking (Harrison & Horne, 2000), underweighting of new information when updating beliefs (Dickinson & Drummond, 2008), rigidity of thinking, and perseverative errors (Harrison & Horne, 1999). These phenomena have been associated with plan continuation errors in aviation accidents (Berman, 1995; Orasanu, Martin, & Davison, 2002).

Mountain Climbing

High-altitude mountaineering exposes humans to certain threats similar to those in space, primarily hypoxia and radiation, which are also of concern to military pilots. The effects of low oxygen levels on the brain, compounded by the effects of sleep deprivation, compromise the ability of even experienced, expert climbers to adjust to changing conditions, to the point of disaster. Problems in motor coordination and personality shifts can also occur. Similar brain damage can result from sustained exposure to radiation in space or on the lunar surface. Everest thus can serve as an analog to study these effects and to develop monitoring techniques that would provide timely alerts to these physiologic and judgmental problems.

While excellent physical conditioning, skill, and experience are essential for successful mountaineering, equally important are teamwork, leadership, cohesion, and trust among the climbing team members. The importance of team support is evident in the case of David Sharp, who had chosen to climb Mt. Everest solo without any support. When he got into trouble 450 meters below the summit of Everest, other climbers failed to assist him, assuming that he was from another party. Another factor was the risk entailed by a rescue attempt, given the exhaustion, lack of strength, and limited oxygen supplies of other climbers (http://en.wikipedia.org/wiki/Everest:_Beyond_the_Limit).

The mountain climbing literature provides many examples of climbers exhibiting poor judgment in deciding to push on toward the summit in the face of delays, injuries, exhaustion, and weather uncertainties. The first-person journalistic account of the disastrous 1996 Everest climbing season, *Into Thin Air* (Krakauer, 1997), illustrates the confluence of factors that contributed to the loss of 12 climbers, the worst since record keeping began 75 years earlier.

Decision Making at Altitude   Perhaps the most mystifying issue in the reported expedition is how one extremely respected and highly experienced expedition leader could fail to adhere to his own golden rule—setting a "bingo time" at which the group would turn back if conditions indicated it would be risky to press on. "Hall's obligatory turn-around time had come and gone a full two hours earlier. Given the guide's conservative, exceedingly methodical nature, many of his colleagues have expressed puzzlement at this uncharacteristic lapse of judgment. Why, they wondered, didn't he turn Hansen around much lower on the mountain, as soon as it became obvious that the American climber was running late?" (Krakauer, 1997, p. 293). The same climber had reached the South Summit the previous year, but had been turned around by the same leader for safety reasons. The leader had encouraged him to join this year's expedition to try again, and so may have felt an obligation to deliver the summit on this mission—despite violating his own safety rule. Unfortunately, both of these men were among the fatalities of this expedition.

The decision-making pattern exhibited by the Everest expedition leader described by Krakauer is similar to what has been observed in aviation, termed plan continuation errors, or failure to change a planned course of action in the face of changing conditions (Berman, 1995; Dismukes, Berman, & Loukopoulos, 2007; Orasanu et al., 2002). At this point we do not have a satisfactory explanation for why these decision errors occur. They tend to be associated with ambiguous operational conditions that are changing dynamically, such as deteriorating weather. They also appear to be associated with underlying goal conflicts: to continue the planned course and get the passengers to their destination on time, even if that means taking a risk, or to take a more conservative course of action that may result in delay and inconvenience for the passengers and cost the company money. Kahneman and Tversky (1984) introduced the notion of "framing," which maps onto this pattern of decision: the conservative course of action is associated with a sure loss (money, passenger ire), while the original course of action is associated with a possible (but not certain) loss (an incident or accident). Loss frames have been associated with increased risk taking.

While the above explanation may account for plan continuation events in aviation and some mountaineering accidents, it is not clear that the same explanation holds for climbers on Everest. Research conducted by Lieberman and colleagues (Lieberman, Kanki, & Protopapas, 1995; Lieberman, Kanki, Protopapas, Reed, & Youngs, 1994; Lieberman, Morey, Hochstadt, Larson, & Mather, 2005) focuses on the role of hypobaric hypoxia on decision making and other cognitive processes.

Hypoxia in Mountain Climbing   Some background information on current views on the brain bases of motor control, thinking, and emotion may serve to explain the effects on performance from the stressors that can occur in extreme environments. The brain no longer is viewed as a conventional computer in which one module controls language, another controls motor responses, while yet another module controls emotion. Rather, independent studies that used different techniques show that the neural bases of motor control, cognition, and other aspects of complex behavior lie not in separate cortical regions but in the linkage of different regions—not only in the cortex—to form larger circuits. Distinct parts of the brain do have different local functions. Separate regions, for example, process stimuli in particular sensory modalities, while others perform operations that regulate aspects of motor control (e.g., coding direction), hold information in working memory, and so on. But each local operation constitutes only a subcomponent of a neural circuit that regulates a complex process such as understanding the meaning of a sentence, or striking a particular key on a computer keyboard. Moreover, a neuroanatomical structure responsible for a particular local operation generally comprises many anatomically segregated groups of neurons. These neuronal populations project to segregated populations in other structures and jointly form a neural circuit. This organization allows a given structure (or set of structures) to carry out a local operation that is part of the set of local operations in different neural circuits that execute seemingly unrelated acts. The "syndromes" that follow from brain damage often reflect the contribution of a local operation performed in a damaged neural structure to different complex behaviors.

Hypoxia, the oxygen deficit resulting from breathing air at the extreme altitudes encountered on Mt. Everest, poses a serious problem. Hypoxia can result in permanent damage to the basal ganglia, subcortical structures of the brain (e.g., Cavaletti, Moroni, Garavaglia, & Tredici, 1987). Recent studies employing MRIs of persons who suffered extreme hypoxic damage at high altitudes show bilateral lesions in the globus pallidus, the principal output structure of the basal ganglia (Jeong, Kwon, Chin, Yoon, & Na, 2002; Swaminath et al., 2006; Wang et al., 2005). It has been evident for more than two decades that compromised basal ganglia activity can result in deficits in motor control, emotion, attention, comprehending the meaning of sentences, and providing cognitive flexibility—manifested in changing the direction of a thought process or plan of action when circumstances dictate (cf. Cummings, 1993; Graybiel, 1997; Lieberman et al., 1994). The basal ganglia also interrupt normally continuous sequences when circumstances demand. Moreover, the basal ganglia support neural circuits involved in sequencing and shifting similar cognitive subelements of language and thought. The basal ganglia complex is not the "seat" of motor behavior or cognition; rather, it releases and inhibits pattern generators that specify the subelements of motor acts and mental processes, including linguistic operations, to different regions of the cortex (e.g., ventrolateral prefrontal and dorsolateral prefrontal cortex) (e.g., Graybiel, 1997; Lieberman et al., 1995; Marsden & Obeso, 1994).

Basal ganglia dysfunction undoubtedly has been a factor in many of the fatal incidents on Everest. Climbers are unable or unwilling to adapt to weather or snow conditions. In the course of the Lieberman Everest study (Lieberman et al., 1994), one tragic instance occurred. When we obtained baseline data at Base Camp (5,300 meters) for one young male climber, his computer-derived speech measures were normal and his cognitive set-shifting performance (the ability to change the direction of a thought process) was error-free. We used the odd-man-out test, a standard psychometric tool to assess his ability to form a cognitive category and then shift to a different category. Two days later, after he had ascended 1,000 meters higher to Camp 2, his speech resembled that of subjects who had bilateral lesions in the caudate nucleus and putamin (major basal ganglia structures). His performance was marked by extreme cognitive perseveration: He had extreme difficulty changing the direction of a thought process. His error rates, when he had to shift the criterion for sorting images from size to shape or from shape to size, exceeded 40% and were in the range seen in serious cases of Parkinson's disease (Flowers & Robertson, 1985). The climber insisted on following his original climbing plan to Camp 3, although the weather had dramatically worsened. Other climbers instead changed their plans and descended back to Base Camp. Despite our advising him that he was impaired, he ascended to Camp 3 alone.

On attempting to descend he apparently was unable to maintain the sequence of fastening and unfastening the two carabiners (snap links) that attached his climbing harness to the fixed ropes that run from Camp 2 to Camp 3 and fell to his death. Researchers were unable to directly intervene in this instance because tests are administered using VHF radio links from Base Camp to Camps 2 and 3. In subsequent years, subjects generally heeded researchers' warnings.

Lieberman and colleagues found that they could monitor cognitive deficits by means of a speech measure that can potentially be incorporated into on-line systems. Computer-implemented speech analysis showed that slower speech, discerned by subtle increases in vowel duration that are not audible, co-occurred with deficits in understanding the meaning of a sentence or changing the direction of a thought process. The correlation between average duration of vowels and response time in a sentence comprehension test was $r = 0.70$, $p = 0.03$ (Figure 1.2) (Lieberman et al., 2005).

The technique that Lieberman and colleagues explored in the extreme environment of Everest does not replace expert knowledge and judgments of hypoxia effects based on experience. It could provide a timely warning of an environmental stressor that clouds these abilities. Other applications include aviation where hypoxic incidents have occurred over the past century and in the extreme environments encountered by astronauts. Missions in deep space and on the lunar surface can result in radiation damage to the basal ganglia and other components of the brain's dopaminergic system, which are particularly sensitive to heavy particle radiation (Rabin, Joseph, & Shukitt-Hale, 2003; Vasquez, 2005). A recent study of the effects of exposure to high-energy ionizing radiation suggests that narrowing of the vasculature occurs, impeding oxygen transfer in the brain (Grabham, Hu, Jenkins, & Gerard, 2007), which may explain the sensitivity of the metabolically active basal ganglia structures of the human brain to radiation damage.

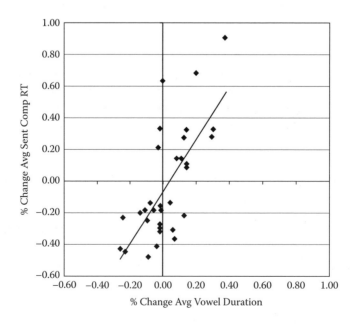

FIGURE 1.2   Change in average vowel duration versus change in sentence comprehension response times.

Lieberman's work highlights the value of monitoring tools that can detect danger-ous neurological states that may interfere with safe judgment and performance. It also increases the generalizability of findings across extreme environments by pro-viding a theoretical foundation that explains the mechanism underlying the cogni-tive deficits. This work serves as a model for examining underlying mechanisms in other extreme environments.

Research Challenges

Individual Differences in Vulnerability to Stress Effects

In all of the extreme environments studied, some individuals are more vulnerable than others to the stresses of the environment, especially over a longer duration. These individual neurobehavioral adjustment issues range from deterioration of mood, loss of vigor, loneliness, and withdrawal to clinically significant depression or other psy-chiatric problems requiring medical intervention. While current astronaut selection procedures aim to "select out" individuals who are more likely to experience these neurobehavioral adjustment problems, knowledge currently is lacking on predictors of who will best adapt to the rigors of a three-year Mars mission.

Research on submariners shows that prior stress exposure, interpersonal attitudes, and routine problem-oriented coping strategies accounted for individuals' ability to maintain well-being during the isolation and confinement of nuclear submarine mis-sions, as well as the acute stress of serious accidents. Research on decision making in the space simulation EXEMSI revealed that while some individuals applied a com-pensatory strategy for maintaining performance levels, others did not (Hockey & Sauer, 1996). Individual differences in vulnerability to sleep deprivation have been recently discovered. A small fraction of the population appears to be able to main-tain high levels of performance with amounts of sleep that lead most people to sig-nificant decrements in alertness and errors (van Dongen, Vitellaro, & Dinges, 2005). Similar observations have been reported for military personnel who were exposed to extremes during training (e.g., continuous operations entailing sleep loss, food depri-vation, cold, high-altitude training).

Resilience in the face of acute stress in many environments, including capsules, depends on cognitive appraisal, that is, how one perceives the situation—as a prob-lem to be solved or as a threat (Tomaka, Blascovich, Kelsey, & Leitten, 1993). The generality of conclusions about individual resilience factors is difficult to determine because investigators working in different extreme environments do not use a com-mon set of research instruments and participant characteristics may vary (Sandal, 2000). In addition, individuals' reactions may be influenced by the social and lead-ership structure of their team (Neubert, 1999; Pearce & Sims, 2002; Schmidt et al., 2004; Wood et al., 2005), their training and skill level, the duration of exposure to the extreme environment, task characteristics, and the severity of the stressors (Paulus et al., 2009).

Indirect Effects on Decision Making

Individual psychosocial or behavioral health decrements or interpersonal tensions can influence crew decision making indirectly by disrupting individual information processing or effective teamwork skills, including team collaboration, cooperation, and monitoring/backup behaviors. In extreme environments, "the safety of each person is dependent on others in the group, necessitating highly adaptive group functioning and optimal behavioral health" (Sandal, Leon, & Palinkas, 2006, p. 282). In all of the extreme environments described in this chapter, mission success depends on effective teamwork. Critical mission tasks are sufficiently complex that a single crewmember cannot accomplish them. Even EVA tasks on the ISS involve two crewmembers: one who performs the task and a second crewmember who reviews the procedure and monitors its execution with the operator. Lunar surface missions will require pairs of astronauts who undertake exploration sorties away from the base while another crewmember monitors their performance and maintains communication with them.

The second finding across studies of many extreme environments is that interpersonal tensions are likely to emerge, resulting in crew conflicts, cliques and isolated members, competition for dominance, and various annoyances. Sustained close personal contact with other individuals, in particular, can be extremely stressful; this condition is exacerbated by additional sources of stress, such as danger, time pressure, equipment malfunctions, and high workloads (or conversely, boredom). The stress is cumulative; behavioral consequences are to be expected if there is no way available to eliminate the source of stress, for example, by removing oneself from the group temporarily. It is impossible to get away from one's comrades when living in isolation and confinement. Clearly, this is what cosmonaut Valery Ryumin meant when he wrote, "All the conditions necessary for murder are met if you shut two men in a cabin measuring 18 feet by 20 and leave them together for two months" (Ryumin, 1980, quoted in Stuster, 1996, p. 165).

These threats to team cohesion, both social and task related, may thus have significant consequences for the safety of the crew and successful completion of mission tasks. Principles of effective teamwork identified in team research over the past two decades emphasize team processes: communication to build shared situation models and to collaborate in solving problems, development of joint plans, task priorities, monitoring and backing up teammates, adjusting workload as needed, and building a sense of trust in each other (Burke, Stagl, Salas, Pierce, & Kendall, 2006; Entin & Serfaty, 1999; Mathieu, Heffner, Goodwin, Salas, & Cannon-Bowers, 2000; Orasanu & Fischer, 1992; Salas, Sims, & Burke, 2005). Communication reinforces social relationships as well as contributing to task performance. Active participation by all team members is a mark of good team cohesion and is associated with effective performance (Fischer, McDonnell, & Orasanu, 2007).

Crew errors stemming from poor communication and coordination of resources led to a number of aviation crashes in the 1970s, leading to the development of crew resource management (CRM) training for aviation. Now, as more people choose to work or play in various extreme environments, this need for training once again becomes paramount. Unfortunately, for many extreme environments, such as long-duration space missions, the basis for predicting specific crew vulnerabilities is limited by the absence of empirical knowledge.

For long-duration missions to Mars, mission planners, system designers, and the crew office responsible for selecting, composing, and training space and ground support teams do not have a robust empirical database to draw upon. A large body of scientific literature exists on human performance under stress (Hockey, 1979, 1986), behaviors that support effective team decision making (Cannon-Bowers & Salas, 1998), teamwork and interpersonal processes (Salas et al., 2005), and how individuals cope with the stressors of other extreme environments (Kanas & Manzey, 2003; Sandal et al., 2006). Analogs provide lessons, but even those data are limited in their commonality with space on a number of dimensions: the environment itself, the habitat, the duration of the missions, crew characteristics, training protocols, procedures, job and decision supports, and operations (Sandal, 2000). Even environments that have been studied extensively, like Antarctica, do not yield clear findings. A recent meta-analysis to understand the effects of overwintering on human adaptation was terminated because essential data were not available from the pool of studies (Shea, Slack, Keeton, Leveton, & Palinkas, 2009). In sum, much of the research conducted to date in extreme environments informs us about what is *not* known rather than providing clear answers.

Conclusions

Empirical data are needed on the impacts of various extreme environments on individual cognitive functioning, psychosocial adjustment, team interactions, and decision making during both nominal and challenging scenarios. These should be related to performance on naturalistic decision tasks that vary in degree of familiarity, complexity, time pressure, and goal conflicts. Individual differences in vulnerability and resiliency factors must be identified, along with effective coping strategies that can be trained. Environmental factors that influence neuropsychological mechanisms underlying components of decision-making processes need to be better understood. These include mechanisms related to, for example, hypoxia, emotion, and sleep deprivation. Tools for monitoring individual and team functional capabilities will be needed, along with supports and countermeasures to maintain both crew performance and well-being.

What is clear from studies in analog environments is that each offers specific advantages and limitations. None is complete as an analog to any environment of interest, such as a three-year mission to Mars in an inhospitable world. NASA has undertaken to develop a framework for evaluating the utility and appropriateness of various analogs based on their characteristics and relations to knowledge gaps—and hence to the purpose of conducting a research study (Keeton, 2009). The importance of features of the environment in shaping naturalistic decision making has been raised since the first efforts to define the nature of NDM (Orasanu & Connolly, 1993), and has repeatedly emerged in discussions of the validity of using laboratory environments to study naturalistic decision processes (Cannon-Bowers, Salas, & Pruitt, 1996). The bottom line is what can be learned from diverse sources. Multimethod approaches in multiple environments promise to yield complementary knowledge and fuller understanding.

Acknowledgments

Preparation of this chapter was supported by the NASA Behavioral Health and Performance Element of the Human Research Program.

References

AGARD (1989). *Human performance assessment methods (AGARDograph 308)*. Neuilly-sur-Seine, France: AGARD.

Antarctica. http://www.usap.gov/

Berg, J. S., Grieger, T. A., & Spira, J. L. (2005). Psychiatric symptoms and cognitive appraisal following the near sinking of a research submarine. *Military Medicine, 170*(1), 44–47.

Berman, B. (1995). Flightcrew errors and the contexts in which they occurred: 37 major U.S. air carrier accidents. In *Proceedings of the 8th International Symposium on Aviation Psychology* (pp. 1291–1294). Columbus, OH: Ohio State University.

Burke, C. S., Stagl, K. C., Salas, E., Pierce, L., & Kendall, D. (2006). Understanding team adaptation: A conceptual analysis and model. *Journal of Applied Psychology, 91*(6), 1189–1207.

Burrough, B. (1998). *Dragonfly: An epic adventure of survival in outer space*. New York, NY: HarperCollins.

Cannon-Bowers, J. A., & Salas, E. (1998). Individual and team decision making under stress: Theoretical underpinnings. In J. A. Cannon-Bowers & E. Salas (Eds.), *Making decisions under stress: Implications for individual and team training* (pp. 17–38). Washington, DC: American Psychological Association.

Cannon-Bowers, J. A., Salas, E., & Pruitt, J. S. (1996). Establishing the boundaries of a paradigm for decision-making research. *Human Factors, 38*(2), 193–205.

Cavaletti, G., Moroni, R., Garavaglia, P., & Tredici, G. (1987). Brain damage after high-altitude climbs without oxygen. *Lancet, 1*(8525), 101.

Cummings, J. L. (1993). Frontal-subcortical circuits and human behavior. *Archives of Neurology, 50*(8), 873–880.

Dickinson, D. L., & Drummond, S. P. A. (2008). The effects of total sleep deprivation on Bayesian updating. *Judgment and Decision Making, 3*(2), 181–190.

Dismukes, R. K., Berman, B. A., & Loukopoulos, L. D. (2007). *The limits of expertise: Rethinking pilot error and the causes of airline accidents*. Aldershot, England: Ashgate Publishing.

Entin, E. E., & Serfaty, D. (1999). Adaptive team coordination. *Human Factors, 41*, 312–325.

ESA (2009). http://esa-mm.esa.int/SPECIALS/Mars500/SEMIS47CTWF_0.html (downloaded May 25, 2010).

Fischer, U., McDonnell, L., & Orasanu, J. (2007). Linguistic correlates of team performance: Toward a tool for monitoring team functioning during space missions. *Aviation, Space, and Environmental Medicine, 78*(5), B86–B95.

Flowers, K. A., & Robertson, C. (1985). The effect of Parkinson's disease on the ability to maintain a mental set. *Journal of Neurology, Neurosurgery, and Psychiatry, 48*(6), 517–529.

Grabham, P., Hu, B., Jenkins, G., & Gerard, C. (2007, July). *Space ionizing radiation effects on tube formation by endothelial cells cultured in 3-dimensional collagen matrices*. Poster presented at the 18th Annual NASA Space Radiation Investigators Workshop, Rohnert Park, CA.

Grant, I. C. (2009). Medicine at the ends of the earth: The Antarctic. In A. H. Buma et al. (eds.), *Conflict and catastrophe medicine, Second edition* (pp. 107–113). London: Springer-Verlag.

Graybiel, A. M. (1997). The basal ganglia and cognitive pattern generators. *Schizophrenia Bulletin, 23*(3), 459–469.

Harrison, A. A. (2001). *Spacefaring: The human dimension.* Berkeley, CA: University of California Press.

Harrison, Y., & Horne, J. A. (1999). One night of sleep loss impairs innovative thinking and flexible decision making. *Organizational Behavior and Human Decision Process, 78*(2), 128–145.

Harrison, Y., & Horne, J. A. (2000). The impact of sleep deprivation on decision making: A review. *Journal of Experimental Psychology Applied, 6*(3), 236–249.

Hockey, G. R. J. (1979). Stress and the cognitive components of skilled performance. In V. Hamilton & D. M. Warburton (Eds.), *Human stress and cognition: An information-processing approach.* Chichester, England: Wiley.

Hockey, G. R. J. (1986). Changes in operator efficiency as a function of environmental stress, fatigue, and circadian rhythms. In K. R. Boff, L. Kaufman, & J. P. Thomas (Eds.), *Handbook of perception and human performance.* New York, NY: Wiley/Interscience.

Hockey, G. R. J., & Sauer, J. (1996). Cognitive fatigue and complex decision making under prolonged isolation and confinement. In S. L. Bonting (Ed.), *Advances in space biology and medicine* (Vol. 5, pp. 309–330). Greenwich, CT: JAI Press.

HPEE. http://www.hpee.org/main/page_about_hpee_statement_of_purpose.html

Jeong, J. H., Kwon, J. C., Chin, J. H., Yoon, S. J., & Na, D. L. (2002). Globus pallidus lesions associated with high mountain climbing. *Journal of Korean Medical Science, 17,* 861–863.

Kahneman, D., & Tversky, A. (1984). Choices, values, and frames. *American Psychologist, 34*(4), 341–350.

Kanas, N., & Manzey, D. (2003). *Space psychology and psychiatry.* El Segundo, CA: Microcosm Press.

Kanas, N., Salnitskiy, V., Grund, E. M., Weiss, D. S., Gushin, V., Kozerenko, O., . . . Marmar, C. R. (2001a). Human interactions during shuttle/Mir space missions. *Acta Astronautica, 48*(2–12), 777–784.

Kanas, N., Salnitskiy, V., Grund, E. M., Weiss, D. S., Gushin, V., Kozerenko, O., . . . Marmar, C. R. (2001b). Human interactions in space: Results from shuttle/Mir. *Acta Astronautica, 49*(3–10), 243–260.

Kanas, N., Salnitskiy, V., Gushin, V., Kozerenko, O., Sled, A., Bostrom, A., . . . Marmar, C. R. (2001c). Crewmember and ground personnel interactions over time during shuttle/Mir space missions. *Aviation, Space, and Environmental Medicine, 72,* 453–461.

Keeton, K. (2009). *Analog assessment tool.* Presentation to the NASA Behavioral Health and Performance Working Group, Houston, TX, Aug 12–14, 2009.

Krakauer, J. (1997). *Into thin air: A personal account of the Mt. Everest disaster.* New York, NY: Villard.

Lebedev, V. (1988). *Diary of a cosmonaut: 211 days in space.* College Station, TX: Phytoresource Research Information Service.

Lieberman, P., Kanki, B. G., & Protopapas, A. (1995). Speech production and cognitive decrements on Mount Everest. *Aviation, Space, and Environmental Medicine, 66,* 857–864.

Lieberman, P., Kanki, B. G., Protopapas, A., Reed, E., & Youngs, J. W. (1994). Cognitive defects at altitude. *Nature, 372,* 325.

Lieberman, P., Morey, A., Hochstadt, J. E., Larson, M., & Mather, S. (2005). Mount Everest: A space-analog for speech monitoring of cognitive deficits and stress. *Aviation, Space, and Environmental Medicine, 76*(6), B198–207.

Manzey, D., & Lorenz, B. (1998). Mental performance during short-term and long-term space-flight. *Brain Research Reviews, 28*, 215–221.

Marsden, C. D., & Obeso, J. A. (1994). The functions of the basal ganglia and the paradox of stereotaxic surgery in Parkinson's disease. *Brain: A Journal of Neurology, 117*(Pt. 4), 877–897.

Mathieu, J. E., Heffner, T. S., Goodwin, G. F., Salas, E., & Cannon-Bowers, J. A. (2000). The influence of shared mental models on team process and performance. *Journal of Applied Psychology, 85*(2), 273–283.

Mollicone, D. J., Van Dongen, H. P. A., Rogers, N. L., & Dinges, D. F. (2008). Response surface mapping of neurobehavioral performance: Testing the feasibility of split sleep schedules for space operations. *Acta Astronautica, 63*(7–10), 833–840.

Nechaev, A.P. (2001). Work and rest planning as a way of crew member error management. *Acta Astronautica, 49*, 271–278.

Neubert, M. J. (1999). Too much of a good thing or the more the merrier? Exploring the dispersion and gender composition of informal leadership in manufacturing teams. *Small Group Research, 30*(5), 635–646.

Orasanu, J., & Connolly, T. (1993). The reinvention of decision making. In G. Klein, J. Orasanu, R. Calderwood, & C. E. Zsambok (Eds.), *Decision making in action: Models and methods* (pp. 3–20). Norwood, NJ: Ablex Publishing Corporation.

Orasanu, J., & Fischer, U. (1992). Team cognition in the cockpit: Linguistic control of shared problem solving. In *Proceedings of the Fourteenth Annual Conference of the Cognitive Science Society* (pp. 189–194). Hillsdale, NJ: Erlbaum.

Orasanu, J., Martin, L., & Davison, J. (2002). Cognitive and contextual factors in aviation accidents: Decision errors. In E. Salas & G. Klein (Eds.), *Linking expertise and naturalistic decision making* (pp. 209–226). Mahwah, NJ: Erlbaum.

Palinkas, L. A. (1990). Psychosocial effects of adjustment in Antarctica—Lessons for long-duration spaceflight. *Journal of Spacecraft and Rockets, 27*(5), 471–477.

Palinkas, L. A., Gunderson, E. K. E., Johnson, J. C., & Holland, A. W. (2000). Behavior and performance on long-duration space-flights: Evidence from analogue environments. *Aviation, Space, and Environmental Medicine, 71* (9, Suppl.), A29–A36.

Paulus, M. P., Potterat, E. G., Taylor, M. K., van Orden, K. F., Bauman, J., Momen, N., … Swain, J. L. (2009). A neuroscience approach to optimizing brain resources for human performance in extreme environments. *Neuroscience and Biobehavioral Reviews, 33*(7), 1080–1088.

Pearce, C. L., & Sims, H. P. (2002). Vertical versus shared leadership as predictors of the effectiveness of change management teams: An examination of aversive, directive, transactional, transformational, and empowering leader behaviors. *Group Dynamics: Theory, Research, and Practice, 6*(2), 172–197.

Rabin, B. M., Joseph, J. A., & Shukitt-Hale, B. (2003). Heavy particle irradiation, neurochemistry and behavior: Thresholds, dose-response curves and recovery of function. *Advances in Space Research, 33*, 1330–1333.

Salas, E., Sims, D. E., & Burke, C. S. (2005). Is there a 'big five' in teamwork? *Small Group Research, 36*(5), 555–599.

Sandal, G. M. (2000). Coping in Antarctica: Is it possible to generalize results across settings. *Aviation, Space, and Environmental Medicine, 71*, A37–A43.

Sandal, G. M. (2004). Culture and tension during an international space station simulation: Result from SFINCSS '99. *Aviation, Space, and Environmental Medicine, 75*(7), C44–C51.

Sandal, G. M., Endresen, I. M., Vaernes, R., & Ursin, H. (1999). Personality and coping strategies during submarine missions. *Military Psychology, 11*, 381–404.

Sandal, G. M., Leon, G. R., & Palinkas, L. (2006). Human challenges in polar and space environments. *Review of Environment Science & Biotechnology*, 5, 281–296.

Sauer, J., Wastell, D., & Hockey, G. R. J. (1997). Skill maintenance in extended spaceflight: A human factors analysis of space and analogue work environments. *Acta Astronautica*, 39(8), 579–587.

Schmidt, L. L., Wood, J., & Lugg, D. J. (2004). Team climate at Antarctic research stations 1996–2000: Leadership matters. *Aviation, Space, and Environmental Medicine*, 75(8), 681–687.

Sells, S. B. (1973). The taxonomy of man in enclosed space. In J. E. Rasmussen (Ed.), *Man in isolation and confinement* (pp. 280–303). Chicago: Aldine.

Shea, C., Slack, K. J., Keeton, K. E., Leveton, L., & Palinkas, L. A. (2009). *Antarctica Meta-Analysis: Psychosocial Factors Related to Long Duration Isolation and Confinement.* Poster presented at the NASA Human Research Program Investigators' Workshop, Houston, TX, February 2–4, 2009.

Strange, R. E., & Youngman, S. A. (1971). Emotional aspects of wintering over. *Antarctic Journal of the U.S.*, 6(6), 255–257.

Stuster, J. (1996). *Bold endeavors: Lessons from polar and space exploration.* Annapolis, MD: Naval Institute Press.

Suedfeld, P. (2005). Invulnerability, coping, salutogenesis, integration: Four phases of space psychology. *Aviation, Space, and Environmental Medicine*, 76(6), B61–B73.

Swaminath, P. V., Ragothaman, M., Muthane, U. B., Udupa, S. A. H., Rao, S. L., & Giovindappa, S. S. (2006). Parkinsonism and personality changes following an acute hypoxic insult during mountaineering. *Movement Disorders*, 21, 1296–1297.

Tomaka, J., Blascovich, J., Kelsey, R. M., & Leitten, C. L. (1993). Subjective, physiological, and behavioral effects of threat and challenge appraisal. *Journal of Personality and Social Psychology*, 65, 248–260.

van Dongen, H. P. A., Vitellaro, K. M., & Dinges, D. F. (2005). Individual differences in adult human sleep and wakefulness: Leitmotif for a research agenda. *Sleep*, 28(4), 479–496.

Vasquez, M. (2005). *Hazards of the deep: Killing the dragons: Neurobiological consequences of space radiation exposure.* Paper presented at 401st Brookhaven Lecture, Brookhaven National Library, February 15, 2005. Retrieved from http://real.bnl.gov/ramgen/bnl/Vasquez.rm

Wang, J., Rao, H., Wetmore, G. S., Furlan, P. M., Korczykowski, M., Dinges, D. F., & Detre, J. A. (2005). Perfusion functional MRI reveals cerebral blood flow patterns under psychological stress. *PNAS*, 102(49), 17804–17809.

Wood, J., Schmidt, L. L., Lugg, D. J., Ayton, J., Phillips, T., & Shepanek, M. (2005). Life, survival, and behavioral health in small closed communities: 10 years of studying isolated Antarctic groups. *Aviation, Space, and Environmental Medicine*, 76(6), B89–B93.

2

Expert Cognition and Sensemaking in the Global Organization Leadership Context
A Case Study

Joyce Osland
San José State University

Globalization and the proliferation of global problems have resulted in greater attention to the growing field of global leadership (GL). In business, the need for increased flexibility and responsiveness has created more networked firms in which not only senior management but also employees farther down the hierarchy perform GL activities related to, for example, global products or project teams or a global supply chain (Osland, Taylor, & Mendenhall, 2009). The scope, importance, and extent of GL are growing in most multinational corporations (MNCs), and developing global leaders is a high priority (Gregersen, Morrison, & Black, 1998; Mendenhall, Jensen, Gregersen, & Black, 2003; Suutari, 2002). Businesses have reported a shortage of global leaders (Gregersen et al., 1998; Charan, Drotter, & Noel, 2001; Mercer Delta, 2006). A Rand Corporation study predicted a future shortage of global leaders in the for-profit, public, and nonprofit sectors (Bikson, Treverton, Moini, & Lindstrom, 2003).

The need for global leadership is better understood than the construct itself, which has no universally accepted definition. This chapter relies on Bird's definition of global leaders as "individuals who effect significant positive change in organizations by building communities through the development of trust and the arrangement of organizational structures and processes in a context involving multiple stakeholders, multiple sources of external authority, and multiple cultures under conditions of temporal, geographical and cultural complexity" (Osland, Bird, Oddou, & Osland, 2007b, p. 2).

Global leaders deal with employees and stakeholders from a range of countries with distinct business and cultural practices. Unlike expatriates who may develop leadership expertise one country at a time, global leaders seldom have the time or luxury to learn about and understand each country and its culture in depth. The complexity of the global context in which they work forces them to develop what can be called metalevel leadership and cultural competencies. These seem to exceed the competencies required in most domestic or expatriate settings (Osland et al., 2009) and constitute an important aspect of expert cognition in global leaders.

This chapter briefly reviews the global leadership literature and presents a case study that typifies how global leaders adapt to the demands of a complex global context and demonstrate expert cognition. It concludes with implications for future research and practice.

Literature Review

Global leadership is a relatively young field of research. To date, there are only 15 empirical studies of GL and its development (for reviews, see Hollenbeck, 2001; Mendenhall, 2001; Suutari, 2002; Jokinen, 2005; Osland, Bird, Mendenhall, & Osland, 2006; Osland, 2008b). Only one study (McCall and Hollenbeck, 2002) used GL effectiveness as a primary selection criteria in determining their sample.* Samples in other studies failed to distinguish between global managers and global leaders and, in some cases, collected opinions from people who were not themselves in global leadership positions. Thus, one of the flaws in some GL research has been a failure to identify and study successful global leaders—that is, experts.

The extant research has focused primarily on determining the right set of GL competencies (e.g., Lobel, 1990; Black, Morrison, & Gregersen, 1999; Ket de Vries & Florent-Treacy, 1999; Rosen, Digh, Singer, & Philips, 2000; Adler, 2001; McCall and Hollenbeck, 2002; Bikson et al., 2003; Goldsmith, Greenberg, Robertson, & Hu-Chan, 2003; Kets de Vries, Vrignaud, & Florent-Treacy, 2004; Moro Bueno & Tubbs, 2004; Cohen, 2007). It is difficult to compare these studies or draw definitive conclusions because GL definitions and samples vary widely (Osland, 2008b). The resultant lists of competencies are overlapping and, according to Jokinen (2005), are distinguished at times only by semantic differences.

Three frameworks (Mendenhall & Osland, 2002; Jokinen, 2005; Osland, 2008b) have been created to organize the approximately 60 GL competencies found in the literature. There is some agreement that global leadership consists of core characteristics, context-specific abilities, and universal leadership skills (Osland, 2008b). These frameworks, however, do not convey the whole picture. There are still very important gaps in our understanding of GL, including whether all competencies are equally important in every global job and situation or whether all of them have to be mastered by global leaders. Only a handful of process models describe how global leaders interact with the environment (Lane, Maznevski, Mendenhall, & McNett, 2004; Osland & Bird, 2006; Beechler and Javidan, 2007), and none have been tested empirically. There is limited agreement and knowledge about the antecedents and outcomes of global leadership and how it develops.

No research has tested whether there are significant differences between global and domestic leadership, although some scholars (Osland & Bird, 2006; Osland, 2008a; Osland et al., 2009) make a conceptual argument for differences of degree and kind. They and others (Weber, Festing, Dowling, & Schuler, 1998) contend that it is primarily the greater complexity of the global context that shapes how global leaders think and behave. Osland and Bird argued that global leadership "differs from domestic leadership in degree in terms of issues related to connectedness, boundary spanning, complexity, ethical challenges, dealing with tensions and paradoxes, pattern

---

* Black, Morrison, and Gregersen's (1999) study also included some nominated global leaders who were viewed as effective by others.

recognition, and building learning environments, teams, and community and leading large-scale change efforts—across diverse cultures" (2006, p. 123).

To date, there have been no direct studies of GL cognition or behavior (Osland & Bird, 2006); only self-report measures have been used. There are obvious linkages between expert cognition and GL. One of the six dimensions Mendenhall and Osland identified in their reviews of the GL literature was cognitive orientation, which consists of environmental sensemaking, global mindset, thinking agility, improvisation, pattern recognition, cognitive complexity, cosmopolitanism, managing uncertainty, managing local versus global paradoxes, and behavioral flexibility resulting from situational analysis (Mendenhall & Osland, 2002; Osland, 2008b). Osland and Bird (2006) delineated the relationship between expert cognition and global leaders in the business field. Building on this work, this case study was designed as part of a larger research project (Osland et al., 2007b) that goes beyond a competency approach to study expert cognition in effective global leaders.

Methodology

Cognitive task analysis (CTA) was used in a case study of the cognitive perspective and process of an expert global leader. CTA focuses on complex cognitive phenomena in the work context (see Chapter 19), and differentiates experts from novices (cf. Hoffman, Crandall, & Shadbolt, 1998; Militello & Hutton, 1998; Crandall, Klein, & Hoffman, 2006). To develop an understanding of GL perspectives and processes, we used the critical incident technique (Flanagan, 1954) and hierarchical task analysis, as described in applied cognitive task analysis (ACTA; Militello & Hutton, 1998). The subject was first asked to describe "a difficult, complex global/international leadership incident involving change." Next, he was asked to "break this experience down into between 3–6 steps," and afterwards to "choose the steps that required difficult cognitive skills." We did not specify the nature of these steps because our goal was to identify how the subject thought about the incident. We then did a knowledge audit on the most complex step he identified by asking structured questions related to expert cognition. The subject also filled out a demographic survey on his educational background and cultural exposure. The interview lasted 2.5 hours and took place on two different occasions.

"Tom" was chosen as the subject of this case study from the sample of the larger study because his incident typifies the complexity faced by global leaders, and most of the strategies he used were also typical. Tom is an American white male in his late forties. An engineer by training, he spent most of his career working in the manufacturing side of the high-tech industry. He had no international experience, such as working or studying abroad; however, he worked for over twenty-five years in a very diverse setting and globalized industry. His company, jointly owned by firms with roots in different countries, had a multicultural senior management team. Tom met the study's selection criteria: "people whose records indicate (a) a global focus in their work; (b) documented success as a change agent; (c) a solid reputation as a leader in their organization's global operations; (d) 10 years of experience as a leader in their field; and (e) demonstrated intercultural competence." Tom was nominated by HR personnel, a consultant, and another global leader in his firm and then vetted by the research team to ensure that he met the selection criteria.

Case Description

Tom, a high-level manufacturing executive, was asked to solve his firm's biggest problem—he had to quickly find a technological solution to salvage a new product before its failure drove his high-tech company into bankruptcy. The new product had languished for a year and was needed urgently to keep the company from going under. Although not an expert in the principal problem domain—design and technology involving customer contact—Tom had a reputation for working across boundaries and pulling people together to accomplish difficult tasks. In this instance, his skill set allowed him to (1) assemble a large, effective global network of multifunctional and multicultural teams; (2) change the way hundreds of employees worked by breaking down departmental silos to work more collaboratively; (3) coordinate simultaneous experiments and prototype creations in various countries; (4) resolve a highly complex problem that involved a technological breakthrough in their industry; and (5) bring the resulting product to market very rapidly. This seven-month global change effort, described in greater detail below, fits our definition of what global leaders do.

Asked to identify the steps in his change incident, Tom noted that as an engineer he relied in large part on a fairly standard problem-solving process along with the social savvy he studied and honed over the years. Normally, the first three steps he identified would occur sequentially; due to the crisis, however, they happened concurrently during 18-hour days.

1. The first step was *gaining an understanding of stakeholder needs and acquiring a deep understanding of the technical problem.* The key stakeholders were company executives, and Tom clarified what they needed from him and also tried to manage down their expectations to a realistic level. Because he could not rely on his own intuition, he spoke with subject matter experts (SMEs) about the problem and solicited opinions about appropriate SMEs who would be able to add value to his own team, the primary task force composed of people from various disciplines and cultures.
2. Tom identified the second step as a *kick-off meeting* that allayed the team's fears, clarified and simplified how the problem was framed, and communicated that he was there to help. He worried that his previous introduction by the CEO as someone who was coming in "to whip them into shape" could harm his ability to work collaboratively with the core task force and might give them the unhelpful impression that they were "losers." In this step, he spent time rebuilding their confidence, clarifying his role, and building trust.
3. The third step was *figuring out the best resources to close the gaps in the problem.* This involved identifying ways to fix the gaps on the technical side as well as analyzing how the current team was functioning. Tom referred to his close observation of team dynamics in this stage as "fly on the wall."
4. In the fourth step, Tom *isolated the team to focus on solving the technological problem* and let others worry about the business ramifications. Given the primary task force's headquarters location and its criticality to the firm's survival, the executive team

had previously micromanaged them. Tom referred to this isolation as the "parenting effect," whereby he provided stability and buffered them by assuming the responsibility of communicating with the executive team and business leaders. Furthermore, he announced that the design team, which had been beaten up for lack of progress, would now be viewed not as the bad guys, but as the customers. "Everybody on this team is here for one purpose, and that is to serve the design team, because at the end of the day, they're the only ones that are going to fix this problem." Tom also helped the design team improve its interactions with other teams.

5. Because more brainpower was needed, the next step consisted of *adding new SMEs to an egalitarian team.* Tom made a point of setting egalitarian ground rules to manage the power differences in the room and gave everyone equal voice, regardless of their title. "We're not about rank, we're not about 'your idea, my idea is better', etc. . . . and that foundation was probably the single most important thing for the team." He held individual meetings with the new SMEs to clarify his expectations of their role before they joined up and to help them feel comfortable. Tom found and recruited one genius SME literally tucked away in the basement whose work on future technology had been ignored in the past. Although this SME was not used to working in a team environment with high-powered people, he soon became a superstar. As Tom commented, "You've got to water them [employees] and feed them fertilizer." Throughout the interview, Tom made frequent references to helping technical people develop their people skills.

6. The last step, which Tom called *assembling the team*, had a heavy emphasis on problem solving. Because this was, in his opinion, the most complex step and difficult task to manage for a novice global leader, it will be described in greater depth. This step consisted of breaking the problem into manageable subproblems, getting people to work across boundaries, brainstorming solutions, "combining and narrowing," expediting the most probable solutions, doing resource mapping, and implementing solutions. Tom quickly realized that the problem could not be solved using a historical, one-dimensional linear method; it required multidimensional thinking and parallel or concurrent generation of concepts, ideas, and solutions. He tried to teach this approach to other team members. In this stage, Tom's lack of technical expertise allowed him to play the "inquiring minds want to know" game and ask innumerable questions that helped identify inconsistencies in thinking and spurred creativity. He identified active listening as a key skill. "In this particular role, I did more listening than I had done in the previous 10 years." Because he was willing to ignore boundaries and kept asking questions, the team was pushed to develop a novel technical application that was formerly viewed as impossible, and they were able to create the manufacturing specifications in nine days rather than the usual three months.

One aspect of global leader expertise is understanding when constraints do and do not matter—and in particular, when culture does and does not matter. In this instance, Tom noted that he wanted to be respectful of the cultural differences on the global team, but he couldn't allow those differences to slow down the process in this crisis. For example, there were powerful cultural groups that desired more communication and consensus building than Tom had time for. Therefore, as a cultural compromise, he established a weekly communication briefing that incorporated their needs, explaining to executives from cultures wanting more involvement: "Look, this mission is critical. Time is the enemy. We're not about consensus [in this project]."

He assigned a lieutenant to listen to their concerns and tried to modify his communications to meet their concerns without allowing them to obstruct progress. It took courage to stand up and insist that the business imperative required ground rules that differed from the normal concern for cultural accommodation. While this may sound like a stereotypical brash American approach, Tom viewed his task and behavior in this critical incident as an exception. He was able to get away with less participation and consensus because he did in fact understand cultural differences and had earned global respect in his previous job. He could rely on the social capital he had acquired and his previous reputation as a collaborative leader to deviate from the decision-making norm. Had his previous reputation been that of an autocratic leader insensitive to cultural differences, his crisis-driven leadership style would have been less acceptable and understood. Generally, he described himself as a facilitator who listens carefully and then occasionally comes in with "Bam, we're doing this!" He referred to this as the good cop-bad cop within the same person—"When there is a moment of clarity, you just have to make the decision, which is not easy for everyone to do."

The most complex and challenging aspect of the last step involved the combining and narrowing of potential solutions—his perception of solution analysis. At this point, there was so much complexity that Tom resorted to hiring a program manager to keep track of details and communications and everything that he was monitoring. The team tried to combine suggested solutions and narrow down the list to the best solution. To take in the big picture amidst competing data and opinions from different company silos and combine them, Tom drew on his intuition, twenty-some years of experience, and capacity for multidimensional thinking. "So when I'm looking at these inputs from all these SMEs, from all these different silos that are just thinking in that silo, I'm creating a new space in my mind that's not in any of their worlds." Furthermore, as he listened to people, he was constantly looking for gaps between the team members' and the executives' perceptions and truth/reality for cues that would help him determine whether their information was valid. "There are very clear warning signs that I've trained myself to look for when you're dealing with an individual that has a high probability of a gap influencing their decision." The warning signs dealt with individual, organizational, and cultural differences in perceptions. Combining also involved eliminating. "Mary, I know you suggested X, but Pete over here very strongly suggested Y, which is 180° out of phase for that. So, effectively the two can't be true. Can we spend a minute determining which of the two is more likely to be true?" "And then you have a candid discussion—two experts debating—and usually one comes to the consensus that one or the other was wrong and rescinds their opinion and their whole investigative path disappears." Tom credited intuition for his ability to find the gaps between perception and truth.

Narrowing refers, for example, to how many different solutions the company could realistically support. This required flexibility and a willingness to constantly assimilate new data and jettison previous plans. In his own words, Tom looked for patterns and knew he had been successful when the team "rejoiced," got excited, and coalesced around a particular solution. He achieved this group consensus by actively listening to their ideas, seeing the pattern, and observing their reactions to his and others' suggestions.

Tom described a key turning point in the team's life that demonstrated combining and narrowing. Some of the team members, junior people in particular, were seeking one solution, "the Holy Grail." Instead, Tom encouraged them to combine two good potential solutions and test whether the combination produced more positive results than their individual tests. The results of the combined solutions came back negative, which validated the team's reluctance to look for more than one "silver bullet" at a time. Everyone else on the team, except for Tom and a junior engineer with a background in statistics, was convinced that combining solutions did not work. Tom's intuition, however, told him that the data were wrong and he continued to study them. He called the junior engineer and asked him to check if the data were gathered wrong or analyzed incorrectly. Because people all over the world were working on very complicated data, Tom was skeptical about the truth of what he'd received in an executive summary. The junior engineer's investigations found that the analysis was in fact inaccurate, proving Tom's intuition correct. This was a defining moment for two reasons. First, it taught people not to blindly accept a set of data without thinking about it. Second, it showed the team that Tom was not an easy person to brush off. Being right in this instance gave him the credibility to insist that they needed to combine all that they had learned—as a result, they solved the problem that same day. When they celebrated later and each team member received an award, Tom accepted his, saying, "I didn't do anything. It was all the team." Subsequently, however, he received an email from a team colleague saying, "If you hadn't made that decision that day, we would all be unemployed!"

It's worth noting that Tom had no inkling about an ideal solution when he agreed to solve this problem for the firm. Buttressed by the self-confidence he'd developed over his career, he assumed that they would figure out the answers as they went along.

Analysis

A closer look at how Tom thought about his work and his leadership style produced the following categories of analysis: shared similarities with domestic leaders, work context, work approaches, and sensemaking.

Leadership Characteristics

Like other global leaders (Osland, Oddou, Bird, & Osland, 2008), Tom possessed some leadership characteristics found in domestic leaders, such as self-confidence, optimism, intelligence, and persistence. He enjoyed and sought out challenges and the opportunity to be creative and learn. Tom found his work intrinsically rewarding.

When asked what a novice would find difficult about his leadership style, Tom identified active listening, understanding the different perspectives of the various stakeholders, and being able to use different styles depending on the situation—what we call managerial code switching (Osland et al., 2008). Molinsky defined cross-cultural code switching as "the act of purposefully modifying one's behavior in an interaction in a foreign setting in order to accommodate different cultural norms for appropriate behavior" (2007, p. 624).

Tom does not completely fit the global leader profile identified in the limited research on GL antecedents (Caligiuri, 2004; Kets de Vries & Florent-Treacy, 2002; McCall & Hollenbeck, 2002). He did not come from a bicultural family, have a long-term expatriate experience, receive mentoring from someone from another culture, or have international exposure and cultural contact during childhood. He had, however, participated in multicultural work teams. In his view, his parochial background was compensated for by his curiosity and being "an unbiased and unprejudiced person who loves dealing with anybody and everybody in the world."

Work Context

Tom characterized his work context in ways that are typical of other global leaders: managing multiplicities, huge challenges, precariousness, and ambiguity (Osland et al., 2008).

> *Managing multiplicities.* The project Tom described required him to manage multiplicities. His job was very complex, with multiple stakeholders, functions, levels, and issues that crossed multiple cultures and countries. Tom had to assemble and lead a large global network of multifunctional and multicultural teams to solve a complex problem. Although the customers' needs were taken into consideration, the stakeholders he dealt with were all internal. Some global leaders, however, also work closely with external organizations and foreign governments, like the high-level Air Force civilian who brokered weapon sales between foreign countries and various U.S. firms, and dealt with the U.S. Congress and numerous government agencies who all had to sign off on sales agreements (Osland et al., 2008).
>
> *Huge challenges.* Tom's assignment represented a huge challenge in that he had to break down the silos within the organization and inculcate a collaborative cross-functional approach, coordinate global efforts around the clock, and produce a novel technological solution in a short time frame. Furthermore, his task was significantly larger than normal, complex, intense, crisis driven, and involved "redesigning on a dime." This is typical of the difficult missions that are assigned to global leaders (Osland et al., 2008). For instance, Osland et al. (2008) report the case of a high-level executive at a major accounting firm who, prior to becoming its CEO, was tasked with moving from individual country earnings to an integrated global financial system. He led a multicultural team with multiple perspectives that crafted a plan that had to satisfy the different partnership and auditing laws in every country of operation. Finally, the executive had to sell the plan to partners around the world and obtain their approval (Osland et al., 2008). In the present case, Tom's challenge was also time limited because of the bankruptcy threat. In contrast, some other global leaders noted that their assignments consumed much more time, in terms of months and years, than was expected (Osland et al., 2008).
>
> *Precariousness.* Had Tom not succeeded at his task, the company would have gone under. His reputation in the industry would also have suffered. Thus, a lot was riding on the results of Tom's performance and the outcome was far from assured. This too is typical of tasks carried out by other global leaders who describe their work as having high risks and high stakes (Osland et al., 2008). For instance, the CEO of a start-up with mathematicians in Switzerland, manufacturing in India, and marketing and sales in the United States knew that his investors would lose

their investment if his team was not successful. In another example, an econo-mist worked to avert the Asian economic crisis by fostering a united approach among Asian nations and trying to convince the International Monetary Fund to accept a different solution than the one it had proposed. In addition to the threat of economic collapse, his personal credibility was at risk as he argued that his solution would result in more positive consequences for the region (Osland et al., 2008).

Global leaders sometimes work with stakeholders who could easily walk away (partners, customers) due to the volitional component of some collaborations. Because the positional authority of some global leaders is therefore limited, they speak primarily of exerting lateral influence and horizontal leadership rather than ramrodding changes through (Osland et al., 2008). Despite a serious organizational crisis and the authority conferred on him, Tom did not describe himself as an auto-cratic leader but as someone who relied on the expertise of his team members and who watched them for cues that signaled consensus.

Ambiguity. No single individual knew the answer to the problem confronting Tom's company. He faced many unknowns, including whether the task was possible. He, like other global leaders, dealt with this ambiguity by using three strategies: relying on a problem-solving process he had learned during his career, getting the right peo-ple on his team, and developing trusting relationships among them (Osland et al., 2008). This response to the ambiguity of sailing in uncharted waters was typical of global leaders who, despite some preparatory background experiences, often talked about "feeling their way" through a global change (Osland et al., 2008). Global lead-ers readily articulate the need for trusting relationships with teams and stakeholders (Osland et al., 2008), which mitigates uncertainty.

Work Approaches

To this point, the analysis has focused on the way Tom and other global leaders describe their work context. This section looks at the themes and subthemes (in ital-ics) related to their work approaches.

Problem solving. In addition to having *confidence in a problem-solving process* on which he had come to rely, Tom also exhibited a great deal of *patience in under-standing the root of the problem.* Like other global leaders, he was not ready to take action until a picture emerged that rang true with his intuition and knowl-edge. Tom also made *decisions predicated on deep domain knowledge.* Because of his manufacturing expertise, he had a better sense than others about what was possible and impossible when it came to production. His intuition told him when data were wrong, despite conflicting views of other team members. When it came to design and technology related to customer input, Tom was operating outside his area of technical expertise. However, his expertise in problem solving, team leadership, critical thinking, and active listening, and his ability to learn quickly compensated for the lack of technical expertise. There were instances when Tom *paid attention to cues that novices would fail to interpret*, especially with regard to his ability to see the gap between peoples' perceptions and truth/reality. Furthermore, Tom was constantly *monitoring, reevaluating, and adjust-ing* the problem-solving process as he requested and received information from around the world on the various experiments and their attempts to combine and narrow solutions. In addition to these typical approaches to problem solving, some global leaders also use *mental simulation to test possible action steps* (Osland et al., 2008).

Strategic thinking. Although Tom felt he was very good at holding a large amount of data in his head, the complexity and size of this task forced him to take on an assistant whose job was simply to keep a record. Thus, Tom recognized the importance of *seeing the global big picture and tracking multiple factors within interrelated systems.* His focus on combining and narrowing reflected a *need to consider alternatives to the present strategy in case it did not succeed.* The time pressure also forced him to *think a step ahead while working on current issues.*

Tom shared these strategies with other global leaders. However, due to the technical nature of his assignment, he did not have to *constantly balance the human implications of decisions and actions with the profit motive or business side of the situation*, as some global leaders do, as illustrated in the following case (Osland et al., 2008): Upper management in a successful biotech firm decided to eliminate their long-time European distributors and ally themselves with a major distribution firm with its own European network. The international sales director, who was previously responsible for building and maintaining relationships with the country distributors, was charged with giving them the bad news. As a further complication, the biotech firm's contract with the distributors committed them to "buying back the inventory" if the relationship were to end but did not spell out how the inventory would be valued. He had to balance the business case against the potential fallout from distributors who had well-established relationships with the biotech firm's major customers, the possibility of lawsuits, and the cost to their reputation. His focus was not simply the profit motive, but a sincere concern for balancing it with good stakeholder relationships and firm reputation.

Boundary spanning and stakeholders. Because of the multiple entities that Tom dealt with, he, like many global leaders, was concerned about boundary spanning. First, he *buffered the team* by creating a protective boundary that allowed them to focus on their most important work. However, he also instituted a weekly communication process that managed this boundary and *met the needs of other stakeholders.* Tom also coached team members to develop the people skills that would allow them to work in cross-functional teams and across team boundaries. He placed great importance on *building trust* with other employees. When Tom sought information about possible SMEs to include on his team, he used *a personal network to expand sources of information and perspectives.* These are all boundary-spanning strategies used by global leaders, in particular the important strategy of building trust among stakeholders (Osland et al., 2008).

A concern for stakeholder relations is a natural outgrowth of dealing with multiplicities. Global leaders who deal with more external stakeholders than Tom also utilize these strategies. They emphasize *treating stakeholders fairly* and *being very clear on company goals and showing simultaneous concern for the overall good of the firm and stakeholder interests* (Osland et al., 2008). They *mediate and educate the various stakeholders* so they can work together effectively. They *assume the role of ambassador* and *visualize how external stakeholders perceive their company.* This means they are capable of taking the perspective of numerous stakeholders. Despite their general respect and concern for all stakeholders, when necessary, they *challenge stakeholder interests* for the good of the company (Osland et al., 2008).

Influencing. Tom spoke about influencing in terms of *persuading others to change their mental models, continually focusing the discussion,* and *clarifying multiple viewpoints.* He also *used social capital to attract followers, maintain commitment, and find common ground.* In addition to these strategies, other global leaders also talked about *continually clarifying the direction of the team, the multiple views of stakeholders, and the status of the work* (Osland et al., 2008).

Intercultural skills. Although expert global leaders share much in common with domestic leaders, some themes are more salient for them as a result of the multicountry, multistakeholder context and the scope and span of their jobs. For example, Tom learned to *"read" people very closely to gauge their reactions.* This is a crucial aspect of bridging differences in intercultural communication and cross-functional work. He also *engaged in perspective taking, mindful dialogue, and active listening in multicultural meetings.* Tom did this in part because he acknowledged his lack of expertise in the primary subject matter. Similarly, global leaders acknowledge that they do not fully understand all cultures, so they work harder at reading people, listening actively, and working to take multiple perspectives (Osland et al., 2008). Tom *took culture into consideration, leveraging and managing it appropriately, and understanding when it does and does not matter.* He found an appropriate cultural compromise and rightly interpreted that the crisis trumped the usual cultural scripts and accommodations. Finally, he engaged *in conscious managerial code switching to be effective in different situations.* Assuming the roles of both good cop and bad cop exemplifies code switching. Other global leaders also work hard to *combat parochial organizational views and coach others to develop a more global mindset* (Osland et al., 2008).

Sensemaking

Sensemaking best describes the global leaders' thought processes as they interact with the global context. Sensemaking entails having a framework to categorize stimuli and enable one "to comprehend, understand, explain, attribute, extrapolate, and predict" (Starbuck & Milliken, 1988, p. 51). Within complex situations people "chop moments out of continuous flows and extract cues from those moments" (Weick, 1995, p. 43). After cues are extracted from the general flow of stimuli, they are embellished and related to a more general idea, most frequently to a similar cue from one's past (Weick, 1995). Klein and his colleagues, in their study of problem detection, wrote that "the knowledge and expectancies a person has will determine what counts as a cue and whether it will be noticed" (Klein, Pliske, Crandall, & Woods, 2005, p. 17). They maintain, in their data/frame model of sensemaking, "that data are used to construct a frame (a story or script or schema) that accounts for the data and guides the search for additional data. At the same time, the frame a person is using to understand events will determine what counts as data. Both activities occur in parallel, the data generating the frame, and the frame defining what counts as data" (Klein et al., 2005, p. 20).

Osland and her colleagues (Osland et al., 2008, 2009) argue that the characteristics of the global context result in several variations of sensemaking by global leaders. The characteristics (Lane et al., 2004; Osland et al., 2009) are shown in the first column in Table 2.1, and resonate with some of Tom's description of his work (e.g., complexity, multiplicities, and ambiguity). *Complexity* concerns the number of factors,

TABLE 2.1   The Global Context and Global Leadership Sensemaking

Global Context	Global Leadership Sensemaking
Complexity	Metalevel sensemaking (higher-order)
	• Requisite variety in mental models
	• Understanding of paradox
	• Influencing and changing mental models (defragging)
	• Creating the correct shared vision
Multiplicity	Inclusive sensemaking
	• Determining whom to include
	• Perspective taking
	• Determining which perspectives to heed
	• Collaborative decision making
Interdependence	Systemic sensemaking
	• Engaging in stakeholder dialogue
	• Coordinating multiple sensemaking
	• Collaborative decision making
Ambiguity	Confident sensemaking
	• Seeking clarity from trusted relations
	• Narrowing the sensemaking focus
	• Gauging when enough is known to make decisions
	• Collaborative decision making
Flux	Quick sensemaking
	• Refocusing the vision based on what's important
	• Innovative responses
	• Realignment
	• Rapid decision making
Cultural variations	Intercultural sensemaking
	• Decoding culture
	• Bridging cultural differences
	• Decisions that leverage culture

Source: Adapted from Osland, J., et al., in R. Bhagat and R. Steers (Eds.), *Handbook of Culture, Organizations, and Work*, Cambridge University Press, New York, NY, 2009, p. 264.

stakeholders, trends, challenges, and relationships that need to be taken into consideration and tracked. *Multiplicity* exists across a range of dimensions, such as more and different ways of doing business and organizing, more and different competitors, customers, governments, stakeholders, and contexts that add up to "many voices, viewpoints, and constraints" (Lane et al., 2004, p. 9). *Interdependence* is present within and without the organization, along the value chain, in alliances, and among a host of stakeholders, sociocultural, political, economic, and environmental systems. *Ambiguity* results from a lack of information clarity, failure to understand cause and effect, equivocality, and difficulty in interpreting cues and signals, as well as identifying appropriate actions and pursuing plausible goals. *Flux* relates to quickly transitioning systems, shifting values, and emergent patterns of organizational structure and behavior. *Cultural variations* exist with respect to patterns of values, habits, expectations, language, and perspectives.

Complexity leads to *metalevel sensemaking* and requires mental models that match the requisite variety (Ashby, 1958) in the environmental context, understanding paradox, giving up obsolete mental models and encouraging others to do the same, and creating an appropriate shared vision. Multiplicity requires *inclusive sensemaking* that incorporates the views and voices of whatever stakeholders need to be included. Perspective taking and figuring out which perspectives can be trusted or hold the most importance eventually lead to collaborative decision making. Interdependence results in *systemic sensemaking*. Stakeholder dialogue is needed to ensure that the interdependencies are well understood, and naturally leads to collaborative decision making. Systemic sensemaking also involves understanding and coordinating the ways in which various entities make sense of their own context. Ambiguity leads to *confident sensemaking* in the face of uncertainty. Global leaders seek clarity from people in their networks whom they trust. The sensemaking focus is gradually narrowed, and a determination has to be made regarding when enough information is known to serve as the basis for collaborative decisions. Flux requires *quick sensemaking*, which involves refocusing the vision based on what's important and coming up with innovative responses. It also means realigning the organization quickly and making rapid decisions.

Intercultural sensemaking is a result of cultural variations. It can be triggered when people are surprised by novel cultural variations, when they observe unexpected cultural behavior, or when they make a deliberate attempt to learn more about another culture (Osland, Bird, & Gundersen, 2007a). Cultural trigger events, which are perceived differentially by individuals, can lead to intercultural sensemaking once they pass a certain threshold. Intercultural sensemaking is an ongoing process involving an iterative cycle of events: framing the situation, making attributions, and selecting scripts that reflect various constellations of cultural values and cultural history (Osland & Bird, 2000). It rests on the assumption that culture is both contextually based and paradoxical in nature (Kluckholm & Strodtbeck, 1961; Osland & Bird, 2000; Fang, 2006; Gannon, 2007). Osland and her colleagues (Osland et al., 2007a) hypothesize that intercultural sensemaking can lead to various outcomes: schema development, automaticity, cue identification, pattern recognition, increased mindfulness, emotional earmarks, and ascending restabilization at a higher level of cultural understanding. All of these characteristics are visible in Tom's case study. He employed metalevel sensemaking to understand a very complex problem and to influence the mental models of his followers. One of his goals was to develop and increase their cognitive complexity to match that of the problem. Tom used inclusive sensemaking when determining whom to place on the team and ensuring that all the voices were heard in an egalitarian setting. He spent a good deal of time figuring out whose perspectives to trust.

Tom also used systemic sensemaking by pulling together the views of various teams and stakeholders. He served as the fulcrum for this project and continually tracked what was happening with different stakeholders. Tom clearly manifested confident sensemaking by engaging in collaborative decision making and seeking clarity from trusted sources. He was compelled to use quick sensemaking by the urgency of the project and changing conditions, which resulted in innovative responses. In this case study, intercultural sensemaking was mentioned the least despite the multicultural nature of all the teams Tom worked with. It is possible that he is so accustomed to adapting to cultural differences in global work teams in a multicultural firm that it did not bear mentioning. His only verbalized acknowledgment of culture, however, was an exception from the norm of cultural accommodation—resorting to a cultural compromise on decision making when cultural preferences were incompatible with the overwhelming business imperative. Tom exhibited cultural sensitivity, but he never had to stop and make sense of cultural behaviors in this incident.

Research Implications

This case study is part of the first examination of cognition in expert global leaders and the first time CTA has been employed in the job domain of global leadership. By focusing on the cognitive demands of the extreme nature of the global context, it provides a novel addition to a field characterized heretofore primarily by competency studies and an occasional case study concerned more with description than analysis.

The cognition Tom described appears to illustrate many characteristics of expert thinking. As Sternberg and Davidson (1994) found, experts, like Tom perceive the world differently and use more sophisticated processes of insightful thinking than do novices. It is a sign of expertise to distinguish perception from truth/reality or to engage in the parallel thinking that Tom described. Tom, like other experts, possesses an encyclopedia of knowledge that is more extensive than that of novices and is better at "gauging the importance of different types of knowledge and the difficulty of problems" (Klein & Hoffman, 1993, p. 209). An extensive knowledge base serves as a foundation and threshold requirement for global leaders. Knowledge alone, however, is not sufficient to develop expertise (Klein & Hoffman, 1993). When experts like Tom look at a problem, they can differentiate more readily between relevant and irrelevant information (Sternberg & Davison, 1994), or between perception and truth/reality, as in Tom's case. Tom, in accordance with other experts, organizes relevant information—sets of cues—into meaningful patterns to allow for a more accurate diagnosis of the problem (Sternberg & Davison, 1994). Pattern recognition functions as an index for the expert's knowledge base (Simon, in Hayashi, 2001), much like a hyperlink between a pattern and the relevant knowledge. Novices perceive fewer patterns, and those patterns are distinguished by more superficial characteristics. Experts like Tom are better than novices at reacting to nonroutine situations (Klein & Hoffman, 1993) and making decisions under pressure. Tom was under tremendous pressure but had no difficulty making the required decisions rapidly. Experts like Tom complement their analytical skills with intuitive reasoning (Prietula & Simon, 1989), as he did when he quickly perceived that the data were incorrect. There are no doubt other examples of expert thinking in global leader samples, but these examples are highlighted here as they relate to Osland and Bird's (2006) delineation of the relationship between expert thinking and global leadership.

Limitations and Future Directions

No substantive conclusions can be generalized from a single case study. While cognitive task analysis is designed to measure cognition and goes into greater detail than a typical interview, it is a form of self-report that is not confirmed by other subjects. This case study does, however, provide ideas about the focus of future research that directly observes and measures GL behavior. It also prompts a closer look at previous research findings concluding that global leaders tend to have international backgrounds (Kets de Vries & Florent-Treacy, 2002; McCall & Hollenbeck, 2002; Caligiuri, 2004) and suggests different developmental profiles (Osland et al., 2008). In the case of expert global leaders without an international background, future research could determine whether compensatory competencies, functionally equivalent experiences, motivation, and the ability to learn may be more salient preconditions of GL (Osland et al., 2008).

Given the dearth of process models of global leadership, the sensemaking approach is a first step in describing how global leaders interact with their environment. It also sheds more light on the cognitive dimension of global leadership. However, more research is needed to elaborate on the various types of sensemaking and the possible linkages with the categories of expert cognition described in the analysis section of this case study.

More foundational research is needed on the construct definition of global leadership, antecedents and effectiveness outcomes, factors that promote or impede GL development, empirical tests of extant models, effectiveness tests of development methodologies, and longitudinal studies of the developmental process (Mendenhall, Osland, Bird, Oddou, & Maznevski, 2008; Osland et al., 2009). A comparison study of expert cognition in global versus domestic leaders would be extremely helpful. We contend that the complex global context places unique demands on leaders and results in the development of a particular set of competencies as well as the ability to engage in sophisticated, complex sensemaking. As the local context becomes more complex and diverse, perhaps differentiation between global and local leadership will eventually disappear and the term *global leader* will no longer be limited only to people who work across cultures. In the absence of a conclusive answer, we can still benefit from the remedies Tom and other global leaders have found for dealing with complexity and ambiguity: a reliable problem-solving process, good intuition, team facilitation skills, and the abilities to think critically, listen actively, observe closely, get the right people on the team, and develop trust.

References

Adler, N. J. (2001). Global leadership: Women leaders. In M. Mendenhall, T. Kuhlmann, & G. Stahl (Eds.) *Developing global business leaders: Policies, processes and innovations* (pp. 73–97). Westport, CT: Quorum Books.

Ashby, W. R. (1958). Requisite variety and its implications for the control of complex systems. *Cybernetica, 1*(2), 83–99.

Beechler, S., & Javidan, M. (2007). Leading with a global mindset. In M. Javidan, R. Steers, & M. Hitt (Eds.) *Advances in international management: Special issue on global mindset* (Vol. 19, 131–169). Oxford, UK: Elsevier.

Bikson, T. K., Treverton, G. F., Moini, J. S., & Lindstrom, G. (2003). *New challenges for international leadership: Lessons from organizations with global missions.* Santa Monica, CA: Rand Corporation.

Black, J. S., Morrison, A. J., & Gregersen, H. B. (1999). *Global explorers: The next generations of leaders.* New York, NY: Routledge.

Caligiuri, P. (2004). *Global leadership development through expatriate assignments and other international experiences.* Paper presented at the Academy of Management, New Orleans, LA.

Charan, R., Drotter, S., & Noel, J. (2001). *The leadership pipeline.* San Francisco, CA: Jossey-Bass.

Cohen, E. (2007). *Leaders without borders.* Singapore: John Wiley & Sons.

Crandall, B., Klein, G., & Hoffman, R. R. (2006). *Working minds: A practitioner's guide to cognitive task analysis.* Cambridge, MA: MIT Press.

Fang, T. (2006). From 'onion' to 'ocean': Paradox and change in national cultures. *International Studies of Management & Organization, 35*(4), 71–90.

Flanagan, J. C. (1954). The critical incident technique. *Psychological Bulletin, 51*(4), 327–359.

Gannon, M. J. (2007). *Paradoxes of culture and globalization.* Thousand Oaks, CA: Sage Publications.

Goldsmith, M., Greenberg, C., Robertson, A., & Hu-Chan, M. (2003). *Global leadership: The next generation.* Upper Saddle River, NJ: Prentice Hall.

Gregersen, H. B., Morrison, A. J., & Black, J. S. (1998). Developing leaders for the global frontier. *Sloan Management Review, 40*(1), 21–32.

Hayashi, A. M. (2001). When to trust your gut. *Harvard Business Review, 79*(2), 59–65.

Hoffman, R. R., Crandall, B., & Shadbolt, N. (1998). A case study in cognitive task analysis methodology: The critical decision method for the elicitation of expert knowledge. *Human Factors, 40*, 254–276.

Hollenbeck, G. P. (2001). A serendipitous sojourn through the global leadership literature. In W. Mobley & M. W. McCall (Eds.), *Advances in global leadership* (pp. 15–47). Stamford, CT: JAI Press.

Jokinen, T. (2005). Global leadership competencies: A review and discussion. *Journal of European Industrial Training, 29*(2/3), 199–216.

Kets De Vries, M., & Florent-Treacy, E. (2002). Global leadership from A to Z: Creating high commitment organizations. *Organizational Dynamics, 295*(309), 1–16.

Kets De Vries, M. F. R., & Florent-Treacy, E. (1999). *The new global leaders.* San Francisco, CA: Jossey Bass.

Kets de Vries, M. F. R., Vrignaud, P., & Florent-Treacy, E. (2004). The global leadership life inventory: Development and psychometric properties of a 360-degree feedback instrument. *International Journal of Human Resource Management, 15*(3), 475–492.

Klein, G., Pliske, R., Crandall, B., & Woods, D. (2005). Problem detection. *Cognition, Technology and Work, 7*, 14–28.

Klein, G. A., & Hoffman, R. R. (1993). Seeing the invisible: Perpetual-cognitive aspects of expertise. In M. Rabinowits (Ed.), *Cognitive science foundations of instruction.* Hillsdale, NJ: Lawrence Erlbaum Associates.

Kluckhohn, F., & Strodtbeck, F. (1961). *Variations in value orientations.* Evanston, IL: Row, Peterson.

Lane, H. W., Maznevski, M. L., & Mendenhall, M. E. (2004). Hercules meets Buddha. In H. W. Lane, M. Maznevski, M. E. Mendenhall, & J. McNett (Eds.), *The handbook of global management: A guide to managing complexity* (pp. 3–25). Oxford, UK: Blackwell Publishing.

Lobel, S. A. (1990). Global leadership competencies: Managing to a different drumbeat. *Human Resource Management, 29*(1), 39–47.

McCall, M. R., & Hollenbeck, G. P. (2002). *Developing global executives: The lessons of international experience.* Boston, MA: Harvard Business School Press.

Mendenhall, M. (2001). New perspectives on expatriate adjustment and its relationship to global leadership development. In M. Mendenhall, T. Kuhlmann, & G. Stahl (Eds.), *Developing global business leaders: Policies, processes, and innovations* (pp. 1–16). Westport, CT: Quorum Books.

Mendenhall, M., Jensen, R., Gregersen, H., & Black, J. S. (2003). Seeing the elephant: HRM challenges in the age of globalization. *Organizational Dynamics, 32*(3), 261–274.

Mendenhall, M., & Osland, J. S. (2002). *An overview of the extant global leadership research.* Symposium presentation at the Academy of International Business, San Juan, Puerto Rico.

Mendenhall, M., Osland, J., Bird, A., Oddou, G., & Maznevski, M. (2008). *Global leadership: Research, practice, and development.* London, UK: Routledge.

Mercer Delta. (2006). The global leadership imperative. Presentation to the Human Resource Planning Society, New York, NY.

Militello, L. G., & Hutton, R. J. (1998). Applied cognitive task analysis (ACTA): A practitioner's toolkit for understanding cognitive task demands. *Ergonomics, 41*(11), 1618–1641.

Molinsky, A. (2007). Cross-cultural code-switching: The psychological challenges of adapting behavior foreign cultural interactions. *Academy of Management Review, 32*(2), 622–640.

Moro Bueno, C., & Tubbs, L. (2004). Testing a global leadership competencies (GLC) model. *The Business Review, 1*(2), 11–15.

Osland, J. S. (2008a). The multidisciplinary roots of global leadership. In M. Mendenhall, J. S. Osland, A. Bird, G. Oddou, & M. Maznevski (Eds.), *Global leadership: Theory and practice.* London, UK: Routledge.

Osland, J. S. (2008b). An overview of the global leadership literature. In M. Mendenhall, J. S. Osland, A. Bird, G. Oddou, & M. Maznevski (Eds.), *Global leadership: Theory and practice.* London, UK: Routledge.

Osland, J. S., & Bird, A. (2000). Beyond sophisticated stereotyping: Cross-cultural sensemaking in context. *Academy of Management Executive, 14,* 1–12.

Osland, J. S., & Bird, A. (2006). Global leaders as experts. In W. Mobley & E. Weldon (Eds.), *Advances in global leadership* (Vol. 4, pp. 123–142). Stamford, CT: JAI Press.

Osland, J. S., Bird, A., & Gundersen, A. (2007a). *Trigger events in intercultural sensemaking.* Philadelphia, PA: Academy of Management Meeting.

Osland, J. S., Bird, A., Mendenhall, M. E., & Osland, A. (2006). Developing global leadership capabilities and global mindset: A review. In G. K. Stahl & I. Björkman (Eds.), *Handbook of research in international human resource management* (pp. 197–222). Cheltenham, UK: Edward Elgar Publishing.

Osland, J. S., Bird, A., Oddou, G., & Osland, A. (2007b). *Expert cognition in high technology global leaders.* Paper presented at Proceedings of the 8th Naturalistic Decision Making Conference (NDM8), Monterey, CA.

Osland, J. S., Oddou, G., Bird, A., & Osland, A. (2008). *Global leadership in context* (Working paper). San José, CA: San José State University.

Osland, J. S., Taylor, S., & Mendenhall, M. (2009). Global leadership: Challenges and lessons. In R. Bhagat & R. Steers (Eds.), *Handbook of culture, organizations, and work.* New York, NY: Cambridge University Press.

Prietula, M., & Simon, H. (1989). The experts in your midst. *Harvard Business Review, 89*(1), 120–124.

Rosen, R., Digh, P., Singer, M., & Philips, C. (2000). *Global literacies: Lessons on business leadership and national cultures.* New York, NY: Simon and Schuster.

Starbuck, W. H., & Milliken, F. J. (1988). Executives' perceptual filters: What they notice and how they make sense. In D. C. Hambrick (Ed.), *The executive effect: Concepts and methods for studying top managers* (pp. 35–65). Greenwich, CT: JAI Press.

Sternberg, R., & Davidson, J. (1994). *The nature of insight.* Cambridge, MA: MIT Press.

Suutari, V. (2002). Global leadership development: An emerging research agenda. *Career Development International, 7*(4), 218–233.

Weber, W., Festing, M., Dowling, P. J., & Schuler, R. S. (1998). *Internationales personalmanagement.* Wiesbaden, Germany: Gabler Verlag.

Weick, K. E. (1995). *Sense-making in organizations.* Thousand Oaks, CA: Sage Publications.

3

Focused Cognition

Information Integration and Complex
Problem Solving by Top Inventors

Harald A. Mieg
Humboldt-Universität zu Berlin

To date, only a few psychological studies on inventors have been conducted, most of them case studies (e.g., Weber, 1992a; Weisberg, 2006). From a psychological point of view, invention seems to be an instance of creativity and innovation, creativity being considered a personal characteristic or trait (Boden, 2003) and innovation the product of teamwork (West, 2002). So far, scant attention has been paid to the study of inventor cognition. An obstacle seems to be the broad range of subjects and fields in which we find inventors, reaching from relatively low tech (bicycles) to very high tech (lasers), encompassing all domains of human activity (e.g., health, leisure, traffic, etc.).

The most immediate and practical way of operationally defining inventors is in terms of patents. Patents are temporary, exclusive rights that are granted to an inventor for claims regarding technical features that are new, inventive, and useful or industrially applicable. In this context, inventiveness refers to an "inventive step" (European Union) or "nonobviousness" (United States) of the patented technical feature. Thus, an inventor can be defined as a person who holds a patent.

More generally speaking, invention is "a creative activity, bringing into being what was not there before" (Perkins, 2004, p. 38). In contrast to the arts or sciences, invention has a strong "functional emphasis," as "invention produces ways and means of doing things: bottle openers for opening bottles; microscopes, optical and electronic, for seeing the very small; cell phones for handy communication; supercomputers for predicting the weather" (p. 38). Inventors change reality.

The *rationale* of this chapter is to contribute to an understanding of the cognitive side of inventors' perseverance. The core argument of this chapter is that in order to study inventor cognition in any domain, we have to switch from the level of content-specific processes and heuristics to a metacognitive and long-term perspective. The evidence in the literature and our own studies shows that inventor cognition is *focused*. From a short-term perspective, focused cognition refers to a form of metacognitive control of cognitive information processing, focused on an idea or envisioned invention. From a long-term perspective, focused cognition refers to extraordinary *perseverance*: Inventors stick to ideas that "normal" people, faced with the amount of problems involved, usually would abandon. The long-term cognitive facet of this perseverance—besides the motivational and developmental implications for self-control, goal setting, etc.—can be described as a "possibility filter" (Weber, 2006) that defines trajectories of learning and technological problem solving.

Without this long-term facet of invention, we would not understand how expert inventors manage knowledge and adapt to complexity. Artur Fischer, the most successful German inventor of the twentieth century in terms of the number of personally held patents, spoke of "permanent supererogation" (Fischer, 1987). For Fischer, any series of inventions and patents already held—he has over 1,080 personal patents—should enable an inventor to enter new domains in order to solve one by one the small and large technology-based problems faced by humanity. In 1949, Fischer started out with a patent for a photo flashlight that became his "cash cow" for further inventions. His most famous invention is the grey "S Plug" dowel. He was also granted patents for construction kits he made for his children and then produced under the label "Fischertechnik." More recent inventions by Fischer are plugs used to fix bone fractures and biodegradable and edible children's toys from potato starch.

This chapter is organized as follows. First, the research on inventors in general is summarized. Second, cognitive approaches to invention based on heuristics and metacognition are discussed. Third, a *long-term* cognitive perspective of invention is introduced.

Research on Inventors

With logic alone, we cannot explain inventions; otherwise, we would be able to predict and anticipate them. The predicted invention wouldn't be an invention any longer. However, we can attempt to explain inventiveness and to study inventors at work.

General Approaches to the Study of Inventors

One of the earliest studies on inventors was by Rossman (1964). He collected statistical data demonstrating, for instance, the often underestimated contribution of freelancing inventors to the national stock of innovations. Since then, additional studies with inventors have been conducted, most of them outside psychology and based on interviews or statistical data. For instance, the interviews by Brown (1988) with American inventors underlined inventors' perseverance: They are completely dedicated to their ideas. For example, one top inventor said: "To be an inventor you not only must have the idea, but also must believe in it so strongly that you're not going to take 'no' for an answer" (p. 289). Or another one: "An inventor may try hundreds of things that don't work, and that gives most people the impression that he is somewhat crazy" (p. 85).

Another line of research concerns the study of inventor productivity. This research most often refers to studies with scientists showing that the productivity distribution in science is skewed (e.g., Lotka, 1926; Price, 1963; Simonton, 1988). Similarly, only a few inventors display high productivity, and most of them have comparatively low productivity (e.g., Ernst, Leptien, & Vitt, 2000; Huber, 1998; Narin & Breitzman, 1995). In a survey by Huber (1998), the top 10% of inventors produced over 40% of all patents (p. 233). Even more extreme, in the Narin and Breitzman (1995) sample, the most productive inventor accounted for more than half of the patents in any of the four semiconductor companies from Japan and the United States (p. 511). Highly productive inventors seem to be rare.

A new level of research on inventors was reached by the so-called PatVal project examining the value of European patents (Giuri et al., 2007). The PatVal survey was launched in May 2003 and ended in January 2004. A questionnaire was submitted to the inventors of 27,531 patents granted by the European Patent Office between 1993 and 1997. The inventors returned 9,216 questionnaires covering 9,017 patents from France, Germany, Italy, the Netherlands, Spain, and the United Kingdom; 2.8% of the inventors were female, 76.9% had a postgraduate education, and 26% a PhD (p. 1111). The PatVal study demonstrated the importance of large enterprises; only one-third of the PatVal patents involved a single inventor (p. 1114).

The PatVal survey highlighted some characteristics of inventors. For instance, it revealed the sources of knowledge that inventors rely on: Customers and users were ranked first, and universities and public research laboratories ranked seventh and last (p. 1117). As to rewards, the inventors clearly preferred the functional aspect ("satisfaction to show that something is technically possible") to monetary rewards. A series of subanalyses were conducted on the PatVal data. Regarding employed inventors, we learned that top performers change their employment frequently—until they find a match between the organizational working environment and their particular needs (for instance, suitable laboratory facilities) (Hoisl, 2007).

The Lemelson-MIT Workshop: "The Architecture of Invention"

In August 2003, a workshop on the architecture of invention was held at the Massachusetts Institute of Technology, supported by the Lemelson-MIT Program and by the National Science Foundation. The workshop was chaired by David Perkins and comprised psychologists who were studying invention—such as Robert Weber (Oklahoma State University)—as well as scholars representing a broad range of sciences, such as physics, engineering, history, or sociology. A top inventor, William P. Murphy Jr., was also among the participants. The workshop's goal was "to define what was known and outline what needed to be known concerning the fundamental nature of the inventive mind and the fundamental processes of invention" (Lemelson-MIT Program, 2003, p. 3).

The report of the workshop defines 12 basic principles of the processes of invention (pp. 28–32):

1. "Invention is an extended process" that may take years (the telephone), or decades (the steam engine), and sometimes centuries (the airplane).
2. "Invention is a highly purposeful activity, but purposes vary."
3. "Both problem finding and problem solving figure centrally in the process of invention."
4. "Invention is a knowledge-generating process."
5. "Inventors use a rich variety of representations and move nimbly among them."
6. "Inventors sustain a dialog between ideas and instantiations—instantiations being, for example, prototypes, experiments, trials, tinkering, etc."
7. "The process of invention depends on iterative cycles of evaluation."
8. "Successful inventors learn from failure."
9. "Inventors override past experience and abandon prior knowledge."

10. "Invention requires boundary transgressions"—drawing upon knowledge and resources from any available source, "irrespective of disciplinary or other boundaries."
11. "Chance plays a significant role in invention, but not in a haphazard way."
12. "The process of invention is self-generating but resource-limited."

The report is a rich scientific source of insights on invention. It defined the standard set of phenomena that need to be explained by any theory on human invention. In the following sections, the *cognitive* interpretation of these findings is explicated.

Cognition: From Divergent Thinking and Heuristics to Metacognition

In general, psychological research on inventors is embedded in or derived from creativity research, with invention regarded as a "distinct form of creativity" (Lemelson-MIT Program, 2003, p. 12). Thus, we will set out by reviewing psychological research on the creative *and* inventive mind.

Psychological Research on the Creative and Inventive Mind

An interpretation (and measure) of creativity that is often used is "divergent thinking" (Guilford, 1967). Divergent thinking consists of opening paths and looking in different directions when solving a problem. Its opposite is convergent thinking: narrowing the search space successively. A simple measure of creativity as divergent thinking is the number of ideas produced per some period of time working at a problem (e.g., King, McKee Walker, & Broyles, 1996; McCrae, 1987). In innovation research, Kirton (1976) argued similarly, using the distinction between adaptors and innovators. Innovators stand for new ideas and products, while adaptors fit them to current processes.

Applying this understanding of creativity, we would expect inventors to be innovators who tend toward divergent thinking. We find this interpretation, for instance, with Huber (1998, pp. 328–329) who makes reference to Simonton (1988) and Kirton (1994), and distinguishes between an "analytical-adaptor type" and an "intuitive-innovator type," the first being characterized by convergent thinking, and the second by divergent thinking. According to Huber (1998), top inventors are intuitive innovators. The report on the "The Architecture of Invention" workshop mentioned divergent thinking only once, in the context of collaboration: Collaboration "can feed divergent thinking" (Lemelson-MIT Program, 2003, p. 35). In his summary of the workshop, Perkins (2004) used the term *transgressive cognition* in order to emphasize that innovative cognition is not just simply creative but also crosses borders: "The cognitive processes of inventive thinking are full of boundary transgressions—they cross boundaries all the time in various ways" (Perkins, 2004, p. 40).

Besides this very general characterization of inventive cognition as divergent or transgressive, there have been several attempts to identify the heuristics of a set of inventors. The word *heuristics* originates from Greek and fits perfectly with our context of inventive cognition, as "the art of discovery." Duncker (1935) introduced the concept of heuristics into psychology (cf. Newell, 1985). Newell and Simon (1972) made it popular within the scientific community. They described heuristics as mental procedures that explain human problem-solving behavior. Since then, a heuristic means a rule of thumb for efficient and effective problem solving; heuristics are "methods of solution which, in contrast to an algorithm, do not guarantee that a solution will be found" (Mieg, 1993, p. 31). Table 3.1 provides an overview of selected scientific papers that address the role of heuristics for inventive thinking. In particular, Robert Weber studied heuristics for different inventions, starting with frame analysis (Minsky, 1975) as his general approach. "In principle, each of these heuristics is generalizable beyond the context of the particular invention that is examined" (Weber, Moder, & Solie, 1990, p. 321).

Most of the heuristics sampled in Table 3.1 deal with the combination of objects, with search or the use of analogy. There are some heuristics, such as "repurposing" or "do not be constrained by nature," that address one of the most common and striking phenomena in inventors: learning from failure.

In our interviews with Artur Fischer about his methods of invention, we tested the set of heuristics presented in Table 3.1. For Fischer, any invention commences with a requirement (*Bedarfsfall*). An invention originates in more or less explicit needs of people or industry, and therefore requires permanent feedback from possible users and the market. Thus, the 1996 model by Weber (Table 3.1, 4th column), which describes cycles going from requirements and necessary specifications to the final evaluation of generated alternatives, fits best with how Fischer characterizes his own inventions. The most important single heuristic Fischer mentioned is analogy; analogies transpose insights from one domain to another. Crossing boundaries or similar notions did not play a role in Fischer's experience. For him, the core of any invention is a technical or practical problem to be solved. The list of inventing heuristics in Table 3.1 is certainly incomplete, and more importantly, such a list does not provide a clear idea of how exactly the set of inventors' heuristics can or should be distinguished from heuristics of everyday cognition and reasoning.

Metacognition in Inventors

To study inventor cognition in a controlled context of complex problem solving, we conducted a study with 46 German inventors using a computer-simulated microworld (Wolf, 2006; Wolf & Mieg, 2010). In addition to the simulated task, we employed the Fragebogen für kognitive Prozessvariablen (FKP), a questionnaire examining variables of cognitive processes. This questionnaire has been developed specifically for the study of problem solving in complex microworlds and assesses aspects of cognitive processes, such as divergent thinking (Kreuzig, 1981). In particular, we wanted to reveal inventors' ability to make deliberate use of divergent *and* convergent thinking. This ability seemed to be an important skill in solving complex problems (Dörner, Kreuzig, Reither, & Stäudel, 1983).

For the computer-simulated microworld, we used a program by Wagener (2001) called FSYS. It consists of 85 variables that are partially connected with each other (covariants). The simulated microworld is opaque, in the sense that some aspects and internal relations of the system are not transparent to the player and need to be inferred. In the FSYS scenario participants have to run a forestry business for a simulated 50-month period: They need to plant and cut down trees, apply fertilizers, and fight pests in five different territories. All tasks need to be accomplished within a certain time frame, with the aim of asset maximization. The FSYS scenario is one

TABLE 3.1 Inventors' Heuristics Identified in the Scientific Literature

Weber et al. (1990, p. 321) on an Invention for Applying Herbicides[a]	Weber (1992b, p. 218) on the Evolution of the Swiss Knife	Perkins and Weber (1992, p. 332), General	Weber (1996, pp. 364–365) on Inventing the Chair	Lemelson-MIT Program (2003, p. 33), General
"Frame description": describing purposes, materials, procedures, etc.	"Joining" of previously independent elements to form a new element	"Organize search by parsing"	Find and describe "requirements or specifications"	"Subgoaling"
"Systematic min/max table": minimize some variables, maximize other variables	"Adding": adding features "to increase functionality"	"Find the boundaries and cross them"	Find and describe "constraints"	"Repurposing"
"Systematic constraint table"	"Fine-tuning"	"Attain goals through a backward search, especially when a forward search does not work"	"Generate alternatives"	"Combining"
"Visual imagery"	"Using an abstract element" on which "spatial transformations and heuristics operate"	"Do not be constrained by nature"	"Evaluate each alternative in the light of the functional requirements or specifications"	"Analogy"
"Metaphor or analogy"		"Minimize search by using a theory or a metaphor or a mental model to work from"		"Identifying variables"
		"When all else fails, do a systematized big search"		"Deliberate evaluation"
				"Exhaustive search"

[a] Provided are the five main heuristics.

program in a line of computer-simulated microworlds that attempt to assess partici-pants' complex problem-solving abilities (Dörner et al., 1983; Dörner & Schölkopf, 1991; Frensch & Funke, 1995; Funke, 1998). FSYS provides information on a partici-pant's problem-solving ability measured along 15 scales.

In our study, we used the following measures:

1. The total FSYS score (total capital earned) as an overall measure of the inventor's ability for complex problem ability
2. The number of granted patents (self-assessed by the inventors)
3. The number of marketed patents for which the revenues were higher than the total investments (self-assessed by the inventors)
4. Degree of divergent thinking (assessed with FKP scale 2)
5. Controllability of divergent and convergent thinking (FKP scale 1), defined as the degree to which an inventor makes deliberate use of divergent and convergent thinking

Data analysis revealed that the complex problem-solving ability of inventors, as measured by the total FSYS score, did not differ from the FSYS norm sample involv-ing students. Surprisingly, the best problem solvers were inventors with exactly one patent granted. Successful inventors (success measured by number of patents) do not seem to excel at general complex problem solving.

The correlation between inventors' success and divergent thinking ability (as mea-sured by FKP scale 2) also was not significant. In contrast, controllability of divergent and convergent thinking (FKP scale 1) was found to be a significant predictor of an inventor's success ($F(3, 40) = 3.86$, $p < .05$). As can be seen in Figure 3.1, this variable distinguished top inventors from inefficient inventors. Invention efficiency (IE) is a measure based on the number of marketed patents. Accordingly, inefficient inventors

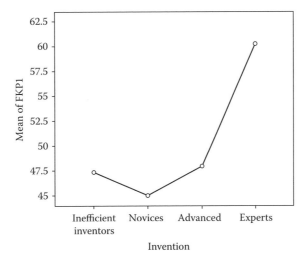

FIGURE 3.1   Group means for FKP1 ($N = 46$ inventors). Note: FKP1 measures controlled usage of divergent and convergent thinking. Invention efficiency (IE) is a weighted ratio of marketed patents to granted patents. This measure was used to identify groups of inventors: inefficient inventors: IE < 1 ($n = 12$); novices: IE = 1 ($n = 13$); advanced: IE > 1 and IE ≤ 10 ($n = 17$); experts: IE > 10 ($n = 4$).

were those who had granted patents but no marketed ones, or inventors who had almost no marketed patents but considerably more granted ones (see Wolf & Mieg, 2010).

Controllability of divergent and convergent thinking is a form of *metacognition*, as it implies metastrategies that govern more basic cognitive processes. Metacognition in general refers to knowledge about one's own knowledge and capacity and is generally considered to be a core cognitive characteristic of top experts (Feltovich, Prietula, & Ericsson, 2006, p. 55). With respect to inventors, the deliberate control of divergent and convergent thinking involves both sparkling creativity *and* goal-oriented, systematic processes. From a metacognitive perspective, the variety of heuristics in Table 3.1 suggests that inventors cross boundaries to combine elements of reality in new ways *and* work on fine-tuning and deliberate evaluation. For instance, Artur Fischer's first step was to create the border-crossing idea of using plugs to fix bone fractures or potato starch to produce edible toys. In addition, hard work, deliberation, and refinement were required to turn these ideas into products. We can suppose that this kind of metacognition is goal oriented and governed by the specific idea or invention that an inventor is attempting to realize. Metacognition seems to be a necessary requirement in order to track the unconventional. As we will show in the following paragraphs, however, inventiveness cannot be reduced to a type of metacognition.

Long-Term Perspective: From Inventors as "Intellectual Bridges" to the "Possibility Filter"

In interviews, top inventors often claim that inventiveness is a "characteristic of a person" (Brown, 1988, p. 39). The concept of metacognition alone does not suffice to explain the long-term perseverance of inventors. From a psychological point of view, we have to look for sets of enduring psychological factors, such as personality or the development of expertise.

Personality Characteristics: Emotional Stability?

The report on the "The Architecture of Invention" workshop (Lemelson-MIT Program, 2003) lists several personality characteristics of inventors:

> Although there is no formula for the inventive mind, a number of abilities and dispositions are associated with inventive productivity. Effective inventors tend to display personality characteristics including resourcefulness, resilience, nonconformity, and a range of others, including passion for their work, unquenchable optimism, high persistence, a sense of play, high tolerance for complexity and ambiguity, willingness to delay gratification, a critical stance toward their own work, embracing failure as a learning experience, not the enemy, and a commitment to making things better through practical action. (Lemelson-MIT Program, 2003, pp. 22–23)

In his workshop summary, Perkins (2004) tried to systematize the personality characteristics, distinguishing between (1) central elements, such as transgressive cognition; (2) supporting elements, such as technical knowledge; and (3) societal elements, such as collaboration or entrepreneurship. Almost the same list of personality characteristics are included in the German DABEI inventors' handbook, which was edited by major German inventors in 1987, including Artur Fischer (DABEI, 1987). The authors mention one further central element: self-awareness about one's own knowledge and abilities as the first step toward successful invention (p. 3). However, some of the personal characteristics mentioned both by Perkins (2004) and DABEI (1987) cannot be generalized to all inventors. For instance, many successful inventors employed in R&D laboratories do not display any entrepreneurial ambition (Kassicieh, Radosevich, & Banbury, 1997).

There are only few empirical studies on inventors' personality characteristics. Some evidence can be derived from creativity studies using the Big Five personality factor approach. In these studies, openness to experience (King et al., 1996; McCrae, 1987) seems to be a success factor for creative work, sometimes in connection with extraversion (Ng & Rodrigues, 2002).

To collect more evidence on this issue, we conducted a study with freelancing inventors, using a set of standard personality tests. We tested the Big Five personality factors, risk behavior, efficacy, and self-concepts (Braun, Mieg, & Neyer, 2009) to examine the possible influence of self-awareness on inventors. We were not able to find strong confirmation of any of the personality-based assumptions concerning risk behavior, efficacy, or self-concepts. Though inventors showed somewhat elevated scores for openness to experience, top inventors did not. The only robust result concerned the emotional stability of inventors, as they displayed very low scores for neuroticism. This characteristic seems to be a necessary condition to tolerate the high levels of frustration involved in inventing. Nonetheless, it is insufficient to explain inventiveness.

Theorizing About Inventors: The Possibility Filter

An often-cited requirement in the context of innovation is collaboration. In the Lemelson-MIT workshop, collaboration was considered so essential that one participant called inventors intellectual bridges: "Because invention is so contextual, inventors can be thought of as intellectual bridges" (Lemelson-MIT Program, 2003, p. 19).

The metaphor of inventors as intellectual bridges allows for several interpretations (see Table 3.2). One option is based on the psychology of expertise (Ericsson, Charness, Feltovich, & Hoffman, 2006). According to this view, top inventors are invention experts—or masters of invention. Indeed, as interviews with inventors revealed, successful inventors demonstrate a very strong motivation toward mastery (Henderson, 2004). For instance, they may serve as intellectual bridges insofar as they change their employment more frequently than average R&D personnel (Hoisl, 2007). Thus, they bridge the work environments of invention and may serve as role models for novices.

A second interpretation of inventors as intellectual bridges is derived from situated cognition (Clancey, 1997; Resnick, Pontecorvo, & Säljö, 1997). This approach examines inventors in the context of socially distributed work and socially shared knowledge. The concept of situated cognition is well suited, for instance, to explain expertise in laboratory settings (e.g., Collins, 1985). In this case, becoming an inventor consists of a productive adaptation to a particular social and technological setting. One presupposition of situated cognition is that knowledge, theories, and language are *tools* or instruments that are socially shared. Accordingly, any invention is contextual, and innovation processes

TABLE 3.2   Theorizing About Inventors

	Expertise	Situated Cognition	Possibility Filter
Concept of inventor	Expert in invention (mastery)	Productive mutual adaptation of a person and his or her sociotechnological environment	Inventor as the instrument of sociotechnological development
Level of explanation	Individual	Networks (individuals *and* social situations)	Individual and sociotechnological
Studies (examples)	Henderson (2004), Hoisl (2007)	Hakkarainen et al. (2004)	Weber (1996)
Open issues (examples)	Domain specificity of expertise does not seem to hold for inventors	The concept of situated cognition better explains innovation than invention	Measuring the success of individual inventors

are best explained via networked expertise (Hakkarainen, Palonen, Paavola, & Lehtinen, 2004). Thus, the role of the individual expert inventor is to complete a task in a time-efficient manner, while others would need much longer to do so (Mieg, 2001).

Both approaches leave some issues unresolved. The psychology of expertise has collected rich evidence for the domain specificity of expertise. However, inventors systematically cross borders. Even today, young entrepreneurial inventors such as Alexander Olek (Berlin) have major inventions in different domains, such as high-tech biomedicine, farming, and Internet encyclopedia. The situated cognition approach explains processes of innovation at an organizational or community-of-practice level (firm, cluster, a nation) much better than the expertise approach, with its focus on the individual process of invention. From this point of view, the use of individual invention might be a case of "blind variation and selective retention" (Campbell, 1960). Both approaches, however, underexpose the *technological* side of invention. An invention ought to *function*, and inventors feel compassion towards this end. In "The Architecture of Invention" workshop, the inventor Murphy spoke of his own compulsion to be creative: "It's not because I wanted to be creative, but because I see things around me that aren't accomplishing what they are intended to accomplish. And I have a compulsion to try to do something about that" (Lemelson-MIT Program, 2003, p. 23).

A third approach is provided by the concept of the possibility filter, introduced by Robert Weber (2006): "In my interviews with inventors, and in the case of the Wrights, the inventors tend to view the world in an unusual way: through the eyes of possibility" (p. 5). The central element of this concept consists of the technological vision, in the case of the Wright brothers, "the flight problem" of achieving powered and sustained heavier-than-air human flight. This technological vision defines a *directed, cognitive space*. The possibility filter "means that the inventor sees the world in a different way: not as it is but as it might be" (p. 6). Thus, the possibility filter leads to the:

- Selection and integration of new information (even failure)
- Generation of knowledge (via metacognition)
- Definition of developmental paths/trajectories (personally and technologically)

In particular, the possibility filter recognizes a common phenomenon reported in interviews (e.g., Brown, 1988), namely, that *inventors try to integrate or test any type of information from any source (technological, private, social, etc.) in order to realize their technological vision.* It is for that reason that analogy is an important heuristic in invention. The notion of a possibility filter also fits well with a view often expressed about designers: They are constantly thinking about comparisons and seeking to take immediate advantage of solution opportunities (cf. Hoffman, Roesler, & Moon, 2004). The concept of the possibility filter makes it possible to describe invention at both the individual level and the sociotechnological level, for instance, in the case of the historical perspective of the flight problem. The concept of the possibility filter implies a contextualization of invention: The inventors provide technological visions. We can even say: The inventor becomes an instrument of the realization of his or her vision. Therefore, possibility filters are not domain specific; rather, a possibility filter creates its own domain. Inventors serve as "domain pioneers."

Presently, the possibility filter seems to be the most powerful cognitive concept to explain inventor behavior from both a long-term and a cognitive perspective. As inventor behavior is a complex phenomenon embedded in an even more complex cultural and organizational context, research will perhaps never find a minimal and sufficient set of inventor heuristics or personality factors for invention. From the perspective of the possibility filter, the open question is how to measure success of such long-term projects, such as technological visions. A broader and richer understanding of inventors could contribute to science and technology education and workforce issues.

References

Boden, M. A. (2003). *The creative mind: Myths and mechanisms* (2nd ed.). London, UK: Routledge.

Braun, A., Mieg, H. A., & Neyer, F. J. (2009). Sind Erfinder anders als es die Kreativitätsforschung erwarten lässt? [Do inventors differ from how psychological research perceives them?] *Wirtschaftspsychologie, 11*(1), 69–79.

Brown, K. A. (1988). *Inventors at work: Interviews with 16 notable American inventors.* Redmond, WA: Tempus/Microsoft.

Campbell, D. T. (1960). Blind variation and selective retention in creative thought as in other knowledge processes. *Psychological Review, 67*(6), 380–400.

Clancey, W. J. (1997). *Situated cognition.* Cambridge, UK: Cambridge University Press.

Collins, H. M. (1985). *Changing order.* London, UK: Sage.

DABEI (Deutsche Aktionsgemeinschaft Bildung - Erfindung - Innovation) (Eds.). (1987). *DABEI-Handbuch für Erfinder und Unternehmer* [DABEI handbook for inventors and entrepreneurs]. Düsseldorf, Germany: VDI-Verlag.

Dörner, D., Kreuzig, H. W., Reither, F., & Stäudel, T. (Eds.). (1983). *Lohhausen: Vom Umgang mit Unbestimmtheit und Komplexität* [Lohhausen: On dealing with uncertainty and complexity]. Bern, Switzerland: Huber.

Dörner, D., & Schölkopf, J. (1991). Controlling complex systems; or, expertise as "grandmother's know-how." In K. A. Ericsson & J. Smith (Eds.), *Towards a general theory of expertise: Prospects and limits* (pp. 218–239). New York, NY: Cambridge University Press.

Duncker, K. (1935). *Zur Psychologie des produktiven Denkens* [The psychology of productive thinking]. Berlin, Germany: Springer.

Ericsson, K. A., Charness, N., Feltovich, P., & Hoffman, R. R. (Eds.). (2006). *The Cambridge handbook of expertise and expert performance*. Cambridge, UK: Cambridge University Press.

Ernst, H., Leptien, C., & Vitt, J. (2000). Inventors are not alike: The distribution of patenting output among industrial RandD personnel. *IEEE Transactions on Engineering Management, 47*(2), 184–199.

Feltovich, P. J., Prietula, M. J., & Ericsson, K. A. (2006). Studies of expertise from psychological perspectives. In K. A. Ericsson, N. Charness, P. Feltovich, & R. R. Hoffman (Eds.), *The Cambridge handbook of expertise and expert performance* (pp. 41–67). Cambridge, UK: Cambridge University Press.

Fischer, A. (1987). Erfolg ist das Produkt stetiger Mehrleistung [Success is the result of permanent supererogation]. In DABEI (Ed.), *DABEI-Handbuch für Erfinder und Unternehmer* (pp. 390–392). Düsseldorf, Germany: VDI-Verlag.

Frensch, P. A., & Funke, J. (Eds.) (1995). *Complex problem solving: The European perspective*. Hillsdale, NJ: Lawrence Erlbaum.

Funke, J. (1998). Computer-based testing and training with scenarios from complex problem solving research: Advantages and disadvantages. *International Journal of Selection and Assessment, 6*, 90–96.

Giuri, P., Mariani, M., Brusoni, S., Crespi, G., Francoz, D., Gambardella, A., ... Verspagen, B. (2007). Inventors and invention processes in Europe: Results from the PatVal-EU survey. *Research Policy, 36*, 1107–1127.

Guilford, J. P. (1967). *The nature of human intelligence*. New York, NY: McGraw-Hill.

Hakkarainen, K., Palonen, T., Paavola, S., & Lehtinen, E. (2004). *Communities of networked expertise: Educational and professional perspectives*. Amsterdam, Netherlands: Elsevier.

Henderson, S. J. (2004). Inventors: The ordinary genius next door. In R. J. Sternberg, E. L. Grigorenko, & J. L. Singer (Eds.), *Creativity: From potential to realization* (pp. 103–125). Washington, DC: American Psychology Association.

Hoffman, R. R., Roesler, A., & Moon, B. M. (2004). What is design in the context of human-centered computing? *IEEE Intelligent Systems, 19*(4), 89–95.

Hoisl, K. (2007). Tracing mobile inventors: The causality between inventor mobility and inventor productivity. *Research Policy, 36*, 619–636.

Huber, J. C. (1998). Invention and inventivity is a random, Poisson process: A potential guide to analysis of general creativity. *Creativity Research Journal, 11*(3), 231–241.

Kassicieh, S. K., Radosevich, H. R., & Banbury, C. M. (1997). Using attitudinal, situational, and personal characteristics variables to predict future entrepreneurs from national laboratory inventors. *IEEE Transactions on Engineering Management, 44*(3), 248–257.

King, L. A., McKee Walker, L., & Broyles, S. J. (1996). Creativity and the five-factor model. *Journal of Research in Personality, 30*, 189–203.

Kirton, M. J. (1976). Adaptors and innovators: A description and a measure. *Journal of Applied Psychology, 61*, 622–629.

Kirton, M. J. (1994). *Adaptors and innovators: Styles of creativity and problem solving*. New York, NY: Routledge.

Kreuzig, H. W. (1981). Über den Zugang zu komplexem Problemlösen mittels prozessorientierter und kognitiver Persönlichkeitsmerkmale [An approach to complex problem solving via process-oriented and cognitive personality traits]. *Zeitschrift für experimentelle und angewandte Psychologie, 28*, 62–91.

Lemelson-MIT Program. (2003). *The architecture of invention* (Report of the workshop, held in August 2003). Boston, MA: School of Engineering, Massachusetts Institute of Technology. Retrieved February 14, 2009, from http://web.mit.edu/INVENT/n-pressreleases/downloads/architecture.pdf

Lotka, A. J. (1926). The frequency distribution of scientific productivity. *Journal of the Washington Academy of Science, 16*, 317–323.

McCrae, R. R. (1987). Creativity, divergent thinking, and openness to experience. *Journal of Personality and Social Psychology, 52*(6), 1258–1265.

Mieg, H. A. (1993). *Computers as experts? On the non-existence of expert systems.* New York, NY: Lang.

Mieg, H. A. (2001). *The social psychology of expertise.* Mahwah, NJ: Lawrence Erlbaum Associates.

Minsky, M. (1975). A framework for representing knowledge. In P. H. Winston (Ed.), *The psychology of computer vision* (pp. 211–277). New York, NY: McGraw-Hill.

Narin, F., & Breitzman, A. (1995). Inventive productivity. *Research Policy, 24*, 507–519.

Newell, A. (1985). Duncker on thinking: An inquiry into progress on cognition. In S. Koch & D. E. Leary (Eds.), *A century of psychology as a science* (pp. 392–419). Oxford, UK: Oxford University Press.

Newell, A., & Simon, H. A. (1972). *Human problem solving.* Englewood Cliffs, NJ: Prentice-Hall.

Ng, A. K., & Rodrigues, D. (2002). A big-five personality profile of the adaptor and innovator. *Journal of Creativity Behaviour, 36*(4), 254–268.

Perkins, D. N. (2004). Mapping the inventive mind. In Lemelson-MIT Program (Ed.), *Invention: Enhancing inventiveness for quality of life, competitiveness, and sustainability* (Report, pp. 37–45). Boston, MA: School of Engineering, Massachusetts Institute of Technology. Retrieved February 14, 2009, from http://web.mit.edu/Invent/n-pressreleases/downloads/report.pdf

Perkins, D. N., & Weber, R. J. (1992). Conclusion: Effable invention. In R. J. Weber & D. N. Perkins (Eds.), *Inventive minds: Creativity in technology* (pp. 317–336). New York, NY: Oxford University Press.

Price, D. J. S. (1963). *Little science, big science.* New York, NY: Columbia University Press.

Resnick, B. L., Pontecorvo, C., & Säljö, R. (1997). Discourse, tools, and reasoning. In B. L. Resnick, R. Säljö, C. Pontecorvo, & B. Burge (Eds.), *Discourse, tools, and reasoning: Essays on situated cognition* (pp. 1–20). Berlin, Germany: Springer.

Rossman, J. (1964). *Industrial creativity: The psychology of the inventor.* New Hyde Park, NY: University Books.

Simonton, D. K. (1988). *Scientific genius: A psychology of science.* Cambridge, UK: Cambridge University Press.

Wagener, D. (2001). *Psychologische Diagnostik mit komplexen Szenarios* [Psychological diagnostics with complex scenarios]. Lengerich, Germany: Pabst Science Publishers.

Weber, R. J. (1992a). *Forks, phonographs, and hot air balloons: A field guide to inventive thinking.* New York, NY: Oxford University Press.

Weber, R. J. (1992b). Stone age knife to Swiss army knife: An invention prototype. In R. J. Weber & D. N. Perkins (Eds.), *Inventive minds: Creativity in technology* (pp. 217–237). New York, NY: Oxford University Press.

Weber, R. J. (1996). Toward a language of invention and synthetic thinking. *Creativity Research Journal, 9*(4), 353–364.

Weber, R. J. (2006). *The Wright Brothers and the heuristics of invention.* Paper presented at the Expertise in Context Conference, Berlin, July 26–28.

Weber, R. J., Moder, C. L., & Solie, J. B. (1990). Invention heuristics and mental processes underlying the development of a patent for the application of herbicides. *New Ideas in Psychology, 8*(3), 341–336.

Weisberg, R. W. (2006). *Creativity: Understanding innovation in problem solving, science, invention, and the arts.* Hoboken, NJ: John Wiley.

West, M. A. (2002). Sparkling fountains or stagnant ponds: An integrative model of creativity and innovation implementation in work groups. *Applied Psychology, 51*(3), 355–424.

Wolf, K. (2006). *Complex problem solving and divergent thinking of inventors.* Paper presented at the Expertise in Context Conference, Berlin, July 26–28.

Wolf, K., & Mieg, H. A. (2010). Inventors as experts in complex problem solving? *European Journal of Cognitive Psychology, 22*(3), 443–462.

4

Large-Scale Coordination of Work
Coping With Complex Chaos Within Healthcare

Shawna J. Perry
Virginia Commonwealth University Health Sciences System

Robert L. Wears
University of Florida School of Medicine, and Imperial College

In complex joint cognitive systems, work is subdivided into assigned subtasks that bring workers together ostensibly when there is a need for subtasks to interact and not necessarily specific individuals (Nemeth, 2003). Such collaboration among workers becomes large in scale when the scope or the work extends beyond what small, stable groups can accomplish within limited time spans (Obradovich & Smith, 2003), for example, when the task requires additional input or expertise from other groups. During normal operations, the interdependency and adaptive capabilities of these complex cognitive systems are "hard to see," embedded in the work for which the system is organized to perform (Hutchins, 1996; Wears, 2005). The study of such systems in context is challenging as one is attempting to learn about visible and invisible activities of coordinated and collaborative work and how these are shaped by the artifacts, goals, and constraints of the organization and the work domain (Woods, 2000). This chapter will discuss three cases where large-scale coordination was needed in a joint cognitive system in which groups were forced beyond the "horizon of tractability" (Voß, Procter, Slack, Hartswood, & Rouncefield, 2006) into situations of increasing risk, growing unpredictability, and expanding complexity. Each case provides a glimpse of the embedded and generally invisible adaptive dynamics that were made visible during off-normal operations and irregular functioning.

Working Big: Large-Scale Coordination of Work

Large-scale coordination is central to large operations such as the military, disaster response, or transportation, such as railroads or aviation, with a growing interest in understanding how these systems interact (Klein, 2000; Salas & Fiore, 2004; Smith, McCoy, & Orasanu, 2001). In such settings, workers must share pertinent knowledge, beliefs, and assumptions in support of interdependent activity (Clark, 1996). Maintaining common ground has been characterized as a dynamic process that requires continual communication, testing, updating, tailoring, and repairing of mutual understandings (Brennan, 1998), with the expectation that participants will work together and be mutually predictable and directable (Klein, Woods, Bradshaw, Hoffman, & Feltovich, 2004).

Effective human-human communication is a critical feature for successful coordination on a large scale, for it not only establishes common ground, but supports effective decision making, especially for highly consequential and time-pressured situations (Johansson & Hollnagel, 2007). The resilient behaviors necessary for effective interaction in large coordinated systems are not readily apparent, usually occurring informally and in undocumented ways. Research into railroad operations (Roth, Multer, & Raslear, 2007) has demonstrated a number of such strategies for building and maintaining situational awareness and safety across this widely distributed work environment. Because groups at work within the railway system are physically unable to work simultaneously (a moving train and a track worker cannot occupy the same space at the same time), they must work at a cooperative distance, allowing the transition of track control based on the needs of the system and problems at hand. The frequent juggling of track control between trains and groups of workers elicited proactive *ad hoc* behaviors, such as track workers calling a passing train to tell them of other crews they may pass in the coming miles, or dispatchers notifying rail crews of the status of their protected time on track. The majority of these behaviors were found to be voluntary, undocumented in operational rules, yet readily adopted by railway workers because of their obvious contribution to safe operations across the joint system. Such adaptive behaviors modify how the joint system works, is grounded in experience, and seeks to achieve antientropic ends, for example, avoidance of train derailment and passenger injury or death, or death of workers struck by a train (Hollnagel, Woods, & Leveson, 2006).

The potentially brittle nature of large distributed systems is rarely apparent until they are required to respond emergently, for instance, to a natural disaster or major system failure like a blackout. In these instances, large-scale joint activity is expected to be successful, assumed by observers to be tightly choreographed and prescribed by policies and procedures. Failures of such endeavors commonly play out in a spectacular fashion, for example, Mann Gulch Fire (Weick, 1993) or Hurricane Katrina (Cooper & Block, 2006), in which work did not proceed as envisioned, even for the workers involved in the response effort. In these instances, workers are called upon to create *ad hoc* strategies in real time to support crucial components of their joint activity for which common ground was not well established and which is not backed up by adequate human-human communication and decision making.

Joint Work Systems in Healthcare: Work at a Cooperative Distance

Healthcare organizations are complex institutions composed of guilds of specialized workers (i.e., clinicians, allied health staff, administrative personnel) who work fairly independently to provide or support medical care. The successful completion of their mission to care adequately for the sick and injured (Lasagna, 1964) requires large-scale coordination of work *among* and *across* these groups. These groups may be comprised of individuals from the same skill group or different ones, depending upon the circumstance (e.g., operating room team will have physician(s), nurses, and technicians; yet an internal medicine admitting team may consist of only a physician and a physician's assistant). Coordination of work on such a scale in the sociotechnically rich environment of healthcare requires various degrees of coupling between work activities, decision making, and patient care that are generally underappreciated by healthcare workers and opaque to the patients under their care.

In the hospital setting, workers traditionally work within a vertical organizational structure that minimizes the appearance of interdependence, establishing fairly rigid boundaries for responsibility and authority in medical decision making and provision of care. Each guild of healthcare workers (physicians, nurses, respiratory technicians, pharmacy, etc.) organizes its work to appear independent, despite the fact that patient care, of course, requires their collaboration. This arrangement minimizes the apparent complexity of the work, as communication and task handoffs are more efficient, and it is also easier for financial management of the organization (Jenny W. Rudolph, personal communication). As a result, each guild addresses only issues specific to its group without considering their impact on other groups, providing a locally bounded view of the hospital operations—like the proverbial blind men all touching different parts of the elephant, with different perceptions and interpretations of the realities of the organizations (Jenny W. Rudolph, personal communication).

This illusion of separateness leads to work groups having no insight into their interdependence. This shortcoming is seldom challenged as there are few opportunities for groups to explicitly coordinate their interactions. Assessment and care is provided at a "cooperative distance," in a serial fashion, with only one group "working" on the patient at any given time. The result is limited face-to-face communication on joint problem solving by teams that manage the same patient. Communication instead occurs through a cognitive artifact, such as the medical record. In the United States this sequential delivery of care has become more entrenched as a result of the growing sociotechnical complexity of clinical care, increased subspecialization, and more prescriptive rules for billing and reimbursement (Maloney, 1992). "Siloed" or standalone behavior within the distributed system of healthcare is particularly evident among physicians who typically do not seek to cross boundaries, and opportunities to do so rarely occur, except for short periods. In these few instances, interactions take place in a formal and stereotypically choreographed fashion; for example, anesthesiologists and surgeons must work simultaneously on the patient, or an emergency physician will provide procedural sedation while an orthopedist reduces a fracture. During these interactions, the boundaries between specialties are maintained and limited to communication on a "need to know" basis; for example, the anesthetist informs the surgeon that the patient's blood pressure is dropping after unexpected bleeding has occurred, but there is no discussion of what the appropriate intervention should or will be.

Subspecialization has also taken its toll among physicians, resulting in narrower views of a patient's care and impoverished understandings of other domains and opportunities for collective simultaneous clinical work (Hashem, Chi, & Friedman, 2003; Swarztrauber & Vickrey, 2004). Below we will contrast two cases in which medical workers were required to bridge their cooperative distance to manage situations of increasing risk, growing unpredictability, and expanding complexity with variable success.

Peace and War

CASE 1 (PERRY, WEARS, ANDERSON, & BOOTH, 2007, P. 2)

A 33 year old 37-week pregnant woman presented to the Emergency Department (ED) complaining of chest and abdominal pain of 24 hours duration. She was sent to the labor and delivery (L&D) floor per hospital protocol for evaluation of pre-term labor and fetal monitoring. Initial assessment by the Obstetrics and Gynecology (OBGYN) resident found no significant problems, but during the night the patient developed increasing chest and abdominal pain and an unstable blood pressure. The OBGYN resident called his supervising attending physician for assistance in the early evening, some 9 hours after the patient checked into the hospital.

Repeat assessment by the OBGYN attending strongly suggested a heart attack as the cause of the patient's worsening condition, and she was moved to L&D for immediate Cesarean section (C-section) to reduce the stress of the pregnancy on her heart and decrease the risk of fetal demise. The attending anesthesiologist expressed concern about sedating the patient, citing the high mortality rate associated with heart attacks in pregnancy, should that be the problem. He felt that a more definitive diagnosis should be obtained before proceeding.

Several failed attempts were made to reach a cardiology resident and the increasingly anxious OBGYN attending called the ED attending on duty to ask for assistance. Upon hearing the story, the ED physician recommended treating the patient as if it were a heart attack, physically located the cardiology fellow and proceeded to the patient's bedside in the operating room. After a very brief review of the data collected so far, the cardiology attending on-call was contacted at home for guidance in managing a possible cardiac event in a pregnant woman; he voluntarily came from home to the hospital.

Three life threatening diagnoses were entertained: a heart attack, an aortic dissection (splitting of the major artery leading from the heart), or a pulmonary embolism (blood clot in the lungs). Each specialty advocated different action plans: the OBGYN attending wanted to deliver the baby immediately due to increasing fetal distress; the anesthesia attending remained reluctant to anesthetize the patient for C-section until the diagnosis for her chest pain became clearer; the ED attending advocated stabilizing the patient with intubation due to her increasing agitation and confusion and to support her during further, more extensive evaluation; the cardiology attending wanted to take the patient to cardiac catherization for definitive diagnosis and treatment if this were a heart attack. Definitive diagnosis could also be made with a computed tomography (CT) scan, however, it was not clear the patient would tolerate being moved several times (operating room to CT scan to intensive care unit (ICU)) and there was concern about the high dose of radiation to the fetus.

Over a short period of time (less than one hour), the group decided to prioritize the treatment of the mother over the child and to perform an alternative test (ultrasound) to evaluate for aortic dissection (the condition with the highest mortality), avoiding a move of the patient to CT scan. The ED attending persuaded the group to intubate prior to the procedure and to make one move to the ICU where all of her needs could be met.

Once moved, a bedside ultrasound demonstrated a massive aortic dissection *and* large heart attack. Following discussion with cardio-thoracic surgery and the family, it was decided to perform an emergent C-section, during which it was found that the dissection had resulted in extensive dead bowel which would be fatal to the patient. The baby was delivered and the patient subsequently expired once removed from life support.

CASE 2 (PERRY, WEARS, ANDERSON, & BOOTH, 2007, P. 3)

A 28 year old woman, recovering in labor and delivery (L&D) after a C-section a few hours earlier for severe pre-eclampsia (elevated blood pressure) suddenly became unresponsive with agonal respirations. A "Code Blue" was paged out across the hospital to mobilize the resuscitation team. The overnight ED attending responded along with one of her resident in their assigned role of airway management for the code team. Upon arrival, she found several members of the L&D staff at the bedside of the patient who was now in full cardio-pulmonary arrest. The staff was watching a certified nurse anesthetist (CRNA) frantically attempting to intubate the patient while shouting orders into the air that no one was following. The ED attending introduced herself and her resident openly to the room and assumed control of the code, assigning tasks to specific staff, such as beginning chest compressions and administering IV medications. An ED nurse arrived to assist (despite having been directed to remain in the ED when the code was paged out), stating that she came upstairs anyway to see if they needed any help, as "codes up here can be a mess." A pulse and blood pressure were quickly regained following the clinical interventions and the patient was intubated and placed on a ventilator by the CRNA.

Despite initial stabilization of the patient, the CRNA continued to give orders for medications and became angry when the ED attending informed her that the medications she was ordering were not needed at that time. The CRNA abruptly left the code and sought out the anesthesia attending (who is not part of the code team). The anesthesia attending arrived and began shouting orders, behaving as if she were assuming care. The EM attending told her that she was willing to transfer care as she needed to get back to the ED but wanted to announce the transfer to minimize staff confusion over who they should take orders from. At this point, the nursing supervisor (who is responsible for administrative operations at night) stepped in and blocked the transfer of care and requested that the ED attending remain in charge to ensure continuity and quality of care because the ED attending had more experience running cardiac resuscitations. The anesthesiologist became very angry but acquiesced under protest and left the area.

The ED attending continued to resuscitate the patient, who had developed a precipitous drop in her hemoglobin and platelet counts in the few hours following the C-section with no evidence of active bleeding. Suspecting HELLP syndrome, an uncommon but life-threatening complication of eclampsia that can occur within hours of delivery, the ED attending asked to speak to the OBGYN attending who performed the surgery and who was the patient's physician of record. The OBGYN attending did not participate in the resuscitation, and only briefly entered to answer a few questions when requested and promptly left. The EM attending ordered a massive transfusion protocol for the patient, but the L&D staff were unfamiliar with this protocol. The ED nurse called the ED to request several units of O negative blood be brought upstairs immediately. The patient was transferred to the first available intensive care bed in the hospital, which happened to be in the surgical intensive care unit (SICU), and prepared to transfer care to the medical ICU (MICU) resident (who was present for the code), as has been customary for critically ill obstetric patients.

When the MICU attending was contacted at home to inform her about the case, she refused to accept the patient because the patient had undergone a surgical procedure (C-section) four hours earlier. She directed the MICU resident to transfer care to the SICU residents, who agreed to accept the patient. This transfer was not communicated to the ED attending, in the expectation that she would soon be returning to the ED.

As the ED attending sat in the SICU finishing her documentation of the code blue, the SICU attending arrived, irate that the patient had been accepted into the SICU without consulting her, in violation of surgery department customs. Critical of the care provided thus far, she accused the other clinicians of abandoning the patient in the SICU. While expressing her criticism, the patient again descended into cardiopulmonary arrest. The ED attending and SICU attending both supervised resuscitative efforts; however, the patient expired. Autopsy found the patient's death resulted from HELLP syndrome, which had caused a large hemorrhage in the liver.

The two cases have similar clinical and social contexts, with both involving obstetric patients in critical condition, characterized by substantial uncertainty, and ultimately requiring the simultaneous rather than sequential involvement of clinicians from different specialties. Both involve "pickup" teams composed of clinicians who rarely work together and in some cases had never seen each other before. There is increasing complexity as the patients deteriorated; however, despite these similarities, the interactions of the medical teams were very different.

Case 1 is a striking demonstration of the emergence of collaborative behaviors and resilient interactions in support of decision making and action for a remarkably complex clinical problem. The simultaneous work of multiple clinical specialties (OBGYN, emergency medicine, anesthesia, and cardiology) is a deviation from the normally bounded work environment in the hospital and expected work routines of those involved. Methods for adapting to the changing clinical course of the patient were unplanned, informal, and outside the normal chain of command (such as the OBGYN attending calling the ED for help), and novel to the individuals involved. The involvement of some of the individuals was necessary (OBGYN required anesthesia to perform a C-section), yet others were voluntary (the ED attending physically locating the cardiology fellow and leaving the ED to come to the bedside; the cardiology attending coming in from home). The primary actors recognized that their individual expertise was necessary but not sufficient for managing this evolving clinical and ethically complex case (whether to prioritize mother or child).

The final action plan in Case 1 was the result of collaborative behavior by the physicians rather than serial interactions with the patient, and it was decided upon jointly once common ground was established (mother first, baby second). Interestingly, very specific actions took place to support the distributed decision making and the necessary human-human interactions important for effective coordination (the ED physician physically located the cardiology fellow and took him to the patient's bedside; the cardiology attending voluntarily came into the hospital from home in the middle of the night). These conversations could have been held by telephone (and usually are). The decisions of the physicians to be physically present during the joint decision making suggests an implicit understanding of the benefits of human-human interaction in the face of high risk and growing complexity.

The four physicians and nurses involved in Case 1 represented four specialties and formed a distributed cognitive system, exhibiting important adaptive properties (Hollnagel & Woods, 2006). Specifically, by mutual deference to expertise they supported the requirement of *directability*, where strategic directions were changed based on current events, past history, and anticipated future directions. Similarly, they supported the facility of *shifting perspectives*, in which each could articulate important but local goals that served to point out alternatives for action and kept the team from being trapped in a narrow view of the problem.

In marked contrast, Case 2 is characterized by sharply drawn lines of responsibility and authority that resulted in little collaborative work or decision making across the five specialties involved in the patient's care (ED, OBGYN, anesthesia, MICU, and SICU). The clinicians were unable to form a distributed cognitive system due to the dominance of silo thinking and territorial behavior. Opportunities for collaborative, adaptive decision making were overwhelmed by competition for power and a failure to recognize the need for barriers to be crossed during a rapidly changing, unclear, and unstable situation. Many of the physicians failed to acknowledge the necessary expertise of others present at different times during the case (e.g., the CRNA becoming angry after the ED attending told her there was no need for certain medications; the SICU attending being critical of care provided prior to her arrival). These rigid boundaries even manifested in clinicians physically leaving treatment areas despite their potential value to the situation at hand (e.g., the anesthesiologist leaving under protest when the nurse supervisor stated the ED attending should run the code; the OBGYN attending standing in the hallway during a code on his patient, until asked for consultation by the ED attending; the MICU attending refusing a customary admission of the critical OBGYN patient because of the recent C-section). The ED attending, a recent graduate, may also have lacked the experience and necessary skill to repair and build consensus or to bridge a perceived authority gradient in the fractured work environment. The time course for this case, however, was much shorter than for Case 1, which may not have allowed for effectively overcoming any of these boundaries by the actors. The resulting fractious interplay smothered opportunities for joint problem solving.

One important obstacle to establishing adaptive behaviors in distributed work is overcontrol by any single individual or group (Brehmer, 1987). The actors in Case 1 were able to avoid overcontrol by one individual as the situation became more critical. Formality, in the form of medical-legal responsibility, seniority, and organizational hierarchy, was supplanted by the reality of the complexity of the case and the dire consequences for mother and baby. The result was shared decision making and negotiated solutions rather than actions being taken along the traditional lines of responsibility and authority. In Case 2, various individuals actively competed for control, and refused to be involved in care if they could not have it (CRNA, anesthesiologist), or avoided responsibility and involvement (OBGYN, MICU).

Some resilient behaviors did occur in Case 2 in an attempt to adapt to the situation, but these actions did not change the overall tone of the group interaction. These included the ED nurse coming upstairs to see if she could be of assistance based on her experience with codes in labor and delivery, the nursing supervisor blocking the transfer of care from the ED attending to the anesthesiologist based on level of expertise in running codes, and the shared resuscitative efforts by the ED and SICU attending. Each of these acts was an attempt to establish common ground around placing the needs of the patient first, and to redirect the group toward more cooperative and resilient interactions that were predictable and directable, rather than fractious and disorganized.

The reasons for these remarkable differences in group interaction and decision making in these similar cases are not clear. One possible contributor to the failure of medical workers in Case 2 to sustain resilient, collaborative interactions may have been that their mental models were inappropriate for emergent problem solving. A rigid adherence to the chain of command and bounded interactions are seen in the behaviors of the CRNA, anesthesiologist, and SICU attending, who all challenged the role of the ED attending in the provision of care, despite her demonstrated expertise (e.g., rapid organizing of patient's care and stabilization). Providers' attempts to impose structure were likely grounded in their belief that these were necessary to manage critical incidents. Their belief was further strengthened by the behavior of the OBGYN, who abdicated responsibility despite the fact that he had performed the C-section and had been the physician of record. This mindset, however, does not allow for the flexibility necessary in situations when decisions have to be made based on inadequate, uncertain, or ambiguous data. While the clinical outcome for the patient in Case 2 likely would not have been any different, providers' insistence on a rigid structure in their relationships and decision making impacted safe operations and system resilience. One may be tempted to argue that the events of Case 2 were the result of the unfamiliarity of participants, who were, for the most part, strangers professionally and personally, coming together for the first time under highly stressful and unusual circumstances. The ensuing conflict-ridden situation would accordingly not seem surprising, given that everyone was out of their element. This view, however, is contradicted by Case 1, which occurred under essentially the same circumstances yet resulted in transactive communication and resilient interactions with joint, distributed decision making in a very complex clinical, as well as ethical, situation.

These two cases compare and contrast features of distributed coordination that may occur at the micro-system level among and across frontline workers. The following case illustrates how these same properties can manifest at the unit level, when different units are challenged with an evolving situation of rapidly expanding complexity and high risk.

Free Fall: Another Exercise in Resilient Distributed Work

Emergency departments (EDs) are dynamic, open, high-risk cognitive systems that operate under considerable uncertainty, yet most have been engineered or designed for their work to only a limited extent. EDs must continually adapt to and accommodate multiple types of variation in their work (e.g., in numbers of patients, or in the kinds of diagnostic or therapeutic problems encountered), as well as account for constraints of economics and human work limits that tend to push them toward their maximum capacity (Leveson, 2004) and the boundary of the safe operating envelope (Cook & Rasmussen, 2005). Many of these adaptations serve as readily available solutions to the "expected, normal and natural troubles" with which workers have become familiar through experience and word of mouth (Voß et al., 2006).

For the most part, the usual solutions to the usual problems in the ED are contained within a *horizon of tractability* (Voß et al., 2006). Actions are skillfully and unconsciously, almost invisibly, performed (Woods & Hollnagel, 2006). The resilient capacity of EDs, however, is finite. Its limits are not commonly reached—if they were, the organization would cease to exist—so they are typically exceeded only by circumstances beyond operational experience. In such cases, the resulting events offer insight into the ways in which people in the system are sensitive to the possibility of failure, know where to look for evidence of failure and for the resources to cope with it, choose strategies to regain control of the system, and decide which goals to sacrifice in order to meet more important goals and maintain system integrity.

In the following case, the resilient capacity of the ED was exceeded, leaving the system in an uncontrolled state (called free fall by the individuals experiencing it), and it demonstrates how workers adapt independently but in a distributed, coordinated fashion to threats to the operational integrity of the system.

CASE 3 (WEARS, PERRY, ANDERS, & WOODS, 2008)

At the start of the evening shift, the entire 52-bed ED was boarding 43 patients awaiting an inpatient room; 28 of these filled the unit reserved for boarders, the remaining 15 were split among the other two areas and the hallway separating the units. Seven were held in the hallway; all four of the acute care unit's critical care bays were filled with admitted patients on ventilators. As the shift change rounds began, the ED received a critically ill ambulance patient. Over the course of the next four hours, an additional five critically ill patients requiring ventilator support and other intensive measures arrived, in addition to multiple additional seriously but not critically ill patients (e.g., chest pain suggestive of heart attack). All treatment spaces were filled; all temporary spaces to hold stretchers were filled; the unit ran out of stretchers and began "storing" incoming patients in chairs near the nursing station. Congestion was severe, making it physically difficult to move around in the treatment area. This was particularly a problem when new critical patients arrived, since they needed to go to specific treatment spaces for needed equipment, and the patients occupying those spaces thus needed to be moved to other locations on very short notice.

The staff later described this situation as a feeling of "free fall," in which they did not know the numbers, types, or problems of the patients in their unit. The crisis continued until approximately 2200, by which time the staff felt they had finally gained control of the situation (in the sense of having a clear picture of which patients were present, where they were located, and at least a vague idea of the nature of their problem) and that the system had stabilized. No adverse events were associated with this episode, as far as is known.

This case represents an episode where the horizon of tractability was exceeded by conditions beyond the range of previous operating experience. The resources and coping strategies for the ED that would normally provide resilience against variation and the unexpected were exhausted, compelling workers to invent new strategies "on the fly" and to make sacrifice decisions, abandoning clinical operations in order to regain control of the situation (Cook & Nemeth, 2006). The workers invoked progressively less familiar adaptations, shifting to "irregular reduced functioning" as the volume of patients grew (see Figure 4.1).

Initially the staff coped with this rapidly expanding workload of critical patients by sacrificing some lower-level goals, such as timely performance of EKGs, customer service activities such as allowing visitors into the area, and reduced administration of all but essential medications. In effect, this strategy identified patients who

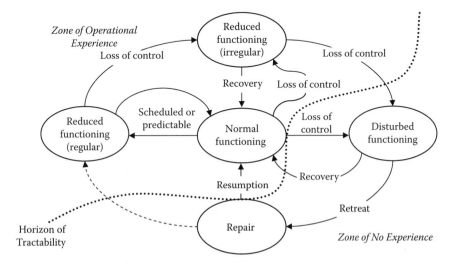

FIGURE 4.1 State-space diagram for service organizations. (Modified from Hollnagel, E., and Sundström, G. (2006). States of resilience. In Hollnagel, E., Woods, D.D., and Levenson, N. (Eds.) *Resilience engineering.* Aldershot, UK: Ashgate, pp. 339–346. With permission.)

were believed to be physiologically more resilient, and "borrowed" some of their resilience to provide additional capacity to support higher-level goals and operations. This strategy provided compensatory buffers to manage the disturbance and was a routine first-line approach for the unit. Workers rapidly migrated to progressively less familiar adaptations, for example, placing patients in chairs. As the number of patients grew rapidly (and seemingly without limit), additional space was located; for example, a small office was used to perform ECGs, because it had a door that could be closed for privacy. Similarly, a small closet was used as a blood drawing area, and newly arrived patients were managed in the hallway when space was exhausted.

Ultimately, the ED was forced to retreat entirely from any semblance of routine operations for all but the most time critical of patients. This was a strategic decision to stop operations and regroup, and led to a shift in operations from medical content to simple tracking—identifying patients, the (irregular) spaces to which they were assigned, and a vague categorization of problem type. This move was aided by creating a second status board within the main status board, used for patients without assigned treatment areas (e.g., waiting in chairs). In terms of goal states, the adaptive strategy sacrificed most lower- and intermediate-level goals (e.g., feeding patients, requiring attending review of all lower-acuity patients) in order to preserve resources to restart the system once the disturbance had passed.

Once the repair was successfully accomplished (in that workers now knew which patients they had responsibility for, where those patients were physically located, and what their basic problem type was), and the system stabilized (aided by the decrease in the numbers of incoming critical patients), then normal operations gradually resumed. This was done cautiously; it took some time to build up confidence that the current assessments were accurate and complete—the "continuing expectation of future surprise" (Rochlin, 1999) led to a conservative and gradual restarting of routine operations.

This case illustrates a complex pattern of performance degradations: acute decompensation (very rapid influx of ED patients) superimposed on chronic problem (boarding inpatients occupying ED treatment spaces) (Miller & Xiao, 2006). The ability of the staff to compensate during the period of chronic decompensation masked the drift toward the boundary of failure. Coping with this evolving emergent situation required the crossing of boundaries from all parts of the hospital system (e.g., physicians performing traditionally nursing duties, such as drawing blood and checking vital signs; EKG and radiology technicians transporting patients) in order for nurses to attend to more critical patients. The suspension of hierarchical rules was done *ad hoc* and was essential for redistribution of work necessary to counter the growing risk to operations.

Resilience in response to circumstances beyond operational experience is dynamic and adaptive, but finite in capacity. In Case 3, the ED began in its normal state of reduced function as a result of a number of inpatients present in the ED awaiting open beds on the wards. The influx of patients moved the ED beyond its zone of operational experience into a further reduced state or irregular functioning that degraded further into disturbed function. When the operational state left the zone of "normal, natural troubles" or function (see Figure 4.1), workers shifted on the fly to progressively more extreme and untested strategies in an attempt to compensate. Some of the

subsequently adopted into the repertoire
e placement of patients in chairs to wait
y of the system during reduced regular
ategies were associated with failure and
n patients in a small storeroom that did
ovel strategy of all—retreat and repair—
isodes of free fall. Its utilization by ED
professional competence and failure of
rks of emergency care.

essful impromptu distributive decision
ustrates a mixed pattern within work-
groups. The ability to engage in these sorts of joint decision making in dynamic
uncertain situations seems fragile, at least in the healthcare domain, with nominally
similar situations resulting in dramatically different group dynamics. Several factors
may contribute to this brittleness.

First, the organization of normal work into medical guilds to minimize interdependence leads to the assumption that optimizing the parts (a specific workgroup's
work) will automatically optimize the whole (the care of the entire patient over time).
Thus, intergroup collaboration is seldom practiced, nor are effective strategies discussed, making its necessity difficult to recognize.

Second, when actors extend their efforts outside their domain, they typically anticipate that their actions are or will be reciprocated, that is, that they will be returned in
kind or in some future case. Initial contact across groups can easily have an opposite
and negative effect on this anticipation of reciprocity. Future situations that require
intergroup collaboration or comanagement may be difficult or impossible to establish
based on previous negative experiences.

Finally, although medicine originated as, and at its core still is, a humanistic profes-
sion, it has become highly technological. Consequently, skills in managing complex
dynamic relations among disparate groups under conditions of stress and uncertainty
are not specifically articulated, taught, or rewarded in healthcare organizations. Case 2
in particular illustrates a form of threat rigidity—a retreat to formal boundaries under
stress. Its presence can severely limit the establishment of common ground among
caregivers and may suppress important adaptive behaviors, further complicating the
already effortful work of this complex, highly consequential joint cognitive system.

References

Brehmer, B. (1987). Development of mental models for decision in technological systems. In
    J. Rasmussen, K. Duncan, & J. Leplat (Eds.), *New technology and human error* (pp. 111–
    120). Chichester, UK: John Wiley & Sons.
Brennan, S. E. (1998). The grounding problem in conversations with and through computers.
    In S. R. Fussel & R. J. Kreuz (Eds.), *Social and cognitive psychological approaches to inter-
    personal communication* (pp. 210–225). Mahwah, NJ: Erlbaum.

Clark, H. H. (1996). *Using language.* Cambridge, MA: Cambridge University Press.

Cook, R. I., & Nemeth, C. (2006). Taking things in one's stride: Cognitive features of two resilient performances. In E. Hollnagel, D. D. Woods, & N. Leveson (Eds.), *Resilience engineering* (pp. 205–221). Aldershot, UK: Ashgate.

Cook, R. I., & Rasmussen, J. (2005). "Going solid": A model of system dynamics and consequences for patient safety. *Quality & Safety in Health Care, 14*(2), 130–134.

Cooper, C., & Block, R. (2006). *Disaster: Hurricane Katrina and the failure of Homeland Security.* New York, NY: Henry Holt & Company.

Hashem, A., Chi, M. T. H., & Friedman, C. P. (2003). Medical errors as a result of specialization. *Journal of Biomedical Informatics, 36*, 61–69.

Hollnagel, E., & Sundström, G. (2006). States of resilience. In E. Hollnagel, D. D. Woods, & N. Levenson (Eds.), *Resilience engineering* (pp. 339–346). Aldershot, UK: Ashgate.

Hollnagel, E., & Woods, D. D. (2006). *Joint cognitive systems: Foundations of cognitive systems engineering.* Boca Raton, FL: CRC Press.

Hollnagel, E., Woods, D. D., & Leveson, N. (2006). Resilience: The challenge of the unstable. In E. Hollnagel, D. D. Woods, & N. Leveson (Eds.), *Resilience engineering* (pp. 9–14). Aldershot, UK: Ashgate.

Hutchins, E. (1996). *Cognition in the wild.* Boston, MA: Bradford Books.

Johansson, B., & Hollnagel, E. (2007). Pre-requisites for large scale coordination. *Cognition, Technology and Work, 9*, 5–13.

Klein, G. (2000). Cognitive task analysis of teams. In J. M. Schraagen, S. F. Chipman, & V. L. Shalin (Eds.), *Cognitive task analysis* (pp. 417–429). Mahwah, NJ: Erlbaum.

Klein, G., Woods, D., Bradshaw, J., Hoffman, R., & Feltovich P. (2004). Ten challenges for making automation a "team player" in joint human-agent activity. *IEEE Intelligent Systems, 19*(6), 91–95.

Lasagna, L. (1964). Modern Hippocratic oath. Retrieved February 1, 2009, from http://www.aapsonline.org/ethics/oaths.htm#lasagna

Leveson, N. (2004). A new accident model for engineering safer systems. *Safety Science, 42*(4), 237–270.

Maloney, J. V. (1992). The resource-based relative value scale. *Journal of the American Medical Association, 268*, 3363–3365.

Miller, A., & Xiao, Y. (2006). Multi-level strategies to achieve resilience for an organisation operating at capacity: A case study at a trauma centre. *Cognition, Technology and Work, 9*(2), 1–16.

Nemeth, C. (2003). How cognitive artefacts support distributed cognition in acute care. In *Proceedings of the Human Factors and Ergonomics Society 47th Annual Meeting*, Denver, CO, pp. 381–385.

Obradovich, J., & Smith, P. (2003). Design concepts for distributed work systems: An empirical investigation into distributed teams in complex domains. In *Proceedings of the Human Factors and Ergonomics Society 47th Annual Meeting*, Denver, CO, pp. 354–358.

Perry, S., Wears, R., Anderson, B., & Booth, A. (2007). Peace and war: Contrasting cases of resilient teamwork in healthcare. In *Proceedings of the 8th International Naturalistic Decision Making Conference*, Pacific Grove, CA, pp. 225–229.

Rochlin, G. I. (1999). Safe operation as a social construct. *Ergonomics, 42*(11), 1549–1560.

Roth, E. M., Multer, J., & Raslear, T. (2007). Shared situation awareness as a contributor to high reliability performance in railroad operations. *Organization Studies, 27*(7), 967–985.

Salas, E., & Fiore, S. M. (Eds.). (2004). *Team cognition: Understanding the factors that drive process and performance.* Washington, DC: American Psychological Association.

Smith, P. J., McCoy, E., & Orasanu, J. (2001). Distributed cooperative problem-solving in the air traffic management system. In E. Salas & G. Klein (Eds.), *Linking expertise and naturalistic decision making* (pp. 367–382). Mahwah, NJ: Erlbaum.

Swarztrauber, K., & Vickrey, B. G. (2004). Do neurologists and primary care physicians agree on the extent of specialty involvement of patients referred to neurologists? *Journal of General Intern Medicine, 19*, 654–661.

Voß, A., Procter, R., Slack, R., Hartswood, M., & Rouncefield, M. (2006). Understanding and supporting dependability as ordinary action. In K. Clarke, G. Hardstone, M. Rouncefield, & I. Sommerville (Eds.), *Trust in technology: A socio-technical perspective* (pp. 195–216). Dordrecht, NL: Springer.

Wears, R. L. (2005). *Studying hard to see things: Shift changes and safety.* Keynote address at University of Sheffield, Sheffield, UK.

Wears, R. L., Perry, S., Anders, S., & Woods, D. D. (2008). Resilience in the emergency department. In E. Hollnagel, C. P. Nemeth, & S. Dekker (Eds.), *Resilience engineering perspective: Remaining sensitive to the possibility of resilience* (Vol. 1, pp. 193–210). Aldershot, UK: Ashgate.

Weick, K. (1993). The collapse of sensemaking in organizations: The Mann Gulch disaster. *Administrative Science Quarterly, 38*(4), 628–685.

Woods, D. D. (2000). *Studying cognitive systems in context: The cognitive triad.* Retrieved March 5, 2009, from http://csel.eng.ohio-state.edu/woods/foundations/triad_intro.html

Woods, D. D., & Hollnagel, E. (2006). *Joint cognitive systems: Patterns in cognitive systems engineering.* Boca Raton, FL: CRC Press.

5

The Role of Cognition in Team Collaboration During Complex Problem Solving

Susan G. Hutchins and Tony Kendall
Naval Postgraduate School

Introduction

Macrocognition is an emerging field within the area of cognitive engineering that describes the way cognition occurs in naturalistic, or real-world, decision-making events (Cacciabue & Hollnagel, 1995). When studying macrocognition, the focus is on the mental activities that must be successfully accomplished to perform a task or achieve a goal (Klein et al., 2003). These cognitive functions are generally performed during collaborative team problem solving, where the emphasis is on building new knowledge. Macrocognition is differentiated from microcognition in several ways. Microcognition places an emphasis on experimental control of tasks and theoretical accounts of specific phenomena, while macrocognition emphasizes cognition and performance under actual working conditions. Macrocognitive phenomena generally occur over longer time periods, have ill-defined goals, and do not focus on the basic cognitive functions of microcognition (e.g., attention and memory). Macrocognition encompasses cognitive processes involved in detecting problems, developing and sharing situation awareness, generating options, using analogs, mentally simulating courses of action, planning and replanning, maintaining vigilance, and assessing risk (Klein et al., 2003). Several groups of researchers maintain that research on macrocognition is needed to better understand the cognitive functions employed by teams when they collaborate to solve challenging, information-rich, time-compressed problems (Klein et al., 2003; Fiore, Smith, & Letsky, 2008; Letsky & Warner, 2008). This understanding can then be applied to improve cognitive engineering of future systems.

One goal for studying macrocognition is to understand the complexity entailed in inter- and intraindividual cognition. For the research reported in this chapter, we focus on cognition in problem-solving teams who collaborate while performing real-world tasks, in line with the view of macrocognition that seeks to describe cognitive work as it naturally occurs (Klein et al., 2003). We seek to better understand how cognition emerges in problem-solving teams engaging in tasks involving short-term situations that require rapid action to be taken toward specific mission goals. Macrocognition is defined, for this research, as the internalized and externalized high-level mental processes employed by teams to create new knowledge during complex, one-of-a-kind, collaborative problem solving (Burke, 2007; Letsky, Warner, Fiore, Rosen, & Salas, 2007). High-level mental processes refer to the cognitive processes involved in combining, visualizing, and aggregating information to resolve ambiguity in support of the discovery of new knowledge and relationships.

Internalized processes, that is, processes occurring inside the head, are those higher-level mental (cognitive) processes that are not expressed externally (e.g., writing, speaking, gesture), and can only be measured indirectly via qualitative metrics (e.g., questionnaires, cognitive mapping, think-aloud protocols, multidimensional scaling, etc.), or surrogate quantitative metrics (e.g., pupil size, galvanic skin response). These processes can become either fully or partially externalized when they are expressed in a form that relates to other individuals' reference/interpretation systems (e.g., language, icons, gestures, boundary objects) (Letsky et al., 2007).

Externalized processes (processes occurring outside the head) are those higher-level mental (cognitive) processes that occur at the individual or team level, and which are associated only with actions that are observable and measureable in a consistent, reliable, repeatable manner, or through the conventions of the subject domain that have standardized meanings (Letsky et al., 2007).

The framework of collaborative problem solving developed as part of the Office of Naval Research Collaboration and Knowledge Integration (CKI) Program (Letsky et al., 2007) provides the conceptual foundation for this research. The emphasis on macrocognition in teams was initiated as part of a larger issue of how to understand and facilitate complex, collaborative activity—specifically in quick-response *ad hoc* teams. Both commercial and military communities are evolving in response to an increased reliance on sociotechnical systems, globalization, and ubiquitous information accessibility—a development that leads to changes in the dynamics of team activity (Letsky & Warner, 2008). The CKI Program seeks to develop a better understanding of internalized, nonquantifiable, mental processes at work as teams collect, filter, process, and share information for problem-solving purposes.

The objective of the CKI Program is to respond to emerging needs in both the military and business environments to better understand and improve the effectiveness of team decision making in complex, data-rich situations. As part of this effort, a model of team collaboration was developed that emphasizes the cognitive aspects of team collaboration and includes the major human decision-making processes used during team collaboration (Warner, Letsky, & Cowen, 2005). The long-range program objective is to develop cognitive science-based tools, models, computational methods, and human-agent interfaces to help attain common situation awareness among distributed team members, engaged in asynchronous, quick-response collaboration for issue resolution, or decision making.

The goal for the research reported here is to understand the role of cognition in teams who are collaborating to solve challenging, ambiguous problems. Our objectives are (1) to empirically evaluate a model of team collaboration (Warner et al., 2005) by analyzing the macrocognitive processes used by teams during real-world complex decision-making events, (2) to refine the model as necessary, and (3) as a result of our analysis, to develop a better understanding of the cognitive processes involved in team collaboration.

Team Collaboration

Many definitions of collaboration are found in the different bodies of research literature (see Wood & Gray, 1991). At the most fundamental level, collaboration refers to the joint effort of two or more agents to achieve a common goal where collaborating members construct judgments and then act on these judgments (Nosek, 2004). A definition more aligned with the research reported here states that collaboration occurs "when a group of autonomous stakeholders of a problem domain engage in an interactive process, using shared rules, norms, and structures, to act or decide on issues related to that domain" (Wood & Gray, 1991, p. 11). This interactive process is performed in a collaborative team environment, with *collaborative* defined as the "cognitive aspects of joint analysis or problem solving for the purpose of attaining shared understanding sufficient to achieve situational awareness for decision making or creation of a product" (Letsky & Warner, 2008, p. 4). Collaboration provides increased information processing capacity where more minds are enlisted to handle complex problems (Hocevar, Thomas, & Jansen, 2006). Team members offer several perspectives on an issue for generating, choosing, and implementing action plans. A collaborative approach also ensures greater flexibility and innovation in situations where human judgment and experience are leveraged (Hocevar et al., 2006).

In this chapter, we examined team collaboration in three distinct task domains: maritime interdiction operations, air warfare decision making, and the fire-fighting response to the 9/11 attacks.

Team Types

The present analysis focused on distributed teams who employed asynchronous or synchronous communications during joint problem solving. Teams were heterogeneous as each team member played a functionally distinct role and contributed specialized knowledge and expertise. These teams are often formed to deal with rapidly emerging critical situations where consequences for error are severe and problem solving calls for diverse expertise. Teams operate in complex sociotechnical settings that require considerable technical expertise from team members. Moreover, teams work within an organizational setting that may impose conflicting goals.

Teams have been defined as a social entity consisting of "two or more people who interact dynamically, interdependently and adaptively toward a shared goal" (Salas, Dickinson, Converse, & Tannenbaum, 1992, p. 4). Their interdependence necessitates that all team members share their knowledge about the situation, and contribute their respective expertise, to develop and maintain an accurate understanding of the dynamically unfolding situation. In many real-world situations, teams are also required to make decisions and to implement them in a timely manner to effectively deal with a given problem.

Decision Making

A decision can be defined as a "mental event that occurs at a singular point in time . . . that leads immediately or directly to action" (Hoffman & Yates, 2005, p. 77). From this perspective, a decision is a commitment to a course of action. Other researchers view decision making as a macrocognitive process that both supports and is supported by deciding (Klein et al., 2003). A complex problem-solving situation typically entails many decisions. These decisions include implementing actions in response to prior conditions or to the existing situation. As a situation unfolds, it will likely present new events requiring a decision.

Dynamic Decision-Making Tasks

Dynamic decision-making tasks, such as the decision domains investigated for this research, are characterized by situations where:

1. A series of decisions is needed; that is, the problem-solving event comprises many decisions to effectively deal with the problem as it unfolds.
2. Decisions are not independent because current decisions are constrained by earlier decisions, and in turn constrain later ones.
3. The problem state changes during the decision process both autonomously—as the situation continues to unfold—and as a consequence of the decision maker's actions.
4. Decisions are made in real time (Brehmer, 1992).

It is necessary for the practitioner to consider how the current decision will solve the immediate problem, as well as how it will impact future aspects of the overall problem-solving task. More importantly, it is not sufficient to make correct decisions "in the correct order, they also need to be made at the correct moment in time" (Brehmer, 1992, p. 16). Dynamic decision-making situations are inherently stressful in part because the decision maker cannot control when these critical decisions have to be made.

Dynamic decision-making tasks are found across the spectrum of problem-solving domains, including process control plants, patient management in hospitals, managing a business, and fighting a battle. All the tasks we examined were dynamic decision-making tasks, as opposed to planning tasks.

Model of Team Collaboration

In this chapter we report on research conducted to empirically evaluate and, if necessary, refine a model of team collaboration developed by Warner et al. (2005), depicted in Figure 5.1. The model consists of general inputs (e.g., task description), collaborative stages that the team goes through during the problem-solving task, the cognitive processes used by the team, and final outputs, such as the selected course of action. This conceptual model emphasizes the cognitive aspects of team collaboration and includes the major human decision-making processes used during team collaboration. Four unique but interdependent stages of team collaboration are included in the model: (1) knowledge construction, (2) collaborative team problem solving, (3) team consensus, and (4) outcome evaluation and revision. The focus of the collaboration model is on knowledge building among the team members and developing team consensus for selection of a course of action (Salas & Fiore, 2004; Warner & Letsky, 2008).

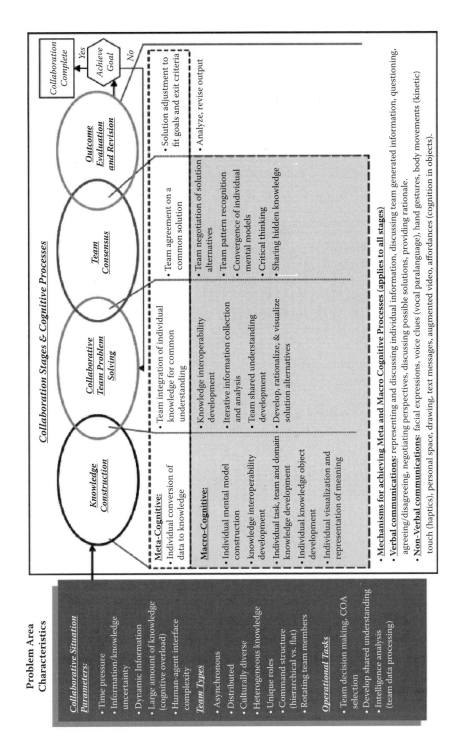

FIGURE 5.1   Model of team collaboration. (From Warner et al., in *Proceedings of the 49th Human Factors and Ergonomics Society Annual Meeting,* Human Factors and Ergonomics Society, Santa Monica, CA, 2005, pp. 269–273. With permission.)

Empirical research (Warner & Wroblewski, 2003, 2004) suggests that teams solving complex, one-of-a-kind, time-critical collaborative problems go through the four stages of collaboration included in the model of team collaboration; however, these stages are not necessarily sequential and are iterative. Cognitive processes within each stage are represented at two levels: metacognitive processes, which guide the overall problem-solving process, and macrocognitive processes, which support team members' activities within the respective collaboration stage. For example, as depicted in Figure 5.1, the metacognitive process during the *knowledge construction* stage involves individual conversion of data to knowledge. Definitions of the macrocognitive processes (Warner et al., 2005) included in the model are listed in Table 5.1,

TABLE 5.1   Cognitive Process Definitions With Examples From Air Warfare

---

Knowledge Construction

Individual mental model construction (imm): Individual team members, using available information and knowledge to develop a coherent representation of the problem situation.

- I am showing 8044 at 400 knots and about 27,000 feet, possible comm-air type profile.
- 2017 is squawking a comm-air mode 3. In company with 2025, but that track is much lower than the comm-air. One at 37,000, one at 8,000 just came in low.

Individual task knowledge development (itk): Individual team member collecting and processing data or information, or responding to clarification requested by other team members.

- Do we have the track number for his CAP? I would prefer to have the track number for his CAP.
- Did you illuminate him?
- Since he is turning to the east, do you still want us to continue with level 1?

Team knowledge development (tk): All team members participate to clarify information to build common team knowledge.

- Rainbow is sending Desert Eagle 101 and Desert Eagle 102 over to investigate track 8037 [7034].
- He looks like he is on a [air] corridor, Kuwait City to Bushehr.
- I don't have mode 3 or any other type of IFF [identification friend or foe] available to me right now.
- They're going too fast for that.

Knowledge object development (ko): Pictures, icons, representations, or standard text, developed by an individual team member or the whole team, that represents a standard meaning to the team.

- [No coded examples for air warfare.]

Individual visualization and representation of meaning (vrm): Visualization—use of knowledge objects (e.g., graphs, pictures) to transfer meaning to other team members. Representations—artifacts (e.g., note pads) used to sort data and information into meaningful chunks.

- [No coded examples for air warfare.]

Collaborative Team Problem Solving

Knowledge interoperability development (kio): Process of exchanging and modifying a mental model or knowledge object such that agreement is reached among team members with respect to a common understanding of the topic's meaning.

- It looks like the AWACs are feet dry. The CAP [combat air patrol], composition 2, appear to be headed feet dry now.
- Doctrine won't work for 2017, make unknown assumed enemy.

Iterative information collection and analysis (ica): Collecting and analyzing information to come up with a solution but no specific solution mentioned.

- We need a report from CAP as to whether, upon intercept of those suspected Pumas, they are armed or not.

TABLE 5.1   Cognitive Process Definitions With Examples From Air Warfare (continued)

- Track 2017 deviated from known flight path still maintaining altitude and still squawking the same mode 3.

Team shared understanding development (tsu): Synthesis of essential data, information, or knowledge, held collectively by some (complementary understanding) or all (congruent understanding) team members working to solve a common task.

- Track 8061 bearing 027 Princeton at 25 miles, 5,000 feet, heading south, covering with birds.
- Track 8061 appeared to originate from Iran. When we picked him up he was already off the coast, but he was coming south from close to the Iranian coast. I can't confirm that he came from Iran, but he was coming from that direction.
- Continue to track sections of Iranian F-1s and F-4s. Approached the force with an attack profile. Interrogated level 1 with no response. They turned away from the force at a range of about 30 miles. Continuing to track.

Develop, rationalize, and visualize solution alternatives (sa): Team member or the whole team using knowledge to justify a solution.

- I would like fire control lock up on 7010, and I'd like to make sure he is designated as a gun target. I'd like to have two rounds of illumination prepped on mount 52.
- My intentions are to issue a warning shot with a flare if the helo proceeds to within 10 nautical miles.
- Indicate to 7010 that if he continues to close he can expect defensive actions.
- Track number 7010 continuing inbound, request permission to engage at three nautical miles, no response to all measures, so far.

Convergence of individual mental models to team mental model (cmm): Convincing other team members to accept specific data, information, or knowledge with the emergence of a single common mental model that all team members accept or believe.

- OK, we need to make them assumed enemy and cover them, AAWC.

Team Consensus

Team negotiation of solution alternatives (tn): The give-and-take process whereby team members agree on a final solution or issue.

- Request batteries release on track 7010, it is continuing inbound, he is at three nautical miles, request permission to engage, over.

Team pattern recognition (tpr): The team, as a whole, identifying a pattern of data, information, or knowledge.

- [No coded examples for air warfare.]

Critical thinking (ct): Team working together toward a common goal, whereby goal accomplishment requires an active exchange of ideas, self-regulatory judgment, and systematic consideration of evidence, counterevidence, and context, in an environment where judgments are made under uncertainty, limited knowledge, and time constraints.

- [No coded examples for air warfare.]

Sharing hidden knowledge (shk): Individual team members sharing their unique knowledge through prompting by other team member(s).

- Yes sir, we ID'd him as a com[mercial] earlier, we will go ahead and talk to him.
- I've got track 7011 ID'd as comm-air. He started out at 35,000 feet, now he is descending.

Outcome Evaluation and Revision

Analyze, revise solution options (aro): Team members analyze final solution options and revise if necessary.

- Ah Rainbow's holding track number 7011, low and slow and inbound. Do you desire me to cover with birds also?

together with examples of communications by air warfare team members that refer to these macrocognitive processes.

Team Collaboration Tasks

The types of problem-solving situations accounted for by the model of team collaboration are ill-structured decision-making tasks that are characterized by time pressure, dynamically changing conditions, ambiguous and incomplete information, high uncertainty, and high cognitive workload (i.e., a large amount of knowledge is brought to bear to solve complex problems), as well as human-system interface complexity. Team collaboration is challenging because team members possess highly specialized knowledge that must be synthesized. Moreover, information from multiple sources needs to be considered, requiring collaborative analysis, to ensure team members come to a shared understanding of the task, the environment, and reach consensus on a course of action.

Method

We evaluated the model of team collaboration by using the macrocognitive processes included in the Warner et al. (2005) model to code the communications of New York firefighters responding to the events on September 11, 2001, a Coast Guard boarding party conducting maritime interdiction operations, and air warfare teams on a Navy ship. These domains were selected because they present the types of complex collaborative problem-solving scenarios the model seeks to explain. In all three problem-solving tasks, situation assessment was particularly difficult due to time pressure, high workload, and incomplete or ambiguous information.

Task Domain I: Maritime Interdiction Operation (MIO)

A series of field experiments was conducted on ships in the San Francisco Bay to test the technical and operational challenges of developing a global maritime domain security test bed (Bordetsky & Hutchins, 2008). A wireless network was developed for data sharing during an MIO scenario to facilitate expert reachback for radiation source analysis, imagery, and biometric data analysis. Subject matter experts at geographically distributed command centers collaborated with a boarding party in near real time to facilitate situational understanding and course of action selection.

Participants

The six boarding party members were comprised of two personnel from Lawrence Livermore National Labs and four graduate students from Naval Postgraduate School. The boarding party boarded the suspect vessel equipped with laptops and radiological and other detection devices to gather data and to collaborate with their team. Some members of the distributed team were located on the ship, but were in different areas (while searching for contraband material and obtaining fingerprints of crew members); others were virtual members—the experts who were located at reachback centers.

Task

The three scenarios used for this research focused on detecting, identifying, and interdicting nuclear materials in open waters. Scenarios differed with respect to the radiological material that was hidden and its respective hiding place. The critical task involved the cognitively complex issue of discriminating contraband radiological material against a background containing multiple benign radiation sources, such as smoke detectors, radiant signs, and a container load of bananas (Schwoegler, 2006). Team members had to collect data on suspicious material, equipment, and people and send them to specific experts for analysis at distributed reachback centers. A MIO typically involves a high level of time pressure, as political and economic considerations require that a vessel is not unnecessarily delayed.

Task Domain II: Air Warfare Decision Making

A series of high-fidelity laboratory experiments was conducted with shipboard personnel at a Navy laboratory in San Diego to gain insight into the decision strategies employed by air warfare teams. Air warfare decision making takes place in the combat information center (CIC) of a Navy ship. The CIC team is responsible for identifying and responding to any aircraft approaching a battle group.

Incoming information arrives via various sensor systems (radar, electronic support measures system, identification friend or foe, etc.) and various reports, for example, intelligence reports, passed by other platforms in the area. Communications between team members are passed as soon as information is received, and updated reports are passed as soon as new information is obtained for any track. Verbal reports on specific tracks are interleaved with reports on other tracks.

Participants

Data from four six-person teams were analyzed. Team members were active duty military personnel, including the commanding officer (CO) and tactical action officer (TAO), from a Navy Aegis ship and four enlisted personnel from a local training command in San Diego. The CO and TAO work as a dyad and are the key decision makers. Roles of the enlisted personnel included the air warfare coordinator, electronic warfare supervisor, identification supervisor, and the tactical information coordinator. These six collocated team members communicated with several distributed information sources (simulated by a confederate), such as the battle group commander, the Saudi air tower, assets passing intelligence reports, and other ships and friendly aircraft in the vicinity of the battle group, to obtain additional information and to keep them apprised of the unfolding scenario.

Task

The task of air warfare teams involves identification and responding to numerous contacts. When an aircraft is detected, CIC personnel work as a team to determine its identity and to determine whether it poses a threat. The high degree of ambiguity associated with contact information can often make threat assessment very difficult because many pieces of data can fit multiple hypotheses. Response choices (that is, do nothing, monitor, take various actions to determine intent, or engage) are largely governed by the ship's orders (e.g., rules of engagement) and the current geopolitical situation. Specific actions to be taken depend on the local conditions and the relative positions of the inbound contact of interest and own ship. Air warfare involves a very high level of time pressure due to the speed of the inbound, potentially hostile aircraft.

One of the most challenging aspects of the CIC team's job is the high mental work-load that is entailed when a constant stream of information must be continuously evaluated, particularly when the information—as it often does—pertains to several different air contacts (or tracks). Relevant data and information items must be associated with the right track number, then analyzed, synthesized, and aggregated (Hutchins, 1996). The air warfare team must assess, compare, and resolve conflicting information, while making difficult judgments and remembering the status of several evolving situations.

Task Domain III: Fire Department of New York
Responding to Events on September 11, 2001

The present analysis is based on the transcribed communications between the units of the Fire Department of New York (FDNY) that responded to the attacks on the World Trade Center (WTC), and the Manhattan dispatcher and additional inbound units. The FDNY units were performing search and rescue in the WTC and tried to extinguish the fire while continuously providing the dispatcher with up-to-date information on the evolving situation. This required a high level of communication as the dispatcher was—and typically is—located at a remote site (in Central Park). The FDNY also had a high level of communication with the many field units who were called to the scene to bring additional capabilities and support, such as fire trucks, ambulances to set up triage areas, breathing apparatus, and so on. Fire fighting involves an extremely high level of time pressure due to the intense speed with which a fire can destroy lives and property. High ambiguity is another dominant factor, as cogently stated by firefighters: "There are no routine fires."

Coding of Team Communications

Communications between the air warfare teams and personnel at other sites were captured as audio recordings and subsequently transcribed. Chat logs were used from the MIO. These included the communications between members of the boarding party and remotely located experts. The transcripts of the communications between the FDNY units, their dispatcher, and additional units during the 9/11 events were obtained from the Fire Department of the City of New York (2001). Two researchers coded the firefighter data to establish the reliability of our coding method (Hutchins, Bordetsky, Kendall, & Garrity, 2007). Subsequently, one of the authors coded the MIO and air warfare team communications.

Macrocognitive process categories developed by Warner et al. (2005) were used to code team members' communications. Communications were segmented into utterances, that is, elliptic or sentential constructions that referred to a distinct macrocognitive process. Each utterance was typically given a separate code; however, in some instances, two utterances referred to the same cognitive process and were thus grouped under one code. One week prior to coding the FDNY communications, two raters coded team communications data from a MIO simulation not included in the present data set. Raters discussed their respective coding with one of the authors to calibrate their use of the macrocognitive process categories. Following this training period they independently coded the FDNY transcript, subsequently reviewed their coding, calculated percent agreement, and resolved any differences in coding.

Interrater Reliability

A total of 1,626 utterances were coded for the FDNY. Interrater agreement was 89.32%. In 6.31% of the cases in which they disagreed, coders were able to reach agreement on a final code. For the remaining 4.37%, they agreed to disagree. Almost half of the disagreements concerned the use of *team knowledge development* (tk) instead of another code. In most (83.3%) of these cases, coders decided to use a code other than tk.

Coding Example

Table 5.2 illustrates an example of the coding process with an excerpt of the communications from one MIO scenario. As can be seen (first entry in Table 5.2), individual

TABLE 5.2   Excerpt From MIO Communications Coding: Developing Solution Alternatives

MIO Team Communications		Code	Macrocognitive Process Coding
Speaker			
DTRA	Cesium 137 can be used to make an RDD. If there are no explosives, then it is not configured as a weapon yet. Recommend material be confiscated.	sa	Develop, rationalize, and visualize *solution alternatives*, using knowledge to justify a solution.
		tsu	*Team shared understanding development*: Synthesis of essential data, information, or knowledge to solve a common task.
BO	Roger. Will confiscate.	itk	*Individual task knowledge* development; individual TM collects and processes data or information, or responding to clarification requested by other TMs.
BO	Make sure you handle carefully. Cs-137 is an external gamma hazard.	kio	*Knowledge interoperability*: Exchanging and modifying a mental model or knowledge object so agreement is reached with respect to a common understanding of the topic's meaning.
BO	Roger. Will take precautions.	kio	*Knowledge interoperability*: Exchanging and modifying a mental model or knowledge object so agreement is reached with respect to a common understanding of the topic's meaning.
SOCOM	Does CG ship have proper storage area for material confiscated?	itk	*Individual task knowledge* development: Individual TM collects and processes data or information, or responding to clarification requested by other TMs.
SOCOM	Search team will report size of material and its current containment condition, then make recommendations.	cu	Team integration of individual team member knowledge for *common understanding*; one or more team members combine individual pieces of knowledge to achieve common understanding.

Note: DTRA, Defense Threat Reduction Agency; RDD, radiation detection device; BO, boarding officer; LLNL, Lawrence Livermore National Lab; SOCOM, Special Operations Command; CG, Coast Guard.

team members (TMs) generate a solution alternative by using knowledge regarding the level of threat posed by the radiological material found on the ship. Team members also develop a shared understanding of the situation by synthesizing essential data regarding the degree of danger inherent in the material discovered. They use this information to justify a solution; that is, the material needs to be confiscated. In the third entry, the team develops knowledge interoperability based on information provided by an expert at one of the remote centers (the material needs to be handled carefully). A distributed team member from Special Operations Command (SOCOM) acquires individual task knowledge (fifth entry) regarding the Coast Guard ship by asking whether it has a suitable storage area for the confiscated material. Finally, in the last entry, TMs integrate their individual knowledge to reach a common understanding of their next action to be taken.

Results

The number of utterances varied across teams: Communications in the four air warfare teams comprised 96, 131, 187, and 233 utterances, respectively; for the three MIO teams, 73, 40, and 118 utterances were discerned; and for the FDNY units, 1,627 utterances. Table 5.3 presents the distribution of macrocognitive processes in communications of the air warfare, MIO, and fire-fighting teams. As can be seen, a large number of team members' communications concerned knowledge construction highlighting the importance of this process for all three task domains. For seven of the eight teams, more than 50% of the speech turns involved the macrocognitive processes related to knowledge construction. These macrocognitive processes are used by team members to develop an understanding of the complex problem and to refine and maintain their understanding as the highly dynamic situation evolves. Of particular interest is the large number of speech turns coded as *individual task knowledge development* (itk): Itk refers to a communication in which a team member collects and processes data or information, or responds to clarification requests by other team members. The large number of requests for information or clarification in the form of questions between team members is consistent with the high degree of uncertainty inherent in all three decision-making tasks and suggests that these teams devoted much effort to reducing this task uncertainty in a rapidly changing situation.

Across the three decision-making domains, all five macrocognitive processes of the *collaborative team problem-solving* phase (categories 6 to 10 in Table 5.3) were observed. That is, in all three domains we found evidence that teams integrated individual knowledge to develop a team shared understanding. In contrast, far fewer utterances were coded as representing processes included in the *team consensus* phase of collaboration (categories 11 to 15) and *outcome evaluation and revision* (16).

Team's Use of the Macrocognitive Processes

Utterances indicating team members' understanding of the problem situation (= *individual task knowledge development*) were the most frequent communications by air warfare teams, followed by utterances in which team members synthesized previously shared data or information (= *team shared understanding*). Air warfare team

TABLE 5.3   Percentage of Macrocognitive Processes Used by Teams for Three Tasks

	Air Warfare				MIO			Sept. 11
Macrocognitive Process Coding Categories	Scen D Run A	Scen D Run B	CG 59	DDG 54	Nov. 06	June 06	Sept. 06	FDNY 9/11
Knowledge Construction								
1. Individual mental model (imm)	16	14	14	36	05	30	07	02
2. Individual task knowledge development (itk)	43	29	24	17	53	18	40	42
3. Team knowledge development (tk)	19	05	14	01	05	13	07	27
4. Knowledge object development (ko)	—	—	—	—	—	05	07	—
5. Visualization and representation (vrm)	—	—	—	—	—	—	—	—
Subtotal	**78**	**48**	**52**	**54**	**63**	**66**	**61**	**71**
Collaborative Team Problem Solving								
6. Knowledge interoperability (kio)	—	11	—	01	06	15	14	01
7. Iterative collection and analysis (ica)	02	11	—	—	09	10	12	—
8. Team shared understanding (tsu)	02	16	22	20	05	05	03	03
9. Solution alternatives (sa)	—	03	—	—	09	—	—	02
10. Convergence of mental models (cmm)	02	—	—	—	01	—	—	03
Subtotal	**06**	**41**	**22**	**21**	**30**	**30**	**29**	**09**
Team Consensus								
11. Team negotiation (tn)	—	—	—	—	06	—	—	01
12. Team pattern recognition (tpr)	—	01	—	—	—	—	—	<01
13. Critical thinking (ct)	—	—	—	—	—	—	—	<01
14. Sharing hidden knowledge (shk)	—	01	—	—	—	—	—	<01
15. Solution adjustment against goal (sag)	—	—	—	—	—	—	—	—
Subtotal	**0**	**02**	**0**	**0**	**06**	**0**	**0**	**01**
Outcome Evaluation and Revision								
16. Analyze, revise solutions (aro)	—	—	—	—	—	—	—	<01
17. Decision to take action[a] (dta)	17	07	27	26	02	05	11	19
Miscellaneous[b]	40	21	30	26	08	—	—	52

[a] "Decision to take action" is a new category that emerged during data analysis.
[b] Miscellaneous communications were removed prior to calculating the percentage of communications coded as representing each of the macrocognitive processes.

members seem to focus on their individual tasks to ensure that their interpretation of incoming data is correct and an accurate report is forwarded to the key decision makers, the TAO and CO, who then will synthesize the various pieces of information.

The macrocognitive processes dominating the communications of the MIO teams were *individual task knowledge development, developing knowledge interoperability,* and *iterative collection and analysis.* Developing knowledge interoperability was critical for the highly distributed MIO teams. The boarding team members who were dispersed throughout the ship related their findings, which were then analyzed by several remotely located experts. MIO teams emphasized iterative data collection, and receiving feedback on their data analysis, which in turn led to additional data collection until they were certain regarding what types of materials had been found on the vessel.

Firefighters relied on all but the following four processes: *knowledge object development* (ko), which requires pictures and icons; *individual visualization and representation of meaning* (vrm), which requires visual aids; *iterative information collection and analysis* (ica), which entails collecting and analyzing information without mentioning a solution; *agreement on a final solution*; and *solution adjustment against goal and exit criteria* (sag). These processes either did not pertain to the firefighters' task context (ko and vrm) or were inconsistent with their standard operating procedures (ica and sag).

Most of the communications between fire-fighting units and dispatch concerned *individual task knowledge development*, indicating participants' need for information. The second most frequent type of communication reflected the macrocognitive process of *team knowledge development*; that is, the team members volunteered task-relevant knowledge. In addition, *decision to take action* was the third most prominent macrocognitive process in the team's collaboration. This process was apparent in many communications in which a team member asked a fellow firefighter to perform some action.

New Coding Category

The most important finding during analysis of the team communications for the three problem-solving domains was that a new macrocognitive process—decision to take action—emerged. It includes two subcategories: (1) issue an order regarding a course of action, and (2) request that a person take some action. These two subcategories are differentiated by the status of the speaker relative to the addressee (i.e., superior to subordinate, versus peer to peer), and the criticality of the desired action regarding the overall outcome. A *request to take action* is not a direct order, and the action to be taken is less likely to impact the outcome of the problem-solving task. Issuing an *order regarding a course of action* could include warnings, statements specifying some future action by another team member, or explicit commands. Table 5.4 provides examples of the two subcategories of decisions included under "decision to take action."

Pattern of Team Collaboration by the 9/11 Firefighters

Insight into the cognitive processes of team members during their collaboration can be gained by examining the pattern of macrocognitive processes apparent in their communications. To illustrate this type of analysis, we will focus on the team collaboration of the FDNY units and their dispatcher during the 9/11 events. We divided the 2 hours and 20 minutes of the coded team communications into four phases, corresponding to the four major events on 9/11 in New York City (each of the two aircraft hitting the towers of the WTC and each of the towers collapsing). We excluded the 849 utterances from the analysis that were coded "miscellaneous," leaving 777

TABLE 5.4   Examples of Two Types of Decision to Take Action

Issue a course of action (coa): A superior in the chain of command issues an order regarding a course of action (i.e., tells a team member to take a specific action).

- Cover 8032 (TN 7013) with standard missile; also generate a SWG 1A solution on him.
- Cease illumination.
- Send every available ambulance, everything you've got, to the World Trade Center.
- Transmit a second alarm and start relocating companies into the area.
- Search team will report size of material and its current containment condition, and then make recommendations.

Request take action (rta): Team member requests that another team member take some action.

- Let's investigate with CAP.
- Confirm that tracks originating from Iranian air space are designated unknown assumed hostile.
- Go ahead and tag 8037 as F-1s.
- Shift your focus air to 8070, inbound helo.
- Please have ambulances respond to West Street.
- Mark material for confiscation.
- Given multiple radiation hits and suspect equipment, recommend divert of entire ship to friendly port [if we are under way] or detained and moved to a safe location [if in the United States].

utterances. Next, a subset of the communications was selected to graphically depict the team's pattern of collaboration. This analysis includes only the macrocognitive codes of utterances in which the speaker introduces a new topic. Typically, each time a new topic was discussed, there were several exchanges between team members on that topic—anywhere from 2 to 12—to ensure all concerned (firefighters on different floors of the WTC, the dispatcher, and incoming units) were aware of the new piece of information. One of the authors read through the transcript and marked the location where a topic shift occurred, or a decision to take action was transmitted. The second author reviewed these segmentations and made some minor adjustments.

This analysis is meant to be a "60,000-foot view" of the team's collaboration because the inclusion of every code would be too detailed for our purposes. We developed this macro-level view to represent how quickly team members moved between the stages of the Warner et al. (2005) model of team collaboration. Additionally, we wanted to show where decisions to take action occurred relative to the other stages in the model.

Figure 5.2 depicts the pattern of the firefighters' collaborative activity as they responded to the first event—when the first plane hit the North Tower of the WTC. This figure represents the macrocognitive processes employed by the FDNY team during the first 16 minutes of this event. The transcript includes 209 utterances; that is, there were 13 utterances per minute, indicating that the rate of communications was fairly dense. We see in Figure 5.2 that the collaborative process was highly iterative in that the team moved back and forth many times between the knowledge construction stage and the other stages of the model. The team also initiated several actions (*courses of action/request take action*), as depicted in the last column: "decision to take action."

The lines in Figure 5.2 represent the order in which the team moved through the macrocognitive stages specified in the Warner et al. (2005) model. For example, with his first utterance recorded at 8:47, "We just had a plane crash into upper floors of the

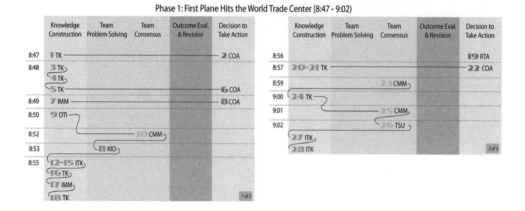

FIGURE 5.2   High-level view of pattern of team collaboration for Fire Department of New York during first 16 minutes of Sept 11, 2001 attack.

World Trade Center," the fire chief shares *team knowledge* (tk). In the same turn, he issued the *course of action* to "transmit a second alarm and to start relocating companies into the area" (Fire Department of the City of New York, 2001). The initial sizing up of the situation resulted in the immediate decision to do something about the situation, specifically, to bring more fire-fighting assets to the scene. Once on site, it became clear to the firefighters (8:49) that the crash might have been an intentional terror attack (*individual mental model construction* (imm)). When the onsite firefighters communicated their assessment to the other, distributed team members (Manhattan dispatcher and the inbound units called to the scene), the mental model of the team at large changed accordingly (8:52) (*convergence of individual mental model* (cmm) to a team mental model). Due to the highly unanticipated nature of the September 11 attack, there was initially a great deal of confusion. Moreover, the onsite firefighters provided the most up-to-date information to the dispatcher, who relied on these reports to stay abreast of the developing situation. In a matter of minutes the FDNY moved through four stages of the Warner et al. (2005) model of team collaboration: from *knowledge construction* and *team problem solving* to *team consensus* and *decision to take action*.

The highly iterative pattern of moving back and forth between different stages of the model shown in Figure 5.2 is representative of the FDNY's problem-solving behavior during the entire 9/11 events (Hutchins, Kendall, & Bordetsky, 2008). Information gathering and taking action based on new information was an ongoing process throughout the 9/11 series of events. When a firefighter in a decision-making role noticed some significant change in the environment, he immediately issued a course of action consistent with his updated understanding of the situation. This pattern reflects the highly refined standard operating procedures (SOPs) that have evolved over more than 100 years of use. Note that this pattern is also consistent with recognition-primed decision making (Klein, 1993). Firefighters are trained to size up a situation, and their SOPs dictate that their situation reports are to include a specification of their intended responses.

Teams Focus on Problem Understanding and Solving

As was the case with air warfare and MIO teams, the 9/11 firefighters' communications were predominantly concerned with knowledge construction ("What is the problem we are dealing with?") and team problem solving ("What are we going to do about it?"). A much smaller percentage of their communications were devoted to team consensus and outcome evaluation and revision, the two phases that, according to Warner et al. (2005), occur late in the team collaboration process. Initial results, based on analysis of the air warfare and firefighters' team collaboration, indicate that team agreement on a common solution is not done collaboratively, presumably due to the inherent time constraints of their tasks.

Discussion

Orasanu (1994) observes that team members communicate to accomplish joint tasks and to let others know what they are thinking. Following Orasanu, team communications serve three main functions related to problem solving: sharing information, directing actions, and reflecting thoughts. In the three decision-making domains examined in this chapter, team members used communication to stay abreast of the evolving status of the situation. Depending on the decision-making domain (e.g., FDNY), much of their communication relied on standard operating procedures, which prescribe not only standardized ways of communicating, but also the types of information that are to be shared, and predefined actions to be taken in response to specific situations.

Directing action is the second critical function of team communications, and includes direct commands for routine actions for a wide variety of situations. It also includes action commands to support problem understanding, such as gathering additional information prior to a decision. In line with Orasanu's analysis, the third function of team communications is sharing what one is thinking, "as opposed to passing on information obtained from an external source." This type of communication is essential to developing a shared problem model among team members.

Several common features of team collaboration were observed across the three decision-making domains. First, the majority of team members' communications concerned *knowledge construction,* reflecting team members' efforts to make sense of what they were experiencing. Sensemaking is a process that entails framing and reframing of data and information in response to additional observations (Klein, Phillips, Rall, & Peluso, 2007). The attack on the WTC was a very unique situation that did not resemble anything the FDNY had previously experienced and typifies the decision-making scenario in which sensemaking is critical. The high level of novelty most likely contributed to the fact that the team devoted much time to constructing a mental model of the situation that accurately accounted for the events.

Second, consistent with past naturalistic decision making (NDM) research (e.g., Fischer, Orasanu, & Montalvo, 1993; Klein, 1989, 1993; Mosier, 1991; Orasanu & Connolly, 1993; Rasmussen, 1993), we found that problem solving by the 9/11 firefighters and the air warfare and the MIO teams comprised a series of decisions. That is, decisions were made iteratively throughout the entire problem situation, as opposed to problem solving culminating in team members agreeing on one big final decision (course of action). Based on these findings, the Warner et al. (2005) model of team collaboration had to be revised to include a new category: decision to take action.

Very few of the cognitive processes included in the team consensus stage of the Warner et al. (2005) model were evident in the team communications examined in the present study. This finding may reflect characteristics of the tasks performed by the teams. These tasks were all of a tactical nature and required that operations were conducted within a very short time period. Decisions had to be made within minutes, or even seconds, due to the speed of a potentially hostile aircraft, political/economic pressure to conduct the MIO quickly, and for obvious reasons for the firefighters. In contrast, the macrocognitive processes of the team problem-solving and consensus phases are more likely to occur in task contexts, such as operational and strategic planning, where team members have the luxury of time to discuss alternatives and arrive at a consensus on the recommended plan.

Conclusions

"Decision to take action" is recommended as a new category to be added to the set of macrocognitive processes included in the Warner et al. (2005) model of team collaboration. Deciding to take action is viewed as both a macrocognitive *process* and a *product* of team collaboration. We maintain that decision making is a critical element of team problem solving when a team is executing a task, in contrast to conducting a planning task. When team members collaborate to solve a problem, they make decisions and implement those decisions as part of performing the task. Team communications often entail asking or telling a team member to perform some action that will move the problem further along toward completion. This contrasts with a team who is collaborating on a planning task, where deciding on and implementing decisions may not be evident. This is the case for problem-solving domains in the military, government, and private sectors. For example, we predict this same pattern would be evident for a surgical team, a humanitarian assistance scenario, and a variety of other task domains.

Decision Making Is Part of Problem Solving

Many critical tasks that involve team problem solving include decision making; that is, team members take action in addition to developing new knowledge and agreeing on a final solution. Actions are frequently part of the overall information gathering process and have diagnostic functions (Orasanu & Connolly, 1993; Orasanu & Fischer, 1997). For the task domains discussed here, a constant interplay exists between sharing information—to develop new knowledge and maintain situation awareness—deciding on actions, and implementing actions, followed by monitoring the situation and continuing to build new knowledge on the unfolding situation. Execution of the mission, or problem-solving task, would come to a screeching halt without this continual, iterative cycle of developing knowledge of the situation and responding to the current situation.

Research Challenges

Challenges associated with analyzing this type of data include:

1. The coders need to be familiar with the domain to understand the processes employed and the associated jargon.
2. Subject matter experts may have to be consulted to decipher jargon and understand standard operating procedures.
3. Coders also need to understand the relationships between team members from different organizations and the hierarchy of the organizations.
4. Utterances cannot be coded in isolation. Coders need to follow the different "threads" being discussed by team members.
5. Resolving differences in coding is a collaborative process where coders express their interpretation of an utterance.
6. In some cases, listening to the audio recordings of team interactions may be helpful, as intonation may disambiguate utterances.

Through the use of a cognitive systems engineering approach, researchers can gain insight into the cognitive processes involved in team collaboration. This insight can then be used to support the cognitive requirements of teamwork. The research reported here represents one aspect of a larger effort with the long-term goal of contributing to the design of tools that support collaborating teams.

References

Bordetsky, A., & Hutchins, S. G. (2008). Plug-and-play testbed for collaboration in the global information grid. In M. Letsky, N. Warner, S. Fiore, & C. Smith (Eds.), *Macrocognition in teams* (pp. 365–384). London, UK: Ashgate.

Brehmer, B. (1992). European approaches to the study of decision making: Focus on process. Paper presented at *27th International Applied Military Psychology Symposium: A Focus on Decision Making Research* (Office of Naval Research Europe Reports, Number 92-4-W).

Burke, C. S. (2007, June). *Panel discussion on macrocognition*. Presented at the 8th International Conference on Naturalistic Decision Making, Asilomar, CA.

Cacciabue, P. C., & Hollnagel, E. (1995). Simulation of cognition: Applications. In J. Hoc, P. C. Cacciabue, & E. Hollnagel (Eds.), *Expertise and technology: Cognition and human-computer cooperation* (pp. 55–73). Hillsdale, NJ: Erlbaum.

Fiore, S. M., Smith, C. A. P., & Letsky, M. P. (2008). Macrocognition Research: Challenges and Opportunities on the Road Ahead. In M. P. Letsky, N. W. Warner, S. M. Fiore, & C. A. P. Smith (Eds.), *Macrocognition in teams*. Burlington, VT: Ashgate.

Fire Department of the City of New York. (2001, September 11). *Manhattan dispatcher radio transcripts*. New York, NY: FDNY.

Fischer, U., Orasanu, J., & Montalvo, M. (1993). Efficient decision strategies on the flight deck. In R. Jensen (Ed.), *Proceedings of the 7th Symposium on Aviation Psychology* (pp. 238–243). Columbus, OH: Ohio State University.

Hocevar, S. P., Thomas, G. F., & Jansen, E. (2006). Building collaborative capacity: An innovative strategy for homeland security preparedness. In M. M. Beyerlein, S. T. Beyerlein, & F. Kennedy (Eds.), *Advances in interdisciplinary studies of work teams: Innovations through collaboration* (Vol. 12, pp. 263–283). New York, NY: Elsevier JAI Press.

Hoffman, R. R., & Yates, J. F. (2005). Decision(?)Making(?). *IEEE Intelligent Systems*, Vol. 20, No. 4, July/August, pp. 76–83.

Hutchins, S. G. (1994). Decision-making errors demonstrated by experienced naval officers in a littoral environment. In C. E. Zsambak & Klein G. A. (Eds.), *Naturalistic decision making* (pp. 207–215). Hillsdale, NJ: Erlbaum.

Hutchins, S. G. (1996). *Principles for aiding complex military decision making* (NOSC Technical Report 1718). San Diego, CA: Naval Command, Control, and Ocean Surveillance Center, RDT&E Division.

Hutchins, S. G., Bordetsky, A., Kendall, A., & Garrity, M. (2007, October). Evaluating a model of team collaboration via analysis of team communications. In *Proceedings of the 51st Human Factors and Ergonomics Association Annual Meeting*, Baltimore, MD.

Hutchins, S. G., Kendall, T., & Bordetsky, A. (2008, June). Understanding patterns of team collaboration employed to solve unique problems. In *Proceedings of the 13th International Command and Control Research & Technology Symposium*, Bellevue, WA.

Klein, G. (1993). Sources of error in naturalistic decision making tasks. In *Proceedings of the 37th Annual Meeting of the Human Factors and Ergonomics Society* (pp. 368–371). Santa Monica, CA: Human Factors and Ergonomics Society.

Klein, G., Phillips, J. K., Rall, E. L., & Peluso, D. A. (2007). A data-frame theory of sensemaking. In R. Hoffman (Ed.), *Expertise out of context* (pp. 113–155). New York, NY: Lawrence Erlbaum Associates.

Klein, G., Ross, K. G., Moon, B. M., Klein, D. E., Hoffman, R. R., & Hollnagel, E. (2003). Macrocognition. *IEEE Intelligent Systems, 18*(3), 81–85.

Klein, G. A. (1989). Recognition-primed decisions. In W. R. Rouse (Ed.), *Advances in man-machine systems research* (Vol. 5, pp. 47–92). Greenwich, CT: JAI Press.

Letsky, M., & Warner, N. (2008). Macrocognition in teams. In M. Letsky, N. Warner, S. M. Fiore, & C. Smith (Eds.), *Macrocognition in teams* (pp. 1–13). London, UK: Ashgate.

Letsky, M., Warner, N., Fiore, S. M., Rosen, M., & Salas, E. (2007, June). Macrocognition in complex team problem solving. In *Proceedings of the 12th International Command and Control Research & Technology Symposium*, Newport, RI.

Mosier, K. L. (1991). Expert decision making strategies. In R. Jensen (Ed.), *Proceedings of the Sixth International Symposium on Aviation Psychology* (pp. 266–271). Columbus, OH: Ohio State University.

Nosek, J. T. (2004). Group cognition as a basis for supporting group knowledge creation and sharing. *Journal of Knowledge Management, 8*(4), 3–18.

Orasanu, J., & Connolly, T. (1993). The reinvention of decision making. In G. A. Klein, J. Orasanu, R. Calderwood, & C. E. Zsambok (Eds.), *Decision making in action: Models and methods* (pp. 3–20). Norwood, NJ: Ablex.

Orasanu, J. M. (1994). Shared problem models and flight crew performance. In N. Johnston, N. McDonald, & R. Fuller (Eds.), *Aviation psychology in practice* (pp. 1–22). Aldershot, UK: Ashgate.

Orasanu, J. M., & Fischer, U. (1997). Finding decisions in natural environments: The view from the cockpit. In C. Zsambok & G. Klein (Eds.), *Naturalistic decision making* (pp. 343–357). Hillsdale, NJ: Lawrence Erlbaum Associates.

Salas, E., Dickinson, T., Converse, S., & Tannenbaum, S. (1992). Toward an understanding of team performance and training. In R. Sweezey & E. Salas (Eds.), *Teams: Their training and performance* (pp. 3–29). Norwood, NJ: Ablex.

Salas, E., & Fiore, S. M. (2004). *Team cognition: Understanding the factors that drive process and performance*. Washington, DC: American Psychological Association.

Schwoegler, D. (2006, September 29). *Marine experiment tests detection capability*. NEWSLINE, Lawrence Livermore National Laboratory, Livermore, CA.

Warner, N., & Letsky, M. (2008). Empirical model of team collaboration focus on macrocognition. In M. Letsky, N. Warner, S. Fiore, & C. Smith (Eds.), *Macrocognition in teams* (pp. 15–33). London, UK: Ashgate.

Warner, N., Letsky, M., & Cowen, M. (2005). Cognitive model of team collaboration: Macrocognitive focus. In *Proceedings of the 49th Human Factors and Ergonomics Society Annual Meeting* (pp. 269–273). Santa Monica, CA: Human Factors and Ergonomics Society.

Warner, N., & Wroblewski, E. (2003). Achieving collaborative knowledge in asynchronous collaboration: Murder mystery collaboration experiment. In *Collaboration and Knowledge Management Workshop Proceedings* (pp. 327–340). Arlington, VA: Office of Naval Research.

Warner, N., & Wroblewski, E. (2004). Achieving collaborative knowledge in asynchronous collaboration: NEO collaboration experiment. In *Collaboration and Knowledge Management Workshop Proceedings* (pp. 63–72). Arlington, VA: Office of Naval Research.

Wood, D. J., & Gray, B. (1991). Toward a comprehensive theory of collaboration. *Journal of Applied Behavioral Science, 27*, 149–162.

6

Decision-Making Processes of Leaders in Product Development

Petra Badke-Schaub
Delft University of Technology

Introduction

The growth of technology has significantly influenced the well-being of our society; however, a by-product of the benefits associated with technological development is that we are more than ever dependent on reliable products, product systems, and services. As a response to that dependency, we can state an interesting paradox: Due to safety concerns, there is an ever-increasing interest in building systems that aim to decrease the influence of human operators in favor of the apparent reliability associated with increased automation. In contrast, there is relatively little interest in affecting the behavior of the human actor who is responsible for the design of these products. This chapter addresses the latter issue.

Most often we associate the failure with the *use* of a technical product, but more frequently the primary reason for the failure lies in the *design* and development of the product. Certainly, product design and development are not restricted to issues of mechanics and materials but involve knowledge and skills as well as creativity, experience, and decision making throughout the design process. Thus, when confronted with technological, economic, and cognitive challenges, it is important to take into account both limits on resources and the limitations of the human actors who are in charge of developing products, product systems, and services. Failures in design may be extremely expensive in terms of cost and even in terms of life (Hales, 1995; Reason, 1987). Human beings are often limited in regard to their ability to predict and prevent failures (Tversky & Kahneman, 1974). Therefore, efforts should be made to improve the processes and techniques used to reduce the probability of failures in complex, technological systems.

We know that design failures can be explained as caused or at least contributed to by humans. However, the occurrence of design failures does not provide an understanding of the underlying human failures—and the occurrence of human failures does not provide enough knowledge to forecast how, when, and in what context design failures will occur. A promising way to gain insight into designers' thinking and actions is through the analysis of their decision making as it occurs in the natural environment. From this analysis, information concepts, methods, or training guidelines can be derived to ensure that human actors deal with the complex requirements of a design project in a more reliable and effective way.

Unfortunately, more than 150 years of research in classical decision theory—if we accept Bernoulli (1738) as its founder—has not delivered concepts that explain decision making in complex and dynamic situations. Much research has primarily focused on decisions with well-defined alternatives in a static environment, thus equating decision making with choice (i.e., the selection of the best option). This view has been broadly criticized because it reduces our understanding to a limited element and neglects the decision-making process (Beach, 1993; Beach & Lipshitz, 1993; Dörner, 1996; Dörner & Schaub, 1994; O'Hare, 1992). In contrast, researchers in naturalistic decision making (NDM) have focused on how professionals make decisions in real-world contexts and collect empirical data in a number of domains, such as aviation (Kaempf & Klein, 1994; Orasanu & Fischer, 1997), the military (Drillings & Serfaty, 1997; Serfaty, McMillan, Entin, & Entin, 1997), and fire service (Klein, Calderwood, & Clinton-Cirocco, 1986). Klein (1993) defines NDM as a framework that describes how experts make decisions in ambiguous and uncertain situations under conditions of time pressure, dynamic goals, and high risk. As each of these conditions are present in the design and development of complex, technological products and systems, it appears that product development may be appropriately studied using the NDM framework.

The first part of this chapter outlines the main characteristics of design activity in product development and compares this domain to the operational environments mentioned above. It also describes different requirements and constraints for the designer as decision maker. In the second part of the chapter an interdisciplinary study is presented in which psychologists and engineers investigated the daily decision-making processes of leaders in product development departments.

Factors Affecting Decision Making and Leadership in Product Development

Product development processes, also new product development (NPD), encompass the engineering, form-giving and business activities from the first idea for a new product to the market launch including market research and marketing analysis.

The product development process can be described by three characteristics: *complex, dynamic, and multidisciplinary.*

Product development is complex. Product development is a complex task in terms of both the actual products and the process leading to their development. Products range widely in complexity, and their complexity is ever increasing as products include new and continuously evolving technology. Moreover, the development of products is less structured than aircraft flight operations or work in other prototypical NDM fields, often involving tasks that can carry on for days, weeks, and sometimes even for years. Although the number of instruments and controls in a cockpit is large, and in emergency situations the cognitive load on the pilot is extremely high, the number of variables is finite in comparison to the design realm, where the problem can be made even more complex by adding features and components, or by integrating other disciplines, such as electronics and material sciences. As a result, leaders of design teams need to focus on the big picture in order to integrate knowledge from different disciplines; yet, at the same time, they also need to be able to notice interdependencies between the elementary parts of the product or service on a very detailed level of analysis.

Product development is a dynamic process. In product development the designer is embedded in a constantly changing environment. The situation can also change without the designer taking action. Therefore, the designer needs to continuously assess the situation and adjust his or her decision making to the current situation. There are not many rules and regulations, and no standard operating procedures or preplanned responses to provide guidance. As dynamic changes may have multiple causes, continuous monitoring and adjustment of goals, information, knowledge, and resources are most important in product development.

Design problems also exemplify ill-defined and wicked problems with unclear or even contradicting goals (Rittel & Webber, 1973; Simon, 1957, 1996) as a result of the social embeddedness of the design process. The dynamic characteristics of goals can be caused by different interests of the diverse stakeholders involved in the product development process, such as the marketing department, the client, the supplier, and other collaborating partners. Furthermore, during long-term development processes resources often change due to reduction or reallocation of money or personnel. However, possibly the most relevant dynamic is caused by changes of knowledge due to new information introduced into the process. For example, the information that a supplier cannot deliver the material as ordered can lead to a complete change of a design concept. Thus, coping with the dynamic aspects of the design process requires leaders who establish and maintain a process-related view of the essential activities, such as planning, monitoring, and adjusting resources.

Product development involves multidisciplinary teamwork. Situations in product development are multidisciplinary, as project teams are usually composed of people from different functional departments. The core idea in NPD is to involve key functions as early as possible in the design process, which means many decisions have to be made by teams consisting of people with different backgrounds and, often, diverse goals. Managing the multidisciplinary perspectives in product development projects requires leaders who can communicate effectively in order to coordinate the different stakeholders involved.

Leadership as Integration of Three-Level Knowledge

Facing the pressures of globalization and the complexity of technical innovation, competent leadership is recognized as a key factor in organizational effectiveness. That statement is also true for leadership in the engineering environment. However, even though there is general agreement on the importance of competent leaders, we are still far away from science-based applications, such as the development of training courses. In order to support leaders, it is important to determine, when and under which conditions the behavior described above is successful. Furthermore, there is a need for more concrete knowledge and understanding of how a successful leader implements these actions. Research on expertise highlights the importance of experts' ability to synthesize and interpret information in *context* (see, for example, Chapters 3 and 4 in this book). This finding has implications for a theory of leadership. It suggests that leaders have to synthesize and integrate knowledge not only on a content level but also on a managerial and people level (Mintzberg, 1973). On the managerial level, knowledge integration is required for planning; on the social level, a leader's synthesizing ability is needed to inspire his or her staff to balance their individual goals with the company's or the projects' objectives. The latter requirement is especially important in a multidisciplinary context, where different disciplines need to arrive at a shared understanding and add to a common result (Badke-Schaub, Neumann, Lauche, & Mohammed, 2007). Mumford, Zaccaro, Harding, Jacobs, and Fleishman (2000), summarizing research on leadership skill requirements, proposed a concept of leadership that is comprised of the following four skills (see also Zaccaro, 2001): cognitive skills, interpersonal skills, business skills, and strategic skills. Most of this work involved surveys and questionnaires rather than observations of real-life behavior. Observational studies, however, are needed to identify key patterns of behavior displayed by leaders in different types of situations.

The present study was performed to gain a deeper understanding of decision making in product development. In particular, we wanted to address the following goals: (1) detail the requirements for leadership in design, (2) develop a typology of critical leadership situations analogous to the typology of critical situations in design practice developed by Badke-Schaub and Frankenberger (1999), and (3) determine which leadership strategies are successful versus unsuccessful in different situations. Research questions included: What are the decision-making requirements in the daily work of product development leaders? How do these leaders make decisions in response to different requirements, and how successful are they in doing so? Are there patterns of correlation between leadership strategies and success in product development?

Method

Participants

Leadership activities in product development teams, including meetings and talks with customers and suppliers, were observed in three engineering design departments. Two design departments were part of medium-sized enterprises (in total <1,000 employees), which provided automotive devices and system solutions to the automobile industry and its suppliers. The third company produced various industrial equipment and facilities, commercial vehicles and engines, with more than 75,000 employees worldwide.

Design and Procedure

In each of the companies, the study proceeded in five consecutive steps (see Figure 6.1). In the first phase (A), the leaders of the product development department were interviewed about the products and processes of their specific work environment. In the next phase (B), a two-week-long on-line observation of the real-life working environment of the leaders was conducted by an engineer and a psychologist. After analysis of the data (C), a feedback session (D) was provided by the researchers that formed

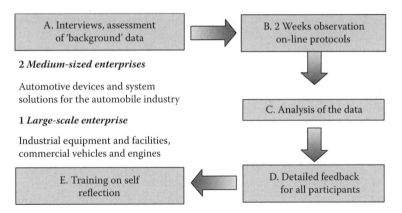

FIGURE 6.1   Design of the study.

the basis for a self-reflection training course (E), completing the investigation in each of the three companies. In the present chapter only the analysis and the results of the on-line protocols will be presented.

The primary method of the study was continuous, nonparticipatory observation. A laptop-based protocol system derived from well-established protocol systems (Badke-Schaub & Frankenberger, 1999) was used to document the observations in real time. In each company the leader of the R&D department was observed, including all the contacts he had during the day. The observation period was two weeks. The final protocol consisted of a word-by-word transcription of dialogues and a description of the observed processes. The continuous protocol of the observed process allowed for multiple and repeated analysis, in particular facilitating the identification of critical leadership situations and the categorization of leadership requirements.

Table 6.1 provides an example of a critical leadership situation and illustrates our categorization system. In this situation, the leader of the R&D department (AW) discusses a sample order with the engineer (CF) of the testing department. Due to time constraints, they will not be able to complete and deliver a customer's order on time. AW knows that there are still components from an earlier order by a competitor of the customer that are constructed in the same way as the ordered ones, but they are labeled with another number. He proposes to change the numbers of the old components and to deliver them to the customer. CF feels uneasy about this idea but AW reassures him: "This is an arrangement between us. If you don't tell anybody, nobody will know!"

This short example is one of 344 situations identified as critical. A situation was defined as critical when a decision was made by the leader that had serious consequences for the development process. Thus, the main criterion for identifying a leadership situation as critical was its relevance to this process. The relevance of a situation was judged *post hoc* on the basis of the on-line protocol. A situation was defined in terms of topics in the conversations between a leader and others; that is, a situation started with the introduction of a distinct problem and ended when a decision had been reached. Consequently, situations could extend over several days. A critical situation could arise during a phone call or in a meeting; two or more individuals could be involved; the individuals could be from the same department or from different departments, or they could be a client or a supplier.

Each critical situation was described in terms of a set of parameters, such as type of interaction (see Table 6.1). Thus, the unit of evaluation was a situation identified in the protocols of the on-line observation. Situations were identified by either one of the two observers and subsequently validated by the other; some of the situations were also confirmed with the leader during the feedback session.

Each of these critical situations presented problems that leaders had to solve and that required particular activities from them, such as goal clarification, conflict management, or the allocation of resources. Nine different types of activities could be distinguished (see Table 6.2) that were grouped into three categories: activities that concerned product-related, process-related, or interpersonal decisions.

Product-related decisions occurred in situations that required the clarification of goals—for instance, concerning the size, weight, material, and function of the

TABLE 6.1   Example of a Critical Situation and Its Classification Based on the Transcribed Protocol

Documentation	Persons	Interaction	Requirement	Action	Quality
• Situation • Protocol lines • Name	• Leader • Others	• Face-to-face • Meeting • Email • Phone call	• Product • Process • Interpersonal	• Goals • Solutions • Failures	• Function • Self-evaluation • Consequences • Side effects • Long-term effects
Sit16g06 Lines 471–484 "Nobody knows"	AW CF	Face-to-face	Process	Decision Planning	Function fulfilled Side effects

TABLE 6.2   Categories of Critical Leadership Situations and Associated Leader Activities in Product Development

Product-Related Decisions	Process-Related Decisions	Interpersonal Decisions
Goal elaboration • Specifies/sets goals • Clarifies tasks • Negotiates design changes related to the requirements	**Planning** • Assigns activities: who does what and when • Designates responsibilities • Develops and initiates long-term opportunities	**Interpersonal influence** • Generates and pursues strategies to increase own influence • Disseminates or withdraws relevant information
Solution development • Decides about the subsolutions and alternatives • Sets the criteria about the final solution(s)	**Monitoring** • Supervises and controls relevant procedures to secure the accomplishment of milestones	**Conflict management** • Solves disagreements about the task • Unfolds hidden differences that negatively affect the team process
Failure analysis • Gives feedback and decides how to proceed with (unexpected) design failures	**Resource management** • Allocates resources, such as money, people, and material	**Coaching** • Motivates and supports staff • Promotes identification with the company's goal

product—the generation and analysis of design solutions, as well as the analysis of design failures. Situations that presented problems concerning the management of material, personal, and financial resources, and that accordingly required decisions about planning, monitoring, and allocating equipment, people, money, and time, were categorized as process-related decision situations. Finally, situations involving interpersonal decisions required answers to such issues as how best to interact with others and influence them, how to manage interpersonal conflict, or how to motivate and support subordinates and colleagues.

This typology of critical leadership situations differs from the required leadership skills that Mumford, Campion, and Morgeson (2005) propose, who, in addition to cognitive and interpersonal skills, also mention business and strategic skills. In contrast, in our study we were not able to distinguish between situations requiring strategic versus business-related decisions, and consequently classified both as process-based decision situations.

The quality of leaders' decisions was evaluated by the researchers; some evaluations were also validated by the leaders themselves during the feedback session. Due to the complexity of most design problems, successful decisions often also include less unsuccessful elements. Thus, we developed a binary rating system for decision quality successful versus unsuccessful concerning the outcome of the situation, according to the following questions:

- Was the problem solved completely?
- Were subtasks/problems solved?
- Were nonintended side or long-term effects created?

For example, in a conflict situation with a designer, the leader forced him to realize a different solution than the one the designer preferred. The new solution had no direct advantages, but the designer was unhappy with that new solution and was demotivated to further elaborate and work on this solution. Thus, this conflict situation was not solved successfully because the designer would not bring in his motivation and commitment to solve the problem, and the solution itself did not show advantages over the designer's solution idea.

Results

Altogether, 344 critical leadership situations were identified. Descriptive analysis revealed that nearly half of these (47%) involved activities related to process requirements, whereas the remaining situations were almost equally distributed between product-related (26%) and interpersonal decisions (27%).

Figure 6.2 provides a more detailed analysis of leadership decisions in terms of required activities. When leaders of product development departments made product-related decisions, they most often were occupied with finding solutions to unforeseen problems, such as sudden changes of the delivery times of components, or the analysis of failures. Although the observations were focused on leaders of design departments, only 2% of all relevant decisions were concerned with goal elaboration. These decisions are usually most important because they determine what the result

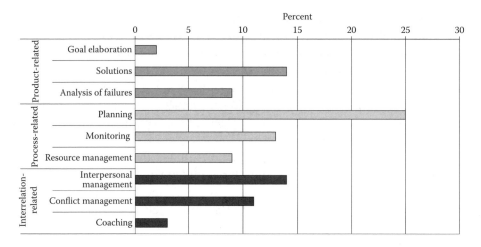

FIGURE 6.2   Distribution of activities associated with different leadership decisions.

(the product) will be and will define further milestones for the project. By far the most frequent activity was planning, which made up 25% of all observed decisions. Almost equally frequent were situations with interpersonal management and conflict resolution activities. Coaching activities refer to the support of persons and were observed only in 3% of all situations.

The distribution of critical situations sketches a picture of the daily work of leaders in design departments, but these numbers do not tell us anything about the outcomes or success of the designers' activities in these situations. In order to address this question, two raters independently evaluated the outcome of each situation in terms of its success. A situation was classified as successful if the observed activities that were associated with the leader's decision brought the team closer to their stated goal(s). Of the 344 critical leadership situations, 13 could not be evaluated since their outcomes were ambiguous. For the remaining situations, an overall success rate of 60% was observed (see Figure 6.3).

Figure 6.3 further indicates that leadership situations involving planning were associated with a high success rate. In contrast, situations that concerned goal elaboration and conflict management had predominantly poor results. In the reminder of the chapter we will take a closer look at these types of situations and explore issues associated with leadership decisions, especially relating to planning, goal and task clarification, and conflict management.

Planning

Planning activities encompassed situations that required scheduling decisions, the coordination of actions by individuals, or strategic decisions. The results reveal that strategic planning decisions seem to be the most difficult ones, as half of them were rated as unsuccessful (see Table 6.3). Decisions concerning staff actions were the most frequent and the most successful ones. The reason may be that this type of planning, when done by an experienced leader, provides clear instructions to subordinates and is easier to perform than strategic planning decisions. Remarkable is also the high

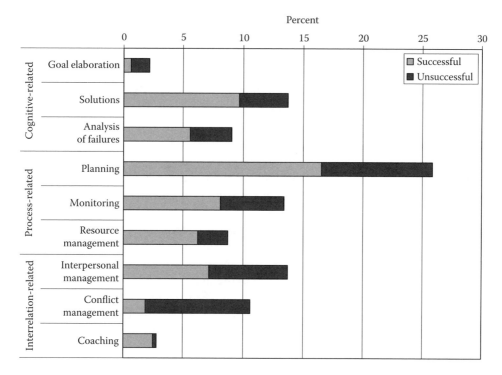

FIGURE 6.3   Percentage of leadership activities associated with successful and unsuccessful results.

TABLE 6.3   Distribution of Planning Situations by Type and Outcome ($n = 83$)

	Successful	Unsuccessful
Time scheduling	23%	17%
Coordination of staff	33%	11%
Strategic planning	8%	8%

percentage of unsuccessful time scheduling; most of these unsuccessful decisions were due to overly optimistic assessments by the leader, leading to various negative consequences, such as unsatisfied customers.

Goal Elaboration

A surprising result was the extremely low number of decisions that involved goal elaboration ($n = 7$), or addressed failures to reach goals ($n = 5$). Detailed analyses of these situations revealed that leaders failed in goal elaborations because they went through the situations without making sufficiently clear how tasks and responsibilities are to be allocated; that is, no one was assigned to tasks and subtasks. Inadequate allocation of responsibility led to a diffusion of responsibility. This tendency was even stronger when the leader did not specify the importance of a goal or subgoal.

Another major obstacle to comprehensive goal elaboration was the lack of a standardized procedure for developing a thorough task clarification. The observed decisions involving goal elaboration were mostly *ad hoc* decisions; that is, they were not preceded by detailed planning or thorough information gathering. On the other hand, goal decisions in highly complex environments are often strategic decisions with long-term consequences. As a result, decision making that is not based on appropriate information about the situation at hand and possible constraints can jeopardize the survival of the whole company.

Conflict Management

Conflicts occur in various forms, such as cognitive, affective (socioemotional), and process conflict (Jehn, 1995), and may have positive or negative consequences (Badke-Schaub, Goldschmidt, and Meijer, 2010).

Moreover, conflicts are a crucial force for change (Carnevale & Probst, 1998). Thus, conflict management covers a broad area of decision making referring to coping with opposite values and contradictory goals and interests. In the present study, conflict management situations were characterized as involving decisions where two different opinions or interests were stated and a decision was needed. Activities by the leader in conflict management situations were divided into three main categories: personal feedback, consensus seeking, and striving for a rational solution. Their success was rated based on whether or not the group progressed toward task completion. In addition, all conflict management situations were rated as to whether the leader tried to solve the conflict at the expense of his or her positive relationship with the disagreeing team member. Figure 6.4 depicts how conflict management strategies were associated with a positive or negative person orientation.

Although few conflict management situations were observed, the results indicate some interesting phenomena. Striving to resolve conflicts with rational arguments was unsuccessful in five out of the six cases. Even though rational conflict resolution is often recommended as the strategy of choice (Hambrick, Finkelstein, & Mooney, 2005; Mintzberg, Raisinghani, & Theoret, 1976), in most of the observed cases this approach did not move a team closer toward solving the conflict at hand. In contrast,

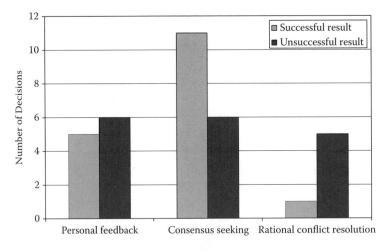

FIGURE 6.4   Leaders' strategies to manage conflict and their associated successes.

consensus seeking was found to be the most effective conflict resolution style. It supported task completion and, in most situations, had a positive impact on the relationship. One reason for the success of consensus seeking may be that this strategy is conducive to a cooperative orientation, while rational conflict resolution imparts a response orientation that puts one's own ideas in the foreground.

Personal feedback proved a successful conflict management strategy in some cases; however, in other cases it did not lead to the desired outcome with respect to the project's goal. This finding suggests that the success of personal feedback is dependent on additional factors, such as the relationship between the leader and the person who receives the feedback. Furthermore, conflict situations may have characteristics that personal feedback alone does not resolve; further actions have to be taken.

Conclusions

In the present study we observed the behavior of leaders in three design departments and analyzed their decisions. Decisions were categorized in terms of the activities they involved, and whether or not they advanced the design team in its task.

Analyses revealed that the majority of leadership decisions in design departments are planning activities, and are mainly concerned with coordinating the decisions of the different stakeholders involved. Obviously, these activities are of key importance in dealing with the complex issues encountered in product development. Planning is a strong strategy to cope with a changing environment, to ensure that everybody knows what to deliver, when, and how to do so. Thus, planning reduces uncertainty and increases the alignment of team members' mental models (Badke-Schaub et al., 2007).

Although planning is their main activity, our data indicate that leaders in design may not be completely occupied with managerial tasks; in fact, more than 20% of their decisions were concerned with product-related issues, such as solution development and analysis of failures. This finding has two interesting theoretical implications for NDM research:

1. According to Klein et al. (1986), NDM is a valuable framework in settings such as aviation or fire fighting, where decision makers have little time for conscious deliberation. These work domains provide predefined rules and standard operating procedures for decision and judgment tasks, thus limiting the amount of choices considerably. One of the most influential models within the NDM framework (Beach & Lipshitz, 1993), the recognition-primed decision making (RPD) model (Klein, 1993, 1998), was the result of cognitive task analyses of firefighters. It has been proven as a reasonable explication for decision making in situations with ill-defined goals and under time pressure, where the decision maker has a considerable amount of experience to rely on.

   Lipshitz, Klein, Orasanu, and Salas (2001) distinguish three variants of recognition-primed decision making, which refer to different levels of complexity. The first variant concerns situations in which the decision makers generate an immediate response based on cases they have accumulated through their professional experience. The second variant applies to situations that are not clear to the decision maker. In these instances, decision makers will mentally simulate events that may have led to the current situation (Kaempf, Klein, Thordsen, & Wolf, 1996). The third variant describes how decision makers can evaluate a course of action without undergoing a detailed comparison with other options (Klein & Crandall, 1995; Pennington & Hastie, 1993). In these situations, decision makers run a mental simulation of the proposed action to see intended as well as unintended consequences. Freud already referred to this kind of mental simulation as *internes Probehandeln* (1984).

The work domain of product development is embedded in a complex, dynamic, and multidisciplinary environment where no single optimal decision can be made. Our observations of leaders in design departments—who can be considered as formally acknowledged experts—revealed that they displayed skill-based and rule-based behavior (Rasmussen, 1986) in routine situations, that is, behavior consistent with the first variant of the RPD model.

However, nonroutine situations required leaders of design teams to conduct a thorough analysis of the product and design process and to generate new knowledge. None of the three RPD variants describes this kind of knowledge generation decision.

2. Obviously, there are not only differences but also commonalities between the more operational environments traditionally studied by NDM researchers and the more knowledge generating environments, such as product development. The NDM framework could be expanded to account for expert behavior in both routine and nonroutine situations.

Because NDM focuses on experience and experts, the role of domain-specific knowledge is seen as especially crucial. The present study demonstrated that leaders in product development need to have skills in team building, motivation, and conflict management. For example, process-related activities that made up nearly 50% of all leader activities required a combination of domain-specific knowledge, methodological knowledge, and managerial knowledge. Leaders in design departments need to be not only experts in the knowledge domain, but also coordinators and planners as well as conflict moderators—that is, they need additional (social and management) knowledge and skills.

References

Badke-Schaub, P., & Frankenberger, E. (1999). Analysis of design projects. *Design Studies, 20,* 481–494.

Badke-Schaub, P., Goldschmidt, G., & Meijer, M. (2010). How does cognitive conflict in design teams support the development of creative ideas? *Creativity and Innovation Management, 19,* 119–133.

Badke-Schaub, P., Neumann, A., Lauche, K., & Mohammed, S. (2007). Mental models in design teams: A valid approach to performance in design collaboration? *CoDesign, 3,* 5–20.

Beach, L. R. (1993). Broadening the definition of decision making: The role of prechoice screening of options. *Psychological Science, 4,* 215–220.

Beach, L. R., & Lipshitz, R. (1993). Why classical decision theory is an inappropriate standard for evaluating and aiding most human decision making. In G. A. Klein, J. Orasanu, R. Calderwood, & C. E. Zsambok (Eds.), *Decision making in action: Models and methods* (pp. 21–35). Norwood, NJ: Ablex Publishing.

Bernoulli, D. (1738). Specimen Theoriae Novae De Mensura Sortis. *Commentarii Academiae Scientrum Imperialis Petropolitanae, 5*(1738), 175–192. (English translation by Sommer, L. (1954). Exposition of a new theory of the measurement of risk. *Econometrica, 22,* 23–36.)

Carnevale, P. J., & Probst, T. M. (1998). Social values and social conflict in creative problem solving and categorization. *Journal of Personality and Social Psychology, 74,* 1300–1309.

Dörner, D. (1996). *The logic of failure: Why things go wrong and what we can do to make them right.* New York, NY: Metropolitan Books.

Dörner, D., & Schaub, H. (1994). Errors in planning and decision making and the nature of human information processing. *Applied Psychology: An International Review, 43,* 433–453.

Drillings, M., & Serfaty, D. (1997). Naturalistic decision making in command and control. In C. E. Zsambok & G. Klein (Eds.), *Naturalistic decision making* (pp. 71–80). Mahwah, NJ: Erlbaum.

Freud, S. (1984). *Vorlesung zur Einfuhrung in die Psychoanalyse.* Frankfurt, Germany: Fischer TB.

Hales, C. (1995). Five fatal designs. In V. Hubka (Ed.), *Proceedings ICED 95, Prague, WDK 23* (pp. 662–667). Zürich, Switzerland: Edition Heurista.

Hambrick, D. C., Finkelstein, A. C., & Mooney, A. C. (2005). Executive job demands: New insights for explaining strategic decisions and leader behaviors. *Academy of Management Review, 30,* 472–91.

Jehn, K. A. (1995). A multimethod examination of the benefits and detriments on intragroup conflict. *Administrative Science Quarterly, 40,* 256–282.

Kaempf, G. F., Klein, G., Thordsen, M. L., & Wolf, S. (1996). Decision making in complex command-and-control environments. *Human Factors, 38,* 206–219.

Kaempf, G. L., & Klein, G. A. (1994). Aeronautical decision making: The next generation. In N. McDonald, N. Johnston, & R. Fuller (Eds.), *Aviation psychology in practice* (pp. 223–254). Aldershot, UK: Avebury.

Klein, G. (1998). *Sources of power: How people make decisions.* Cambridge, MA: MIT Press.

Klein, G. A. (1993). A recognition-primed decision (RPD) model of rapid decision making. In G. A. Klein, J. Orasanu, R. Calderwood, & C. E. Zsambok (Eds.), *Decision making in action: Models and methods.* Norwood, NJ: Ablex Publishing.

Klein, G. A., Calderwood, R., & Clinton-Cirocco, A. (1986). Rapid decision making on the fireground. In *Proceedings of the 30th Annual Human Factors Society* (Vol. 1, pp. 576–580). Dayton, OH: Human Factors Society.

Klein, G. A., & Crandall, B. W. (1995). The role of mental simulation in naturalistic decision making. In P. Hancock, J. Flach, J. Caird, & K. Vincente (Eds.), *Local applications of the ecological approach to human-machine systems* (Vol. 2, pp. 324–358). Hillsdale, NJ: Erlbaum.

Klein, G. A., Orasanu, J., Calderwood, R., & Zsambok C. (Eds.). (1993). *Decision making in action: Models and methods.* Norwood, NJ: Ablex Publishing.

Lipshitz, R., Klein, G., Orasanu, J., & Salas, E. (2001). Focus article: Taking stock of naturalistic decision making. *Journal of Behavioral Decision Making, 14,* 331–352.

Mintzberg, H. (1973). *The nature of managerial work.* New York, NY: Harper and Row.

Mintzberg, H., Raisinghani, D., & Theoret, A. (1976). The structure of unstructured decision processes. *Administrative Science Quarterly, 21,* 246–275.

Mumford, M. D., Zaccaro, S. J., Harding, F. D., Jacobs, T. O., & Fleishman, E. A. (2000). Leadership skills for a changing world: Solving complex social problems. *Leadership Quarterly, 11,* 11–35.

Mumford, T. V., Campion, M. A., & Morgeson, F. M. (2005). The leadership skills strataplex: Leadership skill requirements across organizational levels. *Leadership Quarterly, 18,* 154–166.

O'Hare, D. (1992). The ARTFUL decision maker: A framework model for aeronautical decision making. *International Journal of Aviation Psychology, 2,* 175–191.

Orasanu, J., & Fischer, U. (1997). Finding decisions in natural environments. In C. Zsambok & G. Klein (Eds.), *Naturalistic decision making* (pp. 434–358). Hillsdale, NJ: Erlbaum.

Pennington, N., & Hastie, R. (1993). A theory of explanation-based decision making. In G. A. Klein, J. R. Orasanu, R. Calderwood, & C. Zsambok (Eds.), *Decision making in action: Models and methods* (pp. 188–201). Norwood, NJ: Ablex.

Rasmussen, J. (1986). *Information processing and human-machine interaction: An approach to cognitive engineering.* Amsterdam, Netherlands: North Holland Press.

Reason, J. (1987). The Chernobyl errors. *Bulletin of the British Psychological Society, 40,* 201–206.

Rittel, H., & Webber, M. (1973). Dilemmas in a general theory of planning. *Policy Sciences, 4,* 155–159.

Serfaty, D., McMillan, J., Entin, E. E., & Entin, E. B. (1997). The decision-making expertise of battle commanders. In C. E. Zsambok & G. Klein (Eds)., *Naturalistic decision making* (pp. 233–246). Mahwah, NJ: Erlbaum.

Simon, H. A. (1956). Rational choice and the structure of the environment. *Psychological Review, 63,* 129–138.

Simon, H. A. (1973). The structure of ill-structured problems. *Artificial Intelligence, 4,* 181–204.

Tversky, A., & Kahneman, D. (1974). Judgement under uncertainty: Heuristics and biases. *Science, 185,* 1124–1131.

Zaccaro, S. J. (2001). *The nature of executive leadership: A conceptual and empirical analysis of success.* Washington, DC: American Psychological Association.

7

Expert Cultural Sensemaking in the Management of Middle Eastern Crowds

Winston R. Sieck, Jennifer L. Smith, and Anna Grome
Applied Research Associates, Inc.

David A. Rababy
Rababy & Associates, Inc.

In June 2003, a team of U.S. soldiers, Kuwaiti police, and an Iraqi guide were investigating mass grave sites to search for Kuwaiti missing persons. The team learned of a Ramadi cemetery that likely contained some missing persons, and they went to investigate. The U.S. soldiers waited outside the Muslim cemetery with the vehicles, while the others entered to investigate. Local kids began to gather near the vehicles, and then more people stopped as they walked by. As more adults approached, the kids melted to the background. Approximately 30 to 40 people gathered within 15 minutes, and the team was hemmed in. At this point, an older, grizzled man made his way to the front of the crowd and greeted the team leader. The other members of the crowd deferred to him when he talked. The grizzled man asked the team leader if there were Kuwaitis in the cemetery and why they were there. The team leader answered the questions calmly, and the grizzled man then began to loudly describe many bad things that Kuwaitis were responsible for. More people joined the crowd.

In order to successfully deal with crowds in host nations, American personnel must be able to understand the situation from the perspective of the crowd members. This claim is based on the assumption that crowd reactions depend in large part on how the relevant players (i.e., crowd members and security forces) interpret the situation. Past research in naturalistic decision making highlights the importance of mental models for how people make sense of situations (Klein, 1998; Klein, Phillips, Rall, & Peluso, 2004). According to Rouse and Morris (1986), mental models are "mechanisms whereby humans are able to generate descriptions of system purpose and form, explanations of system functioning and observed system states, and predictions of future system states" (p. 351). People's mental models describe how they understand physical things like mechanical devices, but also their understanding of social and cognitive phenomena, such as crowd behavior, that tend to differ across cultures (Gopnik & Wellman, 1994; Lillard, 1998; Sieck, Rasmussen, & Smart, 2010).

In the past, crowd theorists popularized notions that minimized the importance of interpretations in crowd situations. Particularly, suggestions that crowd membership drives people toward irrationality and destructiveness do not leave much room for mental models, at least on the side of crowd members (Le Bon, 1947). However, more recent theories have been developed that do take into account the role of mental models in crowd situations. One such theory is the social identity model (Drury & Reicher, 1999). The social identity model emphasizes the self-concepts of crowd members, and explains how conceptions of the self and related outcomes, such as feelings of power, change through participation in crowd events. According to the model, social identity is a mental model of one's position in a set of social relations along with actions that are possible and legitimate given such a position. Social identity thus drives decisions in crowd situations. Conflicts can arise when the various groups within a crowd, such as security forces and crowd participants, have distinct models of the crowd members' social identity (i.e., roles within the event, and society more generally) that guide their interpretation of the situation (Drury & Reicher, 2000). With its emphasis on mental models, the social identity model enables an important link between analyses of crowd situations and the cultural analysis that is required to understand interactions between Middle Eastern crowd members and American personnel who find themselves in positions of needing to manage those crowds.

One important issue that the social identity model of crowd behavior has not yet addressed concerns the differences in the mental models of crowd functioning that U.S. security forces and crowd members from Middle Eastern cultures most likely have due to their distinct cultural backgrounds. That is, Americans who are expected to manage Middle Eastern crowds must also be adept at cultural sensemaking (Osland & Bird, 2000; Sieck, Smith, & Rasmussen, 2008). Cultural sensemaking refers to the processes by which people come to understand and explain the behavior of others with distinct cultural backgrounds. A major research issue is to determine what cultural aspects are most important and helpful for making sense of behavior in a context such as crowd events.

Before addressing culture in protests or other crowd situations, we first need to define *culture*. As expected in any highly interdisciplinary field, there exist a variety of conceptions of culture (Atran, Medin, & Ross, 2005). Our conception is distinctly cognitive in nature, following an epidemiological perspective (D'Andrade, 1981; Sperber, 1985). As such, a fundamental assumption about culture is that members of geographically proximal groups share experiences growing up in similar, but not identical, ecological and social contexts. These shared developmental experiences lead to significant commonalities in individuals' mental models and other representations. Such distributions of representations, in turn, ground the distribution of behavioral norms, expectations, interpretations, and affective reactions in a population (Sperber & Hirschfeld, 1999).

An important property of these mental representations is that they are highly specific to particular domains (Hirschfeld & Gelman, 1994). That is, social activities, such as participation in protests or providing security during protests, are supported by mental models that are tailored to those specific activities. Hence, the culturally shared mental models comprise values, beliefs, and concepts that are salient to members of a particular culture in those contexts, and may well not generalize to other situations. Multiple cultural values are reflected in peoples' mental models, and certain values may be more important than others, depending upon the situation, a phenomenon sometimes known as value trumping (Osland & Bird, 2000). For example,

Americans typically place a high value on freedom of speech; however, they may also support censorship or restricted access to information at certain times (e.g., extremely violent or sexually explicit content).

The upshot is that it is difficult to understand the cultural considerations that are relevant within a particular context, such as crowd management in the Middle East, by starting with preexisting lists of domain-general cultural values (Hofstede, 2001; Schwartz, 1994). In the present study, we take a different approach. Here, we investigate the experiences and mental models of Middle Eastern cultural and military experts who have direct experience in managing Middle Eastern crowds. Our aim was to uncover their cultural expertise, with a special focus on the mental models they used to make sense of the behavior of others in crowd situations. By capturing and modeling the expert cultural knowledge specific to crowd situations, we were then able to identify particular dimensions of cultural variation that are relevant in this context. This knowledge also formed the basis for a cultural education package situated in crowd contexts, and other recommendations for the improvement of cultural sensemaking in crowd situations.

Method

Participants

We interviewed 12 experienced military personnel in the United States and Lebanon. We conducted interviews with Lebanese commandos in Beirut who had a native cultural perspective on the Middle East, and had personally provided security at crowd demonstrations in Lebanon. We also interviewed U.S. military personnel (e.g., foreign area officers, civil affairs, and human intelligence officers) who had advanced cultural knowledge of the Middle East, typically including Arab language fluency, as well as specific crowd management experiences in Iraq. All of the interviewees were men. Though most of the Lebanese participants spoke English, a translator was needed and available during those interviews. The experts were strictly volunteers, and did not receive compensation for their time because of their military status.

Interview Guide

The critical decision method (CDM) was used as the basis for the interviews used in this study. The CDM is an incident-based interview method for uncovering information about the knowledge, goal structures, cues, and judgment and decision processes underlying observable actions in a particular context (Hoffman, Crandall, & Shadbolt, 1998; Klein, Calderwood, & MacGregor, 1989). The CDM was originally developed based on an earlier technique for uncovering critical incidents that come from direct experience (Flanagan, 1954). Sieck, McHugh, and Smith (2006) provide more detail on the use of the interview technique for examining cultural issues, including a comparison between CDM and more traditional ethnographic methods.

The CDM interviews used a case-based approach, and were organized around an initial, unstructured account of a specific incident. Once the participant identified a relevant incident, he was asked to recount the episode in its entirety without interruption from the interviewer. The expert's account of the incident provided the basic structure for the remainder of the interview. The interviewers then conducted additional sweeps through the incident to elicit further details. Examples of questions included:

- What cues alerted you to changes in the crowd?
- How did you recognize when the crowd was changing in some way?
- What were your concerns at that point?
- What was it about the situation that let you know what was going on?
- Can you describe what the crowd was like at the beginning, at the middle, and then again at the end of the gathering? How was it different at these different points?
- What if you had taken action X? How would things have turned out differently?

Interview Procedure

Interviews were conducted by a pair of trained interviewers with one expert at a time. In a given session, one interviewer led the questioning and took notes on key points, while the other interviewer focused on taking extensive notes. Occasionally, the lead interviewer would pause and ask the second whether he or she had any questions for the expert. The military participants declined permission to audio record the sessions, so notes were relied upon as the data record. As soon as possible after each session, the second interviewer would type up the main body of notes. The first interviewer would then review the notes against his or her records, and use track changes to fill in any gaps or highlight inconsistencies. The interviewers would then discuss and settle the differences by consensus. No major disagreements were encountered; in that event, the interviewers would have consulted the expert. An Arabic translator was available during all of the interviews with Middle Easterners, and the translator joined the interview to facilitate communication between the interviewer and interviewees as necessary. The duration of each interview was approximately 1.5 to 2 hours.

Analysis

A decision requirements analysis was conducted in order to understand the critical cognitive and cultural elements pertinent to crowd management. The first step was to code each incident for decisions, critical cues, factors, challenges, strategies, novice errors, goals, and cultural considerations mentioned in each incident. Two raters coded the data independently, and then met to compare their coding, to ensure that they fully captured the decision requirements for each incident. Disagreements were resolved through discussion. Tables of the decision requirements were created as an intermediate step. Finally, an expert model of Middle Eastern crowds was developed that highlighted the key considerations present across incidents. The model is reported in the next section, along with supporting segments from incidents.

Results

Consistent with past research on expertise, we found that the experts in the current study held elaborate mental models of dynamic crowd situations that consist of a set of various kinds of concrete and abstract concepts, bound together with intricate causal relationships. Past research on expert-novice differences has shown that experts' knowledge representations are richer conceptually, possessing more abstract concepts and higher-order relationships between concepts, and being more organized than novices' (Chi, Feltovich, & Glaser, 1981; Larkin, McDermott, Simon, & Simon, 1980). In addition, the expanded knowledge bases of experts have also been found to enhance aspects of perception and cognition, such as judging typicality, noticing cues that novices miss, and visualizing antecedents and consequences of actions and events (Christensen-Szalanski & Bushyhead, 1981; Klein & Hoffman, 1993). Klein and Hoffman (1993) argued that experts could be identified based on the way they see relationships between concepts, especially causal relationships. One useful way of graphically representing expert knowledge relevant to key judgments and decisions in a particular domain is the influence diagram (Howard, 1989). Influence diagrams are especially useful for depicting sets of complex causal relationships that enable experts to see how a situation developed into its current state, as well as how it is likely to progress.

Figure 7.1 illustrates a consensus of the experts' mental models in the current study, as extracted from the interview data. We have represented the expert mental model in the form of an influence diagram (Bostrom, Fischhoff, & Morgan, 1992). The circles represent basic concept nodes of variables the experts kept in mind, the arrows illustrate experts' beliefs about causality, and the final concept nodes under "social effects" show the end-state values that they attempted to influence (i.e., decrease immediate threat and increase positive civilian attitudes). The expert mental model guides the types of information that security forces attend to when they make sense

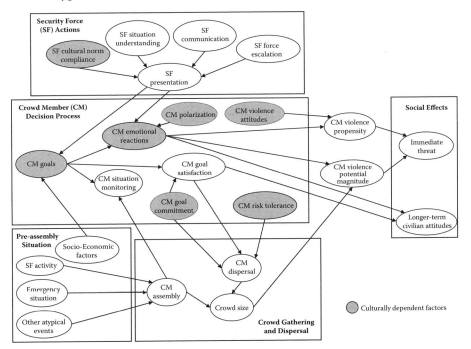

FIGURE 7.1   Expert mental model of crowd dynamics in the Middle East.

of crowd situations and assess the causal relationships between factors. As shown in Figure 7.1, experts considered the following variables: the preassembly situational factors, crowd gathering and dispersal processes, crowd member decision-making processes, security force presentation and actions, and resulting social effects. The preassembly situation referred to relevant contextual factors, including the event that caused people to begin to gather in a crowd (e.g., a fire, presence of security forces, etc.). Crowd member decision-making processes were believed to be influenced by background contextual factors, and to vary culturally in several ways. Security force actions, such as displays of force, wearing helmet and body armor, and acting according to cultural norms, were also believed to influence aspects of the crowd member decisions. Finally, the experts considered the effects of the crowd management efforts on longer-term civilian attitudes, in addition to immediate threat level and rate of dispersal. We next provide specific incident results that corroborate and elaborate aspects of the model.

The findings suggest that the experts made several important judgments during crowd management; in particular, as shown in Figure 7.1, they informed and updated their baseline models with details of the situation at hand. Key assessment categories included:

- Goals and motivation of crowd members
- Crowd members' goal commitment and tolerance for risk
- Security force presentation with respect to cultural norms
- Crowd members' use of polarizing language
- Crowd members' emotional expressions

Goals and Motivation of Crowd Members

Goals, needs, and wants are all concepts that explain peoples' motivations for specific behavior. The experts from our interviews attempted to determine the goals and motivations of the crowd members in order to identify leverage points for influencing the crowd. They implicitly understood that crowd members would disperse once their goals were satisfied. For example, an Arab-American Marine officer was ordered to disperse what appeared to be an angry mob forming outside of the Palestine Hotel in Baghdad, in 2003, just after major combat operations had ceased:

> The Marine officer climbed up onto a car inside the compound and looked at the crowd. He didn't have a flak jacket or helmet. He learned that keeping a helmet on kept the crowd more aloof, while not wearing it drew them in. He expected to be hit with stones or even bullets, but the crowd was just yelling. There were approximately 1,000 people, both men and women. It was noisy; he couldn't tell what was being said. He didn't see any guns. He spoke some Arabic, and it was like a light switch; everyone stopped yelling. Then, the people started screaming questions at the officer. He realized that the people weren't angry with the United States; they were just starved for information. He held a Q&A session and answered the questions one at a time. He could only talk to the people in front. He addressed questions from elders and the most vocal crowd members. Most of their questions focused on Saddam and missing family members.

For example, "Where is my family?" "When is the electricity coming on?" "Where is the food?" "Where's Saddam?"

When he talked to the crowd, he switched to an Arab mindset. He didn't know if his responses were true, but he said what he needed to in order to calm the crowd. He told them what they wanted to hear, for example, "Saddam released all of the prisoners. We're looking for your family." "Saddam turned off your electricity, but we're trying to turn it back on. First we're going to turn electricity on in your neighborhood (pointing) and then we'll get electricity turned on in their neighborhood." "You'll have food when the roads to Jordan open up. We're working on this." "Saddam's dead. We bombed his bunker over there."

The reality was that the United States did not know where Saddam was at this point. The officer said he was dead because he knew the main fear of many Iraqis was that Saddam was hiding and would punish everyone once the United States left—like he did in 1994. Also, he never wanted to say "I don't know" in the Middle East, because it brings shame upon you. It's looked upon as a personal weakness. The crowd liked what they heard.

The more he talked, the calmer the crowd became. The crowd was the most quiet when he spoke, but it was never very quiet. As their appetite for information was satisfied, the people began to disperse.

In addition to assessing the crowd members' goals and using that to influence them, the officer was also able to judge the level of threat by looking for arms and rock throwing. It also shows how the officer attended to his own presentation, both his physical stance (no helmet) and by answering questions in accord with Arab cultural norms.

Crowd Members' Goal Commitment and Tolerance for Risk

In addition to the goals themselves, the experts we interviewed also assessed the level of commitment to those goals, including the extent to which crowd members would risk physical harm. They used the information to determine how strong a stance they could take in directing crowd members, while avoiding significant backlash. For example, extremely high-risk tolerance and commitment in protestors was reported by a Lebanese Army officer who was appointed to a security detail during protests against Syria in 2005, following the assassination of Prime Minister Rafic Hariri:

The demonstrators included men, women, and children from all religious groups. The people were angry, and wanted to vent their anger in public. They were not dangerous—he did not see any sticks, arms, stone throwing, or anything. He had arranged his soldiers behind concertina wire, with an officer on a pile of stones with a bullhorn. The officer was in charge of talking to the crowd. His job was to calm them down, and repeat that they were not allowed to come in. The crowd reaction was shouting slogans, walking over the concertina wire, and pushing the soldiers. He saw women and children walking over two layers of concertina wire. He saw that as an indication of the strength of their determination. He felt that attempting to block them completely at that point would end in disaster, so he let a few enter the area, a little at a time.

As with the first incident, this one again shows the expert's ongoing assessment of threat level, in addition to reading cues regarding the behavior and appearance of crowd members in order to judge their commitment and tailor his crowd management strategy accordingly.

Security Force Presentation With Respect to Cultural Norms

As illustrated in the first incident, the experts were aware of their presentation to the crowd. They also took cues from crowd members, who were observing events, and determined whether people were playing by the rules of society or whether security forces or other crowd members were stepping out of the bounds set by cultural norms. Consider the following example described by a U.S. officer who was part of a team that had intercepted some bank robbers in Baghdad in 2003:

> The Iraqis were standing there quietly watching the events; they seemed curious ... then some of the men began saying "Haram"—meaning "shame" or "it's too bad." This started spreading throughout the crowd. The crowd told the security force officer that he needed to go see the old man. He understood what the problem was as soon as he walked down the sidewalk to the old man. The bank robbers, cuffed and lying on the concrete sidewalk, were not comfortable. One of these men was in his late 50s or 60s—he was a gray hair. He was a little frail. The crowd could clearly see that he was in pain. The crowd began complaining about the way that the gray hair was being treated. The elder was in obvious discomfort. They told the security force officer that he should let the old man go. Crowd members started shouting, "Let him go." The crowd started to become more agitated and angrier. The officer treated the elder with respect, and decided to let him go. He helped the elder stand up, brushed off his clothes, and cut off the elder's flexicuffs. He then picked the elder's belongings up off the ground and put them back into his pocket. He walked the elder to the edge of the crowd and said, "You're free to go, Uncle." The elder was very grateful. He kissed the security force officer on his cheeks and shook hands with him. The crowd immediately applauded.

In this case, the officer recognized immediately that the emotional reaction from the crowd occurred because the U.S. treatment of the old man violated Middle Eastern norms regarding respect for the elderly. He used that understanding to turn the situation to his advantage; by freeing the old man, he was able to reverse the emotional reaction. After the crowd event, some people from the crowd pulled the officer aside and gave him information on some locations of weapon stores, suggesting that his actions fostered positive attitudes among the Iraqis who were present. In the next incident, a U.S. officer leveraged a cultural norm violation by the crowd members themselves as a way to manage the crowd:

> The officer noticed an old woman being pushed into the concertina wire surrounding the base. The first thing he yelled at the large crowd was, "What's wrong with you? You're hurting mama!" The crowd stopped and listened to what he was saying. Starting at the back of the crowd, the crowd began to back up and give the woman some room.

The gray hairs are important. They command a lot of respect through age. No one in the crowd wanted to hurt the old woman.

Crowd Members' Use of Polarizing Language

Another common theme that emerged from the interviews was the attention experts paid to crowd members' use of exacerbating language to inflame emotions. In these Middle Eastern crowds, the security forces acted quickly, attempting to counter such language before it could cause strong emotional reactions. In some cases, instigators in the crowd used language to highlight in-group/out-group differences between the crowd members and security forces. Unfriendly crowd leaders attempted to engender hostile emotional reactions among their fellows by proposing images of opposite social identities between security forces and the crowds, as in the example below, which describes a situation during a Hezbollah-led demonstration in Beirut. The Lebanese security forces were able to counter polarizing efforts by emphasizing commonalities between themselves and the protesters, and by providing evidence to back up their claims:

> The lead protestors would call out arguments that created a distance between themselves and the security forces. For example, the instigators argued that the protestors were Muslims, and the security forces were Christians. They also brought Israel into the picture, suggesting that the security forces were working on behalf of the Israelis. The security forces attempted to talk to the crowd in ways that would calm them down and find commonalities between them. They would say things like, "Calm down," "we are not the enemy," "we're just doing our jobs here—have to clear the area." They also had some Muslims in their ranks who stepped forward to directly counter the argument about religion. By pointing out the commonalities, they were able to defuse the situation.

In addition to attending to and countering polarizing language, this example provides yet another illustration of security force awareness and shaping of their presentation to the crowd—in this case with the purpose of defining common social identity with crowd members. In another portion of the bank robbery incident described above, the U.S. officer noticed a change in the language being used by some women in the crowd and recognized the need to engage them in dialogue:

> The 50 or so people weren't expressing emotion—neither happy nor sad. The Iraqis were standing there quietly watching the events. The officer interpreted this as meaning that the crowd gathered because they were curious and wanted to see what was going on.
>
> At first the people were just talking to each other, then they started to talk to the Marines. When the officer exited the building the second time the crowd was louder than they had been when he went back in the building. At this point he started noticing what they were saying. The loudest voices were coming from a group of women dressed in full abaya and niqab at the front of the crowd on the left. This was where the officer's attention was focused, because they were the most vocal. There were some children mixed in with the women. This subgroup kept getting closer and closer to the bank. The rest of the crowd appeared to support these women. The women and the rest

of the crowd started blaming Saddam for the robbery—Saddam made the people poor and they were only taking money because they didn't have any. It was all Saddam's fault. They were very sympathetic to the robbers. At this time, there was a lot of looting going on (e.g., the museum was robbed, banks were closed). This bank robbery was not unusual. This is the first time that the officer noticed what the crowd members were saying, and that they were becoming more vocal. At this point he wasn't feeling that the crowd was hostile, but he was thinking about the threat. The crowd was twice as large as it had been, and there are only three on his team. The officer decided to address the loudest in the crowd first— the group of women in the front. He told the crowd that the robbers were taking the crowd's money, not Saddam's money. The women/crowd quieted and thought about this. Then, they were less vocal, but they didn't stop talking. The women wanted to talk to the officer about his background and about how evil Saddam was. He stayed engaged in communication with them at this point, so as to form a bond with the crowd members.

Crowd Members' Emotional Expressions

The experts' reports consistently suggested that Middle Eastern crowd members tended to be very expressive, with extensive use of body language and gesticulation. As one U.S. officer described, "Arabs talked with their hands. The most vocal people exhibited the most body language, the most flailing of limbs." The Americans thus felt they needed to recalibrate their interpretation of emotional expressions so as not to overrespond to those cues. For example, one officer noted, "Arabs tend to speak more loudly than Americans, often causing Americans to think they are angry when in fact that is just how they speak." Another U.S. Marine described an incident that shows how crowd members sometimes managed their emotions:

> A Sheik felt threatened by another village leader, and ordered his son to use the Mosque loudspeaker to tell his followers to come to his house. Hundreds did come, and then they became the problem. It was the officer's first night in the city, and he had just taken over the civil affairs lead. His team was in the police station, on the top floor. He hears the Mosque blaring something, but doesn't understand. A little while later, droves of people are walking with purpose down the road, past the police station, and converging on the Sheik's house. The team went to investigate, and when they rounded the corner to the Mosque, the officer's first reaction was, "Oh my God, this was stupid. What am I going to do?" He felt fear because of their numbers, and also because they seemed so angry. The crowd was in a frenzy, and actively working themselves up. They were jumping up and down, yelling, dancing around, chanting, and looking threatening. This was not directed toward the Marines; many probably didn't see them. The officer yelled (and his translator joined in) at the Sheik and son to get the people out of the street. The sheik did, and the people calmed down quickly. The officer was surprised at how fast the frenzied people calmed down and started home.

In this case, the Marine felt that his original assessment of threat was overly influenced by the level of emotional display, and that the Middle Eastern crowd members were not feeling the intense anger that he had perceived.

Discussion

Overall, the analysis revealed that experts have complex mental models of crowd dynamics that are sensitive to Middle Eastern cognition and decision making. As indicated in Figure 7.1, security force members must ultimately determine whether the crowd currently poses a threat, whether its members' attitudes can be improved at least minimally and the crowd dispersed, or whether the crowd is likely to become more hostile over time. This assessment can be particularly difficult for personnel who are new to the region and have little experience interacting with its inhabitants. Cues, such as the five kinds described above, that can be used to determine crowd members' intentions and level of threat are substantially culture specific. The theoretical and practical implications of these findings are discussed further in the following sections.

Theoretical Implications

The cultural perspective that we have adopted proposes that cultures cannot adequately be described in terms of a small set of domain-general values. Rather, the primary aspects of culture that are salient and significant to an interaction will be situation specific (Hirschfeld & Gelman, 1994). Hence, we started our research by characterizing the nature of the intercultural interactions between U.S. and Lebanese military personnel and Middle Eastern crowds. Incidents on crowd control were elicited from experienced U.S. and Lebanese military personnel and examined to determine the cultural aspects that are critical in these contexts. Our stance is that the a priori application of cultural dimensions is of little use if one seeks to predict which cultural norms or values will be critical to an accurate understanding of specific real-world situations. However, our position does not deny the usefulness of basic research examining particular aspects of cultural differences, once analysis of naturalistic situations has identified culturally relevant aspects. This approach is taken in the following section. We will consider domain-general cultural research as it pertains to the five cultural aspects that, according to our analysis, are most relevant to an understanding of Middle Eastern crowd behavior. In addition, we will suggest avenues for future research.

Goals and Motivation of Crowd Members

Cultural variation in individuals' goals, values, and needs has been the subject of extensive research (Schwartz, 1994). For example, Grouzet et al. (2005) found that personal goals in 15 countries comprised 11 categories falling along two dimensions:

1. Intrinsic goals (psychological needs) versus extrinsic (external rewards and praise) goals
2. Self-transcendent (spiritual needs) versus physical (pleasure and safety) goals

This two-dimensional model provides a theoretical framework that may prove useful for representing and describing differences in goal structures across cultures. Similarly, research on crowd types has provided frameworks for characterizing crowds on the basis of members' goals and intentions, such as crowds who are expressive, acquisitive, escapist, and aggressive (Varwell, 1978). However, these frameworks do not explicitly include some of the goals, such as a "need for information," that the cultural experts in the current study identified as motivating crowd members' behavior. This finding suggests that further research should be conducted on the nature of goals within crowd situations.

Goal Commitment and Tolerance for Risk
Studies of cross-cultural differences in risk tolerance or risk-taking behaviors have primarily compared the United States and China. Far fewer studies address attitudes toward risk in Middle Eastern cultures, especially how risk attitudes prevalent in these cultures impact individuals' physical safety behaviors. This issue clearly would be most applicable to understanding risk-taking tendencies of crowds. A comparative study of traffic accidents suggests greater risk taking in the Middle East (Bener & Crundall, 2005). Bener and Crundall (2005) reported a significantly higher accident rate in Arab countries than in other developing countries with similar vehicle ownership levels. The largest single cause of accidents in the United Arab Emirates was careless driving, followed by excessive speed, both of which might be classified as high-risk-taking behaviors. These results suggest that Western and Middle Eastern cultural variations in tolerance for physical risks would be a fruitful area for further investigation.

Security Force Presentation With Respect to Cultural Norms
Although norms involve a large class of cultural phenomena, one cultural norm salient to the cultural experts in the current study was respect. Respect is a key concern in Middle Eastern cultures. How one appears to others, and how that image reflects on one's family, is an important determinant of individuals' perceptions and behavior. One's honor, or "face," is an important measure of a person's worth (Feghali, 1997). This aspect of Arab culture has been studied fairly extensively (Gregg, 2005; Patai, 2002; Peristiany, 1966). For example, Sieck and colleagues have recently examined the role of honor in understanding crowd reactions in the Middle East (Sieck, Smith, Grome, Veinott, & Mueller, 2009). However, further research is needed to explicate the cultural beliefs linking violence and respect (Nisbett & Cohen, 1996), perhaps with more emphasis on understanding concepts of subcultures in which violent reactions lead to loss of respect.

Polarizing Language and Emotional Expression
The use of polarizing language has been described as especially prominent within the Middle East (Patai, 2002). A recent study found that sampled Middle Eastern societies exhibited the highest levels of polarized judgment in a comparison of 47 nations (Minkov, 2009). Minkov (2009) further linked the results to the propensity for dialectal thinking, such that "societies whose members are more likely to have dialectical selves are also more likely to suppress expression of strongly formulated quality judgments that are likely to cause social polarization" (p. 241). These results are also reminiscent of basic research that has been conducted on cultural variations regarding overconfidence in probability judgments, that is, people's tendency to overestimate the extent to which their judgments are correct. Most cross-cultural research

on this issue has compared East Asian and U.S. populations (Yates, Lee, Sieck, Choi, & Price, 2002). The typical finding across studies using a variety of procedures and materials is that Chinese tend to express greater overconfidence than Americans, whereas Japanese tend to be the least overconfident (and leaning toward underconfidence). Yates and colleagues also related the overconfidence results to decisiveness, and found a direct relationship between the size of the overconfidence effect and participants' reasoning, in particular, the extent to which they expressed balanced views on available options (Yates et al., 2010). Given the importance of polarizing language and its effects on crowd member decisions as revealed by the experts in the current study, further research is warranted to clarify the precise relationships between patterns of polarized thinking, language, and decision making in crowd situations.

Similarly, albeit limited, some ethnographic research suggests that Middle Easterners tend to show more emotional expressiveness than Westerners (Patai, 2002). Though a sizable literature base exists on emotional expressions across cultures, the majority of this work has been limited to the study of Western and East Asian cultures. These studies provide substantial evidence for the universality in physiological responses to emotions (Bond, 2005). Cultural differences tend to emerge with respect to subjective emotional experience and measures of expressive behavior, such as facial expressions. Research on culture in crowds should further examine the relationships between polarized language, emotional expression, and violent actions. The incident below, which is the continuation of the situation mentioned at the beginning of this chapter, provides a good illustration of this issue. As described, a team of Americans, Kuwaitis, and an Iraqi were about to enter a cemetery to extract DNA of missing Kuwaitis from Saddam's invasion of Kuwait.

> As the crowd began to form, the American team leader wanted to let the Kuwaitis do their job, while the United States drew the crowd's attention. It's a sensitive issue for Kuwaitis to be in Iraq. It's commonly believed by Iraqis that the Kuwaitis paid the United States money to destroy Baghdad in revenge for the Iraqi destruction of Kuwait City. The conversation between the older man and American team leader began in a very cordial manner. Just discourse, there was no sign of trouble. But the situation escalated as outrageous statements were made by the grizzled man, about Kuwaitis and then Israel. The American leader attempted to counter the arguments, but without effect. The crowd started to become more heated and the old man would throw in comments as the situation escalated. The American leader felt that the situation was starting to become dangerous for his team. At this point, there wasn't necessarily anything that the American could do to de-escalate the situation, so he gathered up the Kuwaitis and left.

Practical Implications

Based on the findings from this study, we developed an educational package for use by American personnel who may need to manage crowds in the Middle East. The educational package focuses on providing learners with the specific cultural knowledge that is needed to make sense of Middle Eastern behavior in crowd situations. The educational content is delivered on a Web-based platform, and is organized into five modules. In Modules 1 to 4, the user is first presented with discussions of a particular topic, followed by brief exercises to reinforce the lessons. Module 5 contains a capstone exercise that incorporates lessons learned in the previous four modules. A description of each module follows.

Module 1 provides an overview of culture and crowd management. It addresses high-level concepts, such as an introduction to culture and cultural considerations in crowd situations. The cultural sensemaking approach to understanding crowd situations is discussed. In addition, the user is presented with a summary of the main elements of a crowd situation and crowd types. Module 2 teaches the user how an understanding of the culturally based goals of crowd members can lead to accurate predictions of their behavior as the situation unfolds. This section addresses a cultural theory of goal structures and its application to reading intent in Middle Eastern crowd situations. The impact of situational factors on crowd goals is also discussed. Module 3 focuses on cultural underpinnings of decision making in crowd situations. This section discusses cultural variations in decision making between U.S. and Middle Easterners with application to making sense of crowd situations. Topics include crowd member mental models, the framing of situations, attitudes toward violence and physical risk, and emotional reactions and expressions. Module 4 presents security force strategies for managing crowds in the Middle East. Teaching points include ways to avoid common norm violations, and other incidental actions that can inflame a situation, actions for diffusing tensions, as well as techniques for countering inflammatory or polarizing tactics by hostile crowd members. Module 5 contains a capstone exercise that uses a cognitively authentic scenario to test the user's comprehension of teaching points.

Beyond providing this specific educational package, our research led us to formulate a systematic approach to cultural training that seeks to provide learners with specific cultural knowledge needed in particular situations, as well as general strategies for improving their ability to learn from their cultural experiences. This cultural sensemaking training approach is not concerned with educating the participant about high-level general cultural differences (Hofstede, 2001), nor does it focus on teaching domain skills, such as crowd control skills. Instead, the purpose of cultural sensemaking training is to provide the necessary cultural knowledge and strategies that learners need to be more successful in intercultural interactions in any number of specific situations, such as crowd situations in the Middle East (Sieck et al., 2008).

In addition to implications for cultural education and training, our results also bear on issues of technology development for the purposes of supporting crowd management in other cultures. Currently, much progress in the development of nonlethal weapons has emphasized technologies that increase the capability to apply physical force against crowds without killing. One strategy that experts in the present study repeatedly mentioned was the importance of communicating with crowd members in order to understand and influence the crowd situation. This result suggests that more emphasis should be placed on the advancement of communication technologies in crowd control. For example, crowd organizers are finding ways to use cell phones and fourth-generation wireless technologies to orchestrate and manage crowd events, for instance, by communicating destinations and slogans, or by providing directions. An important area for future research and development is to determine how communication technologies can be used by security forces to assess and shape crowd events in ways that promote positive social effects.

During modern military operations that emphasize the provision of humanitarian assistance, stability, and other support to local populations, it is common for personnel to encounter and attract crowds of local civilians. These crowds can quickly escalate into angry riots when they are not handled properly. But when managed correctly, crowd situations provide opportunities to make gains on "winning the peace" (Petraeus, 2006). The manner in which American personnel interact with crowd members influences the crowd members' beliefs about and attitudes toward the United States and its mission. This chapter aimed to provide an understanding of how cultural experts make sense of crowds and crowd behavior in the Middle East, with a special emphasis on the cultural issues that arise in crowd situations. It is hoped that the results and recommendations provided here will assist in improving American military interactions with culturally different civilians in such situations.

References

Atran, S., Medin, D. L., & Ross, N. O. (2005). The cultural mind: Environmental decision making and cultural modeling within and across populations. *Psychological Review, 112*(4), 744–776.

Bener, A., & Crundall, D. (2005). Road traffic accidents in the United Arab Emirates compared to Western countries. *Advances in Transportation Studies, Section A, 6,* 5–12.

Bond, M. (2005). Emotions and their expression in Chinese culture. *Journal of Nonverbal Behavior, 17*(4), 245–262.

Bostrom, A., Fischhoff, B., & Morgan, M. G. (1992). Characterizing mental models of hazardous processes: A methodology and an application to radon. *Journal of Social Issues, 48*(4), 85–100.

Chi, M. T. H., Feltovich, P. J., & Glaser, R. (1981). Categorization and representation of physics problems by experts and novices. *Cognitive Science, 5,* 121–152.

Christensen-Szalanski, J. J. J., & Bushyhead, J. B. (1981). Physicians' use of probabilisitic information in a real clinical setting. *Journal of Experimental Psychology: Human Perception and Performance, 7*(4), 928–935.

D'Andrade, R. G. (1981). The cultural part of cognition. *Cognitive Science, 5,* 179–195.

Drury, J., & Reicher, S. (1999). The intergroup dynamics of collective empowerment: Substantiating the social identity model of crowd behavior. *Group Processes & Intergroup Relations, 2,* 381–402.

Drury, J., & Reicher, S. (2000). Collective action and psychological change: The emergence of new social identities. *British Journal of Social Psychology, 39,* 579–604.

Feghali, E. (1997). Arab cultural communication patterns. *International Journal of Intercultural Relations, 21*(3), 345–378.

Flanagan, J. C. (1954). The critical incident technique. *Psychological Bulletin, 51,* 327–358.

Gopnik, A., & Wellman, H. M. (1994). The theory theory. In L. Hirschfeld & S. Gelman (Eds.), *Mapping the mind: Domain specificity in cognition and culture* (pp. 257–293). New York, NY: Cambridge University Press.

Gregg, G. S. (2005). *The Middle East: A cultural psychology.* New York, NY: Oxford University Press.

Grouzet, F. M. E., Kasser, T., Ahuvia, A., Dols, J. M. F., Kim, Y., Lau, S., … Sheldon, K. M. (2005). The structure of goal contents across 15 cultures. *Journal of Personality and Social Psychology, 89*(5), 800–816.

Hirschfeld, L., & Gelman, S. (Eds.). (1994). *Mapping the mind: Domain specificity in cognition and culture.* New York, NY: Cambridge University Press.

Hoffman, R. R., Crandall, B. W., & Shadbolt, N. R. (1998). Use of the critical decision method to elicit expert knowledge: A case study in cognitive task analysis methodology. *Human Factors, 40*(2), 254–276.

Hofstede, G. (2001). *Culture's consequences* (2nd ed.). Thousand Oaks, CA: Sage.

Howard, R. A. (1989). Knowledge maps. *Management Science, 35,* 903–922.

Klein, G. (1998). *Sources of power: How people make decisions.* Cambridge, MA: MIT Press.

Klein, G., Calderwood, R., & MacGregor, D. (1989). Critical decision method for eliciting knowledge. *IEEE Transactions on Systems, Man, and Cybernetics, 19*(3), 462–472.

Klein, G., & Hoffman, R. R. (1993). Seeing the invisible: Perceptual-cognitive aspects of expertise. In M. Rabinowitz (Ed.), *Cognitive science foundations of instruction* (pp. 203–226). Hillsdale, NJ: Lawrence Erlbaum Associates.

Klein, G., Phillips, J. K., Rall, E. L., & Peluso, D. A. (2004). A data/frame theory of sensemaking. In R. R. Hoffman (Ed.), *Expertise out of context: Proceedings of the 6th International Conference on Naturalistic Decision Making.* Mahwah, NJ: Erlbaum.

Larkin, J., McDermott, J., Simon, D. P., & Simon, H. A. (1980). Expert and novice performance in solving physics problems. *Science, 208,* 1335–1342.

Le Bon, G. (1947). *The crowd: A study of the popular mind.* London, UK: Ernest Benn.

Lillard, A. (1998). Ethnopsychologies: Cultural variations in theories of mind. *Psychological Bulletin, 123,* 3–32.

Minkov, M. (2009). Nations with more dialectical selves exhibit lower polarization in life quality judgments and social opinions. *Cross-Cultural Research, 43*(3), 230–250.

Nisbett, R., & Cohen, D. (1996). *Culture of honor: The psychology of violence in the South.* Boulder, CO: Westview Press.

Osland, J. S., & Bird, A. (2000). Beyond sophisticated stereotyping: Cultural sensemaking in context. *Academy of Management Executive, 14*(1), 65–79.

Patai, R. (2002). *The Arab mind.* Long Island, NY: Hatherleigh Press.

Peristiany, J. G. (Ed.). (1966). *Honour and shame: The values of Mediterranean society.* Chicago, IL: University of Chicago Press.

Petraeus, D. H. (2006). Learning counterinsurgency: Observations from soldiering in Iraq. *Military Review, 14,* 2–12.

Rouse, W. B., & Morris, N. M. (1986). On looking into the black box: Prospects and limits in the search for mental models. *Psychological Bulletin, 100,* 349–363.

Schwartz, S. H. (1994). Cultural dimensions of values: Towards an understanding of national differences. In U. Kim, H. C. Triandis, C. Kagitcibasi, S. C. Choi, & G. Yoon (Eds.), *Individualism and collectivism: Theory, method, and applications* (pp. 85–119). Newbury Park, CA: Sage.

Sieck, W. R., McHugh, A. P., & Smith, J. L. (2006). Use of cognitive field research methods to investigate cultural groups: The case of individual decision making in Middle Eastern crowds. In R. Sun & N. Miyake (Eds.), *Proceedings of the 28th Annual Conference of the Cognitive Science Society* (pp. 2164–2168).

Sieck, W. R., Rasmussen, L. J., & Smart, P. (2010). Cultural network analysis: A cognitive approach to cultural modeling. In D. Verma (Ed.), *Network science for military coalition operations: Information exchange and interaction* (pp. 237–255). Hershey, PA: IGI Global.

Sieck, W. R., Smith, J., Grome, A. P., Veinott, E. S., & Mueller, S. T. (2009). *Violent and peaceful crowd reactions in the Middle East: Cultural experiences and expectations.* Paper presented at the International Academy for Intercultural Research, Honolulu, HI.

Sieck, W. R., Smith, J., & Rasmussen, L. J. (2008). *Expertise in making sense of cultural surprises.* Paper presented at the Interservice/Industry Training, Simulation, and Education Conference (I/ITSEC), Orlando, FL.

Sperber, D. (1985). Anthropology and psychology: Towards an epidemiology of representations. *Man, 20,* 73–89.

Sperber, D., & Hirschfeld, L. (1999). Culture, cognition, and evolution. In R. A. Wilson & F. C. Keil (Eds.), *The MIT encyclopedia of the cognitive sciences* (pp. cxi–cxxxii). Cambridge, MA: MIT Press.

Varwell, D. W. P. (1978). *Police and public.* London, UK: MacDonald and Evans.

Yates, J. F., Ji, L.-J., Oka, T., Lee, J.-W., Shinotsuka, H., & Sieck, W. R. (2010). Indecisiveness and culture: Incidence, values, and thoroughness. *Journal of Cross-Cultural Psychology, 41,* 428–444.

Yates, J. F., Lee, J.-W., Sieck, W. R., Choi, I., & Price, P. C. (2002). Probability judgment across cultures. In T. Gilovich, D. Griffin, & D. Kahneman (Eds.), *Heuristics and biases: The psychology of intuitive judgment* (pp. 271–291). Cambridge, UK: Cambridge University Press.

8

Managing Complex Military Planning

*Processes and Techniques Used by Experienced
and Less Experienced Commanders*

Peter Thunholm
Swedish National Defense College

The purpose of this study was to explore and describe the thought processes of military commanders faced with traditional battle planning tasks and required to plan a course of action (COA). One key issue was to explore the strategies used to merge new information with knowledge in the COA planning process. Another key issue was to study whether there were differences in the thought processes of experienced and less experienced officers. The goal of the project of which this study was one part was to develop new planning models and supporting technology, and for that reason, it was important to study how planning is done by military commanders without restricting them to following a formal process.

The military planning process (e.g., NATO, 2004; U.S. Army, 2005) is a highly structured and step-by-step process, designed to receive, interpret, and transform an assigned task from headquarters (HQ) into a fixed-format operational order (OPORD) that gives guidelines and tasks to subordinate units. The following brief description of the military planning process is based on the traditional Swedish Army planning manual (Swedish Army, 1995), but there is little difference to other Western army planning processes. The initial phase is *task analysis*, in order to interpret the meaning and the intentions of the mission received from HQ. The second phase is *situation analysis*, in order to understand the current state of the situation in which the task is to be fulfilled. This includes analysis of one's own and an opponent's available forces and capabilities, force comparisons, terrain, weather and visibility analysis, and analysis of the civilian situation. Traditional planning manuals prescribe that each aspect of the situation is analyzed separately and exhaustively, in a noniterative way, and that conclusions in terms of restrictions and capabilities are made for each aspect of the situation. The third phase of the planning process is to *generate* a set of options (normally three) concerning how to act (i.e., COAs), covering all main activities taken until the assigned task has been fulfilled. The fourth phase is a formal *evaluation* of these COAs, either in the form of a simulation (called wargaming) comparing own COAs against those of a probable enemy, or in the form of a formal comparison of one's own COAs against a set of predefined selection criteria, derived from the task and situation analysis. The fifth phase of the planning process includes the *selection* of a course of action, and subsequent further detailing of the COA and a transformation of the COA into a fixed-format concept of operations.

There is ample evidence indicating that this noniterative and step-by-step formal process is seldom followed in detail by experienced military planners (Fallesen, 2000; Klein, 1993; Pasqual & Henderson, 1997; Schmitt & Klein, 1999). Instead of developing and comparing several options simultaneously, experienced (and often also less experienced) planners arrive at a single option without much formal situation analysis. This option comes to the mind of the planner as a result of the planner recognizing the situation as familiar, or seeing an analogy with known previous similar cases, or drawing on previous personal experience. The planner subsequently evaluates this option by mentally simulating how it would be implemented and what effect it may have. If it is assessed to be workable in the present situation, the planner implements it without further analysis of other options. If mental simulation indicates that the option will not work, then another option is developed and mentally simulated, until a working solution has been identified.

Klein and Crandall (1995), based on an extensive literature survey, defined mental simulation as "the process of mentally enacting a sequence of events" (p. 325). Mental simulation projects situation development over time, from the present into the future. The simulation allows the decision maker to anticipate the look and feel of ensuing events and to adequately prepare for them, for example, by adopting/adjusting a plan. Klein and Crandall (1995) found that mental simulation was used by decision makers and problem solvers for several different purposes. Relevant to this chapter is mental simulation that serves a planning/anticipation function (i.e., testing actions) and mental simulation that serves the function of modeling or discovering a situation (i.e., generating actions).

Previous descriptive studies on military planning (e.g., Schmitt & Klein, 1999) have focused more on the option generation and evaluation phases of planning and less on planners' task and situation analysis, and the question of how they combine their knowledge with situation-specific information in order to derive a COA. Moreover, no previous studies have investigated differences in the thought processes of experienced versus less experienced military decision makers as they go through a battle planning procedure in order to generate a COA. The objective of the present study was to fill these gaps in the extant research literature. As in previous research, the focus was on discovery and not on testing hypotheses.

Method

Participants (all male) were two Swedish Army brigadier generals, one Army colonel, and three Swedish Army captains. All three high-ranking officers had experience as mechanized brigade commanders; one of the generals also had several years of experience as a division commander. Their level of experience concerning participation in battle planning at the division level ranged between 50 and 100 planning processes. Every captain had experience as a commander of a mechanized company. Their level of planning process experience at the division level ranged between 2 and 15 processes.

Participants were tested individually and received three battleground planning scenarios: two were army corps level and one was division level, resulting in a total of 18 data cases. Participants' level of *expertise* regarding tactical planning was not assessed. Instead, the research interest was on whether *experience* in conducting substantially more planning processes (i.e., exercises where planning was done) would impact participants' behavior. Prior to the study, participants were informed that its purpose was to examine tactical mission planning processes.

The study was explorative, but included the person variable "experience" at two levels (*low* = captains, *high* = senior officers). The participants' task was to take on the role of commander and use a maximum of three hours to plan a course of action (COA), stated as a (reduced) concept of operations (CONOPS). The CONOPS was to include (1) a written outline and intention of the COA and (2) a sketch of the COA for the army corps (or the division in Scenario 2) on a map overlay. Using U.S. Army (2005) terminology, this is equivalent to a commander's intent and concept of operations.

In order to capture the effect of experience, the scenarios were traditional battle scenarios of the type familiar to the participants from training and exercises. The scenarios were constructed by experienced teachers at the Swedish National Defense College to be realistic and complex; two of the scenarios were modeled on real-life battles. The hierarchical level in the scenarios (army corps and division) was normal for the high-ranking officers, but above the level for which the captains were trained. Participants were provided with a realistic amount of information, comprising an operational order (OPORD) from HQ and a specific scenario information concerning the current battlefield situation, called an intelligence summary (INTSUM), supplemented by a situation map (SITMAP), which was a map on the scale of 1:50,000 or 1:100,000 covered by an overlay showing positions of one's own and enemy units and other important information, such as destroyed bridges, mine fields, and so forth. The OPORD and INTSUM included facts (e.g., numbers, locations, etc.), estimates (e.g., how long something will take), and more formal assumptions (e.g., the assumption is that the enemy . . .). Participants also had access to eight different documents with detailed reference materials (facts) concerning the battlefield systems available to them and to the enemy. They were also provided with a staff officer who role-played any other actor or staff functions with whom the participant wanted to communicate as a part of the planning scenario (e.g., subordinated or lateral commanders). The participants could ask the staff officer any questions, but they could not task him to do the plan development or write any documents that they had been assigned to produce. The purpose of having the staff officer was to make the participants' task realistic (no high-level military mission is planned by a single commander without any staff assistance) and to prevent participants from getting stuck if they needed clarification of some data in the scenario documents. The instruction to the staff officer (who knew each scenario well) was to assist the participant (i.e., the commander) by providing an answer to his questions, but not to do any actual planning work or give advice on how the plan or parts of it should be designed.

Participants received no additional training on planning procedures before the study; however, during their career they had of course been trained to plan according to the battle planning procedure of the Swedish Army. Participants were instructed that they were free to use any decision process they preferred, and asked to think aloud as they proceeded through the planning process. Instructions also mentioned that their planning process was videotaped, as well as timed and observed, with notes being taken. The think-aloud procedure followed the recommendations by Ericsson and Simon (1980). After each session participants were given a questionnaire, and subsequently a follow-up interview concerning their planning process. Questionnaire items and interview questions will be presented below in the "Results" section.

The videotapes were transcribed, and the resulting verbal protocols were coded. The purpose of the coding was to map all the utterances captured in the protocols onto *units of meaning* in terms of planning process activities. Each such unit of meaning consisted of one to several consecutive statements that referred to a certain purpose/activity. For example, one statement uttered during the initial phase of Session 2 was: "Okay, what type of terrain do we have in this area? Some wooded areas, it is a little bit mixed." This utterance was coded as T (= stating a fact regarding the terrain). Such an utterance is represented as a light gray square in Figure 8.1. All utterances were coded in this vein and are represented as different squares in Figure 8.1. A (non-exhaustive) list of codes and definitions is provided in Figure 8.1.

The initial list of coding categories was developed by a military officer (the author) based on the different substep activities prescribed in the Swedish Army planning process (Swedish Army, 1995). This list was then extended and refined during the process of coding all six protocols from participants' first planning sessions. No new codes emerged during the coding of protocols from Planning Sessions 2 and 3. After all protocols were coded, a second military rater was trained on the coding definitions and then independently coded one of the protocols. The second rater agreed with the first rater on 92% of the codes.

Results

Manipulation Check

Participants rated the scenario and task realism for each scenario, using a 6-point Likert scale ranging from *very low level* (scored as 1) to *very high level* (scored as 6). Ratings concerned the following four aspects (scores averaged across participants are given in parentheses): (1) realism of the scenarios/the story of events ($M_{scenario 1} = 5.17$, $SD = .75$; $M_{scenario 2} = 5.50$, $SD = .56$; $M_{scenario 3} = 5.33$, $SD = .82$); (2) realism of the amount of available information ($M_{scenario 1} = 4.83, SD = 1.60$; $M_{scenario 2} = 4.83, SD = .98$; $M_{scenario 3} = 4.67, SD = 1.51$); (3) realism regarding the amount of available time for solving the task ($M_{scenario 1} = 5.33$, $SD = 1.21$; $M_{scenario 2} = 5.50$, $SD = .56$; $M_{scenario 3} = 5.50$, $SD = .84$); and (4) realism concerning the level of uncertainty in the scenario ($M_{scenario 1} = 5.17$, $SD = 1.33$; $M_{scenario 2} = 4.83$, $SD = 1.83$; $M_{scenario 3} = 5.0$, $SD = 1.09$). There were no substantial differences in the ratings between participants with a low or high degree of experience, respectively. These results indicate that participants, on average, found the scenarios to be realistic concerning all measured aspects.

After each scenario, two questions were asked during a follow-up interview: (1) Was the process you followed in the planning scenario a normal one for you? (2) Did you feel disturbed or influenced by having to think aloud during your planning process? After the first scenario, one of the senior officers mentioned that he initially

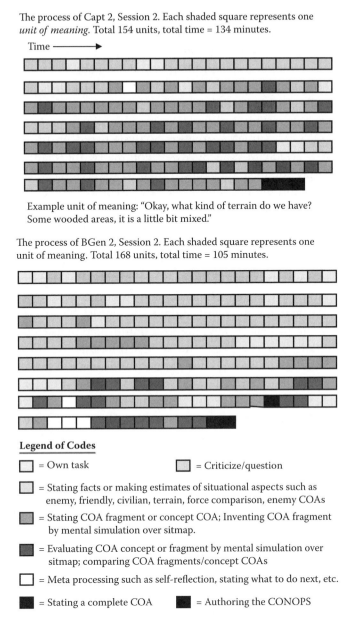

The process of Capt 2, Session 2. Each shaded square represents one *unit of meaning*. Total 154 units, total time = 134 minutes.

Time ⟶

Example unit of meaning: "Okay, what kind of terrain do we have? Some wooded areas, it is a little bit mixed."

The process of BGen 2, Session 2. Each shaded square represents one unit of meaning. Total 168 units, total time = 105 minutes.

Legend of Codes

☐ = Own task   ☐ = Criticize/question

☐ = Stating facts or making estimates of situational aspects such as
     enemy, friendly, civilian, terrain, force comparison, enemy COAs

▨ = Stating COA fragment or concept COA; Inventing COA fragment
     by mental simulation over sitmap.

▦ = Evaluating COA concept or fragment by mental simulation over
     sitmap; comparing COA fragments/concept COAs

☐ = Meta processing such as self-reflection, stating what to do next, etc.

■ = Stating a complete COA   ■ = Authoring the CONOPS

FIGURE 8.1   Two participants' planning processes expressed in codes.

was disturbed by the think-aloud instruction, but except for that occasion, all participants reported that the planning process felt natural to them and that they did not feel disturbed or influenced by the think-aloud procedure.

Evaluation of the Planning Process

Participants' planning processes were reconstructed from all the different data sources. The process notes and the verbal protocols presented a somewhat different picture of what had happened compared to participants' accounts of their planning processes (in the follow-up interview) directly after each session. The difference was that to the observer, the planning process appeared to be far more complex, with repeated iterations between different planning process activities, than reported by the participant himself.

Two examples illustrating participants' planning processes are given in Figure 8.1; shown are participants' activities throughout the planning process until they started to author the CONOPS. Initially, situation analysis based on information mainly from the OPORD, INTSUM, and SITMAP dominated the planning process (cf. Figure 8.1, light gray squares), interrupted by task analysis (i.e., participants interpreted the meaning and implications of the task issued by HQ; cf. Figure 8.1, lightest gray squares). The situation analysis was iterative in nature, oscillating between different aspects of the situation (i.e., the enemy, friendly forces, terrain, etc.). In this manner, there was always progress toward a deeper and broader understanding of the situation, the task, and plan to be developed. The information from the different documents that was available to the participants was thus digested in small portions at a time, and integrated with participants' knowledge and present situation understanding. Participants apparently did not distinguish between facts, estimates, and assumptions, but instead seemed to treat all information as facts (i.e., implicitly accepted assumptions as true). They often returned to analysis of their own forces, the enemy and terrain, and so on, however, not to the same details, but to another aspect, resulting in a more enriched understanding of the situation. Also, participants tended to start early with the process of analyzing the task given from HQ in order to understand what the final state should be. This analysis reoccurred several times during the planning process, and tended to deepen toward the end of their deliberation, when participants already had a fairly developed COA.

The planning process was sometimes guided by the order in which situation information was given in the OPORD and INTSUM, and sometimes, especially later in the process, it was guided by an idea in the form of a concept COA (i.e., a high-level or low-detailed statement regarding a course of action; cf. Figure 8.1, medium gray squares) because this idea initiated a search for facts. As their current situation became clearer to the participants, their planning process included longer periods of COA generation (cf. Figure 8.1, medium gray squares) with subsequent evaluation (cf. Figure 8.1, dark gray squares) and modification of concept COAs.

Generation of a COA always involved a dialogue between the participant and himself in the course of which he presented actions and arguments as he was looking at the SITMAP. While the COA was generated, it was often evaluated as illustrated by the following example from Capt1. At this moment, he was looking at the SITMAP, starting to form his plan, but still without mentioning any specific units:

> Right now it feels like if I can fight myself over the existing bridges. I have a feeling that it can be done, but it will cost a lot, and I am not so sure that the [enemy-controlled] bridges will still be there.... And I must assume that they are not.... And that means that I can also launch an attack on a place where it suits me, and lay my own bridge...and try to create favorable conditions for that instead [of trying to capture the enemy-controlled bridges]. And then push forward deeply [after crossing the river] and then disrupt the enemy lines from behind...and let that cost me instead. But then I am accomplishing both the purpose

according to the doctrine and what I regard to be most clever in this situation. To take the fight against their [enemy] mechanized brigades is rather stupid. And then I must decide what units [...] I can use to make the enemy believe that I am attacking somewhere else. Then it is about creating a diversion. Then I think the smartest would be to divert him up into the northern area....

In this example, the COA is still conceptual, but later it becomes more detailed, and subsequently is discussed further in order to generate more details. This step is illustrated by the following excerpt from the planning process of Capt2:

I could actually let 6th Division attack down here [referring to the map]. Around 5th, or between 5th and 9th. Fifth is blocking were they are. Ninth could also attack down here [referring to the map]. Over that [enemy] regiment.... That's stupid. Then we have...Sketching a little bit [on a map overlay]. This line should be held in any case. That is my mission. That line [pointing at the map]. I am already there with two divisions. That enemy feels uncomfortable. I should at least find out what it is. Counterattack, disrupt, prevent an enemy attack down here [pointing at the map]. The question is, how to do such a thing....

And Capt2 went on like this for several minutes.

In both of these examples the main purpose of the map-based self-discussion was to *generate* a COA. Another type of self-discussion predominantly served the purpose of *evaluating* a COA. This type of discussion was apparent in the planning process of Capt3, as illustrated in the excerpt below. The COA he favored at that moment (about halfway into the exercise) was to launch a main attack with one division followed by another one in the central area, and at the same time to launch diversionary attacks, with one division each on the northern and southern flanks in order to prevent the enemy from reinforcing the central area:

I am trying to find something to counteract it [the COA]. If this battle is not successful for the enemy [pointing at the central area], they [the enemy] still cannot leave his blocking position [pointing at the southern flank]...then my division can slip through [in the south], and he only has one division here so I don't think he will leave this area. It is the same thing up here [looking at the northern flank]. Sure, I arrive, he [the enemy] realizes: "This is a diversion, this may not be the main attack, so I will regroup to the south."...That, he cannot do, because then I can cross the river in that area. So, the enemy will probably be blocked....It is a risk I take, but....It feels correct anyway.

Such phases of generating and evaluating self-discussions dominated participants' planning process after about 30 to 60 minutes. The self-discussion mainly occurred while participants looked over the situation map. This activity continued for another 40 to 70 minutes with increasingly shorter breaks to consult the OPORD or the scenario description to find some facts, until a complete COA was produced to a satisfying level (cf. Figure 8.1, near black square) and a participant started to write his plan (cf. Figure 8.1, black square). A satisfying level of detail was reached when the participant had developed his COA with sufficient detail to tell his directly subordinate units *what* he wanted to do and for *what purpose, when* he wanted to do it, *how* it should be done, and the *specific task* for each of his main subordinate units.

In all cases the final COA (the CONOPS) emerged in a stepwise fashion. This finding was also confirmed by all participants (except for one participant in one of three sessions) when they were asked to describe how they had arrived at their final COA. Initially, the COA was more like a feeling, a principle, or an idea. One example is from Col1: "There seems to be some kind of chaos in the line of command [on the enemy side] right now, which is an argument for us to do something now...attack." Later the idea was developed into a more generally stated concept COA, often without mentioning any specific units. One example for this is by Capt1: Infantry to the East, own artillery [pointing at the map]. Diversion.... Move the enemy tank units to one direction while we are doing something in the other.... Many units in a small area.... Find weak points.... Use bridges [to cross over to the enemy side of the river].... Should be two [bridges]." After that, his discussion of his COA moved to the question of how his own directly subordinate units should be used—these units concerned the divisions in the army corps scenario and the brigades in the division-level scenario. Finally, a fully detailed COA was developed to the level necessary in order to author the CONOPS. To conclude, what we see here is a progression from (1) intuition to explicable knowledge, and (2) abstract to specific.[*]

Moments of choice or decision occurred at all levels of detail of a COA, such as the choice between two different principal concepts, for example, whether or not one should attack. The choice could also concern which option to include in a specific COA. Decisions of this kind often followed a chronological order and occurred at a level where the different options were not yet detailed, as exemplified in the following protocol by BGen2. At this point in the planning process, BGen2 was considering how to advance his division while studying the map:

> I am thinking a lot about the task [...] Stockholm is the key. If I hold Stockholm I can rest easy. The question is how to capture Stockholm. If we look at the key point, advancing on the north side of Lake Malaren is more tempting right now [= Option 1]. On the other hand, it can be quite crowded on the north side [studying the roads on the north side of Lake Malaren, evaluating Option 1]. If I run into trouble I am considering advancing both in the north side and the south side of the lake [= Option 2]. I think this has clear advantages [studying the roads on the south side, deciding to go with Option 2]. One is to increase security if the enemy does something. If he alters his direction of attack, we can have air drops all over the area. There is also enemy air force, and these bridges can be destroyed [= studying the map and mentally simulating what can happen when the division is approaching Stockholm].

Later, after studying the march plan of the division, he had to make another choice. This time he considered whether two brigades advancing on the north side of Lake Malaren should use only one (Option 1) or both (Option 2) of the two available main roads. These choices did not contrast one complete COA with another complete COA; rather, they concerned different COA fragments within a COA. These decisions were also made in chronological order, building up the final COA from the starting point (where the units were positioned at the start) to the completion of the mission. No participant proceeded in the reverse direction.

---

[*] I thank Ute Fischer for making me realize this.

Differences Between Experienced and Less Experienced Commanders

It is important to say that each individual used his own personal style. This individual style changed considerably between the first and second sessions for a few participants, but was rather stable from the second to the third session. This indicates that a certain familiarization occurred, at least for some participants. Two examples of individual application of the planning process are provided in Figure 8.1. They are both from Session 2 and illustrate a principal difference between experienced and less experienced participants, which will be elaborated further in the following.

Three different process time measurements were taken. The first concerned how long it took until the participant for the first time mentioned a COA fragment, that is, an idea about how to use his own resources in terms of action. For example, as done by Capt2: "I could actually let the 6th Division attack down here." The second measurement concerned how long it took, from the start, until the participant had a final COA worked out, that is, a course of action with a sufficient level of detail in order to start authoring the CONOPS. The third measurement concerned how long it took, from the start, until the CONOPS was finalized. In most cases the writing of the CONOPS resulted in a need to go back and rethink, or further detail some part of the COA, so it was not only a matter of writing.

Compared to less experienced officers, senior officers took 10 minutes less time to introduce the first COA fragment (M_{high} = 35.33, SD = 8. 19; M_{low} = 46.0, SD = 12.58). They were 30 minutes faster to formulate a complete COA (M_{high} = 71.44, SD = 5.42; M_{low} = 101.56, SD = 23.57), and 38 minutes faster to produce the final (M_{high} = 107.67, SD = 2.33; M_{low} = 145.44, SD = 36.98).

Protocol analysis suggests that these differences were mainly due to differences in the amount of COA generation/evaluation participants used to come up with a final COA (see Figure 8.1). Both groups of participants used the same decision process in general, but less experienced officers spent substantially more time than senior officers with generating and evaluating COA details in order to develop their preferred COA (cf. the medium gray squares in Figure 8.1). The same behavior was observed when they authored the CONOPS.

Potential Weakness in Participants' Planning Process

One potential weakness in participants' planning behavior concerns their inclination to accept, or at least not question, assumptions about the enemy that HQ expressed in the OPORD and INTSUM (for example, "the assumption is that the enemy will not have the capacity for reinforcements within the next 48 hours"). Participants seemingly viewed most of these assumptions as facts and not as judgments. None of them treated assumptions as uncertainties in the plans they developed, and none of them asked themselves questions such as "What if this assumption is wrong?" This meant that participants' plans depended on the belief that assumptions and estimates made by HQ would prove to be correct.

Discussion

This study concerned the planning processes of commanders who had received a new mission from a superior commander. The results indicated that planning was an iterative mental process that started with a new mission order and ended when the commander had transformed his own mission into missions or tasks for his subordinate commanders. The iterations between what was given (facts and estimates about the situation) and what was required (a representation of the mission being solved) closely resemble behavior observed in studies of problem solving (e.g., Duncker, 1945; Wertheimer, 1945/1959; Lipshitz & Adar Pras, 2005). The findings of the present study suggest that the military mission planning process is more of a problem-solving process than a decision-making one (as defined by traditional judgment and decision-making research). More specifically, the process is action oriented; that is, its purpose is for commanders to make sense of their own missions in terms of *actions/activities* (a COA) that should be taken by their subordinate commanders. This finding is in line with definitions of sensemaking (e.g., Brehmer, 2007).

The purpose of this study was to explore how complex military planning is managed by experienced and less experienced army commanders. The participants of this study had to deal with several kinds of complexity, and the results indicate that commanders of both levels of experience coped with different complexities in a number of ways.

First, the complexity of the *planning process* was handled by relying on a learned/ trained planning procedure as a guideline, to inform both how to conduct a planning process and how to author a plan with a sufficient level of detail (i.e., acquired knowledge determined what a good CONOPS looks like, or what information to consider). However, the learned planning procedure was only followed regarding the aspects (e.g., enemy situation, force comparison, etc.) that should be analyzed, but not regarding the order or content of the steps (i.e., how to conduct the analysis of each aspect). In that respect, participants adhered to a highly iterative, somewhat idiosyncratic process that also simplified the formal COA analysis compared to a formal Western army planning manual. This finding suggests that the formal planning procedure emphasized repeatedly in training sessions was of limited use to the officers participating in the present study.

Another type of complexity concerns that of the *battlefield situation*, which stems from the different entities on the battlefield, such as several of one's own and enemy forces, units with different capacities, and units deployed in different types of terrain. Adding to the complexity is a time perspective regarding the current situation and how it may evolve. All this information and background knowledge has to be analyzed, and integrated into a coherent interpretation of the specific situation commanders face. To this end, the "Task" section in the OPORD seems to elicit suitable mental models of *tactical concepts* underlying commanders' situation analysis. A tactical concept can be viewed as a fragmentary mental model, guiding both situation analysis and COA formation. These mental models are fragmented because they concern one specific aspect of the situation at a time, for example, how to cross a river, or how to accomplish air defense at a local object, or how to support an attack with enough artillery. As a result, the officers in the present study handled the total complexity of the battlefield situation by taking in pieces of situation-specific information related to a tactical concept and integrating these pieces into an action-oriented understanding, yielding conclusions such as: "Because of this information, I must carry out this action."

A third type of complexity is that of the *CONOPS*, or the plan (as compared to the complexity of the tactical situation). This complexity was handled by sequencing the plan, and thus developing and comparing COA fragments or partial COAs in order to build up a complete COA (i.e., a CONOPS). A COA was always constructed by starting from the present geographical position of the subunits and moving forward in time and space toward the end state. This buildup and evaluation of a COA from fragments was done in a generating and evaluating self-discussion, or mental simulation (c.f. Klein & Crandall, 1995). It is interesting to note that this process is neither consistent with traditional planning manuals nor corresponds to findings reported by previous descriptive research on military planning (e.g., Klein, 1993). Traditional manuals prescribe a formal comparison of complete COAs; this behavior was not displayed by the officers in the present study. The recognition-primed decision (RPD) model that has been used to describe military decision making (e.g., Klein, 1989) assumes that a decision option (e.g., a COA) comes to mind as a result of situation analysis, and that this option is evaluated and, if necessary, modified based on mental simulation. The results from the present study suggest that a COA is developed in steps, not as a whole. Moreover, the planning process was found to involve several decision points where officers had the choice between different COA fragments (details/parts of a complete COA) before they reached a final COA. Also, the phases of COA generation were interspersed with situation analysis. This finding may have been a result of the complex and time-stretched task; that is, it was difficult for the officers to grasp the whole situation in one step and to come up with a single recognition-primed decision, as suggested by the RPD model. Nonetheless, the frequent development and comparison of options (COA fragments) during the process of generating a complete COA seems to be inconsistent with the RPD model.

One possible explanation for the inconsistency of the present results with the RPD model is that none of the officers participating in this study may have been a true expert, and therefore may not have been able to instantly see a preferred COA or COA fragment as a result of matching the situation to vast knowledge base (as is predicted by the RPD model). More experienced officers, in contrast, might have done so. On the other hand, the officers in the present study were most likely about as experienced as most other senior officers in any army. Real-life military experience at that level of command and that type of mission is very rare; rather, military experience concerning high-echelon mission planning (and associated tactics) normally stems from training and exercises, as was the case with the participants in the present research. An alternative explanation centers on the fact that the present study used a different method than earlier studies of military decision making (e.g., Klein, 1993). It may be that the think-aloud method is better able to capture the planning process of military officers in contrast to interviews or observations.

Another interesting finding was that the *way* the plan was developed and tested did not differ between experienced and inexperienced officers; rather, differences only concerned the *amount* of time spent generating and evaluating COA details.

Moreover, although the experienced planners spent less clock time on situation analysis, they spent proportionally more of their total planning time on situation analysis than the less experienced planners. This finding is in line with earlier research (e.g., Klein, 1989). The finding that the experienced officers worked faster overall is consistent with earlier research on expert-novice differences (Herbig & Byssing, 2004).

This study has several limitations. The first limitation is its small sample size. There were only six participants, and these may not reflect all possible process differences among military officers. Other preferred ways of conducting military planning may be possible that are not captured in the present study. The second limitation is methodological. The instruction to think aloud may have altered participants' planning behavior, or at least may have made them more self-aware regarding their thought processes. This effect cannot be completely excluded despite participants' reports that they were not affected by the think-aloud instruction and that the process was natural to them. The third limitation concerns the fact that the study contained only one kind of traditional battle scenario. This limitation was necessary because the scenarios needed to be familiar in order to capture the influence of experience. On the other hand, another kind of scenario may have elicited a different planning process. The fourth limitation concerns the military training of study participants. All of them had been trained (as part of their professional education) to use a multiple-option evaluation process. While they did not mimic that doctrinal approach in the planning sessions of the study, it may still have affected their behavior, even though they were instructed to use any process they liked.

Future studies using the think-aloud technique could focus on other planning scenarios and different aspects of the planning process. The present study involved military commanders engaged in battle planning within the context of familiar scenario types. Follow-up studies could use more novel scenario types to examine how novelty affects the planning process. It could also be interesting to study specific aspects of planning or execution, such as risk management.

References

Brehmer, B. (2007). Understanding the functions of C2 is the key to progress. *International C2 Journal, 1,* 211–232.

Duncker, K. (1945). On problem solving. *Psychological Monographs, 58*(5), ix, 113.

Ericsson, K. A., & Simon, H. A. (1980). Verbal reports as data. *Psychological Review, 87*(3), 215–251.

Fallesen, J. (2000). Developing practical thinking for battle command. In C. McCann & R. Pigeau (Eds.), *The human in command* (pp. 185–200). New York, NY: Plenum Press.

Herbig, B., & Byssing, A. (2004). The role of explicit and implicit knowledge in work performance. *Psychology Science, 46*(4), 408–432.

Klein, G. (1993). A recognition-primed decision (RPD) model of rapid decision making. In G. A. Klein, J. Orasanu, R. Calderwood, & C. E. Zsambok (Eds.), *Decision making in action: Models and methods* (pp. 138–148). Norwood, NJ: Ablex Publishing.

Klein, G. A. (1989, May). Strategies of decision making. *Military Review,* pp. 56–64.

Klein G. A., & Crandall, B. W. (1995). The role of mental simulation in naturalistic decision making. In P. Hancock, J. Flach, J. Caird, & K. Vicente (Eds.), *Local applications of the ecological approach to human-machine systems* (Vol. 2, pp. 324–358). Mahwah, NJ: Lawrence Earlbaum Associates.

Lipshitz, R., & Adar Pras, A. (2005). Not only for experts: Recognition primed decisions in the laboratory. In H. Montgomery, R. Lipshitz, & B. Brehmer (Eds.), *How experts make decisions*. Mahwah, NJ: Lawrence Erlbaum.

NATO. (2004). *Allied command operations, guidelines for operational planning (GOP) Rev 1* (1100/SHOPJ/101321-101321PE). Brussels, Belgium: NATO HQ, Military Committee.

Pasqual, R., & Henderson, S. (1997). Evidence of naturalistic decision making in military command and control. In C. E. Zsambok & G. Klein (Eds.), *Naturalistic decision making* (pp. 217–227). Mahwah, NJ: Lawrence Erlbaum.

Schmitt, J., & Klein, G. (1999). A recognitional planning model. In *Proceedings to Command and Control Research and Technology Symposium 1999* (pp. 130–132). Newport, RI: Naval War College.

Swedish Army. (1995). *Arméreglemente del 2 TAKTIK* [Army Regulations Part 2: Tactics]. Swedish Armed Forces, Solna: Forsvarets bok- och blankettforrad.

U.S. Army (2005). Army planning and orders production (Field Manual 5-0). Washington, DC: Headquarters, Department of the Army.

Wertheimer, M. (1959). *Productive thinking* (rev. ed.). New York, NY: Harper & Row. (Original work published 1945)

Part II

Technological Support and Training
for Knowledge Management

9

The Design of a Distributed Work System to Support Adaptive Decision Making Across Multiple Organizations

Philip J. Smith, Amy L. Spencer, and Charles Billings
The Ohio State University

The focus of this chapter is on the design and use of new strategies for (1) distributing the work of managing traffic flows through the National Airspace System (NAS) in the United States (an FAA function), while (2) providing operators in the NAS with increased flexibility to manage their particular operations. These two issues in traffic management highlight the importance of designing an architecture for distributing cognitive work that takes into consideration the distribution of knowledge, expertise, data, processing capabilities, and motivations among a diverse set of organizations and individuals so that effective system-level performance emerges. At a more detailed level, they also emphasize the need to:

- Support effective communication, information exchange, and information display in order to enable appropriate shared situation awareness, while recognizing that appropriate shared situation awareness does not imply that everyone needs to have an identical depth and breadth of awareness regarding the overall situation.
- Design an architecture for distributing work that limits the demands in terms of cognitive complexity for any one individual.
- Provide computational support to deal with cognitive complexity and enable asynchronous coordination.
- Support the initiation of effective real-time, synchronous collaboration to deal with unanticipated situations that require the interaction of individuals with different goals, perspectives, and areas of expertise (Baecker, Grudin, Buxton, & Greenberg, 1995; Caldwell, 2005; Hinds & Kiesler, 2002; Orasanu & Salas, 1993; Rasmussen, Brehner, & Leplat, 1991).

With its emphasis on the support of a large-scale distributed work system that is enabled by advanced decision support and communication technologies, this chapter thus complements and extends the coverage provided by the chapters by Perry and Wears (Chapter 4, dealing with large-scale coordination of work) and Thunholm (Chapter 8, emphasizing knowledge management and the use of mental simulations).

The Use of Airspace Flow Programs as a Distributed Traffic Management Strategy

There are a number of considerations that are relevant to making decisions about air traffic flows when widespread convective weather is expected to develop in en route airspace over the northeastern United States, but not at the major airports themselves. These considerations include how to:

- Develop a plan that covers the range of uncertainty associated with the weather (i.e., the set of possible alternative scenarios that could develop).
- Safely maintain the highest possible throughput regardless of how the weather develops.
- Provide flight operators with the flexibility to make trade-offs based on their business priorities and constraints.
- Provide equitable treatment across the different flight operators.

Below, we define the "rules of the game" (Smith et al., 1997) for a new traffic management strategy based on Airspace Flow Programs (AFPs), which was first employed during the summer of 2006.

An example is provided below based on an actual day in the NAS (June 13, 2007). This example is used to define AFPs and to illustrate the issues and requirements for setting up this type of traffic management initiative. We refer to this example throughout the chapter to illustrate the use of AFPs and other programs to manage traffic flow, and the effective sharing of knowledge and expertise in a collaborative and distributed fashion. We then discuss a number of factors considered in the development of AFPs to manage traffic flows, including the need for tools to support collaborative work (Olson & Olson, 2003).

Rules of the Game: Ration by Schedule

To help provide equitable treatment across all flight operators, AFPs apply a "ration by schedule" strategy (Smith, Geddes, & Beatty, 2008) to delay those departures whose planned trajectories cross a set of geographically defined lines within a given time interval and altitude range. As an example, on June 13, 2007, two AFPs in the northeastern United States were designated as AFPA05 and AFPA08. The geographic locations of these two AFPs are shown in Figure 9.1. Flights were subject to control by these AFPs if they were expected to cross either one of the AFPs at altitudes between 12,000 and 60,000 feet from 1600Z (Zulu or Universal Coordinated Time) on June 13 to 0259Z on June 14 (using trajectory predictions based on historical data), and if they were scheduled to arrive at airports in the Boston Air Traffic Center (ZBW), in the half of Washington Center (ZDC) east and north of AFPA08, or in New York Center (ZNY).

The reason for employing AFPs on this day was that thunderstorms were predicted to occur across the northeastern United States. Based on the weather forecast (which is provided in more detail later), it was decided that 90 flights should be allowed to cross AFPA05 into the Northeast during the first hour (1600 to 1659Z) of the AFP and 75 per hour for the remaining hours. As Table 9.1 indicates, these decisions were made by

FIGURE 9.1   AFPs to control traffic into the northeastern United States on June 13, 2007.

TABLE 9.1   Decisions Made in Managing Traffic Flow Using AFPs

Decision	Decision Maker	Collaborator	Medium for Collaboration
Create AFP	ATCSCC Traffic Manager	Airline Dispatcher; Center Traffic Manager; Airport Traffic Manager	Phone and shared software display
Set parameters for AFP	ATCSCC Traffic Manager	Airline Dispatcher; Center Traffic Manager; Airport Traffic Manager	Phone and shared software display
Route flights out of AFP	Airline Dispatcher	Airline Air Traffic Control Coordinator	Phone or face-to-face
Cancel flights	Dispatcher	Airline Air Traffic Control Coordinator	Phone or face-to-face
Swap slots for flights in AFP	Airline Air Traffic Control Coordinator		
Swap slots for flights in AFP to fill empty slots	Flight Schedule Monitor		
Set Mile-in-Trail Restrictions	En route Traffic Center Manager	ATCSCC Traffic Manager	Phone and digital message dissemination
Set departure time for flight controlled by a Mile-in-Trail Restriction	En route Traffic Center Manager	Airport Tower Supervisor or Traffic Manager; Pilot	Phone and radio
Release a flight from an airport prior to its Expected Departure Clearance Time	ATCSCC Traffic Manager	Airline Dispatcher; Pilot; Airline Ramp Controller	Phone and digital message dissemination

traffic managers at the FAA Air Traffic Control System Command Center (ATCSCC) in consultation with traffic managers at the affected regional air traffic facilities and airports, and with dispatchers representing the affected flight operators.

The use of the ration by schedule strategy meant that 90 equally spaced time slots were allocated for included flights to cross AFPA05 during the first hour of the AFP, 1600 to 1659Z. These AFP arrival slots (arrival time at the controlling AFP, not at a destination airport) were allocated to the first 90 included flights predicted to cross AFPA05 at or after 1600Z. For example, if there were originally 125 flights expected to cross AFPA05 in the 1600Z hour, the first 90 would be allocated the available slots in that hour. The next 35 would be given the first of the 75 AFPA05 arrival slots allocated to the 1700 to 1759Z hour. In this manner, AFP arrival slots were assigned to all of the included flights. Departure times for these flights were then adjusted by working backward from the AFP-assigned arrival slots to calculate a corresponding airport departure time for each flight. (This assigned departure time is referred to as an expected departure clearance time.)

Establishing an AFP: Distributed Decision Making and Technological Support

In order to initiate an AFP as a type of traffic management initiative, several things need to be decided or calculated:

- Decision 1. Determine whether an AFP (or set of AFPs) is the appropriate traffic management initiative to meter traffic flows through some airspace region given the predicted weather and traffic situation.
- Decision 2. Determine the parameters for this AFP (or set of AFPs):
  - Start and end times
  - Altitude floor
  - Altitude ceiling
  - Arrival centers to include
  - Flow rates through AFP(s) per hour
- Decision 3. Identify the flights to be included and assign slots (entry times into an AFP).

Decision 1 requires consideration of the predicted weather and traffic forecasts. The primary weather forecast is a consensus prediction developed by weather forecasters working for the FAA, National Weather Service, and a number of airlines. These weather forecasters, who are distributed around the country at different sites, use shared displays and teleconferences to develop what is referred to as the Collaborative Convective Forecast Product (CCFP), as shown in Figure 9.2 for this date. This particular CCFP shows the consensus forecast for 1900Z made at 1300Z. To interpret this forecast, see the included legends. For example, the hash-marked polygon outlined in bold (blue on the actual interface display) in the center of the country indicates an area that is forecast with high confidence to have 25 to 49% coverage with thunderstorms sufficiently strong to require an aircraft to deviate around the weather. Note also that each such polygon is numbered. The numbers correspond to information below the map, providing more details on the forecast for weather within each polygon.

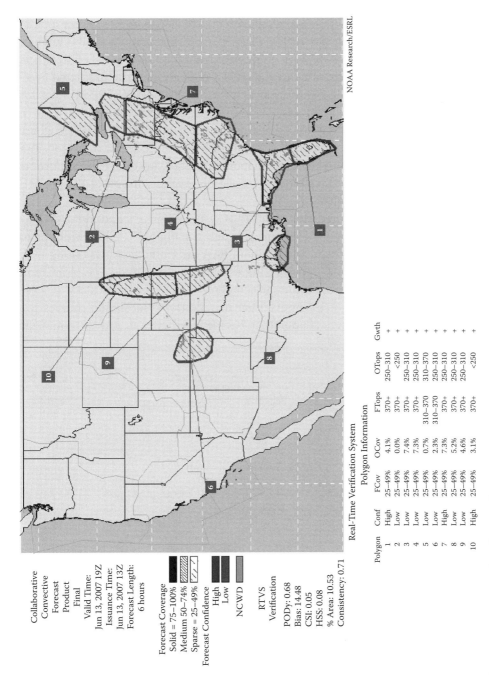

FIGURE 9.2 Convective weather forecast for June 13, 2007.

Traffic forecasts are presented to traffic managers and airline air traffic control coordinators by a tool known as the Flight Schedule Monitor. This tool displays the predicted traffic volume through a given AFP as a function of time into the future using a bar chart. By varying the parameters for the AFP (size, location, altitude boundaries, and included arrival centers), the decision maker can look at the expected impacts for alternative flow rate settings. This includes feedback about the average and maximum delays for flights controlled by the AFP. For instance, the settings for the AFP illustrated in Figure 9.3 indicate that the predicted average delay per flight will be 52.2 minutes, with a maximum delay of 92 minutes for one flight. Note that this way of assessing different options contrasts at least in part with the military planning tasks described in the chapter by Thunholm, where commanders relied heavily on mental simulations. While the traffic managers and dispatchers described here certainly think about potential variability through some form of mental simulation, the baseline simulation shared with all of the participants is completed by the software.

This information about predicted weather is available on a stand-alone display (Web site), and traffic volume is available through the Flight Schedule Monitor to traffic managers at the ATCSCC and regional FAA air traffic facilities, along with air traffic control coordinators representing different airlines and general aviation operations. During a strategic planning teleconference, staff members at all of these organizations must look at these inputs, plus any additional local data sources relevant to their operations, and collaborate to decide whether to use AFPs to manage

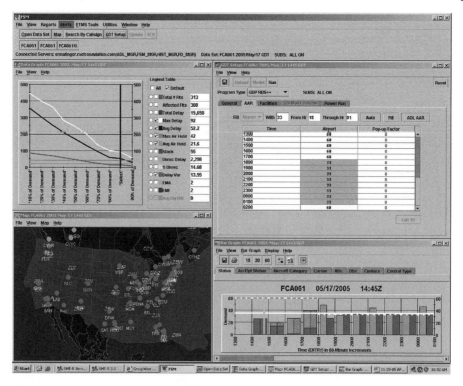

FIGURE 9.3   Sample display from the Flight Schedule Monitor.

the situation (with ATCSCC staff making the final decision based on this discussion). These collaborative teleconferences are held every two hours throughout the day.

Decision 2 (the parameters for this AFP or set of AFPs) is based on analyses of historical performance and the personal experiences of the decision makers. Research is under way to develop more objective methods for determining which AFPs, if any, to use, and for setting the flow rates for those AFPs. However, at present the cognitive processes involved can at least in part be characterized as some form of case-based reasoning or recognition-primed decision making, as the expert decision makers frequently make statements indicating that they try to remember similar days where AFPs were used successfully, and repeat the strategies used on those days, with minor adjustments to the flow rates and start times based on differences between the current situation and the weather associated with those previous days.

Once the parameters are set for an AFP, the Flight Schedule Monitor automatically calculates and assigns slots (AFP entry times) to individual flights based on the "ration by schedule" strategy, and back-calculates to estimate the controlled departure times (expected departure clearance times) for each of these flights (Decision 3, identify the flights to be included and assign slots). This information is then distributed to all of the flight operators via a secure network.

While this sounds straightforward, the design of AFPs to manage traffic is by itself quite a complex decision task, along with the challenges associated with deciding whether and how to apply AFPs to deal with a particular scenario. The major considerations are described below.

Weather Uncertainty

When convective weather develops in en route airspace in the Northeast, it is necessary to reduce air traffic flow through this airspace. Given the high volume of traffic involved, this cannot be done in a purely tactical manner by vectoring or rerouting airborne flights once the weather has developed. Rather, to reduce the overall flow through this airspace, thus providing enough "wiggle room" to safely vector the remaining flights around the weather, some of the flights that intend to use this airspace need to delay their departure. This means that these decisions need to be made very early, at a time when there is still considerable uncertainty about the location, timing, and severity of the weather event. As described earlier, Figure 9.2 provides an illustration of such uncertainty for June 13, 2007, and represents the type of weather for which AFPs were designed. This forecast was produced at 1300Z, predicting the coverage for regions of the United States at 1900Z.

Equitable Treatment of Airspace Users

Philosophically, the development of AFPs was based on the assumption that, to provide more equitable treatment to all flight operators, departure delays should be spread across all flights that traverse the weather-impacted airspace, rather than focusing on a few major flows or arrival airports. This criterion contrasts with traffic management practices prior to 2006 in the United States, which relied heavily on three other types of traffic management initiatives, such as the use of ground delay programs (Smith et al., 2008), assigned reroutes, and miles-in-trail restrictions. (Miles-in-trail restrictions require that flights along a given route or flow be separated by more than the minimum separation requirements.)

Ground delay programs and miles-in-trail restrictions were historically used to indirectly reduce flow though weather-impacted en route airspace by limiting arrival rates at a few major Northeast U.S. airports whose arrival flows traversed the affected en route airspace. Thus, they imposed delays only on the users of those airports, rather than spreading the delays across all of the users of the impacted airspace. Assigned reroutes were used for the same purpose, but these reduced flows in the weather-impacted airspace by routing flights around it. As with ground delay programs and miles-in-trail restrictions, such reroutes tended to focus on flights between major hubs, as it was easier to identify and control a large number of flights by applying reroutes to those city pairs. However, both ground delay programs and miles-in-trail initiatives are less effective because they impact only a subset of the relevant flights (an equity problem).

In the case of ground delay programs, there is a second weakness: A ground delay program reduces the arrival rate at a given airport such as IAD (Dulles International Airport near Washington, DC) regardless of the departure airports of the incoming flights. On a day where the convective weather is only to the west of IAD, flights from the south and west of IAD are equally affected, even though those from the south are not flying through weather-impacted airspace. This wastes available airspace capacity.

AFPs were developed to deal with both equity and airspace capacity concerns. Because they apply to all flights entering weather-impacted airspace, they focus on a broader set of departure and arrival airports, creating a more equitable plan and potentially spreading the delays across a larger number of flights (thus reducing the average delay per flight). And because they focus only on those flights entering the affected airspace, they do not impose delay on flights flying through nonimpacted airspace.

Accommodation of Airspace User Constraints and Priorities

A third factor influencing the design of AFPs is the desire to provide airspace users with as much flexibility as possible to accommodate their business concerns (Smith, Beatty, Spencer, & Billings, 2003). In particular, avoiding arrival delays is more important to an airline for some flights than for others (such as a flight with a large number of passengers with international connections). From a traffic management perspective, it doesn't matter (too much) whether the flight using a particular weather-impacted en route airspace is from Chicago or Denver.

Thus, when an AFP arrival slot (time to arrive at the AFP) is initially assigned to a specific flight, that slot belongs to the flight operator (such as an airline). The flight operator can swap flights among its slots for that AFP, as long as those flights can make the assigned AFP arrival times (or cancel a flight to create an empty slot).

Note that this slot swapping does not require any discussion or real-time collaboration between the airline air traffic control coordinator who makes the swaps (with the help of a decision support tool) and the FAA traffic manager who has put the AFP into effect. It does involve direct interaction between the air traffic control coordinator and the dispatcher who has responsibility for that flight (see Table 9.1).

Thus, a key property of this traffic management strategy is the design of an architecture in which FAA traffic managers at ATCSCC have to make only high-level decisions regarding the arrival rates associated with each of the AFPs after phone discussions with the affected centers, airports, and airlines, with each party looking at the weather and traffic forecasts during these discussions. Software (the Flight Schedule Monitor) then uses these arrival rates to create and ration the arrival slots allocated to those flights subject to the AFP, and to inform the flight operators regarding the slots that they have been assigned (see Table 9.1).

The other decisions are then made internal to each flight operator. Each flight operator can decide whether to cancel a particular flight, to route it out of the AFP so it is no longer controlled by that traffic management initiative, or to swap one flight with another in order to reduce the delay for a higher-priority flight. These internal decisions are made either by phone or in face-to-face conversations at the dispatch center for that flight operator (see Table 9.1). Many of the swaps are made using slot-swapping software that looks at the priorities associated with the different flights, but exceptions are handled manually by the air traffic control coordinators.

For instance, a flight from Chicago O'Hare to New York LaGuardia with an arrival slot in AFPA05 of 1715Z could be swapped by the flight operator with a flight from Minneapolis to LaGuardia that had an arrival slot in AFPA05 of 1745Z, assuming the Minneapolis–LaGuardia flight could depart on time to make the 1715Z AFP arrival slot time. As a concrete example of using such swapping tactics, on June 13, 2007, one flight with a scheduled takeoff time of 2001Z was originally assigned an expected departure clearance time of 2136Z (a 95-minute delay), but through swapping was moved up to an expected departure clearance time of 2010Z and actually departed at 2007Z (a final delay of only 6 minutes).

Additional flexibility is provided to the airspace users by allowing them to route themselves out of or under the AFP. Thus, flights included in AFPA05 can file flight plans that take them north into Canada to avoid inclusion in the AFP, and flights included in AFPA08 can file a plan going east over the Atlantic to avoid inclusion (see Figure 9.4 for examples). When a flight is filed around (or under) its AFP or is cancelled, its AFP arrival slot can then be used to move up the departure times and reduce the delays for other flights controlled by that operator. As with slot swapping, this process involving "route outs" does not require any discussion or real-time collaboration between the airline air traffic control coordinator who makes the swaps with the help of a decision support tool and the FAA traffic manager who has put the AFP into effect. It does, however, involve direct interaction between the air traffic control coordinator and the dispatcher who ultimately files the new route (see Table 9.1). In addition, if a slot is left empty because an airline cancels a flight or otherwise leaves the slot vacant, then the Flight Schedule Monitor software will automatically try to move up a flight from another airline into that slot.

Also note that the use of AFPs, unlike the use of assigned reroutes, provides the flight operators with additional flexibility with respect to the route they file within the AFP. As long as a flight can make its assigned AFP slot time, it can be filed on any route through the AFP (subject to weather and normal ATC constraints). As

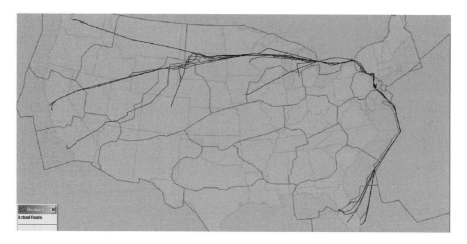

FIGURE 9.4   Actual filed routes for flights to Newark going around AFPA05 or AFPA08 on June 13, 2007.

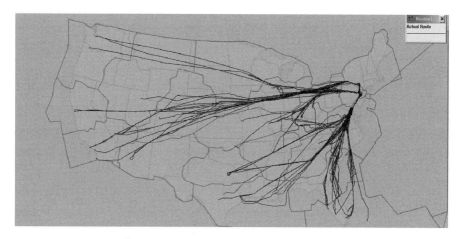

FIGURE 9.5   Actual routes for 137 flights to Newark flying through AFPA05 or AFPA08 on June 13, 2007.

an illustration, Figure 9.5 shows the routes for flights to Newark that actually flew through one of the two AFPs. Finally, note that because expected departure clearance times are assigned well before the scheduled departure time, they potentially provide greater predictability for the flight operator.

Adaptive System Design to Deal With Uncertainty

One of the challenges in using AFPs or any other type of traffic management initiative is that it is not sufficient to design a static traffic management plan that remains in effect as is throughout the day, because weather and traffic constraints do not develop exactly as predicted. As a result, a number of strategies have been either built into the management of the AFPs themselves, or developed as complementary strategies that can be applied along with AFPs.

Providing Reservoirs to Cope With Uncertainty

If there were no uncertainty about when and where convective weather was going to develop, then it would be relatively easy to determine how many flights to schedule through the affected airspace per hour. However, especially given the long planning horizons involved, there is typically considerable uncertainty about what the actual weather will be, and thus about how many aircraft will actually be able to be accommodated in a given time period.

To deal with this uncertainty, four types of traffic management strategies complementary to the use of AFPs may be used. These create "reservoirs" of time and space that can be used to increase or decrease throughput in the airspace in the Northeast relative to the rates originally set in the AFP; these are described below.

Strategy 1: Flights Controlled With Enroute Spacing Program (ESP) Delays

Figure 9.1 shows that Cleveland Center (ZOB) is inside the boundary formed by AFPA05 and AFPA08. As a result, flights departing Cleveland Center destined for Boston, New York, or Washington Center do not cross these AFPs, and hence are not controlled by the associated traffic management initiative. Instead, these flights may be controlled through delays generated by an Enroute Spacing Program, or by miles-in-trail restrictions, which are set by a traffic manager at an en route center, with concurrence from a traffic manager at the FAA Systems Command Center.

These departures from Cleveland Center and controlled by an Enroute Spacing Program are handled using a manual process. Each aircraft departing Cleveland Center and flying to Boston, New York, or Washington Center is required to contact the ATC tower at its departure airport when it taxis out to takeoff, and to ask for a release time (controlled departure time). This release time is assigned by the controlling Center (Cleveland Center in this example) as the flight taxis out, and is based on the current en route weather and traffic situation. If the weather is less severe than expected, the delay incorporated into this release time will tend to be very short. If the weather develops as expected, the average delay for the flights controlled by the Enroute Spacing Program should be about the same as the average delay for flights controlled by the AFP. If the weather is worse than expected, then the Enroute Spacing Program delays could average longer than the AFP delays.

This strategy takes advantage of the fact that the Cleveland Center flights are relatively close to the location of the weather, and that they are asked to taxi out on schedule. Thus, the Cleveland Center flights serve as a reservoir of flights that can be used to either increase or decrease throughput in the airspace based on how the weather actually develops (at the price of less departure predictability for those flights, as they do not have expected departure clearance times). In a similar manner, departures from Boston, Cleveland, New York, and Washington Centers to anywhere serve as a reservoir. This process of coordinating Enroute Spacing Program and AFP delays requires real-time collaboration by radio and phone by the flight crew, airport tower supervisor, and an en route center traffic manager (see Table 9.1), with the center traffic manager looking at a number of displays showing weather and traffic information to determine when a flight can be fit into the overhead stream.

On June 13, 2007, the weather in the northern half of Cleveland Center had largely dissipated by 2100Z. Because there was still storm activity impacting the airspace surrounded by AFPA08 and the southern half of AFPA05, the AFPs were left in place without any revision of the rates until 2347Z. However, Cleveland Center flights were allowed to depart earlier than originally expected in order to make use of the available airspace. As a result, the average delay for the 17 Cleveland Center departures to Newark was 11.1 minutes, while the average delay for the flights to Newark controlled by the AFPs was 31.7 minutes (Smith et al., 2008).

Strategy 2: Flights Released Early at an Airport Through a Suspension of Expected Departure Clearance Times

A second, similar strategy used to provide a reservoir for increasing throughput through airspace when the weather and traffic constraints are less significant than expected is to let flights controlled by an AFP depart early by suspending expected departure clearance times at an airport. Generally, this strategy is used at airports close to the AFP to quickly generate more traffic, such as would occur with the early release of flights from Chicago to go through AFPA05. The suspension of expected departure clearance times is initiated by a traffic manager in the FAA Systems Command Center, who must then coordinate with the responsible airline dispatchers by phone, who must in turn coordinate with their ramp control towers by phone and pilots by radio (see Table 9.1).

Strategy 3: Flights Delayed Through the Use of Ground Stops or Departure Stops

If weather and traffic constraints suddenly increase beyond expectations, all flights scheduled to land at a given airport or depart from a given airport can be stopped on the ground for an indefinite time. This can quickly reduce the traffic flow through a region. On June 13, 2007, four grounds stops were initiated during the course of the AFPs, at Baltimore, Washington National, Washington Dulles, and Teterboro. This strategy was requested by the air traffic control tower at the involved airports, and implemented by ATCSCC.

Strategy 4: Use of Airborne Flights as a Reservoir

Although AFPs focus primarily on control of throughput through departure delays, airborne flights are also used as a reservoir as necessary. If there is a temporary excess of flights entering New York Center through Cleveland or Washington Center, for example, en route flights may be put into no-notice high-altitude holding before they reach the New York Center boundary. This tends to reduce departures in the affected region as well as delay flights along the routes where the holding is occurring. Figure 9.6 shows the flights put into holding while the AFPs were in effect on June 13, 2007. A more extreme strategy for creating a type of reservoir is to divert flights to a different arrival airport if there is no other way to delay these flights until they can safely land at their intended destinations. On the other hand, if the weather is less significant than expected, some flights that filed flight plans around or under the AFP

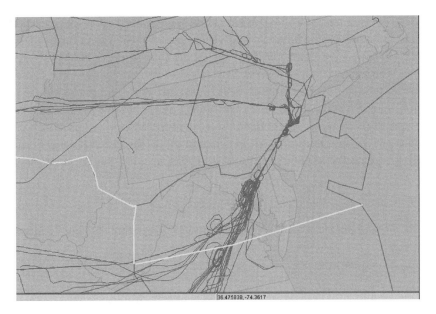

FIGURE 9.6   Flights put into airborne holding while the AFPs were in effect.

may be rerouted through the AFP to make use of the available airspace. (Note: This must be done in a coordinated fashion to make sure the flights don't arrive with too much fuel and thus exceed their safe landing weights.)

Conclusion

This chapter serves to illustrate a number of important points about the design of the highly distributed system for managing traffic flow in the NAS. First, even a seemingly straightforward traffic flow management strategy that has been designed in a very deliberate manner, such as the use of AFPs, in reality involves the interaction of a distributed group of individuals making use of a large, diverse set of traffic management tools or strategies (see Table 9.1). This reality exists because of the complex uncertainties that change over time and across geographic locations, and the need to apply different combinations of traffic management tools as the situation emerges.

Second, relevant knowledge, expertise, data, processing capabilities, and motivations are distributed among a diverse set of organizations and individuals. This includes FAA traffic managers centrally located at ATCSCC, as well as traffic managers at regional en route centers and at airport towers. It also includes air traffic control coordinators and dispatchers working for each flight operator at its centralized operational control center. In many cases, it is clear how and why such resources are distributed as they are. For example, the air traffic coordinator for a flight operator is clearly in a better position than an FAA traffic manager to know about the priorities for its different flights, and to be motivated to cancel, reroute, or swap flights based on these priorities. Similarly because traffic managers typically rise through the ranks of the controllers responsible for the separation of aircraft in the airspace controlled by their en route centers, they have developed considerable center-specific knowledge about how to handle traffic flows through those centers when weather develops.

There are many interesting research questions that could be addressed to better understand the impacts of distributing the resources defined by these five dimensions, and to better predict how they will interact to produce emergent performance in some distributed work system. Because they represent a newly designed and introduced feature of the air traffic system, AFPs offer an interesting opportunity to explore the impact of new designs for distributing work in order to guide the development of models to help with future decisions about how to design complex, distributed work systems.

Acknowledgments

This work was supported by the FAA Collaborative Decision Making Program.

References

Baecker, R., Grudin, J. Buxton, W., & Greenberg, S. (1995). *Readings in groupware and computer-supported cooperative work: Assisting human-human collaboration.* San Francisco, CA: Morgan Kaufmann.

Caldwell, B. (2005). Multi-team dynamics and distributed expertise in mission operations. *Aviation, Space, and Environmental Medicine, 76*(6), 145–153.

Hinds, P., & Kiesler, S. (Eds.). (2002). *Distributed work.* Cambridge MA: MIT Press.

Olson, G., & Olson, J. (2003). Groupware and computer-supported cooperative work. In A. Sears & J. Jacko (Eds.), *Handbook of human-computer interaction* (pp. 583–593). Mahwah, NJ: Lawrence Erlbaum.

Orasanu, J., & Salas, E. (1991). Team decision making in complex environments. In G. Klein, R. Calderwood, & C. Zsambok (Eds.), *Decision making in action: Models and methods.* Norwood, NJ: Ablex.

Rasmussen, J., Brehner, B., & Leplat, J. (Eds.). (1991). *Distributed decision making: Cognitive models for cooperative work.* New York, NY: John Wiley & Sons.

Smith, P. J., Beatty, R., Spencer, A., & Billings, C. (2003). *Dealing with the challenges of distributed planning in a stochastic environment: Coordinated contingency planning.* Paper presented at Proceedings of the 2003 Annual Conference on Digital Avionics Systems, Chicago, IL.

Smith, P. J., Geddes, N., & Beatty, R. (2008). Human-centered design of decision support systems. In A. Sears & J. Jacko (Eds.), *Handbook of human-computer interaction* (2nd ed.). Mahwah, NJ: Lawrence Erlbaum Associates.

Smith, P. J., McCoy, E., Orasanu, J., Billings, C., Denning, R., Rodvold, M., & VanHorn, A. (1997). Control by permission: A case study of cooperative problem-solving in the interactions of airline dispatchers and ATCSCC. *Air Traffic Control Quarterly, 4,* 229–247.

10

An Investigation of Technology-Mediated *Ad Hoc* Team Operations
Consideration of Components of Team Situation Awareness

Laura D. Strater, Haydee M. Cuevas, Sandro Scielzo, and Erik S. Connors
SA Technologies

Cleotilde Gonzalez
Dynamic Decision Making Laboratory, Carnegie Mellon University

Diane M. Ungvarsky
U.S. Army Research Laboratory

Mica R. Endsley
SA Technologies

Technological advances have yielded significant changes in the way people work. Decision makers dealing with complex, ill-structured problems, dynamic environments with significant time stress, shifting or competing goals, and significant consequences for failure are particular targets for technological support. In fact, these same characteristics are key task indicators in naturalistic decision-making (NDM) contexts (Zsambok, 1997). In many environments, the employment of technology has led to teams in which members are more mobile, more versatile, and more distributed in time, space, and purpose. Often these teams are *ad hoc*—they are brought together for a limited time span to address a specific problem and often have diverse backgrounds and technical expertise that form the basis for their selection onto the team. This expertise provides a second key distinguishing characteristic of NDM research; that is, it does not address naïve participants, but rather experienced decision makers.

In this chapter, we present research aimed at investigating factors that influence *ad hoc* team operations and decision processes in technologically sophisticated operational environments, thus providing a third distinguishing characteristic of NDM research—that it addresses complex problem spaces. Finally, due to the complexity of the environment, our research focuses on the situation awareness (SA) of the decision maker, which highlights a fourth and final significant characteristic of NDM research: a concern with situation assessment. We begin with a brief overview of the challenges faced by *ad hoc* teams, then introduce a theoretical framework of team SA, and describe a preliminary study that evaluated elements that may affect factors of this framework.

Ad Hoc Teams in Complex Operational Environments

Organizations, including businesses and military forces, increasingly rely on *ad hoc* teams. These teams are intentionally composed of individuals with diverse skills, backgrounds, and experiences to bring their multiple perspectives and competencies to bear on a problem. *Ad hoc* teams have several defining characteristics, including the following: limited time span, assembled to address a specific problem, limited common training, diverse backgrounds, distributed in space, formed or disbanded asynchronously, and team duties that supplement rather than replace regular duties. Each *ad hoc* team may possess all or a subset of these characteristics.

While these characteristics provide advantages to the team, they can also complicate team operations. Specifically, *ad hoc* team members may be less homogeneous; thus, they may not share common operational vocabularies or fully understand the expertise and capabilities of fellow team members. This may result in poor team communication and collaboration. Furthermore, traditional teams benefit from common training and background, as this allows the development of relationships built on mutual trust and understanding and promotes the ability to accurately assess the input of individual team members. Lacking this background, *ad hoc* team members must rely on one another for critical information in order to quickly develop an understanding of the situation. This understanding, or situation awareness (SA), is formally defined as "the perception of the elements in the environment within a volume of time and space, the comprehension of their meaning and the projection of their status in the near future" (Endsley, 1995b, p. 36), and forms the foundation for decision making and action.

Ad hoc teams are further challenged by the temporal timelines within which they operate. Team members may cycle in and out of the group, which can result in the loss of specific aspects of team SA resident in the departing team member. They may also multitask between duties on other teams. *Ad hoc* teams members may also be physically distributed, and so the means and timing of communication may impact operations. Distributed teams (*ad hoc* or permanent) must rely heavily on technology mediated communications (e.g., voice or text chat, email), and members with different backgrounds may prefer different information exchange strategies. Geographic distribution can create challenges for the team leader in monitoring team status (e.g., which teams are operational, what specific tasks are being done) and team membership (e.g., who is currently on the team and what are their task assignments). While many of these challenges exist to some degree in other types of teams, *ad hoc* teams face a greater number of these issues, and often lack the common background to ameliorate the difficulties.

Investigating Technology Mediated *Ad Hoc* Team Operations: A Case Study

A better understanding of *ad hoc* team operations in complex environments requires evaluating how the implementation of automation and collaboration technology may influence critical team collaborative processes. In this case study, we examined a short-term *ad hoc* team that was formed for the purpose of a military exercise. We used a framework for team SA to direct our investigation of *ad hoc* team operations. Extending the definition of SA presented earlier, team SA is the degree to which all team members have the SA necessary to perform their roles on the team, and ultimately to contribute to achieving the team's goals (Endsley, 1995b). Endsley and Jones (2001) defined a framework for team SA that describes four interacting factors: team SA requirements, team SA mechanisms, team SA processes, and team SA devices (see Figure 10.1).

Team SA requirements are those pieces of critical information needed by each individual team member to perform his or her specific assigned tasks. Team SA requirements are influenced by the mechanisms, processes, and devices utilized by the team. *Team SA mechanisms* refer to internal cognitive structures that drive the process of sharing information, such as mental models and knowledge derived from common training. *Team SA processes* refer to external processes and include standard operating procedures, information sharing strategies, and communication protocols. For both team SA mechanisms and processes, limitations in common training and background are likely to produce a greater degree of variability among *ad hoc* team members than among members of traditional teams. *Team SA devices* describe the physical means by which information is exchanged and include displays, communication devices, and other equipment used for information exchange. Our framework illustrates that an investigation of *ad hoc* team operations relies not only on the information needs of the team (which by themselves are critical to building team SA), but

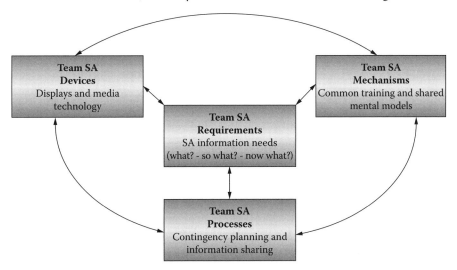

FIGURE 10.1   Framework of team SA. (Adapted from Endsley, M. R., and Jones, W. M., in M. McNeese, E. Salas, and M. Endsley (Eds.), *New Trends in Cooperative Activities: Understanding System Dynamics in Complex Environments*, Human Factors and Ergonomics Society, Santa Monica, CA, 2001, pp. 46–67.)

also consideration of the mechanisms, processes, and devices that enable information transfer.

To investigate forces that may influence these transfer factors, we collaborated in
a large-scale three-part experiment, within a military command and control (C2)
setting that employed a variety of collaboration technologies. The specific team SA
devices (collaboration technologies) were varied between sessions, enabling us to
focus on measuring team SA requirements (objective SA of team members) as well
as constructs related to team SA mechanisms (team mindfulness) and team SA processes (social network analysis) as a function of technology type. The research goal
was to determine whether higher levels of technology facilitated SA in *ad hoc* teams.

Team SA Requirements

SA requirements are those critical information requirements needed to meet
both individual and team goals and are assessed using objective measures of SA.
Developing and maintaining SA involves being aware of what is happening around
you to understand how information, events, and your own actions will impact your
goals in the present and near future.

Team SA Mechanisms

SA mechanisms are the cognitive structures (e.g., mental models) through which
data are filtered to produce the individual's SA. Generally, traditional teams develop
similar mental models through common training and shared experiences, which are
limited for *ad hoc* teams.

Team Mindfulness

At the individual level, mindfulness refers to the ability to be sensitive to information in context. It results from a propensity to draw novel distinctions, notice new
information, consider alternative perspectives, and adapt to new situations (Langer &
Moldoveanu, 1989). At the group level, collective mindfulness has been studied with
respect to the success of high-reliability organizations (e.g., Weick & Sutcliffe, 2001)
and is defined as the organization's ability to respond effectively to novel situations.
Five components of collective mindfulness include (1) preoccupation with examining
and learning from failure; (2) concern with achieving a reasoned, analytical solution;
(3) attention to operations; (4) commitment to success; and (5) dynamic decision-
making structures and deference to expertise. These factors are related to team SA
mechanisms as they define how the team members interact with one another and
what the team values. We hypothesized that team mindfulness would be positively
correlated with SA scores, as team mindfulness scores reflect the individual's assessment of team attitudes, priorities, and values.

Team SA Processes

Team SA processes are those team-related behaviors that team members employ to
enable team operations, such as communication and collaboration, self-checking

and confirming, prioritizing and questioning. Developing efficient processes can be a challenge for *ad hoc* teams.

Social Network Analysis

To investigate team communication, we employed methods and measures from social network analysis (SNA) (Borgatti, 1994; Scott, 1992) to assess team communication and information flow among *ad hoc* team members. In any team, individuals influence not only each other, but also the ideas being exchanged and how those ideas are transferred. Thus, a social network represents not only the organization of team members, but also how they interact with one another. SNA methodology maps entities as nodes in a network, and uses links between nodes to represent relationships or information flow between entities. Many SNA measures are relevant for military *ad hoc* teams (Graham, Gonzalez, & Schneider, 2007), but we calculated the two most common: (1) social network distance, the shortest social path separating two people within a network (Borgatti, 1994), and (2) network density, the number of links observed among the members of an organization divided by the number of possible links (Freeman, 1979). As improved collaboration technologies are introduced, we hypothesized a decrease in social network distance and an increase in network density as indications of increased cohesion, closer communications, and tighter relationships.

Method

Participants

The Urban Resolve experiment involved 86 military personnel (mean age = 49 years; range = 22 to 67 years) brought together from multiple specialties, duty stations, and service branches (Army, Air Force, and Marines) to fill between 52 and 59 roles. Personnel included two retired generals, 70 active duty and retired officers (ranks ranging from captain to colonel), nine warrant officers, and five enlisted soldiers. When possible, personnel were placed in roles related to their past rank and experience, yet this was not strictly controlled due to changes in personnel availability over the course of the experiment. Because only a subset of participants was involved in the entire study, it is the complete data from only those 60 participants that are reported here. Although their data are not reported here due to limited participation, coalition forces (British personnel) were also participants during the second experimental session.

This analysis investigates the study participants as a single team, though they were actually organized into teams of teams. This organization, however, was far more complex than it seems, as many personnel had multiple team membership. As an example, the surgeon had membership both in the headquarters staff team and on the medical support team. Most positions had at least dual team membership, and some had membership on multiple teams. For simplicity, the current analysis considers all participants as members of a single team.

Urban Resolve Simulation

The Urban Resolve experiment employed a distributed military C2 simulation. The operational setting was a joint force (multiple service branches) conducting stability operations (e.g., detect and respond to improvised explosive devices, negotiate with local officials, restore local services, and deliver humanitarian aid) while opposed by an adaptive enemy. The headquarters elements, consisting of the Joint Force Land Component Command (JFLCC) along with four other joint force military organizations, were geographically distributed across the United States. The JFLCC headquarters executed C2 over six maneuver brigades, four support brigades, and eight theater units, ranging in size from the battalion to the command level. The data presented in this study were collected only from the JFLCC and subordinate brigade, theater, and support staff, located at Ft. Leavenworth ($N = 60$). Study participants were distributed across three separate rooms in the Battle Lab at Ft. Leavenworth. Approximately two-thirds of the participants were located in a single room, the JFLCC headquarters. Although a seating chart was developed prior to the commencement of the experiment, personnel were relocated during and between experimental sessions to facilitate collaboration and communication. JFLCC personnel included all major staff functions, such as the commander, intelligence, operations, planning, logistics, knowledge management, and critical liaison personnel, such as those providing support for aviation, medical needs, and space-based assets.

Prior to the beginning of actual data collection, participants completed a one-week training session, which included briefings on the purpose of the experiment, collection of demographic data, familiarization with the simulation, and training on the collaboration technologies to be used. Urban Resolve was then executed over three separate two-week (Monday through Friday) human-in-the-loop (HITL) sessions, one per month for three consecutive months. For nine days of each HITL, participants took part in an eight-hour battlefield simulation exercise followed by an after action review, with the final day of each session abbreviated to four hours. See Table 10.1 for an overview of the experimental design and schedule.

TABLE 10.1   Overview of Experimental Design and Schedule

	HITL 1 2 weeks		HITL 2 2 weeks		HITL 3 2 weeks	
IVs	2005 Technology (C2PC)		2015 Technology (CPOF + space assets and predictive tools)		2015+ Technology (CPOF + additional space assets and predictive tools)	
Administrative Schedule	2 Times/ Day	Weekly (Thursday p.m.)	2 Times/ Day	Weekly (Thursday p.m.)	2 Times/ Day	Weekly (Thursday p.m.)
DVs						
Team attitudes scale		✓		✓		✓
SA audit	✓		✓		✓	
SNA survey	✓		✓		✓	

Collaboration Technology

The primary manipulation across HITLs in the experiment was to modify the technology provided to participants. HITL 1 simulated current technology and employed the Command and Control Personal Computer (C2PC; http://www.ms.northropgrumman.com/). C2PC uses one screen, though another screen is available for additional collaborative displays, such as chats and email. With C2PC, users can view and edit a shared display of the Common Operating Picture (COP), apply overlays, display imagery, and send and receive tactical messages. HITL 2 and 3 were meant to simulate future battlefield capabilities, and employed technologies anticipated to be in use in 2015 (HITL 2) and 2015+ (HITL 3). These technologies included the use of space-based assets, such as real-time satellite imagery and decision support tools with predictive capabilities. The difference between HITL 2 and 3 was in the extent of assets provided, with HITL 3 personnel having access to more assets than HITL 2 personnel.

In addition, in HITL 2 and 3, 31 key personnel (just over half of the participants) received information via the Command Post of the Future (CPOF; http://www.gdc4s.com). The other participants had access to C2PC only. The CPOF employs three screens and provides a shared environment for distributing, manipulating, and displaying information to support the planning of operations. Features included a shared display, Voice over Internet Protocol (VoIP), a graphical user interface (GUI), mapping tools, and enhanced briefing capabilities.

Measures

Objective individual situation awareness was measured using an SA audit questionnaire, administered twice each day. At a predetermined time, participants' display screens were blanked and the questionnaire was presented on participants' monitors. After two minutes, the simulation resumed and any unanswered queries were scored as incorrect. Based on the SAGAT methodology (see Endsley, 1995a), each individual SA audit included 10 items from a total pool of 21 queries about relevant aspects of the situation at that point in time. Unlike traditional SAGAT queries, the SA audit queries were broadly applicable, not tailored to each role. The questions were developed from SA requirements analyses conducted for various Army C2 staff positions using the goal-directed task analysis methodology (see Bolstad & Endsley, 2003; Bolstad, Riley, Jones, & Endsley, 2002; Strater, Endsley, Pleban, & Matthews, 2001). Personnel responsible for designing and running the simulation scenarios selected the queries from a candidate list based upon their broad relevance and applicability across all staffed roles.

In order to obtain a sufficiently large query pool for administration over the six weeks of the experiment, two types of queries were developed: single-response and multiple-response queries. Single-response queries allowed only one response and were scored as either correct or incorrect. Multiple-response queries were multiple-choice queries for which several response options could be correct. Scoring for these queries required assessing whether each response option should have been selected or not selected, and combining scores for each response option into a single score for the query; thus, each query could be fully correct, fully incorrect, or partially correct. The SA audit queries were classified by SA level: Level 1 (perception; 4 queries); Level 2 (comprehension; 11 queries); and Level 3 (projection; 6 queries). Scores were computed for each participant for each administration for overall SA audit, along with Level 1, 2, and 3 SA audit scores. Both Level 1 and Level 3 queries were evenly distributed across single and multiple-response types; Level 2 queries were predominantly multiple response (9 of 11).

Team mindfulness was measured using the team attitudes scale, developed by our research team from the constructs of collective mindfulness. This instrument consisted of 50 statements (both positive and negative) that asked participants to rate their degree of agreement with each statement on a 7-point scale. Questions were targeted for a military C2 environment from each of the five key components of collective mindfulness. Sample positive and negative statements from each component are listed in Table 10.2. Ten statements were created for each component. The scale was administered once per week, on Thursday afternoon. Data from HITL 1 were not included in the analysis, as errors in the survey mechanism resulted in the collection of incomplete data from this HITL.

Social network analysis was assessed using the SNA communication frequency scale, administered twice each day, once in the morning and once in the afternoon. To identify information flow patterns during the simulation, participants identified the person with whom they communicated most frequently, then second, third, fourth, and fifth most frequently. These data were recorded and translated into XML files for use in the ORA social network analysis tool, with each role represented by a node in the network, and the reports of communication frequency represented by lines between the nodes. The data in ORA were then employed to construct social

TABLE 10.2 Sample Team Attitude Items From Each Collective Mindfulness Component (CMC)

CMC	Sample Team Attitude Statements
Concern with learning from failure	• Team/staff members feel comfortable reporting mistakes to other team members. • Team/staff members should fix any problems they find without talking about them; there is no need to discuss mistakes.
Concern with analysis	• Team/staff members focus on finding out what they don't know. • Team/staff members listen more to people with similar backgrounds and experience.
Attention to operations	• Team/staff members listen carefully to each other when talking about military operations. • Team/staff members are concerned with their own tasks, not with operations as a whole.
Commitment to success	• Team/staff members frequently help one other with tasks. • Team/staff members rarely talk about what insurgent groups will do next.
Dynamic decision making and deference to expertise	• When personnel are unable to solve a problem, they seek help from team/staff members with more experience. • Team/staff members sometimes feel uncomfortable expressing their opinions and ideas, especially to those of higher rank.

Note: The second statement listed for each CMC is reverse scored.

network graphs, as well as to calculate social network distance and network density in the networks. Values were then averaged across HITLs.

Results and Discussion

The analysis and interpretation of the results for each of the measures are presented below.

SA Audit

Analyses of the SA audit questionnaire revealed that overall SA declined across HITLs: $F(655, 6) = 4.28$, $p < .01$ (see Figure 10.2). Both Level 1 and Level 3 SA remained consistent across HITLs, and the statistically significant decrease in overall SA was due to the decrease in Level 2 SA (comprehension). As noted earlier, compared to the Level 1 or 3 queries, Level 2 queries were primarily multiple response. Arguably, multiple-response option queries are more difficult than single-response queries, as the participant must evaluate whether each response option is true or false rather than identifying the option that is *most* correct. The decline in Level 2 SA across HITLs may reflect decreasing motivation to answer these more difficult queries. As mentioned earlier, the study occurred over three separate two-week sessions, and researchers noted an apparent decline in motivation for some aspects of the study, including the SA audit questionnaire. The combination of more challenging queries and decreased motivation may account for the decline in Level 2 SA across HITLs.

The objective data contrast with subjective assessments by expert observers at the experiment who believed that SA improved over the HITLs. The decline in SA audit scores may reflect the fact that the queries did not exclusively consist of items of immediate relevance to the participant. The general questions asked in this SA audit may not accurately reflect overall SA in this particular large and diverse *ad hoc* team

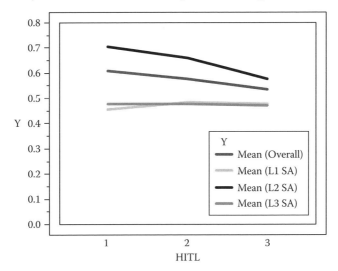

FIGURE 10.2   SA audit scores across HITLs, showing level 1 (perception), level 2 (comprehension), level 3 (projection), and overall SA.

exercise, as the globally relevant items may not have been of interest to participants in all roles and echelons represented.

Team Mindfulness

As the team attitudes scale was a new measure developed for this experiment, the first step was to evaluate the psychometric properties for the overall scale and for the subaggregate component area scores at each point in time. While the overall score for internal consistency revealed high consistency across administration times, in part due to the large number of overall items, the internal consistency scores for the subaggregates were lower than desired. Several items that were negatively correlated with the subaggregates were dropped due to the possibility that the item phrasing may have been confusing. Once all negatively correlated items were dropped, resulting in a 37-item scale, all internal consistency scores for the overall scale and subaggregates improved, indicating that the scale was consistently found reliable over time (see Table 10.3). Only the subaggregate "concern with failure" at Times 1, 2, and 3, and the subaggregate "attention to operations" at Times 2 and 6 yielded insufficient reliability, although the reliability is certainly acceptable for exploratory analyses. Thus, all further data analysis reported here is based on this reduced scale.

Social Network Analysis: Network Distance and Network Density

Both social network distance and network density represent the cohesion, communication, and tightness of relationships among members of an organization. As improved collaboration technologies were introduced across HITLs, we expected that social network distance would decrease and network density increase. Traditional statistical models would not be appropriate for these SNA data, given the dyadic interactions measured in a nominal scale, and the expected low power of the effects in a naturalistic environment. However, as expected, the network density, that is, the number of links observed among team members divided by the number of possible links, increased over the three HITLs, indicating a possible effect of the collaboration technologies introduced. Specifically, density increased from 0.03 in HITL 1, to 0.04 in HITL 2, and to 0.05 in HITL 3. In general,

TABLE 10.3   Revised Internal Consistency Scores With Sample Size for the Team Attitudes Scale at All Six Administration Times

Time	HITL	Overall Scale α (N)	Concern With Failure α (N)	Concern With Analysis α (N)	Commitment to Success α (N)	Attention to Operations α (N)	Fluidity in DM α (N)
1	1	.94 (37)	.63 (8)	.84 (8)	.88 (5)	.76 (8)	.81 (8)
2	1	.92 (37)	.63 (8)	.82 (8)	.83 (5)	.67 (8)	.81 (8)
3	2	.95 (37)	.67 (8)	.83 (8)	.87 (5)	.82 (8)	.81 (8)
4	2	.95 (37)	.76 (8)	.83 (8)	.87 (5)	.77 (8)	.83 (8)
5	3	.95 (37)	.78 (8)	.85 (8)	.84 (5)	.73 (8)	.85 (8)
6	3	.94 (37)	.72 (8)	.76 (8)	.85 (5)	.69 (8)	.86 (8)

Note: α in bold are acceptable scores for internal consistency, as measured by Cronbach's alpha.

this team's network density is low when compared to the network density reported in other studies involving military organizations (e.g., 0.10 in Graham et al., 2007). However, the C2 organization investigated in the present study is *ad hoc*, and is also larger and more diverse than previous organizations studied. It is reasonable to posit that the challenges to communications in an *ad hoc* team would be even greater in a large, diverse, and distributed *ad hoc* team. So, although modest, the increase in density suggests an improved understanding and use of communication technologies across the HITLs.

Also as predicted, the social network distance of this organization decreased across HITLs, indicating that, on average, the shortest path length separating two people within the network decreased over time, and that any one individual needed to go through fewer nodes to communicate with others in the network. Social network distance decreased from 3.4 in HITL 1, to 3.3 in HITL 2, and to 3.1 in HITL 3. Again, in general, these values are low when compared to the social network distance values of previous studies (e.g., 5 in Graham et al., 2007). This decrease, nonetheless, suggests a better use and understanding of the technology across HITLs.

In addition to the quantitative findings presented here, qualitative analysis, reported in depth elsewhere (Cuevas, Caldwell, Strater, Gonzalez, & Ungvarsky, in preparation), revealed that the structure of the network changed over time. With the introduction of the improved collaboration technology, the personnel responsible for updating display information emerged as key nodes in the social network. Because the updating process could be accomplished without the direct team member-to-team member communications captured in the SNA questionnaire, this change indicates the importance of the information updating function and the relevance team members placed on accurate and timely updating. In addition, the network became less fragmented across HITLs, with more alternate routes for information flow. This is important, as busy personnel in key positions can hinder efficient information flow in a fragmented network. It is impossible to attribute this change to the collaboration technologies, as personnel also became more familiar with each other over time and may have developed information exchange strategies to ensure efficient information flow through the team.

Team Mindfulness and Situation Awareness

A correlational analysis was conducted to provide evidence for a relationship between the subjective team attitudes scale (TAS) and the objective SA audit measure. Because of changes in items for both the SA audit and the TAS from HITL 1 to HITL 2, these correlations were performed only for the data collected during HITL 2 (Times 3 and 4) and HITL 3 (Times 5 and 6). Due to the expected positive relationship between team attitudes and SA, all correlations are one-tailed. Overall, some support was found for a relationship between the TAS and SA audit data. Specifically, when correlating the scale subaggregates to overall SA performance, and performance at each SA level (i.e., Level 1, perception; Level 2, comprehension; and Level 3, projection), significant relationships were found across time.

Team Attitudes and SA at HITL 2 (Times 3 and 4)

The subaggregate "concern with failure" at Time 3 significantly correlated with overall SA ($r = .33$, $p = .01$), Level 2 SA ($r = .32$, $p = .01$), and Level 3 SA ($r = .27$, $p = .03$).

At Time 4, "concern with failure" was found to significantly correlate with Level 2 SA ($r = .283$, $p = .04$).

Team Attitudes and SA at HITL 3 (Times 5 and 6)

The subaggregate "concern with analysis" at Time 6 significantly correlated with overall SA ($r = .43$, $p < .01$), Level 1 SA ($r = .36$, $p < .01$), Level 2 SA ($r = .36$, $p < .01$), and Level 3 SA ($r = .32$, $p < .01$).

Team Attitudes Baseline as a Predictor of Future SA Performance

A further analysis was performed to look into the relationship between the first team attitudes scores and the final SA audit scores. This was an exploratory analysis to verify whether or not team attitudes expressed at the beginning of HITL 2, which can be regarded as a baseline assessment, can predict future performance on SA, as measured in Time 6 (HITL 3). The goal was to further establish the diagnosticity of team attitudes for predicting SA performance. Linear regression was performed using each baseline subaggregate (Time 3, HITL 2) as an independent variable, and each level of SA as well as overall SA as the dependent variables. Table 10.4 summarizes the findings, which indicate that all but one baseline subaggregate (commit to success) did predict overall SA at Time 6.

In sum, the team attitudes scale was demonstrated both to be reliable across time and to be valid to the extent that it shows a relationship with actual SA. However, because not all subaggregates consistently correlated with SA, work remains to be done to revise items to further increase the validity and reliability of the scale. Nevertheless, these results highlight the potential diagnostic utility of the team attitudes scale for predicting SA performance.

Implications for Expert Team Performance

As society's problems increase in complexity, *ad hoc* teams will emerge as a valuable organizational unit to engage for finding solutions. Gathering specialized domain expertise when needed most, these rapidly forming teams offer organizations an effective means of dealing with unanticipated and urgent problems (Engwall & Svensson, 2004). Such teams can support organizational productivity across a variety of domains, including military (e.g., military transition teams), healthcare (e.g., coordination of patient services among healthcare providers from varying disciplines), manufacturing (e.g., engineering design teams), and disaster response (e.g., multinational teams responding to disaster relief efforts), among others. Lessons learned from the investigation of *ad hoc* teams can provide insights into how traditional teams respond to emerging unforeseen events.

Researching *ad hoc* team processes in order to better support these teams through automation design and collaboration technology is a vital objective. While a number of collaborative tools exist (Bolstad & Endsley, 2005), few, if any, are focused around the unique needs of *ad hoc* teams, such as dealing with dynamic temporal timelines and changing membership. Lessons learned from our research on the challenges faced by *ad hoc* teams suggest several key design goals to keep in focus: (1) Provide *team SA devices* that facilitate the timely and effective exchange

TABLE 10.4 Linear Regressions Between Team Attitude Subaggregates as Predictors of Overall SA and Level of SA

Predictor	Overall SA				Level 1 SA				Level 2 SA				Level 3 SA			
	R^2	SEB	F	p	R^2	SEB	F	p	R^2	SEB	F	p	R^2	SEB	F	p
Concern with failure	**.17**	**.09**	**6.9**	**.01**	**.20**	**.17**	**8.8**	**.01**	**.11**	**.08**	**4.1**	**.05**	.28	.16	2.8	.10
Concern with analysis	**.11**	**.09**	**4.4**	**.04**	.10	.18	3.6	.07	.02	.09	0.6	.44	.07	.16	2.6	.12
Commit to success	.28	.09	2.8	.10	.01	.19	0.3	.58	.03	.09	1.1	.30	.02	.17	0.6	.43
Attention to operations	**.19**	**.56**	**7.8**	**.01**	**.22**	**.17**	**9.5**	**.01**	.03	.09	0.9	.35	.07	.16	2.5	.12
Fluidity in DM	**.15**	**.09**	**6.1**	**.02**	.04	.19	1.5	.22	.06	.09	2.3	.14	.04	.16	1.4	.25

Note: p-Values in bold are significant linear regressions (two-tail).

of critical task-relevant information among team members, and thus encourage improved *team SA processes*; (2) support *team SA mechanisms* by enabling members to develop a shared understanding of the task environment as well as each other's competencies; and (3) support the team leader's *SA requirements* by improving the ability to monitor and manage the activities of a diverse group of experts across time and space.

Achieving these design goals requires designing automation and collaboration technology that facilitates awareness of shared workspaces (Gutwin & Greenberg, 2004; Vick & McNamara, 2005), which in turn leads to improved team SA and shared SA. In addition, such technologies should support knowledge management and information flow to ensure that members have timely and ready access to the distributed expertise of their a*d hoc* team members (Caldwell, Palmer, & Cuevas, 2008).

Conclusions

This chapter presents preliminary work aimed at investigating the team processes within an *ad hoc* military C2 team with increasing levels of technology. Improvements in team SA processes with higher levels of technology were suggested by decreases in social network distance and increases in density across HITLs. While SA audit scores did not show improvement across HITLs, this may reflect a lack of motivation to accurately respond to the more challenging Level 2 SA queries. In addition, because of the nature of the experimental conditions, some of these queries may have been insufficiently relevant to study participants. Thus, the decline in SA audit scores may reflect an actual decline in SA, or it may reflect that participants were more adept in later HITLs at focusing only on the information relevant to their goals, objectives, and task demands. Additional analysis will investigate the data within varying team structures.

Finally, results from the new team attitudes scale indicate that the scale is consistently measuring a cognitive construct over time, while the correlation demonstrated between the scale and objective SA audit scores indicates that the cognitive construct measured is, indeed, related to situation awareness. These results also indicate that the team attitudes scale provides some diagnostic capability to predict objective SA. Although further research is needed to refine and validate this scale, these results provide promising support for the team attitude scale's potential benefit for investigations of team performance.

Overall, results from this study support the relationship between team SA mechanisms, team SA devices, team SA processes, and team SA requirements as presented in Endsley and Jones's (2001) framework of team SA. This framework may provide utility for guiding future NDM research in team operations.

Acknowledgments

The authors thank Michelle L. Tinsley for her editorial assistance on this paper. Work on this paper was partially supported by funding through participation in the Advanced Decision Architectures Collaborative Technology Alliance sponsored by the U.S. Army Research Laboratory (ARL) under Cooperative Agreement DAAD19-01-2-0009. The views and conclusions contained herein, however, are those of the authors and should not be interpreted as representing the official policies, either expressed or implied, of the ARL, U.S. Army, U.S. Department of Defense, U.S. government, or the organizations with which the authors are affiliated.

References

Bolstad, C. A., & Endsley, M. R. (2003). Measuring shared and team situation awareness in the Army's future objective force. In *Proceedings of the Human Factors and Ergonomics Society 47th Annual Meeting*. Santa Monica, CA: Human Factors and Ergonomics Society.

Bolstad, C. A., & Endsley, M. R. (2005). Choosing team collaboration tools: Lessons learned from disaster recovery efforts. *Ergonomics in Design, 13*(4), 7–14.

Bolstad, C. A., Riley, J. M., Jones, D. G., & Endsley, M. R. (2002). Using goal directed task analysis with Army brigade officer teams. In *Proceedings of the Human Factors and Ergonomics Society 46th Annual Meeting*. Santa Monica, CA: Human Factors and Ergonomics Society.

Borgatti, S. P. (1994). A quorum of graph theoretic concepts. *Connections, 17*(1), 47–49.

Caldwell, B. S. Palmer, III, R. C., & Cuevas, H. M. (2008). Information alignment and task coordination in organizations: An 'information clutch' metaphor. *Information Systems Management, 25*(1), 33–44.

Cuevas, H. M., Caldwell, B. S., Strater, L., Gonzalez, C., & Ungvarsky, D. M. (In preparation). *Exploring the boundaries of command and control models of distributed team performance.*

Endsley, M. R. (1995a). Measurement of situation awareness in dynamic systems. *Human Factors, 37*(1), 65–84.

Endsley, M. R. (1995b). Toward a theory of situation awareness in dynamic systems. *Human Factors 37*(1), 32–64.

Endsley, M. R., & Jones, W. M. (2001). A model of inter- and intrateam situation awareness: Implications for design, training and measurement. In M. McNeese, E. Salas, & M. Endsley (Eds.), *New trends in cooperative activities: Understanding system dynamics in complex environments* (pp. 46–67). Santa Monica, CA: Human Factors and Ergonomics Society.

Engwall, M., & Svensson, C. (2004). Cheetah teams in product development: The most extreme form of temporary organization? *Scandinavian Journal of Management, 20*(3), 297–317.

Freeman, L. C. (1979). Centrality in social networks: Conceptual clarification. *Social Networks, 1*, 215–239.

Graham, J., Gonzalez, C., & Schneider, M. (2007). A dynamic network analysis of an organization with expertise out of context. In R. Hoffman (Ed.), *Expertise out of context: Proceedings of the Sixth International Conference on Naturalistic Decision Making* (pp. 385–402). New York, NY: Lawrence Erlbaum Associates.

Gutwin, C., & Greenberg, S. (2004). The importance of awareness for team cognition in distributed collaboration. In E. Salas & S. M. Fiore (Eds.), *Team cognition: Understanding the factors that drive process and performance* (pp. 177–201). Washington, DC: American Psychological Association.

Langer, E. J., & Moldoveanu, M. (1989). The construct of mindfulness. *Journal of Social Issues, 56*(1), 1–9.

Scott, J., (1992). *Social network analysis*. Newbury Park, CA: Sage.

Strater, L. D., Endsley, M. R., Pleban, R. J., & Matthews, M. D. (2001). *Measures of platoon leader situation awareness in virtual decision making exercises* (Research Report 1770). Alexandria, VA: Army Research Institute.

Vick, R. M., & McNamara, J. E. (2005). *Shared cognition and resource coordination in distributed decision-making teams.* Paper presented at Proceedings of the 11th International Conference on Human-Computer Interaction, July 22–27, 2005, Las Vegas, NV.

Weick, K. E., & Sutcliffe, K. M. (2001). *Managing the unexpected: Assuring high performance in an age of complexity.* San Francisco, CA: Jossey-Bass.

Zsambok, C. E. (1997). Naturalistic decision making: Where are we now? In C. E. Zsambok & G. Klein (Eds.), *Naturalistic decision making* (pp. 3–16). Mahwah, NJ: Lawrence Erlbaum Associates.

11

Planning, Monitoring, and Trouble Shooting
Decision Making in Distributed Drilling Operations

Kristina Lauche
Radboud University Nijmegen

Petra Saskia Bayerl
Delft University of Technology

Ever since Hutchins (1995) proposed the concept of *distributed cognition*, researchers have used it to describe decision-making processes beyond a single human individual in diverse applied settings. Cognition is here seen as a phenomenon mediated via social interaction and technological artifacts that serve as tags or reminders for distributed knowledge. Pitched as "cognition in the wild," it shares the commitment of naturalistic decision-making researchers that to obtain an appropriate understanding of a complex phenomenon, decision making has to be studied as it occurs in the field context rather than be stripped of its complexities in controlled lab studies (Klein, Orasanu, Calderwood, & Zsambok, 1993; Klein et al., 2003). The approach has also inspired researchers working on computer-supported collaborative work to understand how people use their physical environment, including information technology, as external support for their cognitive processes. There is some debate between proponents of distributed cognition and proponents of activity theory whether cognition can reside in inanimate objects such as artifacts or information technology (Halverson, 2002; Nardi, 2002), yet both approaches emphasize that the unit of analysis should be the system level of the activity, including team interaction and artifacts. In our analysis of decision making in distributed teams, we take inspiration from these approaches to conceptualize distributed decision making as it occurs in practice, and to discuss how it can be supported by means of technology.

In this chapter we analyze decision making in different forms of computer-mediated settings in the context of remote operations in the oil and gas industry. Remotely monitored operations have increased over the last decade due to improved technological capabilities and more reliable networks for real-time data transfer. They can be found in a wide range of areas, such as transport management (Heath & Luff, 1992), expert medical advice (Johnsen, Breivik, Myrvang, & Olsen, 2006), aerospace exploration (Patterson, Watts-Perotti, & Woods, 1999), aviation (Fields, Amaldi, & Tassi, 2005), or the coordination of emergency response services (Artman & Waern, 1999; Petterson, Randall, & Helgeson, 2004). Potentially, working remotely can provide huge benefits: It reduces human exposure to risk in hazardous environments, it improves feedback and control over what happens in inaccessible locations, and it makes decision support more readily available without subject matter experts having to travel, which can lead to considerable savings in time and travel costs. However, remote operations also affect how teams interact and make decisions. So far, most research on this topic has been conducted in experimental settings or short-term contexts, while field studies in real work settings are still underrepresented. Yet, for a realistic understanding of processes in work contexts, it is important to observe them in their natural habitat, which is what this study has done for the oil and gas industry.

The authors of the previous sections have identified a number of situational characteristics that impact decision making and, to a large extent, also apply to distributed teams and remote operations. The situation is complex, ill structured, data rich, dynamic, and characterized by time pressure and high workload (Hutchins & Kendall, this volume). Like the medical team that Perry and Wears (this volume) researched, the work of distributed teams is typically carried out at a cooperative distance in that specialists are rarely engaged on the same object of work simultaneously, or in our case, not in the same location. As many actors and a multitude of companies are involved in remote operations, distributed teams also need to address multiplicity in terms of diverse goals and practices, although probably not to the extent that Osland (this volume) found for global leaders.

While there are similarities to other naturalistic decision-making research on an abstract level, most of the studies on teamwork involve collocated teams that rely on face-to-face interaction. In face-to-face settings coordination of processes, relationship building, or even more subtle aspects, such as recognizing stress in others, can be based on the observation of physiological and emotional cues, which is generally not possible in remote work arrangements. With the increasing importance of distributed settings the topic of virtual or distributed teams has received growing attention in recent years, but mostly in the form of controlled lab studies and over short time spans (mostly hours to a few weeks). As a recent review pointed out, the actual team processes of planning and monitoring as well as behavioral outcomes have not yet been studied in any depth (Martins, Gilson, & Maynard, 2004).

Many workplaces, and in particular remote operations, consist of a mixture of face-to-face interactions among collocated and computer-mediated interactions with remote team members. These teams tend to use a hybrid mix of communication technologies and artifacts, including physical documents and maps, email, phones, audio- or videoconferencing, and even radio. Their work environment is related to operations in which a central support facility integrates incoming information and coordinates subsequent actions of distributed teams (e.g., in aviation control, military operations, or police dispatchers). The pragmatic assumption usually is that individuals in the central support facility can maintain an overview of everything that is happening "out there," as they have "all the information" on their displays. The idea is that this kind of technological support should speed up decision making and make services more efficient to require fewer personnel.

Yet, decision making over distances also poses challenges that may not be easily remedied by better technology. As a meta-analysis by Baltes, Dickson, Sherman, Bauer, and LaGanke (2002) suggests, distributed teams tend to be less effective in decision-making tasks. They need more time to complete tasks and are less satisfied with the results than teams in face-to-face conditions. Team members working face-to-face were found to be better informed, more likely to make recommendations predictive of correct decisions, and to show higher confidence in their decisions than their distributed counterparts (Crede & Sniezek, 2003; Hedlung, Ilgen, & Hollenbeck, 1998).

The question therefore remains whether technology and accompanying organizational practices really enable "four eyes to see more than two" (Mark, Kobsa, & Gonzales, 2002) in the sense that team members develop sufficiently shared and accurate situation models (Cramton, 2002; Sole & Edmondson, 2002) to coordinate their activities across distance. Past research has raised some doubts about this. Alge, Wiethoff, and Klein (2003), for instance, demonstrated that restrictions in media capabilities negatively affected information sharing between team members. Also, the continuous separation of groups across different geographical locations may corrode identification with the greater unit, leading to different interests and goals (Fiol & O'Connor, 2005), and introduce faultlines between locations (Lau & Murnighan, 1998; Polzer, Crisp, Jarvenpaa, & Kim, 2006). The positive examples of distributed operations mentioned in workplace studies are characterized by two features: They typically involved an intricate mixture of experienced personnel who practiced specific strategies, such as listening in, and there were diverse media to support awareness and coordination (Artman & Wearn, 1999; Fields et al., 2005; Heath & Luff, 1992).

The specific effects of technological mediation and their interaction with organizational practices are so far underresearched in the NDM literature. The research questions guiding our investigation therefore were: (1) How does the interplay between technology and organizational practices influence decision making across distances? (2) Under what conditions do technology and organizational practices enable four eyes to see more than two?

Research Context

The domain of our research is the offshore oil and gas industry. The current study of decision making in drilling teams was part of a long-term research collaboration with a major globally operating company (Bayerl, Lauche, & Badke-Schaub, 2008; Lauche, 2008). The oil and gas industry has decades of experience with remote operations due to the nature of its task, as hydrocarbons are typically found in remote, hard-to-access locations on land or offshore. While personnel on site are responsible for the actual drilling and extraction of hydrocarbons, the office-based team plans, prepares, and supports the operation. The geographic distribution is therefore not the result of strategic business decisions such as outsourcing or cost reduction, but rather an inherent feature of the domain, comparable to the construction industry, the military, or space exploration. Distributed working is the only possible way to get the job done, and people rely on distributed decision making on a daily basis.

Traditionally, onshore and offshore locations had clearly defined roles and comparatively little direct contact. Direct face-to-face contact between subgroups was very rare, and then usually restricted to management. Discussions and exchange of information were conducted via email, phone, or audioconferencing. Planning decisions and problem solving were the tasks of specialists such as engineers, geologists, and petrophysicists, who would liaise with staff offshore about the implementation of plans and solutions as needed. Asymmetries between the onshore and offshore groups arising from their different responsibilities, task-specific knowledge, and expertise are reinforced through geographical distribution and limited contact and, over time, result in different subcultures (Bayerl & Lauche, 2008; O'Leary & Cummings, 2007).

Recent technological developments have facilitated faster and more powerful communication between offshore and onshore groups. Drilling data and video images can now be transmitted real time via fiber optic cable or satellite communication to the onshore support facility. Figure 11.1 shows a typical setup of drilling operations.

On the left-hand side, typical offshore functions are depicted that involve manual handling and supervision at the sharp end (driller, tool pusher, shaker hand, drilling supervisor). These individuals are kept informed by drilling support staff (such as directional drillers or measurement engineers) and well site geologists–shown in the middle of the diagram to indicate that they can be located either offshore or in onshore support centers. Their task is to continuously monitor drilling operations and to alert and advise their colleagues both onshore and offshore about problems and required adjustments. Typical onshore functions shown on the right-hand side include managerial staff such as the drilling superintendent, and specialist experts such as geologists or well engineers. The dotted line represents the data transmission from downhole to servers, as well as cameras offshore and onshore.

While the drilling itself is controlled offshore, the sensor and logging technology can be manipulated remotely to change settings and to diagnose problems. This technical development has enabled companies to drill more effectively into oil reserves that are increasingly smaller and more difficult to access. But at the same time, it also has created new challenges as to who should make what kinds of decisions. The

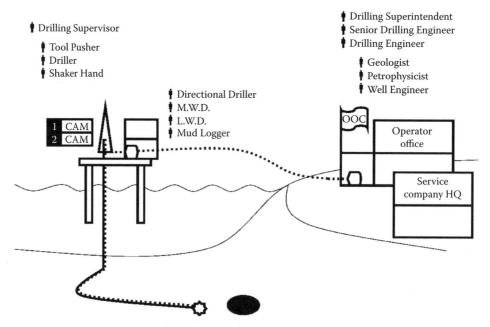

FIGURE 11.1   Hybrid team setting offshore, in support facility, and onshore.

objectives of the present study therefore were to investigate current practices of distributed decision making in drilling operations and, where necessary, to recommend different practices.

Typology of Decision Making in Remote Operations

Based on our ongoing research, we identified three main aspects of team decision making in remote operations: planning, monitoring, and trouble shooting (cf. Bayerl & Lauche, 2008).

Planning refers to proactive decisions on where and how to drill, and determines the length and costs of drilling projects. Planning activities also concern the logistics of materials, technology, and personnel to be transported on and off the platform. Planning is traditionally the responsibility of onshore staff with occasional inputs for fine-tuning and reality checks from offshore staff (see Figure 11.2).

Monitoring refers to overseeing drilling operations using sensor technology and software to visualize their progress. Its goals are (1) to ensure operations are carried out according to plan, (2) to identify and diagnose deviations, and (3) to prevent potential hazardous events. Monitoring used to be carried out by support staff offshore since they had direct access to equipment and could take immediate actions, but is now increasingly being moved onshore. Monitoring constitutes a fast feedback loop that feeds into the slower, more strategic decision making of planning activities (see Figure 11.3).

Trouble shooting refers to the management of unexpected events, such as sudden influx of gas, unpredicted geological formations, or equipment failure. These situations typically require close collaboration between experts onshore and offshore for adequate situation awareness and pooling of expertise. As direct observation of the borehole is not possible, the situation has to be inferred from sensor data, such as pressure, temperature, or torque. If the data indicate a problem, the situation is not at all clear. The irregularity may be the result of sensor failure or of transmission problems, or it may indeed represent a real issue. Information about the situation is compared against geological models and expert knowledge of the area and equipment behavior (see Figure 11.4). As in many domains, most unexpected events are also dynamically changing and time critical: One cannot leave a drilling rig idle and ponder the options—the pipe can get stuck, an influx of gas or water could hinder further

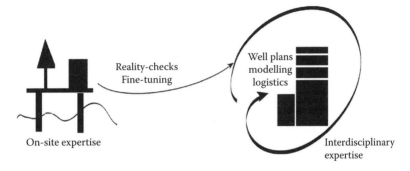

Reality-checks
Fine-tuning

Well plans
modelling
logistics

On-site expertise

Interdisciplinary
expertise

FIGURE 11.2   Planning activities.

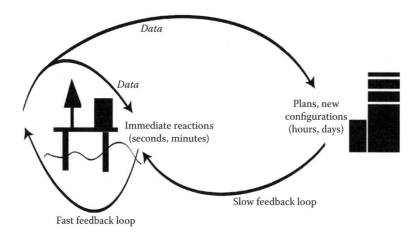

FIGURE 11.3   Monitoring activities.

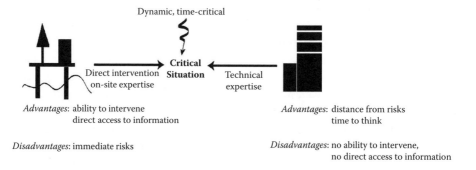

FIGURE 11.4   Trouble-shooting activities.

operations, gas leaks can be potentially hazardous to plant, personnel, and environment, and last but not least, a drilling rig sitting idle is extremely costly. Trouble shooting therefore requires similar skills to those identified for incident management teams in the oil and gas industry, that is, information gathering, projection, problem diagnosis, option generation, risk assessment, response selection, and outcome review, as well as teamwork and leadership skills to communicate and implement decisions (Crichton, Lauche, & Flin, 2005).

These three activities constitute a spectrum of decisions, from tactical decision making (planning) to operational decisions (monitoring) to trouble shooting, as the collective management of unexpected and potentially adverse events. As we will demonstrate in the remainder of this chapter, distributed settings pose specific challenges for these different aspects of team decision making.

Methods

Participants

The sample was drawn from four settings that exemplify different approaches to implementing onshore support centers. They will be briefly described in terms of two dimensions: a sociotechnical versus technical approach, and vertical versus horizontal integration (cf. Lauche, 2008). A sociotechnical approach conceives of the technical possibilities of real-time monitoring as an opportunity to rethink and innovate work processes in terms of a joint optimization of social and technical systems, with the aim to establish a more collaborative and cross-disciplinary way of working. A purely technical approach, in contrast, means that remote monitoring capabilities are installed without fundamentally changing the organization. Limitations such as time and budget constraints or lack of infrastructure on older rigs are taken as a given, rather than seen as a sign that larger investments are needed for bigger gains. Vertical integration refers to cross-disciplinary collaboration of onshore and offshore staff on a given drilling project, while horizontal integration refers to the pooling of expertise across several drilling operations. Figure 11.5 depicts the four possible settings along the described dimensions.

Sample and Data Collection

The data for the present analysis stem from observations of planning, monitoring, and troubleshooting activities in three different settings, the technology-based approach, integrated operations, and the low-cost pilot. These were complemented by 43 semistructured interviews of drilling personnel about the nature of their task, the job design (task variety, process control, time flexibility, physical activity, need for cooperation), and the impact of technology on work practices (Lauche, 2006, 2008). An overview of the settings and the type of data collected for each activity is given in Table 11.1.

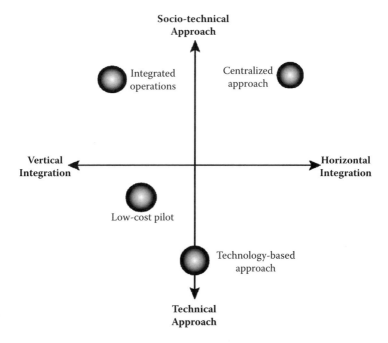

FIGURE 11.5   Different approaches to implementation of onshore support centers.

TABLE 11.1   Overview of the Sample and Settings

Type of Activity	Setting	Data Collected
Planning	Technology-based approach	30 hours of observations (three teams)
Monitoring	Integrated operations	5:48 hours observation
		Interviews with 5 onshore, 3 offshore, and 8 support center staff
	Low-cost pilot	8:11 hours observation
		11 morning meetings (2:35 hours)
		Interviews with 11 onshore, 10 offshore, and 6 support center staff
Trouble shooting	All settings	Five episodes (illustrative of a larger pool of observations)

For *planning* activities, we observed a total of 30 hours in three drilling teams ($n = 24$) onshore. The situations comprised morning calls, normal work situations, and production-critical events. The observations were coded by the second author according to forms, location and means of coordination, and topic (see coding scheme in Table 11.2). For the purposes of this chapter, the preliminary results from one team (approximately 15 hours of observation) are reported.

Monitoring activities in two teams in two onshore support centers during shift handovers, normal shift work, and unplanned problem solving were observed by the first author. Observations were recorded as field notes; action categories were recorded using an online coding system on a handheld PC (Held & Manser, 2005). The categories conceptualized the task as a question of supervisory control of a complex system (Sheridan, 1992), and distinguished between the following activities: communicating, documenting, proactive intervention, monitoring, response to person, response to system, and giving instructions.

Trouble-shooting behavior was noted during our observations of planning and monitoring activities whenever teams had to deal with unexpected events. Unexpected events are by their very nature something one cannot plan for; rather, one only happens upon them, and as in most industries, they occur only infrequently. Our observations of trouble-shooting activities were thus fortuitous events taking place during the time we spent with the different teams. Both authors took field notes during their observations and collected several examples of trouble shooting over the course of four years across the four different settings. Five of these examples were chosen for the present discussion to illustrate team processes during unexpected events.

Results

Planning

Planning decisions were observed in a setting we characterized as technology based because advanced visualization and data sharing tools had been implemented, but roles and functions remained traditionally distributed. Real-time updates of drilling data were presented on flat screens in the onshore support center to facilitate

TABLE 11.2   Coding System

Category	Codes
Forms of coordination	Explicit—collective/group level (e.g., planned or *ad hoc* meetings)
	Explicit—individual level (e.g., face-to-face calls)
	Implicit—collective/group level (e.g., data, shared access to information, reports, and documents)
	Implicit—point to point (e.g., copresence, always-on VC)
Location of coordination	Whole group (onshore and offshore)
	Onshore only
	Offshore only
	External (e.g., contractors, vendors)
Media for coordination	Email, phone, fax, audioconferencing, video-conferencing, face-to-face, documents and pictures, planning and tracking systems, procedures and existing standards
Topic of communication	Open category (e.g., material, equipment, logistics, weather)

coordination during normal operations. Apart from this, onshore and offshore staff continued to communicate using phone, email, and audioconferencing.

In all three teams, planning was treated as a clear onshore task with little involvement from offshore staff. Planning of wells is a long-term activity that can take months or years, depending on the complexity of the field. It comprises a section-by-section plan detailing equipment, personnel, timelines, and responsibilities, as well as risk assessments and action plans for each offshore function. This degree of prescriptive detail arises from the logistic complications of offshore work, where unavailability of resources can render the operation economically unviable. Due to the complexity of the planning process, multiple onshore functions (drilling, completion, geophysics) were involved for the different aspects of the plan, such as the modeling of the (likely) geography, modeling of the best drilling trajectory, required equipment, assembly of the completion string, and so forth.

Decision making in planning, apparently, was not so much affected by geographical distribution, but instead by the quality of cooperation across onshore functions. Most interactions during planning took place between onshore disciplines, while offshore staff were only marginally involved (see Table 11.3).

The majority of observed planning interactions occurred in dyads belonging to the same onshore team; interactions with members of other teams or with third parties were less frequent. The different onshore disciplines mostly discussed questions face-to-face, followed by phone and email exchange.[*] Details on equipment (costs, size, specifications) were requested by phone from vendors to be put in the plan. A number of group meetings were scheduled on a regular basis, such as daily morning calls, weekly team meetings, or biweekly planning, health, and safety meetings, with offshore participation in the morning calls and planning meetings. The outcome of the planning process—the drilling plan—was distributed to all individuals involved in the drilling project to be reviewed and signed off in a joint session between onshore staff, offshore staff, and vendors. As a last stage, so-called drilling-on-paper exercises

---

[*] As only parts of the team's coordination were observed, the category "forms of coordination" was not systematically used for analysis.

TABLE 11.3   Results of Observations on Planning

Category	Observed Frequencies	
Forms of coordination	No frequencies were calculated, as only random sections of team interactions were observed	
Location of coordination	1.12%	Whole team (onshore-offshore)
	66.90%	Within onshore group of the team
	19.01%	Onshore subgroup with individuals outside the team
	12.97%	Onshore subgroup with third parties outside company
	—	Offshore only: not observed due to lacking access to offshore location
Media for coordination	58.64%	Face-to-face
	34.03%	Phone
	7.33%	Documents (also in combination with face-to-face and phone)
	—	Email: no frequencies as only partly observable

were conducted to test the plan. Here, onshore and offshore jointly went through each stage of the process and discussed potential risks and contingencies.

A critical point in the planning process is reached when the plan is transferred to offshore for execution. Generally, both onshore and offshore operations can rely on highly trained individuals with many years of experience, as drilling projects in the same field are often executed by the same people. However, as the following example shows, the translation of the plan by offshore staff was not always without problems, even with detailed planning:

Example 1: Traditional Setting

Running a standard procedure to test the middle part of a newly installed completion string, offshore personnel reported unexpected and unusual results. A joint audioconference between onshore and offshore staff was conducted to investigate possible reasons for the unexpected results. The analysis found that offshore staff had misunderstood the design of the completion string and therefore tested the equipment in an inappropriate manner—resulting in potential damage to the equipment.

Overall, planning decisions in drilling were driven by onshore staff and required little onshore-offshore coordination, but instead relied on considerable cross-functional integration (see Figure 11.2). As the result of a concerted corporate effort to establish a so-called common process across all drilling projects, planning followed a highly standardized procedure with little variation in the overall steps. Coordination between onshore functions or between onshore and offshore staff was mostly conducted explicitly and on an individual basis to obtain missing details. As far as observable, implicit forms of coordination were less frequent and consisted mostly in consultation of documentation and the exchange of drafts for drilling plans. Explicit coordination on a group level took place to confirm information on a draft design, or to clarify or sign-off on important steps.

The main challenge associated with distributing work between onshore and offshore subgroups concerns their shared understanding of task-critical information, as

Example 1 demonstrates. While extensive experience in working with each other on the same oil field may facilitate communication, the near complete separation of planning and execution, together with different practices of describing and presenting information, could lead to potentially severe as well as costly problems, especially in complex, nonstandard situations. In the teams we observed, contact between onshore and offshore staff during planning was restricted to the management levels. Plans thus had to be translated twice—once from onshore to offshore staff, and then again from offshore management to their technicians. Integrating these separate layers during earlier stages of the planning process should help reduce the potential for misunderstandings.

Monitoring

Monitoring activities included operational decisions, such as watching geological and engineering data for possible deviations, responding to alarms, and deciding whether a signal represents a normal deviation or a trend that requires intervention. Monitoring thus constituted a link between the planning process where drilling operations were prepared on a project level, and the execution and adaptation of these plans on the operational level at the drill floor (see Figure 11.4).

Monitoring has traditionally been an offshore task; however, with the advent of real-time data transfer, some monitoring responsibilities have been transferred to onshore support centers. Engineers there can access the same data insofar as it is captured electronically, but they no longer physically experience the vibrations of the rig, the smells, and the touch and feel of geological samples.

The two settings for our observations comprised one team operating in a sophisticated high-tech center that supported a newly built rig offshore with substantial sensor technology; the other team worked in a low-cost pilot version of such a center supporting an older rig from a distance in order to free up bed space on the rig. In both settings, personnel performed supervisory control of the monitoring systems and engaged in proactive interventions to prepare for the following drilling task, and briefed their colleagues on the expected geology and required drilling process. The handovers among support staff were detailed and collegiate and included an extensive briefing about operations and equipment.

Media-related codes indicate that a PC was used in 41%, phone or radio in 20%, and paper in 39% of all communications. PCs were used not only for email but also in documentation and calculations; hand-written notes functioned partly as external memory to aid the preparation of instructions, and partly as a handover record in a logbook for the next shift. While a physical logbook can be a very effective means of communication for collocated handovers, its content needs to be captured digitally to share with team members or colleagues who work on similar wells in other locations.

Given that the task had been labeled as monitoring in job descriptions and interviews, we expected to find personnel interacting with technology in a form of supervisory control. We were thus taken by surprise at the high prevalence of communication in monitoring activities, which by far outnumbered other behaviors (see Table 11.4). This finding suggests that support staff not only were the "eyes and ears of the rig," as one interviewee put it, but also maintained the lines of communication between different actors offshore and onshore, beyond what the job description stated.

TABLE 11.4   Frequency of Activities in Monitoring

Communicating	46.4%
Documenting	7.6%
Proactive intervention	11.2%
Monitoring	23.5%
Response to person	5.7%
Response to system	3.2%
Giving instructions	2.3%

In summary, monitoring decisions were accomplished reasonably well and effectively across distance with the help of real-time data, albeit with an increase in communication to clarify and reconfirm. Our finding that communication plays a crucial role in monitoring resonates with results from workplace studies of coordination centers in transport management and emergency response (Fields et al., 2005; Heath & Luff, 1992; Petterson et al., 2004). There, operators wore headphones over one ear only because the headphone design prevented them from listening to colleagues who worked next to them (Heath & Luff, 1992). In the low-cost pilot setting of our study, phones were not equipped with headsets, and sound isolation at the rig site was problematic. These conditions caused personnel to strain their necks while jamming a handset, or led to desperate attempts to hide from surrounding office noise by hovering under a table to transmit instructions. These ergonomic factors were addressed in the integrated operations setting, but the underestimation of the importance of communication is likely to remain an issue in the drive to automate monitoring.

Trouble Shooting

Unlike planning and monitoring, trouble shooting was found to be an activity that required equal input from onshore and offshore during problem diagnosis and solution generation. One basic problem with distributed working is that while offshore staff members are able to detect and react to unexpected events, they often lack the engineering expertise to solve complex problems. Onshore staff, on the other hand, do not necessarily have all the relevant information to evaluate the situation. In the traditional setting with clear onshore-offshore separation and restricted media, generating ideas and alternatives was thus frequently hampered by the lack of a common understanding of the situation, but also by the different priorities of onshore and offshore functions (see Figure 11.4).

In many cases, a first solution was developed by onshore staff and afterwards discussed with offshore personnel to check feasibility and details. This was often a lengthy process, as procedural details had to be explained over the phone or via audioconferencing, and clarifying pictures or drawings needed to be sent by email. The continuation of the problem described in Example 1 demonstrates that this process could be problematic:

Example 1: Traditional Setting (*continued*)

Because it was unclear whether the equipment had been damaged during the faulty testing, a discussion took place within the onshore team to devise a plan to proceed with equipment tests to ensure that the equipment was still in good condition. During the discussion, onshore staff identified crucial elements of the equipment in a hand drawing, generally referenced as A, B, and C. In an audioconference, offshore staff were then informed of the results of this discussion and the action plan was explained step by step. Onshore staff repeatedly referred to the drawing on the board in their explanation using A, B, and C as terms for specific sections in the completion string. Since offshore staff had not been part of the previous discussion, nor did they have access to the drawing itself, several misunderstandings occurred during the conversation concerning the exact targets of individual actions.

The technical setting we studied aimed to overcome these problems by providing videoconferencing to facilitate communication between onshore and offshore personnel, in particular to enable onshore access to real-time data on big flat screens. The added media capabilities made it easier for the groups to develop a common understanding of the situation, and helped onshore staff to stay informed of the progress.

Example 2: Technology-Based Setting

Four-fifths down the hole, the drill pipe got stuck and could not be removed from the hole. Circulation, however, was possible, so that the hole did not collapse. It was therefore assumed that a physical obstruction from the surrounding rock might be the cause for the stuck pipe. The priority of onshore staff was to resolve the problem as quickly as possible, as the weather was forecasted to get worse. Possible actions were discussed with offshore staff during the morning call. As offshore staff worked on the solution, onshore staff monitored the progress on flat screens showing real-time drilling parameters, such as depth, drag, and torque, and adapted their solution accordingly.

While detailed information about drilling parameters did improve situational awareness for onshore staff, our observations made clear that the effect was somewhat restricted in scope. As they were not familiar with the type of information displayed, subsurface or completion engineers were not able to read and interpret the data, and thus had to ask drilling engineers for clarification. Obviously, they had not received training to familiarize themselves with the displays. This problem was resolved by relocating skilled offshore personnel into the office who were tasked to monitor incoming real-time information and alert onshore as well as offshore staff to possible deviations (centralized approach).

Nonetheless, we observed several episodes that indicated challenges in trouble shooting in the centralized approach. The most critical incidents were due to unclear responsibilities between offshore personnel located in the office and offshore personnel on the rig (see Example 3), conflicts in responsibilities and conflicting tasks (see Example 4), or diffusion of responsibility, or the bystander effect, that is, the reluctance to take action in the presence of many others who might also be expected to act (Darley & Latané, 1968; see Example 5).

Example 3: Centralized Approach

The drilling optimization engineer in the central facility noticed a deviation in the drill drag chart, which pointed to a stuck pipe. To free the pipe, offshore staff ran the drill pipe in and out and continued drilling. The recorded measurements from the original model subsequently showed a deviation of the drag parameters. It was unclear what caused this aberration, and different options were discussed between the drilling optimization engineer and his supervisor onshore. One option was to contact the rig and ask them whether they had noticed anything unusual. The supervisor assumed that contact was not necessary, as offshore staff should have an expert onboard monitoring this situation and thus should already be aware of it. The drilling optimization engineer, in contrast, argued that offshore staff most probably did not have an expert onboard because the rig had been pushed to reduce head count. The supervisor then asked the drilling optimization engineer to send an email message to the rig. The rig ignored this message and no further action was taken.

Example 4: Centralized Approach

During drilling operations the well experienced a sudden severe water influx. The operator in the central facility responsible for monitoring the drilling process and for alerting the offshore drilling team in case of potential problems did not detect the onset of this event. Instead of monitoring, he was trying to solve an unrelated data entry issue for another well that was also monitored by the central support facility in parallel to the first well. Consequently, during the two hours the operator was busy with solving the data problem, the first well was not monitored and the deviation in the parameters not detected. The water influx resulted in the near loss of the well and was associated with considerable time and financial costs. The data entry is not traditionally part of the operator's normal job; instead, he is responsible for monitoring the well parameters. However, because the operator had been moved from offshore to the central support facility onshore, he was expected to monitor more than one well, and complete additional tasks outside his traditional work responsibilities and routines.

The last episode illustrates diffusion of responsibility in the integrated operations setting, which was otherwise well designed for collaboration using always-on video-conferencing and a shared interactive whiteboard. Next to the onshore support center and visible through glass doors was a dedicated meeting room. Here the onshore team could keep an eye on data and video displays during meetings with the offshore team, enabling them to resolve misunderstandings. The video link also discouraged unproductive behavior in meetings, such as parallel conversations or dismissive non-verbal comments that had occurred in other teams. Most team members actively participated in the meetings and problems were mostly discussed right then and there. However, this high degree of participation could also delay decision making, as the following example shows.

Example 5: Integrated Operations

During the morning meeting, the offshore team reported high pressure no one had ever seen before in this area. The problem was not easy to diagnose, and it was first decided to close the well and observe. What would have previously been an offshore problem now became the business of the project leader and senior engineers onshore. They called in all the experts they could muster, such as an experienced driller who knew the geology like the back of his hand, and vendor staff to provide advice on how to replace a tool temporarily so that it could be checked. Over the course of the entire day, onshore staff developed a diagnosis and discussed options. Senior staff were still around when the night shift arrived; nobody had yet made any decision or initiated action. They linked up with the offshore team, who also had spent the day working on a solution, albeit a different one. During the many hours of parallel discussions, the teams could have seen each other on the video screens but seemed completely oblivious of their counterparts. While the technical setup enabled them to deal with challenges that previously had been seen as technically impossible, some team members complained that the habit of always calling in more and more people had led to a very ineffective way of working. Decisions took much longer, and it was no longer clear who was supposed to make them. Team members were possibly falling prey to diffusion of responsibility, which is likely to occur in larger groups with many people qualified to provide input.

In summary, our observations suggest that trouble shooting is most adversely affected by the spatial separation of subgroups, especially in situations that require the on-site expertise of offshore staff as much as the technical expertise located onshore. The dynamic nature of critical situations and their potential for human and financial loss make it paramount that team members reach an adequate understanding of the problem and devise correct solutions. These prerequisites are impeded in distributed teams as members in spatially separated teams do not have access to the same information, and thus face considerable difficulty in distributing in-depth information. Examples 3 to 5 demonstrate that while the implementation of advanced technologies can alleviate these problems, technology alone will not solve them. Facilitating the distribution of information is not sufficient to establish the appropriate team behaviors to utilize this information as a basis for shared situation awareness and collaborative decision making.

Discussion and Conclusions

In this study we addressed decision making in distributed teams in the offshore drilling industry; in particular, we examined the question whether providing onshore teams with access to real-time data facilitates remote support of offshore teams. Our findings suggests that four eyes indeed can see more than two, provided that technological systems support adequate situation awareness, team members are trained in their effective use and know how to interpret the information they display, and onshore and offshore team members' roles and responsibilities are clarified. Given the remoteness of offshore drilling, the industry has long-standing experience and established practices in computer-mediated and distributed work, which has been quite successful in ensuring that the spatial separation of teams does not lead to a breakdown in communication and coordination. Still, our results clearly demonstrate challenges for the effectiveness and quality of decision making by onshore and offshore teams.

Our findings point to different aspects of decision making in spatially distributed teams that involve different thought processes and may need specific tools and practices to support them. Planning as a form of strategic and tactical decision making requires projection and anticipation of possible consequences, as well as coordination among team members. It is currently a matter of cross-functional discussions in the onshore team with dyadic consultations and input from vendors. This process could be aided by visualization tools that illustrate the geological situation and enable the simulation of a proposed drilling plan. Such tools are currently being developed and tested and seem particularly apt to provide a common language, as geologists and drilling engineers traditionally use different forms of visualizations and normally cannot read each other's diagrams. The integration of the two visual languages in a single software tool was welcomed in one of the projects; however, as there are many different software systems in use, the industry is far from a standard solution. Another important caveat is that these tools need to be treated as aids, and not as substitutes for critical thinking. Ideally, their use should be guided by someone with technical and facilitator experience who can probe *what if* questions and make the team aware of the limitations of any given tool.

In current practice, planning decisions are characterized by a rather Tayloristic division of labor, with thinking being done onshore and doing carried out by offshore staff. While this is partly necessitated by the logistic challenges of offshore work, it might be worth considering giving offshore staff a higher stake in planning decisions. Research in other industries has generally shown that while planning can mitigate the impact of variations and unexpected events, it cannot eliminate them. Instead, a higher degree of operator control was found to create more resilient and flexible systems (Hollnagel, Woods, & Leveson, 2006; Norros, 2004; Patterson, West, & Wall, 2004). As communication across spatial distance gets easier, offshore staff could partake more in the planning process.

Operational decisions involved in monitoring can in principle be assisted from onshore support centers, provided that the technology is designed appropriately to enable shared situation awareness and communication among distributed team members. The main issue seems to be that time and budget constraints, as well as the infrastructure on older rigs, often lead to a limited investment in technology rather than to a sociotechnical approach. A low-cost approach to monitoring, however, may create suboptimal working conditions for those in the onshore support centers, rendering remote monitoring less reliable and effective.

Normal monitoring situations can turn into trouble shooting when potentially hazardous events arise that require the involvement of additional expertise. The instances of trouble shooting we were able to observe indicate that teams struggle with the transition from normal to abnormal situations, and that technological support systems are not put to their best use. As the integrated operations example shows, one solution may be to make real-time data and video feed from the onshore support centers available to the onshore engineers. However, engineers think in drawings, and as long as these are not shared, misunderstandings are likely to occur. Consequently, the problem diagnosis should not only be based on visualization of data, but also be facilitated by a shared digital drawing tool or interactive whiteboard that enables team members to sketch what they think is happening.

While trouble shooting by definition concerns unexpected events, technology can also be used to prepare and train for such situations. In a set of pilot interventions, we adapted the concept of tactical decision games to create scenarios for drilling teams to be enacted in an onshore support center (Lauche, Crichton, & Bayerl, 2009). With the help of drilling and technology experts, a previous case was recreated with sample data and a description of the challenge. Members of existing teams worked through the scenario in two video-linked locations. The experience so far indicates that these facilitated exercises helped team members to familiarize themselves with the new technology and to explore a challenging situation in a fail-safe environment.

We are aware that the data presented in this chapter rely on a small sample in a particular industry. However, we believe that both the typology of team decision making and the challenges that we identified could be generalized to other domains in which remote operations play a key role. Comparative research could further substantiate our findings. We hope to have shown that changing the unit of analysis in decision making from individual cognition to the level of the activity system, including team interaction and artifacts such as media and communication technology, is a promising approach.

Acknowledgments

This research was funded by BP plc, and their support is gratefully acknowledged. Thanks are also due to all participants who agreed to take part in this study, to Steve Sawaryn for his continued support, and to the editors and an anonymous reviewer for constructive comments.

References

Alge, B. J., Wiethoff, C., & Klein, H. J. (2003). When does the medium matter? Knowledge-building experiences and opportunities in decision-making teams. *Organizational Behavior and Human Decision Processes, 91,* 26–37.

Artman, H., & Waern, Y. (1999). Distributed cognition in an emergency co-ordination centre. *Cognition, Technology and Work, 1*(4), 237–246.

Baltes, B., Dickson, M., Sherman, M., Bauer, C., & LaGanke, J. (2002). Computer-mediated communication and group decision making: A meta-analysis. *Organizational Behavior and Human Decision Processes, 87*(1), 156–179.

Bayerl, P. S., & Lauche, K. (2008). Coordinating high-interdependency tasks in asymmetric distributed teams. In *Proceedings of the ACM 2008 Conference on Computer Supported Cooperative Work* (pp. 417–426). New York, NY: ACM.

Bayerl, P. S., Lauche, K., & Badke-Schaub, P. (2008). Collaborative environments for distributed teams: Comparing effects of different concepts. In *Proceedings of the Human Factors and Ergonomics Society 52nd Annual Meeting 2008* (pp. 1140–1144). Santa Monica, CA: Human Factors and Ergonomics Society.

Cramton, C. (2002). Finding common ground in dispersed collaboration. *Organizational Dynamics, 30*(4), 356–367.

Crede, M., & Sniezek, J. A. (2003). Group judgment processes and outcomes in video-conferencing versus face-to-face groups. *International Journal of Human-Computer Studies, 59*, 875–897.

Crichton, M., Lauche, K., & Flin, R. (2005). Incident command skills in the management of an oil industry drilling incident: A case study. *Journal of Contingencies and Crisis Management, 13*(3), 116–128.

Darley, J. M., & Latané, B. (1968). Bystander intervention in emergencies: Diffusion of responsibility. *Journal of Personality and Social Psychology, 8*(4), 377–383.

Fields, B., Amaldi, P., & Tassi, A. (2005). Representing collaborative work: The airport as common information space. *Cognition, Technology and Work, 7*(1), 119–133.

Fiol, C., & O'Connor, E. (2005). Identification in face-to-face, hybrid, and pure virtual teams: Untangling the contradictions. *Organization Science, 16*(1), 19–32.

Halverson, C. A. (2002). Activity theory and distributed cognition: Or what does CSCW need to DO with theories? *Computer Supported Cooperative Work, 11*(1–2), 243–267.

Heath, C., & Luff, P. (1992). Collaboration and control: Crisis management and multimedia technology in London underground control rooms. *Computer Supported Cooperative Work, 1*(1–2), 69–94.

Hedlund, J., Ilgen, D. R., & Hollenbeck, J. R. (1998). Decision accuracy in computer-mediated versus face-to-face decision-making teams. *Organizational Behavior and Human Decision Processes, 76*(1), 30–47.

Held, J., & Manser, T. (2005). A PDA-based system for online recording and analysis of concurrent events in complex behavioral processes. *Behavior Research Methods, 37*(1), 155–164.

Hollnagel, E., Woods, D. D., & Leveson, N. (2006). *Resilience engineering: Concepts and precepts*. Aldershot, UK: Ashgate.

Hutchins, E. (1995). *Cognition in the wild*. Cambridge, MA: MIT Press.

Johnsen, E., Breivik, E., Myrvang, R., & Olsen, F. (2006). *Benefits from telemedicine in Norway—An examination of available documentation* (Høykom Report 2006:1). Tromsø, Norway: Norwegian Centre for Telemedicine.

Klein, G., Orasanu, J., Calderwood, R., & Zsambok, C. (1993). *Decision making in action: Models and methods*. Norwood, NJ: Ablex Publishing.

Klein, G., Ross, K. G., Moon, B. M., Klein, D. E., Hoffman, R. R., & Hollnagel, E. (2003). Macrocognition. *IEEE Intelligent Systems, 18*(3), 81–85.

Lau, D., & Murnighan, J. (1998). Demographic diversity and faultlines: The compositional dynamics of organizational groups. *Academy of Management Review, 23*(2), 325–340.

Lauche, K. (2006). Job design for remote collaboration in drilling operations. *Proceedings of the 50th Annual Meeting of Ergonomics and Human Factors Society* (pp. 2497–2501). Santa Monica, CA: Human Factors and Ergonomics Society.

Lauche, K. (2008). Overcoming remoteness: Human factors assessment of real-time monitoring and support in drilling operations. *International Journal of Technology and Human Interaction, 4*(1), 94–112.

Lauche, K., Crichton, M. & Bayerl, P. S. (2009). Tactical decision games: Developing scenario-based training for decision-making in distributed teams. *Proceedings of the 9th International Conference on Naturalistic Decision Making* (pp. 227–234). London, UK: British Computer Society.

Mark, G., Kobsa, A., & Gonzales, V. (2002). Do four eyes see better than two? Collaborative versus individual discovery in data visualization systems. *Proceedings of 6th International Conference on Information Visualization* (pp. 249–255). Los Alamos, CA: IEEE Computer Society.

Martins, L., Gilson, L., & Maynard, M. (2004). Virtual teams: What do we know and where do we go from here? *Journal of Management, 30*(6), 805–835.

Nardi, B. A. (2002). Coda and response to Christine Halverson. *Computer Supported Cooperative Work, 11*(1–2), 269–275.

Norros, L. (2004). *Acting under uncertainty: The core-task analysis in ecological study of work.* Helsinki, Finland: VTT Press.

O'Leary, M. B., & Cummings, J. (2007). The spatial, temporal and configurational characteristics of geographic dispersion in teams. *Management of Information Systems Quarterly, 31*(3), 433–452.

Olson, G. M., & Olson, J. S. (2000). Distance matters. *Human-Computer Interaction, 15*(1), 139–178.

Patterson, E. S., Watts-Perotti, J., & Woods, D. D. (1999). Voice loops as coordination aids in space shuttle mission control. *Computer Supported Cooperative Work, 8*(4), 353–371.

Patterson, M. G., West, M. A., & Wall, T. D. (2004). Integrated manufacturing, empowerment, and company performance. *Journal of Organizational Behavior, 25*(5), 641–665.

Petterson, M., Randall, D., & Helgeson, B. (2004). Ambiguities, awareness and economy: A study of emergency service work. *Computer Supported Cooperative Work, 13*, 125–154.

Polzer, J., Crisp, C., Jarvenpaa, S., & Kim, J. (2006). Extending the faultline model to geographically dispersed teams: How collocated subgroups can impair group functioning. *Academy of Management Journal, 49*(4), 679–692.

Sheridan, T. B. (1992). *Telerobotics, automation, and human supervisory control.* Cambridge, MA: MIT Press.

Sole, D., & Edmondson, A. (2002). Situated knowledge and learning in dispersed teams. *British Journal of Management, 13*, 17–34.

12

Expertise in the Submarine Domain
The Impact of Explicit Display on the Interpretation of Uncertainty

Susan S. Kirschenbaum
Naval Undersea Warfare Center

Problem Description and Background

The submarine environment fits Orasanu and Lieberman's (Chapter 1) definition of an extreme environment: It is inherently inhospitable to human life. In some ways the situation of a submarine voyage is similar to that of a space flight (see Chapter 1). It takes place in a hostile environment, there are many periods when the craft is out of communications, transitioning between environments is dangerous (especially reentry to the "normal" atmosphere), and the vessel is highly specialized and complex. In other ways, the submarine is in an even more difficult environment. The only source of information while submerged is sound, and it is subject to significant uncertainty (see below). Submariners must repair their own problems, whether they are mechanical, electronic, or result from a poor decision. The home base has neither the detailed knowledge of the conditions and current situation nor the means to effect change, although it can give advice and adjust the mission. Submariners are basically alone in the undersea world until they make the dangerous transition to communications/periscope depth.

The Undersea Environment

The undersea environment limits the ability of the submarine to accurately sense objects around it. Sound rather than light is the primary sensory medium, but sound transmission underwater is distorted by temperature, pressure, and salinity. In this environment sound bends and refracts; it reflects at odd angles off a rocky bottom or a temperature layer or front; and it is absorbed by the ocean bottom. Sound channels and paths can produce shadow zones where even a noisy contact* can disappear (Urick, 1983). For a number of reasons (including stealth and whale protection), submarines primarily use passive sonar, which cannot directly determine the distance (range) to a sensed object. Relying on passive sonar is rather like relying on vision in a funhouse of distorted mirrors and optical illusions.

---

* A contact is any moving object that can be sensed. Contacts include vessels and biologics such as whales.

Another sensory problem for submarines is that the sea is not silent. Large surface vessels and tiny snapping shrimp make noise that masks the vital sound of collision risks or hostile submarines. In contrast, when trying to surface, silent sailboats pose a hazard, and the nets from fishing trawlers pose another hazard far from the noise of the fishing vessel itself. All of these problems create uncertainty and risk. Perceiving and understanding the situation in this environment includes knowing what you know, knowing what you don't know, knowing how to find solutions, and knowing how certain or uncertain your solution is.

Two Tasks

Submariners do a variety of tasks. Here we concentrate on two tasks, one done by enlisted sailors and the other done by officers. The enlisted task is localizing a contact after it has been sensed by sonar. This task is known as target motion analysis (TMA). The essence of TMA is to take data received from sonar, analyze them, and determine the location, course, and speed of each contact, that is, the "solution." At any time, the sonar data consist of a bearing and the time it was received. The change in bearing from one time interval to the next gives the bearing rate. Bearings are received at a fixed rate that can be adjusted to circumstances. Thus, the operator must solve a mathematically undetermined problem with two known values (bearing and time) and three unknowns (range, course, and speed).

Initially, the skilled operator does not attempt to analyze the new contact because there are too few data points to show a pattern. He just notes that there is a new contact and enters an initial guess at its course, speed, and range, so that it is recorded in the combat system. Later data can be compared to the past solution. The operator might work on three or four contacts at a time so he can concentrate on the ones with sufficient data. He has many methods and tools at his disposal to analyze the data from any contact. He cycles through the contacts for which he is responsible, using the tools described below. The TMA operator also makes recommendations for a next maneuver to improve the TMA on a contact and makes judgments about the quality of the data and reasonableness of the solutions. If the data are very noisy and scattered, the operator might suppress the outliers to get a better fit.

In contrast to the TMA task performed by enlisted sailors, officers must make decisions based on the full contact picture. These decisions include when and where to maneuver the ship, when to change depth, and when to fire weapons. We concentrate here on two of these decisions: when to fire a torpedo and when to come to periscope depth. Given the uncertainties inherent in the undersea environment, these decisions are risky and can endanger both one's own ship and other vessels. To make these decisions, officers examine the full contact picture, taking into account the TMA solutions developed by all of the TMA operators and the degree of certainty of these solutions.

The Tools

Submariners do have many tools to assist them in localizing a sensed contact (Ferkinhoff, Baylog, Gong, & Nardone, 1991; Ganesh, 1999) and making decisions about it. These include algorithms, displays, and procedures. The analysis tools and techniques are highly specialized, and attempting to describe them in detail would distract from the main point of this section and is not necessary to understand that point. Suffice it to say that the tools differ in their accuracy, precision, and conditions of use. Some need to be used together, while others apply only under certain circumstances or at certain times. Some tools can represent their output in several formats; others are limited. Some tools represent both the solution to the problem and the associated uncertainty; others produce only a point solution. All the tools, even the most automated, require skill and knowledge to produce usable information.

The People

Submarine decision makers are trained (Kirschenbaum, McInnis, & Correll, 2009) to understand that the displayed locations of other vessels are not precise. They must learn how to interpret the results that TMA and decision tools give them and must know when to use which tool. They must also learn about the nature of sound transmission underwater (Urick, 1983). This knowledge allows them to selectively accept or reject solutions, take actions to improve them, and make decisions about when there is sufficient accuracy to make decisions. It takes many years to develop the expertise to know when a contact is sufficiently well localized for current purposes and which tools to use under which circumstances.

The Issue of Uncertainty

Uncertainty can be a product of some unknown in the state of the world (diagnostic uncertainty) or in the consequences of actions (outcome uncertainty). The former describes the relationship between evidence (the patient has a fever and sore throat) and the true state of the world (the patient has strep). The latter describes the nondeterministic relationship between an action (give the patient antibiotic x) and the outcome (the patient recovers within three days). In both cases these are uncertain because the same evidence may come from another cause (cold, mononucleosis, influenza, etc.), and the same action can have a different outcome (allergic reaction, no effect, etc.). This simplified example should include the additional diagnostic steps used to discriminate between possible disease states, and thus increase the probability that the action will have the intended consequence.

This chapter will address only diagnostic uncertainty because that is the primary problem for the submariner. As with the medical example, the evidence—in the submariner's case the signal from sonar (bearing and time)—does not uniquely identify the situation. Many contact locations will fit the data. If he* actually knows the state of the world—and knows that he knows it—then the action decisions are relatively easy and prescribed. Until then, his actions are intended to establish those twin states of knowledge. As in medical diagnoses, the issue during this period is to decide what diagnostic steps to take to improve his knowledge, to interpret the results of these steps, and to decide when his knowledge is good enough.

---

* In the United States all submariners are men. Therefore, only the masculine pronoun will be used to refer to them.

Uncertainty has been emphasized as a major problem for submariners. The research questions are: Whether and how should location uncertainty be displayed? Is it useful or does it add unnecessary clutter? Does the display of uncertainty make the submariner more accurate or faster? What is the most effective way to display uncertainty in this environment? The literature on the display of uncertainty for a dynamic spatial task is sparse and fraught with disagreement. For example, Brolese (2005) found no improvement for students having a graphical display of uncertainty, while Finger and Bisantz (2002) and Brolese and Huf (2006) reported that graphical indicators of uncertainty did improve decision making.

No Display of Uncertainty

While this chapter is about the *display* of uncertainty, many times there is no indication of amount, or even presence, of uncertainty. Weather maps display predictions as if they were a fact, but everyone knows that there is considerable uncertainty around these predictions. Many other kinds of information suffer from a similar problem (i.e., no clarification of whether factual or probabilistic information is displayed), including, sometimes, contact positions on a submariner's display.

When there is no indication of uncertainty, the operator/decision maker must use other means to assess the status of the information he receives and his solution. TMA operators work on only one contact at a time, cycling through a workload of several contacts per sailor. Generally, only one solution for the current contact is displayed at any time. The operators must cycle through the set of solutions for that contact generated by other algorithms, tools, or methods, so as to compare them serially. Of course, this puts a burden on working memory and creates an opportunity for error.

In part because some tools have no associated uncertainty measurement and provide only a partial or point solution to the localization problem, submariners are trained to understand that any solution (bearing, course, speed, and range) is only one of a family of possible solutions. Still, the given location on a chart or computer screen is a powerful and compelling visual cue when no other ones are available. (There is no window to the outside world!) Treating that visual cue as uncertain is more difficult than the reader can imagine.

Textual Display

Textual displays come in two forms. One provides a qualitative moderator such as "good" to each solution. The other consists of a table of possible solutions (see Figure 12.1) coming from several solution methods. The first method is no longer in use. It was found to be a poor guide to the accuracy of the solution (Kirschenbaum & Arruda, 1994) and was generally discounted by users. The second one can provide a way to compare solutions and to judge agreement among solutions; however, a table of solutions is usually not available or is well hidden among the many windows on a combat system. In order to compare solutions, the operator must remember each of them while cycling through individual alternatives.

TMA Soln	1538	193	342	7.8	−3.2	Source: PEP	

Solution	Range	Bearing	Course	Speed	Brg Rate		
LOS C	1557	193	348	10.0	−2.8		
LOS O	1557	193	218	10.0	−3.0		
DRM/S	2043	193	357	10.0	−3.6		
DRM/R	1557	193	345	7.8	−3.6		
MP	1069	193	326	6.2	−3.6		
PEP	1543	193	342	7.8	−3.2		

FIGURE 12.1   Table of target motion analysis solutions for one contact.

Graphical Display

As with textual displays, graphical representations of uncertainty can be derived from a single analysis tool/technique or from several tools/techniques. In the first case, the representations can range from a single (e.g., 95th confidence interval) value to multiple levels of confidence. These are usually captured as a region on a bird's-eye type geographic display, such as that shown in Figure 12.2. When there are many contacts, each with its own ellipses, those uncertainty ellipses can add overwhelming clutter and can obscure information. They are almost always optional and can be turned on or off as a group or on a per-contact basis.

Most recently, a new family of algorithms has been developed to assess the agreement among solutions. This second approach follows a tradition of showing competing solutions (or at least ranges) on a paper plot, now largely obsolete. Today, to compare the full set of solutions, the operator has a display that shows agreement among solutions (see Figure 12.3). The shape of the center-most region tells the knowledgeable operator how well they agree. The more tightly the central region forms a bull's-eye, the greater the agreement. (Normally both of these displays, Figures 12.2 and 12.3, are in color.)

What Are the Effects of These Options on Performance? Do Effects Vary With Experience?

Performance can be defined in terms of accuracy or response time. In the submarine world there are constraints on both. There is no need to be more accurate than required by the task at hand. For example, if the boat is planning to come to periscope depth and the contact is known to be at a safe distance with no possibility of collision, then that is sufficient knowledge. Trying to attain more accuracy is referred to, disparagingly, as "polishing the cannon ball."

Uncertainty usually delays the decision on how to respond to a contact in favor of collecting additional information. As a result, the contact could be lost in the shadows of sound transmission anomalies. Occasionally, more time brings less rather

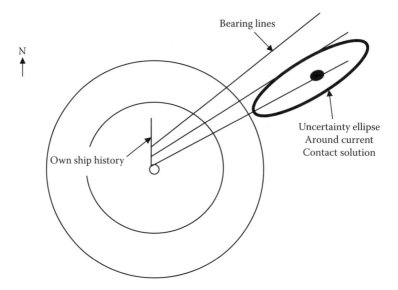

FIGURE 12.2   Graphical uncertainty ellipses of single solution on bird's-eye geospatial display.

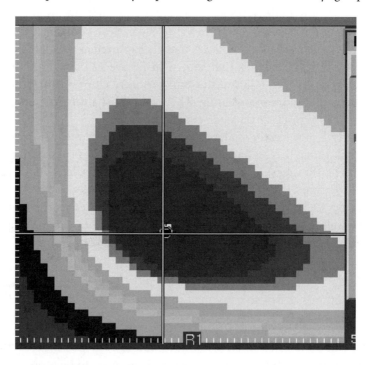

FIGURE 12.3   Graphical display of uncertainty for all solutions. The tighter the bull's-eye, the better agreement among solutions.

than more certainty! Enlisted sailors generally work on one contact at a time, while officers are more likely to assess the picture given all contacts.

Experimental studies involving several of the possible displays of uncertainty have been conducted with senior officers, junior officers, enlisted sailors, and novice college students. All studies used realistic tasks, such as deciding when a solution was adequate for some purpose (shoot a torpedo or come to periscope depth) or judging the closest contact to one's own ship (a possible collision danger). Some also examined the impact of submariners' expertise on decision performance. As our review below shows, studies have included both behavioral and subjective data. In the first section we will review general findings. In the later section we will discuss expertise effects.

General Effects of Uncertainty Representation

In early work, Kirschenbaum and Arruda (1994) investigated the effects of verbal and graphical displays of uncertainty on a submarine command task in which participants had to decide when the solution was adequate to warrant shooting a torpedo. The participants in this study were experienced but not experts. We found that a qualitative verbal descriptor was generally ignored or seen as unreliable. An elliptical display of a spatial area of uncertainty led to more accurate performance, especially when the scenario was difficult in that it involved a high degree of diagnostic uncertainty. We also found that the ellipses could be misleading when the environment was inaccurately represented or the algorithm misused.

A somewhat different finding was obtained by Brolese (2005) in a study in which inexperienced college students had to judge contact proximity to their own ship. Task difficulty was manipulated by the reliability of the algorithm that computed the solution. A textual, tabular presentation of solutions that included no indicator of uncertainty led to marginally faster and more accurate decisions than a geographical display. Moreover, there were no statistically significant differences among different levels of uncertainty, ranging from 99% to 50% containment. These findings seem to contradict the superiority of graphical display found by Kirschenbaum and Arruda (1994); however, one cannot rule out the possibility that the subjects' inexperience led them to misinterpret the graphical display or to be overconfident on the easy task. Additionally, this study did replicate Kirschenbaum and Arruda's (1994) finding that uncertainty ellipses were most useful when the problem was difficult.

The benefits of graphical over tabular displays are further substantiated in a recent study by Kirschenbaum, Trafton, Trickett, Schunn, and Saner (2006). Experienced officers went through the same command task used in Kirschenbaum and Arruda (1994). In addition, eye-tracking data were collected from participants during task performance. Officers at all levels of experience spent more time looking at graphical indicators of uncertainty than tabular ones, and as previously, were more accurate with a geographical-only representation of uncertainty than a tabular-only display.

Lastly, Andre and Cutler (1998) also found that a graphical display of uncertainty supported greater accuracy than a textual or categorical representation. The computer-generated task required participants to pilot an airplane to avoid collision with a more or less erratic meteor. As with other studies, the performance improvement was greatest when the meteor's behavior was very erratic, making the task the most difficult.

While the findings cited above strengthen the case for graphical displays of uncertainty, none of them gave any evidence for how such displays should be drawn or colored. One algorithm suggested for inclusion in the TMA operators' tool set calculates multiple (12) statistical regions of containment of the contact (see Figure 12.4).

In an informal working group evaluation session, Navy experts questioned the use of color (not shown here) and the number of uncertainty regions displayed. As a result, an experimental study was initiated. Employing the task of coming to peri-scope depth, Prouty (2007) investigated the effects of both color and the number of levels of gradations. Behavioral and subjective data from novice and expert officers and enlisted users showed that the original display (Figure 12.4) was often misinter-preted. Usually in probability distributions the largest exterior of the region is the one most likely to enclose the contact (see Figure 12.5). However, in the original display, the centroid (the 1/12 probability region) was displayed as a bright spot, and many

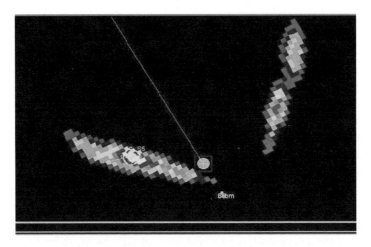

FIGURE 12.4   Graphical display with 12 levels of statistical probability.

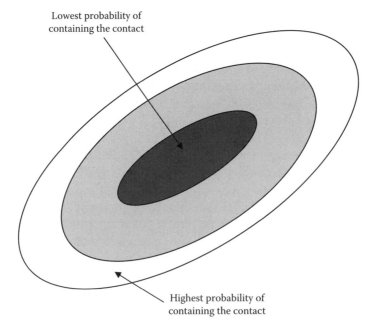

FIGURE 12.5   Revised graphical display with three levels of probability.

users interpreted it as having the greatest probability of containing the contact. In unpublished research extending Prouty's (2007) work, we found that the color of the regions can aid proper interpretation if the brightest (most salient) color is the highest confidence region (i.e., largest region; Kirschenbaum & Beecher, 2005).

The downside of graphical displays of uncertainty is that they can clutter a display, especially when there are many contacts. Control of these displays adds yet another burden to the user's task list. Thus, they are used differently in different circumstances, including depending on the expertise of the decision maker.

Differences Due to Expertise

Expertise is not a dichotomy; it is a continuum. The line between junior and senior officers or between chiefs and lower-ranked enlisted sailors is clear and defined by tradition; the correlation between rank and expertise, however, is imperfect. While it is likely that the most senior officers/chiefs are experts and the most junior officers/enlisted personnel are not, there is a range of expertise between these extremes. Below are some research findings and observations on the effectiveness of explicit graphical uncertainty displays for both groups.

Enlisted Crewmembers

The task of localizing contacts falls to enlisted crewmembers. They employ the algorithms and procedures, and they are the first to view the displays. As their task is to localize only a few contacts, working on one contact at a given time, they are not subject to a clutter problem that can limit the usefulness of uncertainty regions on multicontact displays. Enlisted operators vary in their experience; less experienced men are often teamed with more experienced ones and backed up by highly experienced chiefs. This mentoring helps the junior operators learn which algorithms and tools are likely to give the most accurate answers at any given time. Wright (personal communication) found that the most experienced TMA operators make extensive use of a graphical cumulative solution display (see Figure 12.3) to guide their analysis. However, it should be noted that experienced operators were not necessarily more accurate per se, but rather took less time to achieve adequate accuracy.

Officers

The job of officers is not to perform TMA, but to make decisions based on the locations of all the contacts. To that end, the officers do not consider one contact at a time, but view displays showing their own ship and all active contacts. They must be aware of the status of each contact, including how well it has been localized. Senior officers depend on more junior officers and chiefs to make that assessment, in coordination with the sailors who actually perform the TMA. The most senior decision makers aboard the submarine are well aware of the strengths and weaknesses of their crewmembers and know whose judgment to trust and whose not to trust.

Senior officers are cognizant of the uncertainty associated with all position estimates. They are also knowledgeable about which evaluation methods work best in which situations. Senior officers must deal with the complex decisions of how to respond to the contact picture in order to perform any aspect of their mission. For example, either surfacing or coming near enough to the surface to use the periscope and antennas in a busy environment can put both their own ship and other ships in danger of a collision. Prouty (2007) found that highly experienced officers did not benefit from a display of uncertainty in a coming to periscope depth scenario, even in a complex scenario. Kirschenbaum (in preparation) has found similar results in her lab, confirming the general perception that experts do not need this added explicit display.

In contrast, junior officers can be subject to the illusionary certainty of a visual display of position. They are also more likely to believe what an algorithm or tool indicates and are less able to determine when tool use is inappropriate (Kirschenbaum, 1992). For them, graphical displays of uncertainty are more effective than other representations, in deciding both when to shoot a torpedo and when it is safe to come to periscope depth (Kirschenbaum et al., in preparation). The range of expertise and the traditional military practice of the most experienced individuals standing on the shoulders of their less experienced crewmates argue for the cautionary display of uncertainty information because even the most experienced person can become distracted and misinterpret probabilistic visualizations.

Conclusion

In a highly uncertain and risky world, the dangerous consequences of an error outweigh the hazards (illusionary certainty) associated with displayed uncertain information. It is prudent to include a representation that specifies levels of uncertainty, even when the decision maker is very experienced. Failing to do so is hiding vital information and leaves the entire crew to intuit uncertainty levels. The submarine Navy has made great strides since the early 1990s, when faster computers made it possible to calculate the probability associated with a solution. Today's displays show not only the uncertainty associated with a single solution but the agreement among solutions. The U.S. Navy has used the guidance provided by these and other studies to design uncertainty displays that are useful in even the most difficult situations. They support both decision makers and operators, both highly experienced and inexperienced, especially the latter. We have yet to determine if these displays will help inexperienced people become experts more quickly. That is the next research challenge.

References

Andre, A. D., & Cutler, H. A. (1998). Displaying uncertainty in advanced navigation systems. In *Proceedings of the Human Factors and Ergonomics Society 42nd Annual Meeting* (pp. 31–35). Santa Monica, CA: Human Factors and Ergonomics Society.

Brolese, A. (2005). Graphic representations of uncertainty within sub-surface environments. In B. G. Bara, L. Barsalou, & M. Bucciarelli (Eds.), *Proceedings of the XXVII Annual Conference of the Cognitive Science Society* (p. 2452). Mahwah, NJ: Erlbaum.

Brolese, A., & Huf, S. (2006). Visualizing uncertainty to improve operators' spatial proximity judgments in uncertain surroundings. In *Proceedings of the 2006 Human Factors and Ergonomics Society 50th Annual Meeting* (pp. 294–298). Santa Monica, CA: Human Factors and Ergonomics Society.

Ferkinhoff, D. J., Baylog J. G., Gong, K. F., & Nardone, S. C. (1991). *Feature detection for model assessment in state estimation* (NUSC Technical Report 7064). Newport, RI: Naval Undersea Warfare Center.

Finger, R., & Bisantz, A. M. (2002). Utilizing graphical formats to convey uncertainty in a decision-making task. *Theoretical Issues in Ergonomics Science, 3,* 1–25.

Ganesh, C. (1999). *Fuzzy logic-based information processing in submarine combat systems.* Paper presented at the Fuzzy Information Processing Society's 18th International Conference of the North American. Newport, RI: Naval Undersea Warfare Center.

Kirschenbaum, S. S. (1992). Influence of experience on information-gathering strategies. *Journal of Applied Psychology, 77,* 343–352.

Kirschenbaum, S. S., & Arruda, J. (1994). The effects of graphic and verbal probability information on command decision making. *Human Factors, 36*(3), 406–418.

Kirschenbaum, S. S., & Beecher, M. (2005). *The AOU question and some science.* Unpublished brief to Tactical Control Study Group.

Kirschenbaum, S. S., McInnis, S., & Correll, K. P. (2009). Contrasting submarine specialty training: Sonar and fire control. In K. A. Ericsson, R. Perez, D. Eccles, L. Lang, E. Baker, J. Bransford,... P. Ward (Eds.), *Development of professional expertise: Toward measurement of expert performance and design of optimal learning environments* (pp. 271–285). Cambridge, UK: Cambridge University Press.

Kirschenbaum, S. S., Trafton, G., Trickett, S. B., Schunn, C. D., & Saner, L. D. (2006). *Impact of uncertainty representation on decision making.* Paper presented at the Annual Conference of the Psychonomic Society, Houston, TX.

Prouty, J. R. (2007). *Displaying uncertainty: A comparison between submarine subject matter experts.* MS thesis, Naval Postgraduate School.

Urick, R. J. (1983). *Principles of underwater sound* (3rd ed.). New York, NY: McGraw-Hill.

13

Using High-Fidelity Computerized Training to Prepare Commanders for Operational Decision Making

Laura A. Zimmerman, Jeff M. Sestokas, and Christopher A. Burns
Klein Associates, Applied Research Associates, Inc.

The U.S. Air Force plays a significant role in conducting successful joint and combined operations. These airspace operations are commanded by individuals who plan and support campaigns under time pressure and conditions of uncertainty. Joint Forces Air Component Commanders (JFACCs)* are three-star general officers who are handpicked to command air and space assets comprised of air force components, joint forces, and coalition forces in command posts throughout the world. The main role of JFACCs consists of planning, coordinating, allocating, and tasking joint air operations. Their duties include advising commanders on the proper employment of air and space forces, analyzing various courses of action (COAs), issuing planning guidance, developing operations plans to support joint force objectives, controlling the execution of combined/joint air operations, and coordinating joint air operations with other component commanders and forces (Department of Defense, 2005).

New JFACCs learn the fundamentals of their role during a relatively short formal course of classroom instruction with little opportunity to engage in realistic training simulations that exercise their newly acquired knowledge and skill sets. Thus, they enter their roles without first developing the many specialized skills that would help them direct real-world operations, such as relationship building with host nation officials, accounting for the social, cultural, and economic factors of host communities, and coordinating and negotiating with joint and coalition forces. Those who become JFACCs are already military generals with vast amounts of experience, but the transition to the JFACC role involves new challenges and shifts in operational thinking, planning, and actions. Decision makers at the operational level usually enter their positions with extensive tactical field experience, and must adjust their focus and priorities to make strategic decisions in operational environments (Leland, 1997).

Research investigating performance differences based on levels of experience shows that less experienced decision makers take longer to decide on courses of action (e.g., Klein, 1998; Randel & Pugh, 1995; Thunholm, Chapter 8). One possible explanation

---

* This research includes both Joint and Coalition Forces Air Component Commanders (JFACC/CFACC). In this report we will refer to the JFACC/CFACC job position simply as the JFACC, with the understanding that both the analysis and the design of the system address coalition as well as joint operations.

is that those with little experience in a domain have not developed the mental models necessary to rapidly construct a coherent picture of events (Ericsson & Charness, 1994; Fowlkes, Salas, Baker, Cannon-Bowers, & Stout, 2000; Goodrich, Sterling, & Boer, 2000). Thus, the lack of experience may lead to inefficient or ineffective operations and undesired outcomes. One approach used to address the lack of real-world experience is to create training that not only allows learners to exercise rule-based knowledge, but also fosters development of domain-relevant experience. This type of training seeks to move novices beyond procedurally based thinking toward more situational-based processing that is adaptive and fluid in response to unfolding or novel events (Ross, Phillips, Klein, & Kohn, 2005).

The U.S. Air Force has recognized the importance of leveraging the experiences of their senior members. They have in place a mentorship program that provides new JFACCs with access to retired JFACCs who serve as senior mentors. While the Air Force considers this program valuable, the busy schedules of new JFACCs and senior mentors makes it difficult for them to meet for mentoring. In an effort to increase the interaction between new JFACCs and the senior mentors, the Air Force requested the development of a tool that would provide easier access to senior mentors while also providing new JFACCs with the opportunity to build their own experience bases through simulation-based training.

To meet this request, we developed training that combines high-fidelity computer-based simulations with both active and passive mentoring. This training provides passive mentoring using real-time feedback in the form of consequences to actions and through an automated after action review. JFACC senior mentors provide active mentoring in the form of guidance and feedback to learners during the exercise or by annotating after action review information. The focus of this training was on the development of expertise; thus, the overarching objective was to produce a simulated environment that incorporated the cognitive complexities and challenges faced by experienced JFACCs and allowed new JFACCs to practice the complex duties they will face during critical events. By drawing on the cognitive skills and knowledge of experienced JFACCs, we sought to create an environment where new JFACCs can make decisions and take actions that extend beyond procedural-, or textbook-, level responses. The three main objectives were to:

1. Define the decision-making challenges found in complex environments where JFACCs must consider joint and coalition forces along with the needs of host countries
2. Develop training scenarios that embed cognitive challenges and require experienced JFACC strategies
3. Develop an intelligent mentoring system prototype that supports the development of the cognitive skills (i.e., pattern recognition, sensemaking, adaptive thinking) associated with the JFACC position

This training will provide new JFACCs with the opportunity to engage in the practical application of their skills in realistic environments. The goal of scenario-based training is to develop the mental constructs necessary to process and resolve real-world situations with greater proficiency (Crandall, Klein, & Hoffman, 2006). In order to create a training/mentoring system that accomplishes this, we used cognitive task analysis (CTA) to capitalize on the considerable operational experience that exists among selected Air Force generals and others working in Joint Air Operations Centers (JAOCs). We identified the aspects of mentoring that are most useful to JFACCs, gathered insights into how JFACCs acquire expertise, and clarified key JFACC skills, knowledge, and abilities. From the data, a knowledge architecture emerged that reflected a decision-centered design for implementing a usable, intelligent interface between new JFACCs and the training/mentoring system.

Chapter Summary

This chapter documents the development of the JFACC Simulation and Mentoring System. This system is grounded in the naturalistic decision-making paradigm and blended with instructional systems design techniques. We begin by discussing the fundamental aspects of mentorship and mentor-learner relationships. The discussion then focuses on the challenges to developing realistic training scenarios for high-level command environments, the CTA methodologies used to identify the decision requirements of JFACCs, and the key system components of the training/mentoring programs. We then discuss the development of the training system, present the outcomes of the CTA analysis and program development, and conclude with a summary and recommendations for future training.

Mentorship and Feedback

To embed the mentorship concepts relative to JFACCs, we first conducted a literature review and documented both the functions of a mentor and effective mentoring strategies. From our literature review, we identified several characteristics critical to successful mentoring (cf. Phillips, 2005). These characteristics generally fit into one of four categories:

Definitions of mentor/mentoring
- Mentoring involves teaching, modeling, and counseling.
- Mentoring is the act of reproducing aspects of the mentor in a learner.
- Mentoring requires that the learner be actively involved in the relationship.
- Mentoring is a one-to-one relationship, with a focus on individualized education.
- Mentoring is customizable to individual learner needs.

Mentor-learner relationship
- The learner must trust that information from the mentor is accurate, relevant, and current.
- Mentor and learner develop and share a common set of goals for the learner.
- Mentoring is consensual. Both parties need to want the relationship to work.

Mentoring process
- Mentoring is most effective when executed over time, rather than in one day.
- A mentor is a resource for professional connections and networking.
- Mentors teach learners to construct mental models in the context of real-world situations.
- Mentoring should teach learners *how* to think rather than *what* to think.
- Learners should control the pace of mentoring so it matches their need for support.

Mentoring techniques
- The wisdom and experiences of mentors form the foundation of the mentoring.
- Mentors rely on examples, stories, and anecdotes to pass information on to the learner.
- Mentors should model higher-order strategies and processes to ensure knowledge transfer.
- Mentoring should support learner reflection so learners can gain meaning and insight.
- Mentors account for learners' learning style and their level of proficiency.

Once we identified key mentorship concepts, we turned our attention to other challenges present in the development of command-level simulation training.

New Challenges to Generals Entering Their Role as JFACCs

Our focus was on three challenges JFACCs face that were particularly important to simulate in a computer-based environment.

1. *JFACCs make decisions in joint operation command centers rather than on the ground where the action takes place.* The scope of the JFACC position requires them to make decisions with a big-picture view of events and address larger concerns rather than immediate, singular concerns. Although JFACCs are military generals with years of command experience, they still must guard against narrowing their focus to decisions about mission-specific tactics rather than pushing those decisions down to ground-level responders. When this happens, JFACCs may lose sight of larger goals, and infringe upon the decisions of ground-level commanders who must execute missions based on real-time acquisition of information and changing conditions (Leland, 1997).

2. *JFACCs must synthesize information in complex situations, visualize the course of dynamic environments, and make decisions that lead to successful outcomes for both current and future operations.* Experienced decision makers must sort and assess large quantities of information in order to build coherent stories, or mental representations, of events that map onto their existing mental models (Crandall et al., 2006). JFACCs are not responsible for gathering this information; instead, they must rely on others to communicate key pieces of information. In turn, JFACCs must evaluate the importance and reliability of this information before incorporating it into their assessment of the situation. Efficient information sorting and interpretation depends on how well the team members who operate within the JAOC collaborate with each other. It is JFACC leadership abilities and team-building skills that foster the ability of joint and coalition partners to collaborate effectively on efforts (see, for example, Osland, Chapter 2).

3. *In addition to considering orders and intent from higher commanders, JFACCs must also attend to the needs and desires of host nation officials, nongovernment agencies, the media, joint/coalition military partners, and their staff.* The JFACC is in a demanding position as both a supporting and supported commander, responsible for joint and coalition forces. Not only do JFACCs concern themselves with military operations, but they also need to consider, often for the first time in their careers, other factors of PMESII (political, military, economic, information, infrastructure), using diplomacy, intelligence, military, and economic instruments within their

coalition partners' countries while they establish and maintain joint/coalition partner relationships (Davis & Kahan, 2007). JFACCs need to maintain awareness not only of evolving events, but also of local and international political concerns, changing sociocultural issues, and information flow to and from the media.

Representing Naturalistic Decision Making in Training

The three challenges mentioned above focus on macrocognitive processing in naturalistic decision-making environments. *Macrocognition* is a term used to describe complex cognition at a macro level, such as is necessary when operating in naturalistic environments, as opposed to *microcognition*, which describes the individual cognitive processes that take place within the human mind (Schraagen, Klein, & Hoffman, 2008) (Figure 13.1). In particular, these challenges encompass many of the functions attributed to macrocognition, such as planning, sensemaking, problem detection, and coordination. Supporting these functions are macrocognitive processes such as managing attention, dealing with uncertainty, balancing risk, and mentally simulating events.

To develop scenarios that address the cognitive challenges faced by JFACCs, we sought to provide new JFACCs with the opportunity to engage in the macrocognitive functions and processes that will challenge them in real-world situations. Because these skills tend to develop with experience, we gathered from experienced decision

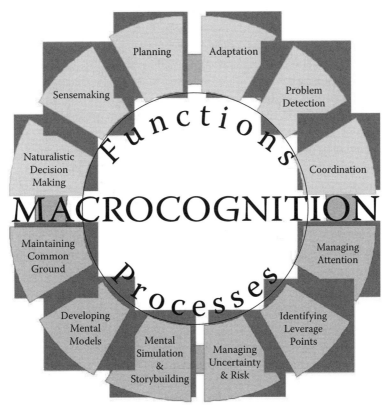

FIGURE 13.1   Macrocognitive functions and processes. (From Klein, G., et al. Macrocognition. *IEEE Intelligent Systems,* May/June 2003, pp. 81–85. With permission.)

makers the cues that signal they should engage in functions such as sensemaking, planning, and problem detection, and we identified the tasks that require processes such as mental simulation, managing attention, and identifying leverage points. This allowed us to incorporate realistic stimuli into training scenarios (Crandall et al., 2006).

Challenges of Simulating Realistic JFACC Operating Environments

Because the duties of JFACCs are complex, we faced several challenges in creating a simulated scenario that matched the decision-making parameters of JFACC operating environments. Typically, computer-based training environments that depict high-stakes events focus on training tactical responders at the scene of critical incidents. Decision makers who must make fast-paced critical decisions "behind the scenes" have less opportunity to engage in challenging simulations that exercise skills such as complex information interpretation, coordination, planning, and decision making while events are continually changing (Pigora, Tamash, & Baxter, 2006). During these behind the scenes situations, JFACCs work from JAOCs and cannot see or respond to the event directly. Our first challenge was to simulate an environment that does not allow firsthand access to information or events at the scene. Instead, we needed to represent the joint operation command environment, which takes place away from the actual action and away from real-time knowledge of information and events.

The second challenge was to provide opportunities for JFACCs to plan and make decisions that have both short- and long-term impacts. When information comes into the JAOC, JFACCs need to assess, plan, and react to both immediate concerns and long-term objectives. The training system needed to allow JFACCs the opportunity to consider both current and future operations and take actions that would demonstrate this thinking within the training system. If JFACCs are reacting only to short-term objectives, without considering the influence of actions on future events, it may result in a reduction of later response options or waylay the overall mission. The simulation needed to provide opportunity for JFACCs to attend to short- and long-term goals as well as presenting short- and long-term consequences to current actions.

Our third concern was the importance of the collaborative aspects of being a JFACC, which are vital to JAOC operations and the overall mission within host countries. JFACCs work with commanders from all branches of military and with coalition partners from host nations. We needed to incorporate these characters into the storyline so JFACCs could practice juggling the conflicting requests of partners who have competing objectives while maintaining productive relationships so that joint/coalition partners will fulfill the JFACCs' requests. Finally, we needed to develop a mentoring system that would allow for constructive feedback and the ability to engage in Socratic questioning that allows learners to practice critical thinking.

Expert Knowledge Elicitation

We overcame these challenges by identifying both the physical and cognitive demands of the JFACC position. To do this, we conducted CTA interviews to elicit the tacit knowledge of seasoned JFACCs. CTA is a set of tools and methods used to elicit general and specific knowledge about the cognitive skills and strategies that underlie performance (Crandall et al., 2006). To elicit expertise from former JFACCs, we used the knowledge audit (Klein & Militello, 2004). This elicitation technique organizes the knowledge into categories that characterize expertise, such as how decision makers diagnose and predict events, attain situational awareness, recognize anomalies, and compensate for system limitations. The semistructured interviews used in CTA are particularly effective in eliciting previous experiences and the tacit knowledge that domain experts develop though their experiences. The interviews were semistructured, which provided interviewers the leeway to form questions based on the previous responses of the interviewees. This CTA technique results in contextually rich accounts of previous events and individual experiences. From these accounts, we identified the macrocognitive functions and processes employed when operating in JFACC environments. The objective during these interviews was to identify key tasks and gather information about the behavioral and cognitive skills with a focus on the macrocognitive functions and processes necessary to perform these tasks. Our goal in conducting interviews with experienced JFACCs was to uncover:

- The complex decisions made during high-stakes critical events
- How JFACCs assess, respond, and adapt in complex environments
- Real-world stories, including lessons learned, strategies, and unique solutions
- Aspects of mentoring that would benefit new JFACCs
- The knowledge, skills, and abilities necessary to operate effectively in real-world environments
- The specific situational and environmental cues and factors associated with sensemaking and decision making when performing JFACC tasks

We used this information to create an experiential learning environment that actively engaged learners in realistic tasks and provided them with opportunities to use analytical skills to resolve situations and reflect on experiences (Herman & Mandell, 2004).

Transitioning Interview Data to Simulation Design

To develop the simulation tool, we identified data from the interviews that indicated aspects of the job where new JFACCs tend to struggle and tasks most difficult to achieve prior to gaining experience. We analyzed and documented the cognitive processes that were gathered during the knowledge audit (Crandall et al., 2006). By documenting cognitive processes, we gained an understanding of the process by which JFACCs make decisions, what task elements are challenging, and what support (i.e., assets, information, and technology) they need. We analyzed the data using decision requirements analysis, which is a method for capturing and categorizing the specific details of incidents provided by domain experts (Crandall et al., 2006; Klein, Kaempf, Wolf, Thordsen, & Miller, 1997). This technique utilizes decision requirements tables (DRTs), an organizing framework that categorizes and highlights the key decisions or assessments in a given domain. The decisions, as well as the factors and strategies, informed the design of the scenario and simulation. We categorized the data according to eight critical tasks, and then identified the key decisions for each task, why each task is difficult, factors that influence decision making in the tasks, strategies used to accomplish the tasks, and other useful comments. The data in each category come directly from the interviews and drive the formation scenario content. Findings from our analysis revealed eight critical tasks that new JFACCs struggle with while on the job (Table 13.1). Table 13.1 shows a sample DRT for the task of managing, balancing, and mitigating risk.

Critical Tasks Performed by JFACCs

Presented here is a general description of the eight tasks and the behavioral indicators associated with task performance. These tasks do not encompass the entire range

TABLE 13.1   Sample Decision Requirement Table: Managing, Balancing, and Mitigating Risk

The JFACC's day-to-day job is managing risk. There is a constant balance between the mission requirements and the risk involved. As one interviewee stated, "There's nothing that happens in U.S. Central Command anymore that's not a risk to someone, but at the same time, there's a risk that if the JFACC doesn't do his job, someone else will get hurt even worse." JFACCs have to mitigate risk as much as possible; however, there are times when the requirement to execute the mission will outweigh the risks. The JFACC has to know when to make that call.	
Decisions and assessments	• How much risk am I willing to take? How much is prudent? • Is the mission requirement critical enough to put people's lives in danger? • What are acceptable losses for conducting the air campaign? • Do we have the initiative? How do we keep it? • What factors (material, personnel, weather, political, time, etc.) will cause us to lose the initiative? • If the red commander has the initiative, how do we take it from him?
Why difficult	• Tragedy (e.g., loss of life) can cause your staff to lose their focus on accomplishing the mission. • There are political consequences for the decisions and actions taken by senior military commanders. • Decisions about time-sensitive targets that deal with the protection of friendly forces are most challenging. • Differential risk tolerance across the military branches (e.g., Air Force vs. Army).
Factors	• Threat/risk to pilots and other operators. • Risk of collateral damage. • Risk of noncombatant injuries. • Tactical mistakes have strategic consequences.
Strategies	• You need to take the lead and not let tragedy or adversity get in the way of mission accomplishment. People will draw strength from what you do and how you handle situations. You need to let them know that the mission continues as planned. • In advance, develop a playbook of contingencies and work through how you would handle each one. Then bring in an expert to walk through the situation and look for likely problem areas.
Additional comments	• There is a perception that the Army is more lax about controlling or minimizing collateral damage than the Air Force. JFACC should be alerted about cultural constraints and opportunities.

of JFACC job responsibilities. Rather, they address areas where new JFACCs tend to struggle and where a mentoring system for new JFACCs can add value. New JFACCs learn the job duties encompassed in these tasks, but do not necessarily learn how to handle the task complexities when attempting to resolve critical events. Instead, they often first encounter these complexities after they begin their JFACC duties and must struggle to adapt their procedural knowledge to unfolding events. Though this initial learning curve is common in many domains, the responsibilities associated with high-level command positions, particularly those where relations with foreign governments and military are vital to U.S. security, make training to reduce the learning curve particularly important.

The simulation provides opportunity for learners to display these key behavioral indicators during the scenario.

1. *Coordinate with joint and coalition partners and nongovernment organizations.* Successful JFACCs spend a significant amount of time coordinating and collaborating with other players to ensure a shared understanding of intent, capabilities, and roles. JFACCs must elicit information from the task force and component commanders and must work closely with coalition commanders and nongovernment organizations (e.g., to provide airlift for humanitarian supplies). Someone who is coordinating with joint and coalition partners and nongovernment organizations might engage in activities such as the following:
   - Discuss intent with joint and coalition forces
   - Assist joint forces when they request support, without neglecting personal interests
   - Communicate with outside agencies and political leaders in the community
   - Hold regular briefings to gather and report information

2. *Build and maintain relationships and manage communications.* JFACCs must develop and maintain relationships with the task force and component commanders. Close relationships with other commanders create mutual trust, which allows the JFACC to cut through red tape and solve problems quickly. JFACCs need to engage in *active* relationship building prior to the mission, if possible. You can expect someone who is building/maintaining relationships and managing communication to:
   - Adapt communication style to fit the audience (i.e., host nation officials vs. support staff)
   - Take actions to support the needs of other commanders
   - Call upon relationships fostered prior to the event
   - Leverage contacts to assist with mission tasks

3. *Know and use assets.* JFACCs must allocate all assets under their control across the spectrum of operations. They need to track the capabilities and limitations of assets that are not organic to the JFACC's branch of service (e.g., an Air Force JFACC must learn Navy and Marine Corps aviation assets). JFACCs must include command and control, information operations, nongovernment organizations, and the media in the array of assets available to them. You would expect someone who knows the assets available and uses them appropriately to:
   - Maintain a realistic assessment of asset availability, including human resources
   - Explore options for obtaining assets
   - Prioritize asset distribution to meet critical and long-term needs
   - Call in support from external agencies when necessary

4. *Gather and assess information and intelligence.* JFACCs need to ensure that staff members collect and analyze the correct information without overlooking anything significant. JFACCs must quickly evaluate and prioritize information, must distinguish bad targeting plans from good ones, and must continually assess ongoing air operations and the functioning of their teams. You would expect someone who is gathering and assessing information and intelligence to:
   - Ask direct, specific questions rather than general questions such as "What is going on?"
   - Attend to specific incoming information and filter out less important information
   - Issue orders or offer guidance to deal with future events, not just immediate concerns
   - Actively try to understand the progress and consequences of earlier decisions

5. *Plan and replan during mission operations.* JFACCs must synchronize their strategies with the strategies of joint/coalition force commanders. JFACCs should meet with core planners to ensure the planners understand their guidance and are able to assess whether plans are operationalized correctly. Without micromanaging, JFACCs must monitor the plan and decide when it is time to replan. You would expect someone who is planning and replanning during mission operations to:
   - Take effective action when new information comes in or when plans do not go as expected
   - Change action and shift priorities in response to unfolding events
   - Plan future operations while conducting current operations
   - Slow down and observe the situation instead of rushing to action

6. *Maintain leadership and delegate tasks.* JFACCs should express their intent and guidance to subordinates in a clear and concise manner. Their guidance needs to be specific enough to direct subordinates toward a goal but flexible enough to let them determine the best way to reach the goal. JFACCs need to stay strong and focused during tragic incidents while keeping others calm. You would expect someone who is actively maintaining leadership and delegating tasks to:
   - Clearly communicate the command structure
   - Know when to relinquish command to the partner more suited to deal with the current situation
   - Empower staff to make decisions and not dictate how to complete each task or micromanage
   - Clearly express intent and mission objectives

7. *Manage, balance, and mitigate risk.* JFACCs must constantly balance mission requirements with the risk involved. JFACCs have to mitigate risk as much as possible, but recognize when the requirement to execute the mission will outweigh the risks. You would expect someone who is managing, balancing, and mitigating risk to:
   - Take action to reduce any negative consequences their actions might have on joint/coalition forces, outside agencies, and the host nation
   - Weigh risks by interpreting information and events beyond observable facts
   - Recognize when events are not immediate threats and take time to weigh risks and benefits surrounding potential actions
   - Execute missions with the intent of preventing long-term, or greater, consequences while allowing for short-term consequences

8. *Apply rules of engagement and legal requirements.* JFACCs must coordinate with components that may have different rules of engagement or interpret these rules differently. There is frequent need for the various components to discuss and negotiate

rules of engagement to ensure common ground, and JFACCs are instrumental in making this happen. You would expect someone who is attempting to apply rules of engagement and legal requirements to:

- Take actions that reflect mission priorities
- Avoid addressing needs outside mission scope
- Accommodate and negotiate with joint/coalition partners who have conflicting mission goals and rules of engagement
- Mitigate consequences of non-mission-specific actions in both the short and long term

We paired decision strategies from the DRTs with key macrocognitive functions and processes (Table 13.2). This table provides a summary of the cognitive processes or functions that support JFACC knowledge, skills, and abilities (Ross, Readinger, & Mills, 2005). Although commanders in many domains are likely required to possess these abilities, the information obtained from experienced JFACCs highlights how they fit within their specialized environments.

Developing the JFACC Simulation and Mentoring System

To create a complex decision-making environment that immerses learners into their roles and provides robust and relevant training simulations, it is important to write challenging scenario content. We did this by incorporating the complex challenges and environmental factors present in real-world situations into the scenario we created for the prototype system.

To focus the training objectives and requirements, we directed the scenario content toward the task "manage, balance, and mitigate risk." Although we highlighted this task in the scenario storyline, other tasks are inherent, to greater or lesser degrees, in the scenario, as they are in any JFACC situation. From the DRTs, we identified the following learning objectives:

1. Take action to reduce the risks associated with current threats to acceptable levels
2. Sort, filter, and evaluate incoming information in the context of a continually changing situation
3. Delegate tasks as necessary to complete a mission
4. Demonstrate ability to manage diplomacy with Joint Forces, coalition partners, and host nations
5. Assess enemy capabilities and limitations and predict potential enemy courses of action

These learning objectives require learners to make specific decisions to achieve task goals (Table 13.3). The actions learners take while completing the simulation reflect these decisions.

We then created training modules that support two phases of learning:

1. The *vignette player* presents text-based scenarios that use low-fidelity scenario inputs (storylines in text) and focused questions to develop the user's critical thinking skills. This program allows users to receive active and passive mentor feedback about their answers to critical thinking questions.

2. The *simulation player* presents scenarios that mimic real-life events using high-fidelity scenario-based exercises (computer-based simulation) that allow users to practice in time-pressured critical situations. This program includes automated mentoring, active mentor feedback, after action reviews, and links to reference materials that promote reflective practice by the learner.

TABLE 13.2   Summary of Cognitive Processes or Functions That Support JFACC Abilities

Cognitive Function or Process	Supported JFACC Ability
Maintain common ground. Common grounding is a process of continually maintaining and repairing the calibrated understanding among team members.	Monitor team awareness and understanding of commander intent and mission goals Know the roles and functions of JAOC personnel Relate to the other component commanders Understand the capabilities of the JAOC Access information acquired through training
Develop mental models. Mental models are preindexed, abstract "packets of knowledge" that are retrieved and applied as the situation requires. People are able to apply schema-driven reasoning in a context-sensitive way to develop a unique, situation-specific mental model.	Monitor and maintain situation awareness in the JAOC Search for relevant examples of situations quickly and accurately Search for relevant cultural and historical data
Coordination. The ability to act in concert with multiple entities to achieve a common goal by carrying out a shared plan.	Manage time, maintain and support an effective battle rhythm Delegate responsibility within the JAOC to the appropriate element or team member Manage the Joint Force Command, maintain consistent mission intent
Sensemaking/situation assessment. The deliberate, conscious fitting of data into a frame. The frame may be a story, script, map, or other form of representation; the intention is to reduce complexity and simplify the world in relation to a particular goal.	Organize information added sporadically or intermittently Maintain strategic-level situational awareness Maintain awareness of local and international media
Decision making. The identification of a feasible course of action from experience accumulated in similar situations; it may involve, but does not require, a comparison of the strengths and weaknesses of alternative courses of action.	Make rapid decisions based on limited information Identify and apportion assets for high-payoff and time-sensitive targets
Planning. The activities required to transform a decision into some future execution by contemplating, prioritizing, and devising actions that involve the use of resources to accomplish a defined end state.	Assess and manage risks Employ reconnaissance, surveillance, and intelligence assets to conduct and assess effects-based operations
Adaptation/replanning. Once execution of a plan begins, progress is monitored in relation to unfolding reality. When reality diverges from the plan, the plan may be modified by cycling back into the planning process, or replanning. Replanning involves modifying, adjusting, and possibly replacing a plan.	Recognize patterns and trends, and use this information to predict future states
Mental simulation. Mental simulation is the process for consciously and mentally enacting a sequence of events, for example, by imagining how a course of action will play out.	Understand ("know") the enemy, his decision cycle, and his tendencies

TABLE 13.3   Learning Objectives Identified From DRTs

Take action to reduce the risks associated with current threats to acceptable levels	**Decisions Associated With Managing, Balancing, and Mitigating Risk** • How much risk am I willing to take? How much is prudent? Is the mission requirement critical enough to put people's lives in danger? • What are acceptable losses for conducting the air campaign? • What factors (material, personnel, weather, political, time, etc.) will cause us to lose the initiative?
Sort, filter, and evaluate incoming information in the context of a continually changing situation	**Decisions Associated With Gathering and Assessing Information and Intelligence** • What are the priority information requirements, or top five critical questions, our intelligence must answer about enemy capabilities or intentions and about friendly capabilities or problems in the next 24/48/72 hours? What decisions will I need to make when these questions are answered? • What are the top five critical questions the red commander will seek answers to about blue capabilities or intentions in the next 24/48/72 hours? What decisions will I need to make to ensure he will not get the correct answers?
Delegate the tasks necessary to complete a mission	**Decisions Associated With Maintaining Leadership and Delegating Tasks** • Is my guidance clear and concise? Does it empower my subordinates to make the right decisions at the right time in my absence? • Do the JFACC's guidance, mission and intent statements, and prioritized target need to be changed to reflect campaign needs? • Determine how to decentralize execution.
Demonstrate ability to manage diplomacy with joint forces, coalition partners, or host nations	**Decisions Associated With Coordination With Joint and Coalition Partners and Nongovernment Organizations** • How do we best use the coalition air forces while remaining sensitive to issues of national pride, sovereignty, diplomatic/political necessities, and U.S./coalition security? • Determine how to manage diplomacy with coalition partners, host nation, and joint forces.
Assess enemy capabilities and limitations and predict possible enemy courses of action	**Decisions Associated With Planning and Replanning** • Determine how to plan for the enemy. • How do I make effects-based decisions to influence enemy behavior?

Vignette Player

We designed the vignette player to engage learners in a scenario that presents them with circumstances they must assess and make specific decisions about (Figure 13.2). The system requires learners to make plans and contingency plans as well as to address issues presented by subordinates, commanders, and the environment. The goal is to place them into a cognitively complex exercise where they must express in detail how they would handle an unfolding complex situation. The vignette presents a general scenario with background information and two segments of an unfolding event, interrupted by critical thinking questions. The questions following each segment require new JFACCs to provide in-depth answers, plans, or strategies.

The vignette is not a timed exercise, so the JFACCs can reason through their answers and request feedback about their answers from the senior mentors. Allowing new JFACCs

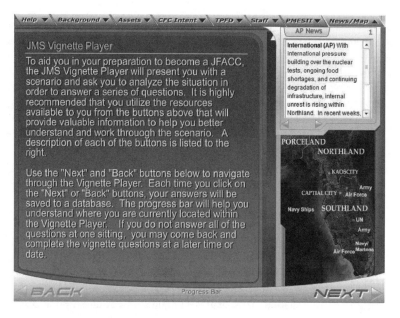

FIGURE 13.2   Example of vignette player.

to make decisions without time pressure gives them time to explore various courses of action, weigh the importance of different situational elements, formulate plans, address challenges, and analyze their solutions. This exercise increases new JFACCs' experience bases and skill sets, further developing cognitive maps that they can refer to during real and time-pressured incidents. This training provides a transition from knowledge-based application by exercising the critical thinking and analytic skills they will need to function effectively in real-time decision-making environments.

Simulation Player

The simulation player allows individuals to make decisions in realistic situations and experience the outcomes and consequences of their decisions. We designed the simulation to build upon the foundational skills exercised in the vignette player by requiring learners to apply these skills in a fast-paced, complex, and ambiguous situation. To depict unfolding events, the simulation presents "injects" such as email, news videos, Web site articles, meetings, face-to-face encounters, and simulated phone calls (see the appendix for module descriptions). Learners handle the incident by responding to messages, communicating with simulated teammates, attending virtual briefings, and giving commands to simulated entities (Figure 13.3).

Unlike the vignette, which has no time limit, the simulation presents a time-pressured environment, where risk management and real-time sensemaking become vital to resolving the crisis. As both relevant and irrelevant information pour into the JAOC, information sorting, intelligence gathering, and aggregation of data become high priorities. The dynamic situation contains ambiguities, multiple pressing needs, information overload, and conflicting priorities, requiring the JFACC to sort and filter large amounts of information, exhibit leadership, communicate and coordinate with

FIGURE 13.3   Example of simulation player.

joint/coalition partners, and delegate tasks to his staff. The following is an example inject that focuses on Task 1: "coordinate with joint and coalition partners."

> Incident: A staff member knocks at the JFACC's office door and states that the Army commander is not allowing coalition forces from the host nation to assist in a rescue and recovery operation after a bombing incident at a nightclub with a predominantly American clientele. The blast also killed citizens of the host country.
>
> Action: The JFACC should make calls to find out why this is occurring and work to clear up any misunderstandings, coordinate efforts between the Army and the coalition partner, and resolve the issue in a manner that creates cooperation between components.
>
> Consequence: If the JFACC does not repair the relationship and foster cooperation, the consequence is that the Army will withhold support to the Air Force as punishment for stepping in, and the host nation will cease cooperating with the Army.

The simulation presents a challenging, flexible environment, allowing for most actions that learners may want to take. By allowing for multiple acceptable solutions to the situations presented, the system provides learners with the flexibility to use their own leadership style and to test different action options. As learners make decisions and take actions, simulated staff members respond and provide input. The simulation tracks learners' actions, decisions, and mistakes throughout the scenario and presents an after action review at the completion of the simulation.

Mentoring and Feedback

This training system demonstrates features and capabilities in exercise design and play that enable both active and passive mentoring to new JFACCs. We developed several avenues for mentorship within the training program, and incorporated the key decision challenges, novel and mundane events, and strategy options into the computer simulation, creating synchronous and asynchronous avenues for passive (automated) and active (human) mentoring. A key component of this system is the feedback learners receive, both from the system and from senior mentors. Feedback is an essential component of efficient decision making and necessary for the development of expertise in a given domain (Ericsson & Charness, 1994; Klein, 1998; Shanteau, 1992). Within the vignette player, senior mentors provide passive mentoring by contributing their expert answers to vignette questions that any new JFACCs can reference anytime. Senior mentors engage in active mentoring by providing detailed annotations to the vignette answers provided by individual JFACC candidates. Their annotations provide direct feedback by highlighting potential errors in thinking, commending innovation, or providing alternative solutions based on their own experiences.

The simulation player immerses new JFACCs in a realistic environment that allows them to see the consequences of their actions in real time. The simulation player provides four levels of feedback during the simulation:

Automated consequences. By incorporating the consequences of decisions, actions, and inactions into the simulation, learners receive instant feedback and must reevaluate the situation and change course of action, take corrective action, or continue on the same course.

Embedded mentoring. Mentors can ask questions during the exercise using an automated assessment feature that pauses the scenario in order to discern the learners' grasp of the situation and their current thought processes.

Automated after action review. After completing the simulation, the system provides an after action review that displays the learner's responses to all injects and provides feedback about the timeliness and consequences of the actions taken. Automated assessment allows immediate feedback that is objective. Within each high-level event, injects prompt the tasks and present corresponding conditions and expected actions. This forms the basis for assessments reported in the after action review. This review indicates learners' responses using ratings that indicate (1) the learner met the assessment criteria for completing the task, (2) the learner met the assessment criteria after prompting by simulated entities, or (3) the learner failed to meet the assessment criteria and complete the task. In addition, all actions, including emails, meetings, and briefing content, are viewable so learners can review and discuss answers with peers, instructors, and mentors.

Facilitated after action review. Senior mentors can provide active mentoring by annotating the after action review with comments and asking follow-up questions about actions taken, decisions made, communication content, and so on. This provides tailored feedback to the individual and allows mentors to assess subjective areas of performance, such as communication content, tone and phrasing of orders, and diplomatic concerns. This provides direct and detailed feedback to the after action review.

Conclusion

The JFACC Simulation and Mentoring System blends several key training components to ensure the learning and development of complex skills associated with experienced JFACCs. We incorporated into this system:

- Key elements of scenario content, including the cues and factors, critical tasks, strategies, and dynamic conditions reported by experienced JFACCs
- Key elements of instructional design built upon defined learning objectives using an experiential and immersive learning environment
- Key factors in the development of expertise, such as critical thinking and problem solving, consistent feedback, and opportunities for self-assessment
- Key mentorship components, such as feedback tailored to learners' needs and the utilization of mentors' experiences to provide a foundation for the mentoring.

By focusing on the cognitive components of expertise to create this program, we were able to incorporate the specialized knowledge and experience of high-level commanders and leaders to create a training program focused on facilitating new JFACCs' progression toward expertise. Incorporating key macrocognitive functions and processes supports the development of critical skills such as sensemaking, information synthesis, and team coordination and collaboration within the context of realistic events. The use of rich scenario content exercises skills such as operating under uncertainty, accounting for novel events, planning and replanning in response to changing conditions, and assimilating data from multiple sources in an operational setting with multiple partners. This exercise builds a pattern base that enhances JFACC candidates' ability to make recognitional decisions when real-world challenges arise and provides progressive training, from acquisition of knowledge through informational presentations, to applying knowledge in a problem-solving environment that requires critical thinking (vignettes), to the application of skills in an individual role with simulated teammates in a realistic simulation.

Limitations

We developed this prototype tool and training content from interviews with past and current JFACCs. Future work in this area should incorporate systematic observations of JAOCs and active JFACCs as well as interviews. Pairing observations with interviews would make it possible to draw direct correlations between decisions and behaviors. Observation of JAOC operations would also provide detailed information about all the staff within the JAOC, allowing for the development of team and joint training.

Because the current state of this training system is a prototype, we have not yet conducted training effectiveness studies. Assessment of this training system would allow for stronger conclusions about the methods used to create this system and the learning that takes place with these training methods. As we further develop this tool, we will conduct effectiveness studies and adjust scenario content, tool usability, and training focus as needed.

Recommendations

From this project, we see many potential future works. In addition to evaluating the current program, we envision several extensions of this training. This computer program has the capability to train multiple players at the same time, which provides excellent opportunities to train teams and partners from multiple agencies, military branches, governments, and so on. By expanding the current training to accommodate all key staff in the JAOC, team cohesion and relationship building can begin prior to arrival at their assigned JAOC. This command-level simulation training system has application across many domains, particularly those in which commanders are transitioning from practical/tactical thinking to conceptual/operational thinking. The capture of expertise and the connection between novices and mentors makes this a desirable program to administrators, commanders, and staff within any organization where decision making must shift from immediate ground-level tactics to higher-level operational planning and strategic decision making.

Appendix: JFACC Simulation and Mentoring System Module Descriptions

After action review reports: The after action review reports provide users tailored feedback about the decisions and actions taken during simulation play.

Community forum/discussion boards: The community forum provides a space where JFACCs, mentors, and JFACC candidates can talk about the JFACC position in both structured and unstructured ways. This forum allows users to schedule formal sessions with mentors, chat informally, post questions and answers, and interact as a group or one on one.

Lessons Learned Database/Navigator: This search capability improves users' ability to access lessons learned, after action reviews, and similar documentation from existing military databases.

Network Builder: The system allows users to manage, maintain, and build their contact lists. This system links to Virtual Officer's Club/Community Forum to enable relationship building.

Resource Recommender: This personalized system allows users to record and reflect upon their experiences. The system provides users with recommendations from resources related to the issues they request. The resource recommender tracks items such as lessons learned, unresolved questions, and developmental plans. If the user chooses, he or she can post diary entries in a module that makes excerpts public so others in the community can discuss them.

Vignette Community System: This system allows mentors and new JFACCs to create an electronic library of vignettes. A mechanism for mentor and peer feedback to both the vignettes and individuals' responses to vignettes is built into the system.

Acknowledgments

We thank the Air Force Research Laboratories for their support through Contracts FA8750-04-C-0077 and AF8750-04-C-0155. And specifically, we recognize our

TPOC, Carl DeFranco, and our collaborative partners, Charles River Analytics and WBNS/ONN-TV for their support.

Finally, we acknowledge our colleagues for their contributions to this research: Holly Baxter, Donald Cox, Eric Geissler, Dave Malek, Jennifer Phillips, Will Readinger, Bill Ross, and Karol Ross.

References

Crandall, B., Klein, G., & Hoffman, R. R. (2006). *Working minds: A practitioner's guide to cognitive task analysis.* Cambridge, MA: The MIT Press.

Davis, P. K., & Kahan, J. P. (2007). *Theory and methods for supporting high level military decision making.* (Technical Report prepared under Contracts F49642-01-C-0003 and FA7014-06-C-01). Santa Monica, CA: Rand Corporation.

Department of Defense. (2005). *Air & space commander's handbook for the JFACC* (June 17 rev.). Washington, DC: Author.

Ericsson, K. A., & Charness, N. (1994). Expert performance. *American Psychologist, 49,* 725–747.

Fowlkes, J. E., Salas, E., Baker, D. P., Cannon-Bowers, J. A., & Stout, R. J. (2000). The utility of event-based knowledge elicitation. *Human Factors, 42,* 24–35.

Goodrich, M. A., Sterling, W. C., & Boer, E. R. (2000). Satisficing revisited. *Minds and Machines, 10,* 79–110.

Herman, L., & Mandell, A. (2004). *From teaching to mentoring: Principles and practice, dialogue, and life in adult education.* New York, NY: RoutledgeFalmer.

Klein, G. (1998). *Sources of power.* Cambridge, MA: MIT Press.

Klein, G., Kaempf, G., Wolf, S., Thordsen, M., & Miller, T. E. (1997). Applying decision requirements to user-centered design. *International Journal of Human-Computer Studies, 46,* 1–15.

Klein, G., & Militello, L. (2004). The knowledge audit as a method for cognitive task analysis. In H. Montgomery, R. Lipshitz, & B. Brehmer (Eds.), *How professionals make decisions* (pp. 335–342). Mahwah, NJ: Lawrence Erlbaum & Associates.

Klein, G., Ross, K. G., Moon, B. M., Klein, D. E., Hoffman, R. R., & Hollnagel, E. (2003, May/June). Macrocognition. *IEEE Intelligent Systems,* 81–85.

Leland, J. M. (1997). *Keeping the JFACC at the operational level* (unpublished manuscript). Newport, RI: Naval War College.

Phillips, J. (2005). *JFACC knowledge report.* (Technical Report prepared under Contract FA8750-05-C-0077). Dayton, OH: Klein Associates.

Pigora, M A., Tamash, T., & Baxter, H. C. (2006). *Training novices and experts: A common assessment mechanism for knowledge, skills, and abilities.* Paper presented at the Interservice/Industry Training, Simulation, and Education Conference, Orlando, FL.

Randel, J. M., & Pugh, H. L. (1996). Differences in expert and novice situation awareness in naturalistic decision making. *International Journal of Human-Computer Study, 45,* 579–597.

Ross, K. G., Phillips, J. K., Klein, G., & Kohn, J. (2005). *Creating expertise: A framework to guide simulation-based training.* Paper presented at the Interservice/Industry Training, Simulation, and Education Conference, Orlando, FL.

Ross, W. A., Readinger, W. O., & Mills, J. A. (2005). *Learning in the hot seat: Mentoring software to support JFACC performance* (Final Technical Report prepared under Contract FA8750-04-C-0155). Dayton, OH: Klein Associates.

Schraagen, J. M., Klein, G., & Hoffman, R. R. (2008). The macrocognition framework of naturalistic decision making. In J. M. Schraagen, L. G. Militello, T. Ormerod, & R. Lipshitz (Eds.), *Naturalistic decision making and macrocognition* (pp. 3–25). Burlington, VT: Ashgate Publishing Co.

Shanteau, J. (1992). Competence in experts: The role of task characteristics. *Organizational Behavior and Human Decision Processes, 53,* 252–266.

Part III

Commentary
Overlooked Issues in Expert Decision Making

14

Naturalizing Sensemaking

David Snowden
Cognitive Edge

> The greatest loss of time is delay and expectation, which depend upon the future. We let go the present, which we have in our power, and look forward to that which depends upon chance, and so relinquish a certainty for an uncertainty.
>
> **—Seneca**

When things go wrong, its common to seek reasons for failure with the intention of using the knowledge gained to prevent similar failures in the future, and at times to allocate blame and responsibility. In management science considerable effort is placed on reducing future uncertainty through research, analysis, forecasting, scenario planning, and the like. We have a basic need to *make sense* of the world around us so that we can act in it. However, despite many investigations, multiple research projects, and an endless stream of popular (and unpopular) books that offer recipes for future mistakes, we still make mistakes; the future remains uncertain, and we are frequently surprised by what we thought were outlier events, so improbable that they could be ignored.

The material in this chapter has been derived from a broad range of projects over four continents in the past decade dealing with intractable problems. Much of the original funding came from the U.S. and Singapore governments in the context of counterterrorism and horizon scanning. Other source projects have included the mass engagement of staff in micro-scenario planning for the Government of British Columbia, the educational impact of museums on schoolchildren in Liverpool, issues of disintermediation for several pharmaceutical companies, as well as staff engagement and cultural mapping in the context of organizational change.

The argument will be made that we need to stop trying to anticipate the future, and instead move to a focus on anticipatory awareness, in which state we have a *resilient* capacity to recover from inevitable surprise. This is contrasted with approaches based on *robustness,* where the emphasis is on prediction and prevention of negative outcomes. To make the argument, we will first draw from complex adaptive systems theory to provide a theoretical base for the essential unknowability of future outcomes. This will lead to an examination of a new research tool based on self-signified micro-narratives to understanding the *evolutionary potential of the present*, which in turn enables a coevolutionary approach to decision making, in which theory, intent, and reality constantly interact through a series of safe-fail experiments (i.e., experiments in which failure is not fatal and from which we can recover quickly and learn), amplifying success and dampening failure, to allow the emergence of novel and beneficial solutions.

Sensemaking is a neologism most commonly associated with the work of Weick (1995), for whom the term defines the various actions and their consequences that emerge from efforts to create order, and to make sense of what has occurred in the past. Weick's work originates in social psychology and emphasizes the importance of language, metaphor, and meaning making through social interaction. While there is much in common between Weick's position and the material discussed in this chapter (e.g., work by Browning & Boudés, 2005), there are also some key differences. First, this chapter challenges the use of retrospective coherence to create models for future action, placing greater emphasis on understanding the present and reducing pattern entrainment that results from past failures. Second, it is in the philosophical tradition of naturalizing epistemology, drawing on natural science, and avoiding the dangers of confusing correlation with causation, which are all too common in management science. Third, the term *sensemaking* is used to emphasize that we are talking about a diverse and constantly evolving collection of processes that synthesize human and machine capabilities.

Different Types of Systems

> Whereas strong dynamic links among components (characterized as nodes) result in a "strong cluster," weak links between strong clusters give rise to a community or a world. Since any node can simultaneously belong both to a strong cluster and to a larger networked community, society, or world, boundaries become diffuse, but also dynamic and creative. Complex dynamical systems thus begin to look more like bramble bushes in a thicket than like stones. And it is extremely difficult, as any outdoorsman will tell you, to determine precisely where a particular bramble bush ends and the rest of the thicket begins.
>
> **—Juarrerro**

Complexity science has its origin in chemistry and biology, but has increasingly been applied in economics and social science (Byrne, 1998; Waldrop, 1992). It is best understood by looking at three different relationships that can exist between a system and agents operating within the system. I am using *system* to mean any network of interaction with coherence, which means it may have fuzzy boundaries. By *agent* I mean anything that acts within the system. That may be a person, a community, a dominant narrative, a process, or a rule.

Based on the constraint relationship between system and agent we can define three types of systems:

- **Ordered systems:** Here the nature of the system constrains the behavior of agents to make that behavior predictable. There are repeating relationships between cause and effect that can be discovered by empirical observation, analysis, and other investigatory techniques. Once those relationships are discovered, we can use our understanding of them to predict the future behavior of the system and to manipulate it toward a desired end state.

- **Chaotic systems:** These are sometimes called random systems, in which the agents are unconstrained and present in large numbers. For this reason, we can gain insight into the operation of such systems by the application of statistics, probability distributions, and the like. The number and the independence of the agents allow large-number mathematics to come into play.
- **Complex adaptive systems:** While these systems are constrained, the constraints are loose, or partial, and the nature of the constraints (and thereby the system) is constantly modified by the interaction of the agents with the system and each other; they coevolve.

The coevolutionary nature of complex adaptive systems means that they have inherent unpredictability, as the system will not return to an equilibrium state after it is disturbed; hence, the phrase *far from equilibrium* is sometimes used to describe them. In such systems the agents are adapting to proximate interactions with other agents and the environment. Any order or structure is emergent and only repeats, if at all, by accident, not by design. Of particular importance is the fact that due to these characteristics, complex systems are highly susceptible to minor changes or weak signals. This is sometimes illustrated by the cliché that the flapping of a butterfly's wings in the Amazonian rain forest causes a hurricane in Texas, but it is poor way of explaining the point, easily illustrated by asking the question: Why don't we just shoot the butterflies? There is no linear causality between the two events; the point is that multiple small perturbations create through their interaction an increasingly coherent storm system.

The phase change between types of system is also important and is more fully treated elsewhere (Kurtz & Snowden, 2003). It is important to realize the constraints in an ordered system can easily produce the conditions under which that system shifts and collapses into chaos. Attempting to exert excessive control through bureaucracy may result in a slow buildup of tension. Because excessive control makes it impossible to get anything done, people find workarounds, which enable the system to work despite itself, disguising failure until the system breaks catastrophically.

Most human systems are complex and adaptable to local interactions. We are constrained to varying degrees by systems, but we are also capable of modifying those systems. Small things lead to unintended and unforeseeable consequences. Once disturbed, any human system is altered irretrievably and will not return to an equilibrium state. When we understand that a system is complex, then our expectations with respect to decisions and decision processes are different. We do not make decisions based on forecasting outcomes and best practice, as both are impossible. We cannot adopt an approach based on *fail-safe design*, but have to switch to *safe-fail experiments* and monitor for the emergence of patterns. Some patterns we amplify and some we dampen, depending on the evolutionary direction we wish the system to take. We thus manage the evolution of the system toward an unknowable future state; we do not waste energy in trying to achieve a predefined system outcome.

Managing a complex system is rather like the effective management of a children's party. We create some boundaries (and if we have any sense, they are flexible, not rigid), either physical (do not leave the garden) or moral (no teasing), and then use catalytic probes (a football, a computer game, or similar) to see if we can stimulate the formation of stable self-organizing form of play. If what emerges is good, we amplify it; if it starts to go badly, we dampen it. The pattern of play is called an *attractor* in complexity theory. Attractors are phenomena that arise when small stimuli and probes resonate with people. As attractors gain momentum, they provide structure and coherence (Snowden & Boone, 2007). *We manage the emergence of beneficial coherence within attractors, within boundaries.* What is beneficial is determined in the light of loose goals rather than precise objectives. This is a highly effective low-energy solution compared with an approach based on learning objectives, project plans with milestone targets, incentives for target achievement, and party mission statements. The potential of complexity is to allow more to be achieved with less, and as importantly, to allow contextually appropriate solutions to emerge.

Managing for that emergent and beneficial coherence requires an effective mapping of the potentialities of the current state. Weak signals are important here, as outlier events represent both threat and opportunity. We are dealing in complex systems with human motivations and attitudes, and as will be argued, these are best revealed through an understanding of the day-to-day micro-narratives of existence.

Micro-Narratives

In order to understand the role of micro-narratives, we shall start with the endpoint of narrative research. Fitness landscapes, shown in Figure 14.1, were originally developed in biology (Wright, 1932) to represent the process of natural selection. With recent developments in computer modeling capability, it is possible to produce a representation of landscapes to demonstrate areas (the hollows) where there is an increased probability that the system will be stable. The deeper the hollow, then the greater the propensity of agents to visit, and the stronger the entrainment once there. The peaks, on the other hand, represent areas the system would normally avoid, but in consequence, these represent areas of unexpected or sudden change. The concept of fitness landscapes was adapted as a representation for large volumes of micro-narratives—in the above example, many thousand. How we produce these types of maps will be explained later in the chapter; however, the concept of fitness landscapes is

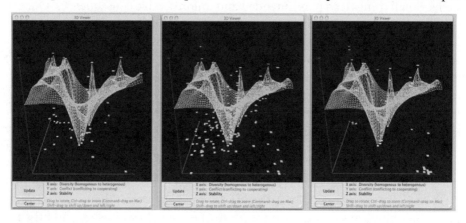

FIGURE 14.1   Fitness landscapes for micro-narratives.

introduced at this stage to demonstrate why new forms of research are needed to support the new dynamics of strategic decision making enabled by complexity science.

The self-signification of narratives (to be discussed later) produces the quantitative data that are captured in fitness landscapes. Hollows represent belief systems that are unlikely to change. If they are beneficial, then little energy is required to maintain them; on the other hand, if they are negative, they will be difficult or impossible to change. The smaller hollows (or "lumpy bits") represent proto-belief systems that could, with stimulus, become stronger attractors, potentially sucking support away from the existing ones.

This type of mapping allows decision makers to sense the evolutionary possibilities (and impossibilities) of the present along with risk assessment. It also allows monitoring of the impact of safe-fail experiments, permitting more rapid, effective, and lower-cost interventions. In Figure 14.1 each frame of the landscape represents a three-month period, and the dots represent outlier events. The third frame shows a new cluster, an interesting emergent possibility for change, comprising less than 10 micro-narratives out of tens of thousands, a weak signal that would normally be ignored as an outlier or exception but now can gain attention.

A New Approach to Narrative Research*

> The model of the human mind has been assumed to be akin to that of a symbol processor, a computer like engine that allows us to manipulate successfully a range of symbols of which language is deemed the most significant.
>
> This view of the human mind is very limiting because it assumes that what we know, and are able to know, is expressible in symbolic form only.
>
> ...because intangibles cannot be captured in the grip of such symbolic representations as questionnaires or surveys. It might rightly be pointed out that there are qualitative means of assessing transformational leadership in terms of interpreting certain leader behaviors, or by applying leader self-reports. These are imbued with their own problems because of the inability of differentiating between competing interpretations, a core problem of interpretive social science and hermeneutics, and by the endemic unreliability of self-reports.
>
> **—Lakomski**

Czarniawska (1998) challenges the assumptions of those who advocate *homo economicus* in organizational studies by arguing for a narrative-based approach to research. Stories are at the heart of our day-to-day discourse and our sensemaking abilities. They form a part of the commonsense world in which intention, interpretation, and interaction are all intermingled in any narrative. The narrator and listener must assume shared context when inferring meaning from narrative statements. Because stories carry with them ambiguity, their meaning can be interpreted in different ways in different contexts. So while few would disagree that narrative creates meaning, the question arises as to how it should be interpreted.

Much effort in recent years has seen the development of a range of formal methods derivative of the assumptions of interpretivism. Others see the interaction between researcher and research subject as an iterative process of inquiry that may be primarily

---

* Some of the material described this section is patent pending (Cognitive Edge Pte Ltd.).

driven by the researcher or the research subject. In the field of narrative this position is exemplified by Boje (2002). It is not the purpose of this chapter to provide a comprehensive summary or criticism of these methods other than to set the scene for what we are attempting with prehypothesis techniques, namely, to provide a quantitative technique that is supported by the rich context of self-interpreted narrative. In its turn, this provides a more objective basis for qualitative interpretative processes by the researcher, and indeed by the research subject, that can lead to sustainable action.

At the heart of this approach is a view of meta-narrative as an emergent property or strange attractor arising from social interaction, which is discoverable and actionable in the sense of quantum mechanics rather than the laws of motion. By taking narrative as a fragmented form of support for cognition, and using the ubiquity of the web and social computing together with the representational and information processing capacity of computers, we can considerably augment and enhance the natural pattern-based intelligence that underpins human decision making, and more so radically reduce interpretative conflict in the process. Further, research so conducted also creates a knowledge base that conforms with the naturalistic principles discussed throughout this volume.

The goal is to utilize the rich context of narrative to inform sensemaking, and also to create objective data in which cognitive bias is minimized and we can place some reliance on the conclusions drawn. In particular, we want to be able to move rapidly from research to action in decision making, allowing the decision maker to move back and forth from an abstract representation of the field as a whole to the raw micro-narrative without mediating interpretative layers.

The micro-narrative approach described below derives from a coevolution of theory and practice. The historical context of this development was as follows:

- The original use of narrative was a source for mapping knowledge. It arose from the deeply practical need to create a rich context from which it was possible to extract decisions and judgments and to ask questions about knowledge in use (Snowden, 1999). Narrative was also shown to be a better recall mechanism for contextual knowledge than questions.
- Subsequent work extended to the field of antiterrorism both before and after 9/11, where the approach was based on the capacity of narrative to elicit disclosure of otherwise hard to understand factors, such as intent and purpose. Also, and more critically, narrative was proposed as a sensory mechanism of weak signal detection. This was based on anecdotal evidence, confirmed by subsequent experiments, that human brains are more sensitized to narrative forms of knowledge about a situation than they are to analytical processes (Lazaroff & Snowden, 2006).

In carrying out work using narrative as a research approach, which has spanned over a decade, the following conclusions were drawn. From the perspective of practice, they seem commonsensical and were subsequently validated by reading in the natural sciences, but at the time they were (and in some circles still are) controversial. In summary:

- Naturally occurring stories come in fragmented anecdotal form. Those with the most meaning are often the most poorly constructed. In one case, when looking at the stories of schoolchildren on leaving a secondary school in Singapore, we found that the most powerful stories were from the least articulate students; there was less disguise in their narratives. Stories with accompanying paintings or pictures often resulted in a better form of narrative expression than a pure story in textual form.

- A story is always told in a context, from a context. If you read it, then it will trigger a reaction, but the reaction is not necessarily sympathetic to that intended or experienced by the storyteller. Each reader has his or her own context and situation. When we also take into account that anecdotes need to be captured in their native language (try telling a story in something other than your mother tongue and you will see the problem), this adds complexity to the process of gathering narratives. There needs to be some common context for any translation to be effective. As will be described in the next section, we determined that the best way to achieve this was for the researcher to create a tagging system of sufficient simplicity to be understood without active interpretation, and for the storyteller to signify the meaning in his or her narrative. In this way the metadata represent a common context.

- If the researcher first looks for patterns in the metadata using statistical or visual tools, he or she is less likely to be biased by content and prematurely converge on an interpretation. Metadata enable larger volumes of material to be scanned, and anomalies and clusters to be more easily detected, including outlier events that are often ignored by conventional research. This allows the researcher to construct and test hypotheses after data capture, using the self-signifiers.

- The material so gathered forms, with simple visual and criteria-based selection, a valuable knowledge asset that allows direct access by the knowledge user to data ranging from an abstraction of the field to the raw self-interpreted narratives. The material reflects a natural knowledge repository. Faced with a difficult or intractable problem, we are unlikely to look up best practice as a structured document. Instead, we seek out people and other sources, such as the Internet, gathering fragmented material that we select and blend with our own experience and the current context to determine how to act.

Self-Signification

> Nor do people pour new wine into old wineskins. If they do, the skins will burst, the wine will spill out, and the skins will be ruined. Instead, they pour new wine into fresh wineskins, and both are preserved.
>
> **—Mark 9:17**

Self-signification, as discussed, refers to the process of "tagging" one's own stories. There are two approaches generally in use to create metadata. One is to adopt a classification system, frequently hierarchical, assigning the material to a category. Within knowledge management the generation of a hierarchical taxonomy has been a frequent starting point. Another option is to use the free form tagging of key words and categories, as in social computing, the aggregation of which creates what is now known as a folksonomy and may be semantically created as well as interpreted.

In practice, due to the inherent limitations of card classification systems (which passed into early computers), hierarchical taxonomies have required an item to be placed in a single unique category. Innovations such as facet analysis (Ranganathan, 1967) allowed for greater flexibility and, to a large degree, form an early evolutionary stage of the approach advocated in this chapter, although the practicalities of such approaches had to await the development of scalable and reliable computing together with the wider awareness of folksonomies generated through social computing. However, the ideas of deep structure in language are under challenge from cognitive science (Deacon, 1997; Freeman, 2000), and this limits the aggregation claims of the semantic web and other technologies.

In a very real sense we are now provided with two limited extremes: the rigidity of hierarchical classification and the anarchy of folksonomies. Neither presents an ideal solution for meaning. A classification system that attempts to remove ambiguity would be subject to the general criticism of such systems as static and nonadaptive (Weinberger, 2007). On the other hand, allowing people to assign whatever tag they wanted would introduce massive uncertainty about the way the material was tagged. In practice, people do not use the same words or concepts consistently even in small groups, let alone larger populations. A pure folksonomy lacks a grammar of meaning between researcher or decision maker and the subject. In more recent years attempts have been made to create controlled vocabularies in social computing environments. This has potential within a restricted population but is not practical for mass capture.

The approach we adopted and refined over several years of experiment was to create a semiconstrained signification system, one that could be created by the researcher to accomplish specific objectives, or through an emergent process if inquiry is more general. The intention and practice of this approach is to create a common interpretative grammar between subject and object.

This is best illustrated by taking a recent case involving the experimental cultural mapping of populations in Pakistan, South Africa, and the United Kingdom. This project is part of a wider program designed to allow lateral transfer of knowledge between communities in different parts of the world using micro-narrative. The principle of a signifier or semiconstrained index set is that it have enough structure to create meaning, but not so much as to confine that meaning to hypotheses.

The method entails creation of a construct with labels (symbolic or language based) into which the tellers of the original micro-narratives position their story. Any shape can be used for this construct (this approach is patent pending), and the anchors are normally linked to the core concepts involved in the field of study. In this case that field was anthropology, so the process involved distilling some of the core concepts of anthropology such as temporalization, law, motivation, reason, and so forth. A triangle was selected as the most natural shape to characterize these concepts. Balancing between three points places enough cognitive load to force the person signifying to think about placement; it also avoids the more traditional good-bad type scale. Two examples are given below, together with their explanations. The italicized phrase provides the guide or constraint for the tagging system.[*]

---

[*] The work of Dr. Beth Mirram, the anthropologist on the project, is acknowledged here.

Temporalization

The lesson in this story applies to...

Temporality is the process of cultural time construction, whereby actors create and plan their activities and their temporal reference points during their life projects, thereby engaging the past and the future in the present (Munn 1992, p. 104). Issues of time (which may be conceived and experienced as linear, cyclical, relative, part of a "dreamtime" or dreaming, social or "emplaced") have often been secondary to other anthropological frames and issues, such as political structures, dissent, ritual, work, narrative, history, and cosmology, and to general theories of anthropological discourse. This triad recognizes the centrality of temporal orientation in cultural life (see also Gell, 1992).

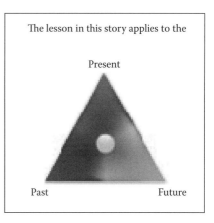

Law

What type of justice is evidenced?

This triad looks at the variance of legal sensibilities, which are embedded in different moralities and understandings about the relative locus of justice, be that formal or informal. This field focuses on how societies—with or without courts and constitutions—manage disputes, and involves finding out how various systems of justice really work in practice.

The modern anthropology of law began with Malinowski's *Crime and the Savage Society* in 1926. Malinowski proposed an ethnographic approach to the study of legal issues, calling for extended fieldwork in order to "study by direct observation the rules of custom as they function in actual life" (1926, p. 126), which is one ethnographic component this triad extends and deepens.

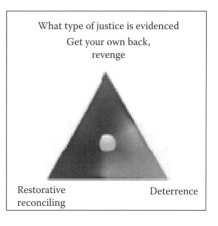

This index does not merely detail a particular set of legal rules, but seeks also to explore the cultural context of law in a given situation, and to appreciate its rationality. As Malinowski put it, "We are met by law, order, definite privileges and a well-developed system of obligations" (1926, p. 21). The spoken feedback channel available in this methodology and signified by the speakers answers Comaroff and Simon's (1981) call for illumination of the processes by which disputes are resolved and norms are elaborated. It also contributes to Riles' (1994) corollary about the alternative regimes and structures of law that inhere in any society. (From Meriam [2010]. With permission.)

These are two examples of the indexing constraints for self-signification; others covered issues of responsibility, worth, motivation, reason, and so on. No major issues or problems completing the process were found with any age group or literacy level. In other projects, symbols or animations have been used as an alternative to words, and various geometric shapes (not just triangles) can be used with the indexing occurring relative to fixed points used to generate scales for use in analysis.

For each triangle in the example above, we can derive three filters or scales, each representing the strength or weakness of one of the labels. These can then be used as axes on the fitness landscapes illustrated earlier, but they can also be used in a range of other interpretative systems, including correlation and *ad hoc* exploration. Here, visualization and statistical instruments allow patterns to be detected in the metadata, and once a pattern is detected, the ability to go to the supporting narrative, immediately and without interpretation, enables more effective decision making with respect to that pattern (e.g., encourage or dampen). Figure 14.1 shows the pattern of the metadata (one of several representations possible), and clicking on a part of that pattern reveals the underlying narrative. The nature of the method also means that capture is continuous and ongoing, and shows an evolving picture of the patterns of possibility. It contrasts with the more rigid planning cycle of annual targets and structured techniques, such as planning for specific scenarios. Ironically, the use of narrative data is both familiar and unfamiliar. In our day-to-day lives we live the unfolding narrative of our various social interactions, and we navigate them with ease. In the context of work, we move into more linear processes. Now that we understand some the natural science of uncertain systems, and we have new methods of research and representation, it is possible, as argued by Lincoln, to think anew, act anew.[*] To do so, however, requires new wineskins—the old cannot contain the new, although the old wine can complement the new vintage.

Conclusions

> For now we see through a glass, darkly; but then face to face: now I know in part; but then shall I know even as also I am known.
>
> **—1 Corinthians 13:12**

This chapter started with a quote from Seneca about the attractiveness of the certainties of the present over the unknowable future. It now concludes with a more poetic quote from St. Paul and the nature of understanding. The use of complexity theory and associated narrative research is new, especially in the fields of social and management science. Its theoretical base and practical workings are still novel, showing potential, but not yet fully known. We see as through a glass darkly, but we can still see.

Most human social systems are complex adaptive ones. They are constrained, but the constraints mostly adapt to changing context. Sometimes that change is gradual; sometimes it results from the catastrophic buildup of tension in an overconstrained system. Heavily bureaucratic organizations (in the author's experience) tend to have dense informal networks that make things work despite the constraints, not because of them. The net result is that failure in the system is disguised and tension builds until the final collapse is sudden and unexpected.

For the decision maker there are multiple problems associated with managing a complex adaptive system. There is no definite future that can be determined, and the most that can be set by way of objectives is a general or aspirational goal. Additionally,

---

[*] Message to Congress, December 1, 1862.

in complex adaptive systems, what has happened in the past may not provide insight for the future. Retrospective analysis may appear coherent but it is dangerous, as *hindsight does not lead to foresight.* The dangers of retrospective coherence, attributing cause in cases where complex historical events represent a unique pattern that will only repeat by accident, are all too obvious. So is the related danger of premature convergence, that is, coming too quickly to a solution for the future when even the present is not fully known. Where accurate anticipation is not possible, the decision maker has to move to a state of *anticipatory awareness* (see also Klein, this volume), operating on a safe-fail approach, assuming micro-failures, and focusing on resilience rather than robustness.

The narrative approach to research outlined above offers one new tool to assist decision makers in complex adaptive systems. By creating fitness landscapes we can direct the decision maker to the evolutionary potential of the present. Understanding what is stable, and what may rapidly or unexpectedly become unstable, allows better focus and the selection of contextually appropriate methods (Snowden & Boone, 2007). The collection of large numbers of self-signified micro-narratives enables not only research capability, but also a means to engage large numbers of staff or customers in the creation of micro-scenarios and to plot the landscapes of what those populations deem possible. Once a pattern is measured, deviations from that pattern can, with technology augmentation, be used to create weak signal alerts; the sooner an early pattern is spotted, the lower the energy cost of amplification or dampening of that pattern.

References

Boje, D. (2002). *Narrative methods for organization and communication research.* London, UK: Sage Publications.

Browning, L., & Boudés, T. (2005). The use of narrative to understand and respond to complexity. *E:CO, 7*(3–4), 32–39.

Byrne, D. (1998). *Complexity theory and the social sciences.* London, UK: Routledge.

Comaroff, J., & Roberts, S. (1981). *Rules and processes: The cultural logic of dispute in an African context.* Chicago, IL: University of Chicago Press.

Czarniawska, B. (1998). *A narrative approach to organization studies.* Thousand Oaks, CA: Sage Publications.

Deacon, T. (1997). *The symbolic species.* Penguin.

Gell, A. (1992). *The anthropology of time.* Oxford, UK: Berg Publishing.

Freeman, W. (1999). *How do brains make up their minds?* London, UK: Weidenfeld & Nicholson.

Kurtz, C., & Snowden, D. (2003). The new dynamics of strategy: Sense making in a complex-complicated world. *IBM Systems Journal, 42*(3), 462–483.

Lazaroff, M., & Snowden, D. (2006). Anticipatory modes for counter-terrorism. In R. Popp & J. Yen, *Emergent information technologies and enabling policies for counter-terrorism.* Wiley-IEEE Press.

Malinowski, B. (1926). *Crime and custom in savage society.* New York, NY: Harcourt, Brace & Company.

Meriam, B. (2010). *Signifier Design for Cultural Mapping Project.* Singapore: Cognitive Edge, Ltd. http://cognitive-edge.com/articledetails.php?articleid=63

Munn, N. (1992) The cultural anthropology of time: A critical essay. *Annual Reviews in Anthropology, 21*, 93–123.

Ranganathan, S. R. (1967). *Prolegomena to library classification*. London, UK: Asia Publishing House.

Snowden, D. (1999). Story telling: An old skill in a new context. *Business Information Review, 16*(1), 30–37.

Snowden, D., & Boone, M. (2007, November). A leader's framework for decision making. *Harvard Business Review,* 68–76.

Waldrop, M. (1992*). Complexity: The emerging science at the edge of order and chaos*. New York, NY: Simon & Schuster.

Weick, K. E. (1995). *Sensemaking in organizations*. Thousand Oaks, CA: Sage.

Weinberger, D. (2007). *Everything is miscellaneous: The power of the new digital disorder*. New York, NY: Henry Holt.

Wright, S. (1932). The roles of mutation, inbreeding, crossbreeding, and selection in evolution. *Proceedings of the Sixth International Congress on Genetics* (pp. 355–366). Austin, TX: Genetics Society of America.

15

Anticipatory Thinking

Gary Klein
Applied Research Associates, Inc.

David Snowden
Cognitive Edge Pte Ltd.

Chew Lock Pin
Defence Science & Technology Agency, Singapore

Anticipatory thinking is the process of imagining how unexpected events may affect plans and practices. We engage in anticipatory thinking when we suspect that the margin for error has become too small, or that a vulnerability has become exposed. Anticipatory thinking lets us guard against or forestall potential threats. It is a form of sensemaking. Sensemaking often involves explaining events and diagnosing problems, a retrospective process (e.g., Weick, 1995). It can also consist of formulating expectancies about future events (e.g., Weick & Sutcliffe, 2001). It is this future-oriented aspect of sensemaking that interests us here—anticipatory thinking.

The ability to perform anticipatory thinking is a mark of expertise in most domains. For example, de Groot (1946/1978) provided protocols of grandmasters studying chess positions and trying to find the move to play. Many of their comments show instant reactions upon considering a possible move, such as recognition that a move is promising, or else "Take it away," to reflect immediate disapproval. The grandmasters didn't have to perform progressive deepening to appreciate where they might be able to take control and where they would be getting themselves into trouble.

We distinguish anticipatory thinking from prediction. Certainly, anticipatory thinking overlaps with prediction and relates to the Level 3 situation awareness described by Endsley (1995) as well as to Hawkins and Blakeslee's (2005) formulation of the brain as a device for storing memories in order to make predictions. All of these accounts emphasize the future-oriented nature of human action. They all presuppose a model of humans as actors who are not simply acted on by changes in their environments (either actual or potential), but who act on the basis of their plans. However, we believe it is a mistake to see anticipatory thinking as a means of predicting what will happen. Instead, we are gambling with our attention to monitor certain kinds of events and ignore/downplay others. The ability to blend different concepts, experiences, and stories is a key part of human intelligence and permits us to handle greater uncertainty and ambiguity.

For example, experienced drivers are actively scanning for potential hazards, unlike novices. Pradhan et al. (2005) studied the eye movements of skilled and inexperienced drivers and found that the skilled drivers directed their focus to potential trouble spots. In contrast, the inexperienced drivers ignored these trouble spots, presumably keeping their eyes on the road to make sure their car stayed within the lanes. The experienced drivers aren't expecting the hazards or predicting them, but they are managing their attention. Experience and training have created the right patterns. Therefore, they have heightened sensitivity to weak signals that would be ignored by those with less experience. They have an edge in detecting problems.

Another difference between anticipatory thinking and Endsley's Level 3 situation awareness (making predictions) is that anticipatory thinking is aimed at potential events, including low-probability high-threat events, not simply the most predictable events. Along these lines, Adams and Ericsson (1992) distinguished between routine expertise, marked by a mastery of procedures, and adaptive expertise, which involves anticipatory thinking.

Further, the process of prediction is externally directed and usually concerned with guessing future states of the world. In contrast, anticipatory thinking is functional in that it helps us prepare to act, not just to predict. Klein, Phillips, Rall, and Peluso (2007) studied information operations specialists and found that the more experienced ones engaged in functional sensemaking. They weren't simply noting the content of messages but were interpreting the messages in terms of what information operations they could initiate. Their sensemaking was centered on what they could do. Therefore, we take a functional view of anticipatory thinking. We are sensitive to the affordances in the situation. These affordances stem from our beliefs about our own capabilities. When we anticipate events we are also preparing ourselves to both act and react.

Think about a sports event. Sometimes, when we don't care, we might predict that a favored team will win the game. But when we do care, and our team is the underdog, we say we are anticipating a loss—we are preparing ourselves for the disappointment.

In his book *Fundamental Surprise*, Lanir (1986) showed that in military examples of surprise the signals were fairly strong. The reason for the surprise was that the military officers overestimated their own abilities to react. Thus, we fail to anticipate when we don't prepare ourselves, either because we don't notice the signals or because we don't worry about them and don't bother to prepare ourselves. Anticipatory thinking depends on our capability to prepare, and not just our ability to predict future states of the world.

We also distinguish anticipatory thinking from the concepts of anticipated consequences and expectancies found in judgment and decision-making research (e.g., Keeney & Raiffa, 1976; von Neumann & Morgenstern, 1947). These concepts are attempts to represent future states in the process of making choices, as opposed to anticipatory thinking about how to prepare and position oneself for possible future states and to detect nonobvious demand characteristics of these states.

Varieties of Anticipatory Thinking

In reviewing various examples of anticipatory thinking we found several different forms, and we expect that researchers will identify additional forms in the future. Three common forms are pattern matching, trajectory tracking, and convergence.

Pattern Matching

With pattern matching the circumstances of the present situation bring out similar events and clusters of cues in the past. Experts have developed large pattern repertoires and so can immediately be on guard if they notice something untoward. Anticipatory thinking doesn't only involve problem detection, but one of its greatest values is to provide an early warning system when we are about to run into trouble. We will sense that something doesn't feel right, or that we need to be more vigilant. Greater experience and higher levels of expertise make it more likely that our anticipatory thinking will be accurate and successful. (We discuss anticipatory thinking in the context of recognitional decision making in a later section.) However, they also carry a danger, namely, overconfidence in our experience that may lead us to make a diagnosis, but miss something new or novel that may be seen by the naïve observer.

Trajectory Tracking

Sometimes anticipatory thinking requires people to get "ahead of the curve." The curve is the trajectory of events, and getting ahead of the curve means preparing ourselves for how the events are unfolding and how long it will take us to react. It means noticing and extrapolating trends. But it also requires a functional perspective. Infants have trouble catching a ball that a parent rolls past them because they initiate their reaching response aimed at where the ball is. With age and practice they learn to reach where the ball will be by the time they can move their hand. Beach and Mitchell (1990) have highlighted trajectory tracking as the basis of their account of decision making. Again, anticipatory thinking here blends our assessment of external events with the preparations we make to handle these events.

Trajectory tracking is different than pattern matching. It requires us to compare what is expected with what is observed. The process of tracking a trajectory and making comparisons is more difficult than directly associating a cue with a threatening outcome.

This is one of the areas where we use narrative. By paying attention to the experiences of others, generally expressed through stories, we build additional patterns that we can use to govern our response to future events. Narrative is a fundamental mechanism for meaning making (Kurtz & Snowden, 2003) and is of particular use in trajectory tracking to understand the possible moves of other actors in the decision space.

Convergence

This type of anticipatory thinking requires us to see the connections between events. Instead of responding to a cue, as in pattern matching, or to a trajectory, we also need to appreciate the implications of different events and their interdependencies. Duggan (2007) has described this process as strategic intuition, in contrast to the more reflexive recognition-primed intuition. With convergence, we notice an "ominous intersection" of conditions, facts, and events.

Or, sometimes we don't notice this ominous intersection. Snook (2002) has provided a variety of examples of inadequate anticipatory thinking in his analysis of the 1994 friendly fire incident in which two USAF F-15s shot down two U.S. Army

Black Hawk helicopters over northern Iraq. The F-15s and the helicopters were the only aircraft in the area at the time, it was clear daylight, and both the F-15s and the helicopters were in communication with an Airborne Warning and Control System (AWACS) that served as an air traffic control tower in the sky.

Because the primary mission of F-15s is air-to-air combat with enemy fighter jets, there was little expectation that they might be attacking helicopters. The F-15 pilots received brief training showing the profiles of Iraqi helicopters, but no one anticipated that the USAF pilots might have to visually distinguish friendly versus enemy helicopters. Therefore, the training didn't address ways to tell Iraqi Hind helicopters apart from U.S. Army Black Hawk helicopters.

Two years prior to the shoot-down, the operational security specialists had instituted a procedural change in which U.S. aircraft taking off from Turkey would squawk IFF (Identify Friend or Foe) code until they reached the Iraqi border, and then switch to a different IFF code while they were flying over Iraq. No one anticipated that some pilots might fail to make this shift and would therefore be vulnerable to friendly fire. AWACS crews were not on the lookout for this kind of IFF error. As a result, no one noticed that the Army helicopters flying into Iraq were not switching IFF codes (because no one had ever notified the Army aviation community about the new IFF procedure). Consequently, during the shoot-down incident the F-15 pilots found that the helicopters were not emitting the appropriate IFF code, indicating (incorrectly) that the helicopters were Iraqi.

The weapons directors (WDs) on the AWACS were communicating with all the aircraft. The procedure was for an en route WD to track an aircraft through Turkey, and then transition the aircraft to a tactical area of responsibility (TAOR) WD when it crossed into Iraq. These two WDs sat next to each other, to facilitate their coordination. However, on the day of the shoot-down the radar console for the en route WD wasn't working and he was shifted to an extra console, and away from the TAOR WD. No one anticipated how their separation might degrade their coordination. No one anticipated a need to ensure that they handed off aircraft moving between Iraq and Turkey. As a result, the TAOR WD was not tracking the helicopters as he communicated with the F-15s who informed him of their intent to shoot down two "unknown" helicopters.

Each of these examples contributed to the shoot-down. Each of them represents a failure of convergent anticipatory thinking—a failure to appreciate how problems might arise in the future.

Convergent thinking may require mindfulness. Langer (1989) and Weick, Sutcliffe, and Obstfeld (1999) have discussed the importance of mindfulness for skilled performance and safety. However, many times the relationships forge their own connection without being willed. Whether deliberate or unconscious, we need to notice inconsistencies.

In addition to catching inconsistencies, the convergent form of anticipatory thinking is how we notice connections. Convergent thinking is related to the Level 2 situation awareness discussed by Endsley (1995). The difference is that the convergent form of anticipatory thinking blends inference generation with a future orientation, blurring the line between Endsley's Levels 2 and 3 situation awareness. People who see the connection between events and conditions are not simply generating inferences. Their future orientation anchors the kinds of connections they notice, and they are not necessarily engaged in deliberate thinking. They are sometimes surprised and caught off-guard by the connections they see.

In one high-level Marine Corps exercise (Klein, McCloskey, Phillips, & Schmitt, 2000) the planners had not done a very thorough job and the exercise controllers decided to teach them a lesson. The plan left a very weak defense against an attack from the north, so the controllers got ready to launch precisely this type of attack. They were gleefully awaiting the panicked response of the Marine unit they were going to punish. However, the Marines had augmented their staff with some experienced colonels who had formerly been on active duty but were now in the reserves. These colonels had no real responsibilities. They didn't report to anyone or have anyone report to them, so they could just wander around. One of them noted a situation report that an enemy mechanized brigade had just moved its position. That was odd—this unit only moved at night, and it was daytime. He wondered if it might be on an accelerated time schedule and was getting ready to attack. (The technician who noted this movement had no idea of its implications.) Checking further, the colonel talked to the senior intelligence watch officer, who was also suspicious, not because of any event but because of a nonevent. The rate of enemy messages had suddenly declined. This looked like the enemy was maintaining radio silence. Based on these kinds of fragments, the colonel sounded an alert and the unit rapidly generated a plan to counter the attack—just in time. The colonel didn't predict the enemy attack; he put together different cues and discovered a vulnerability in his unit's defenses.

The pattern-matching form of anticipatory thinking involves recognition and recall processes in which a current situation is perceived as a familiar case. The convergence form involves a story construction process that connects different events and conditions. The trajectory-tracking form appears to be in-between, relying on recognition, recall, and story building, particularly when the trajectory is not a simple extrapolation of a trend but requires us to take additional events and conditions into account.

Aspects of Anticipatory Thinking

Anticipatory thinking is one type of sensemaking; explanation/diagnosis is the other type of sensemaking. Anticipatory thinking is linked to most, if not all, of the other macrocognitive functions and processes described by Klein et al. (2003). It is part of decision making, particularly the generation of expectancies within accounts such as recognition-primed decisions (Klein, 1998). Anticipatory thinking is also the process of mentally simulating courses of action in order to evaluate what sorts of problems they might lead to. Anticipatory thinking is essential to planning and replanning, for preparing to alter the direction taken. It is critical to coordination—effective teams need to have interpredictability so that team members successfully predict each other's reactions and successfully anticipate how they will each react to unexpected events. At the level of team interactions sensemaking depends on the coordination of anticipations.

Anticipatory thinking is a form of problem detection. Klein et al. (2006) showed that problem detection is not simply accumulating discrepancies until some threshold is reached—in many cases it requires a reframing of situational understanding in order to appreciate the significance of the evidence. That means shifting mental models and frames. Anticipatory thinking is also a form of mental simulation and the generation of expectancies.

Anticipatory thinking is expressed through attention management, as illustrated by the research on the eye movements of drivers. It forms the basis of common ground because without anticipatory thinking we couldn't maintain dialogues and we couldn't be surprised by the reactions of others. Surprise indicates that common ground has broken down and has to be repaired.

Barriers to Anticipatory Thinking

Unhappily, the set of barriers that interfere with anticipatory thinking are fairly long. We may fall prey to fixation/pattern entrainment (DeKeyser & Woods, 1993); we may use knowledge shields to explain away inconsistencies (Feltovich, Coulson, Spiro, & Adami, 1994); and we may be overconfident in our own capabilities. On top of these, we also have to contend with team- and organization-level barriers: organizational policies that filter weak signals, perverse incentives, disconnects between the data collector and the data integrator, difficulties in directing someone else's attention. Klein (2006) has described a variety of barriers to problem detection at the team/ organizational level.

We recently completed a pilot study to see if we could improve anticipatory thinking in small teams (Snowden, Klein, Chew, & Teh, 2007). Specifically, we wanted to overcome failures in anticipatory thinking resulting from attention entrainment/ fixation/garden path thinking, dismissal of alarms raised by people noticing weak signals, and confusion about mission intent. We primarily wanted to increase the likelihood of noticing and reacting to weak signals.

The study used military and intelligence scenarios presented to seven small teams (n = 4 to 5 per team) of professionals working in related organizations in Singapore. Each scenario included weak signals—to determine if and when the team noticed these signals and their implications. At predetermined break points each team member wrote individual notes about what was happening. We also observed the team discussions.

We examined a few techniques to improve performance, such as having the team members examine attractors and barriers to their mission, a crystal ball method for considering alternative explanations for events, a ritualized dissent technique, and a prospective hindsight method. Data were collected using narrative capture as well as a method for calibrating situation awareness.

A key finding is that at least one individual in every group did notice the weak signals and their implications, and typically half the group noticed the weak signals, based on the individual notes. However, no team took these early signs seriously. Usually, they weren't mentioned at all. If mentioned, they were dismissed. So the groups themselves did not consciously pick up or act on those signals. Therefore, the challenge shifts from helping people recognize weak signals to helping their groups and organizations take advantage of the anticipatory thinking of individuals.

Improving Anticipatory Thinking

We structure this section by considering the ways that anticipatory thinking may break down and some kinds of interventions to reduce or avoid the breakdown. Some of the common breakdowns result from fixation, weak mental models, organizational barriers, automation, and perspective.

The *fixation* problem has been amply demonstrated and discussed (e.g., DeKeyser & Woods, 1993; Feltovich et al., 1994; Rudolph, 2003). To prevent or overcome fixation, anticipatory thinking needs to be an adaptive response to a changing environment. Lovallo and Kahneman (2003) have suggested the value of an "outside view," using analogs to provide a reality check. Another approach is to bring in fresh eyes that have not yet been captured by the dominant interpretation of the situation. In contrast to a devil's advocate, these fresh eyes bring with them authentic dissent.

Weak mental models serve as a limiting factor for effective anticipatory thinking. One approach is to develop richer mental models that include a larger repertoire of patterns. Klein (2004; Klein & Baxter, 2009) has described a range of techniques for speeding up the growth of expertise.

Snowden (2000) has taken a different tack, exploring techniques for reconceptualization using high-abstraction languages or metaphor. For example, the attractors/barriers exercise seeks to strengthen anticipatory thinking by having people alter their perspectives of a situation. The exercise directs participants to describe their situation in terms of attractors (desirable states that are self-reinforcing) and barriers that must be overcome or neutralized. Participants distinguish between the attractors and barriers they can control versus those out of their control. Snowden also has developed a "future backward" technique to increase the sophistication of lessons learned sessions. In this exercise, participants identify two future states, an ideal one and an unacceptable one. These future states are intended to be incredible, rather than realistic. Using the future state as an anchor, the participants step backwards to the present, identifying decision points that would shift the trajectory from ideal to unacceptable, or vice versa.

Another strategy is for organizations to try to slow down the rapid rotation assignments so that people can gain more experience. And that raises the question of how organizations support or impede anticipatory thinking.

Organizational barriers can take two forms. *Between-organization* barriers impede the flow of ideas, interpretations, and information; *within-organization* barriers discourage people from voicing unpopular concerns. One approach for reducing between-organization barriers is to set up liaison officers or units. However, this stopgap method doesn't overcome the problem that people's primary allegiance is with their home organization, so that organizational rivalries still operate. Perhaps a more intense solution is to truly establish new units, drawing from the rival groups (in order to use their networks and expertise), but with a unified hierarchical structure. Turning to within-organization barriers, methods such as the use of devil's advocates don't seem to work. Snowden et al. (2007) have explored different approaches to ritualized dissent in which the team members are expected to voice unpopular but sincere beliefs; teams using these approaches appeared to perform better. The premortem method (Klein, 1998) is another form of ritual dissent that has gathered at least anecdotal support. Another approach has been described by Weick et al. (1999), who studied high-reliability organizations and found that they took a mindful and active stance toward potential problems, compared to the mindless and dismissive attitude of companies and industries that tolerated higher accident rates.

Complexity

Obviously, high degrees of complexity pose challenges to anticipatory thinking. Military organizations try to overcome complexity by structuring situations. The costs of this structuring process include a difficulty in seeing connections that cut across the boundaries and a vulnerability to situations that don't fit the preexisting structure.

Automation can increase passivity, thereby interfering with the active mindset needed for anticipatory thinking (Mosier, Skitka, Heers, & Burdick, 1998). Cognitive systems engineering methods (e.g., Hollnagel & Woods, 1983; Rasmussen, Pejtersen, & Goodstein, 1994) have been developed to improve the design of information technologies so that they support anticipatory thinking. These methods are intended to ward off "technophiliacs" and to maintain focus on strengthening and supporting the cognitive functions of the decision makers.

Team Coordination

Anticipatory thinking is essential to teams as well as for individuals. Klein, Feltovich, Bradshaw, and Woods (2004) have discussed the importance of interpredictability for teams, and Serfaty, Entin, and Johnston (1998) have described an anticipation ratio measuring a team's implicit coordination in terms of the tendency to send messages before those messages were requested. To improve anticipatory thinking for teams we can use a see-attend-act distinction. Someone on the team has to do the anticipatory thinking to become alert to a possible threat. The commander and other team members have to attend to the cues and the potential threat. And they have to prepare themselves to react.

Requirements for Anticipatory Thinking

A number of the chapters in this volume illustrate the importance of anticipatory thinking. None of these chapters explicitly refers to anticipatory thinking, because it had not been previously identified as a macrocognitive function that is relevant to the naturalistic decision-making community. Nevertheless, the varieties of anticipatory thinking all seem to be relevant to the projects described by the chapters.

Osland (Chapter 2) describes the challenges facing global leaders. These challenges, such as complexity, multiplicity, interdependence, ambiguity, flux, and cultural variations, make anticipatory thinking extremely difficult, but the nature of the job makes anticipatory thinking essential for global leaders. Similarly, Zimmerman, Sestokas, and Burns (Chapter 13) described a training program for Joint Forces Air Component Commanders (JFACCs) that should increase their anticipatory thinking.

DiBello, Missildine, and Lehmann (Chapter 17) describe a knowledge elicitation instrument that differentiates business experts who can quickly learn to anticipate changes in projected sales and revenues from those who are slower to anticipate what is likely to happen in the next quarter.

Anticipatory thinking is critical for effective teamwork, as illustrated by Hutchins and Kendall (Chapter 5) in their analysis of team collaboration by firefighters, Aegis air warfare teams, maritime interdiction teams, and interagency teams. Perry and Wears (Chapter 4) assess large-scale coordination within healthcare and the need that decision makers have to track expectancies and make accommodations on the fly. Strater, Cuevas, Scielzo, and Connors (Chapter 10) examined the role of collaboration technologies for supporting *ad hoc* command and control teams, which face a more severe challenge in anticipatory thinking than intact teams.

Anticipatory thinking is also useful for dealing with neutral or adversarial groups. Sieck, Smith, Grome, and Rababy (Chapter 7) studied the expertise needed to anticipate Middle Eastern crowd reactions. Thunholm (Chapter 8) contrasted military commanders with high or low experience in battle planning and decision making and found that one of the key demands was to anticipate what an adversary might do.

Therefore, we find the requirement for anticipatory thinking embedded in a wide variety of the domains studied by NDM researchers. Hopefully, in the future it will be possible to harvest the discoveries made about anticipatory thinking in these different settings and for these different activities.

Conclusions

Anticipatory thinking isn't just another new term. It is a form of sensemaking, looking forward rather than retrospectively. It is different than prediction. While it intersects with virtually all of the macrocognitive functions (e.g., decision making, planning, and coordination), it is different from each of these functions. It may operate in different ways than the explanatory forms of sensemaking. We believe that anticipatory thinking is critical to effective performance for individuals and for teams. This chapter offers some initial thoughts about the nature of anticipatory thinking, and we hope these will stimulate additional investigation.

References

Adams, R. J., & Ericsson, K. A. (1992, June). *Introduction to cognitive processes of expert pilots.* (Technical Report DOT/FAA/RD-92/02). Washington, DC: Federal Aviation Administration, Research and Development Service.

Beach, L. R., & Mitchell, T. R. (1990). Image theory: A behavioral theory of decisions in organizations. In B. M. Staw & L. L. Cummings (Eds.), *Research in organizational behavior* (Vol. 12). Greenwich, CT: JAI Press.

de Groot, A. D. (1978). *Thought and choice in chess.* New York, NY: Mouton. (Original work published 1946)

DeKeyser, V., & Woods, D. D. (1993). Fixation errors: Failures to revise situation assessment in dynamic and risky systems. In A. G. Colombo & A. Saiz de Bustamente (Eds.), *Advanced systems in reliability modeling.* Norwell, MA: Kluwer Academic.

Duggan, W. (2007). *Strategic intuition: The creative spark in human achievement.* New York, NY: Columbia University Press.

Endsley, M. R. (1995). Toward a theory of situation awareness in dynamic systems. *Human Factors, 37*(1), 32–64.

Feltovich, P. J., Coulson, R. L., Spiro, R. J., & Adami, J. F. (1994). *Conceptual understanding and stability, and knowledge shields for fending off conceptual change* (Final Report, Contract N00014-88-K-0077). Cognitive Science Division, Office of Naval Research. Also CKRP Technical Report 7, School of Medicine, Southern Illinois University, Springfield, IL.

Hawkins, J., & Blakeslee, S. (2005). *On intelligence.* New York, NY: Times Books, Henry Holt.

Hollnagel, E., & Woods, D. D. (1983). Cognitive systems engineering: New wine in new bottles. *International Journal of Man-Machine Studies, 18*, 583–600.

Keeney, R. L., & Raiffa, H. (1976). *Decisions with multiple objectives: Preferences and value tradeoffs.* New York, NY: Wiley.

Klein, G. (1998). *Sources of power: How people make decisions.* Cambridge, MA: MIT Press.

Klein, G. (2004). *The power of intuition.* New York, NY: A Currency Book/Doubleday.

Klein, G. (2006). The strengths and limitations of teams for detecting problems. *Cognition, Technology and Work, 8*(4), 227–236.

Klein, G., & Baxter, H. C. (2009). Cognitive transformation theory: Contrasting cognitive and behavioral learning. In D. Schmorrow, J. Cohn, & D. Nicholson (Eds.), *The PSI handbook of virtual environments for training and education: Developments for the military and beyond: Learning, requirements and metrics* (Vol. I, pp. 50–65). Westport, CT: Praeger Security International.

Klein, G., Feltovich, P. J., Bradshaw, J. M., & Woods, D. D. (2004). Common ground and coordination in joint activity. In W. B. Rouse & K. R. Boff (Eds.), *Organizational simulation.* New York, NY: John Wiley & Sons.

Klein, G., Phillips, J. K., Rall, E., & Peluso, D. A. (2007). A data/frame theory of sensemaking, In R. R. Hoffman (Ed.) *Expertise out of context* (pp. 113–155). Mahwah, NJ: Erlbaum.

Klein, G., Ross, K. G., Moon, B. M., Klein, D. E., Hoffman, R. R., & Hollnagel, E. (2003). Macrocognition. *IEEE Intelligent Systems, 18*(3), 81–85.

Klein, G., Schmitt, J., McCloskey, M. J., & Phillips, J. (2000). Decision making in the Marine Expeditionary Force (MEF) Combat Operations Center. *Proceedings of the International Command and Control Research and Technology Symposium 2000.* Naval Postgraduate School, Monterey, CA, June 26–28.

Kurtz, C. F., & Snowden, D. J. (2003). The new dynamics of strategy: Sensemaking in a complex and complicated world. *e-Business Management, 42*(3).

Langer, E. J. (1989). *Mindfulness.* Reading, MA: Addison-Wesley.

Lanir, Z. (1986). *Fundamental surprise.* Eugene, OR: Decision Research.

Lovallo, D., & Kahneman, D. (2003). Delusions of success. *Harvard Business Review, 81*(7), 57–63.

Mosier, K. L., Skitka, L. J., Heers, S., & Burdick, M. D. (1998). Automation bias: Decision making and performance in high-tech cockpits. *International Journal of Aviation Psychology, 8*, 47–63.

Pradhan, A. K., Hammel, K. R., DeRamus, R., Pollatsek, A., Noyce, D. A., & Fisher, D. L. (2005). Using eye movements to evaluate effects of driver age on risk perception in a driving simulator. *Human Factors, 47*, 840–852.

Rasmussen, J., Pejtersen, A. M., & Goodstein, L. P. (1994). *Cognitive systems engineering.* New York, NY: John Wiley.

Rudolph, J. W. (2003). *Into the big muddy and out again.* Unpublished doctoral thesis, Boston College, Boston, MA.

Serfaty, D., Entin, E. E., & Johnston, J. H. (1998). Team coordination training. In J. A. Cannon-Bowers & E. Salas (Eds.), *Making decisions under stress: Implications for individual and team training* (pp. 221–245). Washington, DC: APA.

Snook, S. A. (2002). *Friendly fire: The accidental shootdown of U.S. Black Hawks over northern Iraq.* Princeton, NJ: Princeton University Press.

Snowden, D., Klein, G., Chew, L. P., & Teh, C. A. (2007). A sensemaking experiment: Techniques to achieve cognitive precision. *Proceedings of the 12th International Command and Control Research and Technology Symposium.* Naval War College, Newport, RI, June 19–21.

Snowden, D. J. (2000). The art and science of story or 'Are you sitting uncomfortably?' Part 1: Gathering and harvesting the raw material. *Business Information Review, 17*(3), 147–156.

von Neumann, J., & Morgenstern, O. (1947). *Theory of games and economic behavior* (2nd ed.). Princeton, NJ: Princeton University Press.

Weick, K. E. (1995). *Sensemaking in organizations.* Thousand Oaks, CA: Sage.

Weick, K. E., & Sutcliffe, K. M. (2001). *Managing the unexpected: Assuring high performance in an age of complexity.* San Francisco, CA: Jossey-Bass.

Weick, K. E., Sutcliffe, K. M., & Obstfeld, D. (1999). Organizing for high reliability: Processes of collective mindfulness. *Research in Organizational Behavior, 21*, 13–81.

16

Uncertainty Management and Macrocognition in Teams
A Multidisciplinary Review and Integration

Stephen M. Fiore, Michael A. Rosen, and Eduardo Salas
University of Central Florida

Uncertainty is a central component of naturalistic models of decision making as well as emerging macrocognitive frameworks, and a defining characteristic of human performance in naturalistic decision-making (NDM) environments. In contrast to traditional decision-making approaches that conceptualize uncertainty in terms of explicit probability assessments, uncertainty in NDM contexts has been defined as a "sense of doubt that blocks or delays action" (Lipshitz & Strauss, 1997, p. 150). In this way, uncertainty is viewed, at least in part, as an affective appraisal, as a *feeling* of uncertainty. However, uncertainty in NDM is still largely viewed as a quantity to be reduced or eliminated, an obstacle to be overcome. While this is no doubt valid in many senses, it is a limited view consistent more with prescriptive decision-making research traditions than with naturalistic ones. As the NDM community of practice expands the type of cognitive performance it investigates, from intuitive decision making to causal reasoning and sensemaking, for example, the issue of uncertainty becomes increasingly important. The sensemaking literature places the affective experience of unexpected events as a central component of performance, so much so that the "*feeling* of order, clarity, and rationality is an important goal of sensemaking" (Weick, 1995, p. 29). Therefore, a more explicit treatment of how affect interacts with or colors the knowledge work of professionals is in order.

Research from parallel traditions studying group and individual knowledge building and problem solving in naturalistic contexts has suggested that reducing uncertainty is only one of several strategies adopted when managing complex tasks (Bradac, 2001). A more comprehensive perspective considers uncertainty as a resource that individuals and teams actively manage through various cognitive and behavioral strategies. This includes reduction at times, and active cultivation at others (Brashers, 2001). For example, perceptions of uncertainty about the likelihood of highly negative events is frequently increased during group discussion. Similarly, an individual or group can actively increase uncertainty about a piece of information by questioning the credibility of the source of that information. Intentional increases in perceived uncertainty can occur when information does not fit a working understanding of the situation.

This chapter attempts to contribute to the understanding of uncertainty and uncertainty management in real-world situations through a critical review of the multidisciplinary literature pertaining to the experience and management of uncertainty by teams and individuals in naturalistic settings. Theoretical and empirical research from group communication theory, organizational sciences, and the emerging emotion regulation and management literature for individuals and groups will be reviewed and integrated with the extant NDM literature on how individuals and teams experience and manage uncertainty in decision-making and problem-solving activities. Specifically, this chapter seeks to provide a review of important perspectives on the experience and management of uncertainty, and propose several summary themes at the team and individual level that solidify the implications of this literature for NDM researchers. Before addressing these issues, we discuss the macrocognition in teams perspective, as this is an area where uncertainty management can contribute significantly.

What Is Macrocognition in Teams?

The NDM tradition focuses on understanding and improving decision-making processes in real-world settings. However, decision making is not the only type of cognitive work done in the wild, and as the NDM community of practice matures, researchers have expanded their focus in terms of cognitive and collaborative performance. Decision making is no doubt a critical aspect of performance in many settings; however, problem solving, planning, sensemaking, causal reasoning, and collaboration all occur in field settings as well and are equally important to organizational effectiveness. The term *macrocognition* has been used, at times loosely, to describe these types of complex cognitive work. Among other things, the growing emphasis on macrocognition represents a shift from what Rasmussen (1983) called rule-based performance to knowledge-based performance (Rosen, Salas, Fiore, Letsky, & Warner, 2008). That is, NDM has traditionally investigated the intuitive routine performance of experts (i.e., people that know what to do in a given situation based on extensive experience in a domain), and macrocognition expands this to include experts working out of context (e.g., Hoffman, 2007), solving problems in novel situations, engaging in knowledge-based performance. There has been a rapid increase in interest in this topic and a growing amount of theoretical work available on both the individual and team levels (e.g., Klein et al., 2003; Letsky, Warner, Fiore, & Smith, 2008; Schraagen, Militello, Ormerod, & Lipshitz, 2008).

Recently, Fiore and colleagues (Fiore, Smith-Jentsch, Salas, Warner, & Letsky, in press) have developed a multilevel model of macrocognitive performance in teams. In their framework, macrocognition in teams is defined as "the process of transforming internalized team knowledge into externalized team knowledge through individual and team knowledge building processes" (p. 8). The Fiore et al. model proposes five main dimensions of macrocognition in teams: internalized knowledge, externalized team knowledge, individual knowledge-building processes, team knowledge-building processes, and team problem-solving outcomes. Each of these dimensions comprises multiple subdimensions. These are summarized in Table 16.1 and described below.

TABLE 16.1   Summary of the Dimensions of Macrocognition in Teams

Dimension	Subdimension	Definition
Internalized team knowledge	Team knowledge similarity	The degree to which different roles understand one another or the important features of the situation (e.g., mental model similarity, shared situation awareness)
	Team knowledge resources	The collective understanding of the team's resources and responsibilities (e.g., task knowledge stock)
Externalized team knowledge	Externalized cue-strategy associations	Collective agreement as to their task strategies and how situational variables modify those strategies
	Pattern recognition and trend analysis	The accuracy of patterns and trends explicitly noted by team members
	Uncertainty resolution	Degree to which a team has collectively agreed upon critical problem variables
Individual knowledge-building processes	Individual information gathering	Actions individuals engage in to increase their existing knowledge (e.g., information search in displays, requests for information)
	Individual information synthesis	Building and comparing relationships between information to develop actionable knowledge
	Knowledge object development	Creating artifacts that represent task knowledge
Team knowledge building	Team information exchange	Sharing relevant information; passing information to the right person at the right time
	Team knowledge sharing	Sharing explanations and interpretations
	Team solution option generation	Proposing solution options to the group
	Team evaluation and negotiation of alternatives	Clarifying decision options by discussing advantages and disadvantages of alternatives
	Team process and plan regulation	Discussing and critiquing the team's performance (i.e., knowledge-building) process
Problem-solving outcomes	Quality of plan (problem-solving solution)	Effectiveness of the plan at meeting the objectives or resolving the problem
	Efficiency of planning process	The amount of time the team takes to arrive at a solution
	Efficiency of plan execution	The quality of the plan

Source: Fiore, S. M., et al., in E. S. Patterson and J. Miller (Eds.) (2010). *Macrocognition Metrics and Scenarios: Design and Evaluation for Real-World Teams*, Ashgate, Aldershot, UK.

First, *internalized team knowledge* is the collective knowledge possessed by individual team members. This includes shared knowledge, as discussed in the team cognition literature, in terms of both overall knowledge and distribution of knowledge across team members. Second, *individual knowledge building* comprises the processes a person engages in to develop a coherent understanding of a situation. This includes internal processes as well as overt actions. Third, *team knowledge building* is a team-level process where team members distribute and synthesize information into actionable knowledge. Fourth, *externalized team knowledge* includes the facts and relationships that have been explicitly agreed upon by the team members and are present in group discussion or shared workspaces. The subdimensions of these processes are defined in Table 16.1. As this framework focuses on the knowledge work of a team and not behavioral coordination, it highlights a slightly different role for uncertainty. For example, in traditional team decision-making literature, behavioral coordination and team decisions are facilitated by accurate and shared mental models of team members, the task, and situation. Team members are able to make compatible assessments of the situation and take coordinated action because they share an understanding of the situation and what it means relative to the team's goals and each member's individual roles. Here, uncertainty can affect either the understanding of the situation (i.e., team members don't know what is happening) or the response to it (i.e., team members know what is happening, but not how to address the issue). If the situation is routine (i.e., team members have shared mental models), then the space of "things to be uncertain about" is limited significantly.

However, in macrocognition in teams, there is not necessarily the precondition of shared mental models of the team, the task, or the situation. When the team's purpose, goals, configuration, and situation are entirely unique, the team must engage in a learning process (i.e., knowledge building) as it performs. In this situation, uncertainty functions at a more fundamental level as the team has to negotiate the process of building knowledge from the ground up and not relying on preexisting shared mental models. In the following sections, we discuss perspectives on uncertainty with ramifications for understanding this type of knowledge-based performance.

What Is Uncertainty in Macrocognitive Contexts, and Why Manage It?

In macrocognitive environments, sources of uncertainty are numerous. Klein (1998) lists the following four categories of sources of uncertainty: missing information (i.e., information is unavailable, has not been transmitted to the decision maker, or simply cannot be located when the decision needs to be made), unreliable information (i.e., confidence in the source of the information is low or the information is actually not credible), ambiguous or conflicting information (i.e., the information can be interpreted in multiple plausible ways), and complex information (i.e., integrating the information is difficult). These categories all describe features of the information or decision-making environment that elicit or precipitate the psychological experience of uncertainty. Uncertainty as a psychological construct is widely discussed in the literature (see Lipshitz & Strauss, 1997), with most conceptualizations falling into one of two categories: objective indeterminance in the environment (see Milliken, 1987, for a review of this debate) and perceptions of uncertainty. The objective indeterminance approach has been employed in relatively abstract and tightly controlled laboratory tasks (see Kahneman, Slovic, & Tversky, 1982) but has proven problematic in those conditions (Gigerenzer, Todd, & the ABC Research Group, 1999), and even more so in real-world situations. Actual and perceived levels of uncertainty are quite different as an individual may (and frequently will) have perceptions that are inconsistent with the true state of the world. Therefore, even if objective measures of uncertainty were plausible from a practical perspective in complex tasks, objective uncertainty is a distinct (but hopefully not orthogonal) construct from perceived uncertainty. It is the perception or psychological experience of uncertainty that this chapter deals with.

As previously stated, in NDM contexts, uncertainty has been defined as "a sense of doubt that blocks or delays action" (Lipshitz & Strauss, 1997, p. 150). This definition emphasizes two important characteristics. First, uncertainty in complex environments is subjective. Second, uncertainty is conceived of in terms of the effects it has on the individual's ability to act. Uncertainty has long been linked to levels of arousal. For example, the experience of uncertainty has been described as a state of general arousal or activation without a clear course of action (Brener, 1987). The decision maker knows something must be done but not what to do, and therefore remains in a heightened state of preparation to act. Researchers increasingly draw on ideas of dual processing systems to explain how people make decisions under conditions of uncertainty and how emotions associated with the experience of uncertainty contribute and in some cases dominate the decision-making process. In general, these theories propose distinct yet functionally and structurally intertwined emotional and cognitive systems that interact and influence one another. For example, Loewenstein and colleagues' (Loewenstein, Weber, Hsee, & Welch, 2001) risk as feelings hypothesis proposes that cognitive evaluations of and emotional reactions to different risky options can diverge (i.e., each system has a preference for different options), and that when they diverge, the emotional system is likely to determine behavior. Slovic and colleagues' (Slovic, Finucane, Peters, & MacGregor, 2002, 2007) affect heuristic proposes that people often rely on a rapid affective appraisal of a situation in order to make a decision. This "affect as information" position, however, describes only one role played by emotions in decision making, and in many situations decision outcomes are reached by an interaction of cognitive and affective mechanisms and not by choice of one form of information over another (Pfister & Bohm, 2008).

So, if uncertainty is an affective experience of a state or situation that blocks, delays, or otherwise modifies action selection, decision makers must come to terms with it before acting. From a deterministic perspective this means improving the amount or quality of information as much as possible before the time to act can no longer be forestalled. However, from a dual processing perspective, it is plausible that the strategies the decision maker uses to manipulate the affective experience of the situation will influence outcomes as well. That is, it is not just the cognitive and behavioral uncertainty management strategies most often discussed that determine effectiveness, but the affective strategies as well. In the following sections, perspectives from several sets of literature are reviewed to provide some insight into this general perspective on the experience of uncertainty.

Perspectives on Managing Uncertainty

This section provides a review of the theoretical and empirical literature pertaining to uncertainty on the team or group level. Specifically, perspectives from group communication theory on the role of uncertainty in group processes will be reviewed. In the following section, implications of this literature for macrocognition in teams will be explored.

Group Communication Theory

Group communication theorists have focused much attention on the topic of uncertainty within group interactions in various situations. In this section, three main theoretical perspectives are reviewed: uncertainty reduction theory (URT), problematic integration (PI), and uncertainty management (UM). These perspectives differ in many regards, such as their conceptualization of the nature of uncertainty and the level of abstraction at which they explain interactions (Babrow, 2001). Additionally, these three theories have been chosen for examination here because they are representative of theorizing on this topic in the group communication literature and because they illustrate the development of an increasingly sophisticated understanding of how people experience and work with uncertainty in real-world environments.

Uncertainty Reduction

Uncertainty reduction theory (URT) was developed to explain the process by which people make sense of initial interpersonal situations. That is, URT posits that people are driven to reduce uncertainty about others in order to increase the predictability of their own behavior and that of others during interaction (Berger & Calabrese, 1975). In this sense, uncertainty is the driving force behind uncertainty-reducing behaviors such as information seeking. This view of uncertainty as a driver of behavior is consistent with the view that uncertainty is an impetus for decision making as well (Beach & Connolly, 2005). Uncertainty in URT is conceptualized in terms of the number of possible alternatives perceived about an interactant's future behavior, explanations of past behavior, or values and beliefs. Increased numbers of perceived alternatives are related to higher levels of uncertainty. In this way, URT adopts a view of uncertainty that is subjective, but very much rooted in a description of the environment (i.e., its perceptions about the number of alternative explanations). URT has been developed and extended by many researchers since its initial proposal. One such extension of particular note is the motivation to reduce uncertainty (MRU) model proposed by Kramer (1999). MRU more clearly articulates the nature of the need to reduce uncertainty underlying URT and outlines a number of important moderators of the effect of this drive on information-seeking behaviors. Specifically, MRU proposes that reducing uncertainty is only one of multiple goals a person can have while interacting with others. People must balance these goals during an interaction and not focus on maximizing one to the exclusion of others (Eisenberg, 1984). In recognizing this, MRU moves beyond the initial conceptualization of URT, where uncertainty is an autonomous or isolated driver of communicative behaviors.

Some common goals that can conflict with reducing uncertainty involve maintaining the coherence and flow of the conversation (e.g., following Grice's maxim of relation; Grice, 1975), avoiding conflict, and maintaining a façade of certainty. The crux of MRU is that the presence or absence of goals that conflict with the goal of reducing uncertainty moderates the relationship between a given level of motivation to reduce uncertainty and the observed information-seeking behaviors. Different levels of motivation and goal conflict (e.g., does seeking information cost anything?) can influence uncertainty-reducing behaviors (e.g., type and amount of information seeking). The four central propositions and uncertainty-reducing strategies of MRU are described in Table 16.2. MRU proposes that the outcomes of these different uncertainty-reducing strategies may not be different. For example, it has been shown that passive information seeking can be just as effective for new employees in organizations as direct methods (Morrison, 1993; Kramer, 1993). Additionally, the effect

TABLE 16.2 Summary of Propositions of the Motivation to Reduce Uncertainty (MRU) Theory

Proposition	Description of Prediction
High motivation and aligned goals → direct information seeking	When someone is highly motivated to reduce uncertainty and there are no competing goals (e.g., saving face or maintaining an illusion of certainty), direct information-seeking behaviors will result. That is, the individual will attempt direct communication with the person from which uncertainty is stemming.
High motivation and conflicting goals → indirect information seeking	In the case of a person with a high motivation to reduce uncertainty in a situation where the pursuit of reducing uncertainty conflicts with other goals, MRU hypothesizes that indirect information seeking will result. This entails going to third-party sources of information in order to reduce perceived uncertainty. For example, if someone is uncertain about another's competence in a given area, but asking this person would be perceived as violating a social norm, third-person information could be sought to avoid causing a personal offense.
Low motivation and aligned goals → passive information seeking	Passive information seeking will result when an individual has a low motivation to reduce uncertainty in situations with aligned goals. In this context, there is no real cost for reducing uncertainty, but there is no strong drive to do so either. Consequently, the individual monitors the situation without expending effort or attention to reduce uncertainty. This situation can arise when one person knows little about another, but does not have a great deal of shared goals or interdependency.
Low motivation and conflicting goals → varied responses depending on the nature of conflicting goals	An interesting prediction of MRU is that conflicting goals can drive an individual to engage in uncertainty-reducing behaviors when there is a negligible motivation to do so stemming from perceived levels of uncertainty. For example, appearing to be cooperative and engaged in the dialogue is a common goal in interaction. This goal can elicit information seeking when there is a low level of motivation to do so based on the experience of uncertainty.

Source: Kramer, M. W., *Management Communication Quarterly, 13*, 305–316, 1999.

of information-seeking behaviors on perceived uncertainty is contingent upon the nature of information received. It is very possible that receiving more information can increase the level of uncertainty (e.g., if the information received is complex or conflicts with previously held information).

Problematic Integration

Problematic integration (PI) is a general theory of communication (Bradac, 2001; McPhee & Zaug, 2001). Three fundamental notions outline the PI perspective in a broad sense. First, people form probabilistic orientations; that is, they generate subjective estimations of the likelihood of events. Probabilistic orientations deal with issues such as the tendency for a person to behave in a specific way or the expectation that some event will occur. These probabilistic orientations are not specific probability assessments, but general senses or feelings. Second, people form evaluative orientations; that is, they associate meaning or value with an event and its probabilistic orientation. Third, probabilistic orientations and evaluative orientations are integrated in complex ways. There is reciprocal influence between people's estimations of likelihood and their evaluations. For example, people tend to overestimate the likelihood of positive events (Weinstein, 1980).

The crux of PI is that the integration of probabilistic and evaluative orientations can be predictably difficult given certain conditions. Specifically, PI outlines four conditions in which integration is problematic. First, *integration is problematic when probabilistic and evaluative orientations diverge*. This occurs when a highly positively valued event is estimated at a very low probability of occurring, or conversely, when a highly negative or adverse event is likely to occur. Second, *integration is problematic when there is ambiguity*. Ambiguity is essentially uncertainty about uncertainty and arises when probabilistic orientations cannot be formed readily, when a person does not know how likely or unlike an event may be. Third, *integration is problematic under conditions of ambivalence*. Ambivalence occurs when a person is choosing between mutually exclusive options that are valued equally. Essentially, the person (or group) has to decide between two options whose outcomes may be different, but equivalent in terms of value. Fourth, *integration is problematic when events or outcomes are impossible or inevitable*. Here, the evaluative orientation can conflict with the certitude of an event (e.g., an impossible event that is highly valued or a highly negative yet inevitable event).

Using the concepts of probabilistic and evaluative orientations, PI clearly identifies cases where assessments of value and fact diverge as critical areas for research and tools for support in practical contexts (McPhee & Zaug, 2001). Additionally, PI proposes that social interaction is the medium in which these integrations are performed. Specifically, problematic integrations are "formed, sustained, and transformed by communication" (Babrow, 2001, p. 556). In essence, PI theory proposes that these conditions in which the two orientations diverge are constituted by and resolved with social interaction. In the following section, these ideas are extended further and methods by which groups attain resolution are discussed.

Uncertainty Management

Uncertainty management theory (UMT) is rooted in the perspectives previously discussed, yet in many ways it represents a departure from traditional thinking (Bradac, 2001). Most fundamentally, the earlier perspectives primarily focused on probability assessments as uncertainty. However, UMT researchers conceptualize uncertainty as "a self-perception about one's own cognitions or ability to derive meaning" (Brashers, 2001, p. 478). This definition is metacognitive in nature and divorces uncertainty from a direct relationship with the probabilistic nature of the environment. If individuals feel uncertain (i.e., they perceive themselves to have a poor understanding of a situation), they are, regardless of whether their understanding is accurate. Engaging in uncertainty management involves the manipulation of uncertainty with various strategies (Brashers et al., 2000). Information can be used to increase or decrease levels of uncertainty, both intentionally and unintentionally. That is, people may seek out information with the intent of reducing their uncertainty, but this new information may ultimately have the opposite effect (e.g., conflicting information is found). UMT also uniquely highlights the intentional creation of uncertainty and does not focus solely on its reduction. People may increase uncertainty around options they do not wish to pursue or events and information they value negatively. This is an integral part of group problem solving. In addition to seeking information for manipulating uncertainty, information avoidance behaviors may be applied as well. These strategies seek to maintain a given state of certainty. There is strong empirical evidence that the degree to which groups discuss the possible negative outcomes of alternative courses of actions is critical to effective outcomes (Orlitzky & Hirokawa, 2001). That is, groups that tolerate a process where uncertainty about the proposed solution is actively cultivated as a means of evaluation reach better outcomes. While the end state of the group may be one of reduced or low uncertainty, the trajectory of the group passes through high levels of internally generated uncertainty.

Group Affect

The literature reviewed in this chapter has primarily dealt with the subjective, or affective, component to the experience of uncertainty. If uncertainty management in teams can be conceptualized in part as an affective management process, then a more nuanced view of emotions in groups is necessary. Based on work in the areas of emotional contagion and group affect (e.g., Barsade, 2002; Kelly & Barsade, 2001), Rosen, Feldman, Fiore, and Salas (2007) proposed a framework describing the core features of uncertainty management in team problem solving. This framework is illustrated in Figure 16.1 and is based on the notion that there are two primary mechanisms for the communication (or spread) of affect in teams. First, there are explicit processes of symbolic communication that team members use to inform one another of their emotional states, in this case feelings of doubt (i.e., uncertainty). These explicit processes also include behavioral or communicative strategies for manipulating or managing this uncertainty, such as information-seeking, avoiding, and adaptive approaches. Second, there are implicit processes for communicating emotions in groups. These processes are mediated by low-level paralinguistic, physiological, and other subsymbolic communication. People have an innate capacity to read subtle cues indicating the emotional state of others (Waid, 1984). However, there are differences in people's ability to sense and transmit this type of information. An implication of the literature previously

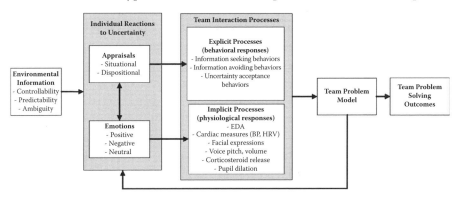

FIGURE 16.1   Framework of core features of managing the experience of uncertainty in team problem solving. (Adapted from Rosen, M. A., et al., *Augmented Team Cognition for Complex Problem Solving: A Framework and Research Agenda*, paper presented at the Augmented Cognition International, Baltimore, MD, 2007.)

reviewed is that the ability of team members to sense and transmit affective information is important to macrocognitive outcomes. While this is an area in need of more research, there is some support for this relationship. For example, groups composed of members with higher emotional intelligence (i.e., the ability to sense and communicate emotion) perform better on collaborative problem-solving tasks than teams comprised of members who are lower on this attribute (Jordan & Troth, 2004).

In sum, the perspectives reviewed above provide insight into phenomena of interest for NDM researchers, specifically incorporating uncertainty management into the five dimensions of macrocognition in teams (Fiore et al., in press). These perspectives are consistent with many of the core characteristics of the NDM community (e.g., a focus on informationally and socially complex situations, collaboration, high-stakes outcomes, stressful or emotionally charged situations). Additionally, these perspectives provide conceptualizations of uncertainty that are distinct yet compatible, and in many ways complementary to the common view of uncertainty as both a sensory and a cognitive experience in NDM. In the following section, implications of these perspectives are discussed relative to macrocognition in teams.

Research Themes and Implications of an Affective-Based View of Uncertainty

Because managing uncertainty is in part an affective experience, understanding and improving how people cope with uncertainty involves understanding not only the cognitive and behavioral strategies, but also the emotion regulation strategies used. In this section, we summarize the preceding discussion by advancing a set of themes. These themes are intended to highlight the overlap in perspectives previously discussed and guide future research. Additionally, this section provides a discussion of the implications of these themes for macrocognition in teams.

Theme 1: The psychological experience of uncertainty is the result of interactions between cognitive appraisals of and affective responses to information in the environment.

While probabilistic information is inherent in most (if not all) real-world contexts, these inherent uncertainties in the environment are distinct from the psychological experience of uncertainty. People can be very certain about uncertain events and vice versa. Similarly, people will have different reactions to the types of conditions generally considered to precipitate the psychological experience of uncertainty (i.e., missing, incomplete, unreliable, and complex information) based on issues such as value motivations. This research theme has implications for understanding many of the macrocognitive processes in teams, specifically the individual knowledge-building processes. As team members integrate information into a coherent understanding of the problem or situation, their behaviors will be regulated in part by their affective experience of the knowledge they possess as well as the information they receive. The sensemaking literature directly addresses this by stating that the feeling of coherence is an outcome of the sensemaking process (Weick, 1995). This highlights the need for a better understanding of the interactions of affect and cognition leading to justified certainty in knowledge-building tasks. This leads to the following proposition.

Theme 2: Individuals manipulate (or manage) their experience of uncertainty via two categories of methods: (1) manipulation of the target of uncertainty and (2) manipulation of their affective response.

The first element of this theme is familiar territory. Decision makers use various information-seeking and sensemaking activities to alter and improve their understanding of a situation or potential course of action. However, much of the literature reviewed in this chapter suggests that decision makers must also manage or manipulate their affective response to the situation. This highlights two potential areas of importance not widely addressed in the NDM literature. First, emotion regulation or emotion management training may provide an important addition to the repertoire of strategies for improving decision-making performance. Training on the knowledge structures underlying expert performance as well as strategies for managing the informational component of uncertainty (e.g., the RAWFS heuristic—reduction, assumption-based reasoning, weighing pros and cons, forestalling, and suppression; Lipshitz & Strauss, 1997; Lipshitz, Omodei, McClellan, & Wearing, 2007) could be augmented with emotion regulation strategies. Second, variability in expert performance in managing uncertainty could be accounted for by individual differences in these emotion regulation skills as well as variables such as tolerance for ambiguity. Although we've adopted the definition of uncertainty as a feeling that blocks action, if this feeling is intense and aversive enough (e.g., as in someone with an extremely low tolerance for ambiguity), action may be taken in order to remove this feeling (e.g., Loewenstein, 1996). In essence, for individuals with low ambiguity tolerance, the proximal need to remove uncertainty becomes more important than meeting a more distal goal of decision making, planning, or collaboration.

Theme 3: Reduction of uncertainty may be a desired end state, but managing uncertainty does not imply a simple linear trajectory with negative slope; increasing uncertainty can be a useful part of the process.

One of the most striking themes, present most dominantly in the uncertainty management literature, is that increasing uncertainty can be useful. This has particular importance for the macrocognitive processes of team knowledge building. When considering knowledge building, the possibility that team members may intentionally increase uncertainty about different options or interpretations is unlikely if a pure uncertainty reduction perspective is adopted. This perspective may be counterproductive, as there may be many plausible interpretations of known information, and only by critiquing and questioning can the group entertain different options and arrive at the one which is most coherent. This is reflected in the evaluation and negotiation of alternatives subdimension of team knowledge building. Here, team members actively cultivate uncertainty between each other in order to test components of their overall knowledge. By engaging in a discussion of possible negative consequences of an action, uncertainty about the appropriateness of the action can be temporarily increased; however, if negative consequences can be mitigated by the resultant alteration of the course of action, then it is likely that a greater feeling of coherence will emerge.

Theme 4: More information is not the cure for uncertainty; the creation of coherent knowledge is.

This theme is linked to the previous one. Early theories of uncertainty in group communication theory proposed that uncertainty motivated information seeking. While this may be true in many cases, it is not true in all cases. Uncertainty can also trigger adaptation strategies if the uncertainty is irreducible (e.g., there is an inherent indeterminate nature about the source of uncertainty or information is not available), or information avoidance behaviors (e.g., refusing to seek or accept new information for fear it will disrupt the current understanding of the situation). In many cases, the situation already involves massive amounts of information. Adding more solves nothing; it does not alleviate uncertainty, it accentuates it. This again highlights the importance of team knowledge-building processes, particularly team knowledge sharing and evaluation and negotiation of alternatives. It is these processes that create "meaning around information in a social context" (Lant, 2002, p. 345). Fundamentally, macrocognition in teams is translating information into knowledge at the group level (Fiore et al., 2010). However, the literature reviewed in this chapter suggests that the affective experiences of team members during this knowledge-building process is as fundamental to the process as the more common perspective of tracing information and knowledge flow.

Concluding Remarks

As the science of team decision making in naturalistic environments grows, it is important to look across disciplinary boundaries. Macrocognition in teams is a novel approach to understanding complex collaborative knowledge work; however, other research traditions have investigated similar types of performance and there is much work to be leveraged. The centrality of the concept of uncertainty to most (if not all) types of performance in complex environments means that the macrocognition in teams literature can gain from previous theorizing and experimentation. There is a rich tradition of conceptual and empirical (qualitative and quantitative) work available to help guide research and ultimately practice for the NDM community. Other traditions that share some of the core characteristics of NDM (e.g., a focus on real-world complexity and interaction) can provide a valuable resource for theory development.

Uncertainty reduction and management theories in group communication theory as well as work in the area of group affect provide a broader framework from which to view the experience and manipulation of uncertainty in complex cognitive work. We hope that this chapter provides an initial bridge between the group communication, group affect, and NDM communities of research. There is much to be gained on all sides from a cross-fertilization of ideas among these domains.

Acknowledgment

The views, opinions, and findings contained in this chapter are the authors and should not be construed as official or as reflecting the views of the Department of Defense or the University of Central Florida. The writing of this chapter was supported by Grant

N000140610118 from the Office of Naval Research, awarded to S. M. Fiore, S. Burke, F. Jentsch, and E. Salas, University of Central Florida.

References

Babrow, A. S. (2001). Uncertainty, value, communication, and problematic integration. *Journal of Communication, 51*(3), 553–573.

Barsade, S. G. (2002). The ripple effect: Emotional contagion and its influence on group behavior. *Administrative Science Quarterly, 47*, 644–675.

Beach, L. R., & Connolly, T. (2005). *The psychology of decision making: People in organizations* (2nd ed.). Thousand Oaks, CA: Sage.

Berger, C. R., & Calabrese, R. J. (1975). Some explorations in initial interaction and beyond: Toward a developmental theory of interpersonal communication. *Human Communication Research, 1*(2), 99–112.

Bradac, J. J. (2001). Theory comparison: Uncertainty reduction, problematic integration, uncertainty management, and other curious constructs. *Journal of Communication, 51*(3), 456–476.

Brashers, D. E. (2001). Communication and uncertainty management. *Journal of Communication, 51*(3), 477–497.

Brashers, D. E., Neidig, J. L., Haas, S. M., Dobbs, L. K., Cardillo, L. W., & Russell, J. A. (2000). Communication in the management of uncertainty: The case of persons living with HIV or AIDS. *Communication Monographs, 67*(1), 63–95.

Brener, J. (1987). Behavioral energetics: Some effects of uncertainty on the mobilization and distribution of energy. *Psychphysiology, 24*(5), 499–512.

Eisenberg, E. M. (1984). Ambiguity as strategy in organizational communication. *Communication Monographs, 51*, 227–242.

Fiore, S. M., Elias, J., Salas, E., Smith-Jentsch, K. A., Warner, N., & Letsky, M. (2010). From data, to information, to knowledge: Measuring knowledge building in the context of collaborative cognition. In E. S. Patterson & J. Miller (Eds.), *Macrocognition metrics and scenarios: Design and evaluation for real-world teams*. Aldershot, UK: Ashgate.

Fiore, S. M., Smith-Jentsch, K. A., Salas, E., Warner, N., & Letsky, M. (In press). Macrocognition in teams: Developing and defining complex collaborative processes and products. *Theoretical Issues in Ergonomics Science*.

Hoffman, R. (Ed.). (2007). *Expertise out of context*. New York, NY: Erlbaum.

Gigerenzer, G., Todd, P. M., & the ABC Research Group. (1999). *Simple heuristics that make us smart*. Oxford, UK: Oxford University Press.

Grice, H. P. (1975). Logic and conversation. In P. Cole & J. L. Morgan (Eds.), *Syntax and semantics* (Vol. 3, pp. 225–242). New York, NY: Seminar Press.

Jordan, P. J., & Troth, A. C. (2004). Managing emotions during team problem solving: Emotional intelligence and conflict resolution. *Human Performance, 17*(2), 195–218.

Kahneman, D., Slovic, P., & Tversky, A. (1982). *Judgment under uncertainty: Heuristics and biases*. New York: Cambridge University Press.

Kelly, J. R., & Barsade, S. G. (2001). Mood and emotions in small groups and work teams. *Organizational Behavior and Human Decision Processes, 86*(1), 99–130.

Klein, G. (1998). *Sources of power: How people make decisions*. Cambridge, MA: MIT Press.

Klein, G., Ross, K. G., Moon, B. M., Klein, D. E., Hoffman, R. R., & Hollnagel, E. (2003). Macrocognition. *IEEE Intelligent Systems, 18*(3), 81–85.

Kramer, M. W. (1993). Communication and uncertainty reduction during job transfers: Leaving and joining processes. *Communication Monographs, 60*, 178–198.

Kramer, M. W. (1999). Motivation to reduce uncertainty. *Management Communication Quarterly, 13*(2), 305–316.

Lant, T. (2002). Organizational cognition and interpretation. In J. Baum (Ed.), *Companion to organizations* (pp. 344–362). Oxford, UK: Blackwell Publishers Ltd.

Letsky, M., Warner, N., Fiore, S., Rosen, M., & Salas, E. (2008). Macrocognition in Complex Team Problem Solving. Proceedings of the 12th International Command and Control Research and Technology Symposium (12th ICCRTS), Washington, DC: United States Department of Defense Command and Control Research Program.

Lipshitz, R., Omodei, M., McClellan, J., & Wearing, A. (2007). What's burning? The RAWFS heuristic on the fire ground. In R. R. Hoffman (Ed.), *Expertise out of context* (pp. 97–111). New York, NY: Erlbaum.

Lipshitz, R., & Strauss, O. (1997). Coping with uncertainty: A naturalistic decision-making analysis. *Organizational Behavior and Human Decision Processes, 69*(2), 149–163.

Loewenstein, G. (1996). Out of control: Visceral influences on behavior. *Organizational Behavior and Human Decision Processes, 65*(3), 272–292.

Loewenstein, G. F., Weber, E. U., Hsee, C. K., & Welch, N. (2001). Risk as feelings. *Psychological Bulletin, 127*(2), 267–286.

McPhee, R. D., & Zaug, P. (2001). Organizational theory, organizational communication, organizational knowledge, and problematic integration. *Journal of Communication, 51*(3), 574–591.

Milliken, F. J. (1987). Three types of perceived uncertainty about the environment: State, effect, and response uncertainty. *Academy of Management Review, 12*(1), 133–143.

Morrison, E. W. (1993). Newcomer information seeking: Exploring types, modes, sources, and outcomes. *Academy of Management Journal, 36*, 557–589.

Orlitzky, M., & Hirokawa, R.Y. (2001). To err is human, to correct for it divine: A meta-analysis of research testing the functional theory of group decision-making effectiveness. *Small Group Research, 32*, 313–341.

Pfister, H.-R. D., & Bohm, G. (2008). The multiplicity of emotions: A framework of emotional functions in decision making. *Judgment and Decision Making, 3*(1), 5–17.

Rasmussen, J. (1983). Skills, rules, and knowledge; Signals, signs, and symbols, and other distinctions in human performance models. *IEEE Transactions on Systems, Man and Cybernetics, 13*(3), 257–266.

Rosen, M. A., Feldman, M., Fiore, S. M., & Salas, E. (2007). *Augmented team cognition for complex problem solving: A framework and research agenda.* Paper presented at the Augmented Cognition International, Baltimore, MD.

Rosen, M. A., Salas, E., Fiore, S. M., Letsky, M., & Warner, N. (2008). Tightly coupling cognition: Understanding how communication and awareness drive coordination in teams. *International Journal of Command and Control, 2*(1). http://www.dtic.mil/cgi-bin/GetTR Doc?AD=ADA513557&Location=U2&doc=GetTRDoc.pdf.

Schraagen, J. M., Militello, L. G., Ormerod, T., & Lipshitz, R. (Eds.). (2008). *Naturalistic decision making and macrocognition.* Aldershot, UK: Ashgate.

Slovic, P., Finucane, M., Peters, E., & MacGregor, D. G. (2002). The affect heuristic. In T. Gilovich, D. Griffin, D. Kahneman, T. Gilovich, D. Griffin, & D. Kahneman (Eds.), *Heuristics and biases: The psychology of intuitive judgment* (pp. 397–420). New York, NY: Cambridge University Press.

Slovic, P., Finucane, M., Peters, E., & MacGregor, D. G. (2007). The affect heuristic. *European Journal of Operational Research, 177*(3), 1333–1352.

Waid, W. M. (Ed.). (1984). *Sociophysiology.* New York, NY: Springer-Verlag.

Weick, K. E. (1995). *Sensemaking in organizations.* Thousand Oaks, CA: Sage.

Weinstein, N. D. (1980). Unrealistic optimism about future life events. *Journal of Personality and Social Psychology, 39*(5), 806–820.

17

How Do You Find an Expert? Identifying Blind Spots and Complex Mental Models Among Key Organizational Decision Makers Using a Unique Profiling Tool

Lia DiBello
City University of New York and Workplace Technologies Research, Inc.

David Lehmann
Workplace Technologies Research, Inc.

Whit Missildine
City University of New York and Workplace Technologies Research, Inc.

The decisive shift from a production-based economy to a knowledge economy over the past half century has forced businesses and management to confront new models of economic success. This knowledge economy, typified by global information and communication technologies, has created a new kind of market volatility. Successful enterprises now prioritize speed and flexibility over the old standards of size and access to resources. Companies now seemingly grow overnight, but they also implode much faster than before when they are not able to maintain their value proposition. For those of us focused on changes in cognition and decision making in business, these conditions require the development of new models of expertise, decision making, and leadership.

Traditionally, studies of leadership have focused on top management as the central organizing force of an organization. Numerous efforts to pinpoint the relevant characteristics of successful leaders were carried out in the hopes that the expertise of effective leadership could be harnessed and reproduced to enhance organizational performance (Hunt, 1999). Leadership studies, particularly those in social and organizational psychology, focused heavily on optimal leader traits, such as charisma, esteem, assertiveness, and type A personality structures (Hollander, 1978; House, Spangler, & Woycke, 1991). However, scores of inquiries showed these models of leadership have little utility in the real world. As early as 1985, Meindl, Erlich, and Dukerich (1985) attributed the fervor around top-down trait approaches to leadership as a "romance" and a "myth" we perpetuate to keep faith in the capabilities of top-level decision makers.

The assumptions we create around leadership most likely have their roots in director-centric, rationalistic Cartesian models of decision making and expertise. These classic models of decision making assume that the expertise (of a business, for example) resides *within* the individuals who control and direct the major decisions.

As an alternative perspective, our work on decision making and expertise is highly influenced by the Vygotskian tradition, including critical psychology and activity theory. This broad framework reverses the classical view of mind and decision making (Cole, Engestrom, & Vasquez, 1977; Vygotsky, 1986). In this view, the mind is not conceived as an internal entity that imposes itself on the world. Rather, cognition is shaped through individuals' participation and performance in the social and physical environment in an ongoing manner. As individuals participate in goal-oriented group activities, they get social feedback as to the appropriateness and the contributory value of their behavior; over time, this kind of reinforcement influences cognitive abilities, and to some extent cognitive development itself (Scribner, 1987).

Newer perspectives, such as distributed cognition (Hutchins, 1996), naturalistic decision making (Klein, 1999), transactive memory systems (Wegner, 1987), and complexity science (Marion & Uhl-Bien, 2001), support a similar view. In the emerging field of naturalistic decision making (NDM), for example, researchers focus on how people make decisions in real-world, real-time settings and perform cognitively complex functions in situations defined by "ill-structured problems; uncertain, dynamic environments; shifting, ill-defined or competing goals; action/feedback loops; time stress and high stakes" (Gore, Banks, Millward, & Kyriakidou, 2006, p. 928). The kinds of volatile environments that require critical decision-making expertise often present unpredictable scenarios and do not allow time for planning, modeling, and optimization (Klein, 1999). Expert decision makers under these conditions cannot rely on deductive processes toward a best course of action; rather, they use heuristics, intuition, and satisficing strategies to make rapid, high-stakes decisions that can be rapidly modified to changing conditions. Similarly, work on distributed cognition, pioneered by Hutchins (1996), argues that, when studying leadership and expert decision making, the unit of analysis is not simply one individual at the top, but rather leadership should be understood as a distributed enterprise embedded within the social relationships and organizational norms and constraints guiding decision-making activity.

New insights from the fields of complexity science and emergence also indicate a need for models of business leadership that are more in line with new economic realities and are providing new ways of understanding the role of leadership in organizational performance. Marion and Uhl-Bien (2001), for example, conceptualize leadership as the ability of top management to *enable*, rather than *control*, the outcomes of organizational interactions. These theoretical models suggest the new "expertise" of top management may be *an ability to anticipate future states of change*, rather than the ability to design and carry out strict objectives and directives. In line with these new theories of cognition and leadership, assuming a well-coordinated team, the "expert" at the helm of a successful profit-oriented company may not be any one person. Rather, running a company may be more of a finely tuned coordination among a leadership team, especially in large companies or in particularly volatile industries.

These insights have not only theoretical but also methodological implications. Three important realities of everyday life in business have methodological significance for assessing enterprise executive-level decision makers: (1) Organizations are composed of distributed cognitive systems, (2) organizations rely on well-coordinated mental models, and (3) expensive mistakes can result from complex blind spots within a distributed team mental model. Researchers must not overlook the fact that decision making at the top is a distributed enterprise, requiring a great deal of coordination within the organization to achieve performance objectives. Assessments of executive decision making may be more effective when we are able to tap into the mental model guiding decisions that evolve over time, rather than looking into specific traits or attributes of the decision makers themselves. The term *mental model* refers to mental structures that instantiate long-term domain knowledge and that are used to reason through a specific task. Mental models develop as a function of experience, and are not based on pure logical deduction. Mental models enable simulation; that is, decision makers mentally "run" the model to make predictions about possible events in the environment or in a system and to prepare for future outcomes (Gentner & Stevens, 1983). In the present discussion, moreover, mental model is understood to be embedded within emergent complexities of an organization, and to be distributed across organizational members.

Furthermore, decision-making expertise may be best understood as a developmental process. Given the volatility of markets and the complexity of team decision making in large organizations, we need not be as concerned with the general cognitive ability of today's executive so much as his or her domain-specific expertise and cognitive agility, which is often associated with the kind of intuitive expertise developed through experience. Cognitive agility is what allows executives to rapidly respond to changing situations and revise guiding mental models to meet performance demands. In sum, these insights require us to shift away from thinking of the cognitive ability of business leaders as fixed and static, and instead to focus on the way in which expertise evolves over time in response to dynamic environments. It also requires us to discard attempts to locate decision-making expertise as a fixed capacity that resides within the individual decision maker.

For this chapter, we present preliminary results of a leadership team assessment using our FutureView™ Profiler. Specifically, this case involves the top eight managers and the CEO of a global biodevice company. The participants were the CEO, and the division presidents from around the world. The Profiler is a tool that assesses expert decision making of executives and top management. In its most basic form, the Profiler allows one to (1) assess the extent to which an individual's guiding mental model can be revised to accommodate novel sources of information relevant to key decisions, (2) identify domain-specific blind spots in key decision makers' mental models of their industry, (3) identify the extent to which a mental model of the business is shared among leaders on the same team, and (4) identify the extent to which a comprehensive mental model of the business exists among members of a leadership team; that is, are all the individual blind spots "covered" by the members of the team collectively? The Profiler is meant only to profile leaders' mental models regarding the major elements of their business sector and examines how they solve real business problems using online tasks similar to those of their actual jobs. It does not evaluate personality traits, the ability to communicate, charisma, or ethics. In contrast, it does address questions such as: How do decision makers approach complex sources of information to make judgments about appropriate courses of action? Exploring the utility of our tool and its implications for executive assessment, this chapter highlights some of our insights, the pitfalls, and some remaining questions from a field test of the Profiler among key decision makers in a medical device firm.

Expertise and Cognitive Agility

Researchers studying highly skilled people have begun to focus on what has been called intuitive expertise, which is the kind of expert knowledge that resides below the threshold of conscious awareness (Klein, 1999; Polanyi, 1967). In general, experts tend to organize their knowledge within a holistic framework that allows them to quickly perceive the significance of events or situations and mentally simulate possible courses of action and the consequences of actions. From their point of view, experts are acting from "the gut," but in fact, a complex framework (or mental model) is guiding their behavior and can be specified by a systematic analysis of their behavior (Dreyfus, 1997). Experts in the same domain easily identify each other. Even if they don't agree with another expert's choices, they easily recognize that they share a common perceptual experience within their area of expertise.

The early expertise literature isolated characteristics of experts by comparing their performance to that of novices, but did not address the development of expertise (e.g., Chase & Simon, 1973; Chi, Glaser, & Farr, 1988). Hubert Dreyfus (Dreyfus & Dreyfus, 1986) advanced the view that expertise is a developmental process. His five-stage model of expertise ranges from *novice* to *expert*, with *advanced beginner, competent,* and *proficient* filling the interim stages. Dreyfus introduced the idea that as individuals become more expert, their thinking evolves from rule based to intuitive. In other words, their thinking gets increasingly organized around a core of organizing principles that comprise an underlying mental model of the domain as opposed to a set of recipes for action. Consequently, with increased expertise in a domain, individuals' thinking gets increasingly agile and responsive to situational cues, rather than being governed by abstract rules. We use Dreyfus's five stages in the Profiler to frame how we look at managers' patterns of decision making (see Table 17.1).

Because expertise is not consciously accessible, it is normally assessed using highly designed work sampling methods, performance in simulators (such as those used with aircraft pilots), or cognitive probes, which require a person to perceive, process, and act on a data set. These kinds of methods have been shown to be more reliable than surveys or self-reports in revealing the underlying mental models or operating heuristics that drive the thinking, holistic situation assessment, perceptual processing, and "gut feel" decision-making characteristic of intuitive expertise (Roth, Bobko, & McFarland, 2005). In contrast, verbal methods, such as tests, surveys, or interviews, rely on conscious awareness and productive verbal skills, and thus risk tapping into only surface dimensions of mental processing.

Dreyfus's developmental model of expertise is most useful for our purposes. In particular, it suggests two features that seem highly pertinent to a characterization of business experts. One is a deep understanding of the underlying forces of business and the ways that they can tip out of balance, or tip each other out of balance. Good examples of this would be the tension between supply and demand, or the changing status and availability of capital. The other characteristic—which may underlie all kinds of expertise—is cognitive agility (DiBello, 1997). While the business landscape

TABLE 17.1   Outline and Description of the Dreyfuses' Five-Stage Model of Expertise

Stage 1: Novice: During the first stage of acquiring a new skill, the novice learns to recognize various objective facts and features relevant to the skill as well as rules for deciding how to act on these facts and features. At this stage, the facts and rules are context-free. That is, they are clearly and objectively defined so the novice can recognize and apply them regardless of the situation or context in which they occur. Novices are usually so caught up in following the rules that they have no coherent sense of the overall task.

Stage 2: Advanced beginner: As the novice gains experience in real situations, performance improves to a marginally acceptable level. This encourages the learner to consider more than context-free facts and fosters an enlarged vision of the world of the skill. Through practical experience in concrete situations, and by noting the similarities between novel situations, the advanced beginner learns to recognize and deal with previously undefined facts and elements. The person also learns to apply more sophisticated rules, to both context-free and situational factors. The rules can offer a sort of framework for storing and shaping experience, so that learning from experience becomes possible. The advanced beginner learns to deal with situational elements but still applies learned rules and procedures.

Stage 3: Competence: With experience, the learner begins to recognize more and more context-free and situational elements. To avoid being overwhelmed by this information explosion, the future expert is taught to adopt a hierarchical view of decision making. By choosing a plan to organize the situation and then concentrating on only the most important elements, the person both simplifies and improves performance and gradually grows in competence. At this stage of the game, objectivity often goes out the door. The competent person appraises the situation, sets a goal, and then chooses a plan, which may or may not involve following the rules, but also has some risk of not succeeding. Whether the plan succeeds or fails, the situation and its outcome are likely to be vividly recalled—an important resource for future expertise.

Stage 4: Proficiency: Proficiency brings with it a new style: rapid, fluid action that does not always stem from detached reasoning. For the proficient performer, usually deeply involved in the task, important elements of the task will stand out clearly, and others will recede into the background and be ignored. As the situation changes, different features may take on importance and different plans may evolve. "No detached choice or deliberation occurs," explain the Dreyfuses. "It just happens, apparently because the proficient performer has experienced similar situations in the past and memories of them trigger plans similar to those that worked in the past." The Dreyfuses call this holistic similarity recognition. Klein calls this recognition-primed decision making.

Stage 5: Expertise: Experts don't apply rules, make decisions, or solve problems. They do what comes naturally, and it almost always works. When they fail, it often is because they are pitted against another expert, as in a world-title chess match. Experience-based holistic recognition of similarity produces the deep situational understanding that leads to the expert's fluid performance. Experts' skills have become so much a part of them that they are no more aware of them than they are of their own bodies. They are also able to innovate a solution to a problem they have not encountered. In a sense, they have a "first principles" understanding of their domain, so they don't actually need a similar prior experience to draw upon when they encounter a novel event.

Source: Adapted from Dreyfus and Dreyfus, 1986.

may look unpredictable and repeated success seems rare, some individuals have proven themselves continually adept at anticipating trends others missed and—when in leadership roles—steering their companies toward continued success.

Building on theories of emergence, adaptation, and flexibility from complexity science and NDM, we use the term *cognitive agility* to refer to the extent to which an individual revises his or her evaluation of a situation in response to data indicating that conditions have changed. The converse is *cognitive rigidity*, where the person is impervious to new data, being dominated by a rigid framework or paradigm that acts to filter out new, possibly relevant, information, creating blind spots (DiBello, 1997).

Cognitive Agility and Assessment

We believe that an instrument that effectively assesses business expertise must (1) be able to draw on the intuitive expertise of organizational members; (2) tap into the specific mental models individuals use to approach problems, rather than basic problem solving or generalized decision making skills; (3) locate individuals within the distributed cognition of an organization, that is, specify the individual's role in the organization; (4) be able to identify strengths and blind spots of the organization's transactive memory system and, in so doing, highlight dimensions of expertise that contribute to high-level decision making; and lastly, (5) measure not only cognitive ability, but also cognitive agility, that is, the capacity to rapidly revise one's mental model in the face of dynamic feedback.

The Profiler is a knowledge elicitation instrument or cognitive probe that we have developed to specifically address these issues. The Profiler measures cognitive agility within business decision makers and renders detailed profiles, helping users locate themselves as decision makers and gain insight into where their organization's weaknesses and strengths may lie. The Profiler, which can be given in both pencil-and-paper and online formats, does not necessarily measure general cognitive ability, but rather profiles the framework, or heuristic, that an individual or team uses to approach problems in a given context, as well as the degree of agility present in the team or individual.

We built the Profiler based on research into how world-class experts approach and solve complex business problems in contrast to less experienced individuals. The instrument and scoring scheme was tested and refined using 48 data points from 10 very highly successful individuals who had repeat successes with large organizations in challenging markets and in highly varied conditions. From their responses we were able to distill the mental model of world-class business experts. The instrument was then retested with faculty from Vanderbilt University, the Rady School of Business at UCSD, and among executive MBA students at the University of Colorado Leeds School of Business. Each participant's results were consistent with his or her professional track record.

The Profiler falls into a category of assessment measures labeled work output sampling. Work output sampling consists of measures that simulate actual job tasks to assess context-relevant expertise without relying on self-report data. In fact, research on work output sampling showed that out of 48 methods used to ascertain or project "fit," only work output sampling resulted in a statistically significant improvement over measuring general mental ability (Schmidt & Hunter, 1998). In other words, it was the only measure that added to the correlation between general mental ability and success on the job. While work output sampling has been lauded as a technique that has high predictive validity and that reduces adverse impact, it traditionally has not been practical.

The Profiler uses work output sampling in assessments for executives in a systematic and automated way, and is what has been called a high-fidelity simulation. The names of the companies are removed in the simulation, but all relevant information needed to make a prediction is retained. Hence, the Profiler is considered a high-fidelity work output sampling design that reflects real decision-making processes. In contrast, many work output sampling techniques are of low fidelity, simulating job tasks that are less representative of actual conditions, and thus suffer from an inability to accurately capture real-life job tasks.

The User Experience of the Profiler

The Profiler requires the user (1) to examine and analyze the same material used by actual experts (e.g., annual reports, 10K's, analyst's reports, etc., from actual companies) to make business decisions, (2) to make predictions about the company with respect to a number of domains (e.g., revenues), and (3) to judge various aspects of the company (e.g., evaluate the management team).

Specifically, the Profiler asks users to answer several questions about the company to predict how its finances will develop over the next five years. Users' answers are evaluated in terms of Dreyfus's five-stage model of expertise (discussed above) to determine their business acumen and level of expertise within the domain of business strategy. The Profiler also helps us identify blind spots in users' thinking; that is, we can discern areas where users seem to miss aspects critical to the company's performance. Moreover, for each prediction or judgment users must indicate the specific materials they relied on, such as discrepancies in annual report statements or the general state of the company's finances. This aspect of the Profiler taps into the heuristics that are guiding users' decision making.

Our research revealed that people who have achieved a high level of business expertise have a deep understanding of the following three core areas: (1) factors involved in effective operations, (2) forces influencing the market, and (3) those driving business finance and economic climates. Consistently successful business leaders have been shown to intuitively understand these areas and their impact on each other, and to pay attention to this fundamental triad in a uniquely dynamic way within a guiding context of business strategy. For example, these experts are able to sense that market conditions change based on environmental indications that others may fail to notice. Further, they foresee the consequences to their business operations and finances, and thus make necessary adjustments proactively. Unlike most business professionals, they are attuned to the early indicators of widespread change. Beyond this, they are expert at keeping the triad in balance, or shifting the balance when external conditions are conducive to do so (e.g., focusing on marketing during favorable economic times). In contrast, competent managers (one level down from experts) tend to be very talented in only one or two of these areas; however, they often do not understand the dynamics between these areas as well as the "superstars" do. Competent managers are likely to be very successful when larger market or economic trends are favorable to their specific skills.

These three core areas are not directly addressed in the questions we ask in the Profiler. Rather, an individual's answers are rated and compared to those of the ideal expert. The questions are based on tangible outcomes and concern the company's performance. The questions ask users to evaluate their company with respect to its strategy, leadership, and finances. These are areas that senior executives would be expected to make valid predictions about and are good ways to reveal their underlying business expertise. For example, a question about finances would be: As the senior manager for the business, which aspect of financial performance most urgently requires your attention? This question would then be followed by a series of options, such as "cost of goods sold," "fixed assets," "receivables," or "R&D." To answer this question—that is, to know what is troubling or of concern in the total context of the company at that time—the user must understand operations, finance, and market trends. Answer options reflect levels of expertise, 1 through 5, corresponding to the five stages in the Dreyfus model. The "correct" answer is empirically determined. Because these are actual cases, the outcomes are known and the root causes of problems have been identified.

In addition to these Dreyfus questions tapping their business expertise, users are asked to provide three predictions that refer to quantitative outcomes in the company's performance. These questions can vary slightly, as the instrument is customized according to a company's needs; however, they will ask about issues, such as profits and revenues, that are indicative of how well a user can synthesize information about the company to predict real-world outcomes. For example, we may ask: What is your prediction of the company's profits for the next 12 months? Users then indicate their answers along a 5-point Likert scale whose points are labeled appropriately, for instance, in the preceding example, options may range from "down 20% or greater" to "up 20% or greater."

Users then go on to Year 2. After reading through the Year 2 materials, they are able to see whether or not their predictions were validated by the company's performance. In other words, they receive feedback as to the accuracy of the previous year's predictions. They repeat this exercise for five years of material, making predictions and getting feedback as to whether or not their predictions have been validated. This iterative process taps into users' cognitive agility, allowing us to assess the degree to which users are able to revise their thinking in the face of feedback about company performance and their own predictions. Cognitively agile individuals learn from their inaccurate predictions or judgments and improve as they go along.

Furthermore, we can see persistent blind spots that may exist and occur consistently across all five years. Thus, the Profiler can provide windows into the acumen, blind spots, mental models, and agility with which users approach complex decision making for a real company. It is important to keep in mind that all of the data provided are from real companies. We do not determine the outcomes, as they are taken from actual annual reports and actual finances over a given period of time.

In addition to evaluating users' direct responses to the Dreyfus and Likert questions, we also ask users to point to sections of the material they reviewed (including statements in the annual reports and financial summaries) that informed their decision on a particular question. For example, the annual report might mention a recent acquisition. This may reflect a strategic turning point for the company. As such, after users respond to the question on strategy, they must indicate what sections of the material influenced their decision. Users are allowed to choose up to five reasons for their decision. In this case, users should be aware that the recent acquisition plays a major role in the company's strategy going forward, even if this is not immediately obvious. As such, when users answer this particular strategy question, they should be pointing to the acquisition as a basis for their decision. This not only allows us to evaluate the expertise and accuracy of their responses, but also gives us a window into the kinds of information they use to approach the decision-making process. Furthermore, this aspect of the Profiler allows us to determine whether users are utilizing information based on the three core areas listed above: supply, demand, and finance. Specifically, we can see whether users approach the questions in an expert manner by evaluating the degree to which they are paying attention to these core areas as they make decisions.

Case Study: Background of a Biodevice Company

For this chapter, we will present a case in which we used the Profiler to assess the senior management team of a medical device company. Our relationship with the company began when the chairman and acting CEO asked us to evaluate his senior staff for succession planning purposes. In particular, he wished to decide who, among the division presidents, would succeed him as the CEO. At the time, the company was growing very rapidly. During the four months we worked with the company between 2005 and 2006, we saw them grow from $300 million to $400 million. A pending acquisition was intended to increase the company's size to $600 million by 2008.

The CEO of the company was aware that there is a qualitative difference between *competent* managers, who do very well in interviews or on personality tests, and *experts*, who can perform under challenging conditions. He wanted to protect himself from competence at a time when his industry was in a high growth phase. He was afraid that a favorable market might be masking a lack of skill—and cognitive agility in particular—among his senior staff.

For this case study, we built the Profiler using data from five consecutive years of a biotech company of similar size and with similar business challenges. The company had experienced rapid organic growth, doubling in size with a major acquisition, while considerable outside investor capital fueled expanded distribution. The company also had similar financial challenges. For example, the profit margins for biotech and biodevice products can be very high (sometimes north of 90%), but the cost of sales and distribution is very high compared to other industries. The managers of the biotech company were competent, but failed to anticipate events that—from our data—an expert would have foreseen. In real life, the end result for the large and successful biotech company was implosion due to poor management decisions. The rationale for using this company's data was to evaluate the biodevice managers' risk for the same lack of foresight.

We assessed eight of the company's top managers (division presidents) and the CEO, thus totaling nine participants in all. All of them took an online version of the instrument. All the managers who participated were highly experienced (15+ years in a senior management role in biotech or biodevice with more than one company). Many had obtained their MBAs from prestigious schools such as Harvard or Cornell. They were also knowledgeable in global business. Not surprisingly, they showed themselves to be at Dreyfus Level 4 or 5 (on a scale from 1 to 5) on some of the key dimensions, such as strategy and leadership (see Figures 17.1 to 17.3 for mean scores).

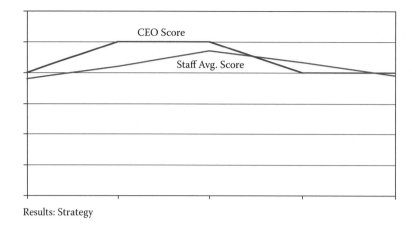

Results: Strategy

FIGURE 17.1 Averaged division presidents' scores compared to the CEO's scores on strategy.

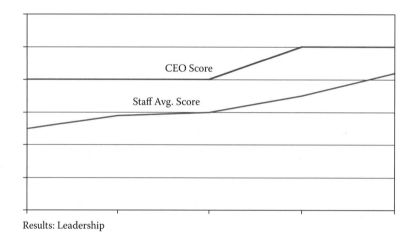

Results: Leadership

FIGURE 17.2 Averaged division presidents' scores compared to the CEO's scores on leadership.

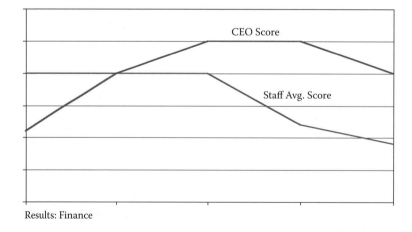

Results: Finance

FIGURE 17.3 Averaged division presidents' scores compared to the CEO's scores on finance.

As a process check, we administered the same instrument to an equal of number of business-knowledgeable controls (BS or MBA business students who were not yet functioning managers or consultants and had not ever actually run a company of any size). Their performance was much lower. This, too, was an expected result.

Because the Profiler is an instrument used to profile the judgments of senior management, we do not use traditional quantitative measures, such as regression, ANOVAs, or other statistical tests. Instead, we rely on basic responses, means, and graphs to get a snapshot of the individual's performance against others' in the group. Our sample sizes are small, and we concentrate on describing the user and how he or she modifies thinking and behavior in response to dynamic conditions. Traditional assessment measures based on traditional statistical techniques are not appropriate for this kind of in-depth, dynamic assessment. Our results, therefore, are presented as descriptive observations only.

Descriptions of Managers' Profiles

We compared the average performance of the division presidents to the performance of the CEO with respect to their level of business expertise. The figures relate the average performance of all eight division presidents to the CEO alone across five years based on the three Dreyfus scored questions: strategy, leadership, and finance. The strategy question captures the user's beliefs about how the strategy of the company will be able to meet projected goals. The leadership question taps the user's confidence in the company's leadership to carry out strategy and vision. The finance question probes the user's beliefs about the contribution of key financial aspects of the company to short-terms goals. These questions reflect key areas of information that would shape a top-level manager's decisions about a company. The biodevice managers showed marked agility on most dimensions. That is, their accuracy increased as they got more information with each "year" of the instrument they completed. In addition, in nearly all cases, they adjusted their thinking when their predictions were off the mark, demonstrating an ability to revise their thinking based on feedback.

On the strategy question, the CEO and staff expertise levels are nearly the same (see Figure 17.1). On the leadership question (Figure 17.2), the CEO performed slightly better than the staff, but in general the staff showed sufficient expertise in line with expectations. However, when we looked at the staff's predictions on the finance question, the results were troubling. All the staff except the CEO performed poorly. On this question, the division presidents performed more like the MBA students in our novice group. As can be seen in Figure 17.3, the division presidents rarely showed expertise above Level 2 or 3. Moreover, their predictions actually got worse over time, indicating that they did not revise their thinking over the years in response to feedback.

In general, financial understanding and financial agility should be the easiest of the three key questions, and a persistent blind spot in this area was not expected among managers at this level of seniority and experience. After discussing the results with the CEO, he indicated that a serious problem was emerging concerning the way finances were being managed, causing the company to lose more and more money as their revenues increased. One reason the CEO wanted to use the Profiler was to determine whether this financial issue was due to a blind spot of his managers, or whether something out of the company's control was the root cause.

The Profiler revealed that the financial mental models of the division presidents had not changed as the company had grown. Their financial strategy regarding sales was to use consignment inventory to entice prospective clients early on to try the products. When the company was small and heavily funded by investors, this was a highly effective strategy. However, with gross revenues approaching $1 billion, this was a lock up of capital that the company did not have and could not afford. The division presidents did not appreciate the negative implications of their strategy. As they lacked a full understanding of the financial dynamics of the uses of capital, and were unaware of the need for additional investment and sustainable positive cash flow and profits, the senior mangers believed they were impacting the right variables with new products and market penetration. However, their growth strategies where actually putting the company's existence at risk.

Conclusions: Pitfalls and Successes of Assessing Complex Distributed Cognitive Systems

Our analysis of the company, along with the results of the Profiler, made clear that the CEO had been "covering" the financial blind spot of his global team, allowing them to focus on penetrating the worldwide marketplace and growing the company. However, as the company doubled in size, this was an unrealistic approach. The CEO's expertise in finances was only sufficient so long as the challenges remained minimal and the company grew at a steady pace. Rapid expansion required the company to draw on the "distributed cognition" and financial skills of the team in a way they had not anticipated. By relying solely on the CEO's financial expertise, the company had created a blind spot that could have led to financial ruin.

We made a presentation on our findings at a board of directors' meeting and got enthusiastic agreement that we had uncovered an important shortcoming, and that those reporting to the CEO could not yet succeed to his position, or rely only on him to cover the financial decision making given the company's current size. The feeling in the room was that the problem had been identified in time and that remedial action could be taken. Furthermore, the staff themselves felt that they had sufficient insight into the problem, and that they knew what steps to take. They realized that they, as a unit, made decisions on the allocation of assets that were putting the company at risk, especially with some acquisition pending. They asked us to evaluate their staff members. As a result, 15 more people, all of whom were directly reporting to the division presidents, used the Profiler. Not surprisingly, the profiled results showed that the identified knowledge gap had spread to the lower levels. Every staff member assessed had a profile similar to his or her boss's.

Unfortunately, coordination among the collective "experts" in the organization was fragile, and the CEO was unable to compensate for gaps in team members' financial expertise. As the company continued to grow and the CEO was more involved in shaping the future of the company, he was less able to steer the financial decisions of his direct reports and the financial problems continued. Within six months, the

CEO and several of his staff were let go by the board of directors and the company continues to struggle under new leadership.

In the end, this case study created more questions than it answered. On the one hand, these data provided support for our model of a business expert's decision-making process. The CEO and his staff of division presidents scored high on two of the dimensions that are critical to expert decision making in business. In these areas (strategy and leadership), the company was healthy. However, the persistent blind spot in the area of finance, in which their thinking was similar to that of an advanced beginner or competent decision maker (on the Dreyfus stage model), led to the company's downfall. This occurred even though all the managers had long track records of professional achievement. On the other hand, when it comes to running large companies, expertise can and perhaps must reside among a group that works closely together to ensure that the situation is well managed, particularly in the face of rapid growth. This case study highlights the importance of identifying blind spots among top decision makers and presented the tools that can enable this process.

In this case study the Profiler uncovered the mental models used by the team and by the CEO. In so doing, we found a persistent blind spot with respect to one aspect of business expertise, despite significant acumen among team members in other business areas. Perhaps most significantly, we found that because the CEO may have been covering for the inadequate mental models of the rest of senior management, he may have enabled the persistence of domain-specific blind spots concerning financial issues. Because the senior management team was unaware of their inadequacy in the financial area and the consequences of their shortcomings, they were unable to identify and modify their strategies in time. Thus, while the Profiler was successful in uncovering a serious issue among senior management, our intervention may have been too late. The blind spots had become so entrenched in the company's strategy that by the time everyone realized what was wrong, change was too difficult to enact.

References

Chase, W. G., & Simon, H.A. (1973). The mind's eye in chess. In W. G. Chase (Ed.), *Visual information processing*. New York, NY: Academic Press.

Chi, M. T. H., Glaser, R., & Farr, M. J. (1988). *The nature of expertise*. Hillsdale, NJ: Erlbaum.

Cole, M., Engestrom, Y., & Vasquez, O. (1977). *Mind, culture and activity; Seminal papers from the laboratory of comparative human cognition*. Cambridge, UK: Cambridge University Press.

DiBello, L. (1997). Exploring the relationship between activity and the development of expertise: Paradigm shifts and decision defaults. In C. Zsambok & G. Klein (Eds.), *Naturalistic decision making* (pp. 17–28). Mahwah, NJ: Lawrence Erlbaum Associates.

Dreyfus, H. (1997). Intuitive, deliberative, and calculative models of expert performance. In C. Zsambok & G. Klein (Eds.), *Naturalistic decision making* (pp. 17–28). Mahwah, NJ: Lawrence Erlbaum Associates.

Dreyfus, H. L., & Dreyfus, S. E. (1986). *Mind over machine: The power of human intuition and expertise in the era of the computer*. Oxford, UK: Blackwell.

Gentner, D., & Stevens, A. L. (Eds.). (1983). *Mental models*. Hillsdale, NJ: Erlbaum.

Gore, J., Banks, A., Millward, L., & Kyriakidou, O. (2006). Naturalistic decision making and organizations: Reviewing pragmatic science. *Organization Studies, 27*, 925–942.

Hollander, E. A. (1978). *Leadership dynamics: A practical guide to effective relationships.* New York, NY: Free Press.

House, R. J., Spangler, D., & Woycke, J. (1991). Personality and charisma in the U.S. presidency: A psychological theory of leadership effectiveness. *Administrative Science Quarterly, 36,* 364–396.

Hunt, J. G. (1999). Transformational/charismatic leadership's transformation of the field: An historical essay. *Leadership Quarterly, 10,* 129–144.

Hutchins, E. (1996). *Cognition in the wild.* Cambridge, MA: MIT Press.

Klein, G. (1999). *Sources of power.* Cambridge MA: MIT Press.

Marion, R., & Uhl-Bien, M. (2001). Leadership in complex organizations. *Leadership Quarterly, 12,* 389–418.

Meindl, J. R., Erlich, S. B., & Dukerich, J. M. (1985). The romance of leadership. *Administrative Science Quarterly, 30,* 78–102.

Polanyi, M. (1967). *The tacit dimension.* Chicago, IL: University of Chicago Press.

Roth, P. L., Bobko, P., & McFarland, L. A. (2005). A meta-analysis of work sample test validitiy: Updating and integrating some classic literature. *Personnel Psychology, 58,* 1009–1037.

Schmidt, F. L., & Hunter, J. E. (1998). The validity of selection methods in personnel psychology: Practical and theoretical implications of 85 years of research findings. *Psychological Bulletin, 124,* 262–274.

Scribner, S. (1987, April 11). *Head and hand: An action approach to thinking* (Occasional Paper 3). Paper presented at the annual meeting of the Eastern Psychological Association, Arlington, VA.

Vygotsky, L. (1986). *Thought and language* (A. Kozulin, Translator and Ed.). Cambridge, MA: MIT Press.

Wegner, D. M. (1987). Transactive memory: A contemporary analysis of the group mind. In B. Mullen & G. R. Goethals (Eds.), *Theories of group behavior* (pp. 185–208). New York, NY: Springer-Verlag.

18

Losing Sight of the "Golden Mean"
Accountogenic Decisions in UK Policing

Laurence Alison, Marie Eyre, and Michael Humann
University of Liverpool

Policing is about living with complexity, including ambiguity, short timescales for action, and appreciation of the ambient context of high-risk decisions (Crego & Harris, 2001). Whether to shoot a potential suicide bomber, storm a building, place a child on an at-risk (child protection) register, or make a grab for an individual teetering on a rooftop during a negotiation requires appreciation of this complexity and an awareness that such decisions hang on a knife edge of uncertainty. Researching the influences on and processes entailed in such decision making is likewise complex. We argue here that making such decisions is not simply a cognitive process but a deeply, personally involving social one that is affect laden. We further contend that these latter aspects have yet to be fully addressed. We believe that the decision-making context is one in which social/organizational identity exerts a powerful influence on the sociocognitive processes.

Consideration of social processes per se is, of course, not new. It appears even in behavioral economic approaches and traditional cost-benefit models, which largely neglect affect in favor of rationality. In other words, the idea that rationality has limits has long been established with the idea of *subjective* utility (Bernoulli, 1738/1954), game theory (von Neumann & Morgenstern, 1944), the concepts of *bounded* rationality and satisficing (Simon, 1972), and (adaptive or otherwise) commonplace heuristics and biases (Gigerenzer, 2000; Kahneman, Slovic, & Tversky, 1982). More specifically, this notion has also been supported within the accountability literature, as reflected by various approaches and findings (Lerner & Tetlock, 1999) and the emerging debates and propositions (Frink & Klimoski, 2004). Thus, contrived distinctions between cognitive and social approaches are unhelpful. Rather, we maintain that the recent focus on cognitive processes is a matter of undue emphasis. There is a synergy between the social and the cognitive, the one inextricably derived from and informed by the other.

Naturalistic decision-making (NDM) approaches have made great strides in understanding the cognitive processes that actually obtain in the field (as distinct from decision making in decontextualized laboratory studies). NDM has firmly established that decisions in these types of contexts cannot be described by traditional search-inference models of decision making (e.g., Klein, 1993). However, NDM has not yet fully appreciated the deeply emotional/interpersonal/organizationally bound aspects of decisions (Alison & Crego, 2008).

It is essential that we define the position of the decision maker before exploring the factors that affect the individual decision-making processes. Tetlock (1992) proposed various metaphors in order to understand decision makers and their motivations. They include the decision maker as *psychologist*, striving for cognitive mastery of the causal structure of the environment, or decision maker as *economist*, with rational economic man focused on maximizing subjective-expected utility. However, it is Tetlock's metaphor of *politician* that best encompasses the cognitive as well as the social considerations within real-world environments. The police decision maker operates in a politicized environment, where he or she needs to balance both cognitive as well as social aspects of the decision-making process. In high-profile critical incidents, in particular, impression management is an important feature of the overall context, and accountability issues feature in many policing environments.

The decision maker who occupies these complex contexts needs to find a "golden mean," where he or she should operate "sensitive to the views of important constituencies, but avoid appearing so chameleonic that one loses their trust and confidence [...] one should be self-critical, but not to the point of paralysis [...] and one should stick by one's principles but not to the point of dogmatism and self-righteousness" (Tetlock, 1992, p. 360). Clearly, this is a difficult balancing act, which can have a detrimental effect on performance as well as perceptions of the accountable individual if it is not fully understood.

A decision maker, then, may fail to attain the golden mean. The authors argue here that such an imbalance may be caused by accountability factors inherent in the broader decision-making context. We have coined the term *accountogenic* to describe the phenomenon where decisions are circumvented or derailed, or unduly and inappropriately influenced by perceptions of accountability. Thus, the term is specific beyond the more general and value-neutral term *accountability*. To draw on Tetlock's metaphor, the politician's accountogenic decisions are fueled by the audience's views. Thus, his or her decisions center on public presentation and impression management at the cost of good government. Accountability may come to dominate operational best practice because decisions that would have otherwise been made differently are unduly skewed by this factor. Thus, given a particular organizational context, some critical incident environments generate risk-averse or risk-displaced (accountogenic) decisions that focus on protecting oneself and the consequences of one's actions rather than generating the best decision for the current environment.

Decision-making factors related to accountability have been researched in a number of different domains (e.g., medicine, management, business) looking at the impact these have on individuals' choice of actions (Lerner & Tetlock, 1999). Accountability has been related to a shift in goals and focus, as well as biases, all affecting cognitive and decision-making processes. These influencing factors relate not only to the actual decision making, but also to the information gathering and interpretation, as well as the defense and reinforcement of decisions individuals commit to in pursuit of particular goals (Gollwitzer & Moskowitz, 1996).

In relation to the source of accountability, research has focused on two key factors: the type of accountability pressures and their timing. Four conditions or facets of accountability that contribute to significant affect factors have been recognized: known versus unknown audience's views, pre- versus postdecisional, outcome versus process, and legitimate versus illegitimate (Lerner & Tetlock, 1999). Working through this multifactorial framework, findings have pointed to optimal conditions of accountability that attenuate errors and biases in decision makers. Predictions state that open-minded, self-critical, and effortful thinking is activated when decision makers are faced with (1) predecisional accountability, (2) from an audience with unknown views, (3) who is interested in the decision-making process, and (4) has legitimate reasons for monitoring the individual (Lerner & Tetlock, 2003). Based on these findings and the progressive understanding gained from operational conditions, a clear picture has emerged on the amplifying and attenuating effect accountability has on cognitive decision-making processes.

A distinction is made between conditions in which the views of the audience are known versus unknown to the individual who is to be held accountable. With regard to these various agent-audience relationships, the police operate within environments that are characterized by known audiences (e.g., supervisors, government, public, media). They are therefore very aware of their accountability obligations prior to any committed decisions, and although these conditions may not have an operational value, they do point to valid reasons for cognitive errors and biases in terms of performance expectations. Where the views of one's audience are known, individuals seek approval from their respective audience, resorting to different tactics in pursuit of that goal rather than any inherent tactics relevant to the task (Baumeister & Leary, 1995). Similarly, Lerner and Tetlock state that individuals "adopt positions likely to gain the favour of those to whom they are accountable, thereby allowing them to avoid the unnecessary cognitive work of analysing the pros and cons of alternative courses of action, interpreting complex patterns of information, and making difficult trade-offs" (1999, p. 256). Here the effort is shifted between focusing on the task at hand and focusing on seeking approval from the audience. Optimally, decision makers would attain the golden mean by balancing attention between the operational requirements of the task at hand and the audience. By contrast, excessive emphasis on gaining favor with those to whom one is accountable would generate accountogenic decisions. These latter decisions would be suboptimal and likely directed by negative affect (for example, fear of blame).

In terms of their awareness about accountability, individuals direct more cognitive energy in self-justification of actions rather than self-criticism (Lerner & Tetlock, 1999). This differentiation points to the fact that effortful thinking is not invested exclusively in evaluating ideas and decisions, but rather in validating and reinforcing committed actions. Further, postdecision accountability perceptions amplify defensive bolstering (Schlenker, 1980) and escalation in resource commitments to failed or unprofitable actions, such as in sunk-cost effects (Arkes & Blumer, 1985). Studies of individual differences indicated that dogmatism and intolerance of ambiguity also reinforce defensive bolstering rather than self-criticism (Tetlock, Skitka, & Boettger, 1989). Accountability, then, affects errors and biases at different levels, and the findings of these studies raise questions about the impact on the decision-making process within complex environments such as critical incident management.

The other two conditions raise further questions, insofar as officers need to defend their processes as well as their outcomes, and do so to legitimate as well as illegitimate audiences. Outcome accountability emphasizes results and is less concerned with how they were attained. Outcome accountability increases decision stress, narrowing attentional capacity and simplifying decision processes (Siegel-Jacobs & Yates, 1996). Process accountability, in the form of regular updates on various alternative decision-making paths, encourages more even-handed evaluation of alternatives and less self-justification. Individuals in conditions of process accountability use more robust decision strategies and are evaluated and monitored on these, regardless of their decision outcome (Simonson & Staw, 1992).

UK police officers are subject to process accountability, as they have a statutory requirement to log all their decisions from the start to the conclusion of an operation. In criminal investigations, these logs are disclosable to the defense. However, performance indicators (aka targets) have been at the core of government drives to make public sector services more accountable. In the UK public sector, policing included, an overwhelming focus on outcomes has prevailed for well over a decade.

The performance culture is not without its critics, and performance targets are thought by some to have little impact on (or even relation to) operational services (Seddon, 2008). Indeed, the UK government's own researchers discovered that public sector leaders are being diverted away from strategically meaningful goals in favor of short-term measurable outcomes (Performance and Innovation Unit, Home Office, 2000). Put prosaically, the tail is wagging the dog. Despite this warning, targets remain a central feature alongside a raft of policy and procedural prescriptions that restrict decision making. These targets are known within the police as statutory performance indicators (SPIs). They currently measure performance over five areas—promoting safety, tackling crime, serious crime and protection, confidence and satisfaction, and organizational management (APACS, 2008)—though they are soon to be streamlined into one catchall target that measures rates of public confidence (Casey, 2008). Although ultimate decision-making responsibility concerning targets lies with leaders, targets will nonetheless filter down to all ranks of decision maker as an influencing factor because they guide strategic plans for policing. Accountability constitutes a significant feature of the social/organizational milieu in which decisions must be made, and the police decision maker needs to be the consummate politician, who must consider and successfully manage much more than operational tasks with due regard for social aspects that will inform affect.

Thus, with the performance culture of target setting in the policing context generally and critical incident management specifically, there has been an increasing emphasis on outcome, not process. Our qualitative research shows that outcome seems to be the more salient factor for officers. With evidence that outcome accountability increases decision stress and narrows attentional capacity (Siegel-Jacobs & Yates, 1996), it may be argued that these contextual organizational factors contribute to police officers straying from the golden mean. A diminishing focus on process accountability may further decrease the opportunity to evaluate options in the even-handed manner needed by the decision maker as politician (Simonson & Staw, 1992). Hence, they tip over into making accountogenic decisions.

The picture is not entirely straightforward. Research within organizations has highlighted that private sector institutions, which stress the outcome accountability, function more effectively than public sector institutions, which stress process accountability (Chubb & Moe, 1990; Wilson & Brekke, 1996). This research offers a possible explanation for the difference between experimental studies and studies in applied settings, which might lie in the flexibility given to private sector employees to achieve goals, while public sector employees are bound by stricter bureaucratic regulations. Clearly, both of these conditions solicit further attention, considering the contrasting propositions that they offer. They also point to the importance of understanding decision-making contexts and the possible nontransferability of applied research.

An individual's perception of the legitimacy and credibility of the individual or audience monitoring his or her behavior also has an impact on accountability effects. Tyler (1997) found that inducing perceptions that legitimized accountability had a positive effect on performance, while illegitimate monitors provoked perceptions that were classified as intrusive and insulting. Field studies have shown that forceful surveillance in organizational settings can overwhelm cognitive and emotional coping and affect task performance (Sutton & Galunic, 1996). Lerner and Tetlock (1999) state that accountability to an audience perceived as illegitimate will reduce decision makers' motivation and also increase stress.

While the differentiation between legitimate and illegitimate accountability may potentially have a significant effect on the decision-making processes, this classification cannot simply be ascribed by external sources; rather, the perception of the accountable individual is key. Moreover, the individual's opinion regarding the legitimacy of the audience to whom he or she is accountable will shift depending on the interactions and decisions he or she encounters. So, even if an audience has a legitimate reason to monitor the decision-making process, the individuals might regard them as illegitimate and focus their effort on defending their decisions and actions, rather than critically reassessing them.

All of these factors have very clear affective qualities beyond strictly cognitive decision-making processes. Given its complexity, it is a challenging area to research. Not only are factors such as perceptions of legitimacy dynamic, but constructs are also nebulous; for example, it is difficult to disentangle factors such as trustworthiness and power, which are regarded as components of the concept of legitimacy (Lerner & Tetlock, 1999). It is essential, therefore, to establish some clear understanding of the operational settings and the policing context. Our own research is building a descriptive picture of UK law enforcement and is just beginning to acknowledge the impact of context on policing (e.g., Eyre, Alison, Crego, & McLean, 2008; Whitfield, Alison, & Crego, 2008). From our regular analysis of debriefs of police operations and observation of training simulations, accountability is emerging as a common contextual feature. It is a recurring theme among a corpus of over 80 operational debriefs and discussion groups involving more than 4,000 police officers, from lowest to highest rank. Indeed, qualitative analyses of these data (gathered via an electronic focus group system called 10kV, which permits anonymous reciprocal discussion; see Eyre, Crego, & Alison, 2008 for details) indicate that the prospect of accountability permeates the organizational context. Moreover, the current (descriptive) phase of our own work suggests that UK police officers make accountogenic decisions.

Accountability and accountogenic decisions are clearly central factors that warrant research attention, though it is recognized that the latter issue may not generalize beyond UK policing. Indeed, in all domains of study, we must avoid subsuming extremely distinctive and diverse organizational and institutional factors into one generic (and rather vague) context, which is assumed to inform situation awareness without elucidating how, to what degree, or by what means it does so. Nevertheless, before getting into details about the contextual factors that characterize UK policing, it is important to keep in mind the established notions surrounding accountability that have garnered significant research attention and place these within the operational settings of critical incidents and the way in which these unfold.

UK policing is a specific organizational context. Within (and because of) this context, decision strategies would incorporate former experiences of accountability, blame, and their legacy on the particular police force. Where cost-benefit analyses are performed, operationally optimal/satisfactory options would be weighed against the costs of being held publicly accountable for an unpopular/incorrect decision. For the individual decision maker, this may manifest as evaluation apprehension (a social process of arousal in which mild arousal can enhance performance but intense arousal can cause performance decrement), bringing the politician's balancing act between the views of the audience, self-criticism, and confidence to the forefront. These ideas have yet to be fully explored in policing research.

In his review of institutional theory, Crank (2003) notes the limitations in decision-making research specifically related to policing. As well as highlighting the focus on normative approaches, he also notes rational decision making's emphasis on the individual's consideration of action. He says, "The field of rational decision making tends to take the many institutional factors . . . for granted" (2003, p. 199), yet the individual decision maker derives (in part) his or her identity from the institution. Similarly, in a phrase borrowed from Giddens (1979), Crank criticizes the failure to consider the "unique aspects of time and space" as elements that contribute to decision making. While NDM has made great strides in incorporating the decision makers' context, such contexts will differ. Lipshitz, Klein, and Carroll (2006) have argued for the greater consideration of organizational context in NDM research and highlighted the potential for links with organizational decision making (ODM) as a promising avenue (also see Alby & Zucchermaglio, 2006; Gore, Banks, Millward, & Kyriakidou, 2006).

NDM work must continue to elucidate specific details of particular contexts in detail. While it is recognized that some findings, models, and approaches will be domain general (e.g., narrative theory, Fiore, McDaniel, Rosen, & Salas, 2007; situated cognition, Shattuck & Lewis Miller, 2006), others will not. Mieg (Chapter 3) steers us toward common metacognitive rather than content-specific decision-making processes; in contrast, DiBello, Missildine, and Struttman note the "great variability both between and within typical NDM environments, which creates a lack of coherence and clarity around generalizable results" (2007, p. 77). In policing, what applies in the United Kingdom may not transfer to the United States (the latter a disproportionate source of police research [Nickels & Verma, 2008]), and vice versa. In the next section we take just one example of culturally specific terminology, where incongruence yields problems of transferability.

What Do We Mean by Critical Incidents?

In the United States and Canada, critical incidents are defined as "sudden powerful events...outside the officer's control" (Anderson, Litzenberger, & Plecas, 2002, p. 403), which are regarded as stressors sufficiently grave to overwhelm reasonable coping mechanisms; cited examples are shootings, sieges, and so on. Inherent to the U.S. and Canadian definition is a description of its probable impact on the police officer (Kulbarsh, 2007; Kureczka, 1996). In the United Kingdom, however, a critical incident is defined in terms of its impact on the public: It is "any incident where the effectiveness of the police response is likely to have a significant impact on the confidence of the victim, their family and/or the community, which has the potential to generate grave public concern at a local, regional, national or international level" (Metropolitan Police, 2003).

The U.S. and Canadian critical incident does not centralize the public in the way the UK definition does. In the United Kingdom, a community consisting of a small street may have no confidence in the police's ability to stop children from playing and causing nuisance to adult residents. Would these circumstances be sufficient to declare a critical incident? Arguably (given that confidence is perceptual and grave concern variable), this meet the terms of the definition, but critical incidents connote an emergency, a life-threatening event, likely to be traumatic for those involved, which is in line with the U.S. definition. The breadth of the UK definition is clearly problematic for officers who have to manage critical incidents. The UK definition is described as deliberately broad in order that incidents that have the potential to become critical are not missed; an appeal is made to common sense in application of the term. A report from Her Majesty's Inspectorate of Constabulary (HMIC) states that "the variation in existing levels of understanding of this term [critical incident] gives cause for concern" (2008, p. 9). However, in the example above, the trivial neighborly disagreement could escalate to serious rioting if copresent with other factors (e.g., racial or religious tensions).

One decision-making challenge, then, is to possess skills that would anticipate public opinion and perception, as well as the configuration of other factors most likely to propel ordinary incidents into critical incidents. The politician metaphor serves again, where the decision maker needs to engage with operational matters as well as accountability issues, which entail cognitive (problem-solving) as well as affect-laden social processes (fear of media blame for poor outcome).

Demands will differ across organizational, cultural, temporal, and national contexts. Within the specific UK context (though yet to be empirically tested), accountability appears to be a core driver for modern UK police, their decisions unduly accountogenic. The nature of police work is likewise shifting in other countries, so this may yet transfer, as some findings around accountability conditions have different cultural settings (e.g., Chen, Shecter, & Chaiken, 1996; Mero & Motodiwlo, 1995; Wu, 1992). Certainly, the political and organizational backdrop to police decision making is becoming a more significant area for academic inquiry. Such research would supplement the more substantial literature on cognitive processes and individuals' decision making, pointing to the effects accountability has on both. We describe the UK picture next.

The Foundation of the UK Policing Context

In the United Kingdom, the Macpherson (1999) public inquiry into the failed investigation into the murder of Stephen Lawrence marked a sea change in the context in which the police work. Stephen Lawrence was an 18-year-old black student stabbed to death in London in 1993 while walking with a friend (also a young black male) to catch a bus home. Due to an extremely flawed police investigation, no one was successfully prosecuted for the murder, despite five white youths as strong suspects. The case became extremely high profile, especially after Nelson Mandela paid a visit to the grieving Lawrence family.

Public outrage was widespread. In the inquest to establish how Stephen died, the jury's choice was essentially restricted to an open verdict if the evidence was deemed insufficient to meet the alternative option of unlawful killing. Instead, jurors insisted that the court record the following rider to their judgment that Stephen had been unlawfully killed "in a completely unprovoked racist attack by five white youths." With the apportioning of guilt explicitly proscribed in inquests (they are explicitly restricted to fact finding in relation to how, when, and where an individual met his or her death), the verdict was completely unprecedented. A national newspaper followed with a front-page spread naming the five white youths as killers, thus challenging them to sue for libel. Finally, the chair of the inquiry, Lord Macpherson, famously described the police service as "institutionally racist."

Of course, one incident cannot be deemed to cause all change, though the case was the catalyst that propelled UK policing into the twenty-first century. It is commonly regarded as a benchmark, and a raft of changes can be traced back to the impact of Macpherson, including massive programs to overhaul and professionalize the service and forego the old style "learning on the job" (including a senior's mistakes). Post Macpherson, police were also required to engage formally with nonpolice, for example, to seek independent advice or assess the community impact of their investigations (Grieve, 2008). In addition, greater transparency in police work was required. Investigative decisions and their rationale are now routinely recorded for subsequent scrutiny and legal disclosure. The greater degree of public accountability in the wake of the Stephen Lawrence inquiry was accompanied by intense media scrutiny and more frequent audits (O'Connor, 2005).

Accountability brings obvious benefits, and scrutiny, of course, is necessary. However, when the organizational context is such that officers cannot attain a golden mean in their decision making because of undue salience of accountability, the balance needs to shift back to its (optimal) fulcrum point. In a sweeping review of UK policing, Sir Ronnie Flanagan reported that "the police service has never been so comprehensively inspected and audited as it is today. The effect of this has been to considerably drive up standards, but it also means that forces invest considerable resources and energy in servicing inspection and audit requirements. A range of 'inspectorates' can 'descend upon' a force at any time" (2008, p. 13).

Flanagan confirmed officer views that accountability checks and balances originally conceived as positive and protective had now become disabling. He reported an organization paralyzed by bureaucracy and paperwork, though, in a meeting of the National Policing Board, the home secretary, Jacqui Smith, acknowledged that fundamental change cannot be wrought simply by a reduction in bureaucracy (National Policing Board Secretariat, May 2008). For example, reducing the paperwork attached to performance indicators (aka targets) does little to reduce the significant impact that targets and the performance culture have.

Perceptions of remote leaders concerned more with public accountability and personal careers than operations or staff was a prominent theme in 10kV debriefs (Hermitage et al., 2007; also see below). Rank-and-file officers are obviously objectively accountable to their seniors. However, the growing perception that senior officers have very different goals may fuel the idea that seniors are illegitimate audiences. The centralization of key decisions may also have fueled dissatisfaction among rank-and-file officers whose decision-making autonomy had diminished. It possibly also contributes to potential de-skilling given that decision-making responsibility lies elsewhere with police leaders.

Stories From the Job

Accountability and Performance Indicators (aka Targets)

Leadership and decision-making skills required to satisfy media and public appraisal of satisfaction in the police service are vastly different from those required operationally, but in both external and internal arenas, accountability is extremely salient to police officers. Discussion of performance indicator targets is the first recourse of officers faced with a challenge. It is clear from analysis to date of the 10kV database the authors are currently building that the first recourse to a challenge of any kind—from the structure of service delivery through policy development to operational and interpersonal interactions—is to suggest that a new target will effect change. That performance targets are perceived to be drivers of organizational change appears to be a ubiquitous position. At the current time, debriefs are building a descriptive picture, which will help to define the research agenda, but in empirical terms, the impact of this performance culture on critical incident leadership and decision making is largely unexplored. It is clear, though, that the prospect of being blamed for poor outcomes is at the forefront of many officers' minds (Alison & Crego, 2008).

Within this context, the perceived justifiability of decisions is an influential factor. In a rare empirical study on accountability in UK policing, Cronin and Reicher (2006) found that accountability directly influenced decisions made. In a simulated public order/crowd control incident, they collected data on the officers' deliberations, through transcripts that reflected their situational and operational concerns. Experienced police participants showed an early situational assessment of significant risk of violence: Immediate consideration was given to intervening to extract agitators *before* violence occurred, but participants would not commit to a decision to intervene until police had suffered injury. Only then did participants conclude it would ultimately be perceived as a justifiable use of force. Failing to prevent injury to officers (with consequent reduction in operational capacity) cannot be regarded as an operationally optimal outcome. It may be a sound decision outcome insofar as public censure for police violence is avoided. We would nevertheless argue that the salience of public accountability generated accountogenic decisions where officers failed to attain a golden mean.

More generally, performance indicators are perceived to be important and very salient drivers of activity. 10kV sessions reveal preoccupation with targets as a consistent theme across different areas of policing (e.g., counterterrorism, Alison, Crego, Eyre, & McLean, 2006; firearms officers, Alison, Eyre, & Condon, 2007; road traffic policing, Alison et al., 2007; neighborhood policing, Crego, Alison, & Eyre, 2008; rape investigation teams, Crego, Eyre, Alison, & Newman, 2008; multiagency child protection, Eyre et al., 2008). Below we include some representative quotations to illustrate participant officers' views on performance indicators driving accountogenic decisions:

> "The pressures to achieve targets become the priority instead of ensuring that individuals are okay."
> "Statistic-based performance undermines victim focus and the quality of investigations."
> "If we get increased confidence and increased reporting [of rapes], it will be seen as a negative performance indicator but is in fact positive."
> "Stats and targets are crippling policing. We spend far too much trying to 'paint' the correct picture! The public may hate the picture painted, but our leaders see it as masterpiece!"

If such findings about the salience of the organization's profile and public ranking are generalizable across all forces, it is likely that more accountogenic decisions will be made by police leaders who arguably occupy the most politically vulnerable positions. Research is required to learn how this future direction for policing (and its evaluation) may shape organizations, and the skills and competencies required.

Relying on Unreliable Policy

The debriefs show that officers are extremely concerned with adhering to policy, while decision logs from simulated counterterrorism (CT) exercises have indicated that extant policy was unable to support the dynamic nature of their decision making in the intensively fast-time phase of an operation. Participants engaged in satisficing behavior (Simon, 1957) and made decisions that met most of the immediate needs of the incident, though there was a considerable degree of discussion that attempted to clarify the protocols and command structure as set out in policy. The delays before committing to a decision may be explained by the gravity of the decision (lethal shot). However, the double-checking of policy rules may have been driven by fears surrounding accountability, especially salient following the 2005 fatal shooting of the innocent Jean Charles de Menezes by police in London (mistakenly identified as a suicide bomber). For some officers, the time delays incurred by seeking clarification and confirmation may mean the ideal window of opportunity for a decision could be missed. Discussions included:

> "Who has the final say?" [In response] "The point at which the command changes ... cannot be prescribed in an SOP [standard operating procedure]."
> "Is it your responsibility to support evacuation plans for the houses around the subject addresses should this be necessary?"

"No protocol could necessarily cover all eventualities."

"Danger of risk-averse DSO [designated senior officer] . . . could be dangerous."

In such extreme contexts, policy is swiftly reviewed to accommodate new learning, but while valuable, such review is likely doomed to be perpetual catch-up. Given the unique nature of many events, policy cannot be exhaustive, and the decision makers who lead these critical incidents must have room for creativity.

Reduced awareness of/focus on accountability in relation to outcomes and reduction in excessive (sometimes perceived as illegitimate) monitoring may help to reduce accountogenic decisions and thereby assist in attaining a balanced golden mean. Contextual factors that induce or impede truly creative and optimally balanced decision making need identification, and research is warranted. Accountability is, of course, just one such factor though. Where it is highly salient, it would take a singularly robust individual to reject organizational pressures to conform (Andras & Charlton, 2005; Eyre & Alison, 2007), and yet decision makers cannot rely on policy as a shield, not least because it is insufficiently resilient. They need nonetheless to have room to make decisions without the specter of blame looming too large.

Accountogenic Decisions and Career Building

External factors such as managing public expectations or media scrutiny (Crego & Alison, 2004) are not the only challenge. The UK police's professional development program requires officers to provide evidence to gain accreditations and eventual promotion. Over several months, they complete a portfolio of day-to-day work activities, which is cited as evidence of the required skills and competencies. Thus, many decision makers seem to be keenly aware of the skills assessor as the audience to whom he or she is accountable. Rank-and-file officers perceive their supervisors as individuals who make accountogenic decisions of this type. Supervisors are thought to neglect operationally optimal decisions in favor of personal advantage. Another organizational factor that impacts these decisions is pertinent here. It is colloquially known as the "dash for cash." Once past a certain rank, officers lose the opportunity for overtime, which may be a substantial source of income supplement. Those who wish to further careers may actually experience an income drop in the medium term as they progress through the ranks. Hence, they must dash to the higher ranks as quickly as possible to compensate for the absence of overtime payments, and thereby preserve their standard of living. 10kV participant comments include:

"I believe that some leaders are only in a particular position for a short while purely to get to the next rank."

"[Leaders] turn up, alter everything so they can tick the management competency box 'Managing change' and get promoted, leaving us to deal with the fall-out."

"Some consistency would be useful. My last team had four managers in three years with no real issues being tackled for our team."

"[Leaders] who are loath to send us to incidents that are obviously jobs for us to deal with. . .. [They] are too cozy in their role and don't want a shooting on their watch" (a firearms officer).[*]

Many of these issues in modern UK policing remain as yet empirical questions, and the size of the research challenge is evident. Research is required that is robust enough to examine police decision making in its cultural and organizational context. The higher-ranking officers—the leaders—may be a promising focus. They are the decision makers held most directly accountable for force performance. Given the ubiquity of targets as themes in our qualitative research, these officers may yield the strongest insights into the impact of such accountability on decision making.

Conclusions and the Future

We have argued that complex domain research requires a broader focus than cognitive processes, though it bears repeating that these social processes are not neglected. Indeed, they permeate other chapters in this volume. In Chapter 7, Sieck, Grome, Smith, and Rababy address the idea with reference to cultural sensemaking among Western and Middle East groups (though it is defined as a cognitive process). Osland (Chapter 2) draws attention to the greater complexity faced by global than domestic leaders. In the most similar nod to our theme of accountability, Perry and Wears (Chapter 4) discuss the performance-shaping measures specific to a healthcare setting. On the whole, however, social processes and interactions, particularly between groups, often remain implicit or atheoretical. Where studies do move beyond the individual, teams tend to be the limit in terms of group size (e.g., Carroll, Hatakenaka, & Rudolph, 2006; Nemeth, O'Connor, Klock, & Cook, 2006; Strater et al., Chapter 10).

Although social psychological theories have been developed to explain intergroup processes (social identity theory, Tajfel & Turner, 1986; self-categorization theory, Turner, Hogg, Oakes, Reicher, & Wetherell, 1987), police studies are largely atheoretical and tend to retain a narrow empirical focus. They rarely embrace the explanatory power of theory to investigate the sociocultural/organizational context in which decisions are made. Given that UK officers' dissatisfactions concern intergroup interactions at different levels of the organizational hierarchy as well as at the interagency level, the UK context seems ripe for a more theory-rich approach.

The details of how relevant factors "funnel down" from the broad context to the individual decision maker require study. In addition to the immediate proximal features of a critical incident or other operation (uncertain information, time pressure, and so on) the ambient context of perceived accountability can provide sociocultural tipping points that provoke different forms of time-related decision error (Alison & Crego, 2008; Cronin & Reicher, 2006). These errors include premature decisions (acting too soon) or overdue decisions (acting too late) or even complete failure to act for fear of blame. These follow from Lerner and Tetlock's (1999, 2003) propositions

---

[*] Recall, UK police are unarmed. Officers with firearms constitute specialist units that need a command decision to be deployed to an incident.

around the various facets through which accountability affects decision-making processes, as emerging from the policing context.

Anderson (2003) proposes a rational-emotional model of decision avoidance and cites the particular role of anticipated regret and blame. There is evidence that decisions made induce more regret than decisions avoided (Mellers, Schwartz, & Cooke, 1998), and also that less culpability attaches to acts of omission than acts of commission (Spranca, Minsk, & Baron, 1991). For those steeped in an organizational culture of public inquiries where individuals held accountable are named and shamed, the risk to effective decision making and the likelihood of decision avoidance is clear. We argue that tipping points that provoke these time-oriented errors include organizational environments, social identity processes, and ambient context. Thus, we need to examine how time-sensitive accountogenic decisions are affected by evaluation apprehension, further transferring findings from the accountability literature and applying them to particular contextual settings. We need to identify the tipping points that define these sequences and the sociocognitive contexts that bring them about.

As theory and methodology develop, research questions must address the context. Not only must we determine the sociocognitive processes that underpin decision-making behaviors, but we must also address the issue of multiple layers of audiences to which decision makers are accountable. In a contemporary performance culture, the notion of audience is fluid given that the UK police service is monitored and scrutinized in fine detail by politicians in central government. A police officer at the rank of chief constable may nominally lead a large force and, for his or her own officers, represents the audience that must be pleased. Chief constables are simultaneously accountable individuals and followers of performance targets who oversee swathes of data submissions to central government agencies in order to change red (bad) to green (good) in the traffic light system of key performance indicators. This broad organizational accountability (and accompanying political vulnerability) funnels down into decision-making processes, shifting the leader from a level of focused decision maker to the level of metaphorical politician.

Performance culture, targets, and token economy style rewards are integral to contemporary public sector decision makers in the United Kingdom. It makes followers of those who ostensibly lead. Police leadership and decision making cannot be divorced from the political context generally and the performance culture specifically. Our initial descriptive work is showing the UK policing context as one in which accountability is highly salient and typically experienced negatively. This highlights the social and affect-driven components of decision making that—compared to cognitive processes—are underexplored. This context is also likely to generate accountogenic decisions and steer decision makers away from an ideal golden mean. We need to research these issues in a naturalistic ecologically valid, theory-rich manner that does not neglect the details of the significant impact of organizational and social contexts that obtain for decision makers.

References

Alby, F., & Zucchermaglio, C. (2006). 'Afterwards we can understand what went wrong but now let's fix it': How situated work practices shape group decision making. *Organization Studies, 27,* 943–966.

Alison, L., & Crego, J. (Eds.). (2008). *Policing critical incidents: Leadership and critical incident management.* Devon, UK: Willan.

Alison, L., Crego, J., Eyre, M., & McLean, C. (2006). *10kV report: Operation Theseus—In the face of adversity.* Internal document for U.K. Metropolitan Police Force.

Alison, L., Eyre, M., & Condon, C. (2007). *10kV report: Stress among firearms and road traffic officers.* Internal document for U.K. Police Force.

Anderson, C. J. (2003). The psychology of doing nothing: Forms of decision avoidance result from reason and emotion. *Psychological Bulletin, 129,* 139–167.

Anderson, G. S., Litzenberger, R., & Plecas, D. (2002). Physical evidence of police officer stress. *Policing: An International Journal of Police Strategies & Management, 25,* 399–420.

Andras, P., & Charlton, B. (2005). *A systems theoretic analysis of structures in organizations.* Retrieved March 2006 from http://www.liv.ac.uk/ccr/2005

APACS. (2008). *Guidance on statutory performance indicators for policing and community safety.* Retrieved March 2009 from http://police.homeoffice.gov.uk/performance-and-measurement/assess-policing-community-safety/

Arkes, H., & Blumer, C. (1985). The psychology of sunk cost. *Organizational Behavior and Human Decision Processes, 35,* 125–140.

Baumeister, R. F., & Leary, M. F. (1995). The need to belong: Desire for interpersonal attachments as a fundamental human motive. *Psychological Bulletin, 117,* 497–529.

Bernoulli, D. (1954). Exposition of a new theory of the measurement of risk (R. Sommer, Trans.). *Econometrica, 22,* 23–36. (Original work published 1738)

Carroll, J. S., Hatakenaka, S., & Rudolph, J. W. (2006). Naturalistic decision making and organizational learning in nuclear power plants: Negotiating meaning between managers and problem investigation teams. *Organization Studies, 27,* 1037–1057.

Casey, L. (2008). *Engaging communities in fighting crime: A review.* London, UK: The Cabinet Office.

Chen, S., Shecter, D., & Chaiken, S. (1996). Getting at the truth or getting along: Accuracy-versus impression-motivated heuristics and systematic processing. *Journal of Personality and Social Psychology, 71,* 262–275.

Chubb, J. E., & Moe, T. M. (1990). *Politics, markets and America's schools.* Washington, DC: Brookings Institutions.

Crank, J. P. (2003). Institutional theory of police: A review of the state of the art. *Policing: An International Journal of Police Strategies & Management, 26,* 186–207.

Crego, J., & Alison, L. (2004). Control and legacy as functions of perceived criticality in major incidents. *Journal of Investigative Psychology and Offender Profiling, 1,* 207–225.

Crego, J., Alison, L., & Eyre, M. (2008). *10kV report: Neighbourhood policing: Learning together—Making neighbourhoods safer.* Internal document for U.K. Police.

Crego, J., Eyre, M., Alison, L., & Newman, F. (2008). *10kV report: Review of rape and serious sexual violence investigation.* Internal document for U.K. Police Force.

Crego, J., & Harris, J. (2001). Simulating command. In R. Flin & K. Arbuthnot (Eds.), *Incident command: Tales from the hot seat.* Aldershot, UK: Ashgate.

Cronin, P., & Reicher, S. (2006). A study of the factors that influence how senior officers police crowd events: On SIDE outside the laboratory. *British Journal of Social Psychology, 45,* 175–196.

DiBello, L., Missildine, W., & Struttman, M. (2007). The long term impact of simulation train-
    ing that holds workers accountable to organizational performance with minimal instruc-
    tion on how to achieve it. In K. Mosier & U. Fischer (Eds.), *Proceedings of the Eighth
    International NDM Conference,* Pacific Grove, CA, June 2007.

Eyre, M., & Alison, L. (2007). To decide or not to decide: Decision making and decision avoid-
    ance in critical incidents. In D. Carson, R. Milne, F. Pakes, & K. Shalev (Eds.), *Applying
    psychology to criminal justice* (pp. 211–232). Chichester, UK: Wiley.

Eyre, M., Alison, L., Crego, J., & McLean, C. (2008). Decision inertia: The impact of organisations
    on critical incident decision making. In L. Alison & J. Crego (Eds.), *Policing critical inci-
    dents: Leadership and critical incident management* (pp. 201–230). Devon, UK: Willan.

Eyre, M., Crego, J., & Alison, L. (2008). Electronic debriefs and simulations as descriptive methods
    for defining the critical incident landscape. In L. Alison & J. Crego (Eds.), *Policing critical
    incidents: Leadership and critical incident management* (pp. 24–53). Devon, UK: Willan.

Fiore, S. M., McDaniel, R., Rosen, M., & Salas, E. (2007). Developing narrative theory for
    understanding the use of story in complex problem solving environments. In K. Mosier
    & U. Fischer (Eds.), *Proceedings of the Eighth International NDM Conference,* Pacific
    Grove, CA, June 2007.

Flanagan, R. (2008). *The review of policing: Final report.* London, UK: Home Office.

Frink, D. D., & Klimoski, R. J. (2004). Advancing accountability theory and practice:
    Introduction to the human resource management special edition. *Human Resource
    Management Review, 14*(1), 1–17.

Giddens, A. (1979). *Central problems in social theory.* Berkeley, CA: California University Press.

Gigerenzer, G. (2000). *Adaptive thinking: Rationality in the real world (evolution and cognition
    series).* New York, NY: Oxford University Press.

Gollwitzer, P. M., & Moskowitz, G. B. (1996). Goal effects on actions and cognition. In E. T.
    Higgins & A. W. Kruglanski (Eds.), Social psychology: Handbook of basic principles
    (pp. 361–399). New York, NY: Guilford Press.

Gore, J., Banks, A., Millward, L., & Kyriakidou, O. (2006). Naturalistic decision making and
    organizations: Reviewing pragmatic science. *Organization Studies, 27,* 925–942.

Grieve, J. (2008.) Understanding critical event learning and leadership: Hydra/10kV immersive
    learning, debriefing and other tools. In L. Alison & J. Crego (Eds.), *Policing critical inci-
    dents: Leadership and critical incident management* (pp. xxv–xxxi). Devon, UK: Willan.

Hermitage, P., Whitfield, K., Alison, L., Long, M., Phillips, J., & Ayling, P. (2007). *10kV the-
    matic report.* Internal document for U.K. Police Force.

HMIC. (2008). *Leading from the frontline: Thematic inspection of frontline supervision and leader-
    ship, at the rank of sergeant in the police service in England and Wales.* London, UK: Author.

Kahneman, D., Slovic, P., & Tversky, A. (1982). *Judgment under uncertainty: Heuristics and
    biases.* New York, NY: Cambridge University Press.

Klein, G. (1993). A recognition primed decision (RPD) model of rapid decision making. In G.
    A. Klein, J. Orasanu, R. Calderwood, & C. E. Zsambok (Eds.), *Decision making in action:
    Models and methods.* Norwood, NJ: Ablex.

Kulbarsh, P. (2007). Crit*ical incident stress: What is to be expected? When to get help?* Retrieved
    October 8, 2008, from http//www.officer.com/web/online/police-life/critical-incident-
    stress/17$38344

Kureczka, A. W. (1996). *Critical incident stress in law enforcement.* Retrieved October 8, 2008,
    from http://www.fbi.gov.publications/leb/1996/f-m963.txt

Lerner, J. S., & Tetlock, P. E. (1999). Accounting for the effects of accountability. *Psychological
    Bulletin, 125*(2), 255–275.

Lerner, J. S., & Tetlock, P. E. (2003). Bridging individual, interpersonal and institutional approaches to judgment and decision making: The impact of accountability on cognitive bias. In S. L. Schneider & J. Shanteau (Eds.), *Emerging perspectives on judgment and decision research* (pp. 431–457). Cambridge, UK: Cambridge University Press.

Lipshitz, R., Klein, G., & Carroll, J. S. (2006). Introduction to the special issue naturalistic decision making and organizational decision making: Exploring the intersections. *Organization Studies, 27*, 917–923.

Macpherson, W. (1999). *The Stephen Lawrence inquiry. Report of an inquiry by Sir William Macpherson of Cluny.* London, UK: HMSO. Retrieved March, 21, 2006, from http://www.archive.official-documents.co.uk/document/cm42/4262/4262/htm

Mellers, B. A., Schwartz, A., & Cooke, A. D. J. (1998). Judgment and decision making. *Annual Review of Psychology, 49*, 447–477.

Mero, N., & Motodiwlo, S. (1995). Effects of rater accountability on the accuracy and favorability of performance ratings. *Journal of Applied Psychology, 80*, 517–524.

Metropolitan Police. (2003). *Guide to the management and prevention of critical incidents.* Retrieved October 9, 2008, from http://www/met.police.uk/foi/pdfs/other_information/archive/2003/management_and_prevention_of_critical_incidents_guide.pdf

National Policing Board Secretariat. (2008). National Policing Board. Full minutes. Home office. Retrieved July 20, 2008, from http://police.homeoffice.gov.uk/publications/police-reform/NPB-minutes-May-2008?view=Binary

Nemeth, C., O'Connor, M., Klock, P. A., & Cook, R. (2006). Discovering healthcare cognition: The use of cognitive artifacts to reveal cognitive work. *Organization Studies, 27*, 1011–1035.

Nickels, E. L., & Verma, A. (2008). Dimensions of police culture: A study in Canada, India, and Japan. *Policing: An International Journal of Police Strategies & Management, 31*, 186–209.

O'Connor, D. (2005). *Closing the gap: A review of the fitness for purpose of the current structure of policing in England & Wales.* London, UK: HM Inspector of Constabulary.

Performance and Innovation Unit, Home Office. (2000). *Strengthening leadership in the public sector: Research study by the PIU.* London, UK: Home Office.

Schlenker, B. R. (1980). *Impression management: The self-concept, social identity and interpersonal relations.* Monterey, CA: Brooks/Cole.

Seddon, J. (2008). *Systems thinking in the public sector: The failure of the reform regime and a manifesto for a better way.* Axminster, UK: Triarchy Press.

Siegel-Jacobs, K., & Yates, J. F. (1996). Effects of procedural and outcome accountability on judgment quality. *Organizational Behavior and Human Decision Processes, 65*(1), 1–17.

Simon, H. (1957). *Models of man: Social and rational.* New York, NY: Wiley.

Simon, H. A. (1972). Theories of bounded rationality. In C. B. McGuire & R. Radner (Eds.), *Decision and organization* (pp. 161–176). Amsterdam, Netherlands: North-Holland Publishing Company.

Simonson, I., & Staw, B. M. (1992). Deescalation strategies: A comparison of techniques for reducing commitment to losing courses of action. *Journal of Applied Psychology, 77*, 419–426.

Shattuck, L. G., & Lewis Miller, N. (2006). Extending naturalistic decision making to complex organizations: A dynamic model of situated cognition. *Organization Studies, 27*, 989–1009.

Spranca, M., Minsk, E. & Baron, J. (1991). Omission and commission in judgment and choice. *Journal of Experimental Social Psychology, 27*, 76–105.

Strater, L. D., Cuevas, H. M., Scielzo, S., Connors, E. S., Gonzalez, C., Ungvarsky, D. M., & Endsley, M. R. (2010). An investigation of technology-mediated ad hoc team operations: Consideration of components of team situation awareness. In K. L. Mosier & U. M. Fischer (Eds.), *Informed by knowledge: Expert performance in complex situations* (pp. 149–164). Boca Raton, FL: Taylor & Francis.

Sutton, R., & Galunic, D. C. (1996). Consequences of public scrutiny for leaders and their organizations. In L. L. Cummings & B. M. Staw (Eds.), *Research in organizational behavior* (pp. 201–250). Greenwich, CT: JAI Press.

Tajfel, H., & Turner, J. C. (1986). The social identity theory of inter-group behavior. In S. Worchel & L. W. Austin (Eds.), *Psychology of intergroup relations*. Chicago, IL: Nelson-Hall.

Tetlock, P. E. (1992). The impact of accountability on judgment and choice: Towards a social contingency model. In M. P. Zanna (Ed.), *Advances in experimental social psychology* (pp. 331–376). London, UK: Academic Press.

Tetlock, P. E., Skitka, L., & Boettger, R. (1989). Social and cognitive strategies for coping with accountability: Conformity, complexity and bolstering. *Journal of Personality and Social Psychology, 57,* 632–640.

Turner, J. C., Hogg, M. A., Oakes, P. J., Reicher, S. D., & Wetherell, M. S. (1987). *Re-discovering the social group: A self-categorisation theory.* Oxford, UK: Blackwell.

Tyler, T. (1997). The psychology of legitimacy: A relational perspective on voluntary deference to authorities. *Personality and Social Psychological Review, 90,* 323–345.

Von Neumann, J. V., & Morgenstern, O. (1944). *Theory of games and economic behavior.* Princeton, NJ: Princeton University Press.

Whitfield, K., Alison, L., & Crego, J. (2008). Command, control and support in critical incidents. In L. Alison & J. Crego (Eds.), *Policing critical incidents: Leadership and critical incident management* (pp. 81–94). Devon, UK: Willan.

Wilson, J. Q., & Brekke, N. (1996). Mental contamination and mental correction: Unwanted influences on judgments and evaluations. *Psychological Bulletin, 116,* 117–142.

Wu, C. (1992). The effects of affective-cognitive consistency and anticipated self-representation on the structure of attitudes. *Chinese Journal of Psychology, 34,* 29–40.

Part IV

Outlook
New Methods and Approaches

19

Systematizing Discovery in Cognitive Task Analysis

Laura Militello
University of Dayton Research Institute

B.L. William Wong
Middlesex University

Susan S. Kirschenbaum
Naval Undersea Warfare Center Division

Emily Patterson
The Ohio State University

CTA and Discovering the Unexpected

A hallmark of cognitive task analysis (CTA) is the notion of discovery. A range of CTA methods are used by many related communities of practice, including cognitive systems engineering, expertise studies, naturalistic decision making, cognitive work analysis, strong ethnography, situated cognition, and human-centered computing (Hoffman & Militello, 2008). CTA methods extend traditional task analytic techniques, focusing primarily on complex cognitive phenomena in the context of work. Although applied from many different perspectives and in pursuit of many different goals, CTA methods are often used as part of the initial phases of the scientific process in which investigators are observing and examining a phenomenon prior to hypothesis testing. This requires investigators to approach the phenomenon of study with an open mind. In contrast to experiments designed to confirm or disconfirm specific hypotheses, CTA methods are designed to aid in the highly contextual exploration of complex phenomena. Of particular interest are data that violate current understanding of the domain of study. In fact, the notion of discovery of unexpected elements has been suggested as a criterion for success for any CTA study (Klein & Militello, 2001).

Discovery happens via varied mechanisms. Clearly, the amount and types of data collected will influence what types of things are discovered. For example, the term *variance sampling* is used to describe the concept of purposefully sampling from an all-inclusive range to ensure examination of the entire problem space or phenomenon of study. In other cases, investigators may choose to target contrast cases, such as ideal versus not ideal, good outcomes versus poor outcomes, expert versus novice approaches, and so forth. When it comes to content analysis, analyzing the same data at different timescales can yield unanticipated insights. Including researchers with different backgrounds in the analysis process can lead to broader interpretations and highlight links that might be invisible to a homogenous group of researchers. In general, allowing ample time and resources for multiple iterations of data collection and analysis will increase the likelihood that the research team will be able to thoroughly examine the topic of study problem from multiple perspectives. The opportunity to refine, reject, and recast interpretations based on an iterative analysis process increases the chances of discovery.

It follows then that a core feature of CTA methods is flexibility—flexibility to probe in depth to allow digressions into interesting and unanticipated lines of inquiry. The abilities to flexibly adapt interview techniques in real time, to shift attention appropriately during observations, and to uncover unexpected findings during qualitative analyses are skills CTA practitioners hone over time and with experience.

A competing goal arises, however, when CTA practitioners are asked by project sponsors to develop strategies for increased formalization or standardization in the data collection and analysis processes. Reasons for this include potential improvements in the discovery yield rate from CTA studies. Increased formalization and standardization of data collection and analysis methods might decrease the likelihood that discoveries might be missed and might also increase the likelihood that CTA studies could be reasonably replicated. Standardized data sets might lend themselves to reanalysis to address a range of research questions, reducing the burden on subject matter experts, who are often asked to participate in repeated interview and simulation exercises. Increased standardization and formalization might also make CTA methods easier to learn and apply, less reliant on the skills of the investigator, and more dependent on proper application of methods. Some researchers have suggested analogs to physical sciences and other disciplines that use primarily quantitative methods applied in a standardized manner.

While goals such as increasing discovery yield, developing methods that can be replicated, and articulating methods that are easier to learn and apply (and thus investigator independent) are appealing, the idea of introducing additional standardization into CTA seems on the surface antithetical. To many experienced CTA practitioners, the idea of standardizing data collection and analysis to increase efficiency sounds risky. In fact, the practice of CTA grew out of a reaction against attempts to reduce complex cognitive tasks to a set of standard procedures. Efforts to reduce CTA methods to a set of easily followed standard procedures runs counter to the philosophy behind such methods.

Reluctance to move toward standardization may be rooted in the fact that reports of CTA projects tend to emphasize innovations in methods, interesting discoveries, and real-world implications over the aspects of CTA that lend themselves to standardization. Often the ways in which methods are adapted to study a specific phenomenon appear more interesting than the aspects of the methods that are standard across studies. A more likely explanation, however, is that CTA methods do not lend themselves to standardization. A more relevant construct for CTA methods may be that of *systematization*. We argue that for qualitative studies, an emphasis on systematically applying methods tailored to a specific study is a more appropriate application of rigor than the standardization of methods across studies commonly seen in more quantitative approaches. In this chapter, we explore evolving practices for systematizing discovery. Three recent studies that have emphasized different aspects of systematization are described, each illustrating strategies for balancing an opportunistic approach with systematic application of methods to facilitate the process of discovery. This is followed by a discussion of rigor, systematization, and validity. The final section provides a summary.

Evolving Practices for Systematizing Discovery

In the context of CTA, systematization is not about the creation of a standard, fixed, and close-ended set of questions that would be asked of an interviewee during data collection. Nor is systematization about performing data analysis in a single structured manner. Rather, systemization during CTA data collection is about the creation of a set of open-ended questions that enable the investigator to be methodical while probing the participant (or collecting observational data) about issues expected to be relevant to the study, and yet to be flexible enough to recognize and explore unanticipated issues that could lead to new discoveries. During data analysis, systematization is about the use of data handling techniques that enable the investigator to analyze data in a clear and orderly way so that both expected and unanticipated elements emerge and are summarized. Careful description of the types of systematization used is provided for readers of the study so they can assess for themselves the validity of the conclusions.

Perhaps the most important point to make about systematization in the context of CTA is that it is not generally straightforward. The reality of qualitative data is that they are "messy" (Wong, 2004). The data can be subjective and ambiguous, where meanings are often highly context dependent. Due to the open-ended nature of the data collection interviews and observations, the data collected can lack any obvious structure, making it hard to find underlying relationships. Unlike quantitative data, it is hard to reduce qualitative data into means or other descriptive measures of central tendency. Of course, it is possible to identify aspects of cognitive work that can be counted or timed, and from there to calculate means. The focus of CTA, however, tends to be on things that are not easily counted or timed. In many cases, it is only after an initial CTA has been conducted that investigators know what can be meaningfully measured in quantitative values.

Data sets consisting of interview and observation records often reveal gaps, leading to questions for a future iteration of data collection. The data set is also likely to include information only distantly relevant to project goals (i.e., interviewees digress, observations generally include activities beyond the scope of the project goals, etc.). From such messy data, the challenge to the investigator is to efficiently identify significant patterns in the data, corroborate evidence across different interviewees, and find an adequate structure from which to ground the findings with the evidence. While this can and has been done effectively, it is important to acknowledge that creating the structure within which to systematically analyze data requires time, skill, and iterations.

The following examples illustrate how systematization was introduced in the context of three distinct studies, each using different CTA methods to addresses different types of problems. These studies were selected for examination because they illustrate the variability and messiness of CTA projects, as well as strategies for systematization within and across data sets. Furthermore, these examples are ones in which the authors of this chapter have firsthand experience and can reflect on the processes used.

Ambulance Dispatch Study

This example is based on a study of the decision-making strategies of emergency ambulance dispatchers at a large ambulance control center in Europe (Wong & Blandford, 2002). At the time of the study, this center received more than 3,200 emergency calls per day and managed a fleet of more than 400 emergency ambulances. Emergency calls for medical assistance were received by as many as 20 trained call takers. They logged the calls into the Computer-Aided Dispatch System, using the Advanced Medical Priority Dispatch System (AMPDS) to establish medical priorities. The call information was communicated to ambulance dispatchers in the same control center. Within this center, the dispatchers were organized into seven sector desks that mirrored the seven geographical regions of the city. In addition, there was also one air ambulance desk and one rapid response desk for controlling specialized assets. For example, the crew of the air ambulance often included a specialist emergency medicine doctor. The air ambulance and rapid response desks controlled only a few assets (e.g., there was usually one or two helicopter air ambulances on duty at any time) and were responsible for supporting operations across the seven geographical sectors of the city. In general, each of these sectors was managed by a sector supervisor and two assistants.

The study used the well-established critical decision method (Hoffman, Crandall, & Shadbolt, 1998; Klein, Calderwood, & MacGregor, 1989), a retrospective interview method, for data collection. Thirteen ambulance dispatchers were interviewed in this study and were asked to think back to a particularly memorable and demanding incident they had experienced in the course of their duty from the perspective of allocating resources. Using the incident as a framework, the participants were interviewed, or probed, about what they attended to, thought about, considered, and how they reasoned through various aspects of the situation, and then were asked to extrapolate to likely mistakes that less experienced workers might make. Investigators collected a large set of rich, qualitative data in the form of audiotapes that were subsequently transcribed. During the interviews, the interviewer and interviewee used Post-it™ notes to jointly develop timelines of the decisions made during each incident. These were also included in the qualitative data set.

Wong and Blandford (2002) applied a method they called emergent themes analysis to analyze data, facilitating the emergence of themes. They describe this as a concept distillation process that systematically identifies broad themes, and then iteratively refines the themes into more specific subthemes that emerge from the data. *Broad themes* are similar ideas and concepts reported within each interview and across interviews. For example, one broad theme identified in this study was assessment. Within this broad theme, *specific themes* were identified by collating or grouping closely related subconcepts together according to some order, such as similarity or temporality, for example, assessment of resources and assessment of the situation. The distillation process, while systematic, must not constrain the emergence of insightful themes. The emergence of themes can be suppressed if strict a priori classification categories are used. Once the specific themes have emerged, the data are then categorized and summarized.

Figure 19.1 presents a schematic of the emergent themes analysis. Qualitative data can be reduced by collating data initially into different groups, and then by dissecting these groups and regrouping in different ways to reveal commonalities and new relationships.

In this study of ambulance dispatchers, investigators began the emergent themes analysis (Wong & Blandford, 2002) by reading through the transcripts and identifying, indexing, and collating a set of broad themes. Figure 19.2 provides a small sample of transcripts relating to the broad theme of goals that guide how a dispatcher carries out his or her job.

Broad themes such as goals, subgoals, priorities, and constraints provided a structure within which investigators could conduct more detailed analyses, such as ordering each broad theme by type, nature, or common features. For example, the investigators collated the goal excerpts into smaller groups of closely related concepts,

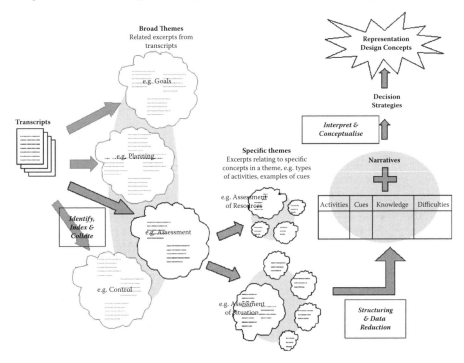

FIGURE 19.1   Schematic of the emergent themes analysis. (From Wong, B. L. W., and Blandford, A., in F. Vetere, L. Johnston, and R. Kushinsky, eds., *Human Factors 2002, the Joint Conference of the Computer Human Interaction Special Interest Group and the Ergonomics Society of Australia, HF2002* (CD-ROM publication), Melbourne, Australia: CHISIG and the Ergonomics Society of Australia, 2002. With permission.)

To get the right number of ambulances to the right place as quickly as possible to ensure a good patient outcome (survivability)
- to get the ambulances there as quick as possible and for a good result" (3/1266)
- maintain um…your [ORCON] standards (3/1274)
- getting the right um…the right response to the um…incident. (4/1513)
- to get an ambulance or ambulances to scene at the quickest possible way…Get the vehicles rolling. (5/1488)
- the main goal is to get the ambulance crews there and get…get patients…to get people treated as quickly as possible. (1/1175)

To ensure that the rest of the sector continues to perform
- the smooth running of the um…sector, um…while all this going on (3/1273)
- smooth running of the service so that other people end up with a reasonable service (6/762)

To keep critical incidents at forefront of considerations
- and for this baby to be…it's always at the forefront of your mind. (3/1277)
- the, um…thing about it is, when something like that happens, although you're still allocating for the rest of West London, it's always forefront in your mind, and it's always…it's always that sort of job, like a suspended baby, or a large road traffic accident will always, although you're just allocating, you're just allocating normally, but then they're always forefront in your mind. (3/49–52)

To understand what is happening in order to assess the need
- what the incident is, what response you need on it, get responses moving. (4/1514)
- to find out exactly what was happening (4/1531)
- until you find out what is happening, you can't mobilize at all (4/1535)
- to find out what was going on…find out what is happening. (5/1488)
- To get the right vehicle to the right amount of patients is difficult. (6/754)

To communicate relevant information to the crews as quickly as possible (radio operator)
- to give [the ambulance crews] the correct information clearly and concisely. (8/1666)
- to keep them informed of the situations (8/1670)
- get updates from the police or the patient, condition might have deteriorated or police have no units to assign (8/1674)
- you're looking after the crews' safety as well, and what they're doing (8/1688)

FIGURE 19.2   Sample of transcripts representing goals that have been collated into more closely related groups.

and further categorized them into *one overall goal*, to get the right ambulances to the right place at the right time; *three subgoals* related to assessment of the situation, planning, and coordination and control; and three other categories that set the *priorities and constraints* of their actions—minimize disruption to the other sectors, control other ambulances simultaneously, and pay attention to critical incidents. This structure provided the investigators with a framework to ask further questions and generate hypotheses. The structure also aided in collating the evidence available to answer those questions, support or disconfirm hypotheses, and elaborate the concepts identified.

For example, the analysis suggested one theme that spanned the different concept groups: knowing or understanding what is happening within and around the sector. The investigators called this *situation awareness* and sought more evidence about this concept. A sample of excerpts thus identified is presented in Figure 19.3.

These situation awareness excerpts were further analyzed for commonalities and grouped under headings such as activities; cues, sources, and consideration; knowledge and experience; and difficulties, likely mistakes, and consequences. Figure 19.4 depicts a data analysis table, and illustrates one way in which a large volume of qualitative data can be systematically reduced and dissected into clear categories that reveal interesting

- Aware of what's going on in and around their sectors so that they can start thinking ahead in case an incident escalates
- "For safety reasons, we need to know who's there...we keep a vehicle movement sheet..." "I know everything that is going on because all info comes through me..."
- Other emergencies occur in a sector despite a major incident, hence still need to keep an eye on situation
- Knowledge of the area on which dynamic movements are tracked
- "we just try and picture everything...everything has to be a picture in your head of what's going on...[anticipating] what else they need,...and what else we can be doing."
- Use a map to help plan how to reach a major incident scene.
- "you're the ones that are talking to the crew on the radio...and they are asking you and telling you the situation"
- 'Control ears'—time and effort minimization strategy for keeping track of what's going on around them
- "It's all up here, you know what's happening, you know what's going on, you know what's been done...its difficult for someone to jump in, cos...you have not got a picture of it, you can't see what's going on, so you can only talk and you can only imagine what's going on"
- Flick through the CAD displays, the tickets, review the box

FIGURE 19.3   Excerpts relating to the concept of situation awareness.

insights about the activities involved in the development of situation awareness, the information used and where it is sourced, the kinds of expertise the dispatcher brings to bear on the problem, and where difficulties are likely to be encountered.

Figure 19.5 shows another example of how the reduction and dissection can be applied to systematically extract different insights, guided by the investigators' intentions. By changing the column categories to reflect new questions or hypotheses, we change the way we filter and organize the information. In this way, we can use the systematic reduction and dissection process to collate the evidence to describe how the different actions associated with situation awareness are carried out—for example, whether they are technology dependent or whether it is a characteristic that is inherent to the process.

In Figure 19.6 we show how the difficulties identified in Figure 19.4 ("difficulties and likely mistakes") can be recast as specific difficulties and then be used to describe how information is handled by the dispatchers. For example, when dealing with duplicate calls, dispatchers like to have the information about the duplicate calls laid out side by side to facilitate rapid visual comparison of important details, instead of relying on memory.

Through this systematic approach to analysis, Wong and Blandford (2002) were able to explore the types of uncertainty dispatchers must contend with and the strategies dispatchers develop to deal with uncertainty. Interestingly, many dispatchers initially described their ability to deal with uncertainty as a sixth sense. Via skillful interviewing and careful analysis of the data, supported by the systematic reduction and dissection procedures described earlier, investigators were able to identify specific cues, sources, and considerations that skilled dispatchers were drawing upon as they applied this sixth sense. For example, one dispatcher reported how he used his knowledge and his sixth sense (e.g., "just doesn't look right") to assess the situation. This very specific piece of information—the description of what sixth sense is—had not been previously articulated and was abstracted into a conceptualization of decision strategies used by dispatchers.

Activities	Cues, sources, and consideration	Knowledge and experience	Difficulties, likely mistakes, consequences
1. Build a mental picture of the problem by integrating situation and incident information. 2. Collate information from many sources. 3. Corroborate evidence with others. 4. Assess if the incident is real. 5. Assess severity of incident (number of casualties).	1. Information that describes the type of incident—call details screen. 2. Information that describes the scene and the situation (e.g. for crew safety reasons)—could be in original call details screen or could be in another ticket. 3. Information from police and fire—on separate tickets. 4. Call rate. 5. Key cues expected—CHALET	1. "Just doesn't look right" or 6th sense—developed from experience and medical (on road) training. This knowledge is used to assess the situation.	1. Uncertain information. 2. Determining if calls are duplicates—flag calls with similar addresses rather than tie in on locations 3. Flicking between summary and details screens to read, collate, compare and mentally integrate information—effortful process, highly memory intensive and therefore requires full attention. Summary display lacks visual discriminators or explanatory information. 4. Information from police and fire not differentiated on summary display.

FIGURE 19.4 A data analysis table for collating observations about behaviors with evidence from excerpts about information, knowledge, and experience used, with difficulties and consequences.

Situation Awareness (1)

Decision stage and decision goals	Actions	Information Source (technology dependent)	Information Used (non-technology dependent)	Knowledge and Experience	Difficulties (technology dependent vs. non-technology dependent)
Keep aware of what's going on around them enables allocators to think ahead and plan for contingencies, and to consider crew safely issues.	Ask for or expect to be updated by Radio Operators and Telephone Dispatchers on any changes in state, or to follow-up on instructions.	Radio Operator Telephone Operator	Verbal or written (history on back of ticket): On-road information e.g., what ambulances are currently doing, what is the outcome of an instruction, emotional state of crews to look after their welfare.	Knowledge of the area is useful for mentally keeping track of the dynamics of who is at which location, and what they are doing or will be doing. (Who, what, where, when)	Building up situation awareness is a continuous process. SA built up by integrating information from a variety of sources. This is difficult as the information and the sources are often randomly organized, and therefore needs to be collated and repackaged.
	"Control ears" used to selectively listen for key things help maintain an awareness of what's going on around them.	Others in control room, and neighboring sector desks	Physical cues: attending to and physically receiving, acknowledging and passing tickets between desk members. Cues to listen for include: when vehicles next become available, e.g., ambulances green-ing at hospitals, and vehicles from another sector but becoming available in one's sector; and reports from the scene; and key words like, "I'm free."		
	Switch monitoring between incidents to keep abreast with all developments in sector.	CAD job summary and job details screen. Tickets on the desktop and in allocators desk.	Looking for changes in reported details, e.g., new information since last "Print acknowledge" (in italics on the printed ticket)		
	Listen in on some calls being received by call-taker (e.g., calls that take a long time) to assess if it is relevant to the sector	Call-taker telephone system and call-taking summary screen showing calls and duration of calls.	Call location and incident description, and why the call is difficult (hence why it is taking such a long time).		

FIGURE 19.5 A data analysis table using different filters for further reduction and dissection to address subsequent questions that arise from the first stage of analysis shown in Figure 19.4. (Adapted from Blandford, A., and Wong, B. L. W., *International Journal of Human-Computer Studies*, 61, 421–452, 2004.)

Difficulty observed	Information handling behavior	Capability needed or exhibited
Duplicate calls. Many occasions when several members of the public call separately to report the same incident. This gives rise to several tickets which are similar but not the same, depending upon the caller's perspective or location with respect to the incident.	*Side-by-side-ability.* Dispatchers place the printed tickets side-by-side so that the incident information can be visually compared. *Share-ability.* Dispatchers may take the tickets and share them with a colleague to help them decide whether the tickets represent the same incident.	*Visual comparison of call details.* Ability to organize information so that duplicate calls are grouped together, or show clear association. Sharing of information and collaborative discussion.
Carrying on to another job. Indicating and remembering intermediate planning stages of many simultaneous jobs. This function is not supported by the computer system.	*Back-to-back.* Tickets from different incidents are being placed back to back in a slot in the allocator's box to indicate that the ambulance is returning from one job (ticket A) and will continue to a second job (ticket B). This acts as both a visual and physical reminder of the intermediate planning decision taken.	*Visual indications of intermediate planning stages, or intentions.*
Jobs still outstanding. Computer system controls the way information is organized and presented on the display, hard to indicate planned intentions, priorities, and position in the task queue.	*Stacking tickets.* Tickets of jobs yet to be assigned are stacked on the desk in a manner that additional *notes* written on the top of the tickets are visible. The notes to provide additional readily visible cues to assist them in planning. The stack can be easily *shuffled* as less urgent jobs are reprioritized as vehicle availability changes. The stack is itself a planning device.	*Planning or plans in progress.* Stacks provide visual cues of the number of jobs still to be assigned. Ease of organization (shuffling) and reprioritization, allows flexibility in planning. Physical placement in the stack allows indication of priority. Annotations to provide quick visual reminders.

FIGURE 19.6   An example showing how outcomes from a data analysis table can be used to create a new line of inquiry about information handling behaviors, using another data analysis table with new filters. (Adapted from Wong, B. L. W., and Blandford, A., in D. J. Reed, G. Baxter, and M. Blythe, eds., *Proceedings of ECCE-12, the 12th European Conference on Cognitive Ergonomics 2004, Living and Working With Technology*, September 12–15, 2004, European Association of Cognitive Ergonomics, York, UK, 2004, pp. 195–202).

Other interesting insights also emerged through this process. For example, three key concepts were used in connection with the word *picture* when describing situations and referring to an awareness of that situation: (1) picture as an understanding of the overall situation (i.e., to know what is going on); (2) picture as a visualization of the geographic area and where fixed assets are located, such as stations and hospitals; and (3) picture as an understanding that is built up over time.

Investigators also discovered difficulties dispatchers encountered in accessing and processing information. This suggested new capabilities that computer displays should support, including side-by-side ability to enable easy visual comparison of information provided by different callers regarding the same incident, and back-to-back ability, or the practice of placing a new job ticket diagonally across the current job ticket to provide visual cues that this ambulance will be carrying on to the next job.

Although emergent themes analysis is still evolving, investigators found that this systematic series of steps (identify broad themes; identify specific themes; identify actions, cues, knowledge, and difficulties, along with representative examples) allowed for easy comparison and collation across different cases. By creating structure in the analysis, they were able to make visible the potential relationships that could exist within the data, thereby making it possible to arrive at new insights.

Primary Care Clinics Study

A study of barriers and facilitators to the use of computerized clinical reminders in ambulatory care clinics was conducted by Saleem et al. (2005). In this study, ethnographic observation was the primary data collection strategy, and upward abstraction was used to increase systematization in the analysis process. Upward extraction is a process by which "details that are specific to the context of a setting are replaced by the underlying strategies and performance criteria that are relevant across settings" (Saleem et al., 2005, p. 440). Three observers collected data at four different hospital sites, spending two days at each site. Several teleconferences were held by the team prior to the visits, and thoughts about what to expect were documented in a centralized game plan document. A guidance document for observers included target areas for observation: the sequence of activities, when the activity begins, when the activity ends, the role of the provider doing the activity, the trigger to initiate activity, the trigger to interrupt activity, and the trigger to complete activity. In addition, a sample field note excerpt was used to guide observers with regard to the level of detail to capture in field notes.

Real-time data collection was somewhat opportunistic in nature. Activities were observed that were not anticipated, such as healthcare providers using clinical reminders prior to and following patient visits, but not during them. Observers shadowed healthcare providers who agreed to be observed as they conducted exams on patients who also consented to being observed. In addition to materials to guide the observations, a set of questions was prepared in advance for use in opportunistic interviews when and if healthcare providers had downtime between exams. These prepared questions were intended to facilitate comparisons across individuals. Questions were asked when the opportunities arose. These questions were:

1. How many patients are you scheduled to see today?
2. How long have you used the clinical reminder system and CPRS?
3. Can you think of a time when a clinical reminder really made a positive difference in the way you treated (or interacted with) a patient?

4. Can you think of a time when a clinical reminder (or the clinical reminder system) got in the way? If yes, please explain.
5. What would you say are the best features of the clinical reminder system?
6. What would you say are the aspects of the clinical reminder system most in need of improvement?

The resulting field notes were copious. In order to systematically explore this context-rich data, investigators began by typing notes into tables that broke observations into meaningful segments with periodic timestamps. Each investigator used his or her own judgment to determine the size and content of meaningful segments. Segments tended to consist of one to four sentences, and each described a segment of activity, interaction, or conversation that took place. The data collectors all participated in the analysis. Each member of the research team reviewed the typed field notes. The members of the research team familiarized themselves with findings from a survey conducted on this topic, as well as a previous study examining computerized clinical reminders in a different clinical setting (Patterson, Ngyen, Halloran, & Asch, 2004). Drawing from prior research and recent immersion in the current study data, the investigator team met to nominate coding categories. A set of 30 coding categories was generated. In an iterative fashion, observations were coded into the 30 categories. Over several iterations, some categories were combined and others were split into logical subcategories. Via this method, emergent themes were identified (e.g., tendency to use the computer while not with the patient). The frequency with which each theme appeared in the data set was recorded, as well as the frequency with which each theme appeared at each hospital site.

Many of the themes translated directly to facilitators and barriers to the effective use of computerized clinical reminders not previously articulated in the literature. The resulting findings guided the development of a set of design concepts intended to increase the effectiveness of computerized clinical reminders (Militello, Patterson, Saleem, Anders, & Asch, 2007).

In this study, an effort was made to introduce appropriate levels of systematization during data collection. Observers shared guidance about level of detail, topics of particular interest, and questions for use in opportunistic interviews. With regard to analysis, detailed and thorough notes allowed for the use of upward abstraction methods as investigators iteratively explored the data for high-level themes. The high-level themes were eventually distilled into a set of barriers and facilitators, which in turn informed a set of design concepts. This approach to data collection and analysis also allowed accurate reporting of how many sites experienced a particular emergent barrier or facilitator to use (including whether it was observed), and included enough detail to place the findings in context. Contextual elements surrounding specific observations, such as the number of patient encounters, whether the provider was a physician or nurse, and the number of clinical reminders, aided investigators in interpretation.

Weather Forecasting Study Using Comparative Cognitive Task Analysis

Comparative cognitive task analysis introduces a strategy for systematically comparing CTA data collected from two or more distinct worker populations. Of the three examples examined in this chapter, this study incorporates the most standardization and also includes quantitative comparison. The standard elements introduced for the comparative study were tailored specifically for the phenomenon of study in order to highlight similarities and differences across two populations of weather forecasting experts.

Kirschenbaum, Trafton, and Pratt (2007) employed comparative cognitive task analysis in a study of Navy weather forecasters. In this case, observational and verbal protocol data were collected from weather forecasters at the U.S. Navy Meteorology and Oceanography center in California, and from forecasters at a Royal Australian Navy Weather and Oceanography center in eastern Australia. The U.S. forecasters participated in an exercise at a high-fidelity simulation facility. The Australians were observed during real-world preparation of forecasts and forecast briefings. Both populations were instructed to think aloud as they worked. Video- and audiotapes were recorded for subsequent encoding and analysis.

The comparative cognitive task analysis technique was developed with a goal of helping investigators disentangle aspects of work practice due to human cognition from those due to organizations and from those due to the tool used. Data were analyzed at two levels of detail. Initial analysis extracted a high-level description of the stages of weather forecasting (i.e., extraction, comparison, deriving, recording). Later analyses focused on developing a detailed description of the information processing procedures used during each stage. Verbal protocols were coded to capture the format of initial information (text, graph, animation, etc.), the way the forecasters used information, output methods (e.g., copy and paste, copy value, derive forecast value, etc.), and the form of the information (qualitative or quantitative) (Kirschenbaum, 2002; Trafton et al., 2000).

The same coding scheme was systematically applied to both data sets, highlighting similarities and differences across the two weather forecasting populations. Investigators discovered that forecast stages were common across sites, and the same methods were used by both groups of weather forecasters. However, the similarity ended there. There were statistically significant differences in the order of method application, the tools used, and the relative frequency with which these methods were used during the different stages of forecast development. Analyses suggested that some key differences in work practice could be attributed to differences in the tools available. The Australian forecasters used two adjacent monitors or adjacent windows on the same monitor for comparison and integration tasks (exploring the satellite and radar pictures). The U.S.-based forecasters did not have the ability to compare data side by side, and thus were required to view one data source, store the data either in memory or on paper, and then view the second data source. This discovery, for example, drove recommendations for better tools and workstation design for U.S. forecasters.

As with both emergent themes analysis and upward abstraction, encoding included general (i.e., stages of weather forecasting) and specific (i.e., information processing procedures) levels of analysis. This multilevel analysis allowed the experimenters to identify key features in the data as a function of the phase of the forecast process.

Systematization Across Three CTA Studies

The types of systematization used in each study were driven in part by study goals. The first study of ambulance dispatchers used a moderate level of systematization in data collection. The critical decision method provided a framework for investigators to collect a set of challenging role allocation incidents from the first-person perspective of the dispatcher. Furthermore, each incident was probed for key contextual elements, such as cues and information sources, as well as aspects of individual expertise that were brought to bear on the incident, such as knowledge and experience. This level of standardization in data collection facilitated the emergent themes analysis. Investigators were able to sift through the data and extract emerging themes related to uncertainty and strategies for coping with uncertainty in the context of role allocation. Each iteration through the data allowed for more fine-grained analysis and increasingly specific findings.

The second study relied primarily on ethnographic observation as a data collection technique in primary care clinics, with a goal of understanding barriers and facilitators to the use of computerized clinical reminders during regular clinic operations. Ethnographic observation allows for less standardization in data collection, as investigators have no control over what types of incidents will be witnessed on a given workday. The resulting data set is thus less focused than a data set derived from critical decision method interviews. As a result, investigators are likely to require additional iterations of analysis to discover important themes relevant to the study goals. Thus, ethnographic observation is generally more time-consuming and costly in terms of both data collection and analysis than more focused data collection techniques. For a study exploring the integration of clinical decision support (computerized clinical reminders) into clinical workflow, however, more focused interview techniques are likely to miss workarounds and workflow adaptations that have become routine to healthcare workers, and thus they are unlikely to be articulated in an interview. In this case, several iterations of analysis were required. Initial passes through the data focused on how to structure the analysis. What information about barriers and facilitators to clinical reminder use was mentioned? How much and what types of context should be retained to drive design seeds and best practices recommendations? An initial framework was developed and refined as some categories were subdivided and others merged. In addition to yielding a set of barriers and facilitators that led to recommendations for technological changes and best practices for integrating computerized clinical reminders into workflow, the study used key contextual elements in the data set to design scenarios for a simulation study assessing the impact of recommended design seeds.

The third study was designed with the intent of comparing work practices across two organizations conducting similar weather forecasting activities. Introducing a level of standardization in data collection that will allow for adequate comparisons is quite challenging given the messy nature of CTA data, and the limited access researchers are likely to have to weather forecasters. In this case, researchers standardized the types of data collected and the analysis process across two sites. Researchers were able to collect data in two comparable contexts, a high-fidelity simulation and real-world operations. Video- and audiotapes were used to record details of tool use, information content, form, and format. Systematic, targeted analyses were then conducted, focusing on the stages of weather forecasting and the information processing procedures used during each stage. These target analyses were likely more standardized and required fewer iterations than the more thematic analyses conducted in the ambulance dispatch and primary care clinic studies.

The Advantages of Qualitative Rigor, Systematization, and Validity

CTA, as with most qualitative approaches, focuses on understanding rather than measuring phenomena. Investigators begin with open-ended research questions (sometimes described as a bottom-up approach) rather than a clearly stated falsifiable hypothesis (sometimes described as a top-down approach). Within this framework, criteria such as methodological rigor, researcher experience and skill, and relevance are used to assess the validity of qualitative findings (Forman, Creswell, Damschroder, Kowalski, & Krein, 2008). Rigor is important for the study design and the research process, both of which are tailored to the study goals, the phenomena of study, and time and resource constraints. While methods are tailored to each study, methodological rigor requires that the methods be systematically applied and that the research process be sufficiently comprehensive to support the findings. It is up to the investigator to carefully document the methods and how they were systematically applied so that the reader may assess the validity and rigor for himself or herself. For qualitative methods focused on understanding complex phenomena, rigor is highly dependent upon the investigator's ability to adapt and apply methods. This is distinct from quantitative approaches for which standard methods and investigator independence are valued.

Forman (2009) suggests that a consensus approach to analysis may be a better strategy for more complex qualitative research than more standard approaches using independent coders and interrater agreement. Efforts to increase agreement across coders might inadvertently stifle discussion of differing assumptions about and interpretation of the data. The consensus approach reflects a constructivist view that there are many possible interpretations of the same data. Validity is therefore increased by considering multiple interpretations and making thoughtful decisions about which are most useful for a given project.

Because cognitive challenges change as new technologies and processes are introduced and as the world in which the system of study operates changes, the idea that one would be able to replicate a CTA study at a later point in time has little meaning. (This is not to be confused with the use of the term *replication* in the classic experimental sense, or to describe the use of the same methods on a different data set with a goal of identifying similarities and differences in work practices across worker populations; Kirschenbaum et al., 2007.) There is no question that the training and experience of the investigators influence what data are collected and what discoveries are made. These elements of variability in method application and solution generation are visible in nearly every discipline aimed at the study of real-world problems and the design of innovative solutions (i.e., engineering, architecture, software design).

How to make systematic observations and conduct systematic analyses are much more meaningful issues in the context of CTA. Addressing these issues has been a challenge in many CTA studies. Systematic analysis is a critical element of CTA. However, given the differing constraints associated with each study (project goals, access to experts, investigator training, time and resources available, etc.), investigators must determine what types and how much systematization will be meaningful in the context of any given study. There is no standard set of steps that will guarantee a successful CTA. Rather, one must determine how to systematically collect data without decontextualizing or distorting the phenomenon of study, and how to analyze large, messy data sets efficiently while allowing for exploration of multiple interpretations and the emergence of unexpected discoveries.

Summary and Conclusions

This chapter posits that efforts to standardize CTA methods must focus on qualitative rigor rather than quantitative standardization. Qualitative rigor requires that methods be applied systematically within the context of a specific study. Experienced investigators devise a data collection plan that can be adapted as needed, incorporating a level and type of systematization appropriate to the phenomenon of study. A similar approach is used during data analysis. Coding schemes are often generated, systematically applied, revised, and systematically applied again. This sort of iteration continues until consensus is reached.

When evaluating the validity of CTA studies, it is important to consider differences between quantitative and qualitative approaches to inquiry. Quantitative approaches tend to focus on measuring, which requires standardization and replication if measurements are to be generalizable. Qualitative approaches, in contrast, focus on understanding complex phenomena that cannot be meaningfully reduced to discrete variables that are easily measured. Qualitative rigor is based on purposeful sampling, selection of appropriate data sources, and systematic and iterative application of methods. The goal is often to understand a complex phenomenon within a specific context, with reduced emphasis on generalizability.

Although debate exists regarding the most appropriate criteria for assessing the validity of qualitative findings, we find the criteria offered by Forman et al. (2008) to be quite applicable to CTA: methodological rigor, researcher experience and skill, and relevance. We would encourage CTA researchers to emphasize systematization over standardization to increase the likelihood of discovery.

References

Blandford, A., & Wong, B. L. W. (2004). Situation awareness in emergency medical dispatch. *International Journal of Human-Computer Studies, 61*(4), 421–452.

Forman, J. (2009, May). *Conducting rigorous qualitative research* (VA HSR&D Methods Cyberseminar Series). Ann Arbor, MI: Ann Arbor VA Center for Clinical Management Research.

Forman, J., Creswell, J. W., Damschroder, L., Kowalski, C. P., & Krein, S. L. (2008). Qualitative research methods: Key features and insights gained from use in infection prevention research. *American Journal of Infection Control, 36*(10), 764–771.

Hoffman, R. R., Crandall, B., & Shadbolt, N. (1998). Use of the critical decision method to elicit expert knowledge: A case study in the methodology of cognitive task analysis. *Human Factors, 40*(2), 254.

Hoffman, R. R., & Militello, L. G. (2008). *Perspectives on cognitive task analysis: Historical origins and modern communities of practice.* New York, NY: Taylor and Francis.

Kirschenbaum, S. S. (2002). Royal Australian Navy Meteorology and Oceanography operations research report (Tech. Rep. 11-346). Newport, RI: Naval Undersea Warfare Center Division.

Kirschenbaum, S. S., Trafton, J. G., & Pratt, E. (2007). Comparative cognitive task analysis. In R. H. Hoffman (Ed.), *Expertise out of context* (pp. 327–336). New York, NY: Erlbaum.

Klein, G., & Militello, L. G. (2001). Some guidelines for conducting a cognitive task analysis. In E. Salas (Ed.), *Advances in human performance and cognitive engineering research* (pp. 163–200). New York, NY: JAI.

Klein, G. A., Calderwood, R., & MacGregor, D. (1989). Critical decision method for eliciting knowledge. *IEEE Transactions on Systems, Man and Cybernetics, 19*(3), 462–472.

Militello, L. G., Patterson, E. S., Saleem, J. J., Anders, S., & Asch, S. (2007). Supporting macrocognition in health care: Improving clinical reminders. In J. M. Schraagen, L. G. Militello, T. Ormerod, & R. Lipshitz (Eds.), *Naturalistic decision making and macrocognition* (pp. 203–220). Aldershot, UK: Ashgate.

Patterson, E. S., Nguyen, A. D., Halloran, J. P., & Asch, S. M. (2004). Human factors barriers to the effective use of ten HIV clinical reminders. *Journal of the American Medical Informatics Association, 11*, 50–59.

Saleem, J. J., Patterson, E. S., Militello, L., Render, M. L., Orshansky, G., & Asch, S. M. (2005). Exploring barriers and facilitators to the use of computerized clinical reminders. *Journal of the American Medical Informatics Association, 12*, 438–447.

Trafton, J. G., Kirschenbaum, S. S., Tsui, T. L., Miyamoto, R. T., Ballas, J. A., & Raymond, P. D. (2000). Turning pictures into numbers: Use of complex visualizations. *International Journal of Human-Computer Studies* [Special issue: *Empirical Evaluations of Information Visualizations*], *53*, 827–850.

Wong, B. L. W. (2004). Data analysis for the critical decision method. In D. Diaper & N. Stanton (Eds.), *Task analysis for human-computer interaction* (pp. 327–346). Mahwah, NJ: Lawrence Erlbaum Associates.

Wong, B. L. W., & Blandford, A. (2002). Analysing ambulance dispatcher decision making: Trialing emergent themes analysis. In F. Vetere, L. Johnston, & R. Kushinsky (Eds.), *Human Factors 2002, the Joint Conference of the Computer Human Interaction Special Interest Group and the Ergonomics Society of Australia, HF2002* (CD-ROM publication). Melbourne, Australia: CHISIG and the Ergonomics Society of Australia.

Wong, B. L. W., & Blandford, A. (2004). Information handling in dynamic decision making environments. In D. J. Reed, G. Baxter, & M. Blythe (Eds.), *Proceedings of ECCE-12, the 12th European Conference on Cognitive Ergonomics 2004, Living and Working With Technology,* September 12–15, 2004 (pp. 195–202). York, UK: European Association of Cognitive Ergonomics.

20

Expertise in Assessing and Managing Risk of Violence

The Contribution of Naturalistic Decision Making

Paul R. Falzer
Clinical Epidemiology Research Center, VA Connecticut Healthcare System

The impact of behavioral decision theory on forensic psychiatry and criminal justice has been felt principally through studies of juror decision making, behavioral economics, and legal reasoning (for example, see Arkes & Mellers, 2002; Ellsworth, 2004; Jolls, Sunstein, & Thaler, 1998; Simon, 1998). However, its greatest potential impact may lie in the practice of assessing risk of violence. (In context and in this chapter, the practice is referred to as risk assessment.) Violence risk assessment is becoming common practice among jurisdictions in North America, the United Kingdom, and Europe, especially for youth who have come to the attention of the juvenile justice system. Risk assessments enable custodial, clinical, and judicial decision makers to achieve the objective of protecting society while placing individuals who have committed criminal or so-called status offenses into appropriate treatment or rehabilitation facilities.

Typically, the practice consists of classifying individuals into discrete categories based on their propensity to commit violent acts, and using the classification scheme to make decisions about detention, treatment, and disposition. Considerable discretion may be permitted regarding the contents of an assessment, how the information is obtained and by whom, and what occurs subsequently. In other instances, a specific procedure is mandated and prescribed. For instance, a designated mental health professional makes a detention or involuntary commitment determination by comparing results of a clinical examination against statutory criteria for dangerousness. Compare the formality of this procedure with the routine administration of a scale, usually by nonprofessional staff, for the purpose of assigning individuals to custodial or security levels. In some instances, risk assessment findings serve as qualifying criteria for placement into community-based programs or treatment services. Risk assessments are also administered to gauge progress in treatment; in some jurisdictions, they are being used as discharge criteria.

There are two principal approaches for assessing risk. *Clinical judgment* procedures rely on professional expertise to render opinions based on interviews, record reviews, and psychological testing. In contrast, *actuarial assessment* uses validated instruments and may include statistical algorithms for aggregating item scores into categories. There are variations and combinations of these two, such as "anamnestic" assessment, which classifies solely on the basis of a record review, and "adjusted actuarial" assessment, which uses clinical judgment to clarify and modify actuarial findings (Otto, 2000). In all instances, classifications of risk are predictions of future behavior; what these predictions are predicated on depends principally on the kind of assessment that is performed, who performs it, and the purpose that it serves.

In some cases, risk assessment begins and ends with classification, and maximizing predictive validity is paramount. In other cases, classification is preliminary to making recommendations or decisions about what to do next. In the latter case, the assessment is likely to gauge both *fixed* and *dynamic* factors. Fixed (sometimes called historical) factors are determined and unchangeable. For instance, that an individual committed a violent act two years ago is an immutable fact. Dynamic factors are potentially modifiable and may prove especially useful in planning medical or psychosocial interventions. For instance, suppose that a violent act was committed when the perpetrator was intoxicated and he demonstrates no propensity for violence when sober. This person may be sanctioned to participate in a substance abuse treatment program, and successful completion may be a material factor in changing his risk classification from high or medium to low (Hanson, 1998). An important subset of the dynamic category is *protective* factors. These are so named because they assess potential for channeling or moderating violent responses. Examples of protective factors include pro-social affiliations, education, and even willingness to use tranquilizing agents.

There is some dispute, particularly among litigators, about the advisability of using instruments to predict future behavior. Concerns about their routine use are balanced against their prospective value in protecting society at large and facilitating efforts at treatment and rehabilitation, while minimizing the insidious influence of factors such as race and ethnicity (Chapman, Desai, Falzer, & Borum, 2006). However, there is significant disagreement about whether risk assessments should be essentially mechanical exercises consisting of standard questionnaires and actuarial scoring algorithms, or whether the task of risk assessment should be performed by qualified professionals who exercise clinical judgment (Borum & Otto, 2000). This issue continues to have a pervasive influence on criminal justice policy, research, and practice (Monahan, 2003). Discussions have escalated into disputes, and over time the disputes have degenerated into what is commonly known as the clinical-actuarial conflict. While some observers believe that the respective parties to the conflict have reached a point of impasse and the current situation is irreconcilable, others are continuing to pursue a solution.

This chapter is based on the hopeful belief that the conflict can be resolved, even though every significant proposal advanced to date seems to have proven futile; in some instances, an already complicated situation has been further polarized. A solution is outlined in this chapter that is guided by naturalistic decision making (NDM), particularly by the way that NDM-based theories and models have addressed the problem of suboptimality. It is argued that this problem, with its genesis in behavioral decision theory, has contributed to creating the clinical-actuarial conflict and continues to pose a stumbling block.

The discussion begins by reviewing the claim that the act of predicting future violence displays the flaws of clinical judgment, and that problems of fallible decision making can be overcome by the use of valid actuarial instruments. The actuarial approach enjoys strong empirical support, and as its popularity grows, so also does its threat to clinical practice. I discuss the most viable prospect for a solution advanced to date, the approach known as structured professional judgment (SPJ), whose instruments offer a distinctive blending of clinical judgment and actuarial assessment. However, efforts to validate SPJ techniques have focused on the predictive validity of their actuarial aspects and have marginalized the importance of clinical judgment, despite intentions to the contrary, illustrating that considerable work remains to be done if the conflict is to be resolved.

While most efforts to address the clinical-actuarial conflict have attended principally to the classification of violence risk, the solution presented in this chapter focuses on the management aspects of risk assessment, specifically on how classifications are used in developing interventions whose purpose is to diminish the incidence and severity of future violent acts. The proposal draws specifically on Beach's image theory (1998) and his narrative behavioral decision theory (2009). The importance of decision-making expertise, especially expertise as described in principles and concepts of naturalistic decision making, is reflected in the solution's four requisite skills: (1) recognizing the overall situation and how general risk of violence indicators manifest in individual cases; (2) formulating and implementing a viable plan for managing risk of violence, given the availability of effective systemic and programmatic resources; (3) monitoring the plan and adjusting it if progress is not sufficient; and (4) implementing the plan through distributed decision making.

The Problem of Suboptimality and the Clinical-Actuarial Conflict

Those who are familiar with NDM would insist that discussions about the putative suboptimality of human judgment as presented in behavioral decision theory raise complex issues, and that facile conclusions can be misleading. For the applied discipline of forensic psychiatry and among practitioners of risk assessment, human judgment is understood somewhat differently: For some, the fallibility of unaided human decision making has been demonstrated conclusively by myriad studies conducted over more than six decades. Ostensibly, these studies demonstrate pervasive suboptimal tendencies, and thus challenge the capacity of expert clinicians to assess risk and forecast behavior accurately (for examples, see Bornstein & Emler, 2001; Elstein, 1999; Goldberg, 1967; Guthrie, Rachlinski, & Wistrich, 2000; Lassiter, 2002). A review by Monahan (1981), frequently cited in the risk assessment literature, concluded that clinical predictions of violent behavior by psychiatrists and psychologists over a several year period are likely to be accurate in no more than one out of three cases, and the accuracy of clinical predictions about violent behavior are no better than chance. Although this claim was based on evidence gathered over 30 years ago, it has been reiterated as recently as 2008 (see Swanson, 2008).

The express need for reliable and accurate measures of violence risk has led to an influx of actuarial instruments to replace human clinical prediction, and several have become mainstays. For adults, there is the Violence Risk Appraisal Guide (VRAG) (Harris, Rice, & Quinsey, 1993) and the Hare Psychopathy Checklist (PCL-R). Youth and adolescent assessment batteries commonly include the PCL-YV and the

MAYSI-2 (Marczyk, Heilbrun, Lander, & DeMatteo, 2003). Monahan and associates (Monahan, 1997; Monahan et al., 2000) are among the leading advocates of actuarial assessment in forensic psychiatry. Their MacArthur-sponsored violence risk assessment study is responsible for revisiting the relationship between mental illness and violent behavior. The study has spurred development of the Classification of Violence Risk (COVR), an instrument that features a sophisticated iterative tree algorithm (Monahan et al., 2001, 2006). In a recent study of violent acts committed by mentally ill adults, the COVR demonstrated a 77% accuracy rate, and with almost identical rates of false positives and false negatives (Monahan et al., 2005, 2006). For a review and analysis of relevant risk assessment instruments, see Cottle, Lee, and Heilbrun (2001). For a discussion of procedures and issues related to constructing and validating mechanical assessment instruments, see Gottfredson and Snyder (2005).

The Conflict Escalates

Even as actuarial assessment has flourished, advocates of clinical judgment have not allowed the claim that their judgments are suboptimal to go unchallenged. Otto (1992) noted that early studies contaminated the limitations of clinical judgment with the unpredictability of the criterion, and that newer, so-called second-generation studies give a more favorable impression about the accuracy of clinical prediction. In a study frequently cited, Mossman (1994) used receiver operating characteristic (ROC) analysis to demonstrate that the predictive accuracy of clinical judgment is considerably better than chance and may approximate the performance of actuarial instruments. However, recent work suggests that using ROC analysis as the sole measure of predictive accuracy is problematic (see Cook, 2007), and the ebullience with which the study's methodology and findings have been endorsed suggests that the interests of promoting a viewpoint can lead to overlooking key issues, such as what exactly constitutes a risk assessment and how comparisons should be made (for examples, see Buchanan, 2008; Rice & Harris, 2005).

Perhaps the definitive comparison of clinical judgment and actuarial assessment was conducted by Grove, Zald, Lebow, Snitz, and Nelson (2000), whose meta-analysis of studies published between 1966 and 1988 included rigorous entry criteria and a sophisticated measure of effect size. They concluded that mechanical assessment is about 10% more accurate than clinical judgment overall, but there is wide variation among studies, and overall differences seem to diminish on closer inspection (also see Grove & Meehl, 1996). The authors interpreted these results as favoring the broad use of actuarial tools. However, this interpretation was substantiated less on grounds of suboptimality than on practical advantages such as ease of administration, low cost, and consistency of results across populations and jurisdictional boundaries. These advantages, combined with marginal differences in predictive accuracy, may indeed lead to questioning whether clinical judgment has a legitimate place in the contemporary practice of violence risk assessment.

Meehl and his associates (Meehl, 1986) believe that clinical judgment should have been replaced by actuarial procedures long ago. He minces no words in claiming that the continued popularity of clinical judgment is testament to a stubbornness and intransigence that deserve to be quashed (p. 374; also see Dawes, Faust, & Meehl,

1989). Kleinmuntz (1990) gives a more sanguine appraisal in suggesting that progress is slow but sure, and resistance to mechanical tools will yield as new instruments come on line. Monahan and associates (2006) promote the interests of actuarial assessment in a slightly different way, by ensuring that clinical judgment will continue to have a viable though secondary role. Their idea is for the two approaches to coexist in complementary fashion, with actuarial assessment informing clinical judgment but not replacing it. They envision a two-stage procedure, in which actuarial assessment occurs at Stage 1. Clinical judgment comes in at Stage 2, for the express purpose of assimilating and interpreting actuarial findings. This proposal is one vision of how the practice of risk assessment might proceed once the clinical-actuarial conflict has been resolved, but it does not propose how to achieve the solution. Nor does it address, on either conceptual or practical grounds, how actuarial findings are supposed to be integrated with other information, including test data, behavioral observations, reports, and recommendations, without threatening predictive validity (see Gottfredson & Moriarty, 2006; Grove & Meehl, 1996; Hilton & Simmons, 2001). Perhaps the principal contribution of Monahan's proposal lies in its sentiment, a desire to resolve the conflict in a manner that enables the two approaches to remain disparate, but to coexist.

Structured Professional Judgment: A Tantalizing Prospect to Resolve the Conflict

Perhaps the best current prospect for a solution to the clinical-actuarial conflict lies in the approach known as structured professional judgment (SPJ), the fifth and most recent approach to risk assessment (see Douglas & Skeem, 2005; Otto, 2000; Webster, Muller-Isberner, & Fransson, 2002). One of the ways that SPJ strikes a "best of both" compromise is by developing specially designed assessment instruments that include both fixed and dynamic factors. Like actuarial tools, SPJ's instruments target specific high-risk populations; they consist of items drawn from current research and guidelines, and the tests are relatively easy to learn and administer. In contrast to actuarial procedures, which tend to focus on fixed or historical items in the interests of maximizing predictive validity, SPJ instruments tap dynamic and protective factors extensively, and they produce findings that can be incorporated into risk management plans. Another key difference is that actuarial instruments use mechanical algorithms to produce summary scores. In SPJ, a summary classification is expressed by a summary risk rating (SRR) that is the product of clinical judgment (see Borum, Bartel, & Forth, 2005, pp. 312–313).

Several SPJ instruments are now widely used, notably the HCR-20 for adults (Douglas, 2004; Webster, Douglas, Eaves, & Hart, 1997) and the Structured Assessment of Violence Risk in Youth (SAVRY) (see Borum, Bartel, & Forth, 2000). The SAVRY is a 30-item instrument that has been translated into more than six languages and is currently used in North America, Europe, and Asia. The 30 items are explicitly defined and have clear scoring standards. For instance, historical item 1 is *history of violence*, where

> violence refers to an act of battery or physical violence that is sufficiently severe to cause injury to another person or persons . . . regardless of whether injury actually occurs; any act

of forcible sexual assault; or a threat made with a weapon in hand. (Borum et al., 2000, p. 29, emphasis deleted)

The standard for the rating this item is as follows:

0   Low risk: The youth has committed no acts of violence.
1   Moderate risk: The youth has committed one or two acts of violence.
2   High risk: The youth has committed three or more acts of violence.

Reliability studies of the SAVRY have obtained internal consistency ratings of .8 or higher, and interrater reliability coefficients that exceed .7.

Some studies examining the SAVRY's concurrent and predictive validity (Olver, Stockdale, & Wormith, 2009; Rennie & Dolan, 2005) have relied on the clinically derived SRR, while others have used an arithmetic sum of scores on the 24 risk items (leaving out the 6 protective factor items), and still others have used both. The use of a mechanically calculated summary disregards the distinctive role that SPJ reserves for clinical judgment. The SAVRY's developers in particular are adamant that it function as a clinical decision tool for professionals and not be viewed as just another actuarial scale. Curiously, even they and their colleagues have been inclined to compare the two summary measures in an effort to validate clinical judgment (see Borum et al., 2005; McEachran, 2001). A recent study (Lodewijks, Doreleijers, & de Ruiter, 2008) using ROC analysis compared the two summary scores in three groups of juvenile offenders. For one group, the area under the curve (AUC) of .65 for the computed summary compares with .71 for the SRR. In the other groups, the probabilities are .70 versus .71, and .74 versus .76. The investigators did not examine these differences for statistical significance and the summary AUC statistic (C) tends to obscure magnitudes (Pepe et al., 2008), but visual inspection of these differences shows only a marginal increment for the SRR.

These findings serve to reinforce the question of whether the SRR—along with the clinical judgment that produces it—offers a meaningful advantage over a mechanical calculation, particularly when the latter uses a simple arithmetic sum. Gauging by conversations at a recent international convention, it appears that the SAVRY is being treated mainly as a predictive mechanical tool and not as a clinical decision aid. The procedure for deriving an SRR is either unknown to some clinicians, researchers, and administrators, or it is not used.

A Solution That Incorporates Naturalistic Decision Making

Despite problems in implementation, SPJ nonetheless is a tantalizing proposal of how to accommodate clinical judgment and actuarial assessment in a manner that minimizes the extant conflict. However, issues related to predictive validity—how to assess the validity of an SPJ instrument without treating it as an actuarial tool—continue to daunt the SPJ approach. Reports of suboptimal clinical judgment in the early risk assessment studies, combined with the considerably lower cost of validated actuarial tools, have resulted in the widespread use of actuarial instruments. Owing to their demonstrable accuracy and their practical advantages, actuarial instruments in risk assessment have enjoyed increasing popularity, and the trend is likely to continue. In the meantime, the value of clinical judgment in classifying risk has become more difficult to defend, and the difficulty extends to SPJ's reliance on the SRR.

Three Elements of Risk Assessment

When we say that an individual who falls into a high-risk category is likely to commit a violent act, we are making a projection based on the assumption that current circumstances will not materially change. This assumption applies regardless of whether the projection is made by an actuarial or clinical procedure. Beach (2009) refers to this projection as the *extrapolated future*. Classifying individuals into categories is an essential exercise, but an assessment that does nothing more is tantamount to the position that the extrapolated future is the only future that should be involved in risk assessment.

The proposal that is presented in this chapter is based on the following principle: Whether a risk assessment is performed by a clinician or an actuarial instrument, it is incomplete unless it contains two elements in addition to a projection of the extrapolated future—a more desirable alternative future, and a strategy for turning the assessment trajectory away from the former and toward the latter. The value of any risk assessment lies less in its ability to classify than in its contribution to developing an intervention to change the extrapolated future into a desirable future. A common mistake of validation studies, particularly those that rely on ROC analysis, is to treat a prediction task as if it were a diagnostic exercise, in which the outcome is known but the clinician or clinical instrument is blinded for the purpose of testing. Risk assessment is an exercise of predicting events that are truly unknown, not only because they have yet to occur, but because of the influence of intervening factors. In the practical arena of risk assessment, the idea is to intervene in a manner that prevents the likely prediction from actually coming to pass.

The practice of risk assessment should not culminate with a projection of the extrapolated future. Its counterpart, the desired future, is no less important, and projecting it relies heavily on individual, dynamic, and protective factors (Grisso, 1998; Hart, 2008; Jessor, Van Den Bos, Vanderryn, Costa, & Turbin, 1995; Wong & Gordon, 2006). While the extrapolated future may be obtained from actuarial measures, there is no analogous algorithm for calculating the desired future. A distinctive feature of SPJ instruments, and perhaps the most significant advantage of the SPJ approach, is its ability to capture in reliable fashion the dynamic aspects of risk, which include mitigating, or so-called protective, factors (Douglas & Skeem, 2005). SPJ instruments can assess the factors that contribute to a desired future more reliably and completely than clinical judgment procedures that focus on problems, impediments, and pathologies and generally do not explore dynamic factors in comprehensive fashion.

For instance, the SAVRY's 30-item scale consists of 6 sociocultural items, 8 individual items, and 6 protective factors, as well as 10 historical items. The sociocultural factor includes items pertaining to peer relationships, coping, parental management, social support, and community organization. The individual factor taps impulsivity, attitude, empathy, attention deficit, and compliance with authority. The protective factor measures pro-social involvement, interpersonal and familial attachments, and commitment to education. The utility of these items in projecting a desired future—a future that is significantly different from the extrapolated future—cannot be overstated.

Two of the three essential elements of a risk assessment can be addressed by extant approaches—actuarial assessment for the extrapolated future and SPJ for the desired future. The third element, formulating a risk reduction strategy, has received comparatively little attention in the risk assessment literature, with the notable exception of Heilbrun's work on risk communication (see Heilbrun, 1997; Heilbrun, O'Neill, Strohman, Bowman, & Philipson, 2000). The task of developing and implementing a strategy has the single overarching purpose of reducing the discrepancy between extrapolated and desired. Expertise in clinical decision making facilitates the performance of this task; expertise that results from knowledge of naturalistic decision-making principles and techniques proves particularly valuable. It is through NDM that a practical solution to the clinical-actuarial conflict can be advanced. The value of decision-making expertise becomes apparent in the course of discussing the proposal's four principal skills of effective strategy development:

1. The ability to recognize the overall situation and how general risk of violence indicators manifest in individual cases
2. The ability to formulate and implement a viable plan for managing risk of violence, given the availability of effective systemic or programmatic resources
3. The ability to monitor the plan and make adjustments if progress is not sufficient
4. The ability to gain concurrence of stakeholders and implement the plan as a distributed decision

The remainder of this section is devoted to discussing the four skills.

The Importance of Recognition

A key contribution of NDM is in turning the attention of experts toward processes that occur early in decision making, and prior to the phenomena, such as option choices that typically draw the interest of decision-making researchers. In NDM (Klein, 1993), decision processes are often dependent on recognition of the decision situation, its constraints, and requirements. A NDM framework that can be applied directly to the task of formulating a risk reduction strategy is Beach's image theory (Beach, 1998), which was so-named to draw an explicit connection between decision making and cognitive psychology (Miller, Galanter, & Pribram, 1960).

In image theory and in Beach's latest work on narrative behavioral decision theory (NBDT) (Beach, 2009), recognition is of a *discrepancy* between the attributes of two entities or processes. In Beach's earlier work, the test of discrepancy was variously known as screening or matching (screening *out* or matching *in*) (see Beach & Mitchell, 1987; Beach & Potter, 1992). For instance, John and Jack are distinguished by their height, color of hair, age, home address, color of shirt, and so forth. We recognize them as two different people when the number of mismatched attributes exceeds an arbitrary sum or threshold. This example has three key features: entities, attributes, and a discrepancy threshold.

Discrepancy analysis by attribute is a general analytic procedure that applies to a host of comparisons, including the classification of individuals into categories. Discrepancy analysis determines whether the respective attributes are different enough so that the prospect that the individual falls into a particular category, such as high risk of violence, can be ruled out. This is a *categorical* discrepancy and the key question is: Does person X fit the criteria for Y? In the actuarial approach to risk assessment, categorical discrepancy analysis is performed by validated instruments that use specific criteria to classify the attributes of individuals and their situations. However, because the algorithms they use can involve sophisticated calculations that are opaque to the individuals who are called upon to use the results, the classifications may be of limited use in developing risk management plans or making disposition decisions.

Monahan and associates (2006) have acknowledged that actuarial findings must be interpreted, and they believe that the task of interpretation requires clinical expertise. However, clinical interpretation of test data will be no less murky than a raw algorithm unless it has the quality that Simon (1978) identified as "procedural rationality" (see pp. 8–9). NBDT's discrepancy analysis can play a significant role here in the classification phase of risk assessment, by giving rationality to actuarial findings. For example, consider this conclusion: "This individual has a strong propensity for violence and belongs in the high-risk category, as gauged by his score on the historical items of the SAVRY and a criminal history that includes three assaults over the past five years using a weapon." Connecting a classification to a specific set of items is a relatively simple task. More difficult, but more meaningful in using the classification as a projection, is creating a clinical summary document that reflects a recognition of the entire situation. It is essential to understand why the items referenced in the summary are critical and why the other scale items do not contribute materially to the classification. This recognition is the first step in the process of strategy development.

Formulating a Plan by Using Available Resources

In Beach's NBDT, recognition is depicted as the most rudimentary decision. While recognition includes specific entities and their attributes, the scope required for plan formulation is broader and encompasses an entire situation. To move from risk categorization to risk management, knowledge derived from classification tools as described above will inform an intervention whose objective is to reduce or eliminate the discrepancy between the extrapolated future and the desired future. Formulating this intervention requires knowledge of community-based, residential, and custodial resources, and the ability to match the needs of an individual with extant programs and services.

Performing this matching activity requires a skill that the NDM literature refers to as epistemic reasoning (see Beach, 1992; Hastie, 2001). The concept draws explicitly on Svenson's (1990) contrast between type A and type B decision problems. A type A problem involves a choice between two (or more) competing courses of action. In contrast, a type B problem focuses on overcoming the discrepancy between present and future, when the present is problematic or undesirable, and a move toward a more desirable future is either contemplated or under way. What is key is that two types of problems lead to different reasoning paradigms. Whereas type A problems are amenable to what Hastie (2001) and Beach (1992) designate as *aleatory*, or calculated, reasoning, type B problems lend themselves to *epistemic* reasoning, which proceeds from problem to solution in goal-oriented fashion.

Beach and Lipshitz (1993) regard the distinction between aleatory and epistemic as crucial for the genesis of NDM theories, which expand the scope of decision making beyond type A decision problems. As Hammond (2000) notes, the pursuit of optimality, that is, the effort to make the best selection from a given set of alternatives, has led the science of decision making down different and oftentimes inconsistent metatheoretical paths. Recent studies have discussed the advantages of NDM in the field of clinical decision making, particularly its value in assisting experts to appreciate the requirements of a clinical situation and to develop the skill of applying general knowledge about effective, evidence-based treatments to specific cases (Falzer, Moore, & Garman, 2008). It is in the application of epistemic reasoning that behavioral decision theory's preoccupation with optimizing yields to NDM's focus on practical problem solving (see Falzer, 2004; Patel, Kaufman, & Arocha, 2002).

Formulating and implementing an intervention plan requires epistemic reasoning because there is no a priori link between problem and solution. The two futures, extrapolated and desired, may not have a common set of attributes, and contiguity must be established deliberately, through a linking strategy. For instance, suppose an individual poses a high risk of violence owing to three factors—one incident of non-life-threatening violent behavior, lack of impulse control, and living in a dysfunctional community and home environment. Both the impulse control problem, which is an individual factor, and the social environment problem, which is a sociocultural factor, must be addressed if future violence is to be prevented. Clinical expertise in risk assessment is required to fashion an appropriate and individualized intervention. This expertise includes the ability to recognize the problem and how it leads to the extrapolated future. It also includes knowledge of available resources that can be brought to bear in redirecting the trajectory, and the ability to structure a link to a future that is both feasible and desirable. This link is what enables a discrepancy to emerge, because without it there is no systematic means of formulating treatment goals and establishing criteria for evaluating progress.

Monitoring and Assessing Progress

Image theory conceives of decision making as a series of events that occur on a trajectory. These events are what the theory refers to as progress decisions, and discrepancy analysis plays a significant role in determining whether the trajectory is on course, or in keeping with the goal of achieving the desired future. In the practice of risk assessment, it is critical to gauge whether an intervention is progressing satisfactorily, and if not, what do to next. In image theory, this type of discrepancy analysis was referred to as image compatibility testing (see Dunegan, 1995). A related but more complex form of discrepancy analysis appears in NBDT, which depicts people as storytellers, whose narratives establish the sensibility of their experience. Decision making is depicted as a series of discernible points that are integral to the unfolding narrative.

When current efforts to achieve a more desirable future are not working suffi-ciently, a *high-level discrepancy analysis* comes into play and considers three principal alternatives, which are neither simple nor mutually exclusive. One alternative is to modify or scale back the goal. The second is to modify or enrich the strategy. The third is to tighten or loosen the assessment criteria. Skill and experience are required to determine where the effort should be directed, what should be changed, by how much, how to gauge whether the change has occurred, and how to determine whether the modification is working.

High-level discrepancy analysis plays a significant role in this proposal, but it should be noted that the ability to practice any form of ongoing progress assessment, particularly the complex form described here, requires expert decision making to gauge whether the plan has been given an adequate trial or whether more time is required before contemplating a change, whether intervening events should put a plan on hold or be incorporated into a revision, whether closer monitoring works against the achievement of a goal or is essential to meeting it, and so on. In medicine and forensic psychiatry, the activity that most closely resembles high-level discrep-ancy analysis is program evaluation. This is a technical assessment function that is performed for the purpose of long-term or strategic planning, frequently because it is mandated by an administrative agency or funding source. In contrast to prog-ress assessment, program evaluation is conducted in a manner that minimizes the possibility of immediate impact. For instance, individuals who have completed an anger management program are monitored for one year, and program effectiveness is determined by comparing the number of individuals who committed a violent act with the total number of program participants. This summative calculation is per-formed retrospectively. It is not a means of assessing progress in individual cases and using the progress assessment to modify the current plan or develop a new plan, unless the discrepancy between extrapolated and desired has been overcome.

Implementing Risk Assessment Plans Through Distributed Decision Making

The multifarious tasks that comprise risk assessment require expertise in recognizing the situation, creating a plan, and monitoring and assessing progress. It is conceiv-able that all of these tasks can be performed by one individual working alone. More commonly, this expert is working for an agency or organization, and the organi-zational entity has a significant voice in what is recommended and how the plan is implemented. A comprehensive risk assessment plan obligates an array of persons, programs, and services. Individuals (whether they are youth, patients, or offenders) must be accepted into programs. Cases are assigned to a lead clinician, team leader, or probation counselor, who is tasked to supervise the collection of data, read and interpret results, and organize a variety of managerial, professional, and staff activi-ties. Some of the activities are routine, but others, particularly in cases that are par-ticularly complex or involve sequenced goals (in which the desired future is attained by a series of contingent steps), can be time-consuming and disruptive. Complex or difficult cases can threaten organizational, historical, discretionary, and disciplin-ary boundaries. Even in the most progressive and amenable settings, the prospect of reviewing previous decisions and making modifications carries an implication, warranted or not, that something or someone has failed.

It is traditional to speak of decision making as organizational or individual, but in the current correctional, healthcare, and social services environment, the decision-making practices that accompany risk assessment can be described more appropriately as distributed (Fischhoff & Johnson, 1997; Rapley, 2008), shared (Hamann et al., 2006), collaborative (Jahng, Martin, Golin, & DiMatteo, 2005), or team based (Orasanu, 2005). Features of effective team-based decision making have been discussed throughout this volume—for instance, in Perry and Wears's chapter on coordination of work, Seick's chapter on crowd management, Strater and Cuevas's discussion of human automation teams, Lauche and Bayerl's chapter on hybrid decision-making teams, and Caldwell and Garrett's account of team coordination. Insofar as the clinical-actuarial conflict is adversely affecting the distributed practice of risk assessment as well as its individual functions, these chapters offer a glimpse into how risk assessments might proceed once the conflict is resolved. However, the conflict is pervasive, and we can only speculate about the prospects of its subsiding. The question for future NDM research is how distributed decision making proceeds as effectively as it does in an atmosphere that is rift by internecine battles, territorial claims, inconsistent objectives, and competing ideologies.

Conclusion

This chapter has been motivated by the belief that while the clinical-actuarial conflict is refractory and its effects are deleterious, the potential benefits of overcoming the conflict make the effort worthwhile. The chapter began by portraying the current status of risk assessment. On one side we have the developers of actuarial tools and their eager consumers, which include agencies, jurisdictions, and policy makers, as well as psychologists, judges, parole counselors, and correctional personnel. On the other side, we have clinicians armed with statistical discrimination models, whose training and experience give credence to the claim they are uniquely able to distinguish genuine causal relationships from chance associations. In the middle there is a dedicated group of practitioners and researchers who are attempting to strike a compromise that capitalizes on the best qualities of both approaches. It is unfortunate, though perhaps not surprising, that the solution they have proffered has been assimilated into the conflict rather than surmounting it.

Against this conflicted situation, a proposal has been advanced that consists of three elements: valid classification, a viable alternative future, and a means of redirecting the current trajectory toward a more desirable outcome. Achieving these objectives requires the use of both actuarial measures and clinical expertise. Experts must develop and implement four NDM-based decision-making skills—recognition, planning, progress assessment, and teamwork—to plot the trajectory of individuals who are at risk of committing acts of violence from problem to solution. The hope is that the proposal outlined here has a reasonable chance of success. Perhaps the ability to project a more desirable future for the discipline of risk assessment will lead to strategies that can bring the current conflict to a close.

References

Arkes, H. R., & Mellers, B. A. (2002). Do juries meet our expectations? *Law and Human Behavior, 26*(6), 625–639.

Beach, L. R. (1992). Epistemic strategies: Causal thinking in expert and nonexpert judgment. In G. Wright & F. Bolger (Eds.), *Expertise and decision support* (pp. 107–127). New York, NY: Plenum Press.

Beach, L. R. (2009). *Narrative thinking and decision making* (online monograph). Retrieved April 12, 2009, from http://leeroybeach.com/sitebuildercontent/sitebuilderfiles/narrative.pdf

Beach, L. R. (Ed.). (1998). *Image theory: Theoretical and empirical foundations*. Mahwah, NJ: Lawrence Erlbaum.

Beach, L. R., & Lipshitz, R. (1993). Why classical decision theory is an inappropriate standard for evaluating and aiding most human decision making. In G. A. Klein, J. Orasanu, R. Calderwood, & C. E. Zsambok (Eds.), *Decision making in action: Models and methods*. Norwood, NJ: Ablex.

Beach, L. R., & Mitchell, T. R. (1987). Image theory: Principles, goals, and plans in decision making. *Acta Psychologica, 66*(3), 201–220.

Beach, L. R., & Potter, R. E. (1992). The pre-choice screening of options. *Acta Psychologica, 81*(2), 115–126.

Bornstein, B. H., & Emler, A. C. (2001). Rationality in medical decision making: A review of the literature on doctors' decision-making biases. *Journal of Evaluation in Clinical Practice, 7*(2), 97–107.

Borum, R., Bartel, P., & Forth, A. (2000). *Manual for the Structured Assessment of Violence Risk in Youth (SAVRY)*. Tampa, FL: University of South Florida.

Borum, R., Bartel, P. A., & Forth, A. E. (2005). Structured Assessment of Violence Risk in Youth. In T. Grisso, G. Vincent, & D. Seagrave (Eds.), *Mental health screening and assessment in juvenile justice* (pp. 311–323). New York, NY: The Guilford Press.

Borum, R., & Otto, R. (2000). Advances in forensic assessment and treatment: An overview and introduction to the special issue. *Law and Human Behavior, 24*(1), 1–7.

Buchanan, A. (2008). Risk of violence by psychiatric patients: Beyond the "actuarial versus clinical" assessment debate. *Psychiatric Services, 59*(2), 184–190.

Chapman, J. F., Desai, R. A., Falzer, P. R., & Borum, R. (2006). Violence risk and race in a sample of youth in juvenile detention: The potential to reduce disproportionate minority confinement. *Youth Violence and Juvenile Justice, 4*, 170–184.

Cook, N. R. (2007). Use and misuse of the receiver operating characteristic curve in risk prediction. *Circulation, 115*(7), 928–935.

Cottle, C. C., Lee, R. J., & Heilbrun, K. (2001). The prediction of criminal recidivism in juveniles: A meta-analysis. *Criminal Justice and Behavior, 28*(3), 367.

Dawes, R. M., Faust, D., & Meehl, P. E. (1989). Clinical versus actuarial judgment. *Science, 243*(4899), 1668–1674.

Douglas, K. S. (2004). *Making structured clinical decisions about violence risk: Reliability and validity of the HCR-20 violence risk assessment scheme*. Vancouver, British Columbia: Simon Fraser University.

Douglas, K. S., & Skeem, J. L. (2005). Violence risk assessment: Getting specific about being dynamic. *Psychology, Public Policy, and Law, 11*(3), 347–383.

Dunegan, K. J. (1995). Image theory: Testing the role of image compatibility in progress decisions. *Organizational Behavior and Human Decision Processes, 62*(1), 79–86.

Ellsworth, P. C. (2004). Legal reasoning. In K. Holyoak & R. Morrison (Eds.), *The Cambridge handbook of thinking and reasoning*. Cambridge, UK: Cambridge University Press.

Elstein, A. S. (1999). Heuristics and biases: Selected errors in clinical reasoning. *Academic Medicine, 74*(7), 791–794.

Falzer, P. R. (2004). Cognitive schema and naturalistic decision making in evidence-based practice. *Journal of Biomedical Informatics, 37*(2), 86–98.

Falzer, P. R., Moore, B. A., & Garman, D. M. (2008). Incorporating clinical guidelines through clinician decision making. *Implementation Science, 3*(13).

Fischhoff, B., & Johnson, S. (1997). The possibility of distributed decision making. In Z. Shapira (Ed.), *Organizational decision making* (pp. 217–237). New York, NY: Cambridge University Press.

Goldberg, L. R. (1967). Research on the clinical judgment process. *Anthropology and Medicine, 15*(4–5), 220–242.

Gottfredson, D. M., & Snyder, H. N. (2005). *The mathematics of risk classification: Changing data into valid instruments for juvenile courts* (No. NCJ 209158). Washington, DC: National Center for Juvenile Justice.

Gottfredson, S. D., & Moriarty, L. J. (2006). Statistical risk assessment: Old problems and new applications. *Crime and Delinquency, 52*(1), 178–200.

Grisso, T. (1998). *Forensic evaluation of juveniles.* Sarasota, FL: Professional Resource Press.

Grove, W. M., & Meehl, P. E. (1996). Comparative efficiency of informal (subjective, impressionistic) and formal (mechanical, algorithmic) prediction procedures: The clinical-statistical controversy. *Psychology, Public Policy, and Law, 2*(2), 293–323.

Grove, W. M., Zald, D. H., Lebow, B. S., Snitz, B. E., & Nelson, C. (2000). Clinical versus mechanical prediction: A meta-analysis. *Psychological Assessment, 12*(1), 19–30.

Guthrie, C., Rachlinski, J. L., & Wistrich, A. J. (2000). Inside the judicial mind. *Cornell Law Review, 86*, 777–830.

Hamann, J., Langer, B., Winkler, V., Busch, R., Cohen, R., Leucht, S., Kissling, W. (2006). Shared decision making for in-patients with schizophrenia. *Acta Psychiatrica Scandinavica, 114*(4), 265–273.

Hammond, K. R. (2000). Coherence and correspondence theories in judgment and decision making. In T. Connolly, H. R. Arkes, & K. R. Hammond (Eds.), *Judgment and decision making: An interdisciplinary reader* (2nd ed., pp. 53–65). Cambridge, UK: Cambridge University Press.

Hanson, R. K. (1998). What do we know about sex offender risk assessment? *Psychology, Public Policy, and Law, 4*(1–2), 50–72.

Harris, G. T., Rice, M. E., & Quinsey, V. L. (1993). Violent recidivism of mentally disordered offenders: The development of a statistical prediction instrument. *Criminal Justice and Behavior, 20*(4), 315–335.

Hart, S. D. (2008). Preventing violence: The role of risk assessment and management. In A. C. Baldry & F. W. Winkel (Eds.), *Intimate partner violence prevention and intervention: The risk assessment and management approach* (pp. 7–18). Hauppauge, NY: Nova Science Publishers.

Hastie, R. (2001). Problems of judgment and decision making. *Annual Review of Psychology, 52*, 653–683.

Heilbrun, K. (1997). Prediction versus management models relevant to risk assessment: The importance of legal decision-making context. *Law and Human Behavior, 21*(4), 347–359.

Heilbrun, K., O'Neill, M. L., Strohman, L. K., Bowman, Q., & Philipson, J. (2000). Expert approaches to communicating violence risk. *Law and Human Behavior, 24*(1), 137–148.

Hilton, N. Z., & Simmons, J. L. (2001). The influence of actuarial risk assessment in clinical judgments and tribunal decisions about mentally disordered offenders in maximum security. *Law and Human Behavior, 25*(4), 393–408.

Jahng, K. H., Martin, L. R., Golin, C. E., & DiMatteo, M. R. (2005). Preferences for medical collaboration: Patient-physician congruence and patient outcomes. *Patient Education and Counseling, 57*(3), 308–314.

Jessor, R., Van Den Bos, J., Vanderryn, J., Costa, F. M., & Turbin, M. S. (1995). Protective factors in adolescent problem behavior: Moderator effects and developmental change. *Developmental Psychology 31*(6), 923–933.

Jolls, C., Sunstein, C. R., & Thaler, R. (1998). A behavioral approach to law and economics. *Stanford Law Review, 50*(5), 1471–1550.

Klein, G. A. (1993). A recognition-primed decision (RPD) model of rapid decison making. In G. A. Klein, J. Orasanu, R. Calderwood, & C. E. Zsambok (Eds.), *Decision making in action: Models and methods* (pp. 138–147). Norwood, NJ: Ablex Publishing.

Kleinmuntz, B. (1990). Why we still use our heads instead of formulas: Toward an integrative approach. *Psychological Bulletin, 107*(3), 296–310.

Lassiter, G. D. (2002). Illusory causation in the courtroom. *Current Directions in Psychological Science, 11*(6), 204–208.

Lodewijks, H. P., Doreleijers, T. A., & de Ruiter, C. (2008). SAVRY risk assessment in violent Dutch adolescents: Relation to sentencing and recidivism. *Criminal Justice and Behavior, 35*(6), 696–709.

Marczyk, G. R., Heilbrun, K., Lander, T., & DeMatteo, D. (2003). Predicting juvenile recidivism with the PCL:YV, MAYSI, and YLS/CMI. *International Journal of Forensic Mental Health, 2*(1), 7–18.

McEachran, A. (2001). *The predictive validity of the PCL-YV and the SAVRY in a popoulation of adolescent offenders.* Unpublished master's thesis, Department of Psychology, Simon Fraser University, Vancouver, BC.

Meehl, P. E. (1986). Causes and effects of my disturbing little book. *Journal of Personality Assessment, 50*(3), 370–375.

Miller, G. A., Galanter, E., & Pribram, K. H. (1960). *Plans and the structure of behavior.* New York, NY: Holt, Rinehart and Winston.

Monahan, J. (1981). *The clinical prediction of violent behavior.* Rockville, MD: National Institute of Mental Health.

Monahan, J. (1997). Actuarial support for the clinical assessment of violence risk. *International Review of Psychiatry, 9*(2–3), 167–169.

Monahan, J. (2003). Violence risk assessment in American law. In P. J. van Koppen & S. D. Penrod (Eds.), *Adversarial versus inquisitorial justice: Psychological perspectives on criminal justice systems* (pp. 81–89). New York, NY: Kluwer Academic Publishers.

Monahan, J., Steadman, H. J., Appelbaum, P. S., Grisso, T., Mulvey, E. P., Roth, L. H., . . . Silver, E. (2006). The classification of violence risk. *Behavioral Sciences and the Law, 24*(6), 721–730.

Monahan, J., Steadman, H. J., Appelbaum, P. S., Robbins, P. C., Mulvey, E. P., Silver, E., . . . Grisso, T. (2000). Developing a clinically useful actuarial tool for assessing violence risk. *British Journal of Psychiatry, 176*, 312–319.

Monahan, J., Steadman, H. J., Robbins, P. C., Appelbaum, P., Banks, S., Grisso, T., . . . Silver, E. (2005). An actuarial model of violence risk assessment for persons with mental disorders. *Psychiatric Services, 56*(7), 810–815.

Monahan, J., Steadman, H. J., Silver, E., Applebaum, P. S., Robbins, P. C., Mulvey, E. P., . . . Banks, S. (2001). *Rethinking risk assessment: The MacArthur study of mental disorder and violence.* New York, NY: Oxford University Press.

Mossman, D. (1994). Assessing predictions of violence: Being accurate about accuracy. *Journal of Consulting and Clinical Psychology, 62*(4), 783–792.

Olver, M. E., Stockdale, K. C., & Wormith, J. S. (2009). Risk assessment with young offenders: A meta-analysis of three assessment measures. *Criminal Justice and Behavior, 36*(4), 329–353.

Orasanu, J. (2005). Crew collaboration in space: A naturalistic decision-making perspective. *Aviation, Space, and Environmental Medicine, 76*(6, Sect. 2, Suppl.), B154–B163.

Otto, R. (1992). The prediction of dangerous behavior: A review and analysis of 'second generation' research. *Forensic Reports, 5*(1), 103–133.

Otto, R. K. (2000). Assessing and managing violence risk in outpatient settings. *Journal of Clinical Psychology, 56*(10), 1239–1262.

Patel, V. L., Kaufman, D. R., & Arocha, J. F. (2002). Emerging paradigms of cognition in medical decision-making. *Journal of Biomedical Informatics, 35*(1), 52–75.

Pepe, M. S., Feng, Z., Huang, Y., Longton, G., Prentice, R., Thompson, I. M., & Zheng, Y. (2008). Integrating the predictiveness of a marker with its performance as a classifier. *American Journal of Epidemiology, 167*(3), 362–368.

Rapley, T. (2008). Distributed decision making: The anatomy of decisions-in-action. *Sociology of Health and Illness, 30*(3), 429–444.

Rennie, C., & Dolan, M. (2005). *Validity of the Structured Assessment of Violence Risk in Youth (SAVRY) in UK Adolescents.* Paper presented at the International Association for Forensic Mental Health Services, Amsterdam, Netherlands.

Rice, M. E., & Harris, G. T. (2005). Comparing effect sizes in follow-up studies: ROC area, Cohen's d, and r. *Law and Human Behavior, 29*(5), 615–620.

Simon, D. (1998). A psychological model of judicial decision making. *Rutgers Law Journal, 30*(1).

Simon, H. A. (1978). Rationality as process and as product of thought. *American Economic Review, 68*(2), 1–16.

Svenson, O. (1990). Some propositions for the classification of decision situations. In K. Borcherding, O. I. Larichev, & D. M. Messick (Eds.), *Contemporary issues in decision making* (pp. 17–32). New York, NY: North-Holland.

Swanson, J. W. (2008). Preventing the unpredicted: Managing violence risk in mental health care. *Psychiatric Services, 59*(2), 191–193.

Webster, C., Douglas, K., Eaves, D., & Hart, S. (1997). *HCR-20: Assessing risk for violence* (Version 2). Burnaby, BC: Simon Fraser University and Forensic Psychiatric Services Commission of British Columbia.

Webster, C. D., Muller-Isberner, R., & Fransson, G. (2002). Violence risk assessment: Using structured clinical guides professionally. *International Journal of Forensic Mental Health, 1*(2), 185–193.

Wong, S. C. P., & Gordon, A. (2006). The validity and reliability of the Violence Risk Scale: A treatment-friendly violence risk assessment tool. *Psychology, Public Policy, and Law, 12*(3), 279–309.

21

A Data-Frame Sensemaking Analysis of Operative Reports
Bile Duct Injuries Associated With Laparoscopic Cholecystectomy

Lygia Stewart
University of California, San Francisco

Cynthia O. Dominguez
Klein Associates, Applied Research Associates

Lawrence W. Way
University of California, San Francisco

Over 750,000 cholecystectomies are performed annually in the United States. During this operation, the surgeon divides the cystic duct, which joins the gallbladder to the common bile duct (CBD), and also divides the cystic artery (Figure 21.1). In rare instances, damage to the CBD or other biliary or arterial structures in the area can occur, with potentially serious consequences. The most commonly injured structures are the CBD and common hepatic duct. Consequences of such injuries are significant; the body cannot function without these two structures, and patients must undergo surgery for repair. The right hepatic artery runs posterior to the CBD (Figure 21.1) and can also be injured if the CBD is transected or injured. The incidence of major bile duct injury is greater during laparoscopic cholecystectomy (0.5%) than during open cholecystectomy (0.1 to 0.2%) (Adamson et al., 1997; Davidoff et al., 1992; Deziel et al., 1993). There are important differences between the open and laparoscopic procedures. With open procedures the surgeons have direct visibility and access to the operative area, while with laparoscopic procedures the operation is done using instruments inserted through small (<1 cm) ports in the abdominal wall. A camera is attached to one of the ports and the anatomy is viewed on a video monitor. This results in a more limited view of the anatomy as well as loss of haptic input.

The pattern of injury associated with laparoscopic procedures is different than with open operations (Martin & Rossi, 1994). The laparoscopic injury is more often an active injury, rather than a passive one, where the common bile duct is deliberately cut because the surgeon thinks it is the cystic duct. In the majority of bile duct injury cases, operative reports suggest surgeons incorrectly assessed the biliary anatomy. The injury usually results from misperception resulting in an incorrect mental model

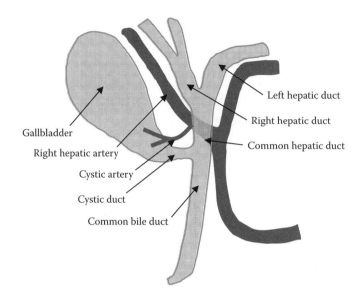

Left hepatic duct

Right hepatic duct

Gallbladder

Right hepatic artery

Common hepatic duct

Cystic artery

Cystic duct

Common bile duct

FIGURE 21.1   Normal biliary anatomy.

of the anatomy (Hoffman, 1998; Stewart & Way, 2007; Way et al., 2003). This sets the stage for an unintended action, whereby the surgeon cuts the common bile duct, thinking it is the cystic duct. Aspects unique to the laparoscopic environment, such as loss of haptic input, the limited two-dimensional video monitor view, magnification, and a fixed viewpoint, contribute to this error. Cutting the incorrect duct has no startling manifestations, so in most cases the illusion is not broken and the injury is not noticed (Stewart, 2002; Way et al., 2003).

The bile duct injuries fall into four groups as defined by the Stewart-Way classification (Stewart & Way, 1995; Stewart et al., 2004; Way et al., 2003) (see Figure 21.2). Class I injuries occur when the common bile duct (CBD) is mistaken for the cystic duct, but the error is recognized when there is an incision of the CBD, but before the CBD is divided. Class II injuries involve damage to the common hepatic duct from clips or cautery used too close to the duct. This often occurs in cases where visibility is limited due to inflammation or bleeding. Class III injuries, the most common, occur when the CBD is mistaken for the cystic duct. The common duct is transected and a variable portion that includes the junction of the cystic and common duct is removed. Class IV injuries involve damage to the right hepatic duct (RHD), because this structure either is mistaken for the cystic duct or is injured during dissection. Bile duct injuries can involve *active* division of a duct due to misidentification of a major bile duct for the cystic duct (Class I, Class III, certain Class IV injuries) or *passive* injury due to working too close to the major bile ducts (Class II, certain Class IV injuries).

It is unclear why a few surgeons detect the injury immediately, while most complete the operation under the impression that it had been uncomplicated. To understand the reasons for the injuries and means of intraoperative detection, we studied 300 laparoscopic bile duct injury cases.We specifically studied the use of the data-frame model of sensemaking by surgeons during laparoscopic cholecystectomy. The question we attempted

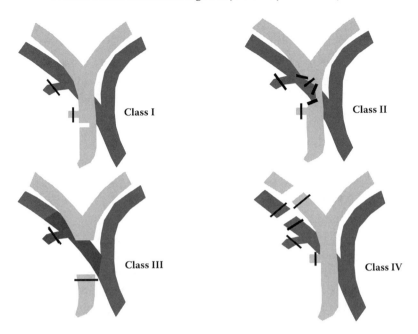

FIGURE 21.2   Stewart-Way classification of laparoscopic bile duct injuries.

to answer was whether this model elucidated the mechanisms of intraoperative surgical decision making.

The literature on perception, judgment, error, and naturalistic decision making offers a number of useful concepts for analyzing the antecedents of bile duct injury, enabling a cognitive researcher to frame the phenomenon in a variety of different ways (Dominguez, 2001; Endsley & Garland, 2000; Hogarth, 2001; Klein, 1998, 2004; Piattelli-Palmarini, 1994; Reason, 1990; Zsambok & Klein, 1997).

Separate but related concepts that we believe are especially helpful are those of sensemaking and metacognition. A data-frame model of sensemaking (Klein, Phillips, Rall, & Peluso, 2007), whereby sensemaking is defined as the deliberate effort to understand events (Klein et al., 2007), raises a perceptual view to a broader contextual view. Sensemaking is the process of fitting data into a frame, and fitting a frame around data. Existing data are used to create a frame of the current situation; in a continuous process, new data will either enrich the current frame or provoke a questioning of that frame. This model is linked to a metacognitive view in laparoscopic surgery in that the act of questioning the current frame could be a way of monitoring and regulating whether the surgery is proceeding safely (Dominguez, 2001). The frame we examine here has to do with the normality of the ongoing surgical procedure, and is specifically concerned with whether the surgeon believes an injury may have occurred.

Methods

Data Set

We examined 300 cases of major bile duct injuries that occurred during laparoscopic cholecystectomy, including 22 in which videotapes of the operation were available.

We analyzed the surgeons' sensemaking process during the operations using the operative report, which is a verbal explanation of the events that is dictated by the surgeon immediately after the operation. The surgeon begins the procedure with a comprehensive mental model of the anticipated situation. When the operative report was dictated, the majority of surgeons believed that the operation had been completed without mishap.

Analysis Procedures

We utilized a data-frame model of sensemaking (Klein, Moon, & Hoffman, 2006) (Figure 21.3) to guide our analysis. Our focus was whether the surgeon questioned the frame of accuracy and noninjury during the procedure to consider the possibility of a bile duct injury. Therefore, the analysis concentrated on whether the surgeon detected disconformatory cues that were inconsistent with the normal frame, how the surgeon utilized these cues, whether the cues were explained away or used to question or reframe, and whether the surgeon acted to generate additional information to support or negate the current frame. We also correlated anatomic details of the bile duct injuries (as subsequently determined) with the verbal explanation in the operative report, to detect cues that were acted on by the surgeon but not described in the operative report.

The Stewart-Way classification (Figure 21.2), which is based on the anatomy and mechanism of injury, was used to group the injuries. In our analysis, operative notes, intraoperative cholangiograms (a dye-based x-ray of the biliary structure), and, when

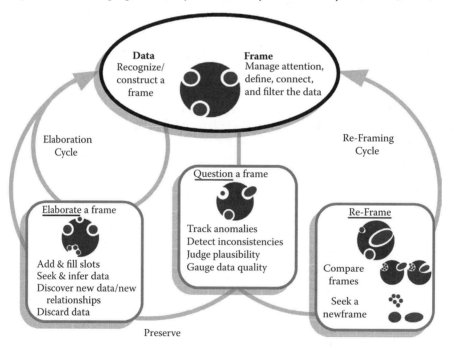

FIGURE 21.3   Data-frame model of sensemaking. (From Klein, G., Moon, B., & Hoffman, R. (2006). Making sense of sensemaking 2: A macrocognitive model. *IEEE Intelligent Systems*, September/October, pp. 88–92. With permission.)

available, videotapes of the procedure were examined for any irregularities during the operation, and how they were interpreted by the surgeon. Discharge summaries, physician's notes, postoperative cholangiograms, and other sources of information were used to determine the extent of the injury.

The following assumptions were made about the surgeons' thought processes during the operation. For Class I, III, and IV injuries that involved misidentification of either the CBD or RHD for the cystic duct, whether explicitly stated or not, we assumed the surgeon believed that the anatomy had been identified correctly. For Class II and Class IV injuries that involved lateral damage to the bile ducts, we assumed that the surgeon considered the dissection to be proceeding safely and without risk to the bile duct, unless otherwise stated. Because the mechanism of injury was different for active versus passive injuries, the cues indicating a potential problem also differed. This was accounted for in the analysis.

Specific discordant intraoperative cues and whether they led to identification of the bile duct injury were noted. The cases were separated into groups based on the postoperative comments of the surgeon and the record of findings during the operation:

1. Unremarkable operation: There was no mention of any unusual findings during the operation that clearly supported the possibility of a bile duct injury. Mentions of inflammation, unless severe, or mild bleeding were not regarded as irregularities.
2. Cues acted on but not mentioned: There was no mention of irregularities in the operative report but the postoperative findings indicated that that surgeon had actively dealt with features not normally encountered in a cholecystectomy. These included cases where the CHD or right hepatic artery was clipped but not mentioned.
3. Cues present but not recognized: Intraoperative findings were reported in the course of the operation that suggested the possibility of biliary injury, but either the significance of these cues was not appreciated or they were interpreted in a way that did not include the possibility of biliary injury.
4. Partial frame change: The surgeon altered his or her surgical approach (e.g., converted to an open operation) but did change to a frame that included the possibility of bile duct injury.
5. Injury suspected or identified: An injury was identified or suspected and the surgeon acted to diagnose the bile duct injury. Diagnostic actions included cholangiography, focused examination of the anatomy, examination of the removed gallbladder, or converting to a laparotomy specifically to clarify the anatomy (not just for inflammation).

To summarize, for cases in the first three groups, the surgeon's perspective was that the operation was proceeding without problem. With the fourth group the surgeon altered his or her approach by converting to an open procedure, but did not consider the possibility of bile duct injury (did not question the noninjury frame). With the fifth group, the surgeon suspected that an injury might have occurred (questioned the frame), and his or her orientation shifted to an active search for evidence, pro or con.

We applied the data-frame model of sensemaking (Klein et al., 2006) (see Figure 21.3) to the extent possible with our data. We could not assess surgeons' elaboration of their frames because we did not have access to verbalizations during the case. However, postoperative reports offered a record of information the surgeon felt was significant enough to note, including whether the case was converted to an open procedure and whether diagnostic procedures, such as intraoperative x-rays, were performed at any point. Converting and using diagnostic procedures indicate that surgeons are questioning their current frame, due to detecting either anomalies or inconsistencies. If there was inflammation present, uncertainties about the patient's biliary anatomy may have led surgeons to question their frame as well, leading to conversion or diagnostic procedures.

One focus of this analysis was on Groups 2 to 4, the groups for which cues were present to possibly indicate that the surgeons *should* question their current frame, but in which surgeons *did not* question their frame to the extent that a biliary injury was considered. We recognize that our interpretation of irregular cues is much more liberal than the surgeon's since we know the outcome (hindsight bias).

Results

In keeping with the exploratory nature of our analyses, most of the results reported here are descriptive. The distribution among classes of injuries was as follows: Class I, 6%; Class II, 23%; Class III, 61%; and Class IV, 10%. The mechanism of injury was active in 74%, passive in 23%, and due to a technical error in 3% of cases. The injury was recognized during the original operation in 28% of cases, and was recognized postoperatively in the remaining cases.

Overall, operative reports reflected that the surgeon continued the procedure without appreciably altering the frame in 60% of cases (Groups 1 to 3), converted to an open operation for reasons other than possible biliary injury in 10% of cases (Group 4), and questioned the frame to consider bile duct injury in 30% of cases (Group 5).

Influence of Injury Mechanism on Framing and Injury Recognition

Cases with a mechanism of injury that involved active transection of the bile ducts were more commonly recognized during the procedure than those with a passive mechanism (33% vs. 13%, respectively). Conversion to an open procedure due to inflammation (a version of frame change) was more common among cases with a passive mechanism (26% vs. 7%, passive vs. active, respectively). In most cases (59 to 65%), surgeons did not seem to shift their frame from that of no injury to one of possible injury; this was true for both passive and active injuries.

Cases With an Active Injury Mechanism (222 of 300 cases)

For cases with an active injury mechanism, there was no apparent change in operative approach (change in framing for any cause) in 59% of cases reviewed. The surgeon converted to an open operation because inflammation limited anatomy identification in 7%. The surgeon questioned the frame and considered the possibility of biliary injury in 34% of cases.

In the groups where surgeons mentioned cues in the operative report, therefore providing a means of comparing the operative report with the case record, we examined specifically how surgeons either questioned the noninjured patient frame or did not do so, in the face of possible anomalies or inconsistencies. The cues examined included routine intraoperative cholangiograms that demonstrated the injury, transected bile ducts in the operative field (which in some cases were not recognized as such but instead were described as accessory ducts, second cystic duct, or tubular structures), unexplained bile leakage, the right hepatic artery in the field (or a large posterior artery), and other abnormal anatomy.

Among active injuries with no questioning of the frame, there were no irregular cues reported or dealt with in 27% of cases. The surgeon dealt with irregularities (clipped hepatic ducts or right hepatic artery) but did not report them in 32% of cases, and irregular findings were reported but interpreted as normal in 41% of cases. Although there was probably some evidence to support questioning the frame in these cases, surgeons did not do so and the injury was not identified in any of these cases.

The injury was recognized in one case where the surgeon converted to an open operation due to inflammation. After opening, this injury was identified with cholangiography. In the rest of the opened cases, the surgeon reported no irregular cues in 40%, dealt with irregular cues but did not report them in 20%, and reported irregular cues but did not recognize the injury in 33% of cases.

Surgeons identified the injury in 95% of the cases when they framed the issue as a possible biliary injury. In 20% of these cases the misidentified anatomy was recognized early enough to limit the injury. Irregular cues that led to identification of biliary injury included cholangiogram findings, identification of an injured duct or second bile duct (the transected hepatic duct), abnormal anatomy, unexplained bile leakage, and examination of the gallbladder specimen with detection of the attached CBD remnant. The same types of cues were reported in the few cases where the possibility of biliary injury was considered but rejected.

Cases With a Passive Injury Mechanism (78 of 300)

For cases with a passive injury mechanism there was no apparent change in the operative approach (framing) in 67%, the surgeon converted to an open operation because inflammation limited anatomy identification in 26%, and the surgeon considered the possibility of biliary injury before opening in 7% of cases.

Passive injuries could conceivably be avoided by earlier conversion to an open procedure to facilitate anatomy identification. The irregular cues usually involved bleeding or some degree of inflammation that obscured the anatomy (to some extent). The case was continued laparoscopically in 67% of cases and opened in 33%. No injuries were identified in those that were continued laparoscopically (no change in framing). The injury was identified (frame change) in 22% of those where the approach was changed to an open operation. The injury was identified in all the cases where the possibility of injury was reported before the case was converted to an open operation.

Discussion

This analysis provides insight into how well-trained, experienced professionals make sense of available cues. Since this analysis does not include a control set of cases without bile duct injuries, we have no way of knowing how often such irregular cues are seen and used to reframe and alter the surgical approach in normal (uncomplicated) cases. That is, we have no denominator. We do know that laparoscopic bile duct injuries are uncommon (0.5%), suggesting that surgeons frequently recognize irregular cues and most likely use this information to guide their dissection.

These injuries are not technical errors. The mistakes conformed to two tight patterns of injury, both resulting from misperception of the anatomy, not from a technical issue during the dissection. The first pattern is one of active errors, whereby the visual illusion that the common bile duct is the cystic duct (facilitated by aspects of the laparoscopic environment) leads to misidentification of a major bile duct for the cystic duct (Way et al., 2003). The second is a pattern of passive errors, whereby the ducts are injured because the surgeon does not realize he or she is working in such close proximity to them. These were not random errors; two types of mistakes were made by all. Our group has previously reported on how the principles of human error analysis can identify means of prevention of bile duct injuries during laparoscopic cholecystectomy, and how normal visual processing can facilitate anatomic illusions in the laparoscopic environment (Hoffman, 1998; Stewart & Way 2007; Way et al., 2003). The current analysis focused on intraoperative injury identification. While prevention would be ideal, early detection can significantly limit the morbidity associated with these injuries (Stewart & Way, 1995). In the 300 cases we examined, only 28% of the injuries were recognized during the operation. The majority were diagnosed postoperatively once clinical manifestations (fever, infection, jaundice, pain, etc.) developed. This means that improving patterns of detection could improve patient outcomes.

A question to ask is whether surgeons are taught to consider the possibility of injury when particular cues are present. Further, what if those cues are only "weak signals" (Snowden, Klein, Chew, & Teh, 2007)? The results suggest that when surgeons consider the possibility of injury, they question their frame and then take appropriate action. In our analysis it seemed that considering this possibility was the key element driving injury recognition and identification. This supports the concept that the data-frame model of sensemaking elucidated the mechanisms of intraoperative surgical decision making. A future step in this analysis will be to determine frequencies of the specific cues surgeons mentioned in operative reports that caused them to question the frame. Identifying those signals, and what constitutes relative weakness or strength, will provide specific material for use in training surgeons when to consider the possibility that an injury has occurred.

The surgeon's description of the irregularities seen provides us with insight into his or her thought processes. Identification of a second bile duct (the transected upper end of the injured CHD) in cases with an active mechanism more commonly led to injury diagnoses. However, when this duct was referred to in a less discriminate way (structure, tubular structure, etc.) or classified as a biliary anomaly (accessory bile duct, etc.), the diagnosis of a bile duct injury was less common. This shows how the same visual image can be interpreted in totally different ways, depending on the surgeon's data frame. The interpretation of cholangiograms demonstrated similar findings.

In any analysis such as this, the possibility of hindsight bias exists. Because we know the outcome, we may give more weight to abnormalities reported by the surgeon than he or she did. Given these reservations, there were potential disconformatory cues reported by the surgeon in 68% of cases. The surgeon used these cues to reframe (convert to an open operation or search for a biliary injury) in 41% of cases. Simply converting the case to an open operation, without considering the possibility of biliary injury, only marginally improved injury identification (by 18%). In contrast, the power of questioning the frame was apparent in that once the surgeon considered the possibility of biliary injury, diagnoses of the injury were almost (95%) universal. In cases where the surgeon acted to generate additional information to support or negate the current frame, the bile duct injury was commonly identified.

In addition, this analysis only includes cases where a bile duct injury occurred. It does not include cases without biliary complications for comparison. We do not know the exact number of anatomic irregularities or irregular cues encountered during uncomplicated cholecystectomy procedures. We do know that this number is not zero. Thus, we have to recognize that many of the irregular cues that we categorized (in hindsight) as those that *should* result in the surgeon questioning his or her current frame may be within the baseline of irregular cues encountered in uncomplicated procedures (hindsight bias).

In conclusion, this study demonstrated that simple recognition of irregular cues is not sufficient for injury detection unless the surgeon reframes the situation to consider that a biliary injury may have occurred. This finding demonstrates the value of a data-frame analysis of sensemaking. Understanding the power of framing has significant implications for the prevention of surgical complications. One possible approach would be to teach surgeons to consider the possibility of biliary injury whenever irregular findings are evident, or to consider that one's assessment of the anatomy might be incorrect when irregular cues are detected. While in general this concept is taught during surgical training, the power of framing is not universally known. Teaching about the benefits of questioning one's current frame could provide surgeons with an additional tool to improve patient safety. There is still additional work to be done, as indicated by the fact that no irregular cues were detected (with very liberal hindsight bias) in over a third of the cases. Teaching surgeons to proactively consider alternative assessments, as well as to actively consider that an injury might have occurred when irregular cues are present, is equivalent to training stronger self-monitoring skills; these metacognitive skills have been found to be stronger in surgical residents who accurately identify irregular cues in an operative field (Dominguez, 2001).

References

Adamson, S., Hansen, O. H., Funch-Jensen, P., Schultze, S., Stage, J. G., & Wara, P. (1997). Bile duct injury during laparoscopic cholecystectomy: A prospective nationwide series. *Journal of the American College of Surgeons, 184*, 571–578.

Davidoff, A. M., Pappas, T. N., Murray, E. A., Hilleren, D. J., Johnson, R. D., Bakera, M. E., ... Meyers, W. C. (1992). Mechanisms of major biliary injury during cholecystectomy. *Annals of Surgery, 215*, 196–202.

Deziel, D. J., Millikan, K. W., Economou, S. G., Doolas, A., Ko, S. T., & Airan, M. C. (1993). Complications of laparoscopic cholecystectomy: A national survey of 4,292 hospitals and an analysis of 77,604 cases. *American Journal of Surgery, 165*, 9–14.

Dominguez, C. O. (2001). Expertise in laparoscopic surgery: Anticipation and affordances. In E. Salas & G. Klein (Eds.), *Linking expertise and naturalistic decision making* (pp. 287–302). Mahwah, NJ: Lawrence Erlbaum & Associates.

Endsley, M. R., & Garland, D. J. (2000). *Situation awareness analysis and measurement*. Mahwah, NJ: Lawrence Erlbaum Associates.

Hoffman, D. D. (1998). *Visual intelligence: How we create what we see*. New York, NY: W. W. Norton & Co.

Hoffman, R. R. (Ed.). (2007). *Expertise out of context: Proceedings of the Sixth International Conference on Naturalistic Decision Making*. Mahwah, NJ: Lawrence Erlbaum & Associates.

Hogarth, R. (2001). *Educating intuition*. Chicago, IL: University of Chicago Press.

Klein, G. (1998). *Sources of power: How people make decisions*. Cambridge, MA: MIT Press.

Klein, G. (2004). *The power of intuition: How to use your gut feelings to make better decisions at work*. New York, NY: Random House.

Klein, G., Moon, B., & Hoffman, R. (2006). Making sense of sensemaking 2: A macrocognitive model. *IEEE Intelligent Systems*, September/October, pp. 88–92.

Klein, G., Phillips, J. K., Rall, E., & Peluso, D. A. (2007). A data/frame theory of sensemaking. In R. R. Hoffman (Ed.), *Expertise out of context: Proceedings of the 6th International Conference on Naturalistic Decision Making*. Mahwah, NJ: Lawrence Erlbaum & Associates.

Martin, R. F., & Rossi, R. L. (1994). Bile duct injuries. Spectrum, mechanisms of injury, and their prevention. *Surgical Clinics of North America, 74*(4), 781–803; discussion, 805–787.

Piattelli-Palmarini, M. (1994). *Inevitable illusions: How mistakes of reason rule our minds*. New York, NY: John Wiley & Sons.

Reason, J. (1990). *Human error*. Cambridge, UK: Cambridge University Press.

Snowden, D., Klein, G., Chew, L. P., & Teh, C. A. (2007). A sensemaking experiment: Techniques to achieve cognitive precision. In *Proceedings of the 12th International Command and Control Research and Technology Symposium*, Newport, RI. www.dodcarp.org

Stewart, L. (2002). Treatment strategies for bile duct injury and benign biliary stricture. In G. Poston & L. Blumgart (Eds.), *Hepatobiliary and pancreatic surgery* (1st ed.). London, UK: Martin Dunitz.

Stewart, L., Robinson, T. N., Lee, C. M., Liu, K., Whang, K., & Way, L. W. (2004). Right hepatic artery injury associated with laparoscopic bile duct injury: Incidence, mechanism, and consequences. *Journal of Gastrointestinal Surgery, 8*, 523–531.

Stewart, L., & Way, L. W. (1995). Bile duct injuries during laparoscopic cholecystectomy. Factors that influence the results of treatment. *Archives of Surgery, 130*, 1123–1129.

Stewart, L., & Way, L. W. (2007). *The prevention of laparoscopic bile duct injuries: An analysis of 300 cases of from a human factors and cognitive psychology perspective*. Paper presented at Proceedings of the Human Factors and Ergonomics Society 51st Annual Meeting, Baltimore, MD.

Way, L. W., Stewart, L., Gantert, W., Liu, K., Lee, C. M., Whang, K., & Hunter, J. G. (2003). Causes and prevention of laparascopic bile duct injuries: An analysis of 252 cases from a human factors and cognitive psychology perspective. *Journal of Gastrointestinal Surgery, 8*, 523–531.

Zsambok, C. E., & Klein, G. A. (Eds.). (1997). *Naturalistic decision making*. Mahwah, NJ: Lawrence Erlbaum Associates.

22

Coordination of Event Detection and Task Management in Time-Critical Settings

Barrett S. Caldwell
Purdue University

Sandra K. Garrett
Clemson University

Coordinated team performance in complex settings often relies heavily on effective information technology use and sharing of knowledge between team members. In a variety of healthcare and spaceflight tasks, there exist challenges in supporting and managing coordination across domains of expertise and complementary task demands. One aspect of these challenges is the ability of teams to perform adaptively and effectively in response to situational events that may threaten mission success and even human survival. Complex, time-critical environments are characterized by emerging and dynamic events that require active monitoring of, interaction with, and response to changing conditions and success criteria. However, different aspects of events have distinct timescales and demands for human response and team coordination.

The research that served as the developmental foundation for this chapter was initially intended to apply a traditional analysis of workflow and task requirements using a traditional industrial engineering approach to healthcare work design and analysis (e.g., Smalley & Freeman, 1966). The specific application of the authors' research was healthcare provider coordination in an outpatient clinic setting, with a goal of improving information flow associated with patient visits. Contemporary work design analysis of nurse scheduling and patient-nurse ratio management often excludes real-time adjustment (i.e., shorter term event dynamics ranging from minutes to hours) as outside of the realm of scheduling focus (Wright, Bretthauer, & Côté, 2006). It is also important to note that, when considering industrial engineering approaches to patient scheduling over time periods of weeks, months, and even years (Kopach et al., 2007), a single patient visit is seen as a point event in a larger sequence of patient management activities.

As our research continued, it became clear that the data being collected regarding healthcare provider task coordination did not align with existing frameworks and definitions underpinning healthcare workflow measurement. Prior assumptions regarding provider task sequences and task analysis classifications derived from the Smalley text (see Overhage, Perkins, Tierney, & McDonald, 2001), and even the study of patient visits as healthcare events, required substantial modification to explain the qualitative and quantitative data from the clinics in our studies. One result of modifying the research goals of the project was the creation of a new framework for describing and analyzing team-based event management and coordination.

Forms of Team Distribution

For the purposes of this chapter, we will distinguish teams whose members are expected to have distinct areas of expertise, task roles, and performance expectations (functional distribution) from those who have different geographic spheres of responsibility (divisional distribution) (Hollenbeck, 2000). A functionally distributed team is one where the team members have specialized roles, possibly due to differing areas of expertise, and therefore are highly dependent on each other to accomplish a task. For example, NASA Mission Control teams are comprised of engineers with different subsystem or disciplinary backgrounds (e.g., propulsion, structures, communications) (Caldwell, 2000, 2005). Similarly, a healthcare clinic team will combine multiple healthcare professionals and support staff (e.g., general practice physician, registered nurse, financial records manager) (Caldwell & Anderson, 1996; Caldwell & Garrett, 2006; Garrett & Caldwell, 2006). Members of a divisionally distributed team can work independently. Thus, team members can be assigned to monitor and conduct tasks addressing different geographical areas, and in many cases, are themselves geographically distributed in order to cover a larger part of their work environment (i.e., increased operational span of control).

These two forms of team structure were studied by Jobidon, Breton, Rousseau, and Tremblay (2006) to determine whether the team structure would have an effect on the team's ability to respond to transitions in workload. Their experimental findings indicated that the overall performance of functional teams was negatively affected by the transition to a higher workload, although they seem to be faster at discovering emerging tasks than divisional teams. The conclusions drawn from this study were that functional teams were more efficient in monitoring for system change, while divisional teams exhibited superior performance in managing the tasks. Jobidon et al. (2006) hypothesize that the performance decrement found in the functional teams could have been due to the need for coordination between team members.

Team-based coordination processes can be very involved depending on the situation complexity, the operational coordination and information flow model used, and the form of distribution within the team structure. In a team-based setting, individual responsibilities for detecting events, obtaining resources, or coordinating task behaviors may also change based on the dynamics of the task setting or event progression. Responsibilities may be defined by the structure and roles of team members, who have specific and predefined requirements for awareness, information, and resource management. In other cases, responsibilities and coordination activities may emerge based on relevant dimensions of expertise within and among team members.

A third form of task distribution in team coordination is that of temporal distribution: Team members may have different responsibilities that occur at different time sequences of tasks, and the tasks of one team member may become an indicator to begin, or a critical input for, the activities of another team member. Two simple forms of this type of distribution include assembly line tasks (where the physical outputs of one operator directly become the inputs of the next operator in the line) and Gantt-style project management dependencies (where information and outcome results from one task must be completed before the next task is allowed to start).

Expanding a Signal Detection Model of Event Management

Event detection is considered a major component of information processing and decision making at an individual level of cognitive performance (Wickens & Hollands, 2000). Even at the level of simple task performance, signal detection and vigilance represent core elements of operator awareness and determining appropriate responses to changing situational or task demands. However, an ongoing issue in ill-constrained, naturalistic environments is determining *which* environmental inputs will actually correspond to important events, and how one's expertise affects the team member's awareness of, response to, and utilization of event-related signals in managing task performance. We encountered this problem when applying a signal detection model to patient visits.

In classical signal detection, an event is most frequently characterized as a signal of a particular strength. Attention, information processing, and vigilance constraints for signal detection and response are based on the ability to detect a signal (usually of short duration) when it appears. From a feedback control perspective, these types of signals are described mathematically as impulse functions, or events with instantaneous onset and decay characteristics. Despite several attempts, however, our attempt to define a patient visit according to an impulse event function proved problematic. When did the patient event begin? The definition of the event depended on which member of the provider team was being studied. For the clerical staff, a patient event begins the night before the visit, when records are pulled and any information needs or gaps in the record are resolved. The nurse only considers the patient event started after the patient arrives, and the folder moves into a location indicating that the patient is actually in the waiting room (a trigger set by the clerical staff). The physician experience of the visit event, however, does not begin until the patient arrives in one of the treatment rooms (a trigger set by the nurse). A production flow model of following a patient through the visit notes delays only as the patient experiencing waiting. However, the physician and nurse are managing multiple patients as an event-triggered task load. They are task shifting and responding to each other's sharing of trigger and priority information regarding the total patient load being managed. Events are not instantaneous, nor are they purely sequential; clinic management seemed to consist of coordination among providers to support multiple overlapping event elements over the course of a day. The reframing of healthcare provider tasks in terms of sequences of dependent events allowed our research to further explore the role of communication between providers in event detection.

A number of real-world events, like slowly degrading operating conditions in a process control plant, or pandemic illness spread (Garrett & Caldwell, 2009), are actually changes in state that accumulate over a distinct period of time. Detection of persistent signals, which last for a perceptually significant period of time, is a separate aspect of classical signal detection, and is often described as a component of dynamic signal detection or even change detection. One aspect of event management, drawn from studies of NASA mission controllers and U.S. National Park rangers (Caldwell, 2005; Garrett & Caldwell, 2002), includes the capability of the task expert to identify an upcoming event, and the rate at which event demands or task load would require expert response. For park rangers, this comparison may be the time requirement needed to answer a visitor question of a given complexity, subject to how busy the visitor center is. For the flight controller, there is an assessment of the severity of a problem, and whether or not it makes sense to try to solve it immediately, or try to "safe" the system to buy additional time to evaluate the situation and develop a more stable solution than is possible in the current time available.

In these cases, the expert does not consider events purely as impulse functions with instantaneous beginnings and ends, varying only by time of arrival or overall demand. Rather, the findings from healthcare providers, park rangers, and spaceflight controllers all suggest that situational event/signal detection also includes a determination of the characteristics of event emergence. From a feedback control perspective, event emergence and duration require an explicit description of the onset and decay functions of the event progression. Examples of different onset and decay functions for different event progressions are presented in Figure 22.1.

In order to effectively coordinate task performance among team members, the issues of signal detection and processing must be supplemented by effective information flow (signal transmission) and shared understanding (knowledge synchronization) (Caldwell, 1997). The ability to recognize and utilize resources, tools, and expertise available to team members to respond to changing timelines of tasks directly impacts the probability of mission success. Being able to detect event triggers and understand the event onset dynamics of a particular situation allows event preparations and early response that may not otherwise be feasible.

Managing Multiple and Dependent Events

An important issue facing teams in complex environments, but not as frequently studied in classical psychophysical or statistical research, is that of dependent sequences of events. The ability of a team member to successfully detect and respond to an event may significantly influence which subsequent events may or may not occur.

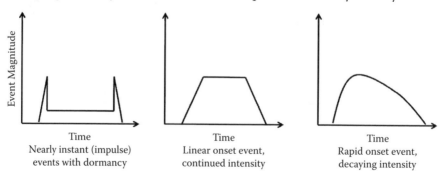

FIGURE 22.1   Examples of different hypothetical onset and decay functions for events of differing onset and progression dynamics. Note: All three examples have similar maximum magnitude and duration of event progression.

Identifying the specific phases within an event (from event trigger detection through event deadline termination) is seen as a critical aspect of managing dynamic task demands (Garrett & Caldwell, 2009). Improved quality, reliability, and timeliness of event identification can help target specific strategic or technology interventions to improve task coordination for crucial aspects of event preparation and response. Situational constraints do affect the sensitivity of experts to delays in information flow that may affect event detection (Caldwell, 2005, 2006). As a result, differences in individual or team processes may affect the ability to detect, resolve, or adapt to events of different onset or decay types.

A critical aspect of coordination for dynamic and evolving tasks is the understanding of how a specific phase of one event relates to or causes another event, which also requires a dynamic response. Helmreich has described this issue as threat error management, where both external events and task activities by team members can affect the experience, demands, and progression of future events (Helmreich & Merritt, 2000). These triggers between events can happen between events on two different timescales, or even between events in two different parts of a geographically distributed system, and will often require different members of the team or organization to respond in distinct but mutually aware ways.

As time pressures for completing required tasks increase, people have less time to react, and consequently need more prior planning, expertise, and available resources. This problem was found in the information technology use of NASA flight controllers (Caldwell, 2005), particularly the desire to trade other resources for time when critical events occurred. However, prior planning is also subject to the probabilistic nature of events, which can limit the effectiveness or utility of advance preparation. Thus, team members must be able to balance appropriate strategies for preparing for, as well as responding to, elements of task events to improve the robustness of team performance. Even in situations with relatively limited coordination demands for divisional or geographical distribution, agents must recognize the demands of providing integrated signal detection and situation assessments within the deadline demands of rapidly changing environments, and managing sensor quality and information flow losses in the sensor network (Kempf, Uzsoy, Smith, & Gary, 2000; Tambe, 1997). In a temporally distributed network, agents must also incorporate issues of time delay between inputs, and determine differences between changes in system state, effects of network delays, and changes in sensor reliability over time. This is, in essence, the challenge of recognizing and understanding the "causal texture" of the turbulent field organizational environment (Emery & Trist, 1965). Finally, integrating functional distributions requires an understanding of differences between stance or perspective of individual experts as an additional source of signal detection and responses among agents.

Dimensions of Event Characteristics and Response Challenges

Our research findings from healthcare providers, park rangers, and spaceflight controllers described consistent patterns of task coordination processes. Members of all groups use information exchange strategies and priorities for task coordination to maintain effective operations and role clarity. These strategies and priorities enable robust response to changing environmental conditions or task objectives. As a result, three important components shaped our research framework for describing and evaluating task performance and response to events.

The first framework component involved a new consideration of the dimensions of expertise that were required for teams of experts to respond effectively in complex task environments. Our work with NASA flight controllers and healthcare providers emphasized that in addition to individual knowledge domains, the team members exhibited several other clusters of individual and team-based skills. Experts in these complex settings also demonstrated competence in utilizing information technology interfaces to develop understanding of the current state of the spacecraft (or patient), and how differing task contexts would affect both the data available for collection and the interpretation of that data. In addition, experts developed skills at recognizing both who would have relevant domain knowledge for problem solving, and the media and timing required to contact that person in a particular time-critical context. These additional dimensions of expertise are presented in more detail elsewhere (Garrett, Caldwell, Harris, & Gonzalez, 2009).

The second framework component regarding expert management of individual and multiple task events is presented in Table 22.1. Task coordination in these applied contexts required experts to detect and resolve multiple forms of uncertainty, and conduct effective planning to acquire resources in light of those uncertainties. Event management requires the ability to successfully recognize and respond to patterns in specific types of signals indicating increasing likelihood of future events. Because

TABLE 22.1   Sources of Uncertainty in Event Detection and Strategic Response Coordination in Complex Team Tasks

Form of Probabilistic Uncertainty	Situation Awareness/Assessment Question to Answer	Strategic Coordination Response Challenge
Single Event		
Event detection	Does a relevant event (or its antecedents) exist in a form that can be detected?	Vigilance and anticipation for likely events, with ability to recognize unexpected events
Temporal arrival	When is the relevant event onset likely to occur?	Response characteristics of increased confidence contrasted with additional time required for gathering resources
Event magnitude	What is the size of the given event?	How many resources are required for response, and can these be gathered in advance?
Event function	What is the temporal behavior function of the event (impulse, ramp, oscillatory)?	When and for how long are resources needed during or after event onset?
Multiple Events		
Event rate	How many events, over what time frame, will occur?	Preparation for multiple events may require integration of tasks and resources over multiple cycles
Event dependence	Will one event (or response to it) affect behavior and characteristics of future events?	Threat error management of event includes forecasting impact of responses on future events

these events are not true impulse functions as described earlier, forecasting their dynamic course requires additional uncertainty resolution.

The multiple sources of uncertainty of event characteristics that must be determined and managed in a complex and dynamic task environment are resistant to simple closed-form mathematical analysis, but do seem to be effectively assessed in high-performing (as opposed to low-performing) teams responding to events (Waller, 1999; Waller, Gupta, & Giambatista, 2004). A summary of those dimensions of uncertainties is presented in Table 22.1, followed by a description of each form of probabilistic uncertainty.

Single-Event Characteristics

Event detection describes the determination that an event has occurred or will occur in the future. It is dependent on the ability to detect and recognize appropriate signals, as well as the awareness that one should be paying attention to this type of event and that the signals observed are related to the event to be detected. The recognition aspect of event detection is closely related to both the physical ability to detect the signals (as defined in classical signal detection) and understanding what various combinations of signal patterns indicate (sensemaking and signal interpretation) (Shannon & Weaver, 1949; Wickens & Hollands, 2000). Awareness of what event types should be paid attention in a given task setting can be improved and trained through experience of what types of events are likely to occur, and through associations of what other events should be monitored.

Temporal arrival is an expression of estimates of when the event will occur. As previously described, the majority of events do not instantaneously occur at one point in time, or as defined in engineering terms, most events are not impulse functions. Rather, most events may begin at some point, but also evolve after they begin (see "event function" below). Thus, temporal arrival more specifically relates to operator awareness of the event's origin, the precipitating factors that lead up to the event, and at what point the deadline for effective performance will be exceeded. Because events operate in a probabilistic environment, an operator must be able to separately determine *that* an event may be occurring, as well as *when* the event may be occurring, in order to develop appropriate response capabilities.

Event magnitude is a description of how large the event is (its maximum complexity, extent, or intensity), and in turn, how much effort will be required for adequate preparation for and response to the event. The larger the magnitude of the event, often the more preparation that is needed and the greater the consequences can be if not successful. In the same way, if the magnitude is determined to be larger than what can be addressed by currently and locally available efforts, a decision must be made on whether it is reasonable to devote effort to mitigating the effect of the event, or rather to devote efforts to other issues and not directly respond to the event at all. In some cases, effort will be allocated to simply stabilizing the event consequences until more resources can be obtained. Prior experience and response capability will mediate the magnitude of events that can be effectively managed. A simple example would be the development of a snowstorm and its effects on snow removal capabilities. A northern U.S. city may be capable of removing snow from a 10-inch (25-centimeter) snowstorm, and consider removal of a 2-inch (5-centimeter) snowfall an easy task and even an inconsequential or trivial event. However, a southern U.S. city without adequate snow removal equipment or experience may be paralyzed by the same 2-inch (5-centimeter) snowfall total. Instead of attempting an inadequate response, the southern city may simply declare an emergency, and cease operations until the snow melts.

Event function refers to the dynamics of how the onset of the event progresses from initial arrival to maximal magnitude or complexity. Returning to the snowstorm description as our example, the event function in terms of the rate accumulation may limit response capabilities. Even if two different snowstorms of 10 inches (25 centimeters) affect a city, snow removal equipment and emergency services personnel may be able to respond effectively to a snowfall accumulation of 0.5 inch/hour (1 centimeter/hour), but unable to cope with snowfall arriving in blizzard conditions and 2 inches/hour (5 centimeters/hour) accumulation. The event function, or rate of accumulation, will also influence the accuracy of predictions for future systems states based on event response capability. The more rapidly an event progresses, the harder it may be for operators to create mental models and accurately forecast event or response dynamics for the task of response planning.

Multiple-Event Characteristics

The above four characteristics define the conditions and uncertainty challenges of identifying and responding to any individual event. In many situations, however, events are neither isolated nor independent. Thus, operators must be aware of characteristics that describe the behavior of clusters of multiple events, and not simply individual events with no temporal or strategic relationships influencing system response.

Event rate describes how many events over what time period occur in a multiple-event scenario. This issue is especially important when event detection and response require depletion of physical or operator resources that require time to replenish. If another new event occurs within that time period (in essence, with an event frequency higher than the response capability of the expert team and other resources), then effective response is not possible.

Event dependence describes the extent to which the characteristics of one event (or the resources and expertise required to effectively respond to it) influence the conditions or characteristics of subsequent events. At the most basic level, Bayesian dependence will describe the probability of an event B given the prior existence of event A or response A. More complex Markov analyses can describe transition probabilities between any number of prior events and behavioral response conditions. In addition, the likelihood of future events may be affected by how capabilities of human responses and resource utilization have been depleted or enhanced by prior events.

Task Coordination and Event Response Strategies in Teams

The third framework component suggested by our research findings describes the methods that teams of experts with differing roles and knowledge bases could use to effectively coordinate their event response strategies. In some cases, expertise served as a workload balancing function and not simply a task delegation effort. For example, expertise at times increased the efficiency with which one provider could accomplish necessary tasks, a strategy used most effectively during time-critical task phases (see also Ignacio, 2008). In those cases, an expert performing a task that could have been performed by another member of the team reduced the time required for the task. When time or other resources were considered in short supply, this strategy effectively increased the amount of time available to the entire team.

Understanding team event response strategies is an important component of improving effective task performance. The first step in this process of understanding is the definition and description of these strategies, and how the suitability of those strategies changes within a specific task context. One activity seen as crucial to success in our studies of outpatient clinics and discussions with healthcare providers was the process of obtaining the appropriate information or resources that were needed to complete a task in a timely manner. Some healthcare providers and administrators have used the term *hunting and gathering* as a description of searching for necessary resources (Brown, 2006). This phrase typically has the negative connotation that the resources are difficult to find, time-consuming to collect, or are only found at random. Thus, the more neutral term *foraging* was chosen to describe these healthcare resource acquisition activities, including the ability to quantitatively describe appropriate and desirable resource gathering strategies.

Specific workflow analysis of healthcare providers highlighted how these experts, especially nurses, developed strategies to acquire the information and resources necessary to respond to dynamic workload. Three distinct foraging strategies were observed (Garrett, 2007):

- Latent foraging for information and resources that are likely to be needed at an unknown point in the future
- Proactive foraging for specific resources in order to prepare for an event that will occur at a known point in the future
- Reactive foraging that is a response to an event that has already occurred

This description of resource gathering strategies, and their relationship to dynamic events, also enables descriptions of how distributed team performance can generate cascading task requirements and coordination requirements. Even for single incidents, our framework for analyzing events and resource acquisition has improved power for describing task coordination and distribution among team members, and the requirements for temporal sequencing or distribution for events that are not impulse functions (i.e., the event takes time to evolve and emerge into its full scale).

In more complex task scenarios with multiple events or task activity that may affect future events at multiple timescales, additional examination of tasks, resources, and coordination performances is required to understand team performance (Patterson, Watts-Perotti, & Woods, 1999; Patterson & Woods, 2001; Watts et al., 1996). The ability to distinguish proactive, reactive, and latent resource acquisition efforts in this type of complex task environment will improve the capacity for analyzing information integration and team coordination across multiple levels of cognitive performance analysis. As shown in the studies of spaceflight controllers, the ability to share real-time references to current knowledge about events and resources also permits improved team synchronization for time-critical tasks.

A dynamic progression of event detection and response can be thought of as a time-line with thresholds that indicate a qualitative change in the environment and event state. Team members who are acquiring resources or information without awareness of a specific event are engaged in latent foraging. Such latent resource acquisition may provide benefits to increase useful stockpiles, but is clearly less efficient than targeted resource acquisition with respect to a known future event, and may limit the useful resources available. If precursor signals can be detected in advance of an event, with sufficient confidence to effectively plan for the future event, team members can engage in a more effective form of foraging known as proactive foraging. A description of the process is presented here; additional detail is presented elsewhere (Garrett, 2007; Garrett & Caldwell, 2009).

Early event trigger detection, before the actual event onset, increases the potential for effective and successful event response success by providing increased time for resource acquisition and planning. On the other hand, if relevant triggers are not available or not detected before the event onset, event detection is limited to reactive response to lagging indicators of the past or current event state. In this case, all additional information gathering and resource acquisition will be done in reactive response to the event (see Figure 22.2).

As the event progresses over time, it approaches the limit after which any further efforts or attempts at performance or resource acquisition will not improve the outcome. This point is defined as the deadline termination, and represents the point at which tasks not completed have failed to achieve task requirements. The minimum time required for an effective response is calculated back from that termination point and provides the operator with the point in time at which the response must be started or the outcome will be degraded. This latest possible start time is defined as the deadline decay trigger in Figure 22.2. The estimates of time available are also subject to uncertainties and the potential for subsequent events also requiring response, especially when signals are weak or team members have limited expertise in evaluating the event timeline or available expertise. In essence, Figure 22.2 presents a visual

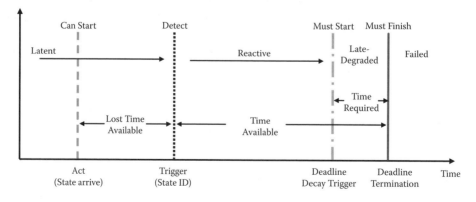

FIGURE 22.2   Event progression, resource acquisition, and task performance response when event triggers lag event start. (From Garrett, S. K., *Dissertation Abstracts International*, 68(10), 177B, 2007 (UMI 3287211).)

description of the consequences of increasing levels of procrastination in response to a task assignment.

Conclusion

This chapter has addressed several important characteristics that influence team performance and coordination in detection and response to complex event dynamics. Successful overall task performance involves an integration of information flow and utilization of expertise to effectively manage both single and cascading series of events. Our goals for this new framework of event management include the development of a set of descriptive parameters that affect team performance in a dynamic task setting. These parameters would describe aspects of team coordination in proactive and reactive forms, mutual awareness and use of multiple expertise domains, and behavioral representations of event sequences. It is expected that this work can extend, rather than replicate or replace, more traditional individual-level information processing, or agent coordination, studies of event detection and response.

An alternative consideration regarding performance in multiple dependent event contexts has been provided by authors such as Reason (1990), who originated a "Swiss cheese" model of human error and system breakdown. The Swiss cheese model emphasizes how critical sequences of errors or missed detection of adverse event precursors create "holes" of degraded system reliability and increased susceptibility to adverse events. More effective performance, from this perspective, can prevent adverse events from processing through the holes of the Swiss cheese. The focus of this chapter, by contrast, emphasizes event awareness, expertise, and information flow among team members. By improving and coordinating expertise, teams can increase the density of the "cheese" of system performance, and thus reduce the size and number of holes.

References

Brown, T. (2006, September 13). Nursing program gets shot in the arm. *Journal and Courier*. Retrieved September 14, 2006 from http://www.jconline.com/apps/pbcs.dll/article?AID=/20060913/NEWS0501/609130328/1152/NEWS

Caldwell, B. S. (1997). Components of information flow to support coordinated task performance. *International Journal of Cognitive Ergonomics, 1*(1), 25–41.

Caldwell, B. S. (2000). Information and communication technology needs for distributed communication and coordination during expedition-class space flight. *Aviation, Space, and Environmental Medicine, 71*(9, Suppl.), A6–A10.

Caldwell, B. S. (2005). Multi-team dynamics and distributed expertise in mission operations. *Aviation, Space, and Environmental Medicine, 76*(6), B145–B153.

Caldwell, B. S. (2006, July 10–14). *Issues of task and temporal coordination in distributed expert teams.* Paper presented at Proceedings of the 16th World Congress of the International Ergonomics Association, Maastricht, Netherlands.

Caldwell, B. S., & Anderson, T. J. (1996). *Design and active phases of medical process improvement systems.* Paper presented at the Examining Errors in Health Care: Developing a Prevention, Education and Research Agenda, Rancho Mirage, CA.

Caldwell, B. S., & Garrett, S. K. (2006, July 10–14). Coordination of healthcare expertise and information flow in provider teams. Paper presented at Proceedings of the 16th World Congress of the International Ergonomics Association, Maastricht, Netherlands.

Emery, F. E., & Trist, E. L. (1965). The causal texture of organizational environments. *Human Relations, 18*(1), 21–32.

Garrett, S. K. (2007). Provider centered coordination, resource foraging, and event management in healthcare tasks. *Dissertation Abstracts International, 68*(10), 177B. (UMI 3287211).

Garrett, S. K., & Caldwell, B. S. (2002). Describing functional requirements for knowledge sharing communities. *Behaviour and Information Technology, 21*(5), 359–364.

Garrett, S. K., & Caldwell, B. S. (2006). *Task coordination and group foraging in health care delivery teams.* Paper presented at Proceedings of the Human Factors and Ergonomics Society 50th Annual Meeting, San Francisco, CA.

Garrett, S. K., & Caldwell, B. S. (2009). *Human factors aspects of planning and response to pandemic events.* Proceedings of the 2009 Industrial Engineering Research Conference, (pp. 705–711). Norcross, GA: Institute of Industrial Engineers.

Garrett, S. K., Caldwell, B. S., Harris, E. C., & Gonzalez, M. C. (2009). Six dimensions of expertise: A more comprehensive definition of cognitive expertise for team coordination. *Theoretical Issues in Ergonomics Science, 10*(2), 93–105.

Helmreich, R. L., & Merritt, A. C. (2000). Safety and error management: The role of crew resource management. In B. J. Hayward & A. R. Lowe (Eds.), *Aviation resource management* (pp. 107–119). Aldershot, UK: Ashgate.

Hollenbeck, J. R. (2000). A structural approach to external and internal person-team fit. *Applied Psychology: An International Review, 49*(3), 534–549.

Ignacio, L. M. (2008). Effect of Workload Transitions on Stress and Performance in a Hospital Inpatient Pharmacy. Unpublished Master's Thesis, Purdue University, West Lafayette, IN.

Jobidon, M.-E., Breton, R., Rousseau, R., & Tremblay, S. (2006). Team response to workload transition: The role of team structure. In *Proceedings of the Human Factors and Ergonomics Society 50th Annual Meeting* (pp. 1769–1773). Santa Monica, CA: Human Factors and Ergonomics Society.

Kempf, K., Uzsoy, R., Smith, S., & Gary, K. (2000). Evaluation and comparison of production schedules. *Computers in Industry, 42*, 203–220.

Kopach, R., DeLaurentis, P.-C., Lawley, M., Murthuraman, K., Ozsen, L., Rardin, R., … Willis, D. (2007). Effects of clinical characteristics on successful open access scheduling. *Health Care Management Science, 10*, 111–124.

Overhage, J. M., Perkins, S., Tierney, W. M., & McDonald, C. J. (2001). Controlled trial of direct physician order entry: Effects on physicians' time utilization in ambulatory primary care internal medicine practices. *Journal of the American Medical Informatics Association, 8*(4), 361–371.

Patterson, E. S., Watts-Perotti, J., & Woods, D. D. (1999). Voice loops as coordination aids in space shuttle mission control. *Computer Supported Cooperative Work, 8*, 353–371.

Patterson, E. S., & Woods, D. D. (2001). Shift changes, updates, and the on-call model in space shuttle mission control. *Computer Supported Cooperative Work: The Journal of Collaborative Computing, 10*(3–4), 317–346.

Reason, J. (1990). *Human error.* Cambridge, UK: Cambridge University Press.

Shannon, C. E., & Weaver, W. (1949). *The mathematical theory of communication.* Urbana, IL: University of Illinois Press.

Smalley, H. E., & Freeman, J. R. (1966). *Hospital industrial engineering: A guide to the improvement of hospital management systems.* New York, NY: Reinhold.

Tambe, M. (1997). Towards flexible teamwork. *Journal of Artificial Intelligence Research, 7*, 83–124.

Waller, M. J. (1999). The timing of adaptive group responses to non-routine events. *Academy of Management Review, 42,* 127–137.

Waller, M. J., Gupta, N., & Giambatista, R. C. (2004). Effects of adaptive behaviors and shared mental models on control crew performance. *Management Science, 50,* 1534–1544.

Watts, J. C., Woods, D. D., Corban, J. M., Patterson, E. S., Kerr, R. L., & Hicks, L. C. (1996). *Voice loops as cooperative aids in space shuttle mission control.* Paper presented at the CSCW '96, Computer Supported Cooperative Work, Boston, MA.

Wickens, C. D., & Hollands, J. G. (2000). *Engineering psychology and human performance* (3rd ed.). Upper Saddle River, NJ: Prentice Hall.

Wright, P. D., Bretthauer, K. M., & Côté, M. J. (2006). Reexamining the nurse scheduling problem: Staffing ratios and nursing shortages. *Decision Sciences, 37*(1), 39–70.

23

"Convince Me"
An Interdisciplinary Study of NDM and Portfolio Managers

Claire McAndrew
University of the Arts London

Julie Gore
University of Surrey

The value of exchanging theory and methods between naturalistic decision making (NDM) and the fields of cognitive science and organizational studies has been growing in recognition (see Chapters 10 and 16; Gore, Banks, Millward, & Kyriakidou, 2006; Lipshitz, Klein, & Carroll, 2006; McAndrew, 2008; McAndrew, Gore, & Banks, 2009; Montgomery, Lipshitz, & Brehmer, 2005). Devoted to this emerging interface, the recent special issue in *Organization Studies* "Naturalistic Decision Making and Organizational Decision Making: Exploring the Intersections" (edited by Lipshitz et al., 2006) is a testament to the mounting appreciation of cross-disciplinary dialogues in NDM across domains as diverse as healthcare (Gore et al., 2006; Nemeth, O'Connor, Klock, & Cook, 2006), design practices in Internet organizations (Alby & Zucchermaglio, 2006), railroad operations (Roth, Multer, & Raslear, 2006), nuclear power plants (Carroll, Hatakenaka, & Rudolph, 2006), and submarine command and control (Shattuck & Miller, 2006). As demonstrated by Strater et al. (Chapter 10 of this volume) and the work of Kester, Badke-Schaub, Hultink, and Lauche (2007), Khoo (2007), and Vanharanta, Easton, and Lenney (2007), the integration of constructs from the organizational and cognitive sciences can be useful in fostering a better understanding of how experts manage and adapt to cognitively complex tasks. For other applications, see the Montgomery et al. (2005) edited volume *How Professionals Make Decisions*, which includes discussions on NDM in relation to recruitment and selection (Gore & Riley, 2005), economic forecasting (Montgomery, 2005), and managerial decision making (Goitein & Bond, 2005). While the work of Strater et al. and of those included in the special issue of *Organization Studies* and recent discussions at the 8th International Conference of Naturalistic Decision Making demonstrate empirical NDM approaches within organizational settings to be undeniably insightful, the work documented in this chapter marks a different approach, preferring to examine the potential of direct methodological exchange.

In this chapter we present a preliminary study that specifically explores the potential of complementing NDM's applied cognitive task analysis (ACTA) (Militello & Hutton, 1998) with methodological advances that have occurred within the fields of managerial cognition and cognitive psychology. We anticipate that this will not only address some of the limitations of the ACTA techniques (as discussed by Hoffman & Militello, 2008, and summarized below), but also set the stage for future interdisciplinary collaborations and methodological exchanges.

The chapter is structured as follows: The first section outlines the ACTA techniques, focusing in particular on both the strengths and challenges of the method. It also considers methodological developments within the field of managerial cognition as alternative techniques for representing and understanding cognition. We use this discussion as a platform for introducing our second method, "convince me," which extends the work of managerial cognition researchers by drawing upon developments in cognitive psychology. The second section of this chapter presents our methodological approach, paying particular attention to the procedures and materials associated with the use of (1) ACTA and (2) "convince me." The third section outlines the results derived from ACTA and then "convince me." The fourth section of our chapter discusses the results and considers the intersections that exist between ACTA and "convince me." Drawing upon these findings, we reflect upon the implications for understanding portfolio managers' decision making and the utility of methodological exchange between the fields of NDM, managerial cognition, and cognitive psychology. We close the chapter with a summary of our conclusions and lessons learned.

Applied Cognitive Task Analysis (ACTA)

The NDM community has been at the forefront of research developing applied methodologies to enable the operative study of decision making in naturalistic environments. One notable contribution has been in relation to cognitive task analysis (CTA). CTA is a set of techniques for identifying the cognitive skills and mental demands required to perform a specific task. However, the resource-intensive nature of CTA has made it difficult for practitioners to use in real-world environments. The ACTA techniques (a streamlined version of CTA) were therefore developed, with the vision that they would make CTA attainable to practitioners in field settings (Militello & Hutton, 1998). Table 23.1 summarizes the key features of ACTA. The aim of the method is to aid the identification of key cognitive components used to perform a task proficiently through a series of three knowledge elicitation and representation techniques: task diagram, knowledge audit, and simulation. These culminate in the construction of a cognitive demands table documenting the critical facets of expertise required to be proficient in the domain, noting specific strategies used to manage and adapt to complexity. Note the similarity of this to Schraagen, Klein, and Hoffman's definition of macrocognition as the study of "cognitive adaptations to complexity" (2008, p. 9) (for recent discussions of NDM and macrocognition, see Klein et al., 2003; Schraagen, Militello, Ormerod, & Lipshitz, 2008). For this reason, ACTA can be useful as a tool to understand the macrocognitive dynamics of cognitive activity: "It can develop a model of the problem space practitioners can face, the factors that make problems difficult, or the demands that any practitioner or set of practitioners need to meet" (Hoffman & Militello, 2008, p. 379).

One of the significant challenges, as discussed by Hoffman and Militello (2008), facing CTA techniques and ACTA specifically concerns the reliability and validity of

TABLE 23.1 Key Features of Applied Cognitive Task Analysis and "Convince Me"

	Applied Cognitive Task Analysis (ACTA)	"Convince Me"
Purpose	To identify characteristics of domain-specific expertise	To understand the overall coherence of arguments within a participant's causal belief map as a product of sensemaking
Theoretical roots	Expert-novice differences (see Chi et al., 1981; Ericsson & Smith, 1991; Hoffman, 1991; Klein & Hoffman, 1993)	Theory of explanatory coherence (Thagard, 1989)
Aspects of cognition	Task-based expertise; cues and strategies	Hypothesis generation and evaluation of evidence
Level of cognitive analysis	Macrocognitive functions and supporting processes (see Klein et al., 2003)	Mid-granularity: Macrocognitive phenomena modeled using microcognitive formalizations

the techniques. The taken for granted assumption that CTA data "really do capture knowledge and reasoning" (p. 382) has been deemed particularly problematic for this class of methods. One approach to dealing with this issue has been to increase the robustness of findings by triangulating CTA techniques such as the critical decision method with both concept mapping techniques (Hoffman, Coffey, Carnot, & Novak, 2002), extensively applied within the field of managerial cognition, and abstraction-decomposition matrices (Bisantz et al., 2002; Rehak, Lamoureaux, & Bos, 2006). The research documented in this chapter builds upon the multimethod approach, borrowing from a methodological development at the interface of managerial cognition and cognitive science called "convince me" (Schank, Ranney, & Hoadley, 1996).

Managerial Cognition

The study of managerial cognition is aimed at exploring "the relationships among mind, management and organization" (Meindl, Stubbart, & Porac, 1994, p. 289). Work within this field has focused upon the development and application of methods for representing and understanding cognition through the use of cause maps (Weick & Bougon, 1986), cognitive maps (Axelrod, 1976), procrustean individual differences scaling models (Hodgkinson, 2005), and multidimensional scaling applications (Ferguson, Kerrin, & Patterson, 1997). Notable contributions include the examination of mental models of competition underpinning team adaptation (Burke, Stagl, Salas, Pierce, & Kendall, 2006) and catastrophic decisions at chemical plants (Vidaillet, 2001). However, as a consequence of the methods employed within these studies, insights into cognitive processes have been solely macrocognitive in nature.

Accordingly, there has been a recent call to expand the catalogue of research tools currently available to managerial cognition researchers (Hodgkinson & Sparrow, 2002). Integrating different developments in the psychological analysis of cognition in organizations has been mentioned as one novel approach (Hodgkinson & Healey, 2008; Hodgkinson & Starbuck, 2008; Hodgkinson & Thomas, 1997; Huff, 1997; Starbuck, 2001); another promising alternative seeks to combine organizational decision making with NDM (Connolly & Koput, 1997; Gore et al., 2006; Lipshitz et al., 2006). It is to one such methodological possibility that we now turn.

"Convince Me"

"Convince me" (Schank et al., 1996) is a mid-granularity computational architecture that is rooted in the notion of causal belief mapping, and applies microcognitive formalizations to represent macrocognitive processes. It is an architecture within which macrocognitive processes such as sensemaking and uncertainty management can be modeled, albeit within a microcognitive framework when microcognition is defined as a "theoretical account[s] of how cognition takes place in the human mind" (Cacciabue & Hollnagel, 1995, p. 57). The interesting mid-level position that "convince me" adopts makes it a novel architecture for modeling NDM and for understanding macrocognitive processes at a more specified level of analysis. See Table 23.1 for an overview of the essential features of "convince me."

"Convince me" operates as a program for generating causal belief maps (characterized as a network of nodes related by explanatory and contradictory links) and analyzing the coherence of their arguments. Each node represents either a hypothesis or a statement of evidence underpinned by subjective ratings of believability or reliability. "Convince me" is composed of two components that are outlined below.

Explanatory Coherence by Harmany Optimization (ECHO)

Explanatory coherence by harmany [*sic*] optimization (ECHO) (see Thagard, 1989) is a connectionist model based on the theory of explanatory coherence (TEC) (see below). It uses an algorithm to compute the acceptance and rejection of propositions on the basis of coherence relations. The coherence of propositions is maximized by spreading activation across all nodes in a given network until all cohering nodes are activated and noncohering nodes deactivated. Four parameters control this connectionist-settling process: excitation (specifying the weight of links between cohering propositions to reflect the relative importance of explanations based upon ratings of believability or reliability), inhibition (marking the relative importance of contradictions determined by the weight given to links between incoherent propositions), skepticism (specifying the percentage of activation a proposition loses at each cycle), and data priority (specifying the weight of links between statements of evidence according to their classification as an acknowledged fact or statistic, observation or memory, one possible inference opinion or view, or whether some reasonable people might disagree). These parameters may be manually adjusted in order to enhance data-model fit. ECHO provides feedback on the coherence of arguments input into the application, summarized as a correlation between ECHO's activations (based on TEC) and an individual's beliefs.

Theory of Explanatory Coherence (TEC)

TEC is a theoretical account of the process by which the plausibility of beliefs asserted in an explanation or argument is established (see Thagard, 1989). TEC is rooted in three fundamental assumptions of reasoning. The first is that the believability of an idea increases with simplicity. This is based on the premise that the generation of lots of assumptions may in fact be counterproductive. Second, statements of belief yield higher credibility when there is more evidence to support them. Finally, people are more likely to believe statements that do not dispute other strong beliefs.

While these demark the broad assumptions of reasoning that underpin TEC, more specific principles that determine the mechanism by which explanatory coherence is determined include symmetry, explanation, simplicity, data priority, contradiction, competition, acceptability, analogy, and overall coherence (Thagard, 2004). These principles are used in conjunction with ECHO's four parameters to establish the local pair-wise relations and weightings among cohering and noncohering propositions. It is this process of establishing coherence (through the propagation of nodes across the causal belief map) that is taken to be reflective of a decision maker's reasoning processes. The resultant correlation is a reflection of the overall coherence of the arguments comprising the mapped decision, on the basis of the decision maker's weightings and those generated by ECHO (which are underpinned by TEC's theoretical postulations).

In previous work we discussed the value of microcognitive and mid-granularity modeling architectures in the study of macrocognitive phenomena (McAndrew, Banks, & Gore, 2008; McAndrew, Gore, & Banks, 2009). In the research discussed here we want to demonstrate the benefits of complementing the macrocognitive insights generated through ACTA with the mid-granularity understanding afforded by "convince me." At the heart of each of these methods (as summarized in Table 23.1) is a concern for understanding the processes through which individuals adapt to and manage uncertainty and complexity. ACTA takes as its starting point the differences that exist between *experts* and *novices* as a catalyst for generating information about the intricacies of practitioners' domain-specific knowledge. By breaking the task down into a number of component parts, particular attention is given to the cues, strategies, and difficult cognitive aspects that shape the task at hand. The resultant data provide insights into an array of macrocognitive functions (and supporting processes), including story building, uncertainty management, decision making, and mental simulation. "Convince me" adopts a slightly different approach, framing the process of adaptation to and management of uncertainty and complexity as one of *hypothesis generation* and *evidence evaluation*, from which the overall coherence of beliefs is established—that is, whether the mental model forms a compelling story as opposed to a set of fragmentary beliefs. These methods intersect insofar as it is the supporting processes (or cognitive capacities) underpinning "convince me" that make possible the achievement of the array of macrocognitive phenomena addressed by ACTA. Indeed, in Klein and Hoffman's (2008) discussion of the connections between the study of macrocognitive phenomena, mental models, and cognitive task methodology, they suggest that there is utility in examining specific criteria such as coherence. Accordingly, we align our approach with Klein and Hoffman's suggestion that the study of macrocognitive phenomena might benefit from methodological exchange: "[But] perhaps the vagueness is a sign that we are thinking about mental models at too abstract a level. Often, when a concept seems too fuzzy to be useful, that means it needs to be examined in specific cases" (Klein & Hoffman, 2008, p. 5).

Method

Participants

Extensive interviews were conducted with two male portfolio managers aged 47 and 53. Both participants worked as independent consultants for organizations that are trading members of the London Stock Exchange and the Association of Private Client Investment Managers and Stock Brokers. Participant A had worked within the investment industry for 35 years and had been employed in his current position for 12 years. Participant B's professional experience in the industry was 24 years, and 1 year in his current position. The principal decision activities of participants were described as portfolio management and discretionary/execution-only stockbroker advice services.

Materials

Applied Cognitive Task Analysis (ACTA)

Both participants completed Stages 1 and 2 of the ACTA techniques (Militello & Hutton, 1998). The instructional format for eliciting and representing knowledge generated from the ACTA techniques as provided by Militello and Hutton (1998) was used.

Stage 1, the task diagram interview, aims to provide a broad overview of the task, identifying areas requiring complex cognitive skills. Participants are asked: "Can you break this task down into between three and six steps?" and "Of these steps, which ones require cognitive skills? By cognitive skills I mean complex thinking skills such as judgments, assessments, or problem solving."

Stage 2, the knowledge audit, focuses on a cognitive subtask from stage 1 identifying cues, strategies, and those elements that may present difficulties for inexperienced individuals. The knowledge audit consists of a set of eight questions, each tapping into a different area of expertise. For example, "past and future" is premised on the assumption that experts know how situations have developed and are able to anticipate where a given situation is going. The knowledge audit seeks to understand this aspect of expertise through the question "Is there a time when you walked into the middle of a situation and knew exactly how things got there and where they were headed?" This is then deconstructed further through the following questions: In this situation, how would you know this? What cues and strategies are you relying on? In what ways would this be difficult for a less experienced person? What makes it hard to do? The other aspects of expertise addressed during the knowledge audit are big picture (experts understand the whole situation and understand how elements fit together), noticing (experts can detect cues and see meaningful patterns), tricks of the trade (experts can combine procedures and do not waste time and resources), improvising/opportunities (experts can see beyond standard operating procedures and take advantage of opportunities), self-monitoring (experts are aware of their own performance and notice when performance is not what it should be and adjust to get the job done), anomalies (experts can spot the unusual and detect deviations from the norm), and equipment difficulties (experts know equipment can mislead and do not implicitly trust equipment).

"Convince Me"

The "convince me" software (Schank et al., 1996) was downloaded from http://www.soeberkeley.edu/~schank/convinceme/index.html. To date, no instructional guidelines exist for the elicitation of expertise prior to input into "convince me." Thus, a detailed research protocol was devised to ensure objectivity in the knowledge elicitation across interviews.

Procedure

Interviews were digitally recorded, each lasting about two and a half hours. During the interview, participants were asked to select a decision task from their own portfolio management practice to complete a task diagram and knowledge audit (= stages 1 and 2 of the ACTA techniques).

Using a second decision task, they then each created a causal belief map identifying task-relevant beliefs, factual knowledge, and their perceived relations, which were subsequently used in "convince me." Participants were asked to state their beliefs and factual knowledge in the form of hypotheses, or statements of evidence, and to identify explanatory (supportive) or contradictory links between them. A participant's hypotheses and statements of evidence were subsequently tabulated and emailed to him for classification. Participants had to use at least one of the following classifiers: acknowledged fact or statistic, observation or memory, one possible inference opinion or view, or some reasonable people might disagree. "Convince me" also required judgments—measured on a scale of 1 to 9—regarding the believability of hypotheses and statements of evidence. These ratings were recorded within the table, as were the participant's judgments of reliability for each statement of evidence, measured on a scale of 1 to 3.

Analysis of Decision Process

Following transcription of the interviews, a content analysis of the knowledge audits was completed to identify common decision processes across participants. Data were coded according to the macrocognitive functions and supporting processes outlined by Klein et al. (2003).

Using "convince me," participant's causal belief maps and their classifications/ratings were input into the modeling architecture. Note that this produced a "convince me" model for each participant. Running the simulations, ECHO's connectionist-settling process used participant's classifications in conjunction with the specified explanatory/contradictory links between nodes to determine the theoretical degree of coherence between propositions (based upon the principles of TEC). Subsequently "convince me" computed a correlation to determine the relationship between participant's ratings and ECHO's activations. Accordingly, the output of each simulation (i.e., the correlation coefficient) is reflective of the overall degree of coherence in the causal belief map. Correlation coefficients are therefore to be taken as an indication of data-theory fit.

Results

Applied Cognitive Task Analysis

First, we present the results from ACTA considering each of its components in turn: (1) stage 1: task diagram, (2) stage 2: knowledge audit, and (3) content analysis of ACTA. We use extracts drawn from participant A to illustrate the results.

Stage 1: Task Diagram
Figure 23.1 provides part of participant A's task diagram detailing the process of constructing a portfolio for a new client with cash to invest.

As can be seen, this process is broken down into four key components. The first component process (know your client: gather background information) is concerned with understanding the financial position of the client. Information gathered typically includes the client's age; annual income; monthly expenditures; any existing holdings, such as savings, pension schemes, and investment funds; and intended purpose of investment, such as retirement fund. The objective of the second component process (construct a risk profile) is to establish the degree of risk appropriate for the client. This risk profile is based on a number of assumptions relating to any existing investments and the client's economic status and financial stability. The third component process (determine purpose of investment) pertains to the client's investment requirements, such as capital growth (an investment strategy that provides capital in the medium to long term through an increase in the price of assets within a fund), income (investing in companies that have dividends), or an intermediary stage (a fund whose aim is to provide both growth and income, achieved by investing in companies that have earnings growth as well as dividends).

The final component process (portfolio construction) provides the basic framework from which participant A works. The construction of an investment scheme for the client is guided not only by the amount of capital available for investment, but also by the total income required and the amount remaining for secure or growth-oriented investments. This framework then influenced his choice in stocks, in addition to his enthusiasm for a particular set of stocks he currently monitored. Participant A also noted that this process was facilitated by the existence of a number of preset portfolios (i.e., international, income, and growth) that had been prepared by the in-firm research team and run by a committee. A final point of informational leverage during the construction of a portfolio comes from peer interaction. This may take the form of discretionary advice, collective investments, or investments in individual stocks other portfolio managers have made. For instance, participant A remarked on the benefits of drawing upon the knowledge base of peers working in collectives who

New client with cash and no previous investments

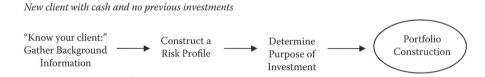

FIGURE 23.1   Illustrative task diagram for participant A.

have significantly closer relationships with fund managers than portfolio managers. The process of portfolio construction was documented as the most cognitively complex aspect by participant A and consequently formed the basis of discussion during his knowledge audit, as outlined in the next subsection.

For participant B the chosen decision task was also the construction of a portfolio for a new client. He highlighted division of an investment strategy and sector allocation as the cognitively most complex areas, and subsequently chose the latter task as the focus of his knowledge audit. Due to limited space, we will illustrate both our analyses and findings with participant A's responses referring to participant B only where differences were apparent.

Stage 2: Knowledge Audit

An extract from participant A's knowledge audit is used to illustrate the type of data ACTA generates during this stage of the knowledge elicitation process. In response to the prompt "Is there a time when you walked into the middle of a situation and knew exactly how things got there and where they were headed?" participant A used the example of being approached by a client with an existing portfolio. While the decision to restructure the portfolio is clear, participant A emphasized that doing so is not a straightforward task, as a "new" portfolio manager likely will view the existing portfolio from a different angle and make substantial changes to it consistent with his or her area of expertise. For instance, understanding the portfolio as it exists (i.e., the *past* aspect of expertise) is challenging given both the narrowed focus of expertise (across stocks and sectors) and the distinct investment style of each portfolio manager. Understanding why the portfolio is constructed as it is requires reconstruction of the underlying investment strategy and extensive simulation of how the portfolio (as it exists) might perform in the future. Equally difficult is the process of repopulating the portfolio and shifting sectoral allocations (i.e., the *future* aspect of expertise), not only in line with one's own expertise, but also to maximize returns while respecting the degree of risk the client is willing to take. Participant A outlined a number of strategies to deal with this challenge, which included ensuring stocks meet current requirements and researching unfamiliar stocks.

Content Analysis of ACTA The analysis of our participants' knowledge audits focused on the decision tasks of portfolio construction and sectors allocation and led to the identification of the following abilities, knowledge, and strategies shared by our two expert subjects:

- Specific expertise: Portfolio managers have specific expertise but know how to compensate for this limitation. While portfolio managers are only knowledgeable of a limited number of stocks—they typically track 100 stocks "hard" and specialize in a subset of 15 to 20 stocks—they have the expertise to reconcile activity in the global market economy and political environment with micro-level stocks and shares. Participant A pointed out that computerized screening software significantly aided him in this task. Through a central research base, the computerized software provides an approved list of stocks that can be included in any given portfolio. This technical support plays a crucial role in narrowing down the potential pool of stocks. However, as participant A noted, there is a need to minimize uniformity, a task that is difficult to achieve if the organization requires stocks to be selected from a predetermined list. Participant A stressed that effective use of these screening tools presupposes that portfolio managers know the appropriate parameters, and understand global markets and the rhetoric of market players.

- Understanding the natural completeness of portfolios: Expert portfolio managers know when a portfolio is complete, when asset allocation and its associated risks cohere across sectors as a whole. The completeness to portfolios is an emergent property that portfolio managers maintain is difficult to explain to clients.

- Metacognition: Expert portfolio managers know when to seek additional information and how to assess the reliability and credibility of information sources. The process of information seeking is also closely related to story building.

- Sensemaking as story building: Expert portfolio managers are able to fashion together cues to create a reasonable "story" to understand past and current developments of markets and funds and to project how investment decisions might play out.

- Use of projections: Expert portfolio managers project future states of investments. Participant A described how during the construction of a new portfolio, he used forecasts of stock performance to gauge if any holes in the portfolio existed. The generation of expectancies was underpinned by both past experience of the performance of sectors and the natural completeness of portfolios.

- Use of heuristics: Expert portfolio managers rely on heuristics, such as a company's price-earnings ratio[*] and its projections, to establish the potential value of selected stocks.

- Use of analogy: Portfolio managers frequently reason by analogy. For instance, participant A mentioned that he made sense of stocks in the United States by comparing them with a familiar market (the United Kingdom).

- Vast knowledge: Expert portfolio managers have vast amounts of general information that they have accumulated over the years and that inform their current decisions. Participant A also drew attention to the intuitive nature of the elements of expertise outlined above.

"Convince Me"

Next, we turn to the analysis of the results derived from "convince me." First, we provide an overview of the correlations that resulted from this analysis. We then present participant A's "convince me" model as an illustrative example.

Correlations: A Test of Coherence

"Convince me" used a participant's classifications and ratings of task-relevant beliefs and knowledge together with his or her specifications of explanatory and contradictory links to determine the degree of coherence between his or her beliefs and factual knowledge. The default parameters built into "convince me" were adopted for the initial run of each simulation. Default parameters were as follows: an inhibition

---

[*] The P/E ratio of a stock is a measure of the price paid for a share relative to the annual net income or profit earned by the firm per share. As such, a higher P/E ratio means that investors are paying more for each unit of net income, so the stock is more expensive than one with lower P/E.

(contradiction) weight of 60, an excitation (explanation) weight of 30, a data priority weight of 55, and a skepticism weight of 40. Correlations between participant's ratings and ECHO's activations (the latter are based upon participant's classifications and explanatory/contradictory links between nodes) were calculated for each hypothesis and statement of evidence. The average of these correlations provides a measure of how well the theory of explanatory coherence fits a participant's data. Overall, a moderate relationship ($r = 0.5$) was found between ECHO's activations and participant A's ratings. In contrast, participant B's ratings could not be adequately modeled by ECHO ($r = -0.04$), even when the program's parameters were changed in subsequent simulations.

An Illustrative Example: Participant A's "Convince Me" Model

Figure 23.2 illustrates the causal belief map "convince me" generated to model participant A's decision to purchase a porterage and lighterage stock* in the developing world. The ellipses represent hypotheses and the boxes symbolize statements of evidence mentioned by participant A. Explanatory relations are represented as solid connecting lines, and contradictory relations as dashed lines. These lines are taken to signify causal relationships, in which statements of evidence inform hypotheses. Note that the strength of the association is not represented visually in Figure 23.2.

Figure 23.2 shows two of participant A's key hypotheses, H17 (global environment fits with the micro-view of this porterage and lighterage stock) and H5 (growth in porterage and lighterage stocks is likely), and their relationships to other beliefs and facts he stated. By forming a component of a client's investment portfolio (under construction at the time of interview), participant A hypothesized the porterage and lighterage stock would add value in the medium to long term. This broad-level expectancy is represented by hypothesis H6 within Figure 23.2. Participant A categorized this hypothesis as an acknowledged fact or statistic, with moderate believability (= rating of 6 on a scale ranging from 1 to 9). Participant A's investment rationale is surmised as follows: Tracking of the stock over a 20-year period revealed that it had reached an all-time low of 60p. This fact is represented by E6, and was rated by participant A as both moderately believable (= rating of 5) and reliable (= 2 on a scale ranging from 1 to 3). He attributed the decreasing value in the share price to the existence of a seller in the marketplace (= E15), and rated this piece of evidence highly in terms of both its believability (rating of 9) and reliability (rating of 3). Participant A employed a number of heuristics to make sense of the existing state of valuation. For instance, he explicitly referred to the seminal work of Benjamin Graham† (= E4) to motivate his conviction that the net asset value will be greater than the share price (= E3). This belief was complemented by price-to-earnings measures that suggested a 7% yield (= E1). Participant A considered both E3 and E1 as acknowledged facts or statistics and rated them highly on believability and reliability.

---

* Porterage and lighterage is the general term used to reflect the maritime services offered by shipping agencies. These include general cargo and containers port operations and ship agency services.

† An American economist and professional investor, Graham is considered the first proponent of value investing. This is an investment approach that attempts to purchase stocks that are trading at a discount to their net current asset value, that is, to purchase stocks currently undervalued and hold them until they are fully valued.

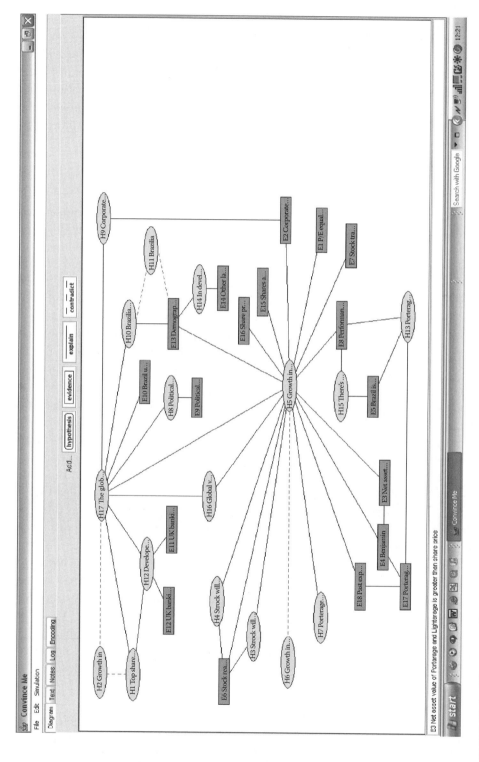

FIGURE 23.2   Illustrative "convince me" model for participant A.

While there was a quantitative undertone to his valuation estimations, participant A's decision making was also complemented by a number of qualitative beliefs that sought to reconcile the micro-view on a stock with global-level activities in the developing world. For instance, H17 reflects participant A's belief that the global environment fits with the micro-view of the porterage and lighterage stock he is considering. This hypothesis was shaped by a number of more specific assumptions, including beliefs regarding the nature of economic growth, such as "top shares in the developing world have good growth prospects" (H1), and "the developed world suffers from a lack of top line growth" (H12).

Participant A's causal belief map also included references to past experiences. For instance, participant A mentioned observed trends in the relocation of large corporations' businesses within developing countries (E14), and suggested that while the share price was about half the price of comparable others within the rest of the market (E16), performance was ahead of its competitors (E8).

Participant A's "convince me" model also contained a number of contradictory relations between nodes. For instance, H1 (top shares in the developing world have good growth prospects) was related through a contradictory link to the suggestion that growth in the developing world may be happening by chance (H2). It is interesting to note that participant A categorized both hypotheses as assumptions with which some reasonable people might disagree and rated them as moderately believable. However, H1 was additionally classified as an observation or memory, a classification that, according to the theory of explanatory coherence (TEC), gives greater weight to a hypothesis.

Discussion

The objective of this study was to explore the utility of a methodological exchange between the fields of NDM, managerial cognition, and cognitive psychology. In addressing this aim, we used ACTA, a specific type of cognitive task analysis, and "convince me," a connectionist model of cognition, to gain insight into portfolio managers' decision making.

The depth of cognitive data obtained with ACTA is the result of its highly structured approach to knowledge elicitation. ACTA's task diagram served as a useful road map for the interview, and facilitated the identification of cognitive components that comprise portfolio managers' expertise.

In order to examine the areas of portfolio construction and sectors allocation in more detail, we adopted the knowledge audit. This method provided a useful mechanism for eliciting the more tacit elements of portfolio managers' expertise, such as the sense of the natural completeness of portfolios. Prompting participants for applied examples during the knowledge audit ensured that participants' responses were grounded in real-world contexts.

Participants' responses during the knowledge audit were further analyzed using content analysis. This approach allowed us to corroborate information across participants and to examine how expert portfolio managers are able to adapt to complexity. The overarching challenge to portfolio managers that our participants identified concerned the reconciliation of macro-economic changes with micro-level activity. The ACTA results suggest that this difficulty is primarily related to portfolio managers' specialization in a few stocks relative to the pool of available stocks. However, our participants mentioned several strategies they use to overcome this limitation. They highlighted the importance of computerized screening software in aiding the selection of appropriate stocks. Expert portfolio managers also know successful heuristics and can rely on extensive domain knowledge to understand unfamiliar phenomena by analogy to familiar cases and to project how decisions at the stock level might play out at the macro-economic level.

These findings were complemented by connectionist models of participants' causal belief maps for a second decision task, which were generated based on their ratings of decision-relevant facts and beliefs. The "convince me" models were met with varied success. The model for participant A had a moderate fit with his ratings, and was in the range expected for a method that was being piloted. Participant B's ratings, however, could not be adequately modeled by "convince me." This failure may suggest that the concept of coherence is an inappropriate framework for representing and modeling portfolio managers' decision making. On the other hand, the contrarian view espoused by participant B—he stated positions opposing the prevailing views in the field—led to a high number of contradictory relations to "perceived industry wisdom," making coherence across the causal belief network difficult to achieve. Given the relative success of participant A's "convince me" model, we consider this to be the most likely explanation of the unsuccessful modeling of participant B's ratings.

The moderate correlation between participant A's "convince me" model and his ratings suggests that there is explanatory potential in both the concept of coherence generally and the use of TEC specifically in understanding how portfolio managers make sense of the macro-economic environment to aid micro-level stock decisions.

"Convince me" has also yielded insights at the microcognitive level of decision making. The concept of coherence underlying TEC and the connectionist-settling process of ECHO suggests that portfolio managers deal with ambiguous and contradictory information by, for instance, de-emphasizing the weight of evidence and lessening the strength of beliefs regarding believability and reliability. Conceptualizing portfolio managers' decision making as a connectionist-settling process was found to provide a particularly appropriate account of the emergent natural completeness of portfolios. Thus, the "convince me" mechanism for integrating judgments regarding the quality and quantity of information seems both appropriate and pertinent to further our understanding of knowledge management in complex environments.

While preliminary, our study nonetheless demonstrated the benefits of complementing NDM methods with approaches in managerial cognition and cognitive psychology. Specifically, we see five important contributions of our work. First, it demonstrates that drawing upon organizational studies and cognitive science can be of value to the NDM community not just conceptually but also methodologically. Second, our work shows how methodological exchange can help address some of the concerns associated with the reliability and validity of the ACTA techniques. Third, we were able to show the utility of complementing macrocognitive insights generated through ACTA with the mid-granularity understanding that "convince me" affords. Fourth, the work replicates characteristics of expertise that have been identified in previous research, however, in very different domains (see Chi, Feltovich, & Glaser,

1981; Ericsson & Smith, 1991; Hoffman, 1991; Klein & Hoffman, 1993). And lastly, our work extends the study of NDM to the domain of portfolio management.

Conclusion

This chapter provides a tentative platform for how research located at the intersection of NDM, organizational studies, and cognitive psychology might progress. Contributing toward our knowledge of how the processes of sensemaking and coherence can be better understood through methodological exchange, our work represents a call for increased interdisciplinary dialogue and further application of these methods to different contexts. As such, we hope that the work illustrated will set the stage for combining new theoretical approaches.

References

Alby, F., & Zucchermaglio, C. (2006). 'Afterwards we can understand what went wrong, but now let's fix it': How situated work practices shape group decision making. *Organization Studies, 27*(7), 943–966.

Axelrod, R. (1976). *Structure of decision: The cognitive maps of political elites*. Princeton, NJ: Princeton University Press.

Bisantz, A. M., Roth, E., Brickman, B., Gosbee, L. L., Hettinger, L., & McKinney, J. (2002). Integrating cognitive analyses in large scale system design process. *International Journal of Human-Computer Studies, 58*, 83–117.

Burke, C. S., Stagl, K. C., Salas, E., Pierce, L., & Kendall, D. (2006). Understanding team adaptation: A conceptual analysis and model. *Journal of Applied Psychology, 91*, 1189–1207.

Cacciabue, P. C., & Hollnagel, E. (1995). Simulation of cognition: Applications. In J. M. Hoc, P. C. Cacciabue, & E. Hollnagel (Eds.), *Expertise and technology: Cognition and human-computer cooperation* (pp. 55–73). Hillsdale, NJ: Lawrence Erlbaum Associates.

Carroll, J. S., Hatakenaka, S., & Rudolph, J. W. (2006). Naturalistic decision making and organizational learning in nuclear power plants: Negotiating meaning between managers and problem investigation teams. *Organization Studies, 27*(7), 1037–1057.

Chi, M. T. H., Feltovich, P. J., & Glaser, R. (1981). Categorization and representation of physics problems by experts and novices. *Cognitive Science, 5*, 121–152.

Connolly, T., & Koput, K. (1997). Naturalistic decision making and the new organizational context. In Z. Shapira (Ed.), *Organizational decision making* (pp. 285–303). New York, NY: Cambridge University Press.

Ericsson, K. A., & Smith, J. (1991). *Towards a general theory of expertise*. Cambridge, UK: Cambridge University Press.

Ferguson, E., Kerrin, M., & Patterson, F. (1997). The use of multi-dimensional scaling: A cognitive mapping technique in occupational settings. *Journal of Managerial Psychology, 12*(3), 204–214.

Goitein, B., & Bond, E. U. (2005). Modes of effective managerial decision making: Assessment of a typology. In H. Montgomery, R. Lipshitz, & B. Brehmer (Eds.), *How professionals make decisions* (pp. 123–134). Mahwah, NJ: Lawrence Erlbaum.

Gore, J., Banks, A., Millward, L., & Kyriakidou, O. (2006). Naturalistic decision making: Reviewing pragmatic science. *Organization Studies, 27*(7), 925–942.

Gore, J., & Riley, M. (2005). Recruitment and selection in hotels: Experiencing cognitive task analysis. In H. Montgomery, R. Lipshitz, & B. Brehmer (Eds.), *How professionals make decisions* (pp. 343–350). Mahwah, NJ: Lawrence Erlbaum.

Hodgkinson, G. P. (2005). *Images of competitive space: A study in managerial and organizational strategic cognition.* Basingstoke, UK: Palgrave.

Hodgkinson, G. P., & Healey, M. P. (2008). Cognition in organizations. *Annual Review of Psychology, 59*(5), 387–417.

Hodgkinson, G. P., & Sparrow, P. R. (2002). *The competent organization.* Maidenhead, UK: Open University Press.

Hodgkinson, G. P., & Starbuck, W. H. (2008). Organizational decision making: Mapping terrains on different planets. In G. P. Hodgkinson & W. H. Starbuck (Eds.), *The Oxford handbook of organizational decision making* (pp. 1–29). Oxford, UK: Oxford University Press.

Hodgkinson, G. P., & Thomas, A. B. (1997). Editorial introduction to the special issue: Thinking in organizations. *Journal of Management Studies, 34*(6), 845–850.

Hoffman, R. R. (1991). Human factors psychology in the support of forecasting: The design of advanced meteorological workstations. *Weather and Forecasting, 6,* 98–110.

Hoffman, R. R., Coffey, J. W., Carnot, M. J., & Novak, J. D. (2002). An empirical comparison of methods for eliciting and modeling expert knowledge. In *Proceedings of the 46th Meeting of Human Factors and Ergonomics Society* (pp. 482–486). Santa Monica, CA: Human Factors and Ergonomics Society.

Hoffman, R. R., & Militello, L. G. (2008). Methodological challenges for cognitive task analysis. In R. R. Hoffman & L. Militello (Eds.), *Perspectives on cognitive task analysis: Historical origins and communities of practice* (pp. 379–398). Hove, UK: Psychology Press.

Huff, A. S. (1997). A current and future agenda for cognitive research in organizations. *Journal of Management Studies, 34*(6), 947–952.

Kester, L., Badke-Schaub, P., Hultink, E. J., & Lauche, K. (2007). *Complex decision making in portfolio management: An exploratory study.* Paper presented at Proceedings of the 8th International Naturalistic Decision Making Conference, Pacific Grove, CA.

Khoo, B. (2007). *How worldviews influence the contemporary management of risks in the business enterprise setting.* Paper presented at Proceedings of the 8th International Naturalistic Decision Making Conference, Pacific Grove, CA.

Klein, G., & Hoffman, R. R. (1993). Seeing the invisible: Perceptual-cognitive aspects of expertise. In M. Rabinowitz (Ed.), *Cognitive science foundations of instruction* (pp. 203–226). Mahwah, NJ: Erlbaum.

Klein, G., & Hoffman, R. R. (2008). Macrocognition, mental models and cognitive task analysis methodology. In J. M. Schraagen, L. Militello, T. Omerod, & R. Lipshitz (Eds.), *Naturalistic decision making and macrocognition* (pp. 57–80). Aldershot, UK: Ashgate.

Klein, G., Ross, K. G., Moon, B., Klein, D. E., Hoffman, R. R., & Hollnagel, E. (2003). Macrocognition. *IEEE Intelligent Systems, 18*(3), 81–85.

Lipshitz, R., Klein, G., & Carroll, J. S. (2006). Introduction to the special issue: Naturalistic decision making and organizational decision making: Exploring the intersections. *Organization Studies, 27*(7), 917–923.

McAndrew, C. (2008). *Cross-fertilising methods in naturalistic decision making and managerial cognition.* Unpublished PhD thesis, University of Surrey, UK.

McAndrew, C., Banks, A., & Gore, J. (2008). Bridging macrocognitive/microcognitive methods: ACT-R under review. In J. M. Schraagen, L. Militello, T. Omerod, & R. Lipshitz (Eds.), *Naturalistic decision making and macrocognition* (pp. 277–300). Aldershot, UK: Ashgate.

McAndrew, C., Gore, J., & Banks, A. (2009). Convince me: Modelling naturalistic decision making. *Journal of Cognitive Engineering and Decision Making, 3*(2), 156–175.

Meindl, J. R., Stubbart, C., & Porac, J. F. (1994). Cognition within and between organizations: Five key questions. *Organization Science, 5*, 289–293.

Militello, L. G., & Hutton, R. J. B. (1998). Applied cognitive task analysis: A practitioner's toolkit for understanding cognitive task demands. *Ergonomics, 41*(11), 1618–1641.

Montgomery, H. (2005). Psychology of economic forecasting: A possibility for cooperation between judgment and decision making and naturalistic decision-making theories? In H. Montgomery, R. Lipshitz, & B. Brehmer (Eds.), *How professionals make decisions* (pp. 119–122). Mahwah, NJ: Lawrence Erlbaum.

Montgomery, H., Lipshitz, R., & Brehmer, B. (2005). *How professionals make decisions.* Mahwah, NJ: Lawrence Erlbaum.

Nemeth, C., O'Connor, M., Klock, A., & Cook, R. (2006). Discovering healthcare cognition: The use of cognitive artefacts to reveal cognitive work. *Organization Studies, 27*(7), 1011–1035.

Rehak, L. A., Lamoureaux, T. B., & Bos, J. C. (2006). Communication, co-ordination, and integration of cognitive work analysis outputs. In *Proceedings of the Human Factors and Ergonomic Society 50th Annual Meeting* (pp. 515–519). Santa Monica, CA: Human Factors and Ergonomics Society.

Roth, E. M., Multer, J., & Raslear, T. (2006). Shared situation awareness as a contributor to high reliability performance in railroad operations. *Organization Studies, 27*(7), 967–987.

Schank, P., Ranney, M., & Hoadley, C. (1996). Convince me (revised computer program (on CD) and manual). In J. R. Jungck, V. Vaughan, J. N. Calley, N. S. Peterson, P. Soderberg, & J. Stewart (Eds.), *The 1996–1997 BioQUEST Library* (4th ed). College Park, MD: Academic Software Development Group, University of Maryland.

Schraagen, J. M., Klein, G., & Hoffman, R. R. (2008). The macrocognition framework of naturalistic decision making. In J. M. Schraagen, L. Militello, T. Ormerod, R. Lipshitz (Eds.), *Naturalistic decision making and macrocognition* (pp. 3–25). Aldershot, UK: Ashgate.

Schraagen, J. M., Militello, L., Ormerod, T., & Lipshitz, R. (2008). *Naturalistic decision making and macrocognition.* Aldershot, UK: Ashgate.

Shattuck, L. G., & Miller, N. L. (2006). Extending naturalistic decision making to complex organizations: A dynamic model of situated cognition. *Organization Studies, 27*(7), 989–1009.

Starbuck, W. H. (2001). 'Is Janus the god of understanding?' In T. K. Lant & Z. Shapira (Eds.), *Organizational cognition: Computation and interpretation* (pp. 351–365). Mahwah, NJ: Lawrence Erlbaum.

Thagard, P. (1989). Explanatory coherence. *Behavioral and Brain Sciences, 12*, 435–467.

Thagard, P. (2004). Causal inference in legal decision-making: Explanatory coherence vs. Bayesian networks. *Applied Artificial Intelligence, 18*, 231–249.

Vanharanta, M., Easton G., & Lenney, P. (2007). *The cognitive iron age: The paradox of NDM in organizations.* Paper presented at Proceedings of the 8th International Naturalistic Decision Making Conference, Pacific Grove, CA.

Vidaillet, B. (2001). Cognitive processes and decision making in a crisis situation: A case study. In T. K. Lant & Z. Shapira (Eds.), *Organizational cognition: Computation and interpretation* (pp. 241–263). Mahwah, NJ: Lawrence Erlbaum.

Weick, K. E., & Bougon, M. G. (1986). Organizations as cognitive maps: Charting ways to success and failure. In H. Sims & D. Gioia (Eds.), *The thinking organization: Dynamics of organizational cognition* (pp. 102–135). San Francisco, CA: Jossey-Bass.

24

Knowns, Known Unknowns, and Unknown Unknowns

Time and Uncertainty in Naturalistic Decision Making

Marvin S. Cohen
Perceptronics Solutions, Inc.

> The longer I live the more I see that I am never wrong about anything, and that all the pains I have so humbly taken to verify my notions have only wasted my time.
>
> **—George Bernard Shaw (Laurence, 1985)**

Time Management

This chapter focuses on a critical issue in naturalistic decision-making (NDM) research—experts' management of the time they take to gather information and verify assessments and decisions—and its implications for training and decision aiding from an NDM perspective. There has been very little research on how, or even if, proficient decisions makers in various domains and task contexts actively manage the time they take to think, and if they do, whether it is a distinctive part of their expertise. This verged on being a nonproblem in early studies of expert problem solving and naturalistic decision making, because performance superiority was attributed to rapid recognition of familiar patterns (e.g., Chase & Simon, 1973; recognition-primed decision making (RPD) Level 1, Klein, 1993). Time management might seem *unnecessary* because the first solutions generated by experts tended to be accurate. Time management might be *impossible* because the relevant processes were largely preconscious.

Time management may become a problem if experts excel along dimensions other than direct recognition. When decision makers mismanage time in these cases, there can be serious consequences. Peters, Jackson, Phillips, and Ross (2008, p. 205), observing a military exercise featuring new displays, noticed that "commanders commonly sacrificed the speed advantage of their lightly armored force in order to satisfy their perceived need for information." Omodei, McLennan, Elliott, Wearing, and Clancy (2005) found experimental support for overuse of unfamiliar information resources by relatively experienced decision makers. General George C. McClellan exemplified this syndrome during the American Civil War, while others, such as Grant and Jackson, warned against it, nicely demonstrating that the phenomenon cannot be blamed entirely on modern technology. Deliberative processes

371

have in fact been observed and acknowledged by NDM researchers: mental simulation (Klein, 1993, 1998), deliberative top-down processes (Endsley, 2000a), critiquing and correcting products of recognition (Cohen, Freeman, & Wolf, 1996; Cohen, Freeman, & Thompson, 1998a; Cohen & Thompson, 2001), and cyclical frame-data interactions (Klein, Phillips, Rall, & Peluso, 2007). Not surprisingly, these researchers emphasize the importance of timely action. Klein's proposed stopping criteria for deliberative processes refer to achieving the *benefits* of reducing *known* uncertainties; for example, sensemaking stops when it has consistently fleshed out a frame (Klein et al., 2007) or when affordances are recognized (Klein, 2000). Endsley (2000a) intentionally abstracts from real-world time constraints when she states that "more SA is always better." I have emphasized a more complex, dynamic picture: Decision makers balance *costs* of delay against benefits, and the benefits of deliberation include both resolving known and discovering *unknown* uncertainties in novel situations.

The assigned mission for this chapter was to identify new directions for naturalistic decision-making research. The management of time and uncertainty in decision making serves this purpose. Some habitual assumptions in cognitive psychology stand in the way of plausible theory: for example, that attention is voluntarily controlled by a "central executive" (for a critique, see Monsell & Driver, 2000), that voluntary processes cannot be explained "mechanistically" (for a critique, see Bargh, 2000; Newell, 1981), and that units of knowledge such as schemas, frames, and mental models are well defined in advance of their use by decision makers (Rumelhart, Smolensky, McClelland, & Hinton, 1986). Some habits in NDM also need to be re-examined: for example, treating macrocognitive phenomena—such as story building, developing mental models, or managing uncertainty (Schraagen, Klein, & Hoffman, 2008)—as primitives that explain rather than merely name the phenomena (for a critique, see Flach, 2008), treating recognition-primed decision making and critical thinking as diametric opposites (e.g., assuming that the former involves no implicit reasoning while the latter is linear and logical), downplaying preference and motivation as determinants of action, and assuming that differences in thinking strategies do not contribute to expertise.

Recognition/metacognition (R/M) theory posits three concurrent and iterative cycles of cognitive activity, as shown in Figure 24.1. (1) In the most basic cycle (left side of Figure 24.1), existing knowledge and preferences interact intimately to interpret the environment and generate actions to influence it. R/M treats recognition-primed decision making as an *anytime* process; i.e., it produces actionable results very quickly, which may then be improved by investment of additional time. (2) A second cycle (inner loop on the right side), conditional on investing time in deliberation, incorporates core recognitional conclusions into a story that explains missing or conflicting evidence, evaluates assumptions required to make the story work, and moves to another core conclusion only if the story requires too much of a stretch. Since critical thinking may be motivated either by *known* uncertainty or by the prospect of *unknown* uncertainty, critiquing and correcting not only answer questions but proactively search for questions to ask. (3) A final cycle (outer loop on the right side) determines how much, if any, time to allocate to deliberation by balancing the potential for improved outcomes against risk and foregone opportunities. This chapter's main focus is on the third cycle, in the context of a connectionist implementation

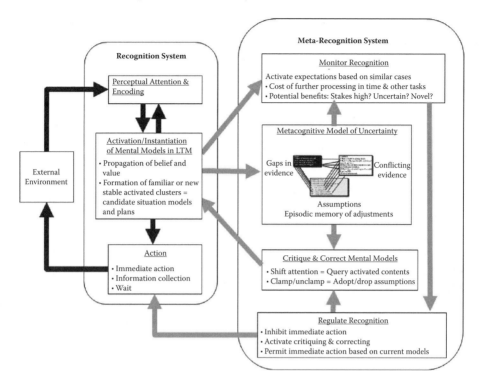

FIGURE 24.1   Overview of recognition-metacognition model.

of R/M (Cohen & Thompson, 2005; Thompson & Cohen, 1999; Shastri, 1999). I will explore the idea that higher-level control is executed by an automatic process called *melioration* (Herrnstein, 1997), in order to illustrate some of the complex dynamics implicit in a realistic "stopping rule." Melioration can lead to premature commitment or to inappropriate delay, but can also improve with the right kind of experience. The chapter outlines some experimental evidence that experts are reliably better at regulating time than nonexperts. The chapter concludes that time allocation affords important overlooked opportunities for naturalistic aiding and training.

Naturalistic Decision Making Is an Anytime Process

An anytime algorithm in artificial intelligence is a computational process that does not need to run to completion in order to provide useful information. The quality of the answer increases with additional time spent computing. In practical reasoning about complex domains, there is no stopping point beyond which improvements are demonstrably no longer possible, but the current best solution can be obtained and used at "any time." The anytime principle plays an important role in Shruti R/M, a connectionist implementation that contends for what might be called the triple crown of simulated automatic or recognition-based reasoning: (1) Shruti is *relational* (Shastri & Ajjanagadde, 1993; Shastri & Mani, 1997). Unlike standard probabilistic systems (i.e., Bayes nets and influence diagrams, which represent events by propositions that lack internal structure) or associative networks (which represent events and objects by conjunctions of features), Shruti reasons with predicates or frames (e.g., *x attacks y at time t*), and uses temporal synchrony of activation to track the objects that fill roles in the relations that predicates represent. (2) Shruti is *probabilistic* (Wendelken & Shastri, 2000). Unlike standard systems for relational reasoning, it propagates uncertainty (i.e., strength of belief) across a network of causally and semantically linked predicates, inferring causal explanations from dynamically changing observations and episodic memories, and predicting future effects from combinations of causes and conditions (Shastri & Wendelken, 1998). More recent enhancements integrate reasoning about belief with reasoning about preferences and actions (Cohen et al., 2000b; Wendelken & Shastri, 2002). (3) Shruti is extremely *fast*. Unlike both probabilistic and relational systems, Shruti draws conclusions from massive knowledge bases in a second or less. In this respect as well as others, it provides a neurally plausible representation of rapid *nondeliberative* human reasoning (Shastri, 2001; Shastri & Mani, 1997).

Shruti R/M explains the early availability of a solution (i.e., the first part of the any-time principle) as the rapid emergence of stable, self-reinforcing cycles of activation in a long-term memory associative network (Shastri & Ajjanagadde, 1993; Shastri & Mani, 1997). In the case of highly experienced decision makers, these cycles of activation tend to include key elements of both a situation model and plan, which can be acted on immediately under conditions that are highly time constrained or routine. Figure 24.2 illustrates some notable features of this process. It depicts the hypothesized spread of activation through an associative network for the tactical action officer (TAO) of a U.S. Aegis cruiser during an incident in which a Libyan gunboat approached his ship in the Gulf of Sidra.[*]

In this example, evidence includes recent observations, now in episodic memory, that *a gunboat emerged from a Libyan port, turned toward own ship,* and *increased speed* (the latter is not shown). Activation spreads up causal chains via query nodes (represented by question marks) to find explanations (*the Libyan gunboat intends to attack own ship*) and explanations of explanations (*Libyans have a motive, the opportunity and means to attack*). In the case of *motive*, it spreads even further to causal preconditions that were already primed (*the gunboat is Libyan, own ship is in Libyan-claimed waters*). When activation reaches facts in episodic memory or perceptual observations, they serve as pathways for activation to flow back to the original predicate's belief collectors (represented by plus and minus signs for truth and falsity, respectively). Simultaneously, activation spreads down causal chains to likely future events: *own ship is within range of the gunboat's weapons*; *the gunboat fires a missile at own ship*; and *own ship is damaged*, a third step that was already primed by an active goal. Preference spreads in parallel with belief, so that when a desirable or undesirable event is predicted (such as *own ship is damaged*), activation travels through the pathway created by a *reward fact* to a positive or negative utility collector. Activation then travels upstream via utility collectors to causes of the predicate, seeking actions that can influence its state for the better. If facts representing feasible actions (e.g., *own ship fires at the gunboat before time t*, when own ship will be within the gunboat's weapons range) are encountered, activation returns over the new pathways provided by performance of the actions, shutting down the circuit generated by the reward

---

[*] This example and other critical incident interviews that motivated the R/M theory are analyzed in more detail in Cohen et al. (1995, 1996, 1998a).

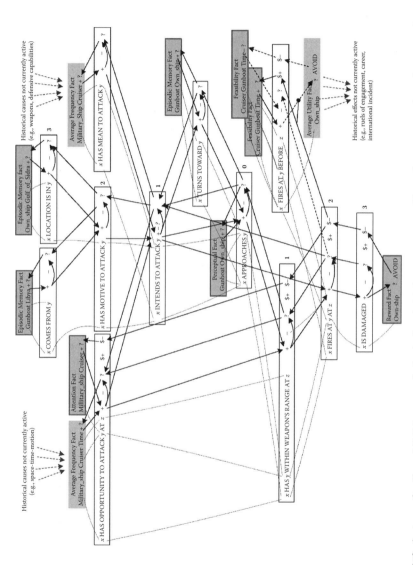

FIGURE 24.2   Simplified view of a Shruti R/M network depicting initial recognition of hostile intent in the Libyan gunboat example. Unshaded rectangles are predicates, each of which has a positive and negative belief collector (+ and −, respectively), a query node (?), a positive and negative utility collector ($+ and $−, respectively, with some not shown to save space), and a node (x, y, z) for each role played by objects in the relation represented by the predicate. Shaded rectangles are facts about objects that instantiate predicate roles. Solid lines represent cycles of self-reinforcing belief and utility activation. Numbers illustrate pathways that activation takes from the perceptual input fact. Faint broken lines represent synchronized activation of objects that instantiate roles and the role nodes that are instantiated by them.

fact. In sum, a single, very rapid process of parallel constraint satisfaction enables the TAO to explain recent and ongoing observations, anticipate the future evolution of events, and find actions to deal with them. There are no distinct processing stages from observations to interpretations to mental simulation to decisions. They emerge together in a process of mutual interaction that does not require a single fixed starting point.

Spreading activation in the Shruti R/M associative network poses questions and attempts to answer them. In Shruti R/M *questions* are predicate instances whose query nodes have been activated by goals, perceptual observations, or focal attention. *Answers* are the activation returning to the predicate instance regarding its truth/ falsity or desirability/undesirability. Activation returns via directly associated perceptual, episodic, or reward facts (e.g., *a Libyan gunboat emerged...*) or indirectly via causally or semantically linked predicates that are directly associated with such facts. Stable situation pictures and plans emerge over very short periods of time if cascading activation returns over multiple fact-created pathways to the same belief collectors of the originally queried predicates. The larger the number of confirming facts, the stronger the returning activation, shutting down weaker pathways corresponding to support for competing causal hypotheses, inhibiting competing goals or actions,[*] and creating a stable self-reinforcing cycle of activated beliefs and intentions. *Knowns* (as in the chapter title) are questions that have received such an answer.

With time and experience, an associative network adapts to the statistical properties of the environment (Brunswik, 1955). A natural outcome of learning is the emergence of clusters of predicates, such as the *hostile intent* mental model in Figure 24.2, whose activation levels covary because of their links in long-term memory, and which reflect the experienced, reported, or inferred co-occurrences of corresponding events (Wendelken & Shastri, 2003). A second natural outcome is the emergence of causal structure among the correlated variables, which both simplifies relationships (Pearl, 1989) and enables effective action (Pearl, 2000). Clusters of this kind are often centered on a structurally definable *core conclusion*. A core conclusion is the current state of a predicate that has a unique organizing and simplifying role in an active network and a significant influence on utility and actions. *Intends to attack* in Figure 24.2 satisfies both conditions.[†] Notwithstanding internal structure, from a connectionist and naturalistic perspective large knowledge structures (e.g., *schemata*, *frames*, or *mental models*) are not fixed or well-defined entities. Each predicate in active memory is typically connected to many other concepts, both active and inactive, which themselves belong to other loosely defined overlapping correlational and causal structures that may be active or inactive on a particular occasion. What makes a situation seem routine or familiar is not its match to a self-contained "pattern," but the conformity of the elements that happen to be recognitionally activated at a

---

[*] For example, strong activation in favor of own ship fires at gunboat suppresses the general reluctance to fire at another ship reflected in the link of the average utility fact to the negative utility collector ($-).

[†] Intends to attack is the most central predicate in Figure 24.2 according to several network measures. It has more incoming ties (i.e., causal precursors, like motive, means, and opportunity) and more outgoing ties (i.e., observable actions, like turning toward own ship and approaching, undertaken to implement intent). In addition, it mediates a larger proportion of the connections between other predicates. These properties reduce the number of connections required to represent the situation.

given time to preexisting correlations among those elements in long-term memory, enabling activation to rapidly spread and cohere. When situation interpretation and action commitment are accomplished without intervention by deliberate attention, they qualify as *automatic*, as defined by Logan (1988): They involve *single-step memory retrieval*. Because experts have more information and have organized it more effectively than nonexperts, their initial single-step recognition of a situation is more likely to be correct (Feltovich, Spiro, & Coulson, 2006), but this is not guaranteed.

Critiquing and Correcting

Shruti R/M accounts for the second property of anytime algorithms—that continued processing can improve results—by the use of skilled attention to *prolong* and *extend* the same types of activation processes as those described in the previous section. Successive shifts of attention widen the sphere of activation and bring new knowledge to bear over multiple retrieval cycles. Attention shifting, unlike general purpose analytical strategies, draws its strength from the same domain-specific knowledge that fuels recognition. It is effective when it stimulates activated regions in long-term memory to expand or coalesce into more coherent and inclusive solutions based on more knowledge (the inner loop on the right in Figure 24.1). Shruti R/M represents a nuanced view of automaticity, according to which processes like spreading activation can be both initiated and guided by deliberate attention, and deliberate attention in turn is influenced by recognized patterns of spreading activation (Bargh, 2007; Logan, 2004; Logan, Taylor, & Etherton, 1996; Wendelken & Shastri, 2005). Success, therefore, depends not only on substantive knowledge but also on the metacognitive skills that mediate this reciprocal interaction (e.g., Dunlosky & Bjork, 2008). The purpose of the following sections is to provide a framework for understanding the skill component of deliberation. This section reviews some of the behavior that is to be explained.

During critiquing and correcting, decision makers attempt to *hold on to* initial recognitional conclusions while at the same time deepening understanding. Rather than discounting or ignoring problematic evidence or prior beliefs, they reconcile evidence and beliefs with their initial conclusions by incorporating them all within a consistent story in episodic memory, ultimately replacing initial core conclusions only if the story requires more of a stretch than they expected. Iterative application of a small set of critiquing and correcting skills accomplishes this:

1. The most basic critiquing skill is finding *known unknowns* in the results of recognitional processing. These are questions that have been asked but not answered, that is, queried predicates whose returning activation is weak, conflicting, or unstable. In the Libyan gunboat example, the captain of the U.S. Aegis cruiser noticed that a causal condition of intent to attack own ship—that own ship was an appropriate *opportunity for attack* based on its being in Libyan-claimed waters—was unstable due to the unexamined assumption that a *better* target was not available.

2. The most basic correcting skill is *shifting attention* to known unknowns in order to expand the scope of activation in the associative network. The aim is to answer relevant questions by activating perceptual observations, episodic memories of

observations, or well-established general beliefs. For instance, the captain shifted attention directly to *opportunity to attack* and noticed that another U.S. cruiser was both closer to the gunboat and closer to Libya. The gunboat had bypassed a better target, casting doubt on its *hostile intent.*

3. If shifting attention does not resolve known uncertainty, correcting includes *clamping* an active predicate (e.g., own ship is a suitable *opportunity for attack*) as a temporary fact in episodic memory. The aim is to bias information retrieval toward evidence supporting the clamped hypothesis, thereby reconciling the core conclusion with observations and prior beliefs. For instance, the best explanation the Captain could come up with was that the Libyans were taking care of the other U.S. cruiser in some other way.

4. If direct evidence is not found to strengthen and stabilize conclusions and explain conflict, correcting includes the retention of clamped, reconciling hypotheses as *explicit assumptions* in episodic memory. The result is a stable and coherent story that consistently combines the core conclusion, observations, and relevant beliefs. To reconcile their assessment of hostile intent with the presence of the other U.S. vessel, the captain and the TAO hypothesized that Libyans would take care of the other ship in some other way. A similar cycle of critiquing and correcting resulted in the adoption of an assumption that the gunboat was a suitable *means of attack* against the cruiser despite the obvious difference in capabilities, because the Libyans were throwing everything they had into the fight.

5. Critiquing includes judgments about the likelihood of significant *unknown unknowns*, that is, hidden issues that, if not managed, might produce surprises down the road. Experts implicitly assess the likelihood of questions whose relevance has not yet been recognized based on the overall unfamiliarity of the situation and the number of assumptions necessary to save the core conclusion.

6. If unknown unknowns are deemed likely, critiquing expands to search for them even in the absence of known unknowns. Unknown unknowns may be exposed as by-products of shifting attention and expanded scope of activation, as in step 2. They may be intentionally sought out by shifting attention to apparent *knowns*, that is, observations or beliefs that apparently support the core conclusion, to find weak evidence, conflicting beliefs, or unstable implicit assumptions underlying the favorable interpretation of the evidence. For instance, as the number of required assumptions increased, the situation seemed more problematic to the captain, and he shifted attention to evidence that seemed to support *hostile intent,* the gunboat's *turning toward own ship.* As a result, the captain recalled that the gunboat was unable to localize own ship at the relevant range. To maintain the hostile intent story, some additional assumptions, such as possible Soviet technical training, or operational assistance, were necessary.

7. Critiquing includes tracking the *overall plausibility* of the set of explicit assumptions in the story. Because residual uncertainties are deliberately translated into assumptions, their collective plausibility serves as a uniform currency for evaluating the story as a whole, and the plausibility of the story as a whole is a basis for judging the plausibility of the core conclusions. It took three assumptions, none of them very compelling, to patch up the *hostile intent* story: that an unknown Libyan plan included taking care of the other cruiser, that the Libyans were willing to sacrifice the gunboat, and that the gunboat was able to localize own ship at the relevant distance before it turned.

8. If the total set of assumptions is regarded as too implausible, correcting may release them and adopt an alternative core conclusion. The captain finally dropped the *hostile intent* story and took a serious look at another core conclusion, that the gunboat was *not hostile*. After several more cycles of critiquing and correcting, a new, *nonhostile* story emerged that also required several assumptions.

9. *Priming* (Shastri & Wendelken, 1999) complements attention shifting by prolonging activation of information that might otherwise have been left outside the radius of activation. Newly activated information can be integrated with information maintained by priming to facilitate new results. A better story or core conclusion may emerge from the spontaneous convergence of ideas primed over repeated rounds of critiquing and correcting. For example, in the gunboat incident the captain and TAO ultimately concluded that the Libyan gunboat was probably looking for targets of opportunity. The *target of opportunity* story required only one unsupported assumption: that *Libya is willing to sacrifice the gunboat*. This became the captain's working hypothesis, and the incident did in fact end with the gunboat's destruction.

Foraging for Surprises

A New Model of the Quick Test

The outermost loop in the R/M model (Figure 24.1, right panel) regulates whether deliberative processing will take place, and if so, where it will focus and when it will stop. According to the R/M theory (Cohen et al., 1996, 1998a), deliberation takes place with regard to some component of a primary task if and only if the stakes are high, the opportunity costs of deliberation (e.g., delayed action or deliberation about other topics) are relatively low, *and* the decision is either uncertain (i.e., there are known unknowns) or unfamiliar (i.e., there are possible unknown unknowns). When these conditions are met, the quick test inhibits immediate action or irreversible commitment to the relevant task component and permits the iterative process of critiquing and correcting described in the previous section. When the conditions fail, critiquing and correcting halt or do not begin. Since most intentional behavior occurs in circumstances that are familiar or pose little risk, by far the most common result is action without even momentary deliberation. One should not be surprised if 80 to 90% (or even more) of decisions described in retrospective critical decision interviews are recognition primed, as reported by Klein and his colleagues. The remaining 10 to 15%, however, tend to be very consequential, and are typically the most salient parts of the incident to the decision makers themselves.

An obvious constraint is that the quick test itself not consume many cognitive resources. Unless it is truly quick, it would consume too much of the time it is meant to allocate, and the costs of delay would overwhelm any possible benefits. This is not to say that deliberation about deliberation is never appropriate, or that it must lead to an infinite regress. Experts often articulate judgments about how much time they have, and effective crews take actions for the explicit purpose of buying more time before action is necessary (Cohen et al., 1996, 1998a; Orasanu & Strauch, 1994). But for thought to be possible at all, *the highest level of "executive control" over mental processes must be simple, automatic, and largely outside conscious awareness* (Son & Kornell, 2005).

Some insight into how a simple, automatic process can produce adaptive decisions about attention allocation comes from ethological studies of animal foraging in the wild (Stephens, 2007; Stephens & Krebs, 1986) and experimental analysis of animal choices in the laboratory (Herrnstein, 1997). Presumably without explicit deliberation, herbivores somehow decide how to allocate their time among patches that vary in the quantity and quality of food they contain; predators know how to allocate time among locations that vary in the incidence of prey. Patches may become depleted over time, are separated by distances that take time to traverse, and may expose the forager to predation. The present model of the quick test is based on an analogy between foraging in the wild and cognitive exploration of idea threads in an associative network under the risks associated with delayed action or other missed opportunities. Unlike so-called *optimal foraging theory*, the Shruti R/M *foraging for surprise* hypothesis does not purport to guarantee an optimal result (Simon & Newell, 1958). Ironically, it provides a pathway for improvement in contexts where some "optimizing" algorithms actually do not. It utilizes implicit metacognitive assessments about knowledge, time, and uncertainty, which I discuss in turn.

Knowledge About Knowledge

While animals forage in patches to discover and consume sources of energy, decision makers forage in predicate clusters to discover and benefit from *surprises* that may lead to more successful actions and outcomes. An associative network like Figure 24.2 naturally decomposes into dynamically evolving patches of information, that is, clusters of predicates that are topically related to one another and whose relevance to decisions is correlated across situations. For example, if the predicate *opportunity to attack* is relevant to a course of action and its outcomes, linked information about spatiotemporal relationships with other potential targets is also likely to be relevant; if the predicate *means of attack* is relevant, so is linked information about relative platform capabilities and availability of better weapons. Patch-like organization of information is an ecological constraint to which deliberation skills may adapt through learning (Pirolli, 2007; Pirolli & Card, 1999). A patch is available for attention only if it is represented by at least one predicate in active memory, which can function as an entry point. As expertise accumulates in a domain, decisions about allocating attention to a predicate in active memory will be shaped increasingly by experience with the patches to which it belongs. This does not imply that decision makers are familiar in advance with all the predicates in a patch, or that patches are well defined enough for such knowledge to be possible. New patch members may be identified dynamically as predicates are encountered during exploration of the associative network.

Three deliberation-related alternatives may exist at any given time: Implement the currently preferred action without (further) deliberation, attend to another active predicate in the currently attended patch, or switch attention to an active predicate in a new patch. Choice is determined by the relative *values* of the available alternatives. An ideal rational model would equate value with the total expected future utility of each choice. In order to globally maximize return from deliberation, it would consider *subsequent* attention shifts, resulting discoveries, their influence on new attention shifts, and so on, to include all possible sequences and durations of deliberation across all available patches and their impact on future decisions and outcome utility. Aside from demanding far more effort than deliberation itself would, the rational approach relies entirely on the model that deliberation is meant to improve. The requirement for explicit modeling assumes the impossibility of unknown unknowns in novel situations (Cohen & Freeling, 1981; Cohen, Parasuraman, & Freeman, 1998b). Optimal foraging theory has produced a simpler rule, the *mean value theorem* (MVT), as its central result (Charnov, 1976), and MVT has been applied to information search by Pirolli & Card (1999; Pirolli, 2007). However, it is not entirely clear how it can be used. Stopping rules based on the MVT presuppose that the current instantaneous rate of return from a patch is known with certainty rather than learned or adjusted (McNamara, Green, & Olsson, 2006), and that the optimal overall rate of return is already somehow known (Green, 1984). In addition, the MVT works only if rate of return always decreases with time in a patch, an assumption which is less plausible for thinking than for foraging.

By contrast, the foraging for surprise model utilizes a process called *melioration*, which is arguably the most psychologically natural and empirically best supported heuristic simplification (Herrnstein, 1997; Herrnstein & Prelec, 1992; Herrnstein, 1982; Davison & McCarthy, 1988). It has very significant advantages over alternative heuristics for attention allocation. Because it bases value on the average rate of return *actually experienced over episodes in an activity*, it makes far more realistic assumptions about what decision makers need to know. Unlike explicit rational models and the MVT, it does not *necessarily* lead to sub-optimality when there is no clear bound on significant information; that is, yet-to-be-discovered unknowns might influence decisions, or returns in a patch may be positively accelerated with time.

The foraging for surprise model works as follows: The value of switching attention to an active predicate summarizes its historical usefulness as a source of surprise and learning: It is proportional to the average absolute change in the predicate's utility activation that has been experienced as a result of switching attention to it and activating new facts. The user may quickly switch attention within the same patch, e.g., to a causally related predicate that became more active because of attention to the first predicate, and so on. In a casually connected cluster, changes in utility activation due to attending to these subsequent predicates propagate through circuits that include the first predicate; thus, a predicate's rate of return takes into account the *patch* of predicates to which it provides entry. Dividing the total change in utility activation at the predicate by the average time during which attention influences it, we get its *rate of return*. The rate of return is updated in the current episode by adding the absolute utility change thus far to the numerator and the amount of time in the episode thus far to the denominator. Thus, the current episode will have little effect if there is extensive prior experience in the patch but may be quite significant if prior experience is sparse (Olsson, 2006; Green, 1984). The updated ratio at the conclusion of the current episode becomes the new baseline.

Knowledge About Time

Since utility gains are seldom linear with time, a decision maker's implicit assessment of an activity's rate of gain is sensitive to the *durations* of experienced episodes over which it was implicitly measured. Some insight into how melioration interacts with selective sampling of episode durations can be obtained by comparing the *value functions* of different activities, that is, the rate of gain that would be experienced if episodes in a patch had a particular duration. The top row of Figure 24.3 illustrates cumulative gains in utility as a function of time in a patch. The bottom row shows the corresponding value functions, obtained by dividing the cumulative gain (y-axis value in the top chart) by time in the patch (the corresponding x-axis value in either

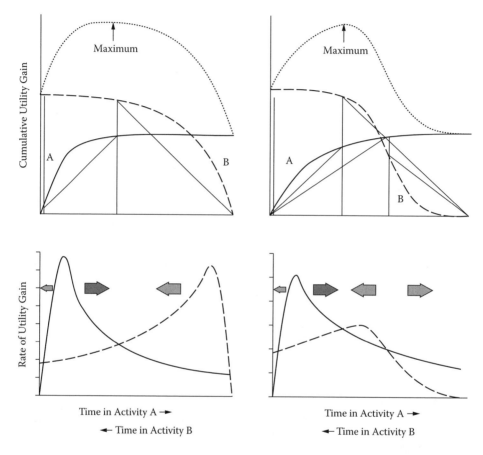

FIGURE 24.3   Value functions. The top row of charts represents *cumulative utility gain* as a function of time in activity A (solid curves, increasing with time in A from left to right) and in activity B (dashed curves, w increasing ith time in B from right to left). Dotted curve is the *total utility* gained from both activities for a given allocation of total time between A and B. Vertical lines indicate equilibrium allocations, for which the two activities have equal rates of gain. (Rate is cumulative gain from the activity divided by time spent in the activity, corresponding to slopes of lines drawn between cumulative utility at the beginning of an activity to cumulative utility at the equilibrium time allocation.) The bottom row of charts shows the *rates of utility gain* for each activity as a function of different allocations of time between them. According to melioration, whenever A's rate of gain is higher than B's, more time will be allocated to A (thick arrow pointing right). Whenever B's rate of gain is higher than A's, more time will be allocated to B (thick arrows pointing left). Equilibria occur when rates become equal, corresponding to intersection of the two curves. The left and right columns represent scenarios with different value functions for B.

chart). Each chart shows two mutually incompatible activities, A and B, that divide a time interval (the length of the x-axis) between them. Because A and B are incompatible (e.g., deliberation versus immediate action, or deliberating in one patch versus another), time spent in one equals the total time minus time spent in the other. A specific division of the interval between an episode in A and an episode in B corresponds to a point on the x-axis. Time to the left of that point was spent in activity A, after which the decision maker switched to activity B; time to the right of that point was then spent in activity B. Notice that Figure 24.3 plots gains in B from right to left. Since B starts when the decision maker switches out of A, this is counterintuitive; however, it enables us to compare the returns from both tasks for every possible allocation of time. For *any chosen time allocation between A and B,* represented as a point on the x-axis, the corresponding y-axis values for the A and B curves show how much utility will have been gained from A and B, respectively, at the end of the time period. The dotted line is the sum, which a rational model would try to maximize.

According to R/M's melioration rule, the allocation of time among activities is governed by a simple preconscious strategy: Spend more time in activities with higher rates of return and less time in activities with lower rates of return. For example, on one occasion, the decision maker switches attention out of patch A into patch B at some point on the x-axis, and spends the rest of the given time in patch B. Suppose that the decision maker receives a higher rate of return from patch A than from patch B. According to melioration, on the next occasion the decision maker will spend a bit more time in A and a bit less time in B; that is, the selected point on the x-axis will shift to the right. (Of course, it would shift left if the decision maker experienced a higher rate of return in B.) If the extra time in A does not produce a proportionate increase in the utility gained from A, its rate of return will decline. If the reduction in time does not result in a proportionate decrease in the utility gained from B, B's rate of return will increase. Repeated over occasions of decision making, these adjustments produce exclusive preference for an activity whose experienced rate of gain remains higher than other activities as more time is allocated to it, eliminate activities whose experienced rate of gain remains lower as less time is allocated to it, and in all other cases, adjust time allocation until experienced rates of gain are equal across the surviving activities.

Because of melioration, decision makers do not need global knowledge of how time affects value. Value functions are ecological constraints that people adapt to by sampling specific durations (i.e., points on the horizontal axis) and learning the results. Melioration is a local adjustment process among activities rather than a rational central executive.

The left column of Figure 24.3 shows that melioration works well when activities A and B both have negatively accelerated returns.* The main thing to notice is the equilibrium represented by crossing lines—equal rates of return, in the lower chart. The equilibrium is (1) stable, because deviations will be corrected, (2) likely to be reached by incremental adjustments regardless of the initially sampled durations

---

* In an associative network, the value of additional periods of deliberation in a patch ordinarily declines both as attention moves further away from decision outcomes and as other predicates in the patch become active. Declining returns may occur for other reasons as well. Marginal benefits will decrease and marginal costs rise as the "low-hanging fruit" is depleted. Animals become satiated with food and people with topics of thought. Additional samples have a decreasing impact on the accuracy of population estimates.

of the two activities, and (3) very close to the global maximum rate of return (i.e., it gives more time to the more productive activity, B); in any case, returns are flat over a wide region near the equilibrium. The same charts (left column of Figure 24.3) can illustrate favorable conditions for choosing among patches and for deciding whether to deliberate or act. With regard to the latter, suppose that A is deliberation that delays irreversible commitment to some action, and B represents irreversible commitment to the action at the expense of A. The value of pushing action B forward by any fixed amount of time is represented by the corresponding size of the increase in B's value from right to left. The benefit of more timeliness declines with increasing immediacy of action (i.e., proximity to the left corner), just as the benefit of more deliberation declines with time attending to patch A (i.e., proximity to the right corner). The appropriate balance will be found by incremental adjustments from virtually any starting sample along the horizontal axis. Decreasing returns are a *necessary* feature of proposed optimizing heuristics. Fu (2007) proposes that they are an "ecological invariant" in representative information-seeking environments. The foraging for surprise model explains why diminishing returns promote effective performance, but it does not *assume* or *need* them.

Returns may increase over time spent deliberating when predicates in a patch depend on one another for value, like pieces of a single puzzle. This may occur because value is not realized until predicates are combined into a single story that is evaluated as a whole, or until later items have been checked to see if they overturn interpretations of earlier items, prompting the emergence of a new story. In addition, when the value of a patch is uncertain, initial results may be useful primarily as indicators of unknown unknowns; that is, they raise previously unasked questions that can be answered by seeking other items in the patch (Olsson & Brown, 2006). In sum, positively accelerating returns distinguish foraging for ideas from foraging for food.

The rightmost column of Figure 24.3 shows that positively accelerating returns for an activity (B) make adaptation more difficult. As before, there is a stable equilibrium involving both A and B that is close to the global maximum. However, there is a much narrower region of starting points from which decision makers can reach this equilibrium. Outside this region, deviations are amplified rather than corrected. As a result, decision makers' initial experiences have a large influence on the size of returns they ultimately realize. If decision makers' initial inclination favors activity A (e.g., deliberating in patch A or pushing forward some action A), episodes of attending to patch B will be short, and hence unproductive; melioration will allocate even more time to A until patch B is neglected altogether. The decision maker will receive a significantly lower total return in the absence of an intervention, like mentoring, that forces exposure to B for periods long enough to realize its value.[*] If we suppose, on the other hand, that A is deliberation and B is pushing action forward in time, the opposite problem occurs. If decision makers initially deliberate too long (proximity to right corner), the costs of further delay may become vanishingly small because the damage has been done; melioration may lead them to deliberate even more on future occasions, until they are virtually incapable of acting effectively (even though they would have done better by not deliberating at all). Yet another occasion for these effects is afforded by the

---

[*] See papers in Fiedler and Juslin (2006) for a discussion of decision errors due to limited experiential sampling.

extra time required to switch attention from one patch to another. If deliberation starts in patch A, the interruption penalty that would be incurred by switching to B may lead decision makers to persist inordinately long in A.

All of these predictions have training implications. Decision makers can be trained to deal with interdependent evidence, in part by learning to base foraging decisions on meaningful patches, and in part by spending enough time in a patch to realize its value. They can practice acting quickly to realize the value of timely action and practice shifting attention to realize the value of deliberation. They should learn how to factor tasks into components with varying degrees of uncertainty and varying costs of delayed commitment.

Knowledge About Uncertainty

As we have seen, the value of an activity reflects previously experienced rates of return updated by current results. It can also be adjusted in the light of other cues, which indicate that rates of return will be lower or higher than average. In the case of deliberation, these cues pertain to uncertainty. Thus, the value of deliberation in the foraging for surprise model is the product of two ratios. The first (as discussed) is the average swing in utility caused by deliberating in a patch, divided by time in the patch; the second is current uncertainty, divided by the average uncertainty for problems of the same type. The first captures the costs of the errors prevented by deliberation (i.e., stakes); the second captures the probability of errors in the absence of further deliberation. Without some uncertainty, the value of deliberation falls to zero, and unless the product of stakes and uncertainty is higher than the associated cost of delayed action, melioration will direct attention away from deliberation.*

Uncertainty is inferred from (1) specific *known uncertainties* in the active predicate that provides entry to the patch, and (2) the *novelty* of the problem as a whole, implying the possibility of *unknown unknowns*. Known uncertainty is the sum of the measures of *incompleteness*, *conflict*, and *lack of resolution* for the active predicate. The possibility of unknown unknowns is based in part on *general cues*, for example, associations of situation and task attributes with lack of experience or poor performance, and in part on the implausibility of the *explicit assumptions* that have had to be adopted thus far to reconcile the current core conclusion with other information.

The model predicts details of proficient decision-making performance observed in incidents such as the Libyan gunboat example. For example, if known uncertainties are resolved by adopting explicit assumptions (as they were for the *opportunity* patch and the *means* patch in the gunboat example), the perceived *novelty* of the situation grows, increasing the chance that the decision maker will continue deliberation even in the absence of *known* uncertainty (as the captain in the gunboat example did by shifting attention to the *localization* patch). A patch's relevance in deliberation can be affected not only by the patch, but also by facts and assumptions elsewhere in active memory. In the Libyan gunboat example, the prioritization of patches based on known uncertainties changed dramatically when a new core conclusion was adopted

---

* The new foraging for surprise formula is roughly consistent with the original qualitative formulation of the quick test: deliberate only if costs of errors outweigh the costs of delay and the problem is uncertain.

(e.g., *opportunity* and *means* were no longer of interest given *nonhostile intent*, but *speeding up, turning toward own ship,* and *ignoring warnings* were of greater interest). If *known uncertainties* are resolved by facts discovered in the patch (and new uncertainties are not revealed at the same time), the value of deliberating in that patch declines. For example, given the core conclusion of *nonhostile intent*, the captain quickly found a satisfactory explanation for *turning toward own ship*, that is, *coincidence*, supported by observations of the large number of U.S. ships in the area. When an innovative solution emerges with significantly fewer assumptions than average (e.g., *the gunboat was looking for targets of opportunity*), the novelty of the situation declines, and the trade-off between action and deliberation shifts in favor of action on the new solution.

Melioration can also be applied to the decision to keep or reject the current core conclusion, yielding more predictions. The value of the core conclusion is inversely related to the implausibility of the assumptions required to make it fit, divided by the time spent deliberating since it was adopted. Because no deliberation has occurred regarding any *new* core conclusion, its value is the inverse of the average of this rate in similarly complex and unfamiliar problems. Melioration implies that the current core conclusion is rejected, and the explicit assumptions supporting it are dropped, when its value falls below this average. (The initial value of a new core conclusion is the average, which is then updated by new results.) This rule takes the novelty and complexity of the situation into account when deciding how long to work with the current solution. The more challenging the situation, the more assumptions that are tolerated in the story supporting a given core conclusion (e.g., the captain stayed with *hostile intent* until three separate assumptions were needed, about *opportunity, means,* and *localization*). Moreover, the expected implausibility of assumptions for an *alternative* core conclusion is only slightly less than that required for the rejected core conclusion. In this case, assumptions required for the *nonhostile intent* story—pertaining to *speeding up, venturing into harm's way,* and *ignoring warnings*—were comparable to those for *hostile intent.*

Each component of the value formula corresponds to a category of factors shown empirically to influence metacognitive assessments, such as *judgments of learning* after studying material to be tested later, *feeling of knowing* prior to retrieving the answer to a question, and *confidence* in answers that have been retrieved (Overschelde, 2008; Reder, 1996). First, these assessments are influenced, to varying degrees, by so-called direct access to memory traces, that is, initial retrieval results and the effort or time required to obtain them. In the foraging for surprise model, these are represented by utility gains and time thus far in the current episode, and by known unknowns in active predicates. Second, metacognitive assessments may be inferred from factors not directly related to traces of the material, for example, the quantity and familiarity of cues pertaining to the task. These factors are represented in the model by novelty and the concomitant possibility of unknown unknowns. Third, assessments are influenced by stored knowledge about knowledge, represented in the present model by the baseline value of deliberating on particular topics and the average rate of required assumptions. The model generates testable predictions about the relationships among all relevant factors that influence metacognitive regulation.

Time Management Is Expert Behavior

Recent studies provide direct evidence that decision makers *learn from their experience in real-world tasks* to monitor and regulate their use of time. Khoo and Mosier (2008) found that pilots with more automation experience took more time and accessed more information about a possible engine fire when time pressure was not severe than when it was. Although they were clearly aware of the time factors, less experienced pilots did not adapt the time they spent or the information they accessed to time pressure. Cohen and colleagues found very similar interactions in two studies in which experienced pilots adapted their time to both time pressure and uncertainty, while less experienced pilots, despite having the requisite information, did not. In one study (Freeman, Cohen, & Thompson, 1998), the costs of delaying a diversion decision were manipulated by varying the amount of remaining fuel. Highly experienced pilots waited longer to divert when the cost of delay was lower (i.e., they had more fuel) and acted sooner when the cost of delay was higher; less experienced pilots took about the same amount of time to act regardless of how much fuel they had (Figure 24.4a). Yet there was no significant difference in the relevant *knowledge* possessed by the two groups (Figure 24.4b). A second study (Cohen, Adelman, & Thompson, 2000) varied *known uncertainty*, represented by inconsistency of reports from different sources (company dispatch, air traffic control, and company airport operations center) about the estimated time of clearance for landing at the destination. More experienced pilots took more time before diverting when reports were inconsistent than when they were consistent. Less experienced pilots took the same amount of time in both cases (Figure 24.4b and c). Uncertainty led more experienced pilots to focus inquiries on factors directly related to the known uncertainty (Figure 24.4d and e) and to postpone inquiries about other matters (Figure 24.4f). Uncertainty led less experienced pilots to delay *all* inquiries. The quick test in R/M predicts the behavior of the experienced pilots: Action is delayed, and active information acquisition and deliberative problem solving occur, when relevant factors are known to be uncertain and irreversible action can be postponed.

Contrasting R/M With Another View of Time Management

The introduction of this chapter mentioned two objectives: identify future directions for NDM research and call certain habitual assumptions into question. To accomplish these, it is necessary to define more sharply than usual some of the *differences* between R/M and other NDM approaches. A recent proposal by Klein et al. (2007) provides an instructive contrast. They hypothesize, as a stopping rule, that "sensemaking usually ceases when the data and frame are brought into congruence" (p. 126). If this were correct, time management would be a by-product of knowledge organization and would not require regulatory skills based on implicit learning about costs and benefits, as described by R/M. A comparison of the two positions will increase understanding of both and bring hidden assumptions to the surface.

Klein et al. (2007) say that any continuation past their stopping rule is "mere grinding out of inferences." The question they do not address is how, in a challenging and novel situation, a decision maker can *know this in advance*. Nothing guarantees that

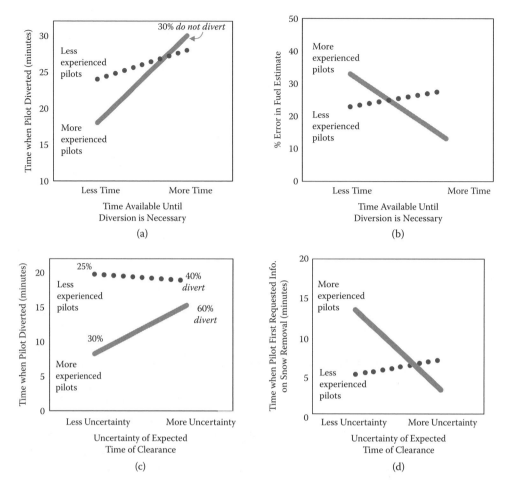

FIGURE 24.4   Results of experiments with commercial airline pilots. (a) With more time available, experienced pilots waited longer before diverting; available time had no effect on diversion by less experienced pilots. (b) There was no significant difference between more and less experienced pilots in accuracy of beliefs about available fuel. (c) Uncertainty led experienced pilots to wait longer before diverting, but did not influence time taken by less experienced pilots. (d) Uncertainty led experienced pilots to inquire earlier about progress of snow removal, but had no effect on such requests by less experienced pilots.

elements outside a frame will not turn out to be relevant, unless we define frames as fixed and isolated patterns, with *no possible connections* to significant unknown unknowns outside themselves. The data-frame congruence stopping rule assumes that decisions are made in an artificial small world—that there is a bright line delimiting the correct and complete theory of the situation (i.e., frame) along with the data it declares relevant. Without that illusion, how does the decision maker know that there is no evidence, hypothesis, or assumption whose importance has not yet been recognized? Klein et al. have gotten the case for a stopping rule backwards. The problem is not that continuation would mean grinding out useless inferences. The true concern is that *it might not*: In realistically complex problems, the possibility cannot be ruled out that another inference might significantly *improve* the response

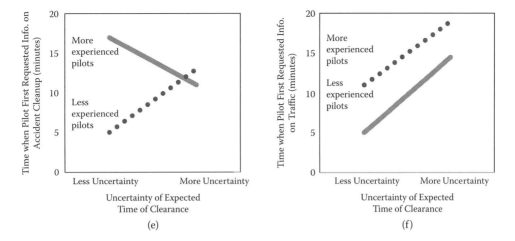

FIGURE 24.4 Results of experiments with commercial airline pilots. (e) Uncertainty led experienced pilots to inquire earlier for relevant information about accident cleanup, but led less experienced pilots to postpone inquiries. (f) Uncertainty led both more and less experienced pilots to postpone requests for less relevant traffic information.

by overthrowing previous assumptions. A stopping rule is needed to balance this possibility against pragmatic demands for timely action. But data-frame congruence ignores both sides of the trade-off between knowledge and timeliness.[*]

Ironically, the data-frame congruence stopping condition contradicts the central constructivist claims of data-frame theory: that data are defined and selected by frames, which are put together on the spot (*just in time*) from smaller "units" (p. 132) and which may be modified and elaborated during sensemaking. If neither data nor frames are fixed in advance, but are dynamically and reciprocally redefined in the course of deliberation (like working memory and primed episodic memory in R/M), data-frame congruence can be no more than a *temporary equilibrium* between data thus far defined and knowledge thus far integrated. Such temporary equilibria can be passed over by proficient decision makers like speed bumps (specifically, interruption delays associated with changing patches in the foraging formula) rather than barriers to pragmatically justified exploration and extension of knowledge. A constructivist account requires that the stopping rule determine the frame, not the reverse.[†]

---

[*] The assumption that there are context-independent criteria for good reasoning, or the sufficiency of an argument, is inherited from the syntactic definition of proof in deductive logic. Although Klein's stopping rule is semantic, it is equally nonpragmatic. Klein et al. (2007) cite plausible reasoning and nonmonotonic logic, but they miss the main point, that real-world (as opposed to small-world) reasoning always remains open to defeat by unsuspected problems. See Cohen, Salas, and Reidel (2001) and Cohen et al. (2006) for a discussion of why stopping rules for "plausible reasoning" must be decision oriented and why the quest for "deduction-lite" argument criteria fails.

[†] Almost as an afterthought, Klein et al. (2007) add a significant qualification to their main account (p. 126): "Note that sensemaking may continue if the potential benefits of further exploration are sufficiently strong." Unfortunately, they do not specify what benefits these are. Similarly, on p. 136, Klein et al. say, "There are times when people try to make sense of events because they believe they can deepen their understanding, even without any surprise" (i.e., known unknowns). But they do not explain when or why "deeper understanding" would or should be sought. They describe the example of a general officer who recognizes a pattern of enemy positions as diagnostic of a particular type of unit. Instead of stopping because of the supposed "data-frame congruence," the general proceeds to look for enemy emplacements associated with larger-scale patterns of higher-echelon units. For R/M, this is expected expert behavior when the costs of errors outweigh the costs of delay and the situation is novel. For data-frame theory, it is inexplicable.

The other half of the data-frame congruence stopping rule—that sensemaking "continues as long as key data elements remain unexplained or key components of a frame remain ambiguous" (p. 126)—is even more puzzling in its neglect of pragmatic considerations. A decision maker might stop deliberating and act before *known* unknowns are resolved, or leave an *undepleted* patch to explore a new patch that promises higher rates of return.

Conclusion

NDM was spawned by the second generation of problem-solving research, when cognitive scientists began to identify expertise with substantive knowledge (Chase & Simon, 1973) or a rich ensemble of finely differentiated frames (Klein et al. 2007) rather than with general purpose reasoning methods. Reasoning methods in this paradigm were assumed to be similar for all levels of expertise. For example, Klein et al. (2007) report in the context of one of their studies that novices and experts "showed no differences in their reasoning processes" (p. 126). In support of this, they cite similarities based on a very coarse first-generation classification of reasoning types: "Both [experts and novices] tried to infer cause-effect connections... both tried to infer effects... both experts and novices were not going about the task in accordance with the precepts of deductive logic." This logic, however, is comparable to arguing that because both expert and novice writers use nouns and verbs, there are no differences in their linguistic skills.

R/M is based on an emerging third-generation view (Holyoak, 1991) that expertise is *adaptation* of both knowledge and reasoning to the requirements of the domain in question, which typically includes both routine and novel situations. The trade-offs that determine how much time to take for information acquisition and reflection originate both in the underlying properties of memory and attention and in the ecologies to which proficient decision makers adapt. Ecologies shape implicit assessments about the potential payoff and time course of deliberation, which in turn shape attentional strategies needed to activate relevant knowledge in novel situations. The foraging for surprise model predicts that thinking strategies will improve as decision makers learn to factor tasks into components that vary in uncertainty and cost of delay, acquire better understanding of how knowledge is organized into patches, sample value functions by deliberating in patches for varying amounts of time, become sensitive to known unknowns, novelty, and explicit assumptions, and learn to update their value assessments accordingly. In short, satisfactory management of time for deliberation requires emphasis not only on substantive domain knowledge but also on strategic skill.[*]

R/M provides a naturalistic basis for critical thinking training that enhances rather than replaces intuition. One variant of such training is called STEPS,[†] in which trainees master the following steps: *story*, to find and reconcile known unknowns with the core conclusion; *test*, to challenge apparently supporting evidence to find and explain unknown unknowns; *evaluate*, to assess a core conclusion in terms of the assumptions required to make the story work; *plan*, to make plans more robust against known or unknown unknowns; and *stop*, to bypass or halt deliberation at any time when costs of delay are higher than potential benefits. Training with STEPS has utilized both tactical decision games (e.g., Cohen et al., 2000a) and live simulator sessions (e.g., Cohen et al., 1998a; Freeman & Cohen, 1996) for practice and feedback. Six different experimental tests of STEPS training, mostly in counterbalanced pretest-posttest comparisons, demonstrated that it successfully influenced targeted behaviors and produced decisions that were more similar to those of experts than the decisions of untrained officers (e.g., Cohen et al., 2000a; Cohen & Thompson, 2001; Freeman & Cohen, 1996). The foraging for surprise model introduced in this chapter suggests some interesting avenues for expansion of this training, such as a more intensive effort to familiarize decision makers with the likely results and pitfalls of specific ways of combining intuition and deliberation, deliberation and action, and deliberation on different topics.

Acknowledgments

The work described here was supported by contracts with Cognitive Technologies, Inc., from the Office of Naval Research, the National Science Foundation, and the Army Research Institute. Thanks to Bryan Thompson and Lokendra Shastri, who were indispensable partners throughout the development of Shruti R/M, and to Shastri for his original development of Shruti.

---

[*] Klein et al. (2007) downplay the importance of their own evidence that experts and novices differ in thinking skills: "A few of the novices…at first seemed reluctant to speculate too much without more data. None of the experts exhibited this scruple." They cite other findings that "novices were less likely to notice when expectancies were violated…novices went down the garden path [held on to an inaccurate interpretation] but experts broke free" (p. 127). Klein et al. attribute the latter to experts' having "more differentiated frames than novices," that is, more expectations to be violated rather than better strategies for handling violations. But the story is inconsistent: They imply that expectancies were violated for both groups. They also state (correctly) in the same paragraph that "a person will not start to question a frame simply as a result of receiving data that do not conform to the frame." In fact, there is abundant evidence that experts take more time to verify their conclusions (Chi, Glaser, & Rees, 1982; Larkin, 1981; Larkin, McDermott, Simon, & Simon, 1980) and have greater ability to correct problems and handle exceptional conditions (Feltovich, Spiro, & Coulson, 2006; McLennan, Pavlou, & Omodei, 2005; Rudolph, 2003; Shanteau, 1992). On a longer timescale, according to Ericsson (2005), experts become experts by intentionally disrupting an achieved level of performance in order to achieve a wider convergence. The destabilization of established equilibria in order to find better ones is a primary engine for creating new knowledge.

[†] The training is called STEP in publications based on the earliest version. The S was added to make the time management aspect more salient, but does not represent any change in content.

References

Bargh, J. A. (2000). Beyond behaviorism: On the automaticity of higher mental processes. *Psychological Bulletin, 126*(6), 925–945.

Bargh, J. A. (Ed.). (2007). *Social psychology and the unconscious: The automaticity of higher mental processes.* New York, NY: Psychology Press.

Brunswick, E. (1955). Representative design and probabilistic theory in a functional psychology. *Psychological Review, 62*, 193–217. Reprinted in K. R. Hammond & T. R. Stewart (Eds.), *The essential Brunswick* (pp. 135–156). Oxford, UK: Oxford University Press.

Charnov, E. L. (1976). Optimal foraging, the marginal value theorem. *Theoretical Population Biology, 9*(2), 129–136.

Chase, W., & Simon, H. (1973). The mind's eye in chess. In W. Chase (Ed.), *Visual information processing* (pp. 215–281). New York, NY: Academic Press.

Chi, M., Glaser, R., & Rees, E. (1982). Expertise in problem solving. In R. Steinberg (Ed.), *Advances in the psychology of human intelligence* (Vol. 1, pp. 7–75). Hillsdale, NJ: Lawrence Erlbaum Associates.

Cohen, M. (1993). The naturalistic basis of decision biases. In G. Klein, J. Orasanu, R. Calderwood, & C. Zsambok (Eds.), *Decision making in action: Models and methods* (pp. 51–99). Norwood, NJ: Ablex. Retrieved from http://www.cog-tech.com/papers/chapters/biases/biases.pdf

Cohen, M., Freeman, J. T., & Thompson, B. B. (1998). Critical thinking skills in tactical decision making: A model and a training method. In J. Cannon-Bowers & E. Salas (Eds.), *Decision-making under stress: Implications for training & simulation* (pp. 155–189). Washington, DC: American Psychological Association. Retrieved from http://www.cog-tech.com/papers/chapters/tadmus/tadmus.pdf

Cohen, M., Freeman, J. T., & Wolf, S. (1996). Meta-recognition in time stressed decision making: Recognizing, critiquing, and correcting. *Human Factors, 38*(2), 206–219. Retrieved from http://www.cog-tech.com/papers/humfac/hf_1996a.pdf

Cohen, M., Parasuraman, R., & Freeman, J. T. (1998). Trust in decision aids: A model and its training implications. In *Proceedings of the 1998 Command and Control Research and Technology Symposium* (DoD C4ISR Cooperative Research Program). Retrieved from http://www.cog-tech.com/papers/Trust/C2_Trust_paper_revised.pdf

Cohen, M., Thompson, B. B., Adelman, L., Bresnick, T. A., Tolcott, M. A., & Freeman, J. T. (1995). *Rapid capturing of battlefield mental models.* Arlington, VA: Cognitive Technologies. Retrieved from http://www.cog-tech.com/papers/mentalmodels/MentalModelsPhaseI.pdf

Cohen, M. S., Adelman, L., Bresnick, T. A., Marvin, F., Salas, E., & Riedel, S. (2006). Dialogue as medium (and message) for training critical thinking. In R. Hoffman (Ed.), *Expertise out of context.* Mahwah, NJ: Erlbaum. Retrieved from http://www.cog-tech.com/papers/Dialogue/DialogueMediumMessage.pdf

Cohen, M. S., Adelman, L., & Thompson, B. T. (2000). *Experimental investigation of uncertainty, stakes, and time in pilot decision making.* Arlington, VA: Cognitive Technologies.

Cohen, M. S., & Freeling, A. N. S. (1981). *The impact of information on decisions: Command and control system evaluation.* Falls Church, VA: Decision Science Consortium. Retrieved from http://www.cog-tech.com/papers/Scanned/Bayesian/Information.pdf

Cohen, M. S., Salas, E., & Riedel, S. (2001). *Critical thinking: Challenges, possibilities, and purpose.* Arlington VA: Cognitive Technologies. Retrieved from http://www.cog-tech.com/papers/CriticalThinking/Phase_I_%20Report.pdf

Cohen, M. S., & Thompson, B. B. (2001). Training teams to take initiative: Critical thinking in novel situations. In E. Salas (Ed.), *Advances in human performance and cognitive engineering research* (Vol. 1, pp. 251–291). Amsterdam, Netherlands: JAI. Retrieved from http://www.cog_tech.com/papers/CriticalThinking/Training%20Critical%20Thinking%20for%20Initiative%20HFES%202002.pdf

Cohen, M. S., & Thompson, B. B. (2005). Metacognitive processes for uncertainty handling: Connectionist implementation of a cognitive model. In M. Anderson & T. Oates (Eds.), *Metacognition in computation: Papers from the 2005 symposium* (pp. 36–41). Menlo Park, CA: American Association of Artificial Intelligence.

Cohen, M. S., Thompson, B. B., Adelman, L., Bresnick, T. A., Shastri, L., & Riedel, S. (2000a). *Training critical thinking for the battlefield: Training system and evaluation* (Vol. II). Arlington VA: Cognitive Technologies. Retrieved from http://www.cog-tech.com/papers/mentalmodels/Vol_IITraining.pdf

Cohen, M. S., Thompson, B. B., Adelman, L., Bresnick, T. A., Shastri, L., & Riedel, S. (2000b). *Training critical thinking for the battlefield: Modeling and simulation of battlefield critical thinking* (Vol. III). Arlington, VA: Cognitive Technologies. Retrieved from http://www.cogtech.com/papers/mentalmodels/Vol_IIISimulation.pdf

Davison, M., & McCarthy, D. (1988). *The matching law: A research review*. Hillsdale, NJ: Lawrence Erlbaum.

Dunlosky, J., & Bjork, R. A. (2008). *Handbook of metamemory and memory*. New York, NY: Psychology Press.

Endsley, M. R. (2000). Theoretical underpinnings of situation awareness: A critical review. In M. R. Endsley & D. J. Garland (Eds.), *Situation awareness analysis and measurement* (pp. 3–32). Mahwah, NJ: Erlbaum.

Ericsson, K. (2005). Superior decision making as an integral quality of expert performance: Insights into the mediating mechanisms and their acquisition through deliberate practice. In H. Montgomery, R. Lipshitz, & B. Brehmer (Eds.), *How professionals make decisions* (pp. 135–167). Mahwah, NJ: Lawrence Erlbaum Associates.

Feltovich, P. J., Spiro, R. J., & Coulson, R. L. (2006). Issues of expert flexibility in contexts characterized by complexity and change. In P. Feltovich, K. M. Ford, & R. R. Hoffman (Eds.), *Expertise in context* (pp. 125–146). Cambridge, UK: Cambridge University Press.

Fiedler, K., & Juslin, P. (Eds.). (2006). *Information sampling and adaptive cognition*. Cambridge, UK: Cambridge University Press.

Flach, J. M. (2008). Mind the gap: A skeptical view of macrocognition. In J. M. Schraagen, L. G. Militello, T. Ormerod, & R. Lipshitz (Eds.), *Naturalistic decision making and macrocognition* (pp. 27–40). Burlington, VT: Ashgate.

Freeman, J., & Cohen, M. S. (1996). *Training for complex decision-making: A test of instruction based on the recognition/metacognition model*. Paper presented at the Proceedings of the 1996 Command and Control Research and Technology Symposium, Monterey, CA.

Freeman, J., Cohen, M. S., & Thompson, B. (1998). *Time-stressed decision-making in the cockpit*. Paper presented at the Association for Information Systems Americas Conference, Baltimore, MD.

Fu, W.-T. (2007). A rational-ecological approach to the exploration/exploitation tradeoffs: Bounded rationality and suboptimal performance. In W. D. Gray (Ed.), *Integrated models of cognitive systems* (pp. 165–179). Oxford, UK: Oxford University.

Green, R. F. (1984). Stopping rules for optimal foragers. *American Naturalist, 123*(1), 30–43.

Herrnstein, R. J. (1982). Melioration as behavioral dynamism. In M. L. Commons, A. Kacelnik, & S. J. Shettleworth (Eds.), *Quantitative analysis of behavior: Matching and maximizing accounts* (Vol. II, pp. 433–458). Cambridge, MA: Ballinger.

Herrnstein, R. J. (1997). *The matching law: Papers in psychology and economics*. New York, NY: Russell Sage Foundation.

Herrnstein, R. J., & Prelec, D. (1992). Melioration. In G. Loewenstein & J. Elster (Eds.), *Choice over time* (pp. 235–263). New York, NY: Russell Sage Foundation.

Holyoak, K. (1991). Symbolic connectionism: Toward third-generation theories of expertise. In K. A. Ericsson & J. Smith (Eds.), *Toward a general theory of expertise*. Cambridge, UK: Cambridge University Press.

Khoo, Y.-L., & Mosier, K. (2008). The impact of time pressure and experience on information search and decision-making processes. *Journal of Cognitive Engineering and Decision Making, 2*(4), 275–294.

Klein, G. (1993). *Naturalistic decision making: Implications for design*. Wright Patterson Air Force Base, OH: Crew System Ergonomics Information Analysis Center.

Klein, G. (1998). *Sources of power*. Cambridge, MA: MIT Press.

Klein, G. (2000). Analysis of situation awareness from critical incident reports. In M. R. Endsley & D. J. Garland (Eds.), *Situation awareness analysis and measurement* (pp. 51–71). Mahwah, NJ: Erlbaum.

Klein, G., Phillips, J. K., Rall, E. L., & Peluso, D. A. (2007). A data-frame theory of sensemaking. In R. R. Hoffman (Ed.), *Expertise out of context* (pp. 113–155). Mahwah, NJ: Erlbaum.

Larkin, J. (1981). Enriching formal knowledge: A model for learning to solve textbook physics problems. In J. Anderson (Ed.), *Cognitive skills and their acquisition* (pp. 311–344). Hillsdale, NJ: Lawrence Erlbaum Associates.

Larkin, J., McDermott, J., Simon, D. P., & Simon, H. A. (1980). Expert and novice performance in solving physics problems. *Science, 20*(208), 1335–1342.

Laurence, D. H. (Ed.). (1985). *George Bernard Shaw collected letters: 1911–1925* (Vol. 3). New York, NY: Viking.

Logan, G. (1988). Toward an instance theory of automatization. *Psychological Review, 95*, 492–527.

Logan, G. (2004). Attention, automaticity, and executive control. In A. Healy (Ed.), *Experimental cognitive psychology and its applications: Festschrift in honor of Lyle Bourne, Walter Kintsch, and Thomas Landauer* (pp. 129–139). Washington, DC: American Psychological Association Press.

Logan, G., Taylor, S. E., & Etherton, J. L. (1996). Attention in the acquisition and expression of automaticity. *Journal of Experimental Psychology: Learning, Memory, and Cognition, 22*(3), 620–638.

McLennan, J., Pavlou, O., & Omodei, M. M. (2005). Cognitive control processes discriminate between better versus poorer performance by fire ground commanders. In H. Montgomery, R. Lipshitz, & B. Brehmer (Eds.), *How professionals make decisions* (pp. 2009–2022). Mahwah, NJ: Lawrence Erlbaum Associates.

McNamara, J. M., Green, R. F., & Olsson, O. (2006). Bayes theorem and its applications in animal behavior. *Oikos, 112*, 243–251.

Monsell, S., & Driver, J. (2000). Banishing the control homunculus. In S. Monsell & J. Driver (Eds.), *Control of cognitive processes: Attention and performance XVIII*. Cambridge, MA: MIT.

Newell, A. (1981). *The knowledge level*. Pittsburgh, PA: Carnegie Mellon University.

Nisbett, R., & Ross, L. (1980). *Human inference: Strategies and shortcomings of social judgment*. Englewood Cliffs, NJ: Prentice Hall.

Olsson, O., & Brown, J. S. (2006). The foraging benefits of information and the penalty of ignorance. *Oikos, 112*, 260–273.

Omodei, M. M., McLennan, J., Elliott, G. C., Wearing, A. J., & Clancy, J. M. (2005). "More is better?": A bias toward overuse of resources in naturalistic decision-making settings. In H. Montgomery, R. Lipshitz, & B. Brehmer (Eds.), *How professionals make decisions* (pp. 29-42). Mahwah, NJ: Lawrence Erlbaum Associates.

Orasanu, J., & Strauch, B. (1994). Temporal factors in aviation decision making. In *Proceedings of the Human Factors and Ergonomics Society 38th Annual Meeting* (pp. 935–939). Santa Monica, CA: Human Factors and Ergonomics Society.

Overschelde, J. P. V. (2008). Metacognition: Knowing about knowing. In J. Dunlosky & R. A. Bjork (Eds.), *Handbook of metamemory and memory*. New York, NY: Psychology Press.

Pearl, J. (1989). *Probabilistic reasoning in intelligent systems: Networks of plausible inference*. San Mateo, CA: Morgan Kaufmann Publishers.

Pearl, J. (2000). *Causality: Models, reasoning, and inference*. Cambridge UK: Cambridge University Press.

Peters, D. J., Jackson, L. A., Phillips, J. K., & Ross, K. G. (2008). The time to decide: How awareness and collaboration affect the command decision making. In A. Kott (Ed.), *Battle of cognition: The future information-rich warfare and the mind of the commander* (pp. 194-211). Westport CT: Praeger Security.

Pirolli, P. (2007). *Information foraging theory: Adaptive interaction with information*. Oxford, UK: Oxford University.

Pirolli, P., & Card, S. (1999). Information foraging. *Psychological Review, 106*(4), 643–675.

Reder, L. M. (Ed.). (1996). *Implicit memory and metacognition*. Hillsdale, NJ: Erlbaum.

Rudolph, J. W. (2003). *Into the big muddy and out again: Error persistence and crisis management in the operating room*. Dissertation, Boston College, The Carroll Graduate School of Management, Department of Organization Studies.

Rumelhart, D. E., Smolensky, P., McClelland, J. L., & Hinton, G. E. (1986). Schemata and sequential thought processes in PDP models. In J. L. McClelland, D. E. Rumelhart, & the PDP Research Group (Eds.), *Parallel distributed processing: Explorations in the microstructure of cognition: Psychological and biological models* (Vol. 2, pp. 7–57). Cambridge, MA: The MIT Press.

Schraagen, J. M., Klein, G., & Hoffman, R. (2008). The macrocognition framework of naturalistic decision making. In J. M. Schraagen, L. G. Militello, T. Ormerod, & R. Lipshitz (Eds.), *Naturalistic decision making and macrocognition* (pp. 3–25). Burlington, VT: Ashgate.

Shanteau, J. (1992). The psychology of experts: An alternative view. In G. Wright & F. Bolger (Eds.), *Expertise and decision support*. New York, NY: Plenum Press.

Shastri, L. (1992). *Neurally motivated constraints on the working memory capacity of a production system for parallel processing*. Paper presented at Proceedings of the Fourteenth Conference of the Cognitive Science Society, Bloomington, IN.

Shastri, L. (1999). Advances in Shruti: A neurally motivated model of relational knowledge representation and rapid inference using temporal synchrony. *Applied Intelligence, 11*, 79–108.

Shastri, L. (2001). A computational model of episodic memory formation in the hippocampal system. *Neurocomputing, 38–40*, 889–897.

Shastri, L., & Ajjanagadde, V. (1993). From simple associations to systematic reasoning: A connectionist representation of rules, variables, and dynamic bindings using temporal synchrony. *Brain and Behavioral Sciences, 16*, 417–494.

Shastri, L., & Mani, D. R. (1997). Massively parallel knowledge representation and reasoning: Taking a cue from the brain. In H. K. J. Geller, & C. Suttner (Eds.), *Parallel processing for artificial intelligence 3*. Amsterdam, Netherlands: Elsevier Science.

Shastri, L., & Wendelken, C. (1998). *Soft computing in Shruti: A neurally plausible model of reflexive reasoning and relational information processing*. Paper presented at the Proceedings of Soft-Computing '99, Genoa, Italy.

Shastri, L., & Wendelken, C. (1999). *Knowledge fusion in the large—Taking a cue from the brain*. Paper presented at the Proceedings of the Second International Conference on Information Fusion, Sunnyvale, CA.

Simon, H. A., & Newell, A. (1958). Heuristic problem solving: The next advance in operations research. *Operations Research, 6*(2), 1–10.

Son, L. K., & Kornell, N. (2005). Metaconfidence judgments in rhesus macaques: Explicit versus implicit mechanisms. In H. Terrace & J. Metcalfe (Eds.), *The missing link in cognition: Origins of self-reflective consciousness*. Oxford, UK: Oxford University Press.

Stephens, D. W. (2007). Models of information use. In D. W. Stephens, J. S. Brown, & R. C. Ydenberg (Eds.), *Foraging: Behavior and ecology* (pp. 31–58). Chicago, IL: University of Chicago Press.

Stephens, D. W., & Krebs, J. R. (1986). *Foraging theory*. Princeton, NJ: Princeton University Press.

Thompson, B. B., & Cohen, M. S. (1999). Naturalistic decision making and models of computational intelligence. In A. Jagota, T. Plate, L. Shastri, & R. Sun (Eds.), *Connectionist symbol processing: Dead or alive?* (pp. 26–28).

Wendelken, C., & Shastri, L. (2000). *Probabilistic inference and learning in a connectionist causal network*. Paper presented at Proceedings of the Second International Symposium on Neural Computation, Berlin, Germany.

Wendelken, C., & Shastri, L. (2002). *Combining belief and utility in a structured connectionist agent architecture*. Paper presented at Proceedings of Cognitive Science 2002, Fairfax, VA.

Wendelken, C., & Shastri, L. (2003). *Acquisition of concepts and causal rules in SHRUTI*. Paper presented at Proceedings of Cognitive Science 2003, Boston, MA.

Wendelken, C., & Shastri, L. (2005). Connectionist mechanisms for cognitive control. *Neurocomputing, 65–66*, 663–672.

Author Index

A

ABC Research Group, 250, 259
Adami, J. F., 240, 244
Adams, R. J., 236, 243
Adamson, S., 329, 337
Adar Pras, A., 132, 135
Adelman, L., 387, 392, 393
Adler, N. J., 24, 37
AGARD 6, 18,
Ahuvia, A., 120
Airan, M. C., 337
Ajjanagadde, V., 373, 374, 395
Alby, F., 280, 288, 353, 367
Alge, B. J., 171, 185
Alison, L., 275, 276, 279, 283, 284, 285, 286, 288, 289,
    290, 291
Amaldi, P., 169, 186
Anders, S., 67, 311
Anderson, B., 58, 66
Anderson, C. J., 287, 288
Anderson, G. S., 281, 288
Anderson, T. J., 340, 349
Andras, P., 285, 288
Andre, A. D., 195, 198
APACS, 278, 288
Appelbaum, P., 327
Appelbaum, P. S., 327
Arkes, H., 277, 288
Arkes, H. R., 313, 325, 326
Arocha, J. F., 322, 328
Arruda, J., 192, 195, 199
Artman, H., 169, 171, 185
Asch, S., 306, 311
Asch, S. M., 306, 311
Ashby, W. R., 35, 37
Atran, S., 106, 119
Axelrod, R., 355, 367
Ayling, P., 289
Ayton, J., 21

B

Babrow, A. S., 252, 254, 259
Badke-Schaub, P., 91, 94, 95, 96, 100, 101, 102, 104, 171,
    185, 353, 368
Baecker, R., 139, 152
Baker, D. P., 202, 219
Bakera, M. E., 337
Ballas, J. A., 311
Baltes, B., 170, 185

Banbury, C. M., 49, 52
Banks, A., 262, 273, 280, 289, 353, 357, 367, 368
Banks, S., 327
Bargh, J. A., 372, 377, 392
Baron, J., 287, 290
Barsade, S. G., 255, 259
Bartel, P., 317, 325
Bartel, P. A., 317, 325
Bauer, C., 170, 185
Bauman, J., 20
Baumeister, R. F., 277, 288
Baxter, H. C., 206, 219, 241, 244
Bayerl, P. S., 169, 172, 173, 185, 186, 324
Baylog, J. G., 190, 199
Beach, L. R., 92, 101, 102, 237, 243, 252, 259, 315, 319,
    320, 321, 322, 325
Beatty, R., 140, 146, 152
Beecher, M., 197, 199
Beechler, S., 24, 37
Bener, A., 116, 119
Berg, J. S., 10, 18
Berger, C. R., 252, 259
Berman, B., 11, 18
Berman, B. A., 12, 18
Bernoulli, D., 92, 103, 275, 288
Bikson, T. K., 23, 24, 37
Billings, C., 139, 146, 152
Bird, A., 23, 24, 25, 29, 35, 36, 37, 39, 106, 120
Bisantz, A. M., 192. 199. 355. 367
Bjork, R. A., 377, 393, 395
Black, J. S., 23, 24, 38, 39
Blakeslee, S., 235, 244
Blandford, A., 298, 299, 301, 303, 304, 310, 311
Blascovich, J., 15, 21
Block, R., 56, 66
Blumer, C., 277, 288
Bobko, P., 264, 274
Boden, M. A., 41, 51
Boer, E. R., 202, 219
Boettger, R., 277, 291
Bohm, G., 2551, 260
Boje, D., 228, 233
Bolstad, C. A., 159, 164, 167
Bond, E. U., 353, 367
Bond, M., 117, 119
Boone, M., 226, 233, 234
Booth, A., 58, 66
Bordetsky, A., 76, 78, 84, 87, 88
Borgatti, S. P., 157, 167
Bornstein, B. H., 315, 325
Borum, R., 314, 317, 318, 325
Bos, J. C., 355, 369
Bostrom, A., 19, 109, 119
Boudés, T., 224, 233

M

Subject Index

A

B